I0816220

PRAISE FOR

How the World Made the West

Named a Best Book of the Year by
The Economist, The Times, The Sunday Times, The Guardian, BBC History Magazine,* and *History Today

"Compelling . . . The book makes a forceful argument and tells a story with great verve: Classical Greece and Rome owed an enormous cultural debt to the societies that preceded them and surrounded them. Therefore, notions that these cultures are the sole and direct ancient progenitors of the modern West are blinkered. We need a new kind of ancient history. . . . [Josephine] Quinn's book points to a possible path forward, toward a more expansive version of ancient history."

—*The Wall Street Journal*

"Those archaic 'Western Civ' classes so many of us took in college should be updated, argues Quinn, an Oxford professor of ancient history. She invites us to widen our scope and see the influence of Phoenicia, Assyria, and India, and to revel in a richer, more polyglot inheritance."

—*The Boston Globe*

"Josephine Quinn ranges wide with [her] broad survey of world history. The Oxford history professor shows how the West has always been remarkably global, detailing examples from the past 4000 years if you doubt it. Your high school teacher may have said it all began with Greece and Rome. But Greece and Rome knew how much they learned by interacting with the rest of the world. From Arabic scholarship (surely we all know their primacy in maths) to Assyrian irrigation, the countless examples of ideas beginning in one place and soon darting all over the world are fascinating."

—*Parade*

"The book is rich in marvellous detail, and succeeds in making the preclassical world come to life. . . . Full of little gem-like shifts of perspective . . . Most of all, the book triumphs as a brilliant and learned challenge to modern western chauvinism."

—Steven Poole, *The Guardian*

"[Quinn's] purpose is to dethrone the 'privileged connection' between the ancient Greeks and Romans and the modern west, and focus instead on the millennia of interaction with other cultures. . . . Quinn pursues this claim with an impressive display of rigorous scholarship lightly worn, successfully covering a huge amount of material. . . . Among Quinn's achievements is her use of advanced discoveries in DNA to scuttle dearly held civilisational myths."

—Tristram Hunt, *Financial Times*

"[Quinn] demolishes the underlying concept of what she calls 'civilisational thinking.' Her argument is simple, persuasive and deserving of attention. . . . An admirable work of scholarship . . . Even seasoned history buffs will find much that is new and fascinating. *How the World Made the West* joins a growing sub-canon of works that explores the broad sweep of history using new intellectual framings, such as Yuval Noah Harari's *Sapiens* (2011), Peter Frankopan's *The Silk Roads* (2015) and *Fall of Civilisations* . . . Anyone who thought history was passé could not be more wrong."

—*The Economist*

"The evidence [Quinn] has accumulated is rich in arresting detail and she delivers it with engaging gusto. . . . Quinn is acutely alive to the ways in which the remote past can serve modern political uses. . . . Her time-scale is immense, and she manages it in quick-quick-slow rhythm. An empire can rise and crumble, four centuries passing, in one sentence. Other times she slows right down to focus on a single encounter. Her geographical reach is equally large. . . . An immense achievement."

—Lucy Hughes-Hallett, *The New Statesman*

"Bold, beautifully written, and filled with insights, *How the World Made the West* demands that we challenge traditional views of the past. An extraordinary achievement."

—Peter Frankopan, bestselling author of *The Earth Transformed*

"As our leaders and pundits glorify 'Western Civilization' and excoriate migration and wokeness, Josephine Quinn offers a momentous correction: The Greeks and Romans were hodgepodge people, and if we are their heirs it is only because of globe-spanning connections that always produce multifarious ways of life. . . . Brilliant and essential."

—Samuel Moyn, author of *Liberalism Against Itself*

"One of the most fascinating works of global history to appear in many years . . . incredibly ambitious and wide-ranging . . . allowing us to understand just how globalized and interconnected mankind has always been."

—William Dalrymple, bestselling author of *The Anarchy*

"*How the World Made the West* is a work of dizzying sweep. Josephine Quinn takes readers on a mesmerizing and frame-shifting journey from the Early Bronze Age to the First Contact. In the process, she deals a magnificently mighty blow to the wrongheaded conceits of civilizational thinking, with all its distortions and misprisions. Weaving effortlessly between literary sources and archaeological evidence, and with an ever-vigilant eye for the fine grain of evocative detail, this book is Big History as it should be written."

—Dan-el Padilla Peralta, author of *Divine Institutions*

"Superb, refreshing, and full of delights, this is world history at its best."

—Simon Sebag Montefiore, author of *The World: A Family History of Humanity*

"Engaging, aspirational, and inspirational, *How the World Made the West* will be devoured by history buffs and should be required reading for those arguing for the supremacy of 'Western Civilization' as well as those arguing for its demise and dismantling, and everyone in between."

—Eric H. Cline, author of *1177 B.C.: The Year Civilization Collapsed*

"No one but Josephine Quinn could have written a book like this—a book of enormous erudition and curiosity; a book that teaches you something new on almost every page."

—Merve Emre, author of *The Personality Brokers*

"The book traces the stories of an imposing array of different early cultures, always focusing on their relations with others and how each of them drew on their predecessors and contemporaries. Quinn makes a point of reexamining many of the familiar landmarks of ancient history. . . . Even readers with a fairly good knowledge of history are likely to learn something new. . . . A fascinating look at world history from the broadest possible perspective."

—*Kirkus Reviews* (starred review)

BY JOSEPHINE QUINN

How the World Made the West

In Search of the Phoenicians

How the World Made the West

How the World Made the West

A 4,000 Year History

Josephine Quinn

RANDOM HOUSE
NEW YORK

Random House
An imprint and division of Penguin Random House LLC
1745 Broadway, New York, NY 10019
randomhousebooks.com
penguinrandomhouse.com

2025 Random House Trade Paperback Edition

Originally published in hardcover in the United Kingdom by Bloomsbury Publishing, London in 2024.

Maps by Michael Athanson

Library of Congress Cataloging-in-Publication Data
Names: Quinn, Josephine Crawley, author.
Title: How the world made the West: a 4,000-year history / Josephine Quinn.
Description: First edition. | New York: Random House, [2024] |
Includes bibliographical references and index.
Identifiers: LCCN 2024006039 (print) | LCCN 2024006040 (ebook) |
ISBN 9780593729793 (hardcover) | ISBN 9780593729816 (ebook)
Subjects: LCSH: Civilization, Western—History. | East and West.
Classification: LCC CB245 .Q487 2024 (print) | LCC CB245 (ebook) |
DDC 909/.09821—dc23/eng/20240716
LC record available at https://lccn.loc.gov/2024006039
LC ebook record available at https://lccn.loc.gov/2024006040

ISBN 978-0-593-72980-9
Ebook ISBN 978-0-593-72981-6

Printed in Canada on acid-free paper

2 4 6 8 9 7 5 3 1

Book design by Ralph Fowler

Chapter ornaments © RainLedy/stock.adobe.com
Title page image © 100choices/stock.adobe.com

The authorized representative in the EU for product safety and compliance is Penguin Random House Ireland, Morrison Chambers, 32 Nassau Street, Dublin D02 YH68, Ireland. https://eu-contact.penguin.ie

For Erich

Our civilization is an immense woven fabric in which very different elements are mixed, in which Nordic rapacity is reconciled to the Roman law, and new Bourgeois conventions to the remains of a Siriac religion. In such a fabric, it is pointless searching for a thread that has remained pure, virgin and uninfluenced by other threads nearby.

—James Joyce, "Ireland, Island of Saints and Sages," 1907

Mélange, hotchpotch, a bit of this and a bit of that is *how newness enters the world.*

—Salman Rushdie, "In Good Faith," 1990

CONTENTS

NOTES TO THE READER

In a book about so many people and places, languages and scripts, consistency of spelling conventions is impossible. My goal has been to avoid unnecessary distraction, and I often use names that are more familiar than strictly correct; my apologies in advance to those who know better. I also prefer to identify people by their geographical origin rather than by a putative ethnicity, itself often created by outsiders or even by modern historians, and for clarity I prefer the concrete to the abstract, so for instance "western Asia" to "Near East." I use BCE and CE rather than BC and AD through training and habit, and in order to avoid the partisan phrase *anno Domini;* I also insist that this notation system still refers not to a truly "Common" but to a "Christian" era. I capitalize West, East, North, and South when I refer to them as concepts rather than cardinal directions. Translations are my own unless otherwise noted.

How the World Made the West

Introduction

Every November I sit on my sofa in my college rooms to read this year's batch of undergraduate applications, and I read the same thing in almost exactly the same words: "I want to study the ancient world because Greece and Rome are the roots of Western Civilization."

I understand why some of my prospective students see things the way they do. Respectable reference sources from the *Encyclopedia Britannica* to Wikipedia describe the development of a distinctive, bounded Western culture built on the ideas and values of Greece and Rome, lost to Europe during the Dark Ages but rediscovered by the Renaissance. Sometimes the story also involves the lands and literature of the Bible, but if other ancient "civilizations" are mentioned at all, it is only to be superseded by the Classical world in an inexorable march of history and culture west.

The predecessors of the Greeks and Romans may be interesting—even impressive—but they are not "ours." Any contribution they make is trumped by that of Greece and Rome, held responsible for all manner of good things from philosophy and democracy to theater and concrete. The neighbors of the Greeks and Romans are ignored altogether, along with later encounters between western Europeans and people to their north, south, and east.

You might think that as a classics professor I'd approve. I've found

Greco-Roman studies rich and rewarding myself, and the place staked out for Greeks and Romans at the heart of ideas about "the West" is one of the reasons my subject still exists. But three decades of teaching and research have convinced me that a narrative focused solely on Greece and Rome impoverishes our view of the past, and impoverishes our understanding of our own world. The real story behind what is now called the West is much bigger and more interesting.

For one thing, Greeks and Romans had their own histories, rooted in other places and older peoples, and they adapted most of their ideas and technologies from elsewhere: law codes and literature from Mesopotamia, stone sculpture from Egypt, irrigation from Assyria and the alphabet from the Levant. They knew this, and they celebrated it.

Greeks were also well aware that they shared the Mediterranean with others—Carthaginians and Etruscans, Iberians and Israelites—and that they lived alongside more powerful empires to the east. Their legends link Greek heroes to the queens, kings, and gods of foreign lands, both real and imagined: Phoenicians, Phrygians, Amazons. Rome's foundation myth meanwhile made the city a place of asylum for refugees, while the Roman poet Catullus can imagine traveling with friends to India, Arabia, Parthia, Egypt, and even to "the Britons on the edge of the world."[1]

For another thing, Greeks and Romans rarely share what are now called "Western values." In fact, much of what these ancients took for granted would seem unfamiliar today, or even unacceptable. Athenians practiced democracy for men, who lauded the seduction of boys while their women went silent and veiled. Romans embraced slavery on a massive scale and they watched public executions for fun.

Finally, there is no privileged connection between ancient Greeks and Romans and the modern "West": the nation-states of western Europe and their settler colonies overseas. The capital of the Roman empire moved in the mid-first millennium CE to Constantinople, and remained there for over a thousand years. Muslims in the meantime combined Greek learning with science from Persia, India, and central

Asia as new technologies streamed around Africa, Arabia, and the Indian Ocean, while sailors on northern seas and riders on the Steppe channeled goods and ideas from China to Ireland.

This is the huge world extending from the Pacific to the Atlantic that the rising nations of western Europe inherited in the fifteenth century CE, as they set out into a new one. These millennia of interaction have however largely been forgotten, drowned out by ideas developed in the Victorian period that organized the world into "civilizations," separate and often mutually opposed.

I want to tell a different story: one that doesn't begin in the Greco-Roman Mediterranean and then re-emerge in Renaissance Italy, but traces the relationships that built what is now called the West from the Bronze Age to the Age of Exploration, as societies met, tangled, and sometimes grew apart. More broadly, I want to make the case that it is connections, not civilizations, that drive historical change.

Civilizations are such a familiar way to see the world today that they can seem like natural facts, a universal model for the organization of human society. They are in fact a relatively recent European invention, part of a phenomenon I call "civilizational thinking."

Well into the eighteenth century, the biblical tradition that the whole earth was populated by the sons of Noah after they survived the Great Flood encouraged an inclusive approach to the past: all humans shared common origins, and they were all members of the same family.[2] The "discovery" of the New World and the spread of Christian missionaries across the globe brought back fascinating stories of new peoples to be worked diligently into this biblical scheme.[3]

Civilization emerged in two stages: singular and plural. When the noun was first used in France in the 1750s, it denoted an abstract concept of advanced society.[4] From the 1760s it was championed by Scottish philosophers who delineated a standard set of evolutions that led to this full realization of human potential, from hunters to shepherds to farmers to merchants and industrialists.[5] As the British liberal John Stuart Mill later explains, progress toward civilization in this sense was measured by the embrace of farming, towns, industry, technology, and trade:

> Whatever be the characteristics of what we call savage life, the contrary of these, or rather the qualities which society puts on as it throws off these, constitute civilization. Thus, a savage tribe consists of a handful of individuals, wandering or thinly scattered over a vast tract of country: a dense population, therefore, dwelling in fixed habitations, and largely collected together in towns and villages, we term civilized. In savage life there is no commerce, no manufactures, no agriculture, or next to none: a country rich in the fruits of agriculture, commerce, and manufactures, we call civilized.[6]

Civilization in this singular sense was in theory a state to which any human society could aspire with sufficient effort and education, and all human societies could be ranked according to their success on this front.* In practice, the standard was set by western Europe. "These elements," Mill explains, "exist in modern Europe, and especially in Great Britain, in a more eminent degree, and in a state of more rapid progression, than at any other place or time."[7]

This abstract concept of civilization provided useful support for western European imperialism too.[8] Mill, who worked for the British East India Company for more than thirty years, took the view that civilized societies had earned a right to freedom and sovereignty that less developed ones lacked.[9] They had a duty to help others on their own journey along the same path, but as Mill put it in 1859: "Despotism is a legitimate mode of government in dealing with barbarians, provided the end be their improvement."[10]

Well into the nineteenth century there were no "civilizations," only

*Not all European intellectual traditions saw "civilization" as the ultimate goal: German scholars, for instance, tended to champion the moral strength of an earlier stage of *Kultur* over the decadent French elegance of the *Zivilisation* that it always threatened to become.

"civilization," and Mill's views represent the culmination of this first stage of civilizational thinking. If civilization could be broken down for him, it was only by degree. By the time he was writing, however, Enlightenment universalism and an idea of constant historical progress were giving way to particularism and cultural relativism. Some scholars had already begun to use the plural form "civilizations" to describe specific human groups in particular places with their own distinct histories and enduring characters, within which development was an internal, self-generated process.

In 1828 the French historian and politician François Guizot gave a series of lectures at the Sorbonne titled A General History of Civilization in Europe. In the first, he discusses "the general civilization of the whole human race."[11] In the second, however, he turns to "civilizations"—individual instances of this general civilization, and in particular to those that preceded the "European" civilization in which he is most interested: Indians, Etruscans, Romans, and Greeks, among others.

They already have distinct characters: "When we look at the civilizations that have preceded that of modern Europe," he muses, "it is impossible not to be struck by the unity of character. . . . Each appears as though it had emanated from a single fact, from a single idea. . . . which universally prevailed and determined the character of its institutions, its manners, its opinions—in a word, all its developments."[12] In Egypt this is theocracy, for instance, in Phoenicia commerce.

This puts them on different paths from the "essentially European" civilization of Guizot's own era, shared by England, France, Germany, and Spain, and distinguished by complexity and freedom: "while everywhere else the predominance of one principle has produced tyranny, the variety of elements of European civilization, and the constant warfare in which they have been engaged, have given birth in Europe to liberty."[13]* Those multiple elements were, in Guizot's view, the Christian

*Like Mill, Guizot notes the special place of his own nation: "The situation in which we are placed, as Frenchmen, affords us a great advantage for entering upon the study of European civilization; for, without intending to flatter the country to which I am bound by so many ties, I cannot but regard France as the center, as the focus, of the civilization of Europe. . . . There is, indeed, in the genius of the French, something of a sociableness,

Church, the Romans, and "the rude barbarians of Germany" who succeeded them.

This exemplifies another aspect of European civilizational thinking: a search for indigenous cultural ancestors. Some, like Guizot, looked to Germany, Rome, and the Roman Church. Others, encouraged by European "philhellenic" support for the Greek War of Independence from the Ottoman Turks (1821–30), looked instead to the Greeks. This approach is neatly illustrated in a startling claim made by John Stuart Mill himself in 1846, that the Athenian defeat of the Persians at the Battle of Marathon was one of the most important events in *English* history:

> The true ancestors of the European nations (it has been well said) are not those from whose blood they are sprung, but those from whom they derive the richest portion of their inheritance. The battle of Marathon, even as an event in English history, is more important than the battle of Hastings. If the Issue of that day had been different, the Britons and the Saxons might still have been wandering in the woods.[14]

Whatever their tastes in historical models, nineteenth-century European intellectuals focused increasingly on civilizations rather than civilization, and on identifying and ranking individual societies' inherent cultural traits rather than on their progress toward a shared human ideal. Cultures in this view were not only quite separate from one other, but had natural ceilings to their development. Over time, this helped to justify harsher forms of imperial rule over what were by that time perceived as irredeemably different and inferior peoples.[15] Empire now had no natural end.

Distinguishing between different peoples was nothing new, of course, nor was the happy discovery that the character of one's own tribe just happened to be the most objectively attractive. But constructing an overall classification of human culture was a novelty. It was encour-

---

of a sympathy,—something which spreads itself with more facility and energy, than in the genius of any other people."

aged by another popular notion that emerged around the same time, that humans could be divided into "races," with differing natural capacities and intelligence, whose evolution was prescribed—or limited—by these innate biological characteristics.[16] These races were then ranked in a variety of color-coded systems that put Australians at the bottom, followed by Africans and east Asians in that order, and Europeans at the top.

The idea of a European civilization could still be problematic. Many European settlers in the new United States saw the American Revolution as a distinct break with the Old World. Concerns about Russia loomed increasingly large meanwhile among those who stayed behind. One attractive alternative was "the West," a more flexible notion that could be used alongside or instead of that of Europe. It could encompass as much of Europe as appealed, and could extend to European settler colonies overseas.[17]

This West operated alongside an equally flexible notion of "the East." In the nineteenth century the boundary between the two often marked political divisions *within* Europe: in 1834 the British foreign secretary Viscount Palmerston described a coalition between Britain, France, Portugal, and Spain as an "alliance among the constitutional states of the west" and "a counterpoise to the Holy Alliance of the east"—Russia, Prussia, and Austria. A similar contrast appears in internal Russian debates between "Westernizers" and "Slavophiles," and the Crimean War of 1854 strengthened the idea of a distinction between Russia (now operating alone) and the rest.[18]

The same binary distinction could be mapped onto race and religion instead, and not only on the border between Europe and Asia. In 1891 Edward Freeman, Regius professor of modern history at Oxford, published a history of Sicily in which he invoked the same fundamental oppositions between its ancient Greek and Phoenician inhabitants and its later Christian and Muslim ones:

> The question had to be fought out . . . whether the central island of the central sea should belong to the West or to the East, to the

> men of Aryan or Semitic stock. And, as ever happens when men of Semitic stock come on the field, the strife of races was from the beginning made sharper by the strife of creeds. Sicily, as an outpost of Europe, had to be guarded or to be won, first from the Phoenician and then from the Saracen.[19]

Civilizational thinking and the West slowly came together in a notion of "Western Civilization" characterized by democracy and capitalism, freedom and tolerance, progress and science.[20] It was fundamentally Christian, and based in biblical tradition, but the Latin Church and the Greek New Testament helped weave Greece and Rome into the heart of the story. By 1912 the Cambridge lecturer J. C. Stobart could proudly begin his popular volume *The Grandeur That Was Rome*—a companion to his 1911 work on *The Glory That Was Greece*—"Athens and Rome stand side by side as the parents of Western civilization."[21]

The imagined borders of Western Civilization continued to shift in the twentieth century. The "Iron Curtain" that fell across Europe in 1945 delineated a new frontier with Russian interests, and the West became a rallying point for alliance between the United States and western European nations.[22] The events of September 2001 helped to realign the East with the Islamic world, but as I finish this book the war in Ukraine is complicating the picture once again.

The way people write about civilizations has changed as well. By the mid-twentieth century straightforward hierarchies had fallen out of fashion, replaced by studies that took a superficially neutral approach, comparing different civilizations rather than ranking them.[23] They were still seen as separate. In 1963 the great French historian of the Mediterranean Fernand Braudel published a school textbook in which he identified a *grammaire des civilisations* ("grammar of civilizations"; a portion was translated into English as *A History of Civilizations*), suggesting that "civilizations" have their own characters as well as a "collective unconscious."[24] He was open to the idea that on a superficial level they were porous: "At first sight, indeed, every civilization looks rather like a railway goods yard, constantly receiving and dispatching miscellaneous deliveries." But the differences between them still "embody more or less permanent characteristics" that are "barely susceptible to gradual change."[25]

A generation later, the end of the Cold War saw a new lease on life for civilizational thinking. In 1996 the Harvard political scientist Samuel P. Huntington made a case for civilizations as the defining feature of a new era, arguing that the most important distinctions between people were now cultural and religious rather than political or economic. He identified nine contemporary civilizations with geographical and religious labels, including a "Western" civilization reaching to the old Iron Curtain, and beyond that "Orthodox" and "Islamic" ones. Most important for us, this state of affairs reflected for him a permanent human condition: "Human history is the history of civilizations. It is impossible to think of the development of humanity in any other terms." Furthermore, "during most of human existence, contacts between civilizations were intermittent or nonexistent."[26]

In such accounts, each culture grows like an individual tree, with its own roots and branches quite distinct from those of its neighbors. Each emerges, flourishes, and declines, and it does so largely alone. Growth and change are the result of internal development, not external connections. Civilizations might change their names in this model, but they don't change their nature.

In the twenty-first century this way of thinking is still the norm, distinguishing "the West," a Christian culture with Greco-Roman or even earlier "Indo-European" roots, from "the East," whether centered on Russia, China, or Islam. Even liberal notions of "multiculturalism" assume the existence, indeed value, of individual "cultures" as a starting point. Civilizational thinking has become civilizational fact.

Ranking is back in fashion too. In its most positive version, the idea of a distinctive, bounded Western legacy built largely on Greek and Roman values takes ancient Athens in particular—rather optimistically—as a model for political participation, creative expression, and free speech. It has new champions in higher education as well, like the Ramsay Centres for Western Civilisation that have opened at three major Australian universities since 2020.[27] In other quarters extremists dressed in

Spartan helmets or tattooed with Roman slogans appeal to the intrinsic value of a white, Western, and European heritage, under threat of a Great Replacement from without.[28]

It's easy to dismiss the idea of Greek and Roman roots to the modern West as old-fashioned, and you certainly won't find it in serious modern scholarship, or even in standard textbooks. But it's still around, it's getting more popular, and it's part of a bigger problem. Civilizational thinking embeds an assumption of enduring and meaningful difference between human societies that does real damage. People die at the hands of zealots for a White West, while the different attitudes expressed in some European countries to refugees fleeing wars in Syria and Ukraine demonstrate the power of civilizational exceptionalism to erase human suffering.

The old model of permanent, separate biological "races" has finally been put to rest by genetic science.[29] Human beings are all closely related to one another—more closely, for instance, than the world's much smaller population of chimps. Genetic differences between groups of people living far apart do of course increase over time. But recent advances in the collection and study of ancient DNA have revealed that the denser genetic groupings you can map in the world today are completely different from those of even the relatively recent past. They are a single snapshot from an ongoing human process of connection and exchange.

Our ancestors traveled often, they traveled long distances, and they frequently encountered new people. Migration, mobility, and mixing are hardwired into human history. As the Harvard geneticist David Reich has put it, a tree "is a dangerous analogy for human populations. The genome revolution has taught us that great mixtures of highly divergent populations have occurred repeatedly. Instead of a tree, a better metaphor may be a trellis, branching and remixing far back into the past."[30]

It is time to make a similar case for human culture. Civilizational thinking fundamentally misrepresents our story. It is not *peoples* that make history, but *people*, and the connections that they create with one another. Human society is not a forest full of trees, with subcultures branching out from single trunks. It is more like a bed of flowers, in need of regular pollination to reseed and grow anew.[31] Distinctive local cultures come and go, but they are created and sustained by interaction—and once contact is made, no land is an island.

I will argue here that there has never been a single, pure Western or European culture. What are called Western values—freedom, rationality, justice, and tolerance—are not only or originally western, and the West itself is in large part a product of long-standing links with a much larger network of societies, to south and north as well as east.[32] The period covered by this book is instead an era of entanglement, in which individuals and societies act and react in relation to one another. These interactions are by no means always positive or peaceful. Indeed, the greatest transformations can occur at times of great upheaval and antagonism—migration, war, and conquest—and people can learn the most from their most bitter rivals.

My story is not a straightforward one of the never-ending expansion of a social or economic network, of the constant forward march of human progress, or of "light from the east" as some nineteenth-century scholars put it, that only reaches full power in the West.[33] There are twists and turns, parallel tracks and occasional switchbacks. Nor is this a book about "influence," a ubiquitous but meaningless concept that gets things the wrong way round: It gives the credit for cultural transfer to the model, not to its adopters. But the past does not act on the future: people choose to interpret, develop, or adapt what they find there.[34]

My book rests heavily on recent historical, archaeological and scientific research including the "genome revolution" of the twenty-first century that is transforming our understanding of human movement and mixing in the past. But it also returns to more ancient ways of thinking about history and how it happens, through journeys, meetings, and relationships. I have been deliberately conservative as well, leaving aside many interesting and plausible theories about contact and cultural transmission between distant societies in order to concentrate on the best-documented examples.

About four millennia separate the two revolutions that bookend my investigation: the adoption of open-sea sailing in the Mediterranean, which provided the first fast link west, and the development of new navigational tools that dramatically extended the western horizon. For much of this period Europe was peripheral to larger cultural, commercial, and political networks, until seafaring states in the far west began to create a new Atlantic world under Christian power—a world that was even more connected over even longer distances, but fostered new ideologies of distance and separation.

Throughout this time, humans traveled for trade, diplomacy, prosperity, adventure, and plunder. They were constrained not by notions of civilizations, but by the real barriers of deserts, mountains, and seas—and, not content to remain alone, they overcame them.

The first contacts between the empires of Egypt and Mesopotamia and the simpler world to their west were made through the region that early European travelers named the Levant, the land of the rising sun, and through some of the oldest urban communities in the world.[35] It is in one of these cities then that our story starts, the city that gave the first seagoing sailing ships their name.

CHAPTER ONE

A Single Sail

BYBLOS, C. 2000 BCE

It is just after dawn on a warm morning about 4,000 years ago. We are at the port of Byblos, built across a promontory below the cool green slopes of Mount Lebanon. The fishing boats are already out, and the front is bustling: barges stream in from merchant ships that dropped anchor the night before, young men joke around as they load up a donkey train with sacks and baskets and, south of the town's stone walls, rafts loaded with tree trunks glide down the river to the coast. High above the harbor stands a new temple with a tower guiding sailors to safe mooring, and with anchors built into its staircase and walls for good fortune.[1] The people of this compact, glittering little town honor their debt to the sea.

A couple of kilometers offshore a handsome sailing ship, larger than the rest, rides at anchor in the shallows. The northwesterly winds have dropped over the last few weeks, the temperature is cooling, and now the boat just awaits its passengers and crew.

Trade has taken these men far and wide across a web of cities and empires, artisans and poets, a network rooted in the river valleys of Egypt and western Asia but connected to a bigger world beyond. They can speak several languages, and if we had run into them last night they

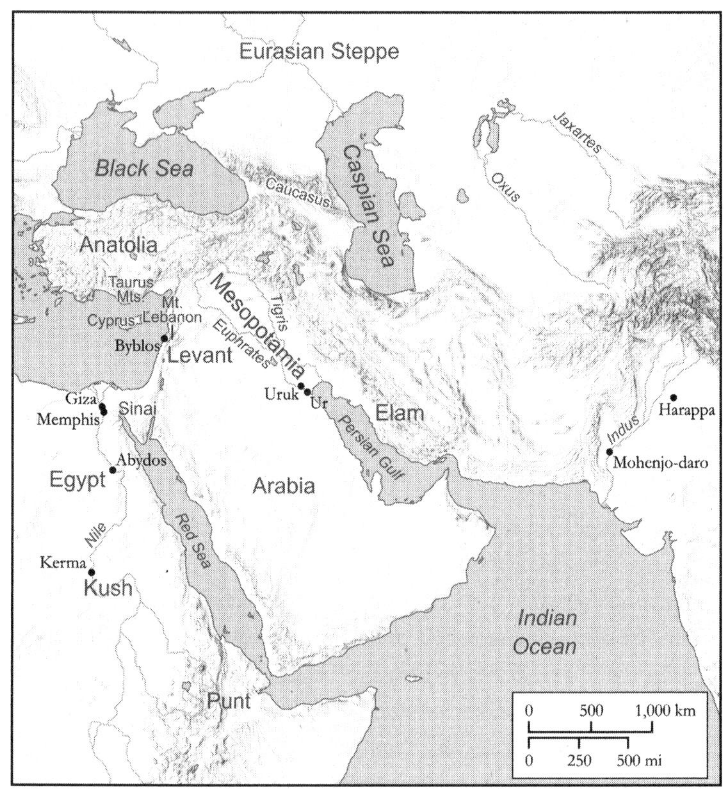

The world of Byblos in the third millennium BCE

could have told us some stories over a jar or two of the excellent local wine.

One of the merchants has sailed down the coast and up the Nile, past more than a hundred of the pyramid tombs built by Egyptian priest-kings, to do business in the sandy trading city of Kerma, capital of the gold-rich land to the south that the Egyptians called Kush. From there he traveled across the eastern Sahara to the Red Sea, where he joined a convoy of ships traveling south to the Horn of Africa, in search of ivory, ebony, incense, and gold.

Two more traders have made the long donkey trek toward Mesopotamia. First they headed north across the mountains through the Akkar Gap (today guarded by the Crusader castle Krak des Chevaliers) then east on flatter lands toward the Euphrates. One carried on overland to the Tigris to break bread with men who had hiked south through the Caucasus, leading fine horses and loaded with furs, and who told him of a flat plain farther north, stretching for months of riding time. The other shipped his wares down the Euphrates to the walled city of Ur just north of the Persian Gulf coast, a port far bigger than Byblos.

There he visited the sacred precinct in the northwest of the city dedicated to the moon god Nanna and his consort Ningal, filled with temples and courtyards, government offices and the king's great palace. In the far corner he climbed the triple staircase of the new ziggurat, a stepped temple-mountain built of bitumen and brick; from the top he watched ships depart for Arabia and the Indian coast and return laden with copper and precious stones. Down at the harbor itself he compared notes with an old man who had been sent to the Gulf from the Indus decades earlier to run his family's trading interests, and listened to his stories of a great green valley far to the east, with strange humped cattle and five enormous cities built of baked red clay.[2]

The conversation in Byblos that night transports us around a vast connected world in constant flux, full of travelers to whom civilizational thinking would make little sense. When the crew head off in the morning they will head in a new direction, toward the setting sun. Before we follow them ourselves, however, we have to go back to the beginning, to find out how much human history depends on human contact, and how they got this far.

Humans have always sought one another out, even at species level: as a result of such encounters—friendly or otherwise—Europeans all have a small but significant percentage of Neanderthal heritage in our genes, and the DNA of at least three other archaic human species survives in modern populations.[3] Once *Homo sapiens* had supplanted other varieties across the planet, she kept on walking—and sometimes paddling too. Hunter-gatherers traveled with their prey and with the seasons, and they traveled to find one another, building mysterious megaliths together in the Taurus Mountains and celebrating feasts in halls made of mammoth bones along the Dnipro and the Don.[4] They swapped raw materials: people in Cyprus and on the Red Sea obtained obsidian, a shiny, hard volcanic glass that made excellent cutting tools, from central Anatolia. They exchanged technical information as well: new designs for arrowheads spread quickly across a wide area from Mesopotamia to Syria.[5]

As the global climate settled and warmed at the end of the Ice Age 12,000 years ago, exchange became even more important in the so-called Fertile Crescent (which really looks more like a boomerang). There in the new temperate conditions, abundant local game and wild plants prompted the first experiments in agriculture. Pioneers took local wild grasses with small, easily dispersed seeds and by careful and repeated selection they nudged them into producing fat, firmly attached grains, easier for humans to harvest, eat, and process into flour but now in need of human intervention to reseed.[6] Another form of selective breeding turned wild animals into human servants: dogs had long been bred from wolves for hunting companions, but now aurochs were transformed into cows, boars into pigs, and sheep were coaxed out of their natural aggression.[7*]

Farming required a more sedentary lifestyle, but it still depended on contact and communication. Each domestication took place in a specific area of the Fertile Crescent—wheat, cattle, and sheep in the north-

*The aurochs stood up to two meters tall and weighed up to 1,000 kilos, with broad shoulders and long, curved horns. The last survivor was shot in Poland in the seventeenth century CE.

ern hills, barley and pigs in different areas west of the Euphrates, and goats in what is now Iran. By around 7000 BCE, however, all the new breeds are found throughout the region.[8] This involved more than just swapping seeds and stock: people had to explain to one another how to sow, cultivate, harvest, and cook the new plants, and how to breed, feed, and care for the new animals.

Farming a wider range of crops and animals considerably reduced the risks of the agricultural lifestyle, dependent as it was on the weather and the gods. Agriculture still wouldn't have appealed to everyone: it is harder work than hunting and foraging, and a sedentary workforce is a breeding ground for infectious disease. But the returns promote population growth, which encourages migration in search of new land. From the seventh millennium BCE agriculture expanded across a vast swath of the world. Farmers took their animals, seeds, and skills south to Egypt, east to Iran and the Indus Valley, north to Anatolia, and from there west into Europe. They established themselves wherever they could sustain crops by good luck or human ingenuity, and at the expense of the people who used to hunt and herd across the new fields.

The most successful experiments took place in the dry river valleys of Mesopotamia, the "land between the rivers," tucked inside the arc of the Fertile Crescent itself. Farming the rich alluvial soils between the Tigris and the Euphrates required the construction of an intricate network of canals and water channels, and rewarded the farmers with dramatic yields. They could now grow enough food to support others to become potters, priests, or administrators, and by the fifth millennium BCE towns had emerged. By the late fourth millennium BCE Uruk on the Euphrates was a true city of 250 hectares—about the size of London's Soho—with canals, temples, and a population of between 20,000 and 40,000 people.[9*]

The administrative requirements of managing a large agricultural territory beyond the city walls meant that Uruk also developed the world's first known system of standard weights and measures, based on

*A hectare is ten thousand square meters, about the same size as a rugby union pitch, and equivalent to 2.5 acres.

the load an average man could carry (a talent) and on the length of his forearm (a cubit).[10] The first writing appears here too. Initially this was just a counting system—circles for tens, lines for ones—but then scribes added pictograms to show what was being counted. By the end of the fourth millennium BCE, they had extended this code to record the local language and then literature in signs imprinted into clay tablets with a stylus and now known as cuneiform, from the Latin for "wedge-shaped."[11]*

By the mid-third millennium BCE a patchwork of cities ruled by kings covered southern Mesopotamia, some with tens of thousands of inhabitants. We can tell a similar tale about Egypt, where farming arrived on the Nile in the sixth millennium BCE. Complex irrigation technology was needed here too to trap and divert the annual floods, and the yields were again impressive. By the late fourth millennium large cities had grown up along the Nile, and around 3000 BCE the communities of Upper and Lower Egypt came together under the "Old Kingdom" dynasties that wrote in hieroglyphs, built the pyramids, and ruled over more than a million people.

This is a story so familiar that it can sound like fate: the first steps on the ladder of progress assembled in the eighteenth century whereby hunters become herders become farmers, who build cities and acquire rulers, rules, and institutions—in short, civilization. But in fact it reveals the holes in the traditional narrative of self-development.[12] Like earlier, smaller communities, the kingdoms of Mesopotamia and Egypt did not make themselves. Nor were they the only societies of interest in this era.

Even the earliest cities needed to import building materials—timber, stone, and metals—from far away, creating economic links between kings, miners, and lumberjacks across thousands of kilometers. And in the third millennium BCE the invention of bronze inaugurated a new era of regular long-distance exchange. Ancient smiths created this new substance by combining copper with an alloy to make a stronger and

*Sumerian, the world's first written tongue, has no surviving relatives. Like many later languages it operated on the basis of grammatical "genders," but these were not male, female, and neuter; instead Sumerian-speakers organized their world into people (including gods) and non-people (including animals).

harder metal with a lower melting point that allowed easier casting and sharper cutting edges.[13] It was soon used for everything from cooking pots and ornaments to weapons and armor, but it came at a cost. Copper itself is hard to find outside mountain regions, and good-quality bronze was alloyed with tin, which is very rare indeed between the Atlantic coast and central Asia, where it was sourced by Elamites—"highlanders" in Sumerian—based in southwestern Iran, who then supplied it to Mesopotamia and lands beyond.[14]

Travel and trade on an ever greater scale required new modes of transport, and these too were imported from elsewhere, the work not of crop farmers in the famous ancient "civilizations" of Egypt and Mesopotamia, but of herders to the north and south: the wheel and the donkey.

The wheel first came into its own on the cold, grassy plain of the Eurasian Steppe, which runs for thousands of kilometers from Manchuria to the lands above the Caspian and Black seas. Flat and with few rivers to cross, the landscape invites long-distance travel, as does the climate. Cattle and sheep could provide nutrition and clothing on the hoof, but to transport heavier items the only options were to roll them on a line of logs or to pull them on a sled, ideally with the help of oxen.

This changed with the invention of the wheel and more importantly the axle. Thousands of wheeled wagons are found in Steppe graves dating to the third millennium BCE.[15] These early wheels were made from solid wood, cut not as slices across the trunk, which would be weak and uneven, but out of a lengthwise plank. They were ideal for ox-drawn carts, and by the late fourth millennium BCE they had rolled into Mesopotamia, where they were used to throw pottery as well.[16]

Wooden wheels are only an option if you have enough wood of the right kind, and the right animals to pull them. Cattle herders in the eastern Sahara and the Horn of Africa had neither, but recent genetic studies suggest that they tamed the African wild ass in the fourth millennium to invent the donkey.[17] By 3000 BCE the animal had reached Egypt to the north, where the reverence it rightly inspired can be seen in the elaborate burial rites given to ten donkeys at the city of Abydos.[18]

Unlike a horse or ox, the donkey is a low-maintenance companion. It is easy to train and care for, sure-footed on rough terrain, will eat anything, can go without water for several days and can carry up to a third of its weight.[19]

This is still less of course in total than an ox-drawn cart, but for long-distance transportation, east Africans had the Nile, a river that runs swiftly north while the prevailing winds blow south. This made it an ideal laboratory for another new technology that allowed efficient travel along the river in both directions. Depictions of boats with sails first appear in the late fourth millennium on objects made in northern Kush, and they soon appear in Egypt too.[20]

Sailing must at first have been confined to the river: the sails depicted in these early images are set too far forward to maneuver in open water. Donkeys got farther: the cuneiform sign for "donkey" appears on tablets at late-fourth-millennium Uruk, and by the third, remains of the animals themselves are found there.*

Dangerous seas, forbidding mountains, and arid desert still obstructed direct contact between the farming river valleys of Egypt and western Asia. Connections ran instead along a more sheltered but much longer and more indirect route through the harbors, plains, and mountains of the western Levant, a narrow strip of coastal land hemmed in by the bulk of Mount Lebanon that has always connected east and west, north and south.

The first journeys through the Levant happened overland. Those donkeys must have trudged across the Sinai Peninsula and up the Levantine coast before turning inland toward the rivers.[21] Even slow and indirect connections can have dramatic effects, however, and they may explain the writing system that appeared in Egypt in the late fourth millennium, now called hieroglyphic from the Greek for "sacred writing." It is entirely unrelated in formal terms to Mesopotamian cuneiform, but the appearance of written language for the first time in the world at more or less the same time in two different places would be a remarkable coincidence.

This connection sped up in the mid-third millennium, as Egypt's

*Egyptians by contrast had little use for the wheel, or indeed for bronze.

sailing technology developed and its vessels began to explore the Mediterranean. Around 2600 BCE Egyptian records start to document regular sea trade with Levantine ports.[22] A century later Egyptian sculpture depicts seagoing ships with sails and rigging that could have handled wind and waves.

Sculptures and images of boats with sails begin to appear at sites in the Persian Gulf by the middle of the third millennium as well. There is no evidence for sailing around the Arabian Peninsula until the first millennium BCE, and images of early Mesopotamian and Egyptian boats suggest that they were not based on the same model, but as with the hieroglyphic script even indirect reports of seagoing sailing ships in one area may well have given people in the other a good idea.[23]

However it arrived, sailing gave traders in Mesopotamia too access to new worlds. Around 2400 BCE wealthy tombs found at the port of Ur fill up with exotic stones from far-flung places: lapis lazuli from Afghanistan and turquoise from Uzbekistan, as well as carnelian from the Indus Valley, where farmers had created immense urban landscapes with fortified citadels, street grids, monumental baths, and drains connected to every house.[24]

Back in the Mediterranean, Byblos was the main port for Egyptian shipping heading north, to the extent that in Egyptian records all seagoing sailing vessels are called "Byblos ships" even when they were built on the Red Sea to sail south to the gold mines of the kingdom of Punt on the African horn.[25] The primary cargo traveling south from Byblos was always the hard, durable cedarwood cut on Mount Lebanon. It was used to fit out Egyptian tombs and temples as well as to build Egyptian boats, including the forty-meter-long funerary barge of King Khufu (Cheops) that was buried alongside his Great Pyramid at Giza.[26]

On the back of this special relationship, Byblos itself grew from a small coastal village built around a natural spring to a bustling port, filled with Egyptian styles, goods, and inscriptions, where images of the local deity the Lady of Byblos depicted her as a version of the Egyptian goddess Hathor.[27]

Even with ships arriving regularly and plenty of people to ask, the art of sailing itself must have taken Byblos sailors themselves a while to perfect: you have to learn how to rig the vessels, as well as how to build them in the first place, which involves making ropes and sails as well as carpentry.[28] Then there is the problem of handling them. Until the mid-second millennium BCE sailing boats had no keels to keep them stable in strong seas, and they had a single square sail, which meant that they needed an offshore wind to leave port and a side or following wind to make progress—although the use of oars no doubt helped.[29]

Eventually however the people of Byblos and neighboring ports began to build their own ships, and to develop techniques for sailing west in a sea full of westerly winds. This signaled far more than incremental improvements in maritime skill and technology: it marked a new start. Ships under sail can travel 100–150 kilometers a day, two or three times the distance of the fastest canoe or rowing boat, with much less effort, more room for cargo and a more stable design.[30] Contacts across the Mediterranean had come and gone for millennia, but now with sailing they stuck.

Down at the harbor, the time has come to leave again. Our own Byblos sailors are among the first to set off toward the west. There they will find a very different world, one with no states, no cities, no temples, and no written literature at all. In what we now call Europe people lived sparsely for the most part in fortified villages and scattered farms, feeding themselves from farming their land. Their lives were not in their own terms primitive, nor distinctively poor: they had not read the great European intellectuals of the eighteenth century, and they did not know that history was supposed to be a march forward toward urbanism, commerce, and the law.

They were not entirely isolated. Wheels are found in central Europe in the fourth millennium, but they were less useful in hills and mountains than on the flat plains of the Steppe or Mesopotamia, and they don't seem to have reached far western regions at all.[31] People stayed in touch instead by water, travelling in small rowing boats and canoes that could do twenty kilometers on a good day: slower than a donkey train, and much slower than walking unladen.[32] They sometimes still traveled great distances. But far from the mainstream of technological, commercial, and political exchange, people lived with less complexity, and more things stayed the same.

That was about to change.

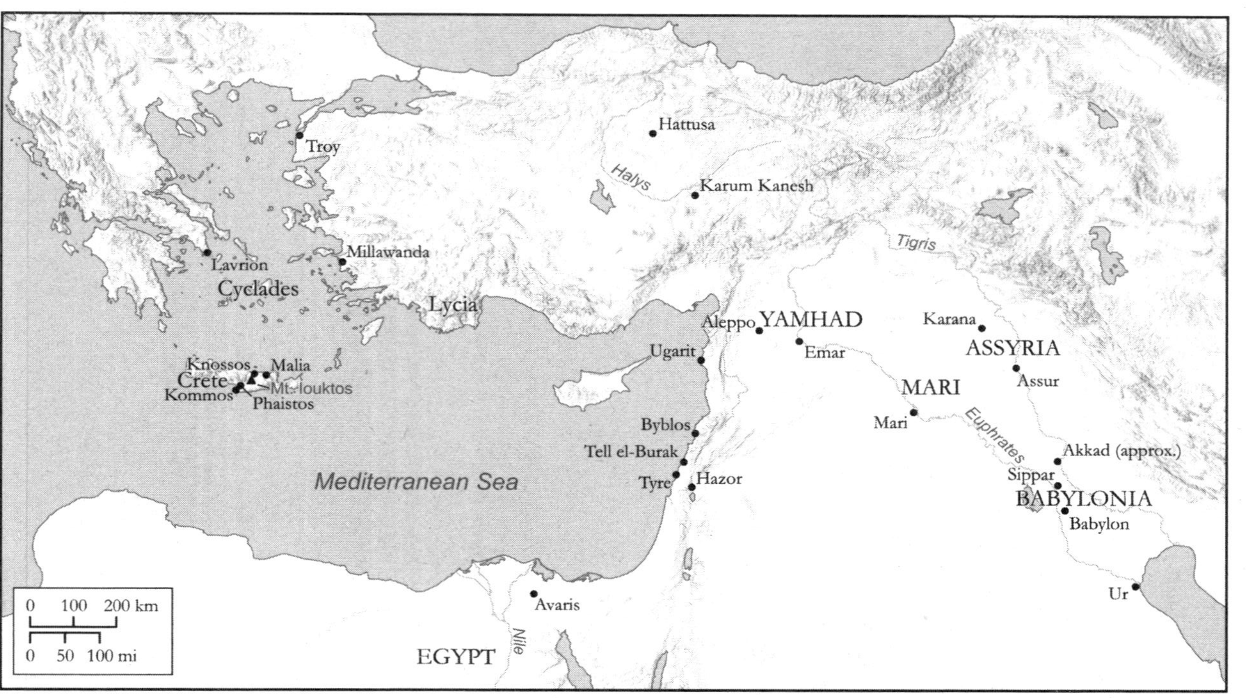

The world of Europa, c. 2000 BCE

CHAPTER TWO

The Palace of Minos

KNOSSOS, C. 1700 BCE

After a tiring donkey ride uphill from the northern coast of Crete, the palace sprawling across the plateau of Knossos must have been a wonderful surprise. Having stabled your animals, you approach it from the west, climbing a broad staircase as its walls rise in front of you. Pierced by huge windows and topped with horned battlements, the buildings gleam orange in the light of the low sun. After crossing a paved courtyard to circle round the compound to the left, you enter through a pillared hallway on the northern flank. Then you turn immediately right and make your way up a narrow passageway to the bright sunlight of a vast internal courtyard built to hold banquets and festivals. Fifty meters long by twenty-five wide, it can hold 5,000 people.[1] To your left, a grand staircase connects at least two floors above ground with two or more cut into the slope of the hill below. Looming above the stonework straight ahead is Mount Iouktas, a colorless round bulk against the yellow sunset beyond.

The whole complex reflects the wealth, success and imagination of the people who built it. The public areas are covered in frescoes of fantastic animals, giant plants, and athletes leaping over bulls, bright with blues, reds, and yellows. Wooden columns painted deep red frame the window spaces, open to the island air. Downstairs is a more private world: cozy rooms decorated in rich geometric patterns, with windows and terraces looking out over a stream to the hills beyond. Colonnaded courtyards let in light and air, but can be closed off in winter by wooden partitions that fold into vertical notches in their elegant pillars. Tucked out of sight are the kitchens, workshops, and storage magazines that power the whole operation, as well as archives of clay tablets covered in mysterious signs.[2]

It is Byblos ships that have brought us to Crete. The earliest image of a sailing boat with a mast and rigging found west of the Levant was carved on a seal and buried in a Cretan tomb in about the year 2000 BCE, right around the time that new metals start arriving on the island, along with new technologies and luxury goods from western Asia and northeast Africa.[3] Crete, then, is the next stop in our story of contact and connection, but we aren't the first to get there.

Ancient Greek authors told their own tale about the first journey from the Levant to Crete. In this version it was a Levantine princess who bridged the gap between two worlds, and she traveled on a seagoing bull. The tale is set in the vague and mystical times before the Trojan War, and it begins in the city of Tyre, which had in more recent times supplanted Byblos to the north as the largest of the Levantine ports.[4]

Europa is the daughter of the Tyrian king, an Egyptian named Agenor. At the start of the story she is picking flowers along the shore. In the distance she catches a glimpse of a beautiful white bull: Zeus, king of the gods, in elaborate disguise to conceal him from his wife's keen eye. As the beast comes closer, the girl is entranced. She talks to him, strokes him, and eventually climbs onto the gentle animal's back—at which point he turns and gallops into the sea, carrying her west across the waves to Crete. There he abandons her with their children, not his first offense of this kind.[5]

Europa makes the best of things by marrying the Cretan king, but trouble continues in the next generation, as her sons fight for control of the island. In the end Sarpedon leaves with his mother and his followers, known as the Termilae, to rule the region of Lycia in southern Anatolia, while his brother Minos becomes king on Crete, with a capital at Knossos.[6]

Minos is less fortunate in his domestic affairs: like her mother-in-law, his wife, Pasiphaë, falls in love with a bull. In this case the attraction is not mutual—perhaps because he is a real bull—so Pasiphaë persuades an inventor and craftsman called Daedalus to make her a wooden cow to climb inside so that she can fool the beast into mating with her. The ruse succeeds, but the resulting infant is born half man, half bull, and so the versatile Daedalus is re-engaged to construct a vast and complicated prison, now better known as the Labyrinth. The poor Minotaur lives a wretched life, his only distraction a feast every nine years of fourteen young men and women sent as tribute by Aegeus, king of Athens, until Aegeus' son Theseus kills the creature with the help of his own half sister, the treacherous Ariadne.

These interwoven stories sketch their own labyrinth of journeys and relationships between Egypt, the Levant, Crete, Anatolia, and Greece. They reveal the gulf between modern and ancient ways of thinking about the human past, between civilizational thinking and what we will come to recognize as a standard ancient preference for explaining historical change through journeys and relationships.[7]

One thing the stories weren't about was Europe. We can see this in the work of Herodotus of Halicarnassus, who wrote the first major work of history in Greek around 425 BCE. To him the continent's name was a mystery, "unless we are to say that the land takes its name from Tyrian Europa . . . but it is clear that she was from Asia, and never came to this land which Greeks now call Europa, but only from Phoenicia to Crete, and from Crete to Lycia."[8]

Crete was to the ancients not a part of Europe but a place of connection between the Levant and points west. This was not the view taken by the archaeologists who rediscovered the island's ancient monuments, as well versed in civilizational thinking as in Greek myth.

It all began in 1878, when a Cretan soap manufacturer named Minos Kalokairinos excavated a small section of a huge, rambling, and very ancient building in the north of the island, then under Ottoman occupation. Well versed in the story of Europa and her sons, he naturally—and correctly—identified the site as Knossos, and he called the maze of small rooms and corridors he had found there "the Royal Palace of King Minos." As early as 1880 the American journalist William J. Stillman labeled it the "Labyrinth of Daedalus."[9]

The new find caused great excitement: this was the oldest building so far found in the Mediterranean. For Europeans who saw Crete as part of their own Christian culture, it could act as a rival to the famous ancient monuments of Egypt and western Asia that had captured the public imagination ever since the scholars who had accompanied Napoleon's invasion of Egypt in 1798 published lavish images of its ancient temples and pyramids in the *Description de l'Égypte* (1809–28).[10*] As an idea of a distinctive and superior European civilization took hold, fascination with the exotic antiquities of what was beginning to be called the Near East combined easily with a sense of distance and even disgust that underlined the otherness of these regions and their decline in Ottoman hands.[11**] Now the Palace of Minos offered a chance to settle the score.

In 1894 an English visitor arrived to view Kalokairinos' site, a man of fixed opinions and unusual habits: from his school days Arthur Evans had refused to wear glasses for his short sight and relied instead on a cane he called "Prodger."[12] As an undergraduate at Oxford he had acquired a taste for exploration in the Balkans, then divided between the Austro-Hungarian empire and Ottoman Turkey. He published an account of his travels in the region with a grant from his father in 1876, an anti-Ottoman work heavily inflected by the new thinking about racial difference. "I believe in the existence of inferior races," Evans informed his readers, "and would like to see them exterminated."[13]

*In the ensuing "Egyptomania," even New York's new water-distributing reservoir on Fifth Avenue was built in 1842 in the guise of an Egyptian temple. This site is now occupied by the New York Public Library, completed in 1911 in a more conservative, classical style.

**Nineteenth-century Europeans could talk of a Near, Middle, and Far East, all naturally nearer or farther from Europe. In the twentieth century this geographical division yielded to a chronological one, with the ancient "Near East" becoming the modern "Middle East," with reference to the same (hazy) region.

After several years working as a journalist in Ragusa (Dubrovnik), where he was repeatedly arrested as a spy or plain troublemaker, Evans returned to England and turned his versatile talents to archaeology. In 1884 he was appointed keeper of the Ashmolean Museum in Oxford. When he arrived on Crete a decade later in search of portable antiquities, he was forty-three years old and at another turning point after the death of his beloved wife Margaret.*

At Knossos Evans found a new love that would last the rest of his life. He had a hard time getting hold of it: the Palace of Minos was a great prize for any archaeologist, but for political reasons was off-limits. Evans' visit to Crete came at a time of rising friction between the Ottoman authorities and the local Christian population, and there was considerable local opposition to further investigation of the ancient remains while the island was under Turkish rule, in case the spoils ended up in Istanbul.[14]

Evans nonetheless managed to purchase part of the site from a local family, and he returned to the island twice over the following two years as a local uprising against Ottoman rule gathered pace. His own sympathies in the matter were clear, as was his adherence to civilizational thinking. In an 1896 address to the British Association for the Advancement of Science, he drew his audience's attention to ancient Crete's "European spirit of individuality and freedom" and proclaimed that "Crete stands forth again today as the champion of the European spirit against the yoke of Asia."[15]

After more than a year of brutal war between the island's Christian and Muslim populations, Crete became an independent state in 1898. The following year Evans invited subscriptions for his new Cretan Exploration Fund, and he bought the rest of the Knossos site just days before beginning excavations there on March 23, 1900.[16] After a week on site he found an ancient writing tablet, within a fortnight he had more than 700, and over the next eight years he revealed the largest palace in the ancient Mediterranean in its full glory.

*Margaret's father was Evans' Oxford tutor Edward Freeman, whose historical vision of a Sicily riven by race and religion between East and West we have already encountered.

. . .

Knossos was the jewel in the crown, but archaeologists from all over Europe and the United States were soon exploiting their new access to independent Crete to uncover ancient towns, palaces, and villas all over the island. Evans himself had no doubt that what they were revealing was "a high early civilization on Cretan soil" that rivaled that of the Egyptian kings. It lacked only a label, but that was easy to fix. As he explained in his sumptuous account of his excavations: "To this early civilization of Crete as a whole I have proposed—and the suggestion has been generally accepted by the archaeologists of this and other countries—to apply the name 'Minoan.' "[17]

With that he invented a culture entirely unattested in antiquity.[18] It was one that mattered too: "this comparatively small island, left on one side today by all the main lines of Mediterranean intercourse, was at once the starting-point and the earliest stage in the highway of European civilization."[19]

It was a very British idea, of course, that Europe owed a great deal to a sea power based on an offshore island. And over time Evans' nostalgic British sensibilities increasingly influenced his interpretation of "Minoan" society as a peaceful and artistic society ruled by kings.[20] As his half-sister Joan later wrote, "Time and chance had made him the discoverer of a new civilization, and he had to make it intelligible to other men. Fortunately it was exactly to his taste."[21]

It also fitted firmly into the nineteenth-century civilizational thinking that tied a particular and enduring culture to a specific place, and tied modern Europe to the ancient Aegean. Evans did allow the Egyptian and, to a lesser extent, Mesopotamian kingdoms a little influence on the island.[22] But, as his Australian student Vere Gordon Childe explained in 1925, this was a superficial phenomenon:

> the Minoan spirit was thoroughly European and in no sense oriental. A comparison with Egypt and Mesopotamia will make the contrast plain. We find in Crete none of those stupendous palaces that betoken the autocratic power of the oriental despot. Nor do

> gigantic temples and extravagant tombs like the pyramids reveal an excessive preoccupation with ghostly things.[23]

Like the ancient legends, however, the archaeology tells a different story, and one closer to the ancient version: not of a separate civilization but of a new relationship that fueled change on Crete and opened a conduit between continental Europe and a larger web of world culture and commerce.

Crete is a mountainous island with hot summers, but it also has large expanses of fertile land and plenty of rain. By the third millennium BCE it was peppered with villages, workshops, and potteries.[24] It was still only an outlying member of the main Aegean trading circuit, which in that era was centered on the Cyclades, where men with a fondness for daggers and wine paddled among their close-packed islands in long, thin canoes with fish totems on their sterns.[25*]

The Cyclades alone would have taken about a fortnight to cross, island to island.[26] The rewards of longer journeys were worth it. By the later third millennium these islands were in frequent contact with the Anatolian coast, trading in Aegean metals including copper and silver, which was much in demand as currency across western Asia, and the standard against which other goods were measured.[27]

Cycladic sailors were regular visitors to the port of Troy, strategically located at the end of a caravan route from Mesopotamia through Anatolia and on a bay at the entrance to the Black Sea, where shipping could shelter as it waited for the wind that would carry it through the Dardanelles Strait.[28] Anatolian pottery appears on the islands in this period, and even the odd piece of carnelian worked in the Indus Valley; the same routes also brought the tin and probably also the techniques required to make "true" bronze, stronger than the copper alloy long de-

*On land they carved the elegant marble "Cycladic" figurines, often scrubbed in museums into unnatural whiteness, but originally painted with faces, hair, jewelry, and tattoos.

rived in the Aegean from arsenic.[29] Other new arrivals suggest the emergence of more complex industry and administration in the Aegean in this era: the potter's wheel, stamp seals, and the donkey.[30]

Crete was even farther away from the Cyclades than Troy, a lengthy voyage south of the islands in a canoe, an even longer journey back against the prevailing winds. With no good metal supplies of their own, however, Cretan farmers needed to import them, and they must have arrived at first on Cycladic canoes.[31]

By the late third millennium, however, there are signs on Crete of direct eastward links as well. The islanders adopt Syrian-style goblets for wine, quite different from Anatolian two-handled cups found in the Cyclades. They import small amounts of gold, hippopotamus ivory, and beads made in Egypt of blue faience, a fine form of pottery made from sand and glazed with bright colors.[32]

Such small, light luxuries could still have been carried by canoe, probably passing through several hands along the way.[33] Soon, however, the quantity and weight of the imports confirm the arrival of the sailing ships depicted on contemporary seal stones, in search of Aegean silver as well as Crete's own arts and crafts: fine metal vessels and weapons, and elegant pottery characterized by white, red, and yellow designs on a black background.[34]

In return they brought new metals, especially tin, as well as African ivory, Egyptian bowls and scarabs, and decorative ostrich eggs half the size of a rugby ball.[35]* Even the Egyptian material must have traveled west from Levantine ports: the currents of the eastern Mediterranean draw shipping in a circle counterclockwise, while the prevailing winds blow northwest to southeast all year round. Although it would in theory already have been possible to sail south from Crete to Egypt, a direct journey north was out of the question.

This is when the wheel appears on Crete, both on vehicles and in

*These were not culinary delicacies: the shells were blown and dried, and then painted, carved, or decorated to make exotic ornaments. They were especially highly valued for the difficulty in stealing them: there was no extensive ostrich farming in antiquity, and wild ostriches were notoriously swift and violent, with very sharp beaks (Tamar Hodos et al., "The origins of decorated ostrich eggs in the ancient Mediterranean and Middle East," *Antiquity* 94, no. 374 [2020]).

pottery workshops, as does the house mouse, a stowaway from the Levantine coast that first disembarked at Cretan ports like Kommos in the early second millennium BCE.[36] It is also when Cretans began to write things down.

About 2,000 documents survive in undeciphered early Cretan scripts, starting around 2000 BCE.[37] The earliest, now called "Cretan Hieroglyphic," has signs that look like little pictograms but for the most part represent syllables. They were scratched into or stamped onto small clay seals, bars, crescents, and medallions at northern sites including Knossos. A different syllabic script then appeared first at the southern site of Phaistos, with more abstract, linear signs that were easier to write on a wider range of objects, from clay tablets to stone offering tables.* Perhaps as a result, "Linear A" replaced Cretan Hieroglyphic across the island by about 1650 BCE.

Shared signs show that these two writing systems were related to each other, but they bear no resemblance to the cuneiform writing used in Mesopotamia and the Levant, nor—despite the shared modern name—to the hieroglyphs employed in Egypt.[38] As in Egypt a thousand years earlier, however, it is unlikely to be pure coincidence that experiments in writing began across the island just as sailing connected it to literate western Asia.[39]

The arrival of Byblos ships in the Aegean helped to seal the fate of the trading network based in the Cyclades, where there were few sheltered anchorages for deep-hulled sailing vessels, along with that of the slower Anatolian overland route east.[40] By contrast, it coincided with a new era of prosperity and development on Crete—and while Byblos ships weren't solely responsible for that, they certainly helped.

With reliable supplies of tin, islanders began to manufacture bronze

*There are also various experimental texts such as the mysterious Phaistos disk, whose spirals of forty-five pictograms may record the same local language as Linear A (Brent Davis, "The Phaistos disk: a new way of viewing the language behind the script," *Oxford Journal of Archaeology* 37, no. 4 [2018]), or perhaps an attempt to capture the power of writing itself rather than to convey specific meaning (Helène Whittaker, "Social and symbolic aspects of Minoan writing," *European Journal of Archaeology* 8, no. 1 [2005]).

in substantial quantities for the first time.[41] Metalworkers on the island developed the first swords out of daggers, as bronze recipes became stronger and allowed for longer blades.[42] Large buildings that had already started to appear in the late third millennium expanded into the palaces tourists visit today, not just at Knossos but at Malia on the northern coast and Phaistos in the south as well.[43] The towns around them grew larger too: Knossos was a small village of just over five hectares in 2500 BCE, but by the eighteenth century it covered a hundred, comparable with all but the very biggest settlements in contemporary Mesopotamia and Anatolia.[44]

Although the new building complexes on Crete may have responded to vague reports of palaces and monuments overseas, they would have looked unfamiliar to men from Levantine kingdoms.[45] It isn't clear in fact that they were really "palaces" at all: they were certainly centers of administration, craft production, and agricultural storage, but we don't know if Cretan communities even had kings in this era.[46] Instead, they reproduced earlier gathering places in permanent form: the central courts at both Knossos and Phaistos are built on the site of open areas that had been used for communal activities as far back as the fourth millennium BCE.[47] Much of the second millennium pottery recovered from these compounds is table crockery, and the enormous vats of oil and pits full of flour also found there suggest large-scale catering operations—and that they were still places for the local community to come together.[48] Despite the arrival of Byblos ships, these communities looked primarily to their own past for inspiration, not to people overseas.

The remarkable rise of Crete in the early second millennium BCE, the appearance of monumental buildings, the first towns and the first writing in the Aegean or anywhere farther west, was undoubtedly fueled in part by contact with new places and people; it exploited new ideas and increasingly specific technologies borrowed from overseas; but it continued to respond above all to local cultural practices and local needs.

Cretans were now traveling east themselves. We can see this in the archives at the palace built around 1800 BCE at the ancient trading center of Mari on the Euphrates in modern Syria. These have yielded 20,000 cuneiform tablets from the first half of the eighteenth century alone, many of them lengthy, and detailed letters between the palace and its representatives elsewhere. One tablet reports a consignment of tin that Mari's king Zimri-Lim acquired from the highland Elamites across the Tigris and had transported west to Aleppo, Hazor, and the Mediterranean port of Ugarit. There his agents sold it on to other people, including a "Kaphtarian": someone from Crete. They also gave a significant cut to "the interpreter of the chief merchant of the Kaphtarians in Ugarit," phrasing that suggests an institutionalized Cretan presence in the harbor.[49] Other tablets record the arrival of gold and silver vessels, weapons, and a belt made in Cretan workshops, as well as a pair of leather shoes "in the Kaphtarian style."[50] The footwear was sent on by Zimri-Lim to King Hammurabi—more properly Hammurapi—of Babylon, who for unspecified reasons sent it back: as we shall see, he was capricious.

By the seventeenth century BCE Cretan artists and artisans were finding inspiration to the east. Abstract painting in the "palaces" yields to vivid imagery of humans, animals, plants, and gods in a style also found at Mari, and the first known versions of fresco painting, long thought to have been a Cretan invention, have now been found in a palace built around 1900 BCE at Tell el-Burak on the coast of modern Lebanon.[51] At this early stage only the preliminary drawings were added to the wet plaster, not the pigments themselves, so the result was less resilient. It was however a step on the way to the "true" fresco technique developed over the following centuries by artisans working at sites across the Levant and Aegean, using increasingly similar techniques and iconography, motifs, and colors.[52]

Tablets from Mari again reveal how this worked in practice. They describe circuits of skilled artists and artisans who worked for wealthy patrons across western Asia, moving from one kingdom to another, traveling by land and sea, river and canal.[53] Doctors and diviners were in the greatest demand, but we also hear of traveling scribes and barbers, smiths, masons, and stone dressers. Kings kept a close eye on their neighbors' projects, too, and tried to keep up: one official reports back to Mari on a palace at Karana on the Tigris to the east, while farther west the king of Ugarit asks to visit Zimri-Lim's own famous home.[54]

These working relationships brought Cretans closer to the Levant and the great kingdoms beyond, but they were still not blind mimics of what they heard and saw overseas. To take just one example, no matter how many Cretans traveled to west Asian cities full of sculptures covered in inscriptions, on Crete itself art and text remained entirely separate realms.[55] The cultural isolation implied by civilizational thinking doesn't work for these so-called Minoans, but models of cultural "diffusion" from one region to another can be equally misleading: like the concept of "influence," they get the action back to front. Overseas exchange meant that Cretans could now pick and choose from different cultural options, and they did.

At the same time, Cretans were still very much on the margins of bigger networks extending to their east, where written records document societies operating on a different scale. They also reveal an era of experimentation in economics, politics, and culture that saw the first signs of much of what is now seen as most distinctive of Western Civilization, and rooted in Greece and Rome: literature, science, entrepreneurship, the rule of law, and some level of popular government. Evans was looking for European civilization in the wrong place.

One place to look instead would be imperial Ur. Around 2100 BCE the city's king Ur-Nammu conquered southern Mesopotamia and western Iran. He also wrote the world's first surviving law code, building on a regional legal tradition of edicts and contracts that already went back a millennium.[56] The fifty-seven clauses of this partially preserved document establish monetary fines for most crimes, but prescribe capital punishment for murder or robbery or rape—unless the victim is an enslaved woman, in which case a fine of five shekels will suffice. The fruits of empire fueled a golden age of literature. Court poets sang Sumerian hymns to the gods and composed eulogies of their kings that emphasized their military victories, their sexual prowess, and, in one poem celebrating Ur-Nammu's son Shulgi, their neat handwriting.[57]

Another archive established in the twentieth century BCE at what is now Kültepe in central Anatolia gives us a vivid picture of private enterprise, venture capitalism, and popular government.[58] It contains the records and letters of merchants from the ancient city-state of Assur on the Tigris in northern Mesopotamia who had established a trading enclave they called Karum ("Port of") Kanesh a thousand kilometers north of their hometown.* This was the largest of around forty Assyrian trading colonies in Anatolia, and it operated as the Assyrian administrative center in the region. The tablets are written in a simplified version of the Assyrian script that the merchants introduced into a region where writing was previously unknown.

They tell us that commerce was in the hands of great families at rocky Assur, whose members established joint-stock companies to fund their individual enterprises alongside other complex credit arrangements. Kanesh was a six-week trek north in caravans of 200 or 300 black donkeys. They carried textiles made in Mesopotamian workshops and ferried to Assur by Babylonian merchants, tin brought by Elamites from sources farther east, and lighter luxuries tucked in between: lapis lazuli from Afghanistan, for instance, or saffron from the Indian Ocean. All this they sold at Kanesh along with the donkeys for gold and silver: tin cost almost twice as much in Anatolia as at Assur.

This archive tells us a lot about the internal workings of the colony, including its governing structure: decisions are always recorded as being taken by collectives, either the "big men"—some kind of council of elders or leading families—or the whole community itself, in assembly. Relatively egalitarian norms are not unusual when new settlements are set up by a small group of people with similar interests. These records also describe the political arrangements back at Assur itself, however, where alongside the limited powers of the king or "overseer," whose main responsibility was to the city's patron god, the city was run

*The material culture—the buildings and objects—found at Karum Kanesh is entirely Anatolian; if it wasn't for the Assyrian documents in the archive, we would not know that the inhabitants were not locals. It is in fact a standard feature of small independent foreign settlements that they take on the material culture of their new neighbors, for practical reasons if nothing else. In the United States the famous windmills, thatched roofs, and "Danish façades" of the town of Solvang founded by Danish-speaking immigrants near Santa Barbara in 1911 all postdate the Second World War.

by a council of elders and a broader voting assembly that operated as the ultimate political authority in the state.

Assur also selected a chief magistrate or *limum* by lottery from among the leading families, who served for a year. He was responsible for financial matters including taxes, fines, and long-distance trade, and he managed the "City Hall" at the heart of the city; no mention is made in this documentation of a royal palace.[59] Since the Assyrians also named the year after this official—like election by lot itself, a practice more usually associated with Classical Athens 1,500 years later—we know the names of more than a hundred of these men, at least half a millennium before we could name a single person living in Europe.[60]

Popular participation in politics wasn't new in western Asia, at least in theory.[61] The poets of Ur told epic tales of their kings' ancestors, the legendary rulers of Uruk, including stories of King Gilgamesh (known in Sumerian as Bilgamesh) that described assemblies and councils that the king had to consult on matters of state.[62] How far these related to practice at Ur itself is another question: as a contemporary proverb says, "The palace bows down, but only of its own accord."[63]

In the same era as the Karum Kanesh archive, however, the main trading city in Babylonia, Sippar, also concentrated political authority in an assembly. Meanwhile elders in towns dependent on Mari could oppose or replace their local kings, and Emar on the Euphrates had no kings at all.[64]

Even after Hammurapi, king of Babylon, rose up against his former friends and neighbors and conquered almost all the other city-states of Mesopotamia as well as the larger kingdoms on its outskirts including Ebla, Mari, and Elam, there is still documentary evidence for magistrates, city elders, and assemblies in his realm, as well as for towns themselves acting as a legal entity, spending funds, issuing leases, and taking loans.[65]

There is also a great deal of evidence for scholarship and culture. Hammurapi's Babylon—Bab-ili or "Gate of the Gods"—is lost under the water table, but we know that it was a center of scientific learning, with a particular focus on mathematical inquiry. Babylonian mathematicians already knew that the square of the hypotenuse of a right-angled triangle was equal to the sum of the squares of the shorter sides more than a millennium before the Greek mathematician Pythagoras was born.[66] Their counting structure was based on the number sixty, which is especially useful for calculating fractions because it has an unusually large number of factors: it can be divided by 2, 3, 4, 5, 6, 10, 12, 15, 20, and 30, as well as 60 itself. For that reason, it is still used to count the sixty seconds of the sixty minutes of our twenty-four-hour days, as well as the 360 degrees of a circle.

Hammurapi's court also saw the flourishing of literature in Akkadian, a Semitic language spoken in ancient Akkad and other northern Mesopotamian cities that was now becoming the international lingua franca of western Asia. Works from this era include not only a full-length epic poem about King Gilgamesh, but also the story of Atrahasis, "Extra Wise," the only human to survive a great flood, along with his family and animals, with the help of a friendly god. Written down around 1700 BCE, the story introduces us to a bickering set of senior gods who, after failing to palm off the difficult but necessary local work of canal digging on to a group of lesser gods, invent humans to do the work instead. Unfortunately they forget to invent natural death, so soon there are far too many humans, and they become very noisy. Attempts to mitigate the problem with plagues and famine fail, and the chief god Enlil decides to send a flood to get rid of these humans once and for all. The other gods are sworn to secrecy, but soft-hearted Enki tells his human friend Atrahasis what is going to happen, and how to escape on a boat with his family, birds, cattle, and wild animals. When this glitch in their scheme comes to light, the other gods grumble but content themselves with imposing mortality and miscarriage on Atrahasis and his descendants, and leaving to them the hard work of irrigation.

In Egypt meanwhile a "Middle Kingdom" based at Thebes on the Upper Nile (modern Luxor) brought prosperity and stability to the river for several hundred years after a difficult period in the late third millennium. Egyptian kings—not regularly called pharaohs for another thousand years—now extended their control south along the Nile beyond the traditional limit of the first cataract. They colonized parts of northern Kush as a base for more intensive trade with the city of Kerma, which controlled the fertile lands of the river basin, a vast cattle-raising operation in the plains of northern Sudan, and trade along the Middle Nile.[67]

A written literature emerged in Egypt too, later than in Mesopotamia, and rather different.[68] Egyptian stories are written sparingly, and in relatively simple language, but they contain complex and often uncomfortable reflections on social and economic relations, justice, and ethics. The power of the gods is assumed, but humans are the center of attention here, and these stories often take the part or perspective of the lower classes: the Tale of the Eloquent Peasant, for instance, relates the desperate attempts of a small trader from a desert oasis to get justice from the Egyptian state when he is robbed. Sympathy only went so far: the Dialogue of Ipuwur and the Lord of All imagines for its prosperous audience a terrifying dystopia where the poor have triumphed over the rich, and "no one at all sails north to Byblos today; what shall we do for cedarwood for our mummies, with whose products are priests buried, with whose oil are officials embalmed? From as far as Crete they do not come!"[69]

Byblos and Crete were the northern limits of this nineteenth-century Egyptian world. By then, however, the search for metals for use and trade had begun to drive sailors from Crete farther into the Aegean: finds of Cretan pottery and sealings (the impressions made by seals) as well as writing in both Linear A and Cretan Hieroglyphic reveal that as early as the nineteenth or eighteenth century Cretans had adopted the new sailing technology to make connections with northern Aegean islands like Samothrace, near mainland silver mines.[70]

By the seventeenth century BCE Cretan ships were reaching the Greek mainland, where these now urban, literate and bureaucratic sailors encountered another society changing fast. One town in particular provided a new link to another network farther north that has now been almost forgotten.

CHAPTER THREE

The Amber Routes

MYCENAE, C. 1650 BCE

The small craggy settlement of Mycenae perches on a low hill in the northeastern Peloponnese, about ninety kilometers southwest of Athens. A natural fortress furred with green between two higher peaks, it looks southwest across a flat river valley to gray-green mountains ten kilometers away. To the left are the low white buildings of Argos, a smaller settlement down in the plain, and just beyond that the glint of the Aegean Sea fifteen kilometers south.

For a long time Mycenae was just one of many new villages that came together near water and farmland in the hills and valleys of southern Greece in the early second millennium BCE.[1] The technology to make bronze with tin had reached the mainland through the Cycladic circuit in the third millennium, as had the donkey and the wheel, but even in the late seventeenth century BCE, when Crete was already covered in towns and palaces, Mycenae had no walls and no monumental buildings. Its wealth was hidden underground.

It was a German businessman who found it. Heinrich Schliemann had taken early retirement by 1868 and set out at the age of forty-six to follow his dreams, which were about the Trojan War. Most scholars at the time believed that the great conflict between the kings of Greece and Anato-

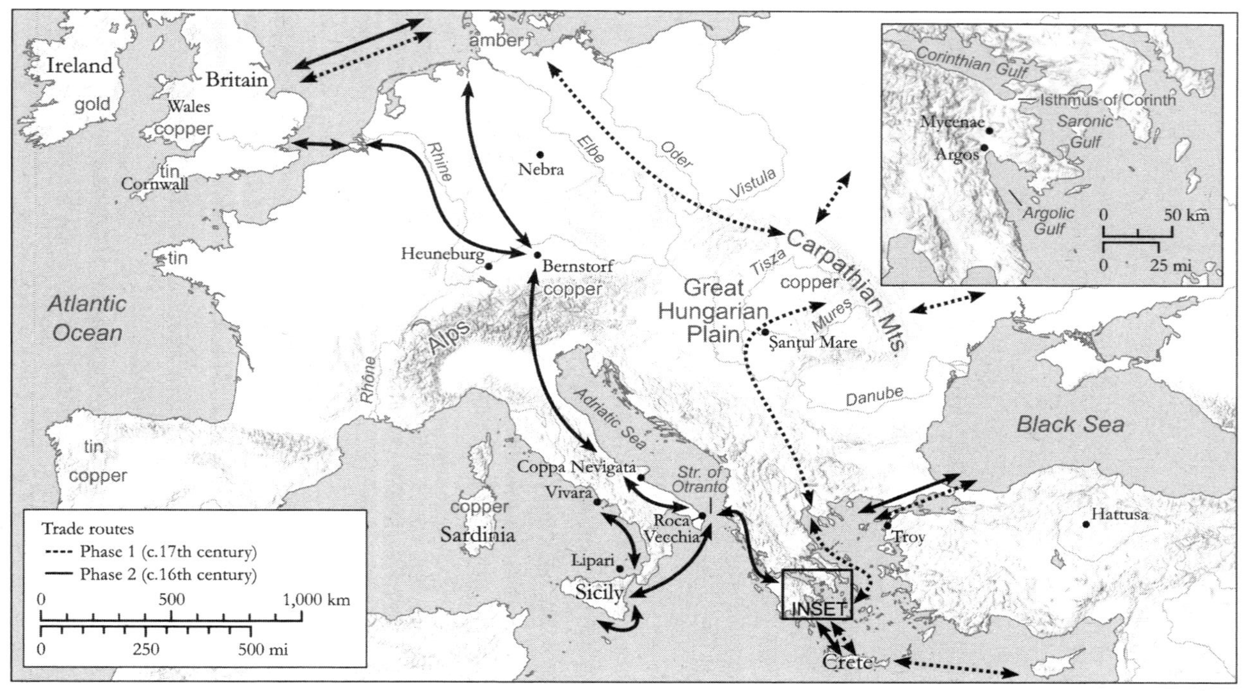

European trade routes in the early second millennium BCE

lian Troy, immortalized in Homer's *Iliad* and *Odyssey,* was the product of poetic imagination. Schliemann wanted to prove them wrong.[2]

He started by identifying the ancient site of Troy itself. He even got permission to dig there in 1871, a year after he had in fact begun excavations. But after an awkward run-in with the local authorities over a cache of ancient treasures that he had removed from the site without remembering to mention them, he turned his attention to Mycenae, whose legendary king Agamemnon led the united Greek forces. Here the issue was not identifying the site: Mycenae's standing remains and in particular its Lion Gate were famous.* Instead, the question was what, if anything, it really had to do with the Trojan War.

One clue came from a guidebook to Greece produced by the Roman travel writer Pausanias in the second century CE, which described a set of five graves inside the city walls as the resting places of Agamemnon and the city's other ancient war heroes.[3] By the time Schliemann arrived these tombs had long disappeared, but he found them in characteristic fashion by sinking test pits across the whole of the site without permission. When he was allowed to begin formal excavations in 1876, he also found that despite their ancient renown they had not been robbed.[4] When he himself opened them up, he struck gold.

These "shaft graves" were large stone-lined trenches cut into the ground and furnished with wooden slats to allow multiple layered burials: functional rather than imposing. They contained the corpses of grand personages all the same, men and women of unusually large size and good health by the standards of their own era.[5] They sported heavy gold death masks and shrouds with gold trimmings, and they were buried with astonishing quantities of precious metals, jewelry, armor, and weapons.[6]

How does a hamlet become a treasure house? The site of Mycenae

*In 1802 Lord Elgin had visited the site with his family, admired the large Bronze Age tomb outside the walls now known as the "Treasury of Atreus" and had his agent ship him several of its large marble slabs in London. Unfortunately for the avaricious earl, the Lion Gate itself was judged too large and too far from the sea to meet the same fate (Dudley J. Moore, Edward Rowlands, and Nektarios Karadimas, *In Search of Agamemnon: Early Travelers to Mycenae,* Newcastle upon Tyne: Cambridge Scholars Publishing, 2014, 55).

seems of little interest in its own right—it's a nice enough spot, and there's a convenient spring, but it doesn't have local mines or other natural resources. What it does have is location, up an easily defended hill just off the main track that winds across the Argolid Plain. White against the green of the valley, the track leads from the Argolic Gulf where ships arrived from the southern islands past Mycenae and on up and over the mountains to the narrow Isthmus of Corinth. There a traveler could turn right toward the Saronic Gulf, for the northern Aegean and Black Sea, or left to the Corinthian Gulf for the Adriatic and points west. This trail had become a trade route; the people of Mycenae could exploit or perhaps even control traffic along it, and it brought them riches from all points of the compass.

From Crete the lords and ladies of the shaft graves acquired silver cups, gold signet rings, stone vases, and ostrich-egg drinking vessels made from raw materials obtained farther afield, and lapis lazuli from as far away as Afghanistan. They were also buried with plenty of locally made pottery and metal vessels based on Cretan models and made with Cretan technologies, as well as Cretan-inspired daggers and swords.[7] There are whetstones too: these weapons weren't just for show.

So far this looks like just another stage in the extension west of the commercial and cultural network that had long linked the valley kingdoms of Egypt and Mesopotamia and now included Crete as well. But there is also bridle gear from the Carpathian Mountains and the European Steppe, and a great deal of gold, which was almost nonexistent in the southern and central Aegean.[8] Gold is always special: its brilliant sheen, rarity, and lack of reactivity are reliably fascinating—it doesn't tarnish or corrode—while it is also unusually easy to work. It just needs hammering, not heating, and a small amount beaten into gold leaf can cover a huge surface. Most remarkable of all, however, the graves contain Baltic amber, a fossilized orange tree resin that shines, feels warm to the touch, floats on water, burns with a perfume, and produces static when rubbed with a cloth.[9] Even today it feels strangely alive; thousands of years ago it must have seemed supernatural.*

*Its Greek name *elektron* is the root of the modern word electricity.

The problem for Schliemann was that style and technique placed many of these "grave goods" far earlier than the traditional date of the Trojan War, fixed by ancient scholarship in the early twelfth century BCE. In the seventeenth century BCE, it now became clear, this small and unprepossessing community already had a wealthy and well-connected ruling class.

What he had found was not the remains of a great conflict between Europe and Asia, East and West, but evidence for a new connection between the network we have already encountered at Byblos and on Crete and another set of sophisticated and prosperous new communities that had emerged in the early second millennium BCE, on the back of another great east–west axis of commerce and culture. It will take our story of exchange and change to new places, places often forgotten by the civilizational thinking that overvalues familiar-looking societies and underestimates less recognizable ones.

Some 1,250 kilometers north of Crete are the gray-green peaks of the Carpathian Mountains. Full of wolves and bears, they form a ring around the Great Hungarian Plain to create an island of their own with the Danube cutting through it.[10] Land that lies between them in modern Romania, Hungary, Slovakia, and Ukraine offered good living: fertile fields in the river valley, timber, salt, and copious sources of copper in the mountains. There were even tin ores on the Transylvanian Plateau in the east of this region, where miners also harvested gold with antler picks from open-cast mines.[11] Small villages filled this landscape in the third millennium, ancient metalworking communities that are never dignified with the label of "civilization" by modern scholars, but had a lot in common with contemporary Crete.

As on Crete an intense phase of economic expansion began around 2000 BCE, with the opening of new copper mines and a huge increase in bronze production. The trees fell, the sound and fury of smelting and casting filled the plains, and people began to build substantial settlements fortified with ditches, especially along rivers. There was so much metal that there was no point trying to control mining itself, but you could control traffic, especially where it met a choke point or a convenient overlook.[12]

And as on Crete, these internal developments were buttressed by goods, techniques, and ideas that arrived from the east. The crucial relationship in this case was with the societies of the Eurasian Steppe, still a corridor of very-long-distance exchange: wheat developed in the Fertile Crescent reached China in the second millennium, while millet domesticated in the Chinese Yellow River region arrived in Europe.[13]

The people of the Steppe had continued to develop new technologies as well. This was one of the few regions where large equines survived the Ice Age, and a recent study of 273 ancient horse genomes suggests that the ancestors of the modern horse were first domesticated in the third millennium in the western Steppe, between the Volga and the Don. They then spread fast throughout Eurasia from around 2000 BCE.[14]

Horses weren't used primarily for transportation: they can only carry about 20 percent of their body weight—perhaps around one hundred kilos—and they aren't strong enough to haul a heavy cart. Furthermore, although they are fast on level ground, they struggle in hilly territory without good trails. Their main purpose, it seems, was to look good—especially when pulling a chariot, another new technology developed on the Steppe. These chariots—in the earliest examples just platforms with front and side rails carried on two large spoked wheels—first appear around 2000 BCE east of the Ural Mountains.[15] Unlike the old oxcarts and battle wagons with their solid wooden wheels, the new conveyances were fast and light, and could be drawn by just two horses. They were more use in battle or on parade than for cargo.

By around 1800 BCE men in search of copper and gold were bringing both horses and chariots west to Transylvania and the Great Hungarian Plain, in effect the final flourish of the Steppe itself west of the Carpathian mountains. They brought new equine accessories with them, including distinctive bone bridle parts with circular disks for cheek pieces. It seems likely that they brought new ideas as well, turning on individual glory, military might, and conspicuous consumption: horses and chariots were not cheap.[16]

Such notions would have taken easily in the Carpathian Basin, already so similar to the Steppe proper with its huge plain, fortified villages, and metal workshops. As on the Steppe, powerful local leaders began to be buried with heavily decorated bronze armor and weapons, horses, and chariots.[17] Stock-breeding centers appear in the region too, identifiable by the age/sex ratio of the remains of horses found there.[18] Local artisans became expert bone workers themselves, covering harness pieces and whip handles with distinctive circles and spirals drawn with a compass, designs that then became popular back on the Steppe.[19]

And again like Cretans around the same time, these communities bolstered their new prosperity by extending their own networks, in this case through the European river systems. Around 1700 BCE Carpathian copper appears in modern Denmark, along with new Steppe technologies for working bronze: spearheads with built-in sockets, for instance, cast using the lost-wax method usually associated with Classical Greek art, meant that the wooden handles no longer needed to be tied on with rope.[20]

The far north of Europe in this era was a world of herding, fishing, and farming communities that lived in relative isolation even from the rest of the continent; agriculture itself had only reached what are now Norway and Finland around 2500 BCE.[21] No doubt the boats that now paddled north carried more than copper: salt, millet, sheep, cattle, horses, textiles, and opium poppies would also have been welcome.[22] Much of the quotidian return cargo has disappeared as well—flints, furs, skins?—but the amber from Jutland and the Baltic preserved in Carpathian graves was a way to touch another world.

Looking south, Carpathian goods of the kind found in the shaft graves probably first reached Mycenae via the Black Sea and ports like Troy, where European gold appears in the eighteenth century BCE. Once the link was established, however, a more direct route from the Carpathians to mainland Greece led down the rivers of the Balkans to the Thermaic Gulf.[23] A new trading connection like this can't have been based on amber and horse gear alone and the latter would have been no use without the horses and chariots themselves. Transylvanian mines meanwhile must have provided the fifteen kilos of raw gold that local craftsmen worked into the jewelry, drinking vessels, and masks found in the Mycenaean tombs.[24]

It's harder to work out what traveled in the other direction: textiles perhaps, or even slaves. It wasn't Aegean silver: isotope analysis now shows that there is far more silver from the Carpathians in the shaft graves than there is from Lavrion just across the Saronic Gulf from Mycenae itself.[25] The northerners were however in the market for weapons, and Cretan-style swords with bronze blades attached to hilts of wood, bone, or ivory are found in the seventeenth century BCE both in shaft graves at Mycenae and in Carpathian burials.

Relatively weak in themselves, these swords inspired further experimentation in the Carpathian Basin that produced more effective full-metal weapons, able to slash as well as thrust without falling apart.[26] Curiously, the new Carpathian sword design included fake rivets, imitating the older wooden-hilted swords from the Aegean: although the locally made swords were better weapons, they were less prestigious than foreign imports. In the ancient Carpathians as in the Aegean, connectedness counted for a lot. Swords of this kind then traveled on through the northern network as far as Denmark, replacing the daggers, battle-axes, and halberds that had long been the weapons of choice across northern Europe.[27]

In the first centuries of the second millennium BCE, then, the sun-pierced palaces of Crete and the chariot-riding chiefs of the Carpathians were both building long-distance networks linking lands to east and west. New paths snaked slowly across new landscapes to feed universal desires for metals, masculinity, and magic, and at little towns like Mycenae they started to cross.

We don't know exactly how it happened, but trade with new partners often begins on the initiative not of an established power, fixed in its ways and owing to its size and complexity dependent on reliable and trusted relationships, but of people on the edges of such powers, who have less to lose and more to gain from seeking out new opportunities.[28] Some of those buried in the shaft graves could have been community elders in receipt of gifts from visitors seeking information, trading privileges or other forms of alliance. Others were probably traders themselves.

However that may be, they made cultural as well as commercial connections with their closest contacts in both directions. Some of the men wear the same outfits we see in Cretan paintings, down to their necklaces and armlets.[29] Some of the grave markers meanwhile depict horse-drawn chariots: the skill required to drive them, let alone fight from them, provided an ideal form of competition between wealthy men in societies without much formal, stable hierarchy who sought to promote their own prowess against their peers. The shaft graves however are still group burials: the tombs of individual leaders are not elevated above everybody else as in the Carpathians. And on Crete in this era there is little evidence for burial at all. Exchange does not prompt mindless imitation.

The people of Mycenae weren't the only ones making new connections north and south in this era. More elaborate tombs now begin to appear outside settlements across the Greek mainland, and an increasing number of people are buried with Cretan weapons and ornaments, Baltic amber, and, in the case of a very wealthy few, decorated Carpathian bridle gear.[30]

At the same time other Aegean traders start to explore new routes to European resources that lead them farther west. Sailing moves slowly across new seas, as new routes, winds, and currents require new tactics and new skills. All the same, by around 1600 BCE sailors were arriving in Italian ports carrying wheel-made and painted pottery from mainland Greece and the Aegean.[31]

The journey would have taken them about three weeks. Traveling across the Isthmus of Corinth, through the Corinthian Gulf and then north up the coast, they would have headed across the Ionian Sea at its narrowest point, the difficult Strait of Otranto, before tracing their way along the sole of Italy's boot, passing an unfamiliar landscape of small hill forts, farms, and fishing villages. Then the path forked: they could either continue to the south coast of Sicily or, more often, thread their way up through the Strait of Messina on their way to Lipari in the Aeolian Islands and Vivara in the Bay of Naples.[32]

The original attraction may have been the raw materials available on the Italian islands themselves such as alum, which was used for tanning and dyeing, and volcanic sulfur (once known as brimstone), which served as medicine, fumigator, and bleach.[33] But these island ports also seem to have controlled access to the metals of the nearby mainland, and harbors around the peninsula now offered a useful shortcut to sources of metal farther north.

Long-established routes led from Italy over the Alps, where new copper mines opened in this era. As in the Carpathians a few hundred years before, mining brought new prosperity and opportunities to regions at the foot of the mountains which controlled traffic in the precious metal, and large towns like the Heuneburg and Bernstorf grew up in what is now southern Germany alongside ostentatious burials under tumulus mounds for local leaders.

Like the Carpathian settlements, these Alpine communities were not civilized by Victorian standards: there is no surviving sign of bureaucracy, literacy, or monumental architecture. They nonetheless formed a powerful new metal-trading hub with commercial relationships reaching along rivers not only as far as Scandinavia, but even to Britain and Ireland, where miners had built one of the oldest bronze-working traditions in Europe on generous local supplies of copper and tin.[34]

The Carpathian communities meanwhile went into decline. The major centers on the plain disappeared and the long-distance riverine routes were abandoned. People retreated to fortified sites off the beaten track.[35] Deforestation to fuel the metal furnaces was partly to blame. But they were outcompeted too by the new mines to the west.

All this explains why most of the amber found at Mycenae and elsewhere in mainland Greece from the sixteenth century BCE onward came through a new and more westerly route from Scandinavia across Europe via Britain, the Alps, and Italian ports, a path that has left traces in distinctive beads of Baltic amber found in the Mycenaean shaft graves.

These particular beads were produced not in Scandinavia but in Britain, where specialist workshops carved the raw material and strung it with beads of local black jet into chunky crescent-shaped necklaces that are found in the richest British tombs.[36] Their components are easy to recognize: British artisans kept the multiple strings of the necklace separate with distinctive rectangular spacer plates, large flat beads with holes bored through from side to side to keep the strings of the necklaces apart. These worked beads did not return to Scandinavia itself and they never reached the Carpathians: the only certain examples are found in Britain, in the new mining settlements of southern Germany, and in the Greek Peloponnese.[37]

What traveled with them to Mycenae, to make the journey worth it? Copper from the Alps is one obvious possibility, but tin might have come from as far away as Britain, where Cornwall boasted the most important tin mines west of Asia in the Bronze Age. We know that the river systems of western Europe were regularly used in later periods for transporting metals despite the inconvenience of carrying them across the European watershed. Long-distance transfers weren't necessarily a problem either: isotope analysis suggests that a small amount of Cypriot copper was already reaching Sweden in the sixteenth century BCE.[38]

Aegean metalworkers had reason to seek new sources of tin in this era, as the traditional trade routes from central Asia were threatened by trouble in the river valley kingdoms. Around 1700 BCE a group based at the fortified hilltop site of Hattusa had managed to unite much of central Anatolia. They called themselves people of Hatti and their language Neshite; we know both as "Hittite." Over the following century powerful kings extended their realm south to Aleppo before conquering Babylon itself. This seems to have brought about a power vacuum in both regions for another century, leading to a dramatic decline in urbanism, production, and regional exchange. Administration collapsed across a large part of Mesopotamia, and even writing all but disappeared.[39]

In the mid-seventeenth century BCE, furthermore, Egypt had undergone one of its periodic revolts against unified rule. With the end of the Middle Kingdom, different dynasties established themselves along the river. Kings based at Thebes ruled the south, and the mysterious Hyksos (*heqa khaust*, "rulers from foreign lands," perhaps the Levant) controlled Lower Egypt from the Delta port of Avaris.

Whether or not tin really traveled with amber all the way from Britain to Mycenae, it must have been very rare for people to make the whole journey. It would have taken several months by foot, river, and sea. And even as commerce came to connect the edges of Europe, there is no evidence for meaningful cultural communication across such distances, any more than there is with the central Asian sources of the lapis lazuli that was also buried in the shaft graves.

The way the amber beads were buried is a case in point. Amber left Britain in the form of necklaces, but these did not reach Greek tombs intact. Instead, the beads are found in different combinations, sometimes with beads of other materials, and often in positions that suggest they were recycled for sword belts. Glowing with vague impressions of faraway places cold, rich, and strange, amber could act in the Aegean as a talisman against the enemy in a way quite alien to its connotations in Britain of pure luxury or its everyday familiarity in Scandinavia itself.[40]

Amber is still found only in the richest Mycenaean graves, nestling against other foreign imports from far to the north, south, and east. Its faraway origins and mystery were what made it most valuable, advertising and emphasizing these local families' connections with distant realms along routes lit up by magic stones from the end of the world.[41]

This investment in connectivity was not a message that reached the nineteenth century CE. In the decades after his discoveries at Mycenae Schliemann and other archaeologists identified many other Bronze Age sites on the Greek mainland and neighboring islands. Like Arthur Evans a few years later they concluded in the spirit of the times that they were revealing not just culture but *a* culture, and they called this one "Mycenaean," after its first excavated and most famous site.

In 1893 the Greek archaeologist Christos Tsountas, who had taken over the excavations at Mycenae, described it as "a distinct and homogeneous civilization" that "has left its landmarks . . . from one end of Greece to the other, as well as on the islands and coasts of the Aegean."[42] To the extent that it had models they were to be found among Germans, Celts, and Italians in Europe, rather than farther east, as some other scholars had proposed. And it is no coincidence that Tsountas' Mycenaean "civilization" itself mapped closely onto the modern nation-state of Greece, then just sixty years old, along with Crete and the Greek-speaking regions of western Anatolia, to which Greek nationalist politicians had laid claim throughout the nineteenth century.[43]

A wider implication of this approach was drawn out by J. Irving Manatt, professor of Greek literature and history at Brown University, in an augmented English translation of Tsountas' book published in 1897. In a passage missing from the Greek original he declares: "The Mycenaean world was of the West, not so much geographically as in its whole spiritual attitude. It was forward looking and forthputting. It had in it the promise and potency of what Europe and America have now wrought out in the complex of modern civilization."[44]

With both Minoans and Mycenaeans now at large, the stage was set for a clash of civilizations quite at odds with the increasing connectivity we have seen in the ancient evidence.

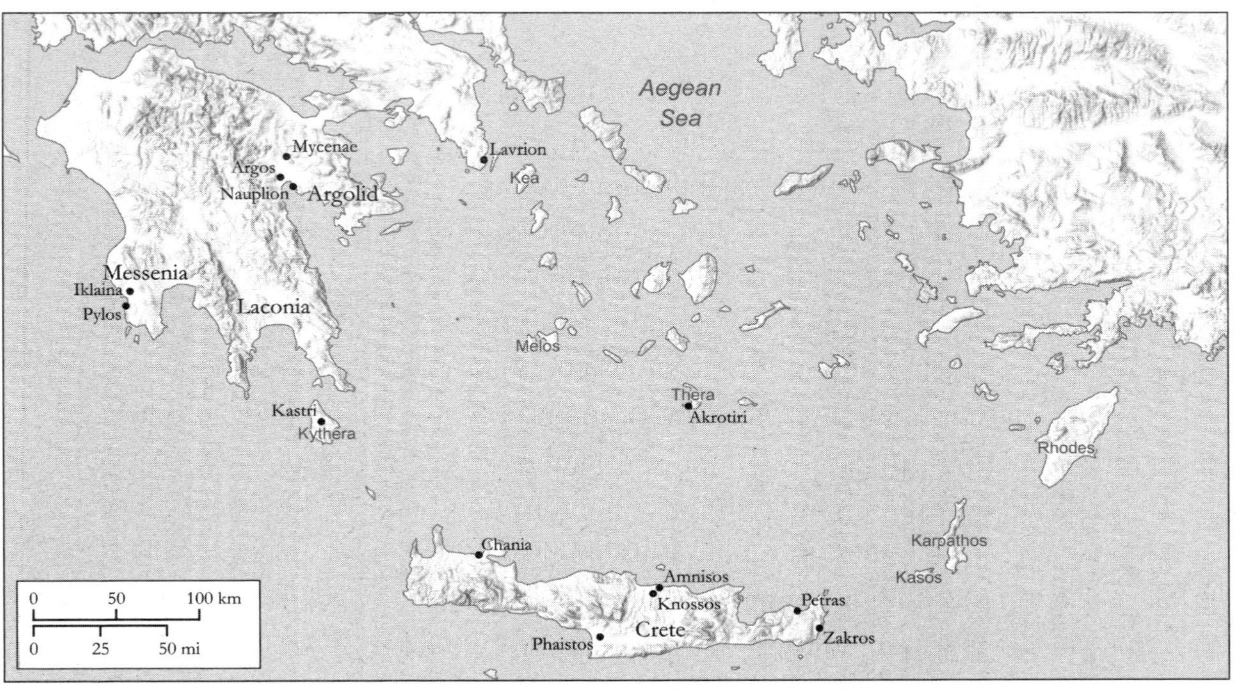

The Aegean in the sixteenth century BCE

CHAPTER FOUR

The Erupting Sea

AKROTIRI, C. 1560 BCE

In the little harbor town of Akrotiri on the south coast of Thera (modern Santorini) a handsome townhouse still stands two stories high more than 3,500 years after it was built. Storage occupies the ground level, and the floor above is the main living space. At the front of the house a large window illuminates a room that archaeologists found filled with loom weights: this must have been where the women spent time together weaving, perhaps the source of the family's wealth.[1] Behind this room is a pantry; beside it, a small painted bathroom contains the remains of a tub as well as a prehistoric toilet connected via a drain and odor trap to the public sewer running beneath the paving of the main street. On a clear day there would have been views from the roof terrace all the way over to Crete, one hundred kilometers to the south.

On this particular summer day, however, the family living in what archaeologists now call the West House would have been looking north, toward the center of their island, where fumes had been rising for days.[2] Now the tremors underground were getting stronger as well, a reminder of an earthquake that had recently devastated Akrotiri, causing damage that the town's inhabitants had been doing their best to clear and repair.

It was time to pack up and get out. Neighbors were already jostling through the little triangular piazza in front of the house. Carrying their possessions in bags and sacks, they were heading down the narrow street to the port. On the quay captains filled their boats as fast as they could, as desperate to get away as their frightened passengers. The volcano belched out pumice like hard hot rain.

When Thera finally exploded, the column of ash reached a height of around forty kilometers. The eruption was several times bigger than Krakatoa in 1883, and perhaps a hundred times bigger than Mount Saint Helens in 1980. It could have been heard thousands of kilometers away.[3]

On Thera itself hot magma reacted with sea water to create surges of volcanic debris across the entire island, and its rim was blown apart and left floating in pieces. Tsunami waves raced across the Aegean, destroying any shipping in their path.[4] A cloud of pumice and ash spread over 200,000 square kilometers to the east, dumping deposits a meter high on Rhodes, and leaving traces from the Black Sea to the Nile Delta.[5]

The event was probably recorded on a stele at the Temple of Karnak at Thebes by the Egyptian king Ahmose, who had recently defeated a number of rivals to reunite the Nile in a "New Kingdom." The displeasure of the gods, he said, had brought a huge storm on the land, a tempest of rain and darkness, flooding both Upper and Lower Egypt for days, and causing the collapse of temples and even pyramids.[6]

Fragments of Thera's prehistoric past came to light again in the 1860s, when the island's volcanic ash was mined to make concrete for the construction of the Suez Canal. It was only in the 1960s however that Spyridon Marinatos, director of the Greek Archaeological Service under the country's military junta, began formal excavations at Akrotiri. As the ancient settlement re-emerged, it looked as if it had been abandoned just a few hours before. Across the site elegant houses built of plastered mud bricks were still decorated with fragments of beautiful frescoes. The fleeing population had left their daily lives behind, down to their crockery—but there was no jewelry, no metal, and no skeletons. The people got away.

. . .

The eruption of Thera has long fascinated scholars. Could it have inspired the story of Atlantis, the land that sank below the waves—despite the fact that Plato's imaginary utopia was situated in the Atlantic Ocean? Might it explain the tale told in the biblical Book of Exodus about a plague of darkness over Egypt, or even the parting of the Red Sea?[7] A third theory first suggested in 1939 by Spyridon Marinatos himself has remained popular ever since: that the volcano on Thera brought about the "destruction of Minoan Crete." Marinatos proposed that the eruption caused a series of fires that destroyed most of the Cretan palaces in the mid-fifteenth century BCE, dealing an "irreparable blow" to Minoan culture and leaving the island ripe for conquest or colonization by a bellicose rival, the "Mycenaeans" of mainland Greece. This caused "a considerable change in the hitherto peaceful character of the Cretan people" as graves filled with weapons became the norm on the island. In return, he suggested, the Mycenaeans found "music and poetry" on Crete, as well as the rudiments of law.[8]

His theory was wrong. For one thing, the timing was off. Scholars originally dated the eruption on Thera to the fifteenth century BCE by comparing the styles of pottery caught up in it with similar examples in supposedly better-dated contexts elsewhere. Dating by pottery style is however notoriously imprecise, and more recently scientists have clarified the situation by carbon-dating seeds and olive branches caught up in the eruption, a process that calculates the decomposition of radiocarbon, also known as carbon-14 because it has fourteen nucleons.

Most of the carbon in our bodies and all other living organisms is carbon-12, but carbon-14 is constantly produced by cosmic radiation interacting with nitrogen in the earth's atmosphere. It enters the food cycle through photosynthesis and then takes up residence in organic matter, from trees to human bones. As long as the host is alive, this radiocarbon is continually replenished, and the ratio of carbon-14 to carbon-12 is more or less the same in all living things. When they die, however, new supplies of radiocarbon cease to be absorbed, and the existing stock begins to decay at a predictable rate: after around 5,750 years you'd expect half of it to have disappeared. Normal carbon by contrast does not decay, so measuring the ratio of carbon-14 to carbon-12 left in an organic sample should tell you when something died.

The problem is that the level of cosmic radiation is not constant. Many factors affect it, from the hemisphere in which the material is found to the open-air nuclear tests of the 1950s and 1960s. Samples are therefore calibrated against the results of carbon-testing wood that can itself be dated by tree rings that mark each passing year with a wide, pale band of growth in the spring and early summer and a darker rim laid down in the late summer and autumn. In the last few years it has been possible to calculate the appropriate calibration curves for different regions ever more precisely, down to an annual basis, and the most recent work suggests that the Theran eruption happened sometime between 1600 and 1520 BCE—still compatible, just about, with a dating from pottery style, but at least two or three generations before the fifteenth-century fires on Crete.[9]

Another difficulty with Marinatos' hypothesis is that the volcano did not have devastating effects beyond Thera itself. It may well have caused environmental damage on Crete—poisoned water supplies, perhaps, or a ruined harvest—but decades of investigation have concluded that the deposits of tephra found across eastern Crete were around ten centimeters at most, too shallow to have caused long-term damage to health or agriculture. The only real evidence for tsunami flooding caused by the eruption comes from a single site in the far east of the island.[10] In fact, Crete continued to flourish in the decades that followed: new "palaces" were built at Phaistos and at Zakros on the east coast, and by 1500 the population of Knossos was 25,000–30,000.[11]

More important, Marinatos' theory was based on a false contrast between two "civilizations" invented more than 3,000 years after they are supposed to have existed: artistic Minoans who lived on the profits of trade with no need for defenses, and philistine Mycenaeans who filled their graves with weapons, and their minds with war.[12] Not only are both these "civilizations" modern inventions, but the idea that the Mycenaeans and Minoans were *separate* civilizations is less than a century old.

They were initially just rival names for the same Bronze Age Aegean culture seen from different perspectives. For Schliemann and his colleagues excavating mainland sites in the late nineteenth century, the even earlier sites that were starting to reappear on Crete were logically "Proto-Mycenaean."[13] Arthur Evans' spectacular finds at Knossos turned the tables, at least in his own mind, and he advocated instead the use of the term "Late Minoan" for the mainland remains: "in spite of slight local divergences in the domestic arrangements or costume, the 'Mycenaean' is only a provincial variant of the same 'Minoan' civilization."[14]

It was only after the First World War that a new generation of archaeologists began to champion the distinctiveness of Greek mainland culture, attributing the special character of these Mycenaeans to the arrival of a more warlike "race" or "stock" in mainland Greece around 2000 BCE that then largely replaced a population related to the Cretans.[15]

One enthusiast for this theory was the American archaeologist Carl Blegen, who directed excavations at Troy and Pylos, and dexterously combined his job as professor of archaeology at the University of Cincinnati with domestic life in an Athens townhouse with his wife, her lover, and her lover's husband. In 1940 Blegen praised the "Minoan Civilization" for its "delicacy of feeling, freedom of imagination, sobriety of judgment, and love of beauty," as opposed to the "Aryan lineage" of the Mycenaeans, that provided "the antecedents of that physical and mental vigor, directness of view, and that epic spirit of adventure in games, in the chase, and in war, which so deeply permeate Hellenic life." Together with the remnants of an earlier Stone Age population of the region, they produced the "Greek people" who constituted "an early stage in the evolution of the culture from which our western civilization is directly descended."[16]

The burgeoning field of ancient genetics gives the lie to Blegen's racial fantasies. Until recently ancient DNA was useless: too degraded, too hard to recover, and too expensive to "sequence" or process into information that scientists could analyze. Meanwhile, extrapolations backward from modern genetic profiles often produced dubious results. But now a combination of better extraction techniques—DNA survives especially well in the dense structure of the petrous bone in the inner ear—and faster, cheaper technology is opening up a new world of information about the movement of people in the past taken directly from their own remains. Sample sizes from the ancient Aegean are small but growing, and the results are consistent. In 2022 the largest study so far reported that Bronze Age Crete, the Aegean islands, and mainland Greece "were inhabited by genetically similar populations that traced most of their ancestry to the Neolithic [Stone Age] inhabitants of the region."[17]

At the same time, archaeology has debunked the distinction between militaristic Mycenaeans and pacific Minoans.[18] The fact that community leaders at Mycenae were buried with weapons in the seventeenth century BCE and Cretans were not is hard to compare with the evidence from Crete, where burial of any kind was, as we have seen, uncommon. Cretan sites are still full of weapons, and Cretan art depicts duels, military processions, and hunting scenes, while the imagery of battle on the weapons and seals found in the shaft graves at Mycenae comes from Crete itself. And while Knossos was indeed unfortified, so was Mycenae in the same period. There were no separate trading blocs either: copious imports from both Crete and the Greek mainland were found in the ruins of Akrotiri.[19]

This illustrates one of the central problems with civilizational thinking: it obscures the real-life connections between the "cultures" it identifies. It also obscures differences within them, differences that can be especially striking in the Aegean, where mountains divide the landscape of the mainland and islands into many small and separate natural regions.

We have no idea what people living on Crete, the Greek mainland, or any of the islands in between called themselves, nor if they had any sense of shared identity above their own towns and villages. Despite the best efforts of Victorian-era intellectuals, however, used to thinking in terms of "civilizations" and keen to set them against each other, in archaeological terms the "Minoans" and "Mycenaeans" did not constitute two distinct, homogeneous, and stable cultural blocs. Nor did they all participate in a single Aegean civilization. Instead, the populations of tiny cities and petty kingdoms across the Aegean traded, competed, and exchanged ideas with one another, and with others as well.

. . .

If we return to the West House at Akrotiri, we get a glimpse through the eyes of these Aegean islanders, looking out across the waters that surround them.

Behind the bathroom, at the back of the first floor, was a remarkable square corner room facing northwest. It was paved with slabs of volcanic stone and flooded with light from continuous windows on both exterior walls; at the end of the day sunset would have filled the space with warmth. And above the windows and doors ran a colorful frieze, just forty centimeters high in its tallest sections and preserved only in fragments from three sides.[20]

The section that ran along the top of the south wall is a crowded seascape, depicting seven ships accompanied by leaping dolphins making their way from one town to another, larger one, where men are running from a lookout post to alert the inhabitants to their arrival. There is no sense of alarm: perhaps the little fleet is returning home from a successful trading mission or military campaign, or maybe we are just looking at a local festival. The whole scene has a Cretan flavor: the design of the townhouses, one with horns of consecration, recalls the architecture of Knossos as well as that of Akrotiri itself, and many of the townsmen seem to be wearing the loincloths seen in Cretan paintings.

The scanty remains of a series of vignettes on the north wall opposite complicate the picture. There is a council or embassy, in which some participants again wear loincloths. There is also a scene of men leaving a city sporting boar's-tusk helmets, which are more characteristic of mainland arms and armor.[21] And there is a sea battle or shipwreck which bears a distinct resemblance to one depicted on a silver drinking horn found in one of the shaft graves at Mycenae—itself however a product of Cretan art.[22]

Along the east wall a larger maritime world intrudes, in the form of a snaking half-height riverscape lined with palm trees and papyrus plants, through which a griffin and a handsome blue spotted wildcat are chasing an unconcerned duck. This is a generic, fantastical "Nilotic" landscape of a kind popular across the eastern Mediterranean in this era, including at Mycenae, where a dagger buried in another shaft grave depicts a feline attacking a duck amid papyrus plants.[23]

The people of Akrotiri did not see their neighbors in terms of separate civilizations based on separate landmasses, and neither should we. The notion of a civilization cuts people off from those around them, and that is the opposite of what was happening in this corner of the Mediterranean in the sixteenth century BCE, as the island-filled waters of the Aegean linked its ports ever closer to one another as well as linking them to other places and people farther afield. Just as at Byblos, at Knossos, and then at Mycenae, the people of Akrotiri looked out on a wide world and made it their own.

The Theran volcano may not have destroyed a Minoan civilization to the benefit of a separate Mycenaean one, but it did change the shape of economic and cultural relationships within the Aegean, and it offered new opportunities to mainland communities.[24]

To understand how this happened, we need to consider the "sailing day."[25] Within a day's sail, direct trading and other relationships are straightforward; more than that and they become more complicated, and often less cost-effective. Even a modern boat traveling downwind under sail would be lucky to make 175 kilometers a day; Byblos ships probably averaged about 110 kilometers—the distance as it happens from Akrotiri to Knossos' port of Poros (modern Heraklion).

As a relatively isolated island, Crete's sailing-day options were always limited, and Thera was a crucial hub to the north between the island and the rest of the Cyclades, where ships could sail more easily up a "western string" of islands including Melos and Kea toward the silver mines beyond. Once Thera was out of the picture, and that fast link north with it, Cretan dealings with Aegean ports would have become more time-consuming and expensive.

This new gap between Crete and the Cyclades was a gift for Mycenae and its neighbors, as reduced access to Cretan wares created greater demand in the Aegean for mainland pottery, and even for imitation Cretan pottery made on the mainland.[26] This was not however a zero-sum game, and the following centuries also saw a new level of overseas contact on Crete, where the focus of trade and contact shifted instead to other harbors around the island and to other overseas ports.[27]

To the east the small islands of Karpathos and Kasos continued to provide convenient stops on the route toward Rhodes, Anatolia, Cyprus, and the Levant, and increasing traffic was encouraged by a revival in state power in Egypt and western Asia.[28] Over the course of the sixteenth century, Egypt's New Kingdom had subdued the Levant and installed garrisons there; by the fifteenth it even controlled Kerma, the capital of Kush. Around the same time the Hittites re-emerged as a major force in central Anatolia and a new dynasty came to power in Babylon with roots in a local people known as Kassites. By 1450 BCE different kings famous for chariot warfare had established rule over the region of Mittani in northern Mesopotamia.

Archaeologists have found remarkable quantities of imported ivory and gold on Crete from this era, and recent analysis of an ingot found in a foundation deposit for a building constructed in the eastern Cretan port of Mochlos shortly after the Theran eruption suggests that the tin route from central Asia was back in full operation.[29]

This may also be when bull leaping arrived on the island. This dangerous-looking sport has been associated with Crete ever since Arthur Evans excavated magnificent frescoes of bull leapers from late phases of the palace at Knossos. There's no reason to doubt that it really happened: rodeo sports tend to develop wherever cattle are domesticated, and bull leaping is still popular today in parts of Spain and France. We don't know whether the leapers were noble youths, hired specialists, slaves, or sacrifices. It seems likely though that the first were traveling professionals, like the fresco painters themselves, and that they came from overseas. Bull grappling of some kind is depicted on little bull-shaped jugs made in Crete in the later third millennium, with tiny humans hanging off the horns, but the earliest images of men leaping over bulls appear on seventeenth-century Syrian seals and Anatolian vases.[30*]

*The first surviving description of something like bull leaping comes in the eighteenth-century BCE Babylonian epic of Gilgamesh, when the king's friend Enkidu confronts the Bull of Heaven—whose snort has just opened ravines in the earth, killing 200 people—by grabbing its horns and jumping on its back, before Gilgamesh grasps its tail and kills it (*Gilgamesh* SBV [Standard Babylonian Version] VI.125–46).

Direct links finally appear between Crete and Egypt in this era too, documented in rock paintings in grand tombs at Egyptian Thebes on the upper Nile. In the Theban tomb of Rekhmire, vizier to Thutmose III who reigned in the mid-fifteenth century BCE, one painting depicting delegations of foreigners who have come to pay homage to the king includes a group of figures wearing kilts and loincloths familiar from Cretan painting.[31] They bring gifts ranging from raw metal ingots to bull-headed drinking horns, and they are labeled "The coming in Peace by the rulers of Keftiu-land [the Egyptian term for Crete] and the chiefs of the Islands in the Middle of the Great Green [the Egyptian term for the Mediterranean], bowing down and bending the head to His Majesty's might."[32] These Cretans and their neighbors are depicted as participating not just in interstate trade but in interstate diplomacy, joining delegations from Syria, Kush, and the great southern kingdom of Punt on the African horn.[33]

Egyptians visited Crete during Thutmose's reign too: Egyptian records begin to mention "Keftiu ships."[34] These are not literally "Cretan": one of the Egyptian documents relates to the import of materials for shipbuilding and repair, and another lists Keftiu ships alongside Byblos ships.[35] Like the latter, these must have been boats designed and built in Egypt to sail to a particular place, and in this case to make the lengthy and difficult journey south across open sea from Crete to make landfall in Marmarica and then follow the African coast east to the Nile; the difficulties of the direct passage north from the Nile Delta to Crete would still have necessitated a detour via the Levantine and Anatolian coasts.[36] Perhaps they already went even farther than Crete: annals carved on the wall of the Temple of Amun at Thebes under the same king record for the first time gifts from a chief of "Tanaja," the Egyptian term for the Greek mainland.[37]

To the west meanwhile it was still an easy sail from the Cretan port of Chania to Kastri on the island of Kythera, and on to the "Mycenaean" southern Peloponnese.[38] We can see the intensity of cultural connections between Crete and western Greek ports in this era at ancient Pylos, a hilltop village in Messenia overlooking the Bay of Navarino, where in May 2015 Sharon Stocker and Jack Davis of the University of

Cincinnati began excavations for the first time since 1969. When a local farmer refused to sell the site they wanted to investigate, they decided to open a trench instead in an olive grove just outside the ancient city wall. On the very first day they discovered a shaft grave in which a man in his early thirties had been buried some time around 1500 BCE.[39]

He took with him spectacular quantities of precious metals, stones, and other luxury goods, much of which must have come through Crete. Stocker and Davis call him the "Griffin Warrior" after a carved ivory plaque buried with him depicting that mythical beast, a winged lion with a falcon's head found originally in the art of Egypt and Iran and recently arrived in the Aegean in this era.[40] There are also hundreds of beads made of gold, glass, amber, Indian carnelian, and Egyptian amethyst; gold, silver, and bronze vessels; and bronze tools and weapons. Four gold signet rings—a breathtaking luxury, especially since seals were not yet used on the Greek mainland for functional purposes—are carved with scenes taken from contemporary Cretan iconography, including one scene of bull leaping and another of five women in typical Cretan dress at a shrine.

At the same time, many of the seals, vessels, and weapons the tomb contains find parallels at Mycenae, while the shaft-grave design itself borrows from Mycenae and other settlements in the eastern Peloponnese.[41] This still doesn't reflect an alternative set of overland connections: travel between Pylos, Crete, and the Argolid would all have been by water, much easier and faster than overland in the ancient and medieval periods, much, much cheaper—by a ratio of around 20:1—and at least as safe.[42] The inhabitants of Pylos lived not in a shared land, but on a shared sea.

What, then, should we make of the events on Crete around 1450 BCE, once blamed on the eruption of Thera? Over a relatively short period of time—two generations at most—almost all the palaces burned down, as well as parts of some towns.[43] Most palaces were never rebuilt, many settlements were abandoned, and grand residences across the island disappeared. The palace at Knossos survived and continued in use, and records kept there reveal that Knossos now became the capital of much of Crete, incorporating formerly independent palatial centers across the island into a single administrative system.[44] Around 1400 BCE the language of the administration at Knossos changed to the Indo-European tongue spoken on the mainland that we call Greek. We can see this shift in the appearance there of "Linear B," a script invented on Crete to write Greek down for the first time. This syllabic writing system was adapted from Linear A, which now disappears, along with the language it recorded, at least from the archives.[45]

The adoption of Greek as an administrative language means that "Mycenaeans" still often get the blame for the trouble—whether for burning the palaces themselves or for taking advantage of the subsequent confusion to commandeer Knossos, and through Knossos the island.[46] There is however no positive evidence on Crete for invasion, conquest, or external occupation, or even for significant levels of immigration. Languages meanwhile can be inherited, adopted, or imposed for all sorts of reasons, and they don't necessarily mark out specific ethnic groups, as a glance at a map of the English-speaking world will confirm.

There is no doubt that much of the damage was deliberate: selective targeting is one clue, and so is the evidence for simultaneous plunder at different places and the wanton destruction of specific art objects.[47] Before the invention of bombs, fire was usually the most efficient way to reduce your enemies to rubble. The survival of Knossos might suggest that it was behind the attacks itself, but internal revolt would better explain the patterns of arson in some places. At Petras in the far east, for instance, the administrative buildings were torched, but not the surrounding town.[48]

There was reason enough for discontent: as overseas connections intensified, economic activity had become centralized in towns and palaces, pottery production was standardized, and smaller and more rural sites increasingly abandoned. Traditional lifestyles on Crete were changing, no doubt in many cases for the worse, and conspicuous consumption by the newly rich would have added insult to injury: globalization always has its victims.

Whoever lit the fires, and whatever devastation they wreaked on people's lives on Crete itself, they didn't in the end make much difference to that global picture. Crete remained the favored destination of ships bringing goods from eastern Mediterranean ports well into the fourteenth century BCE: more than six times as many imports from east and south of the Aegean are found on Crete in this period as on the mainland.[49] And the Aegean remained a place of contact, connection, and combat between maritime communities, not territorial civilizations at war.

Farther west, meanwhile, imports of mainland Greek pottery to southern Italian and Sicilian ports peaked in the early fourteenth century BCE. Around the same time, the donkey chuntered into the landscape, and Italian potters adopted Aegean wheel-made pottery techniques. This suggests that master craftsmen came for at least temporary visits to provide the necessary equipment and training, probably during the summer when the weather was warm enough for the pottery to dry out before firing.[50]

In the late fourteenth century tin, amber, and some Aegean pottery began to reach even Sardinia, a mountainous island full of small farming hamlets and thousands of strange and sophisticated multistory tower houses now called "nuraghi." It had until now been relatively isolated from the goods and fashions of the wider Mediterranean world, and interest may have been stoked by its metals: Sardinia was rich in copper as well as lead, a useful addition to bronze to increase pliability.[51]

It is unlikely however that new visitors came all the way from the eastern Mediterranean: surviving Sardinian finds at harbors in southern Sicily, Crete, and Cyprus in the thirteenth century BCE drop in numbers from west to east, and Sardinian copies of Aegean pottery use purely local technology. This suggests that what we are seeing is not long-distance journeys west by individual ships from the Levant or even the Aegean, but the slow spread of sailing technology itself across the sea, and the increasing interaction of regional trading circuits to pass especially desirable goods down the line.[52]

Some technologies traveled even farther: contemporary Danish sites boast folding stools of a kind also found in Egypt and in wall paintings at Knossos and Pylos.[53] And all across Scandinavia men begin to be buried with swords, tweezers, and one-sided razors with a small handle in the form of a horse's head that must have been inspired by very similar items made on Crete. This suggests that they had adopted the practice of shaving too, perhaps after reports of fashionable practices on Crete and the Greek mainland, where men were buried with their razors as well as their weapons, and were depicted in paintings as clean-shaven.[54] None of this suggests direct contact between Scandinavia and the Mediterranean as yet—links still ran through the Alpine mines—but the importance of travel and contact to these communities is underlined by the images of oared ships scratched on rocks at landing points around the Scandinavian peninsula in this era, echoes of long journeys on cold rivers and seas.[55]

As ever, the smallest and most valuable goods traveled farthest of all. Fourteenth-century Scandinavian graves contain glass beads made in workshops in Mesopotamia and Egypt more than 5,000 kilometers away, and lapis lazuli from Afghanistan has recently been found with Cretan pottery off the Frisian coast, no doubt carried up with copper from the Alps.[56] Baltic amber traveling in the other direction is now found in Egyptian royal tombs and used to make sculptures in inland Syria.[57] And when people at either end of this delicate set of connections couldn't get hold of the real thing, they tried to fake it: amber was imitated in western Asia with orange-colored glass, down to the inclusion of pine needles to mimic the organic materials found inside genuine examples, while European workshops in this era produced faience colored blue with copper salts to make it look more like lapis lazuli.[58]

These ever-longer-distance networks across Europe and the Mediterranean were still little known farther east, and of less interest.

CHAPTER FIVE

Band of Brothers

AMARNA, C. 1350 BCE

It is not entirely clear what happened that day in 1887 on a dusty hill on the east bank of the Nile about 250 kilometers south of Cairo. Tales of the rediscovery of ancient artifacts that come onto the antiquities market are not always reliable, and other people may have been involved. But as the story goes, it was a local woman who was digging in overgrown ruins on an artificial mound, or "tell," just outside the small village of Amarna for sun-dried mud bricks when she happened upon a small collection of clay tablets with cuneiform signs etched into both sides.[1] More than 400 of these tablets were eventually recovered, all letters written in the brief period when Tell el-Amarna housed the most important city in Egypt, if not the world.

It was built by a king who was never supposed to rule. But first his elder brother died, and then his father, Amenhotep III, and in 1353 BCE Amenhotep IV succeeded to the throne. A few years into his reign the new monarch rebelled against Egypt's religious system, closed the temples, and devoted himself to the sun god Aten alone. He changed his name to Akhenaten ("Beneficial to Aten"), and with his wife Nefertiti he built a new capital on the Nile that he called Akhetaten ("Horizon of Aten"). He paid less attention to ordinary politics, neglected the empire,

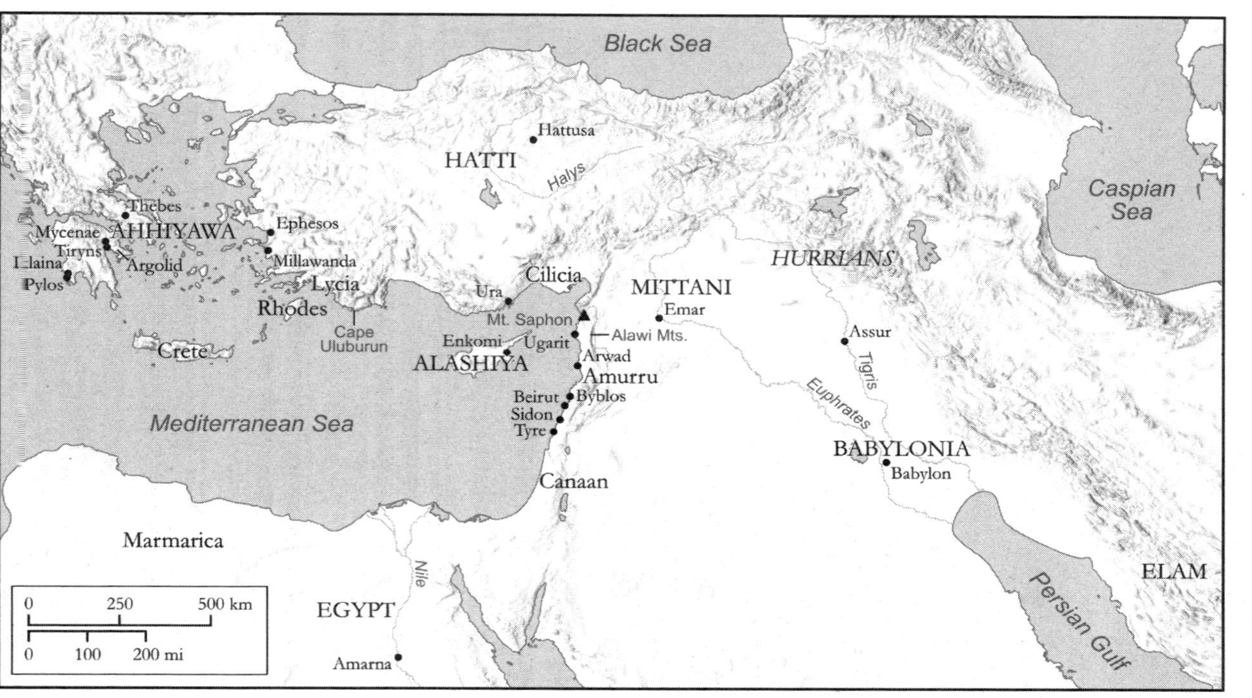

The Brother Kingdoms, c. 1350 BCE

and ruined the economy. When he died after two decades on the throne, his young son swiftly restored the old traditions as well as the ancient capitals of Memphis and Thebes, and changed his own name from Tutankhaten to Tutankhamun.

The correspondence from Amarna tells us nothing of Akhenaten's religious convictions, but it opens a window onto a vast network of economic, political, and cultural connections in the mid-fourteenth century BCE, when urban empires from Egypt to Anatolia traced a shining arc through a galaxy of smaller satellites and challengers ebbing out in all directions. These were the glory days of the Bronze Age, and they brought great wealth and power to a lucky few. From their perspective the Aegean was the far west, with points beyond blinking occasionally in the distance. This isn't the whole story though: the world was getting smaller in this period, with people and places linked ever more closely by goods and letters, trade and war. By the thirteenth century BCE at least one Aegean kingdom was allowed to join the club.

The Amarna letters all come from a building that ancient brick stamps label "The Bureau of the Correspondence of the Pharaoh"—"pharaoh" being a word that meant "royal house" but could by now be used by association for the king as well.[2] They span fewer than three decades, from the final years of Amenhotep III's reign to the first year of Tutankhamun's, and they are mostly written in Akkadian, still the standard diplomatic language of the whole region. The archive preserves about forty letters exchanged among a group of powerful rulers who refer to one another as "Brothers" and "Great Kings."[3]

In addition to the Egyptian king, these include the kings of "Alashiya" (Cyprus), rich in copper; the kings of Hatti, who were extending their holdings into the northern Levant; the kings of Mittani, who controlled land from the Mediterranean to the Zagros Mountains; and the Kassite kings of Babylon to their south, on the all-important routes to the Gulf. The Amarna letters reveal the importance of contact and communication between what are usually seen as separate ancient cultures or civilizations, and they give us an unusually clear view of the practicalities that made it possible.

These kings begin their letters with a polite greeting, asking after the things that matter to them most: "Say to Naphurureya [Akhenaten], the king of Egypt, my brother: Thus Burnaburiash [II], the king of the land of Karaduniash [Babylon], your brother. For me all goes well. For you, your country, your household, your wives, your sons, your magnates, your horses, your chariots, may all go very well."[4] Each king sends his own "greeting gifts" along with the letters: gold from Egypt; copper from Alashiya; lapis lazuli and horses from Babylonia; lapis lazuli, horses, and chariots from Assyria; lapis lazuli, horses, chariots, textiles, and slaves from Mittani. These "gifts" are carefully described by number, weight, and other standardized measures: lapis lazuli comes in "lumps" and "crickets."[5] Metals are often melted down and assessed for quality on arrival.[6]

The letters themselves consist largely of complaints about each other's behavior and etiquette. Some of this can seem petty: we read a lot about missing get-well presents, invitations, or RSVPs.[7] One favorite theme is the stinginess of the king of Egypt, who never sends as much gold with his letters as he used to, or as his father did, or as his correspondent happens to need. In one case the king of Mittani writes to Akhenaten's mother to complain that her son has sent him gold-plated rather than pure gold statues.[8]

Some letters do address more traditional diplomatic concerns. "Brotherhood" with the king of Egypt didn't always mean brotherhood with each other, and Hatti destroys the declining state of Mittani around 1350 BCE, seizing its western territories and allowing an upstart king of Assur—no longer the quasi-republic of the Karum Kanesh era—to seize the old Mittani heartland east of the Euphrates. The Assyrian then makes overtures to Akhenaten for friendship and alliance, which must have been well received, as in his second letter he is already calling Akhenaten his "brother" and complaining that the amount of gold the king of Egypt has provided is not enough to cover the costs of his messengers' journeys. Burnaburiash II of Babylon is less impressed, writing to Amarna: "as for my Assyrian vassals, I was not the one who sent them to you. Why on their own authority have they come to your country? If you love me, they will conduct no business whatsoever. Send them off to me empty-handed." Burnaburiash also finds the time to mention another matter: "At the moment my work on a temple is extensive, and I am quite busy with carrying it out. . . . Send me much gold."[9]

In fact the griping over presents and invitations is just as important as the diplomatic posturing, and between them they reveal the dual driving forces behind this set of alliances: the kings' mutual requirements for political recognition of their imperial conquests, and for raw materials to build the armies and palaces that maintained them. The rulers of these ancient superpowers needed one another to preserve their own power over their subjects both at home and in their wider empires, and they maintained a balance of payments as well as prestige. In this context the complaints about short-weight presents are not so much bad manners as the sensible stewarding of state finances.

The success of the whole system depended on personal relationships, not just among the kings themselves but between many other people as well: the Amarna letters detail journeys, meetings, disputes, trade, and other forms of exchange over very long distances. Some of the people involved were gifts themselves: slaves, specialists on loan—the king of Alashiya asks Egypt for an expert in interpreting omens from the flight of vultures—and above all the kings' female relatives, the ultimate symbol of alliance.[10] Amenhotep III alone married the daughters of two kings of Babylon, two kings of Mittani, and a king of Arzawa in western Anatolia. He gained more from these marriage alliances than women and goodwill. When a royal wedding took place dowry lists were lodged in the Amarna archive, enumerating vast quantities of precious stones, metals, jewelry, weapons, tools, and furniture.

Not all the marriage negotiations were straightforward. In a notably bad-tempered exchange of letters, Kadashman-Enlil the king of Babylon tells Amenhotep III that he is reluctant to send him his daughter, since his "brother" refuses to return the favor with a daughter of his own, he has not sent Kadashman-Enlil the gifts he should and he does not invite him to his parties. Besides, Kadashman-Enlil's sister has already been sent to Egypt as a royal bride and has not been heard of for some time. In response Amenhotep protests, not unreasonably, that the men Kadashman-Enlil sent to inquire after his sister had never met her and so were unable to verify the identity of the woman he produced for them.[11] Eventually the Babylonian king agrees to allow his daughter to risk the new marriage as long as Amenhotep sends him "as much gold as possible, right now, in all haste, this summer" for a new palace he is building.[12] He also pointedly invites the Egyptian king to the opening.[13] It may be this unfortunate girl who writes the only Amarna letter sure to have come from a woman, telling an unknown correspondent back in Babylon, "Do not worry, or you will have made me sad."[14]

A later marriage alliance presents more practical difficulties: Burnaburiash II refuses to supply Akhenaten with a wife until he sends a suitably grand escort, otherwise "my neighboring kings would say, 'They have transported the daughter of a Great King to Egypt in five chariots.' "[15] All gifts between kings, human or otherwise, traveled under escort. Sometimes the escorts were themselves courtiers, but the kings of Babylon and Alashiya describe their messengers as merchants.[16] The missions were time-consuming and often dangerous: as Burnaburiash II puts it, "the journey is difficult, water cut off, and the weather hot"—albeit as a way of explaining to the king of Egypt why "I am not sending many beautiful greeting gifts."[17] On another occasion Burnaburiash's messengers are robbed and killed in Canaan on the way to Egypt.[18] The king's concern for "his" merchants is unsentimental: he asks Akhenaten to have the murderers found and executed because such activities threaten their correspondence.[19] And the kings themselves pose further dangers to their intermediaries: one of Kadashman-Enlil's many complaints to Amarna is that a Babylonian envoy has been detained there for six years.[20]

These Great Kings formed a restricted clique, and their letters rarely look beyond their own and the others' states. They do give us glimpses of people and places on the edge of these kings' vision: a derogatory reference by the king of Babylon to the Kaskaeans, semi-nomads based in the mountainous area south of the Black Sea who had sacked Hattusa itself in the fifteenth century; a letter from the king of Syrian Ugarit to Egypt requesting a doctor and two Kushite attendants.[21] There is however no mention of lands west of Cyprus: for the purposes of this correspondence they do not count. To trace the integration of Aegean communities into the Amarna world, we have to look elsewhere.

. . .

Trade is a good place to start. Large quantities of mainland Greek pottery arrived at Amarna itself in the era of the letters, especially jars that would once have carried wine, olive oil, and perfumes.[22] Thousands of pots made in the Argolid and other regions of mainland Greece in the later fourteenth and thirteenth centuries have been found in the Levant as well.[23] By contrast, by 1300 BCE imitations of mainland Greek pottery in southern Italy significantly outpaced imports as Aegean makers and merchants turned their attention east toward these lucrative new markets.[24]

Most of their wares probably still traveled to their final destinations with middlemen from the island of Cyprus, which prospered greatly on the profits of its plentiful copper reserves, cast in standard blocks of about thirty kilos that were shaped like oxhides with protruding corners to make them easier for a pair of men to carry.[25] Vast numbers of pots made on the Greek mainland are found on Cyprus in this era, while Cypriot ceramics arrive at the same eastern Mediterranean ports as pots from the Aegean, and in far greater quantities. Some of the Aegean pots found in the Levant even have markings in "Cypro-Minoan," a still undeciphered Cypriot script.[26]

At the same time new sailing technologies developed in the Levant did encourage longer and more difficult journeys. These included crow's nests for better visibility, keels that helped keep ships steady even under heavy loads, and brail lines in sails that enabled the crew to control flutter when traveling into the wind, and so to sail much closer to it—especially useful when you need to make a swift escape.[27]

There is good evidence that the kings of Egypt by then knew an increasing amount about the Aegean. Pharaohs were not given to self-effacement, and Amenhotep III was no exception, adorning the mortuary temple in the royal cemetery at Egyptian Thebes where offerings would be left to him after his death with forty or so colossal statues of himself. Five stand on bases listing foreign cities and peoples by region; one is labeled "All of the difficult lands north of Asia."[28]

After the headwords "Keftiu" and "Tanaja"—from an Egyptian perspective the two great islands across the sea to the north—the inscription names fifteen Aegean ports, presented as if they were a set of stops on a single journey. It is difficult to reestablish the full list due to recutting in antiquity and fire damage since the discovery of the bases in the 1960s. It doesn't help either that this is the only time these names appear in Egyptian records. However, they certainly include Knossos, Phaistos, Amnisos, and Chania on Crete, as well as the island of Kythera, and Mycenae and Nauplion in the Argolid.[29]

It is in keeping with the traditional Egyptian symbolism of international relations that all these labels are superimposed on images of bound prisoners, but there is no evidence for Egyptian conquest, or even military interest, in most of the regions concerned. Instead, the lists probably commemorate diplomatic missions, which could also explain the appearance of Amenhotep III's cartouche—his official name written within an oblong frame—stamped on little plaques and small figurines made of Egyptian faience and found at Mycenae, perhaps intended as calling cards or gifts.[30]

Dramatic evidence for the level of exchange between the Aegean and the Amarna world as a whole in this era came to light in 1982, when a young Turkish sponge diver spotted a "metal biscuit with ears" on the seabed. It turned out to be an oxhide-shaped copper ingot, and the first sign in 3,300 years of a twenty-ton, sixteen-meter-long single-mast sailing boat built of wood from Mount Lebanon that had sunk off Cape Uluburun on the southwestern coast of Anatolia. A date in the late fourteenth century BCE has been established by carbon dating, the style of the pottery onboard, and a scarab engraved with the royal cartouche of Akhenaten's queen Nefertiti.[31]

This ship was about as big as they got in the Bronze Age, and the location of the wreck means that it must have been heading for the Aegean: to Rhodes, Crete, or all the way to the Argolid. The hold was full of luxury goods straight out of the Amarna letters, in quantities that would not have been out of place on an Amarna dowry list. There is silver from Anatolia; saffron, nigella, and sumac from Mesopotamia; gold, ebony, and raw ivory—an elephant tusk and fourteen hippopotamus teeth—that must have come via Egypt; and ten tons of copper from Cyprus. Along with the ton of tin on board, which came from both central Asia (modern Tajikistan and Uzbekistan) and the Turkish Taurus Mountains, this would have made more than 300 bronze suits of armor.[32] In fact, the overlap with the gifts and goods discussed in the Amarna correspondence is so striking that some scholars have suggested this was an official mission between kings of the kind discussed in the letters.[33]

However that may be, we can see that it was loaded at a Levantine port: there are also jars full of local olives, glass beads, half a ton of terebinth resin from the pistachio tree, which was used to make perfume and incense as well as to preserve wine, and textiles dyed purple with a distinctive and very expensive dye obtained in industrial quantities in these ports by crushing the innards of the murex, a carnivorous sea snail. The unfortunate mollusks' horn-like feet, a prized ingredient in incense, were also carried aboard. And although the ship would have passed Cyprus before it met its fate, the way the Cypriot pots were stacked in the hold suggests that they were loaded at the port of departure, rather than picked up along the way.

Functional items found on board suggest that the crew was also based in the Levant: four sets of Levantine balance weights and measures, enough for four merchants, as well as Levantine swords, seals, wooden writing tablets, weapons, oil lamps burnt at the nozzle, cymbals, a trumpet for onboard entertainment, and a bronze sculpture of a Levantine goddess the size of a human hand. She may have belonged to one of the sailors, or to the ship herself.

Other personal possessions found aboard came from farther afield: Aegean jugs and drinking vessels, seals, razors, daggers, and knives; jewelry made from Baltic amber; more swords of Aegean and southern Italian type; and an intriguing weapon with parallels in southeastern Europe that combined the functions of a scepter and a mace. Whether sailors, merchants, or diplomats, their owners had wide horizons. They were either from a variety of origins themselves, or some of their offboard interactions went beyond simple barter to encompass the transmission of skills, and no doubt the socializing that went with it.[34] You can't just pick up a sword and use it as you please, unlike a plate or bowl—you need to learn how it was designed to work.

Cultural connections with the wider world in this era were not limited to career travelers and the highest social circles, and borrowings continue to undermine the idea that societies create themselves. The Greek word for wine, *woino-*, comes from *wainu* in the northwest Semitic languages used in the Levant, and it must already have arrived in the language by the mid-second millennium BCE, when Semitic languages replace w- with y-.[35] This is also when the lyre, played in Mesopotamia since the third millennium, appears in the Aegean for the first time.[36] Curious beasts arrive, to feed the mind with ideas of strange and faraway lands: not only the griffin but also the sphinx, a human-headed lion invented in third millennium BCE Egypt and subsequently given wings in the Levant.[37]

Religion becomes more visible in the Aegean in this era as well: idols appear, and shrines with benches and platforms.[38] Ritual practices shared with Anatolia and the Levant suggest a shared cultural community in this respect.[39] Gods across the whole region made similar demands: they need to be tempted up to the human world from below the earth with offerings of wine, milk, and oil, as well as down from the sky with the smell of incense or roasting meat (especially thigh bones). After these sacrifices, Aegean communities held feasts very like those of western Asia, down to a rule that worshippers should not pack their portion to take away.[40] Connectedness has become cultural entanglement.

When one Aegean king did finally join the Brothers' club, it was not through commercial or cultural contact but through conflict. We find the story preserved in scraps of correspondence and documentation preserved in the archives of ancient Hattusa, some written much later than the events they describe, and most now stored at the Ankara Museum.

Things start badly as the Hittite texts begin to mention a troublemaking polity operating in the Aegean called "Ahhiya" and later "Ahhiyawa."[41] In one early-fourteenth-century document a "Man" (*lu*, a standard regional term for a minor prince or ruler) of "Ahhiya" called

Attarissiya is accused of raiding Alashiya. He has also twice attacked Madduwatta, a Hittite client king in southwest Anatolia, the second time with a large force of chariots and infantry. On both occasions Madduwatta had to be rescued by Hittite forces.[42]

Clashes continue. Later in the fourteenth century, a decade or two after letters cease arriving at Amarna, the Hittite king Mursili II's Annals describe a campaign he waged in western Anatolia to put down rebellious clients. These included the coastal city of Millawanda (Miletos) and the Arzawa federation, which held power in southwestern Anatolia. Both had switched allegiance to someone who is now called the "King" (*lugal,* or "Big Man") of "Ahhiyawa"—our first positive indication that at least one Greek mainland city was ruled by someone who looked to outsiders like a king.[43] At the same time, it is worth noting, archaeological evidence suggests increasing interest in fifteenth- and fourteenth-century Anatolian coastal cities like Miletos in imports, styles, and traditions from the Greek mainland.[44]

The name Ahhiyawa must lie behind Homer's later "Achaeans," the collective label usually used in the *Iliad* for the kingdoms that united under Agamemnon of Mycenae against Troy, and Attarissiya is tantalizingly similar to the Atreus whom later Greek legend made king of Mycenae and father to Agamemnon.[45] Nonetheless, the Hittite documentation doesn't tell us whether Ahhiyawa was indeed a confederation, like Arzawa, or a single substantial kingdom. If the latter it was probably Mycenae, though Thebes in Greek Boeotia is another candidate: Knossos was no longer a major player in the Aegean, and other mainland powers were either too small or too far away.

However that may be, Mursili II of Hatti recaptures both Millawanda and the Arzawan capital of Apasa (Ephesos), and the Ahhiyawan king sends him back some refugees.[46] This inaugurates a friendlier phase of relations. By the thirteenth century BCE the kings of Hatti and Ahhiyawa call each other "brother" and "Great King" (*lugal.gal,* or "Great Big Man"), and they exchange Armana-style greeting gifts, if rather small ones: a note sent by a Hittite official to his king reports that a pair of gold and silver drinking horns have been removed from a larger consignment earmarked for the king of Egypt and dispatched instead to

Ahhiyawa.[47] At some point "gods of Ahhiyawa" visit the Hittite capital, perhaps to aid the king at a time of sickness.[48] One letter from an Ahhiyawan king to Hatti is even written in Hittite—probably a translation of a Greek original, but confirmation that Greek–Hittite translators were available in one court or the other.[49]

The integration of Ahhiyawa into a world of Great Kings coincides with a new level of activity at Mycenae and in the wider Argolid, which may have come under direct Mycenaean control in this period, along with the Saronic Gulf and its silver mines.[50] In the fourteenth century walls were built around both Mycenae and the neighboring citadel of Tiryns; according to Pausanias they were the work of the giant Cyclopes, but the circuit at Tiryns incorporates Hittite timber-frame construction techniques and corbeled vaulted galleries. The involvement of Hittite specialists would mirror the passing around of traveling experts between the Great Kings preserved in the Amarna letters, and advertise in itself the participation of local kings in a new and bigger world.[51]

New palaces were built at Mycenae and Tiryns as well.[52] Only the foundations and floors of these buildings are preserved, but they are not based around gatherings in a large open-air courtyard, as in palaces on Crete and later at Pylos and nearby Iklaina in Messenia.[53] Instead they invited visitors to progress through a sequence of internal spaces: a gateway and then a small internal court led into a tripartite complex with a porch, a vestibule, and then a large reception room with an enormous circular hearth platform at the center, and a throne in the middle of the right-hand wall, focusing attention on its sole occupant—the Great Big Man.[54]*

Mycenae was still a small town: the citadel covered only around three hectares. But it now had great prestige. Palaces built in the thirteenth century across mainland Greece borrow heavily from the model pioneered in the Argolid. Even the palace at Pylos was reconstructed around 1300 BCE: Cretan-style ashlars were abandoned, the inner

*Archaeologists labeled this ceremonial set of rooms a "megaron," after the name Homer gave the halls of his Achaean kings (although those sound rather more convivial); it later became the blueprint for the Classical Greek temple.

courtyard disappeared, and the new design was based on the full Argolid gateway, court, and throne-room sequence.[55]

The footprint of the citadel at Mycenae was extended in the mid-thirteenth century to include the western part of the hill within its circuit wall, and its crowning glory, the new Lion Gate, again reveals distinct signs of Hittite art and craft. Monumental sculptural relief of any kind is unknown in the Aegean in this era, but it was common in the Hittite strongholds of central Anatolia, as were grand sculpted gates and stone animal guardians at the entrances to cities. The actual lions above the gateway to Mycenae look nothing like the two that guard the feet of the entrance to the great inland fastness of Hattusa, but a recent study has revealed that the sculptors of the Lion Gate used new stone-cutting methods with central Anatolian parallels, involving the tubular drill and the short convex saw, in addition to more traditional tools from Crete and the mainland.[56]

Another aspect of the same civic reconstruction project sent more local messages about the city's own past glory. The grave circle dug on the edge of the early settlement was now included within the new walls and recast as a historical monument. In an unusual move, its graves were isolated and enclosed by an imposing circular double parapet beside the ramp leading up from the Lion Gate toward the palace, and the original grave markers were re-erected at the new ground level, several meters above the burials themselves.[57] These new arrangements created a window from the city's main road down into its history. Perhaps these tombs were already attributed to war heroes, as Pausanias later heard, or perhaps the early community leaders buried in them had been reimagined as the ancestors of a single powerful king.

Nothing lasts forever, though, and back in the Hattusa archive relations between Ahhiyawa and Hatti were headed downhill. Hattusili III complains in a letter around 1250 BCE not only that his "brother," the Great King of Ahhiyawa, has failed to send him a greeting gift, but that the Ahhiyawan king's (real?) brother Tawagalawa has been helping rebels in western Anatolia escape to Ahhiyawan territory.[58]

By the end of the century, Ahhiyawa was facing relegation from the club of Great Kings. A draft copy of a treaty between the Hittite king

Tudhaliya IV and his nephew the king of Amurru lists as Tudhaliya's only peers the king of Egypt, the king of Babylon, the king of Assyria, and the king of Ahhiyawa, but the latter name was erased by the scribe, and presumably left out of the final version.[59] Ahhiyawa was now surplus to requirements.

CHAPTER SIX

Alphabet City

UGARIT, 1215 BCE

There was more to the Late Bronze Age than Great Big Men. In the Levant a patchwork of smaller vassal kingdoms provides a different perspective on change and exchange. Civilizational thinking promotes a notion of extensive shared cultures, distinct from their neighbors; the historical reality is that distinctiveness emerges on a smaller and more human scale, exploiting resources from elsewhere.

Few archaeological traces of this period have been found in ancient Levantine cities themselves, not least because so many are now modern cities. Instead, many of these little states are best known to us through hundreds of letters Egypt's clients sent to the pharaoh at Amarna, calling him "the sun, my Lord" and themselves "your servant." They pay him tribute, supply him with soldiers, laborers, and hostages from their own households, send him information, ask for help, and play their neighbors off against one another as best they can.[1] We hear a great deal in particular from Rib-Hadda of Byblos, who writes to inform on other petty kings, to bemoan his own lot, and to complain that the Egyptian king is, understandably enough, ignoring him.[2]

One city has however given up its secrets. Less than a kilometer inland from what is now the Syrian coast the ruins of Ugarit spill over a

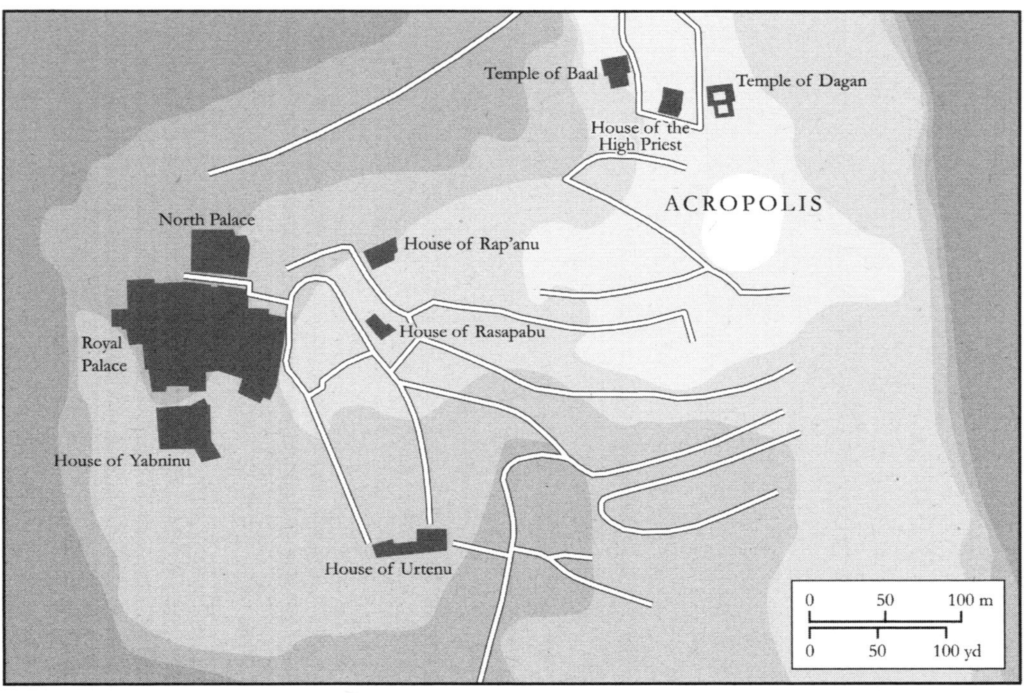

The city of Ugarit in the thirteenth century BCE

great tell rediscovered in 1928 when a local farmer happened upon an ancient tomb in the village of Ras Shamra ("Fennel Hill").[3] When they were excavated, the blocky buildings turned out to be full of clay tablets covered in writing. These texts paint a picture of an innovative small kingdom with wide horizons and a strong sense of its own identity.

The western part of the city is dominated by the royal palace, a warren of public and private spaces interspersed with storerooms for diplomatic correspondence, legal records, and accounts, all kept well above ground level to protect them from flooding. On the eastern acropolis sits the "House of the High Priest" between two tower temples. Here a very different library holds an astonishing collection of poetry and prose, a precious taste of otherwise lost literary traditions of the Bronze Age Levant: myths, epics, prayers, spells, and four medical texts devoted to the treatment of the horse.[4] And scattered through the narrow streets of the city, in densely packed houses, shops, and workshops, are the personal archives of individual merchants and officials.

Altogether we have more than 1,500 documents from thirteenth- and early-twelfth-century Ugarit, in five scripts and eight languages: the old literary language of Sumerian, the Akkadian of foreign correspondence, Egyptian, Cypro-Minoan, and the Anatolian languages of Hittite, Hurrian, and Luwian, as well as Ugaritic itself. The Ugaritic documents in particular reveal new thinking about politics, administration, and culture that distanced the city from the Great Kings who surrounded it.

This shouldn't be a surprise. New ideas rarely come from the center of a system. Empires in particular are intrinsically conservative, and imperial coalitions all the more so. Petty complaints aside, the immense distances and slow speed of ancient communication meant that serious misunderstandings with subjects or brother rulers could be disastrous. The best way for the central authorities to avoid them was to maintain standard practices, long standing relationships, and conventional symbols of power in a traditional language. Innovation happens instead on the borders of larger structures, and in communication with people beyond their control. Contrary to the logic of "civilizations" as self-contained bastions of self-improvement, it is people on the periphery, less set in their ways and with more to gain, who most easily make change. We have already seen this happen at Byblos and Mycenae, in the Carpathians and on Crete and Cyprus, and at Ugarit we see it again in unusual detail.

Ugarit sat between four Amarna kingdoms: Egypt, Hatti, Mittani, and Alashiya. The city's own formal allegiance shifted in line with the changing fortunes of the Great Kings. In early letters to Amarna the king of Ugarit calls himself the king of Egypt's servant, but after the Hittite destruction of Mittani in the mid-fourteenth century BCE Ugarit submitted instead to the victors. Its status as Hatti's vassal was confirmed by treaty, the provision of troops, and a high level of tribute.[5]

All the same, Ugarit was no ordinary client kingdom. The city controlled a large and fertile territory along the coastal plain and its natural harbor was the most important port in the northern Levant, dominating the busy north–south shipping route from Hittite Anatolia to the Egyptian Delta. From there it was just a day's sail to Enkomi on Cyprus, the main commercial hub for western metals: tin ingots from continental Europe and lead ingots from Sardinia found in thirteenth-to-twelfth-century shipwrecks off the coast of modern Israel have markings in Cypro-Minoan, strongly suggesting that they passed through the island's markets. The city of Ugarit itself meanwhile stood below a rare inland pass through the Alawi mountain chain on the overland route heading east to the trading depot of Emar on the Euphrates and central Asian tin beyond.[6]

Ugarit's wealth and strategic position meant that direct orders from Hattusa were rare. Even when they did arrive, the king did not always obey them.[7] He also dealt regularly with other Great Kings. In a letter of around 1220 BCE the king of Alashiya says that he will send Niqmaddu of Ugarit thirty-three copper ingots, and in one bizarre exchange Ugarit's king writes to Egypt to ask for craftsmen to make a sculpture of the pharaoh, but receives instead a gift of ebony, ropes, and 800 whips.[8]

Commerce was central to the well-being of the city, and the king knew it. The palace ran its own large farming and manufacturing operations, but it also took a close interest in trade, acquiring large quantities of raw materials and luxury goods from local merchants.[9] Some traders even resided in the palace, although many were independent operators with their own capital.[10] The biggest commercial operators were also heavily involved in the politics and administration of the kingdom, and they acted as diplomats for the crown.

One king writes to tell his mother that when the powerful merchant Yabninu, who occupied a large mansion near the royal palace, undertook a mission south to the neighboring northern Syrian kingdom of Amurru, he took gold and textiles to the king there and poured oil on the head of his daughter—apparently part of the negotiations over a royal marriage.[11] Another king writes to a merchant named Sinaranu who was importing goods from Crete, exempting him not only from paying import duties in the form of grain, beer, and olive oil, but also from serving as a messenger.[12]

Diplomacy and trade made Ugarit a crossroads of information and ideas. Its merchants operated in Mesopotamia, Anatolia, Egypt, Cyprus, and Crete, and some were even permanent residents in other Levantine ports. One group disgraced themselves by desecrating a temple in Sidon, and were forced to fund a four-day reparation ritual on threat of execution.[13] At the same time the city's own commercial operations attracted visitors and migrants. A significant proportion of the resident population came from outside Ugarit. Civic administrators record the presence of Egyptians, Hittites, and Cypriots who receive food rations from the state, as well as people from Tyre, Sidon, Beirut, Byblos, Arwad, and other cities of the Levantine coast. Some were farmworkers and apprentices; others were organized into guilds of visiting merchants.[14]

This could lead to frictions. Some Cypriot residents appear to have been prisoners, and some foreign traders were robbed and murdered. After a raid in Ugaritic territory on a caravan of merchants from the Egyptian province of Canaan in the southern Levant, citizens of Ugarit were required to pay a large fine to citizens of Canaan.[15] On another occasion certain residents of Ugarit became dangerously indebted to Hittite merchants from the port of Ura in western Cicilia. In response to complaints from the king of Ugarit the Hittite king Hattusili III banned these traders from staying in Ugarit over the winter and from taking land in payment for debt, though payment in human labor remained acceptable.[16]

Despite incidents like this, Ugarit was unusually open to outsiders. The best evidence for this comes from clay tablets that record a local civic ritual for mass atonement to the gods for a variety of personal failings, including anger, impatience, turpitude, and the neglect of sacrifices.[17] This atonement ritual is preserved in at least six versions, more than any other ritual text found in the city. They are written in different hands and found in different places. This multiplicity of examples means that the ritual really happened, and that it was repeated over some period of time.[18]

The atonement itself is accomplished through sacrifices of scapegoat animals: two oxen, two rams, and, in the best-preserved section, two "donkeys of rectitude." The whole performance is strongly marked as a local tradition. While some ritual texts found at Ugarit follow Mesopotamian models very closely—instructions for the interpretation of monstrous births, for example—both atonement rituals and donkey sacrifice are long-standing Levantine customs.[19]

At the same time, the text of the rite repeatedly urges participants to consider the well-being (*npy*) not only of themselves and their city but of "the foreigner within the walls of Ugarit." It also specifies that the trespasses for which they must atone may have been committed against foreigners from seven different places, including Hurrians, Hittites, and Cypriots, as well as against the city's own poor and oppressed.

The wording of the ritual also suggests new notions about the nature of the state itself, and more inclusive notions of political community. With its unusually powerful and stable royal house, there is no hint of popular government at Ugarit. But this atonement ritual is practiced not by or on behalf of the king, as in many other Ugaritic rituals, but by and "on behalf of" the people as a whole, the first and only time to our knowledge that such a group is centered in civic ritual in the second millennium BCE.[20]

Furthermore, within this civic community the ritual includes not only the "Son of Ugarit" but the "Daughter of Ugarit" as well, and although men and women have separate sections in the ritual, sacrificing three animals each, it gives the women of Ugarit equal responsibility for their city. Describing civic populations as "Sons of" cities was an ancient custom in western Asia: traders at Karum Kanesh had called themselves "Sons of Assur," and in this period the "Sons of Emar," another Hittite vassal city, preside over a large number of major rituals.[21] The involvement at Ugarit of the city's daughters probably reflects the relative lack of political power allowed even to male citizens more than it reflects women's liberation, but it does suggest a spirit of egalitarianism and experimentation in the city encouraged by unusual levels of cultural and social interaction.

Inspiration does not necessarily lead to imitation, however, and one of the most interesting things about Ugarit is the distinctively local focus of much innovation in this era, starting with the fact that the atonement ritual itself is written in Ugaritic, a northwest Semitic language closely related to later Phoenician and Hebrew.

Reading and writing in one's own spoken language may seem natural today, especially to native English speakers. It is however an artificial choice, and even in Europe a relatively recent one. In antiquity it was unusual. At Emar, for instance, Akkadian and Sumerian were the preferred languages of local literature and administration. When Ugarit's scribes started to use their own language for almost all local business, politics, and administration in the mid-thirteenth century, they created the world's first written vernacular. It involved a deliberate decision to reject the bureaucratic norms and universal languages of Ugarit's own Hittite overlords and the other Great Kings, and to emphasize the city's local identity.[22]

At the same time, a new script was introduced to write this local language, one that worked completely differently from the writing systems previously in use in the city. To understand how big a change this was, we need some background. Alphabets—writing systems in which a single letter represents a single sound—were not new in the thirteenth century BCE, but they were rare, and they were used only for Levantine languages. It seems more natural for humans to write down syllables than individual sounds: there were several independent inventions of syllabic writing systems across a wide area in the Late Bronze Age—we have already met those invented in Mesopotamia, Egypt, and Crete—but the alphabet was a one-off.

The first certain examples of alphabetic writing appear in the nineteenth and eighteenth centuries BCE, among hired laborers from the Levant living in Egypt. Some of the earliest alphabetic letters are found scratched on rock walls at the royal Egyptian turquoise mines at Serabit el-Khadim in the mountains of Sinai, as well as on sculptures in a shrine to the Egyptian goddess Hathor there.[23] These texts are relatively short—just a dedication to a deity or the name of a person, meaning "I was here," or "this is mine"—but they are meaningful.[24] Their authors weren't used to writing things down, but far from home among foreigners they found a way to communicate with one another and the gods in their own language.

They did so by inventing a script for people who didn't know how to write.[25] That was the job of trained scribes, and for good reason: the cuneiform writing system borrowed by the Bronze Age Levantine kingdoms had close to a thousand signs altogether, each of which could represent a variety of different words, syllables, or "determinatives," silent signs that simply specify the category of what follows: "the next word should be read as a god," for instance, or "a town," or "a kind of duck."

The alphabet cut through this with a clever device. Each "letter" was really a little picture, and it represented the first sound of the word for whatever was depicted. So the sign for "a" was the head of a bull, *alep* in Levantine dialects, "b" was a schematic house (*bayit*), "d" was a door (*dalet*), and so on. You can still see this, just about, by rotating modern "Roman" capitals 90 degrees to the left. Because the "letters" of the alphabet represent sounds, not syllables, there were fewer of them to learn. But in fact you didn't even have to learn the script to get the message; you just needed to know the language and the trick.

Their new surroundings provided these Levantine workers with inspiration in fact as well as motivation. To create the new alphabet, they commandeered Egyptian signs used on the inscriptions they saw around them: all of the letters found in Sinai have models in the Egyptian hieroglyphic script or its simplified "hieratic" version. Ignoring the way these signs operated in the Egyptian writing systems themselves—they probably didn't know—the Levantine laborers treated them simply as images, using some of them backward or upside down.[26] Once again, appropriation and innovation are intertwined.

The new script was not a roaring success back home. Although texts written on wood or papyrus will have vanished in the relatively damp climate of the Levant, the few examples of alphabetic writing found over the following centuries are still for the most part very short texts, with signs that become increasingly schematic.[27]

Perhaps this was the problem: the loss of the pictographic aspect would have made the letters harder to interpret without learning them first. Or perhaps the problem was the opposite: that alphabetic signs weren't hard enough, and so lacked sufficient prestige. Levantine kings certainly preferred the more complex syllabic writing systems etched into clay tablets by specialist scribes for their literature, letters, and bureaucratic records.

The Ugaritic script was the first state-sponsored development of an alphabet.[28] The involvement of formally trained scribes and civic officials in the process may explain some of the more innovative aspects of Ugaritic Alphabetic. The earlier alphabets had been rather informal, with a flexible number of letters written in a variety of ways. They were also technically abjads, marking only consonants. The Ugaritic alphabet was by contrast standardized, and it even marked some vowel sounds, giving it a relatively large number of thirty letters altogether.

In an even bigger shift, Ugaritic Alphabetic was written in cuneiform, transforming the earlier linear signs, easier to write in ink or scratch on rock, into patterns of wedges.[29] This may have been a deliberate effort to distinguish the Ugaritic script from the existing low-status local alphabets and align it more closely with the more prestigious scripts used for interstate communication.[30] It may also have been a purely practical decision, allowing scribes to switch between languages and scripts without swapping out their toolkit. Either way, the new writing system combined the Levantine alphabet with a Mesopotamian technology to produce a new tool for local communication.*

This is a textbook example of "glocalization": the way that the more places became involved in broader economic and cultural networks, the more they tended to emphasize, rediscover, or even invent their own local customs and identities.[31] And the same disruptive, localizing interpretation of broader cultural technologies can be seen in a final innovation of the thirteenth century BCE: a new kind of epic literature composed in the local language and written in the local alphabet.

Although Ugarit itself is not mentioned in any of these stories, the names, gods, geography, and poetic structure of the tales are local, and they reflect a larger oral storytelling tradition in the Levant. They also offer an alternative to the garbled versions of Levantine myth that had made their way into the imperial literatures of the era: one Hittite story even contains a character called "Elkunirsha," a misunderstanding of the phrase "El, Creator of Earth" as the god's proper name.[32] This local poetry allowed a literary class at Ugarit to take control of their own stories.

The longest and best-preserved text is the Baal Cycle, which survives on a single set of tablets. It was inscribed and probably composed as well by one Ilimilku who served as chamberlain to King Niqmaddu in the late thirteenth century BCE.[33] The dramatic and often very funny tale follows the career of the city's patron deity, the hot-tempered weather god Baal, as he defeats his rival the sea god Yam, builds a palace on Mount Saphon, the northern boundary of Ugaritic territory, and is killed and eaten by Mot the god of death but then rescued by his sister Anat.

*It was not necessarily a more democratic form of communication. Although alphabets are obviously faster to learn than syllabic or ideographic scripts, the idea that a smaller number of signs makes alphabets inherently more egalitarian is hard to demonstrate: its use never brought about widespread literacy in the Greco-Roman world, and it still takes schoolchildren some time to learn to read and write an alphabetic language, while children in modern China or Japan do not tend to find their more complex writing systems an insuperable obstacle to literacy.

As in the Hebrew Bible, and in Akkadian literature, Ugaritic poetry works through "parallelism": it is based not on rhyme or meter but on short verses juxtaposing two or three parallel lines. So when we first meet Baal's dashing sister she is doing battle with unknown numbers of mortal men for unknown reasons:

> She smites the peoples [dwelling] on the seashore,
> wreaks destruction on the humans [dwelling] to the east . . .
> She attaches heads around her neck,
> ties hands at her waist.
> Up to her knees she wades in the blood of soldiers,
> to her neck in the gore of fighters.[34]

The delight Anat takes in her activities is typically unsettling. Ugaritic myths do not glorify the deities, kings, and humans they describe. They are instead a riot of badly behaved gods, weak men, and smart, violent women rampaging around the cities and seas of the eastern Mediterranean, feasting, flirting, and generally causing trouble.

In this and other ways they are quite unlike the epics of Sumerian and Akkadian literature that are also preserved at Ugarit, as in many other west Asian cities.[35] Similarly, the story of the Baal Cycle builds on a traditional west Asian tale of a storm god defeating a sea god, but treats the topic in a different way.[36]

One example will suffice, taken from a Babylonian poem written down about a century after the Baal Cycle called *Enuma elish,* or "When, above": the standard ancient titles of literary works in Akkadian are simply their first words. In this work all the other gods support the god of Babylon, the four-eared, four-eyed storm god Marduk, in his battle against Tiamat the goddess of the sea. When he kills her he uses her body to rebuild the universe in a fixed and proper state, including the creation of humans from the blood of her monstrous allies. Here the combat delivers a clear moral and political message about great deeds, natural hierarchies, and the victory of good over evil.

The Baal Cycle turns this whole tradition upside down. The gods are an irresponsible lot, always squabbling about something, the hero is entirely ineffective, and it is often the women who shine. Yam vies for ultimate authority with El, king of the gods, while Baal himself commands little support from the other deities, and has no clear natural or moral legitimacy as a ruler. He is not high-born by divine standards, nor does he acquire his throne by his own efforts: he defeats Yam with the help of magic maces fashioned by the craftsman god Kothar-wa-Hasis. He needs a palace to symbolize his new position among the other gods, but he can get permission from El to build one only with the help of the wily goddess Atirat, whose own favors are of more interest to the king of the gods than Baal's construction project. Baal then requires expert help from Kothar-wa-Hasis to actually build the palace, losing an argument with him along the way about where to put a lattice window. When he finally falls for the tricks of the death god Mot, he is resurrected only after attempts to replace him with other gods fail, and only with the help of his sister Anat, who dismembers Mot with characteristic enthusiasm.

This is not simple storytelling. Despite its mythological subject matter, the Baal Cycle grounds itself in the reality of interstate relations from the start. Like the Amarna kings, the gods in the story are constantly sending messengers to one another, conveying gifts of silver and gold, horses, chariots, and slaves, as well as traveling great distances themselves over land and sea. And when El requires Baal to pay tribute to Yam, the text uses the same terminology as Ugaritic documents relating to the city's subjugation to the Hittite king: Baal is a vassal to El's Great King.[37] The story of Baal's travails is not an upbeat patriotic tale of its god's eventual victory, nor just a lament for Ugarit's vassal status, but a sophisticated and skeptical perspective on the way the world works. The tale not only reflects the fractious and unpredictable reality of the Amarna order, but calls it into question.

In its apparently disrespectful treatment of Ugarit's own principal god as well as of the city's political masters the Baal Cycle fits in with other literary texts in Ugaritic that question political and religious conventions. Kingship in particular is unpredictable.[38] One story about a feast held by El involves him getting so drunk that his sons have to carry him home, and the effects of overindulgence speak eloquently across the millennia:

El fell down as though dead
El was like those who go down into the underworld.[39]

Human kings are just as bad. One poem tells the story of a monarch called Kirta, who is desperate for an heir but has the misfortune to lose seven or eight wives in a row.[40] They all disappear, die, or are killed in a series of tragic and peculiar accidents before they can provide him with a child. El comes to the king in a dream and advises him to acquire a new wife for procreational purposes by blackmailing a neighboring king into handing over his daughter. This project accomplished, Kirta's new wife Hurraya dutifully produces seven or eight sons as well as seven or eight daughters. The king himself then grows old and sick, and his loyal sons mourn his imminent death—at which point El decides to keep him alive after all. When one of his sons still generously offers to take on his sickly father's responsibilities, Kirta offers to break his head—and there the surviving text breaks off.

Commercial success and foreign contact led to dramatic change at Ugarit, and to the assertion of local identities that distanced the city from the larger Bronze Age empires. Ugaritic literature questioned their royal authority along with the city's own. All the same, there came a time when even Ugarit needed help from greater powers.

Around 1190 BCE, enemy ships were bearing down on the city. The king sent a plea for help to the king of Alashiya, who advised him to fortify his towns and gather his warriors and chariots within them.[41] The king's reply is desperate: "My father, now the ships of the enemy have come. They have been setting fire to my towns and have done harm to the land. Doesn't my father know that all my infantry and [chariotry] are stationed in Hatti, and that all my ships are stationed in the land of Lukka [Lycia]?" He suspects the worst is still to come: "Now the seven ships of the enemy which have been coming have done harm to us. Now if other ships of the enemy turn up, send me a report . . . so that I will know."[42]

The second response, this time from the senior governor of Cyprus, is ominous: "the twenty ships which the enemy hadn't yet launched in the mountainous areas have not stayed put. They left suddenly and we don't know where they've turned up [?]. I've written to you to inform you, so that you can take defensive measures."[43] It was too late. The correspondence was baked in the blaze that destroyed the city, left behind with the arrowheads from the final attack.[44]

It wasn't just Ugarit. Over a generation either side of the year 1200 BCE, cities up and down the east coast of the Mediterranean were destroyed by fire. Twelve hundred kilometers to the west, Mycenae succumbed. Over the course of just a few hours the conflagration spread across the citadel, from the Lion Gate to the busy artists' quarter behind the palace, where blacksmiths, goldsmiths, painters, and potters made the luxurious goods of everyday royal life. In the palace itself the bright wall paintings and heavy fabrics of the great throne room went up in flames; whether or not the fire itself was deliberate, the metalwork had already been looted. Everything was destroyed. The same happened at Tiryns, and at Pylos. Altogether more than thirty sites across the Aegean, Cyprus, Anatolia, and the Levant were stripped of their valuables and then burned. The world in which Ugarit made its peculiar mark largely ended with it.

CHAPTER SEVEN

Regime Change

LEFKANDI, 1000 BCE

The sleepy beach resort of Lefkandi on the southwest coast of the Greek island of Euboea is an unlikely setting for a discovery of great historical importance. Above the tourist cafés and beach umbrellas, however, archaeologists have toiled for decades at an anonymous ancient settlement known locally as Xeropolis or "Dry Town." The site sits on a low promontory rising between two natural harbors, facing the hills of the Greek mainland across the wide blue ribbon of the Euboean Gulf, which channeled ancient shipping toward the mines on the mainland farther north. At the dawn of the first millennium BCE, though, two centuries after the fires raged through the Bronze Age palaces, it was a quiet local harbor that had seen few foreign traders in decades.

That made it all the more of a surprise when the ruins of a sophisticated building of this era were found in 1980 a couple of streets behind the beach. Fifty meters by almost fourteen, it boasted plastered mud-brick walls built on stone foundations over a platform of leveled rock, a gabled roof, and a colonnade of wooden posts that ran most of the way around the building. Dated by pottery sherds to the early tenth century BCE, this was the first example of monumental architecture in the Aegean for two centuries, the last for another two, and the remains were

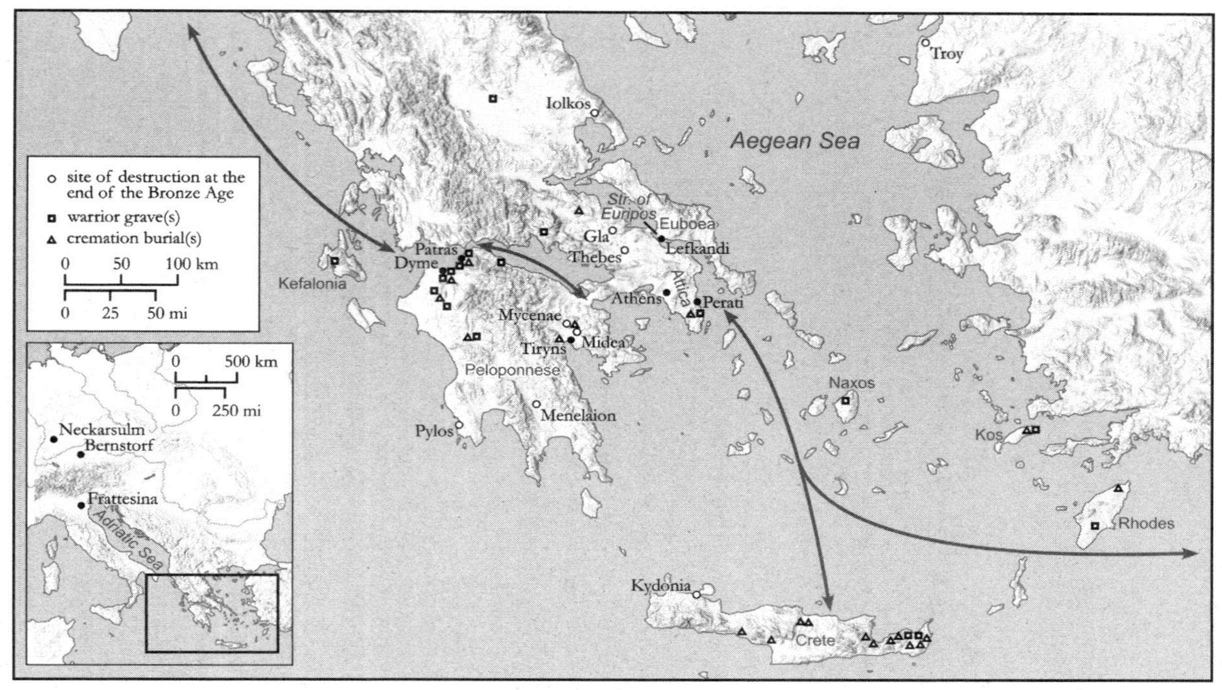

Commercial connections in the twelfth century BCE

almost lost again when the landowner attempted to bulldoze the entire structure before the Greek Archaeological Service could expropriate it. He had only succeeded in taking a large chunk out of one side when the archaeologists stymied his plan to build a summer house on the site and began to excavate instead.[1] What they uncovered suggests a chilling scene.

A few hundred people must have gathered for the ceremonies. First came the cremation, surely at night, when the flames from the great pyre would have lit up the sky around the mourners. Then the ashes of wood and bone were shoveled carefully into a great bronze jar. The man's iron razor, sword, and spear went in too, with a whetstone to keep them sharp. Four of his horses pulled the chariot bearing his remains back to his own house, where two great pits had been dug into bedrock under the central room. There his woman was waiting, dressed in her finest jewelry, with gilt coils in her hair and golden discs covering her breasts. The crossed position in which her hands and feet were found suggests that she was bound. She must in any case have been terrified as she watched them cut the horses' throats and lower their bodies into the larger hole, two buried with their bits still between their teeth. Then she followed the animals. Her body was laid out in the smaller pit beside the urn, the ivory-handled iron knife that had killed her placed gently by her cheek. Shortly afterward the whole structure was destroyed, and a low mound of earth built over the site. Constructing the mound alone would have taken a hundred men at least a week: the "Hero of Lefkandi" had been a person of great importance.

The objects buried with him confirm it: not only were they valuable, but in some cases they were very old, and from very far away. The bronze urn had been manufactured in Cyprus a century or two earlier, the woman wore a necklace made in Babylonia five centuries before that, and the knife's ivory must have come through Egypt or the Levant. The house tomb at Lefkandi gives us a glimpse into a forgotten world, the centuries traditionally known as the Greek Dark Age between the glories of the Bronze Age kingdoms and the wonders of the Classical city-states. It shows us above all the continuing importance of foreign contact in the local imagination even when it had largely disappeared from day-to-day life. These objects were souvenirs of richer times and wider horizons, treasured heirlooms from the town's trading heyday: the people of Lefkandi resisted isolation even when there was little alternative.

In the wake of the destructions around 1200 BCE, fine arts, trade, and writing declined across the whole of the old Amarna system.[2] Individual kingdoms became more isolated and less powerful, and some disappeared altogether. The Hittite empire fell apart in the early twelfth century under pressure from upstart challengers to the south and west and nomadic raids from the north: Hattusa was abandoned by its embattled kings, and around 1185 BCE its palace, temples, and fortifications were torched.[3] Egypt lost its lands in Kush and the southern Levant in the twelfth century, and the ruling dynasty itself disintegrated in the eleventh, taking the New Kingdom with it.

Farther east the changes were less dramatic but still profound: Assyria lost much of its territory, and the Mesopotamian kingdoms more generally were reduced to a smaller and less stable core of cities, cut off from Egypt, Anatolia, and the Mediterranean. Only Cypriot communities proved relatively resilient: the island suffered its own series of attacks around 1200, but its ports recovered and monumental sanctuaries soon appear at Kition and Paphos.[4]

Worst affected was the Aegean, where fire and fury give way to an eerie silence. We hear no more of Ahhiyawa, and the palaces were never rebuilt. Many towns and villages were abandoned. For several centuries everyday life became simpler, and harder for archaeologists to see. Ancient Greek authors are largely silent on this period, and in the twentieth century, English-speaking archaeologists labeled it a "Dark Age," on the model of the later Dark Ages already thought to have descended on Europe after the splendors of Greece and Rome.[5] It made "Classical"

Greece even more of a miracle, emerging as it seemed fully formed out of centuries of poverty and obscurity.

Scholars have traditionally been more interested in who or what was to blame for the "collapse of the Bronze Age" than in the changes that resulted, and there are plenty of theories.[6] Contemporary documents provide some useful suspects: there are Egyptian reports of raiding in the eastern Mediterranean by foreigners collectively known to scholars as "Sea Peoples."[7] In many cases, however, it was only palaces and other public or religious buildings that were burned, not the residential quarters of the cities.

Of all the people who could have attacked the palaces, the local population would have had the most opportunity, and the greatest motivation as well: to escape royal taxes and the demands of royal building works, which for pure ostentation sometimes used larger blocks of stone than were structurally required.[8]

Scholars no longer believe the old picture of the "Mycenaean" kingdoms as highly centralized bureaucracies controlling every aspect of their subjects' lives. Even the king himself usually appears in the administrative records preserved in Linear B in a ritual role, not commanding armies or the economy. Much of the agricultural land meanwhile was administered in the different districts by an independent local body with its own legal standing called the *damos*—the word later used, as *demos,* for the "people."[9] All the same, there is no doubt that these clay tablets—which survive in greatest quantity at Pylos—still describe a world in which the labor of many fed the mouths of a few, and in particular the king. One way or another, most people owed contributions to the palace in kind or in service (including military service), and many were repaid in food or land.[10]

Pirates and political rebels might account for the destruction, but not for the failure to rebuild. Recent attention has therefore focused on more impersonal threats, and above all on natural disaster: an earthquake storm, perhaps, or climate change.[11] Over the last decade, scholars have also emphasized the structural risks that reached through the

Amarna system, and the interdependence of the larger palatial network as a problem in itself, whereby the failure of individual states and kingdoms brought about by a domino effect the collapse of the whole system.[12]

In truth, the craggy landscape and unpredictable climate of the Mediterranean were never ideal for an economic and political system based to any significant extent on the exploitation of agricultural labor. The Amarna kings to the east may be remembered for their gold and their chariots, but their wealth came from the vast flat tracts of good farmland that fed their armies, laborers, and craftsmen. By contrast, smaller and more flexible political communities better suited the limited farmland and poor soils of the Aegean region.

Seen from this perspective, the palaces were simply a failed experiment. And while theories about their demise try to explain what went wrong, for some the changes put things right. In recent decades archaeologists have pushed back against the pessimistic vision of earlier scholarship to reveal more and more evidence for prosperity and creativity during what specialists now call more prosaically the "Early Iron Age."[13]

It would still be wrong to romanticize this era. There is no doubt that it was a period of great upheaval, and life in the Aegean was in many ways pretty bleak. A dramatic fall in both the number and size of detectable sites suggests a considerable drop in population, especially in the vicinity of the old palaces, and a fall in the number of identifiable artifacts suggests lower living standards. There is plenty of evidence for continuing social hierarchy as well: even if the palaces were destroyed by their own subjects, popular revolutions rarely lead to popular rule.

What happened in Greece after 1200 BCE was not so much disintegration as simplification.[14] Kings disappeared along with their palaces. The city walls and royal tombs that symbolized state power—and state control of manpower—disappeared with them. Gods in general survived: many of the deities familiar from Classical Greece had already been mentioned in the Linear B tablets—including Zeus, Hera, Poseidon, Dionysus—although there are some who didn't make it, including Potnia ("mistress") and Diwia (a female version of Zeus?). Below the level of the palaces, some things carried on as before, others somewhat better. Most people now lived in plainer houses in smaller communities, but they still farmed a range of crops, and they still produced wheel-made and painted pottery. Everywhere the local became the main stage.

In perhaps the most striking change, literacy was abandoned at the end of the Bronze Age along with monarchy. There is no trace of writing anywhere in the Aegean for around 400 years. To a modern reader this may seem shocking, or even sad. But Linear B had been a language of accounting and bureaucracy above all, legible only to a few trained scribes. For most people its connotations would have been negative: it had been a tool of privilege if not subjection, the way the palaces counted the wheat, wool, and oil owed to them, and controlled the service and labor they required. Linear B had never been used to record the kind of legends written down at Ugarit, Babylon, or Egyptian Thebes, and as we shall see, local stories survived its loss.

This highlights another problem with modern civilizational thinking: we lose sight of the people who don't fit the model. It is reinscribed in the distinction between "history" and "prehistory," traditionally defined as the study of literate and nonliterate civilizations respectively. Writing isn't in itself though an advance on language, just one thing to do with it. It also has obvious drawbacks as a means of communicating and recordkeeping: anything more than a simple picture-based system takes valuable time to learn, and unlike one's first spoken language at least it requires a conscious effort. Written records are easily lost or—worse—intercepted. Overall, writing works best for those in power, who want to take censuses, collect taxes, and impose law. It's not so obviously in the interests of the rest of us.[15]

The usual focus on the plight of the wealthy and powerful in this era obscures a more interesting story of social, economic, and political experimentation among Greek speakers. What collapsed at the end of the Bronze Age was not a civilization or even the whole of society, but the western edge of a system of rulership embodied in the burnt-out palaces. In the collective refusal to rebuild them we can see a change of priorities.

This hasn't of course gone entirely unnoticed, and some twentieth-century scholars even tried to work it into a civilizational story: the "Mycenaean" kingdoms on this model were mere copies or shadows of authoritarian oriental monarchies of the same era—themselves largely fantastical—and their fall to smaller and less hierarchical communities marked the first steps toward a properly Greek, democratic civilization in which the roots of the West might be found.[16]

In practical terms, it is not at all clear that the kings of the Bronze Age Aegean modeled their economic and political systems on examples farther east, or even had the information required to do so. More important for us though, one of the most striking things about social and political developments in the Early Iron Age Aegean is that, far from creating a pure new culture, they were fueled and inspired by connections with other parts of the world, even after those connections themselves largely faded away.

The rhetoric of "collapse" obscures a more complicated story in the Aegean, of rapid change and then slow deterioration. At first the loss of the palaces brought prosperity to new parts of Greece, above all places on trade routes. While the overall volume of overseas commerce declined in the Aegean, largely as a result of the declining population, more people and places now profited from it.[17] More than three times as many excavated sites in the Aegean imported overseas goods in the twelfth century BCE compared with the thirteenth.[18] And while imports in the Late Bronze Age tended to be concentrated at palatial capitals like Mycenae, Thebes, and Tiryns, twelfth- and eleventh-century imports are found in large numbers only in areas that *didn't* have Bronze Age palaces.[19]

Xeropolis itself was one of the success stories of this era in this sense, and the reason isn't hard to see: it made a natural stopping point for shipping en route to the northern Aegean mines a few kilometers south of the narrow and unpredictable Strait of Euripos that separates Euboea from the mainland, where the tides change direction seven or eight times a day. Another was Perati on the east coast of silver-rich Attica, where graves boast scarabs and faience from Egypt and one amber bead from the Baltic region.[20]

While the export of pottery all the way to the Levant declined and then ceased over the course of the twelfth century, isotope analysis of bronze items made in the Aegean in the twelfth and eleventh centuries demonstrates a continuing copper trade with Cyprus.[21] And this helps to explain a third concentration of imports found at Greek sites along an increasingly popular shipping route from the Isthmus of Corinth and up the Adriatic to continental Europe, a region little affected by the "crisis" that had hit western Asia and the Aegean.[22]

The people who lived there had other concerns in the Late Bronze Age.[23] Where battles had once been fought by bands of one or two dozen men, often over cattle, we now see signs of military conflict on a huge scale. In events almost entirely ignored by recent civilizational history more interested in the burning cities of ancient Greece, the world that had been pulled together by the Alpine metalworking network broke up in flames. Around 1300 BCE the walls of Bernstorf burned down, and 12,000 fragments of human bone mark the site of a clash in the Tollense Valley in the far northeast of Germany, carbon-dated from wooden arrow shafts to the mid-thirteenth century BCE: they represent the remains of at least 140 individuals, which may point to more than 2,000 participants in the battle.[24] Their bones are scarred by trauma, both recent and healed—these men were used to fighting.

Mercenaries were in demand in this era as well, as we can tell from strontium isotope analysis of the teeth of individuals buried at a male-only graveyard at Neckarsulm in southern Germany dated to around 1300 BCE. Strontium is a soft metal that forms naturally in rock all over the world, but its isotopes differ in different regions. When strontium crumbles into the soil, it enters the food supply and eventually the bones and hair of those who eat crops grown there. Most of this material regenerates, so the strontium found in it reflects the isotopes of the region where that person—or animal—most recently lived. When children grow their second set of teeth, however, between the ages of about six and (in the case of third molars or wisdom teeth) their late teens or early twenties, the strontium isotopes in what they are eating at the time are fixed in place and can then tell you where they grew up—or at least where they didn't. In this case the analysis shows that about one-third of the men were not local, but that in addition to being buried in the same graveyard they had shared the same diet as the locals for some time.[25]

We don't know exactly what these wars were about, but they broke out in a period of social change on the continent. Individual grand burials largely disappear in this era, and the practice of cremation spread west from the Carpathian Basin in the thirteenth century BCE into central Europe and Italy. Despite its additional expense and trouble, one attraction of the new rite would have been the dramatic ceremony itself, sending a message to mortals as well as gods. Its adoption may also reflect the arrival of new ideas about death and the divine: in many traditions buried bodies reside with the gods of the underworld, but if they are burned then a soul can ascend in the smoke to the gods of the heavens.[26]

However that may be, war was good for business: European bronze production expanded significantly in these troubled times, bolstered by sheet-bronze technology and fine carpentry techniques pioneered in the Aegean.[27] New swords appear across the continent in the thirteenth century, with a wide, heavy blade designed for slashing more than thrusting, and well suited to man-to-man fighting.[28] These weapons survive in far greater numbers in Europe than earlier types, which must reflect unusually high demand.

From around 1250 BCE the swords also traveled down the Adriatic to the Aegean and points east, along with other bronze weapons and bronze clothes pins (as well as, presumably, the clothes that came with them); in the twelfth century cremation burials begin to appear in Greek cemeteries along the same route.[29] Back went ships that long after the loss of the palaces still carried locally made painted pottery packed in alongside ivory and ostrich eggshells that were still obtained through Cypriot connections, which were evident in the Cypriot imports also found in Greek tombs along all these trade routes.[30]

The same cemeteries reveal that new leaders were coming to the fore in mainland Greece in this period, marked out from the rest in death by the weapons and armor buried with them—a rarity by contrast in Late Bronze Age tombs that have survived intact—along with tweezers, mirrors, razors, and combs, and the majority of the imported goods found in these cemeteries.[31] Their graves are their own: we do not find the communal tombs or family burial plots that marked out ruling families in the earlier era. And these burials are too few in number, just one or two in any cemetery, to represent all of the community's fighting men: these individuals must have had a special standing, acquired as a result of their own personal qualities and their success in attracting followers.[32] It did not pass down to their sons—which is why it makes sense at Lefkandi to turn a leader's house into his tomb.[33]

The new European swords appear in these distinguished warrior graves in large numbers, as both imports and imitations, suggesting that these men's claims rested not only on military skill and personal grooming but on access to foreign goods and techniques.[34] These local heroes were participants in a broader European culture of fighting, metallurgy, and trade, and some may well have served as mercenaries in continental Europe themselves.

Bronze swords were now however becoming vintage goods. As demand for bronze declined in western Asia along with the decline of the Brother Kingdoms, entrepreneurs began to explore new possibilities.

Iron is quicker and simpler to produce than bronze, since it is derived from a single ore found in many more places than copper or tin. The problem is that it melts at a much higher temperature. In the Bronze Age the techniques necessary to smelt iron oxide—heating and reheating it with other agents to free it from its slag—had been the preserve of the Hittites. They probably added carbon to bring the melting point down to a feasible level, but they kept the details to themselves and produced the metal in tiny quantities as a rare luxury.[35]

However they got hold of the secret or solved the puzzle, by the eleventh century BCE Cypriot artisans had perfected the technology to produce iron and introduced it to the rest of the Mediterranean. The widespread availability of iron ore meant that it gradually became the metal of choice for knives, swords, daggers, axes, and even agricultural tools.[36]

This dramatic technological development over a huge area would have been impossible without continuing contacts between distant societies, but in the Aegean it also brought them close to a halt. The new popularity of iron further reduced demand for the distant metals needed to make bronze, and contacts with both Cyprus and continental Europe withered by around 1050 BCE. A century and a half after the Bronze Age palaces collapsed, the people of the Aegean were largely cut off from the rest of the world, and most of their remaining towns disappeared.[37] If the lights were not quite out at this point, they were turned down pretty low.

How long this period of relative isolation actually lasted is difficult to tell: dating the re-emergence of sustained overseas contact usually depends on dating the style of any pottery exchanged, which in many cases depends on little more than a guess. Recent carbon-14 analysis from the northern Aegean and Sidon has however suggested a rather short hiatus, lasting just a couple of generations.[38] Until this is confirmed by further studies, a prudent estimate would still put it at close to a century in many places.

Even so, we have already seen in the remarkable tomb at Lefkandi that even in the depths of their seclusion the people of the Aegean still remembered a wider world, and still used it as a marker of status and power. Their foreign connections don't just matter to us as we reconstruct their history in retrospect; they mattered to them as well. And we can see this even more vividly in the stories people told one another, myths and legends that were passed on by word of mouth and feats of memory until writing returned to Greece in the eighth century BCE.

The best-known examples are found in the *Iliad* and the *Odyssey*, epic tales of superhuman warriors who sacked the city of Troy after a ten-year siege and then fought even harder to get home.[39] Since at least the sixth century BCE both these works have been attributed to a single author named Homer, although later Greeks knew very little about him, and on that they disagreed.[40] Modern scholars remain at odds as to whether the poems were finally committed to writing around 700 BCE by one, two, or many hands. But it has been clear for almost a century that they emerged out of the work of generations of the bards described in the epic songs themselves.[41]

The oral origins of Homeric poetry were conclusively demonstrated in the 1930s, when Harvard classics professor Milman Parry and his student Albert Lord made several trips to Bosnia and Albania to observe the way that local bards sang traditional South Slavic oral epics. They were able to show that their methods shared core characteristics with the Greek epics, similarities emerging from shared practice. Crucially, oral performers of this kind do not memorize their poems by rote: verbatim reproduction is in fact unusual in oral cultures, as there is no fixed text or "original" version for anyone to memorize.[42] Instead they constantly re-create the text for new audiences around a traditional core of characters, stories, and themes, and they do so in more or less predictable ways.[43]

One classic marker of oral recomposition that survives in the *Iliad* and the *Odyssey* is the stock formula—the familiar refrains of "rosy-fingered dawn" and "wine-dark sea" that neatly fit the constraints of the strict poetic meter, easy to trot out and even string together while the performer considers their next move. Another is the type scene: descriptions of typical heroic deeds and encounters from fighting to feasting to sailing almost always follow the same basic structure, so that the singer can concentrate on coloring in specific details to suit the case at hand.[44]

As a result these songs in their final written form contain fragments surviving from different stages of their composition, going back to an era before the Bronze Age palaces themselves and proving that popular culture—and popular memory—survived their fall.[45] Odysseus is gifted a boar's-tusk helmet as found in Bronze Age graves—helmets that by Homer's time had not been seen for centuries.[46] Other warriors carry huge "figure-of-eight" shields reaching from neck to feet that ceased to be useful once warriors began to wear significant amounts of heavy bronze body armor in the fourteenth century BCE.[47] Homer's language as we have it also retains obsolete vocabulary and grammatical forms, and sometimes even treats *r* as a vowel, a feature that had disappeared from the language by the fourteenth century.[48]

Such archaic details didn't just slip through: including them was a deliberate choice, as they helped to create a sense of dramatic distance from the stories being told.[49] They are rare, however. These bards reimagined their stories as they sang: they had to make sense long after the details of everyday life in the Bronze Age world had been forgotten. This means that much of the poems' background scenery reflects times closer to living memory, giving us a window on the Dark Ages they had passed through along the way.

There are no references to standard Bronze Age palace-state phenomena like bureaucracy or industrial production, and there is no certain mention of writing. Even the palaces themselves are usually described in surprisingly simple terms, with earthen floors and pitched roofs, nothing like the grand Bronze Age buildings unearthed by archaeologists.* Central elements of Homeric life meanwhile were unknown in the real Bronze Age: the heroes brandish slashing swords and are cremated in great public ceremonies, while shepherds and plowmen use iron tools.[50]

The poems reveal a fundamentally Dark Age sensibility as well. Their basic premise, that the lord of practically every community in the Aegean spends a decade of their lives on a punitive expedition against the father of a man who has cuckolded one of their number, evokes a world in which hereditary succession is no longer enough. These little kings cannot sit back and await respect: there are always other noble warriors eager to take their place on a man's throne, at his table, or in his bed.

The poems also reveal the extent to which the rest of the world still mattered. From Agamemnon who leads the expedition against Troy to Odysseus who takes another decade to get home, they still have to prove their worth in a foreign war and their ability to survive dangerous journeys. Homer's heroes are men comfortable operating in a larger world, as soldiers and travelers, and as traders or pirates too when the

*Sometimes Bronze Age designs seem to survive for practical reasons. The sorceress Circe, who detains Odysseus for a year on his way home by turning his shipmates into pigs, lives under a flat roof that is crucial for a plot point: the young sailor Elpenor is sleeping drunk on that roof when Odysseus wakes him up so that they can make their escape, and he stumbles off it to his death (*Odyssey* 10.552–60, 11.62–5, with Susan Sherratt, "'Reading the texts': archaeology and the Homeric question," *Antiquity* 64, no. 245 [1990], 814).

circumstances are right. To reach us these stories had to pass through the darkest generations of the Early Iron Age, and they show us that Greek speakers of that era still chose to sing of international kingdoms, intercontinental war, and voyages across broad seas.

In reality, this world was gone for good. The arrival of iron as a cheaper alternative to bronze had wiped out mass demand for copper and tin, and for the vast commercial network that had delivered them. But sailors broke the silence all the same, and in the second half of the tenth century BCE imports appear again in the wealthy graves of a necropolis that grew up alongside the great burial mound at Lefkandi: Cypriot iron knives, Levantine bronze bowls, and a decorative Egyptian bronze bucket.[51]

At the same time, Euboean pottery begins to appear at Levantine ports, and not just any pottery: plates, which were rarely used on Euboea itself, and wide, shallow painted drinking vessels called *skyphoi*, their black glaze buffed to a silver-like sheen and decorated with elegant circles and lines.[52] This wouldn't be enough to sustain a trade route alone, but it still tells us something about the trading relationship; the potters of Lefkandi had found a new market catering to the tastes of a prosperous clientele with an appetite for feasting off luxuries as exotic to them as the handsome bronze bowls they sent back.

We don't know who carried the first Euboean tableware east, whether men of Lefkandi sailed toward Tyre or vice versa. It is clear who set the rules of engagement. One man who looks very much like an armed trader is buried in the cemetery in the early ninth century with a sword, spearheads, sixteen Levantine stone balance weights and an antique Syrian cylinder seal.[53] It is impossible to say whether he was a local or a visitor, but he is working in a Levantine world of trade, with people who hadn't had much of a Dark Age at all.

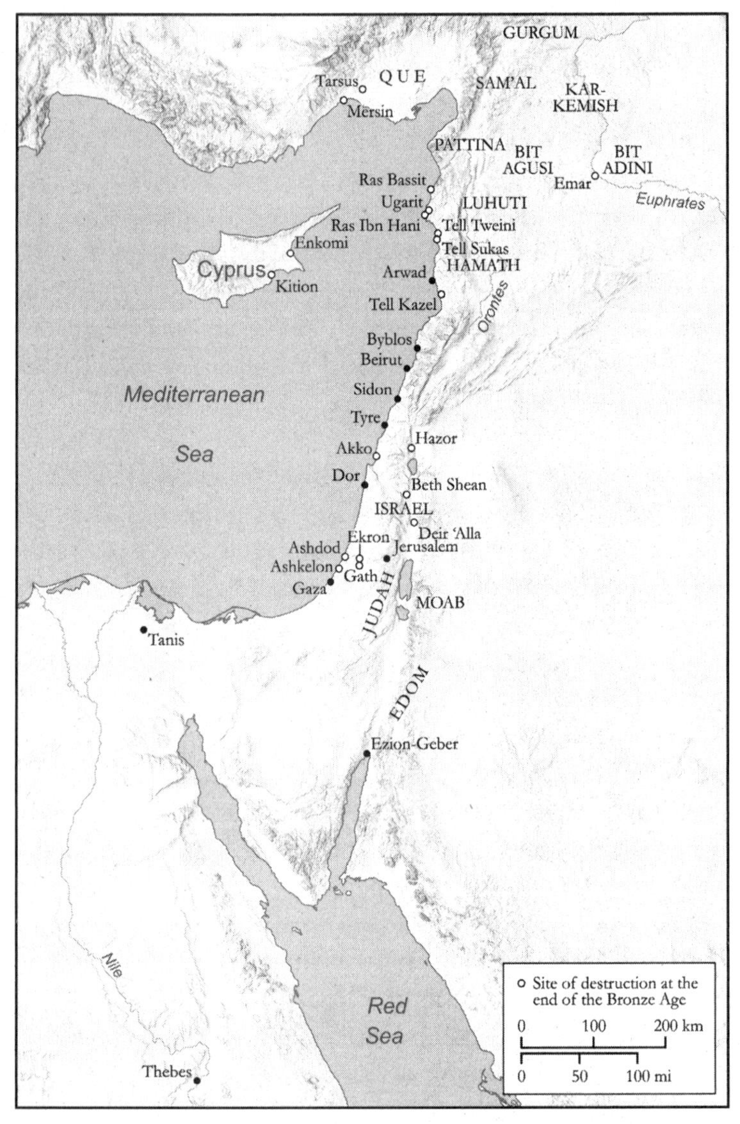

The Iron Age Levant, c. 900 BCE

CHAPTER EIGHT

I Am Not Your Servant

TYRE, 950 BCE

To understand what was going on in the Levant in the tenth century BCE, we need to travel back in time a little, and in good company. The Egyptian "Tale of Wenamun" is a comic account of the misfortunes of an Egyptian temple administrator who undertakes a voyage up the Levantine coast in the eleventh century BCE. Composed no more than a century later, it was found on a single papyrus in Egypt in the 1890s.[1] By Wenamun's time Egypt no longer controlled territory in the Levant, and the united New Kingdom of the Late Bronze Age had ceded power to two separate dynasties in Upper and Lower Egypt. The former was based at the river city of Thebes and was ruled by the high priest of Amon, who decides at the beginning of this tale to send his servant Wenamun to Byblos to buy cedarwood to repair their god's great ceremonial barge.

Wenamun first travels down the Nile to the northern Egyptian kingdom that was based at Tanis in the Delta, where the king and queen receive him kindly and send him on to Dor on the Levantine coast. There he is welcomed again by the local king, Beder. Things only begin to go wrong when a man from Wenamun's own ship steals the silver and gold he had brought with him to buy the cedar. Beder is understandably reluctant to take responsibility for the theft, and fails to find the man responsible. So at some point, somehow—the text here is fragmentary—Wenamun takes matters into his own hands and appropriates a considerable amount of silver belonging to locals.

By the time the story becomes comprehensible again, Wenamun has made his way up the coast via Tyre to Byblos. King Zakerbaal is unimpressed by his Egyptian visitor, and tries repeatedly to expel him, but Wenamun—now without a ship—refuses to leave unless Zakerbaal provides one. Meanwhile, an idol of Amon that he has brought with him gets up to mischief, possessing one of Zakerbaal's entourage. Eventually Wenamun finds a vessel that will take him home but just as he is on the point of leaving, the king summons him to his presence—only to berate him for arriving without proper credentials. Zakerbaal points out to Wenamun that the sum he is offering for the cedar is only a fraction of what his predecessors had paid, gloats over how far Egypt has fallen, and emphasizes his own new power: "I am not your servant! Nor am I the servant of him who sent you!"[2]

The king then sends a demand for further payment to Egypt's Delta kingdom, and receives in return more gold and silver, as well as linen, cowhides, rope, lentils, and fish—a list that highlights how little we usually know about trade and exchange in the distant past: none of the goods that Wenamun brings with him on his journey, or that Zakerbaal later demands, would leave any trace for archaeologists today. It also placates the king, who has the required cedar cut and seasoned, and is about to send it back to Egypt with Wenamun when ships arrive from Dor to arrest the Egyptian for theft. Wenamun flees to a Cypriot harbor where the townspeople attack the new arrivals, and we last see him seeking asylum from a local queen called Hatbi: "She said to me: 'Spend the night . . .' "[3] At this point the text breaks off, leaving us to assume that at some point Wenamun made it back to Egypt, perhaps even with Amon's cedarwood, to make this report.

This is a work of Egyptian literature, not a documentary account, and it is almost certainly a work of fiction. Nonetheless, the setting should have made sense to its original audience: the prosperous maritime world of the eleventh-century Levantine coast, and the busy commercial and political lives of the cities there stand in sharp contrast to the chaotic state of Egypt itself, still in touch with the rest of the world but in too much turmoil to observe the niceties of international diplomacy.

Unlike the Aegean, the Levant had been located at the heart of the Amarna system, as an embattled borderland and transit point between greater powers. After the fall of the Brother Kings and the departure of their soldiers and officials, their old clients became independent states, and new cities and kingdoms grew up alongside them. Together they filled the vacuum left by imperial power with experiments in new political models that would jump-start a new era across the Mediterranean: not despite the collapse of the interstate system, but because of it.

In the mountains of the north, independent kingdoms emerged out of old Hittite provinces and client states.[4] In the southern coastal plain, prosperous industrial cities filled a landscape deserted by Egyptian garrisons later in the twelfth century.[5] Inland, Aramean herders established a series of new tribal states, each conceptualized as the "House of" a legendary shared ancestor: Bit Adini, Bit Agusi, and so on.[6]

Nestled in the middle of these new societies were the biggest winners of all, a string of ancient ports that traced the central Levantine coast from Arwad south to Dor. These were cities like Tyre, Sidon, Beirut, and Byblos, small states left standing among the ruins of the old empires. Nominally vassals of Egypt during the Bronze Age, they had escaped the destructions that signaled its end. The convenient disappearance of Ugarit farther north reoriented regional trade networks in their direction, and their merchants rose to dominate the eastern Mediterranean.

We call these people Phoenicians, borrowing a label used by Greek authors for people from the Levant.[7] The word *phoinix* has a number of different meanings in Greek, including the date palm, a musical instrument, and the immortal bird, but in this case it probably meant "purple" or "crimson"—a reference not to skin color, but to the local specialty craft of producing purple dye from the murex sea snail.

It is not surprising that from a distance these "Phoenicians" looked—or rather sounded—identical: they all spoke similar dialects of a northwest Semitic language very different from Greek.[8] But as far as we know they did not see themselves as a group: on the surviving evidence—which includes more than 10,000 inscriptions from these cities and their overseas settlements—no one ever calls themself a Phoenician in their own language, or uses any similar collective term.[9] Instead, they describe themselves as "sons" of their individual towns, in the regional tradition found earlier at Ugarit and Emar.[10]

The study of antiquity gives the lie to the idea that everyone is born with a natural, fixed ethnic identity, tied to specific other people by ancestry or ancestral territory. The concept is fundamentally incoherent anyway: at some level all humans share the same ancestry and territory, and decisions about where to draw lines across that shared heritage in time and space can only ever be arbitrary. But ethnic identification is also for the most part a relatively modern phenomenon, associated with modern levels of literacy, communication, and mobility. Without these, communal identities tend to form on smaller scales. And despite their physical proximity to one another, links between the "Phoenician" ports were relatively weak.[11]

By land at least, these harbors were curiously remote: they were cut off to their east by a formidable chain of mountains, and most were cut off to north and south as well by multiple fast-flowing rivers running down to the sea. Along with the shortage of farmland on the narrow coastal plain, this encouraged the development of small, autonomous communities, focused above all on the sea: Tyre and Arwad were offshore islands, while their neighbors were located on capes with natural, protected harbors.

It is still hard to say much about the individual Levantine ports in this era: their locations were so well chosen that most have been inhabited ever since, frustrating the efforts of curious archaeologists. But there are few signs of the decline that followed the destructions at the end of the Bronze Age elsewhere: excavations at Sidon, for instance, have revealed a monumental new twelfth-century temple.[12] The eleventh-century site we know most about is Dor, a growing city with large courtyard houses and a lively purple-dye industry. It is situated on what is now a deserted headland in northern Israel with natural harbors to both north and south: prosperity in the Levant was still firmly linked to trade. In an era when Aegean communities had little contact even with their closest neighbors, Dor was exporting pottery to Cyprus, Anatolia, and Egypt, and importing goods like cinnamon from as far away as India.[13]

We get further clues to the scale and organization of merchant shipping at Dor and its neighbors from the Tale of Wenamun, where King Zakerbaal informs Wenamun that there are twenty ships in the Byblos harbor with established dealings with the royal house of the Egyptian Delta, and that another fifty coasters at Sidon have contracts with a private merchant overseas.[14] This tells us something about the relationship between the state and shipping in the region as well: the local traders do business with their own kings, of course, but they also deal with Egyptian monarchs, and with foreign merchants. Merchants in these Levantine ports work not for the state but with it, on a model that we have already seen at Bronze Age Ugarit but that was even more powerful in the absence of foreign imperial control. King Beder's unconcerned reaction to the theft of Wenamun's money by a sailor in his own harbor is very different from the determination of the Amarna kings to control the journeyways of trade.

The Tale of Wenamun is especially interesting for its portrait of Byblos as the most powerful port on the central Levantine coast, since excavations there have so far failed to locate substantial remains from this era. We do have a royal necropolis revealed by a cliff fall in 1922, full of stone sarcophagi covered in the lengthy epitaphs of tenth-century BCE kings. This is the first monumental writing known from any of the Levantine cities, including Ugarit, and it is written in the local vernacular dialect and in an alphabet.[15] Instead of borrowing the cuneiform alphabet of Ugarit, however, which more or less disappeared with that city, Byblos adapted instead the much older linear alphabet that had been used intermittently in the Levant for over a millennium, and was much easier to write without specialized equipment.[16] As is so often the case, increasing contact with a wider world led to increased pride in distinctively local traditions.

Byblos remained a famous center of writing: Greek writers called papyrus rolls *bybloi* after the city, the origin of the modern word "bible." But in the tenth century Tyre to the south came into its own. As usual, we know very little about the archaeology: Tyre is now a busy Lebanese city with a broad headland linking the old island to the mainland, and it offers few opportunities for excavation. A deep sounding near the center of the island has however revealed a large industrial area of potters and metalworkers close to the acropolis, a suggestive glimpse of the inner workings of a prospering city.[17]

Fragments of imported pottery tell us more: large quantities of pottery made on the island of Euboea appear at Tyre in the later tenth century, in the same period that we saw a resurgence of foreign goods in the graves at Lefkandi. The fact that tenth-century Levantine imports to the Aegean outside Crete are almost all found at Lefkandi and that almost all Euboean pots go to Tyre suggests a direct trading relationship between the two ports.[18]

Later Greek historians give us more specifics, claiming to base their work on archival documents from Tyre itself.[19] They describe tenth-century Tyre as a confident and expanding city under the rule of an entrepreneurial king called Hirom who makes expeditions against Tyrian subjects when they fail to pay their tribute, and transforms the appearance of the island itself with major earthworks. He also renovates the city's temples, and builds new ones to Tyre's divine patrons Ashtart and Melqart.

Ashtart was a great goddess identified with Mesopotamian Ishtar, revered throughout the Levant and reinvented in slightly different guises as the primary female deity of almost every city in the region; Melqart by contrast belonged to Tyre alone, literally the *melk-qart* or "king of the city." Between them the pair reflect the familiar double vision of globalization, emphasizing the city's connections across the whole region at the same time as celebrating its own distinctive identity.

The details of these historical accounts can be questioned, but this portrait of Tyre reflects a new attitude toward the state that makes sense in this new context. Smaller kingdoms operating at arm's length from commerce needed new ways to express their power and guarantee their finances, which would explain a new interest in territorial control and regular tribute collection. At the same time there is a shift in emphasis from the palace—which even at Ugarit covered much of the city's surface—to temples, where state wealth benefits the city as a whole.[20] We hear nothing in our sources of a palace at tenth-century Tyre, or any other city on the Levantine coast in this era: we know that there were kings so they surely still existed, but they no longer mattered in quite the same way.[21]

As with Dor and Byblos in the Egyptian Tale of Wenamun, we get another interesting perspective on tenth-century Tyre from stories told a little later by a neighbor. In this case the source is the Hebrew Bible, a collection of poetry, prose, and legal texts relating to the history and rituals of the Israelite people that was compiled for the most part in the seventh or sixth century BCE.

As a whole, the Bible provides another example of the widespread ancient perspective on historical development, which, contrary to modern civilizational thinking, accounts for change in terms of journeys and encounters—friendly or not—with new people. It traces the origins of Israel to a traveling man called Abraham from Mesopotamian Ur, whose god Yahweh persuaded him in extreme old age to move his family west of the Jordan to the land of Canaan, which was promised to him and his descendants; to his grandson Jacob, or Israel, who then moved the clan to Egypt to escape famine, where they fell instead into slavery; and to the prophet Moses, who eventually freed his people and led them back to Canaan, which they then invaded and conquered.

For our purposes here, however, we are interested in what happened next. After their return to Canaan, the story goes, the Israelites were led at first by a succession of generals drawn from their different tribes, who the Bible says "judged" Israel. In the eleventh century BCE a true kingdom emerged, ruled from the stronghold of Jerusalem in the Judean Mountains, and ruled most famously by a shepherd called David and then by his son Solomon. Both these kings, it seems, cultivated a close and convivial relationship with Hirom, king of Tyre.[22] Hirom sent cedarwood, carpenters, and stonemasons to build David a palace, and when Solomon succeeded to the Israelite throne he asked Hirom for wood to build a temple to Israel's patron god Yahweh, a development that echoes the wider regional shift in focus in this era from the palace to the temple.

The two kings made a covenant: in return for grain and oil—useful gifts to an island—Hirom supplied the Israelite king with gold, wood, and craftsmen for his temple. They also collaborated on a fleet built by Solomon at Ezion-Geber (Eilat) at the head of the Red Sea. Hirom supplied experienced sailors to join Solomon's crew, and the fleet sailed every three years to "Ophir," probably the land on the African horn that the Egyptians called Punt. It returned with gold—420 talents on one occasion, or about twenty-five tons—as well as local wood and precious stones.[23]

The reliability of the historical information given in the Bible is variable, to say the least. David and Solomon may have been real people—a ninth-century BCE Aramaic inscription found in northern Israel in 1993 records the defeat of a "king of the House of David" from the kingdom of Judah.[24] And we have plenty of evidence for Judah itself, and Israel to the north, the two kingdoms into which the Bible tells us King David's "United Kingdom" split in the ninth century BCE.[25]

The evidence for a United Kingdom is however less certain, and tenth-century Jerusalem was a hilltop settlement in a sheep-herding society just a quarter of the size of the contemporary Philistine city of Gath, hometown in the Bible of the giant Goliath.[26] Even if it had a king in this era, it seems unlikely that he was, like the biblical Solomon, the richest monarch of his era, and despite the Bible's confidence on this point it is hard to see where he would have found room to house 700 wives and 300 concubines.[27] We may also harbor reasonable doubts about a tenth-century Israelite kingdom's ability to maintain a major naval presence on the Red Sea.[28]

The biblical story of Hirom, David, and Solomon really tells us more about Tyre than about Jerusalem. It inserts legends of early Israel into a larger and better-known Levantine landscape of power, diplomacy, and trade. In this account Tyre is a powerful city-state, a pioneer in commerce and maritime technology, and active in regional diplomacy. It is King Hirom who makes the first contact with both the Israelite kings, and he is the one who provides the rare metals, the raw materials, and the expertise to build their capital in return for local crops, as well as helping them to build an international fleet.

This reading of the stories of Hirom and the kings of Jerusalem gains support from another biblical tale that also emphasizes the importance of long-distance links south from the Levant. Where Hirom and Solomon launch ships down the Red Sea, however, the queen of Sheba leads what must be the first camel caravan known in world literature up to Jerusalem. It is laden with spices, gold, and precious stones, which she presents to Solomon when he proves his fabled wisdom by solving the riddles she sets him.[29]

Again, we cannot take this as historical evidence for Jerusalem's connections with Saba in modern Yemen. There is no evidence outside the Bible for a powerful Sabean queen, and there is no particular reason to think that an Arabian monarch traveling with a trade caravan would have taken a side trip up a Judean mountain to visit a local shepherd lord. Instead, connections with greater powers reassure the reader of Solomon's own accomplishments and fame.

This only works, though, if a tenth-century caravan from Yemen to the Levant is considered plausible. Assyrian records from the early ninth century do document an "Incense Route" running from southern Arabia up through Mecca to ports including Gaza, a journey of more than two months and a little less than 2,500 kilometers. It was from at least the eighth century under the control of Saba, a kingdom blessed with perfume groves of trees producing pale translucent frankincense and woody, opaque myrrh, aromatic tree resins found only here, in Oman, and in northern Somalia. Sabean harbors also imported ivory and gold from Punt across the Bab el Mandeb ("Gate of Tears") Strait, as well as spices and precious stones from the Persian Gulf and points east.[30]

Finally, genetic analysis now confirms what had long been suspected from the increasing number and decreasing size of camel bones found in human settlements: that the world's small population of wild dromedaries, found only in southern Arabia, had been domesticated by 1000 BCE.[31] This made desert crossings much easier: a camel can travel forty to fifty kilometers a day, twice as far as a human on foot, and carry a load of up to 250 kilos. Unlike horses, camels can survive on desert vegetation alone, needing water as little as once a week, or even less often in the cool season.[32]

The trip north across the desert from the Indian Ocean ports of Saba to the Levant would still have taken around two months—about the same amount of time it now took Tyrian sailors to reach the other end of the Mediterranean, the Atlantic seaboard and its hard, ancient rocks full of copper, silver, gold, and tin.

CHAPTER NINE

Through the Pillars

HUELVA, 875 BCE

Our story starts where the Tyrian sailors' journey ended: at Huelva, a small, lively river port on the Atlantic coast of Spain with a strange mix of early-twentieth-century architecture. Elegant art nouveau mansions line the streets of the town center, while ten minutes' walk away in the "Queen Victoria quarter" sit bungalows that would look at home in any British suburb. They were built for the workers of the Rio Tinto mining company, a British consortium that had bought the nearby copper mines from the Spanish government in 1873. Before the company was nationalized in 1954, Huelva was an unofficial British colony, not of pensioners and vacationers but of businessmen and engineers. They scarred the landscape, poisoned the soil, and built the first golf course in Spain.

Archaeological investigations commissioned during the construction of a multistory parking garage in the town center in 1998 revealed that the British were just the latest in a long line of foreign entrepreneurs to arrive in Huelva (ancient Onoba). This was a "rescue excavation," standard practice with major urban building projects. Before concrete can be poured, brief—ideally very brief—explorations must be conducted to recover any information or material of historical inter-

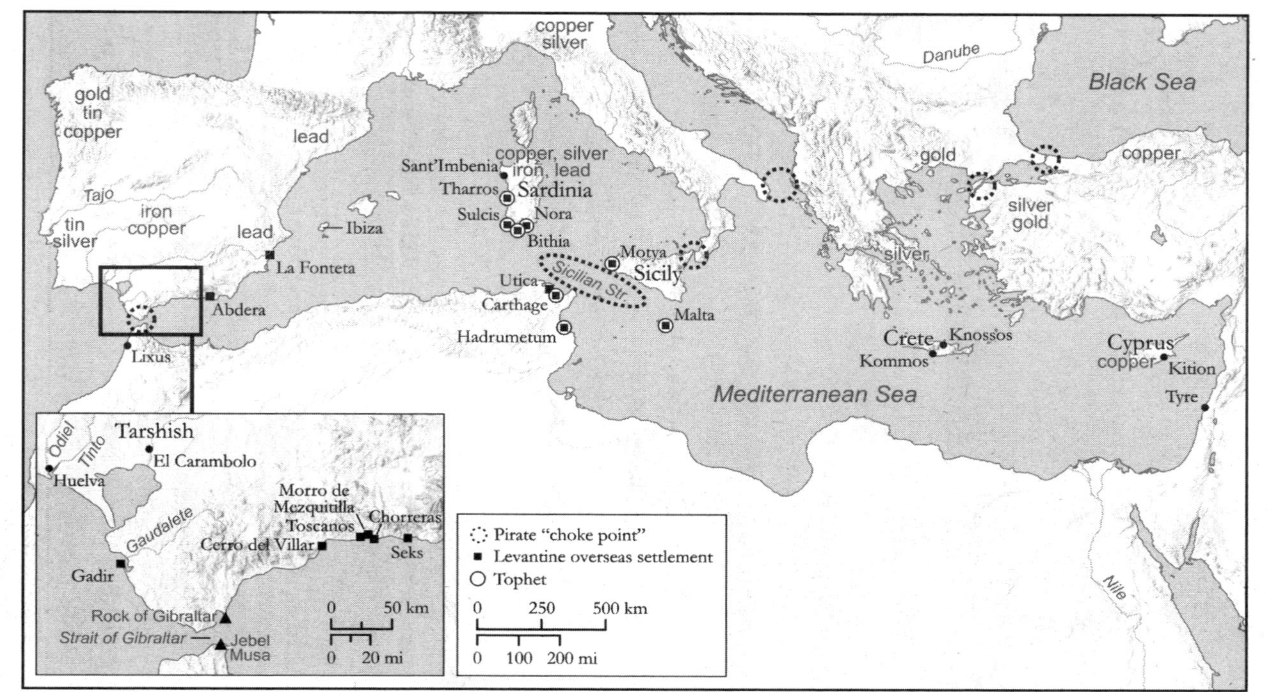

Levantine exploration, trade, and settlement in the early first millennium BCE

est. In this case the archaeologists got lucky: after the contractors had pumped the site dry, they were able to extract soil for the first time from the earliest phase of the city's history, now more than two meters below the water table.[1]

In it they found far more than they were expecting: large quantities of pottery from all over the Mediterranean dating from at least the mid-ninth to the mid-eighth century BCE, mixed in with local ceramics and plentiful evidence for art, craft, and industry.[2] The biggest surprise was that the earliest foreign material was from farthest away: pots just like those found at contemporary Tyre and Dor, almost 4,000 kilometers to the east, and the earliest Levantine pots so far found anywhere in the western Mediterranean.

There was Levantine alphabetic writing too, names and phrases carved on pottery, ivory, and bone, and lead weights manufactured to the half-shekel, shekel, and three-shekel weight standards of the Levant.[3] Murex shells found at the parking garage site suggest experiments with purple-dye production, and there is refuse from the Levantine specialty of ivory carving.

These remarkable finds would not have surprised Greek authors. Homer's Phoenicians were already "famous for their ships" (*nausiklutoi*). One Greek scholar even called them "the first to plow the seas."[4] The Phoenicians were celebrated well into the Roman period for their nautical skills, including their pioneering use of the Pole Star in the Ursa Minor constellation for navigation through the night.[5]

In the modern era, by contrast, archaeologists have traditionally paid far more attention to the evidence for Greek activity in the western Mediterranean, which was long thought to predate the arrival there of Levantine ships.[6] A series of discoveries in recent years have turned this picture upside down, revealing that the Tyrians and their neighbors were sailing and settling in the west long before Greek vessels appeared in the mid-eighth century BCE. They traveled for many reasons too, as we shall see: as merchants and metalworkers, farmers and fugitives, pilgrims and perhaps even pirates.

. . .

The mountains known since Plato's time as the Pillars of Hercules—the Rock of Gibraltar on the Iberian side, Jebel Musa in Morocco—guard a strait that serves as a natural barrier between sea and ocean. The inbound current runs regularly at eleven kilometers an hour, more than enough to deter the casual explorer. On top of that there are strong winds and often fog.

To negotiate it—and to make the journey that far in the first place—would have required sturdy, stable new ships, and we know what they were called: there are nine different references in the Hebrew Bible to Tyrian "ships of Tarshish," the biblical name for southwestern Iberia.[7] Despite their name these vessels are not always found en route to the west: some run down the Red Sea to Ophir.[8] But like ships of Byblos and ships of Keftiu before them, they must have been designed for a specific route: in this case, to cross the Mediterranean and come out the other side.

The route required new skills as well. One traditional idea about ancient navigation is that sailors traveled from port to port along the coast, trying to stay in sight of land, and putting into harbor at dusk.[9] But the fact that the earliest foreign pottery found at Huelva is from Tyre, and that there is no sign of these ceramics anywhere else in the western or central Mediterranean in this era, strongly suggests that the ships of Tarshish headed directly west. Their captains used their knowledge of stars, winds, and currents to cross open sea for weeks at a time, often traveling out of sight of land and stopping, it seems, as little as possible.[10]

These voyages were still difficult and dangerous, as well as time-consuming. The journey from Tyre to Huelva could have taken two months, depending on the winds and weather, and not counting the time spent waiting for a wind at the strait itself.[11] It would have required considerable investment and involved great financial risk. But it was worth it. One of the richest mineral belts in the Mediterranean runs from southwest Spain to southern Portugal, full of iron, copper, silver, and gold. Much of this wealth is concentrated inland of Huelva itself, along the river valleys of the Río Tinto and the Río Odiel.

Ships of Tarshish sailed west carrying clay jars or "amphoras" full of wine and oil, which also acted as ballast on the journey out, packed in with Euboean pottery reshipped from Levantine ports. Presented to the leading men of Huelva brimming with fine wine, these elegant drinking cups could have ensured a warm welcome, and the boats headed home loaded with metals, above all silver.

Silver was used as cash in the Levant: an 8.5-kilo hoard hidden in a jug at Dor in the second half of the tenth century was divided into seventeen separate sealed bags of a standard weight three centuries before the first stamped coins appear in the Mediterranean.[12] Analysis of its composition and isotopes suggests that some of the silver already came from as far west as Sardinia or even Iberia.[13]

There were sources closer to home, in Anatolia's Taurus Mountains as well as in the Aegean, but the downturn in shipping in the eastern Mediterranean had constrained supply: silver found in the Levant from around 1200 to 950 BCE is often heavily adulterated with copper.[14] New connections west helped solve the problem, and by the ninth century silver with certain Iberian origins is found in a hoard buried at ʿEin Hofez, a mountain village a few kilometers inland of Dor.[15]

Phoenician demand for Iberian silver was proverbial to later Greeks: they were so greedy, they said, that if their boats were full but there was still silver to load, they forged it into anchors.[16] According to one story they even obtained it by trickery: when an enormous fire left mountains "running with much silver," the natives did not know what it was or what it was worth elsewhere, and so Phoenicians bought it for a pittance to sell back east.[17]

The tale depends on a long-standing Greek stereotype of Phoenicians as cunning and deceptive—originating in the fact that Greek speakers tended to associate Levantines above all with trade, since it was Levantine traders they tended to meet—and an equally enduring notion of western barbarians as rather slow.[18] The first Levantine sailors to sail through the Pillars of Hercules to Huelva were not however dealing with innocents or fools.

Three thousand years ago the Atlantic seaboard was peppered with small villages of round houses and lively harbors. People communicated by river and sea in large canoes loaded with rare metals: gold from Ireland, tin from Cornwall, Brittany, and Galicia, silver from Tarshish. We can trace their journeys in new types of sword, cauldron, and roasting spit that appear all along the Atlantic seaboard in the late second millennium BCE, both sides of the strait.[19]

Irish cauldrons become especially popular in northern Portugal, while the carp's tongue sword, so called because its blade was for most of its length broad, for slashing, but narrowed dramatically to a thrusting tip, has been found from southern Britain to southern Iberia.[20] Trading links reached down rivers into continental Europe, and bronze shields with a V-notched boss of central European design are found in wood and leather versions in peat bogs in Ireland.[21] They already extended into the Mediterranean as well, delivering occasional Levantine imports through many ports and hands to the Atlantic coast. Finds range from ivory combs to bronze bowls to fragments of musical instruments.[22]

At Huelva itself an enormous dump of bronzes in the harbor carbon-dated to the tenth century BCE includes hundreds of Atlantic-style swords and spearheads, perhaps the arms of defeated enemies dedicated to the gods of the sea, as well as a Sicilian clothespin.[23] Access to these networks must have been a pull factor in itself, but local metals were the main attraction.

Finds under the parking garage from the era of early contact include evidence for metalworking of all kinds: furnaces and Levantine-style crucibles for heating, as well as silver, copper, and iron slag.[24] People at Huelva had long been mining copper and exchanging it for tin from farther up the coast to supply their bronzesmiths. The newcomers helped to scale up production, and to refocus operations on silver: the basic techniques required for producing it from lead ores were already known in the region, but there are few silver artifacts from the second millennium BCE.[25]

Soon ships of Tarshish were making more complicated journeys. By the late ninth century pottery found under the parking garage comes from Cyprus, Sardinia, and central Italy.[26] At the same time Levantine pots and transport jars begin to appear at ports on Crete, Sardinia, and the Mediterranean coast of Iberia, all attractive pit stops on a "Route of the Islands" across the Mediterranean, as well as entry points to smaller regional trading circuits.[27]

The best evidence for the complexities comes from excavations in 2012 at Utica on the northern coast of Tunisia, where Tunisian and Spanish archaeologists discovered a well full of animal bones as well as ninth-century pottery from the Levant, Euboea, Sardinia, Italy, and Iberia. We must be looking at the remains of a feast, perhaps at a stop on the journey home: a little over halfway to Huelva from Tyre by the most direct route, Utica would have offered sailors an excellent opportunity for resupply, rest, and repair.[28]

Before much longer Levantine travelers were sailing west to stay. The first migrants would have been traders and artisans joining existing communities. But before the end of the ninth century BCE we have archaeological evidence for a planned settlement: the earliest certain new foundation yet discovered, earlier than Greek migration by at least two generations, and the very farthest west.

After days or weeks of waiting in the lee of Gibraltar for a wind to help their boat through the strait, the sight of a straggled line of islands a hundred kilometers up the coast must have been very welcome to the Tyrian sailors. It was an ideal spot for a new settlement. To the east, the archipelago sheltered a bay that could provide wood, farmland, and access up the Guadalete River to communities inland. Another day's sailing north would take them to the emporium of Huelva, gateway to copper and silver mines. To the west, the horizon was empty: the next stop, had they known it, was the Caribbean.

The new arrivals chose the northernmost island in the bay, just a little hillock in the ocean, fifteen minutes' walk from end to end, and in the final years of the ninth century BCE they built a tiny village there. Small, neat houses with solid walls and welcoming hearths spilled down the slope toward the little river that separated their islet from a larger, longer island to the south. This became the new settlement's burial ground, and at its far end they built a shrine to the homeland god who had protected their voyage, Melqart.[29] The temple was said in antiquity to contain the god's very bones, as well as timber that never decayed. Its priests were celibate, and statues and images were banned from the sanctuary, along with women and pigs.[30]

According to the Roman historian Velleius Paterculus, writing in the early first century CE, the great western city of Gadir (modern Cádiz) was founded by the powerful fleet of Tyre "on an island surrounded by Ocean at the very end of our world."[31] A fuller version of the tale is preserved by the Greek geographer Strabo, writing around the same time, who attributes it to the people of Gadir themselves.[32]

Strabo's story begins when the Tyrians receive an oracle telling them to found a settlement "by the Pillars of Herakles." The first group sent to scout out possibilities settles on a spot on the Mediterranean coast east of the Pillars, at ancient Seks (modern Almuñécar). When the sacrifices they offer there are unfavorable, however, they come back home. (Examining the entrails of a sacrificed animal, originally a Mesopotamian practice, was the usual way to find out whether it had worked.) A while later, another group goes out to try again, this time sailing through the Pillars and up the Atlantic coast until they get to an island near Huelva. Again their sacrifices are refused, and again they return home. Finally a third group sets out, sails through the strait and finds the archipelago enclosing a bay where they built Gadir, which in their language meant "fence" or "enclosure," and the temple to Melqart.[33] Strabo does not mention whether the new arrivals offered sacrifices: perhaps they had learned better.

Strabo gives no date for his tale, but Velleius puts the foundation of Gadir around 1104 BCE, eighty years after the fall of Troy. This implausibly early dating fits in with a general Greco-Roman tendency to date anything that happened a long time ago in relation to the Trojan War, as well as with the Greco-Roman image of the Phoenicians as maritime pioneers. And until recently the earliest known archaeological remains of ancient Gadir dated from the seventh century BCE. But excavations under the Teatro Cómico in the center of the modern city between 2006 and 2010 changed all that, revealing an ordered settlement that can be dated by Tyrian pottery to the late ninth century BCE.

It also gives us a window into the lives of the settlers themselves.[34] The sandy ground meant that the settlers had to construct retaining walls and terraces, on top of which they laid paved streets, houses, and workshops. The most complete of the houses measures eight meters by eleven, with four rooms of similar size inside, and they were all of a similar design: square-built on the Egyptian royal cubit with mud-brick walls, flat roof terraces, courtyards, and clay bread-baking ovens, all standard Levantine construction techniques.[35]

The new arrivals brought with them writing and the tools of administration: in addition to names and notes scratched onto pieces of pottery, a collection of clay sealings found in a cooking oven would have been affixed to papyrus documents. They brought another technology as well: in one of the little streets, archaeologists unearthed the skeleton of a house cat, a rare find anywhere in Europe in this era. Although wildcats had been tamed in Egypt and western Asia for millennia, it was only at this point that what we recognize as the modern semi-domesticated beasts began to make their way west of Crete along human trade routes.[36] The animal was probably a ship's mouser.*

Establishing a permanent presence on the Atlantic coast of Spain plugged Levantine adventurers more firmly into local resources and Atlantic trading networks, protected their own routes from the Mediterranean, and allowed them to offer new goods and services to passing shipping out of workshops producing pottery and purple dye, and pro-

*He or she was almost certainly a mackerel tabby: the blotched tabby markings characteristic of many domestic cats today originated in the Ottoman empire and only became common in the eighteenth century CE. The word "tabby" itself comes from the Arabic *'attabi,* meaning a taffeta made with a silk warp and a cotton woof, and taken from the name of the 'Attabīya district in medieval Baghdad where it was produced. Much of the coat-color variation in cats today is the product of deliberate breeding in more recent times.

cessing raw metals.[37] Cádiz is still a popular harbor in which to await a favorable wind through the strait.

Over the course of the eighth century BCE, the mines, markets, and fertile land of the far west persuaded thousands more to leave their homeland for good. A string of new settlements grew up inside and outside the Pillars, to north and south: ninth-century Mediterranean material has been found at Lixus on the Atlantic coast of Morocco, said in antiquity to house a shrine to Melqart even older than the one at Gadir.[38]

Not all of them were foreign foundations: all this new activity on the coast attracted people from inland as well. But plenty came from overseas, and they were no longer primarily there for trade-related reasons. At most of these early settlements, there is evidence for intensive metalworking, which previously had been a primarily seasonal activity in the region. This includes the production of iron, lead, and silver, as well as bronze-, gold-, and silversmithing. New farmers meanwhile introduced chickens and donkeys to a landscape previously dominated by cattle herding, as well as peas, chickpeas, lentils, figs, almonds, olive trees, and vines.[39]* Indeed, the introduction of large-scale agriculture to southern Iberia in this period led to significant deforestation.[40]

Some migration may have been enforced. Large quantities of silver slag along the Río Tinto and all across the city of Huelva itself confirm a huge increase in mining from the eighth century BCE.[41] We don't know whether Tyrian entrepreneurs ran these industrial operations themselves, Río Tinto Corporation–style, or simply encouraged them

*Chickens were for a long time rather rare. Descended from the red jungle fowl that lived in trees in southeast Asia, they first started to spend time near humans when the arrival of rice and millet farming provided attractive food at ground level. The earliest bones of fully domesticated animals (identified by the high proportion of juvenile animals among the bones and the fact that they were deposited in tombs as food for the dead along with cows, pigs, and dogs) have been found in central Thailand and carbon-dated to between 1650 and 1250 BCE. In the late second millennium BCE chickens are also found in China and Mesopotamia, where they are associated with wealthy households. They were adopted in the Levant around the eleventh century before appearing in southern Iberia around 800 BCE. By around 500 BCE they reach England and the Black Sea, but it was another millennium before they were fully established in colder climes (Joris Peters et al., "The biocultural origins and dispersal of domestic chickens," *Proceedings of the National Academy of Sciences* 119, no. 24 [2022]).

and then acquired the product. Either way, there is no evidence that the new levels of production enriched the smaller settlements that emerged near the mines themselves in this era, and it is likely that slave labor was involved.

Mining was difficult and dangerous work, and it was now being carried out in Tarshish on an unprecedented scale. At the same time, the relatively slow adoption of new technologies that could have made the process easier, from iron to the lathe, strongly suggests that the additional resources that made this possible were human.[42] Local farming towns and villages cannot have supplied willing laborers in the numbers required, and the opportunity is unlikely to have appealed to volunteers from the Levant.

Scholars often identify Classical Greece as the first true "slave society," where the economy could not have functioned without slavery.[43] It is indeed only then and there that clear evidence emerges for the large-scale use of slaves for mining and agriculture, along with institutionalized slave farming.[44] More than a third of the population of fourth-century BCE Attica may have been enslaved.[45]

Slavery in earlier periods and other places was smaller-scale and more opportunistic: a wealthy household might have a few slaves, a palace rather more, but they'd usually be doing the same kinds of jobs as paid workers might in other contexts—or other unpaid laborers like wives and daughters.[46] There is no doubt however that it existed, nor that Tyrians in particular were enthusiastic slave traders. Homer's heroes complain of Phoenicians selling the people they kidnap on their travels, and Hebrew prophets agree: Amos accuses Tyre of selling Israelite refugees to Edom, Joel accuses Tyrians and Sidonians of selling Judeans to Greeks, and Ezekiel specifically juxtaposes Tyrian imports of slaves from Anatolia and metals from Tarshish.[47]

Others on their own account sailed west to get away. Within a few decades of the foundation of Gadir, a rather different group of travelers established a new home on the coast of modern Tunisia, on a promontory at one end of a bay running around to the mountains of Cape Bon.

They named it simply *Qart-Hadasht* ("New City"). Easily reached by sea, and easily defended by land, Carthage would become the greatest power in the ancient west.

The tale the Carthaginians told of their own beginnings is preserved by a Sicilian Greek historian writing in the third century BCE.[48] It serves as a reminder that people leave home for a host of different reasons, and not always out of choice: in this story the city's founders are refugees, and they are led by a woman.

Elissa was the sister of the king of Tyre, and when her brother killed her husband she fled the city with some of her fellow citizens. After much suffering she reached the coast of Africa, where she founded Carthage. Her new neighbors nicknamed her Dido: in their language, we are told, it meant "the wanderer." When a local African king asked to marry her she at first refused, but her fellow Tyrians forced her to assent to the match—either to preserve good relations with their new neighbors or because they preferred in the end to be ruled by a man. In despair, she lit a great pyre beside her palace, pretending to prepare for a ritual to annul her vows to her dead husband, and then threw herself from the building into the fire.

There is no Aeneas in this legend: it was only centuries later that Roman authors combined the Carthaginian story of Dido with the Greek legend of a Trojan prince who founded Rome. Dido herself may never really have existed. True, a king list later found in the Tyrian archives notes that "in the seventh year of Pygmalion's reign [824 BCE], his sister fled and founded the city of Carthage in Africa."[49] We don't though know when this list was compiled, and the entry could itself have been prompted by the Carthaginian legend. Whatever its historical value, the story does tell us something about Carthage's own self-image. While the foundation story of Gadir foregrounds the gods and government of Tyre, this one emphasizes the new city's independence.

Animal bones from Carthage have been carbon-dated to the final quarter of the ninth century BCE, and there are graves from the early eighth, but the first Levantine settlement itself has probably yet to be unearthed: the earliest houses so far discovered were built on the lower slope of the Byrsa Hill, facing the sea, around 750 BCE.[50] As at Gadir, they suggest eastern Mediterranean origins: square-built with mud-brick walls on stone foundations and little gardens. They are also laid out on a grid, following an example set on Bronze Age Cyprus long before the Greek architect Hippodamos gets the credit for replanning Miletos on a grid in the fifth century BCE.[51]

As at Gadir, there is also plenty of Tyrian pottery in early Carthage.[52] And as at Gadir, Carthage provided processing for raw materials acquired elsewhere: metalworking and ivory-working facilities surrounded the early settlement, and Carthaginians made a particular specialty of converting iron into stronger steel using calcium, in this case obtained from the murex shells that were a product of purple-dye production.[53]

One new development found at Carthage is the sanctuary the settlers established close to the port to the god Baal Haamon, where they sacrificed infants before cremating and burying them.[54] More than 20,000 burial urns were interred over the six or more centuries of the city's existence, signaled above ground by more than 10,000 stone stelae, often carved with images and inscriptions, then plastered and painted in bright colors.

It was these markers that originally led French colonial archaeologists to the site in 1921. They had been turning up on the antiquities market for a century before a misguided dealer offered one for sale to a public official at Tunis, who had him tailed back to the clandestine dig.[55] Official excavations began within days, and scholars quickly made a connection between this strange graveyard and claims by more than thirty Greek and Roman authors that the Carthaginians sacrificed their children to their gods. The fourth-century BCE Greek historian Kleitarchos, for instance, reported that the Phoenicians, and especially the Carthaginians, revered the god Kronos—the Greek name for Baal Haamon—and that "whenever they wish to make a real success of something, they vow one of their children, and if they get what they want, they sacrifice it to the god."[56]

Some scholars now prefer to see Carthaginian child sacrifice as a myth propagated by the city's Greek and Roman enemies, and the sanctuary as a special cemetery for the dedication of stillborn, sick, or disabled infants to the gods. But this is wishful thinking.[57]

It is unlikely that any ancient god would have appreciated the gift of a dead or even sickly child: there are stern prohibitions in written regulations consistent across ancient Mesopotamia, Israel, and Greece on sacrificing animals—or anything else—with imperfections.[58] Furthermore, sheep are buried in the sanctuary too, sometimes separately from the children, sometimes together: they seem to be interchangeable. Again, this would be very unexpected in an ordinary cemetery, and odd in a sanctuary too.

Besides, contemporary Greco-Roman commentary on Carthaginian child sacrifice is not in fact especially judgmental. The practice is treated as an exotic curiosity rather than an outrage.[59] This shouldn't be a surprise: Greeks and Romans themselves simply "exposed" unwanted newborn children, abandoning them to die or, in a best-case scenario, to be rescued for a life of slavery or prostitution.[60]

Finally, the inscriptions on the markers confirm that this was no ordinary graveyard: they do not give the name of the deceased, as in Carthage's other cemeteries, but simply call the child an "offering" to the gods, because "they heard the voice of my words"—which is to say, they answered my prayer. It is hard to interpret the death of a baby as the answer to a common prayer, or something that regularly coincided with other, happier events for which a dead infant could conveniently be offered in thanksgiving. Instead, as Kleitarchos knew, these inscriptions describe the final act of a deal: a request was made, with an offering promised in return; the god came through, and payment was delivered. The standard "vow" at Carthage seems to have been an infant, although if a child was not available at the appropriate time then livestock, especially lambs, made an acceptable alternative.

This peculiar rite may explain the foundation of Carthage itself. The new arrivals didn't invent child sacrifice: they brought it with them.[61] Although no similar infant burial sites have so far been found in the Levant, there is plenty of evidence for child sacrifice there in the early first millennium BCE: archaeologists even call the Carthage sanctuary a "tophet" after the place in Jerusalem where the Hebrew Bible says impious people slaughtered their children and "made them pass through fire."[62]

The Bible reports that this practice aroused disgust among many Israelites, and was eventually banned in Judah by King Josiah in the late seventh century.[63]* We hear of a similar change of heart at Tyre, though without a specific date: when Alexander the Great was besieging the city in 332 BCE, a Roman historian reports an unsuccessful proposal to revive the old tradition of sacrificing a freeborn boy to Saturn (the Roman name for Baal Haamon).[64] He doesn't say when the tradition had fallen out of use there, but increasing opposition to it could explain why, like the Pilgrim Fathers, members of a dissident tradition sought religious freedom in the west.[65]

It might also explain why others joined them in the central Mediterranean, founding about ten more settlements over the next couple of centuries on and around Sicily, Sardinia, Malta, and the Tunisian coast.[66] These people didn't come for the farmland: there is little evidence for large-scale agriculture around these sites for several more centuries.[67] They all however have tophets, with the same infant burials, markers, and inscriptions. These migrants must have been drawn to one another not only by language and cultural familiarity, but also by the unusual cult they shared. It allowed this distinctive group of settlements to maintain its distance not only from Tyre but also from other Levantine migrants farther west, where no tophets have yet been found.

There were other attractions in moving to the middle of the sea. As commercial routes across the Mediterranean became more intensely trafficked, all these ports around a narrows through which almost all east–west shipping had to sail could offer services and supplies to passing trade. Their location offered opportunities for less mutually agreeable forms of exchange as well and some of these early settlers may have been corsairs.

The Sicilian Strait is one of the traditional choke points of the Mediterranean, narrow or difficult passages that tend throughout history to attract pirates, since relatively small groups can effectively harass larger

*The turn against the ritual is encapsulated in the biblical story of Abraham and Isaac (Genesis 22): the father prepares to sacrifice his son in accordance with what he understands to be the wishes of his god, but once he has proved willing to obey, the god stays his hand.

shipping.[68] As we see in Barbary and the Caribbean in later eras, pirates flourish in periods of heavy sea traffic. Historically they find the Mediterranean unusually welcoming, with many islands, inlets, and rocky coasts to conceal their activities.[69] Homer regularly describes Phoenicians as pirates as well as traders in his eighth-century BCE *Odyssey*, which would make sense as a response to recent activity in the central Mediterranean.[70] And pirate cultures throughout history reject or invert social norms, an attitude encapsulated by the story of a city founded by a woman.[71]

CHAPTER TEN

The Invention of Greece

ERETRIA, 750 BCE

Nowadays Greece marks the start of something: culture, civilization, philosophy, and, at least in my own field, even history. Ancient Greeks themselves saw things differently. From their perspective they stood at the end of much longer foreign traditions: Plato has one of his characters declare that Egyptian history goes back 10,000 years, and he has the Egyptians invent mathematics, geometry, astronomy, and literature, while Herodotus reports the origins in Egypt of much of the Greek pantheon and religious culture, with varying degrees of plausibility.[1]

Greek authors wrote themselves into those foreign traditions as well: the legendary founder of Argos came from Egypt via Libya and the founder of Athens married an Amazon queen.[2] They take a particular interest in connections with Phoenicians, who are consistently portrayed in Greek stories and legends as neighbors, teachers, and even ancestors: ethnic purity rarely had the value in antiquity that racists accord it today. They insist that Phoenicians colonized the Aegean, founding settlements on several islands. And they tell particularly vivid tales of King Agenor's Tyrian children, princes and princesses who enclose that sea in a diamond of legendary Phoenician origins.[3]

We have already traveled with Europa from Tyre to Crete, but the

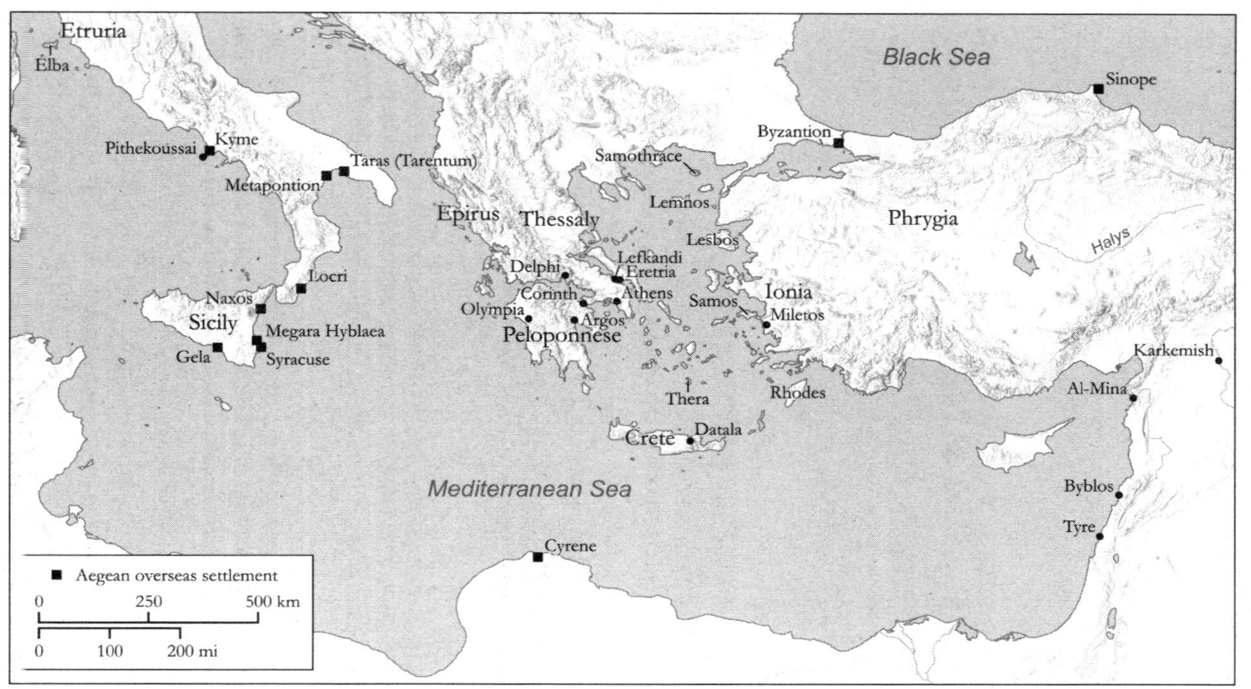

Aegean exploration, trade, and settlement from the eighth century BCE

stories don't end there. After her disappearance, her brothers set out in vain to find her. Where their search ended, they settled. Thasos founded a city on the island of that name in the north Aegean, where he and his followers built a sanctuary to Melqart and a gold mine that Herodotus says he saw himself. Kadmos meanwhile founded the great city of Thebes in Boeotia, where he sired a dynasty that included the Greek god Dionysus, the unfortunate king Oedipus and his misguided daughter Antigone.[4]* Europa's sister Astypalaia was kidnapped meanwhile by another god, Poseidon—in the form of a winged leopard—and abandoned with her children on the island of Samos.[5]

Archaeologists have been unable to locate a gold mine on Thasos or Melqart's temple, and considerable doubt must be cast on the achievements reported of Kadmos by the fact that they also include slaughtering a dragon and growing an army of fierce soldiers from its teeth.[6] In fact, no certain or even very likely Levantine foundations in the Aegean have ever been discovered. Like the biblical tales of King Hirom and the queen of Sheba, Greek authors used these stories of Phoenicians to weave their own history into that of more illustrious neighbors. They helped Greek speakers establish their place in an ever wider world.

By the ninth century, however, there is plenty of evidence for Levantine travelers at least in the Aegean in the Semitic-language inscriptions they left on Rhodes and Euboea, where by around 800 BCE Eretria took over from Lefkandi a few kilometers to the northwest as the island's major trading hub.[7] Meanwhile Euboean pottery was arriving at Tyre and neighboring ports in ever-increasing quantities.[8]

Soon Greek speakers were engaged in long-distance trade themselves again on the coasts of Italy, Anatolia, and the northern Levant.[9] This brought them into contact with Levantine travelers in the west as well, above all at an indigenous trading and metalworking station on the isle of Ischia in the Bay of Naples that they called Pithekoussai, or Monkey Island. This was the central Mediterranean equivalent of

*In an indication of the flexibility of ancient notions of ethnicity, a fragment of a lost play by the fifth-century Athenian tragedian Euripides notes of Kadmos that "born Phoenician, he changed his stock [*genos*] to Greek once he had settled on [the river] Dirce's plain" (Euripides fr. 819 [*Phrixos* B]).

Huelva, where the nearby metals of Etruria and Elba attracted settlers from all over the Mediterranean including the Levant and, from the mid-eighth century BCE, the Aegean.[10]

Today those connections both real and imagined have for the most part been forgotten: they present an inconvenient obstacle to the modern idea that the Greeks themselves invented Western culture from whole cloth. The evidence from the ninth- and eighth-century Aegean suggests however that the legends of Agenor's children got something important right: overseas contacts and borrowings were crucial components of what might otherwise seem a Greek miracle. In particular, the connections Greek speakers made in this era with the people they called Phoenician transformed their own societies both at home and abroad. These connections not only fueled Aegean commerce, they inspired changes in art, religion, and politics that provide core ingredients in the modern myth of Classical Greece.[11]

According to Herodotus, chief among the learned accomplishments that Kadmos and his companions brought to Greece was writing. The settlers taught their alphabet to their new neighbors, who adapted the letters to write their own language and called them "Phoenicians" (*phoinikeia*).[12] The story is set in the Bronze Age, when we now know that Greek was really written down in Linear B, but this much at least is true: even before Herodotus was writing in the fifth century BCE, Greek inscriptions refer to the script in which they were now written as "Phoenician letters."[13]

Sometimes even the act of writing itself was deemed "Phoenician": around 500 BCE the townspeople of Datala on Crete erected an inscription recording the appointment of a man called Spensithios as a *poinikastas,* someone who "does Phoenician," even though the language he was writing down was Greek. Spensithios was given a stipend and rations as well as special legal rights and tax breaks to "both write [*poinikizen*] and remember for the town public matters both sacred and secular."[14]

As with the "Phoenician" label itself, this Greek perspective paints with a broader brush than sources closer to home. Around 800 BCE a eunuch called Yariri who was regent of the neo-Hittite kingdom of Karkemish claimed proudly to know twelve languages and four scripts, including "Tyrian" writing.[15] He was right about the name as well: the Levantine linear alphabet used in tenth-century Byblos had finally been standardized in ninth-century Tyre. The shapes and stances of the letters were now fixed, their number settled at twenty-two, and the direction of travel established as right to left.[16]

They were used in the first instance to write the Tyrian dialect of Phoenician, which was fast becoming standard in Levantine contexts at home and overseas: just as modern Italian is based on the medieval dialect of Tuscany, the ancient language we call Phoenician is based on the speech of Tyre in the late ninth century BCE.[17] But the power and prestige of Tyre in this era meant that Tyrian letters were also borrowed to write other eastern Mediterranean languages, from Aramaic to Hebrew to Phrygian.[18] And when Greeks began to write their own language down again for the first time in more than 400 years, they too chose the Tyrian alphabet.*

Greeks appropriated not only the idea of the alphabet but the whole system. The shapes of the earliest Greek letters derive directly from the letters used at contemporary Tyre, and they represent in most cases the same sounds, with the same names, written out in the same traditional order: Aleph–bet–gimel became alpha–beta–gamma. In early Greek inscriptions they are usually written right to left as well, but the direction didn't much matter, and it was not until the fifth century BCE that Greek writers settled firmly on left to right.

At the same time, the Greek alphabet was not simply a copy of the script used at Tyre, which was technically an abjad. Vowels are rarely

*This makes Tyrian letters the ancestors of almost all modern alphabetic scripts: European writing systems through Greek, and Arabic and Indian ones through Aramaic. The only truly independent alphabet in use today is Korean Hangul, the personal creation of Sejong the Great in the fifteenth century CE to improve literacy levels in his kingdom: it is a completely phonetic writing system that is much easier to learn and read than the Chinese letters previously used in Korea—as long as you already speak Korean.

essential for comprehension in Semitic languages. In modern Hebrew, for instance, they are usually marked only in religious texts and children's books. In Greek, by contrast, vowels are very common, they are often the first letter of a word, and they are frequently added and changed to indicate different numbers, genders, persons, and tenses. It would be hard to understand written Greek without them, and in that respect Phoenician letters posed a problem.

The solution was to recycle letters for sounds that didn't exist in Greek—the glottal stop, for instance, or guttural consonants like the "ch" sound in Scottish "loch." It could not have emerged gradually out of common practice: it would work only if everyone used the same Phoenician letters for the same Greek vowels.[19] So the alphabet must have been invented by someone, or a small group of people, and this must have happened some time around the end of the ninth century BCE, when the forms of the letters in Tyrian inscriptions are closest to those that were borrowed for Greek.[20]

This was probably the work of merchants or other business travelers, people who were already used to reading and writing Phoenician letters and realized that it could be useful, or perhaps just fun, to write down their own vernacular in a similar way. Examples cluster at port towns like Euboean Eretria, where the sanctuary of Apollo has yielded examples of Semitic and Greek alphabetic writing in succession: someone scratched four letters in a Levantine alphabet from right to left on a locally made cup around 800 BCE, and the same sanctuary has yielded more than sixty pieces of pottery with later Greek writing on them, most dating to the second half of the eighth century. Some of these texts were added to the pots by the potters themselves before firing, in other cases they were carved crudely on broken fragments. In neither case was the new technology restricted to an elite class of scribes, and some of these inscriptions are "abecedaria" or practice alphabet lists.[21]

Other early examples of early Greek writing are found at overseas trading posts like Syrian Al-Mina and Pithekoussai off the coast of Italy, where 5,000 to 10,000 inhabitants used pottery from the Levant, Carthage, Iberia, Euboea, and Corinth. They scrawled inscriptions on these pots in Phoenician, Aramaic, and, from the later eighth century BCE,

Greek—although the alphabets were all still so similar that it can be hard to tell which is which.[22]

The Greek alphabet thrived then in commercial contexts, but it was not an accounting script—which would have had little need of vowels.[23] Nor do we find the "public writing" that was common by now in the Levant: Greek inscriptions on stone start to appear only in the seventh century.[24] Of course we are missing everything written with a stylus on leather, papyrus, and wax tablets, themselves all Levantine tools and technologies imported to the Aegean along with the alphabet itself: a writing tablet was a *deltos* in Greek, from Phoenician *daltu*.[25] But the few texts that do survive from this era because they were scratched into pots and other surfaces tell us something about what Greek speakers wanted to say to one another.

A simple name usually means "I own this" or "I am [buried] here"; an additional word or two can indicate that "I made this" or "I dedicated this to god X." Alphabet lists and nonsense strings of letters declare "I can write." And longer inscriptions often say "I can sing": a surprising number of early Greek inscriptions are written more or less successfully in hexameter, the poetic meter of the *Iliad* and the *Odyssey*.[26] They were not however on epic themes: the first surviving literary productions in the Greek alphabet are odes to drinking, dancing, and sex.

One of the earliest Greek inscriptions is found in Athens, an old Bronze Age stronghold that had survived the Dark Age to become a trading center in the ninth century BCE, and where artisans made delicate jewelry using west Asian techniques, including strings of tiny gold beads (granulation) and gold wire openwork (filigree).[27] It is a hexameter verse scratched around 740 BCE from right to left around the shoulder of an elegant ceramic wine jug: "He who, of all the dancers, now performs most daintily. . . ."[28] The jug could be a prize in a competition, or the text may be a joke about the effects of the wine it contains.

Another example of around 725 BCE is written on a drinking cup at Pithekoussai, again from right to left, and reads "I am the Cup of Nestor, good to drink from. Whoever drains this cup, straightaway desire will seize him for beautifully crowned Aphrodite."[29] The first line is a learned joke written in prose, depending on the ironic contrast between this cheap painted pot and a legendarily beautiful golden cup belonging to Nestor, king of Pylos, which is described at length in the *Iliad.* The second line makes a cruder connection in more elevated hexameter between drinking and desire for "Aphrodite"—sex.[30]

Less allusive are graffiti scratched into rocks on the island of Thera, often again in hexameter.[31] They are harder to date—the early seventh century is the best guess—but easy to read, men praising the looks and dancing of other men, and celebrating their joint pursuits: "Krimon fucked Amotion here."[32]

It isn't just the alphabet that is new: "speaking objects" like the Cup of Nestor themselves have no precedent in earlier alphabetic cultures.[33] This brings out a key aspect of how cultural borrowings make change: they make things new again. Ancient Aegean culture would have been very different without the Tyrian alphabet, but the new adopters use alphabetic writing in ways that made most sense to them, to forge connections but also to underline their own differences: different versions of the Greek alphabet develop quickly even in neighboring towns. What matters as ever is not "influence" but choice.

It wasn't only Phoenician letters that reached Greece in this era: words came too. Around a hundred Greek terms have Semitic roots, from animals and plants to foods and religious terminology.[34] Above all they relate to trade.[35] Goods that arrived on a *gaulos* or ship were carried in a *sakkos* (sack) to the *makellon* (market). For ordinary transactions Aegean merchants adopted the Semitic *mina* unit of weight, traditionally used for silver, which they counted in sixties like the Babylonians to make up a "talent," a local measure already attested in Bronze Age Greece. Levantine entrepreneurs meanwhile introduced Greek speakers to west Asian financial technologies such as deposit banking, marine insurance, and bottomry, a high-risk system of financing maritime trade that remained common until the nineteenth century CE in which the ship itself is used as security for the loans that send it to sea.[36]

Ships themselves arrived too: new galleys that are first depicted on sealings on the Levantine coast in the eleventh century are painted on pots buried in graves at Lefkandi by the ninth.[37] These were long, low, fast vessels propelled primarily by oar, and they developed into the biremes and then triremes that fought out the great naval battles of the Classical age. The new design also introduced a bow projection—perhaps originally a cutwater—that would become the ramming device characteristic of later Greek and Roman warships. In this era however these vessels could also have served for cargo themselves, especially where speed was a greater consideration than the cost or availability of labor, or to protect merchant fleets of sailing vessels.

Over the course of the eighth century trading connections between the Levant and Greece expanded, and as Levantine bulk goods—wine, oil, and textiles—piled up at ports all around the Aegean, so did art from west Asian workshops.[38] It is no coincidence that beautiful bronze bowls and ivory seals carved with intricate designs arrive in Athenian graves at the same time as Athenian pottery at Huelva.

This was an era of recovery and growth in the Aegean. From the middle of the eighth century the number of settlements multiplied, and in some cases grew much larger, especially when several neighboring hamlets came together to form a single community, as at Sparta in the central Peloponnese. The population rose dramatically, as did standards of living.[39]

New connections brought new cultural tastes from the eastern Mediterranean. This is when trumpets, castanets, and cymbals appear in the Aegean, as well as the *auloi* or double pipes, which would have needed lengthy training with patient teachers in the circular breathing technique required to produce continuous sound. The rich, vibrating tones of this instrument would provide the backing track for Classical Greece, entertaining guests, accompanying the chorus, and sending armies to war.[40]

Religious ideas adapted too. Universal polytheism made it easier to see equivalencies—or at least close associations—between one's own deities and those of other people. And long before Romans mapped Greek Zeus and Hera onto their own Jupiter and Juno, Greeks did the same to Levantine gods: so Greek speakers called the Tyrian god Melqart by the name of their own hero Herakles, while the Greek goddess of love "Heavenly" Aphrodite was widely equated with Semitic Ashtart, the "queen of Heaven," and was even thought by some Greek authors to have arrived in Greece from the Levant or Assyria.[41]

In some cases Levantine gods do appear to have been straightforwardly adopted into the Aegean: Syrian Adonis, for instance, and the mysterious Kabeiroi or "Great Gods" attested at Emar on the Euphrates in the thirteenth century BCE who now appear on Lemnos and Samothrace, islands well positioned for access to metals on the mainland.[42]

Ecstatic prophecy arrived in this era as well, most famously at Delphi, a sanctuary overlooking the trade route west from Corinth.[43] There Apollo's prophecies were voiced by a priestess transported, by one means or another, to a spiritual realm. Prophesying priestesses had long been a feature of religious life in Mesopotamia, as had the ritual that preceded an audience with the priestess at Delphi, in which a goat was sprinkled with cold water, and only if it shuddered could the consultation proceed.[44] Another innovation of this period that owed as much to new commercial opportunities as to religious ideas was the practice of presenting offerings to the gods of frankincense and myrrh, prepared with Levantine incense burners and poured from Levantine bowls.[45]

The settings of religious ritual changed. Encounters with gods in the early Iron Age Aegean had focused on sacred places and small fires, but by the middle of the eighth century BCE communities started to wall off cult sites, erect altars, and build houses for deities in the form of cult statues with altars outside in the long-standing west Asian tradition.[46] Leaving aside the famous temple attributed to Solomon at Jerusalem, we have seen that a temple was built at Sidon in the twelfth century BCE, others are recorded at Tyre in the tenth, and more sanctuaries appear at Sarepta and Tell Arqa in the eighth.[47] As in the Aegean, they offered fugitives asylum.[48]

The first god houses in the Aegean are found at trading centers, at Eretria around 750 BCE and on Samos around 725.[49] They don't yet look much like Classical Greek temples: the "hundred-footer" at Samos was a long, narrow mud-brick building. These destination sanctuaries still attracted visitors from all over the Mediterranean to commercial centers, where foreigners were expected to pay their respects at the local shrine.[50]

Religion has become a boundary in the modern world, but in antiquity religious sites, rituals, and institutions brought people closer together. Ancient gods were rarely jealous: they had their areas of special competence and their own particular constituencies, but they welcomed donations from anyone, and were happy to serve up favors, prophecies, and protection in return.

More eastern bronzes have been found at the sanctuary of Zeus at Olympia alone than in the whole of western Asia, and foreign objects outnumber Greek ones at Hera's temple on the island of Samos, where the goddess received gifts from Egypt, Syria, Phrygia, and Assyria, as well as Cyprus and the Levant.[51] Some were diplomatic gifts from foreign kings—Herodotus reports that King Midas of Anatolian Phrygia sent a wooden throne to Delphi, and Phrygian bronze work does survive in Greek sanctuaries.[52] Others were offerings from grateful traders brought back from their travels, while homemade luxury goods in west Asian styles must have been dedicated by local hands.[53]

Levantine art provided rich inspiration to Aegean artisans as sculptors adapted, for instance, the elegantly curved volute capitals that crowned Levantine columns into the busier Ionic form of Classical Greece.[54] At a less elevated social level, painted pottery was a cheap and easy way for more people to acquire the eastern styles that arrived on ivory and bronze work imported from western Asia. Greek potters painted sphinxes, griffins, bulls, hunts, and lotus flowers, and arranged them, as on Levantine metalwork, in concentric bands. They also borrowed a technique from eastern metalwork of incising details into silhouettes, giving rise to the "black-figure" vase painting that characterized Greek pottery for almost two centuries, in which images are outlined in black paint before details are incised with a sharp stylus.[55]

The first vases painted in this new fashion were made in late-eighth-century Corinth, now taking over from Euboea as the commercial capital of the Aegean, and where the "oriental" motifs on the vases may have been an advertisement: the pots contained perfumed oils, another product of Levantine supply networks.[56] In an era of increasing east–

west traffic, Corinth profited from its control of harbors at both ends of the isthmus, "of which one leads straight to Asia, and the other to Italy," as the geographer Strabo later put it.[57] More than three-quarters of the dedications found at the harbor sanctuary of Hera Akraia are of Levantine metalwork, and a month in the Corinthian calendar was even named "Phoinikaios."[58]

In the 730s BCE Aegean migrants finally began to found their own communities overseas. They settled first in eastern Sicily and southern Italy, then along the coasts of the Black Sea and what is now eastern Libya.[59] By 700 BCE perhaps 10,000 Greek speakers had left the Aegean.[60] The new arrivals kept their distance from earlier Levantine migrants, however, and for more than a century they settled no farther west than Italy.

Like their predecessors they chose promontories and islands for their new homes, and the mouths of major rivers.[61] Some also chose spots suited to marauding: the coast of Epirus at the foot of the Adriatic, the double entrance to the Black Sea and the Strait of Messina, the last of which may until then have been the safer route to Italian metals if you wanted to avoid the attentions of the Carthaginians and their friends around the Strait of Sicily. No mimicry is required to explain these decisions, but it does seem likely that Greek speakers looked to Levantine models as they built little towns overseas with sanctuaries and square houses, and laid some out on grids long before they are found in the Aegean itself.[62]

The same lessons may have helped to inspire the increasingly urban form of mainland Greek settlements themselves in this era, where public spaces now appear, square-built houses replace oval huts, and burials move outside the built-up area to delineate an area reserved for the living.[63] By the early seventh century BCE Greek authors consider surrounding walls a standard attribute of any self-respecting political community, as illustrated paradoxically by the poet Alcaeus' observation that men, not walls, make a town (*polis*).[64] All this echoes on a smaller scale the older urban landscapes and orthogonal buildings of Levantine ports. Beirut and other cities had fortification walls from at least the tenth century, and Beirut, Tyre, and Sidon all had cemeteries located outside the center.[65]

The same could even be said of the "city-state" itself, often seen as a defining characteristic of Classical Greece, and then of Europe before the rise of modern nation-states.[66] In reality the modern term city-state is somewhat aggrandizing when used of the Aegean, where most *poleis* or "cities" were closer in size to villages in modern terms. Even in the ancient world their size was not impressive: Athens was one of the largest towns in mainland Greece in this era with a population of at least 5,000 by 700 BCE, but this is a lot less than the 30,000 or so inhabitants of the island of Tyre at the time, or the more than 100,000 living at Assyrian Nineveh.[67]

It can also be misleading. Not every Greek *polis* was a state, in the sense of having political autonomy: some were subordinate to larger neighbors like Sparta.[68] And not all Greek states were single towns: in regions from Thessaly to the Peloponnese towns shared responsibility for matters like war and external relations in federal groupings.[69] Nor, of course, were city-states distinctively Greek: autonomous urban political communities are found all over the world in many eras, not only in the contemporary Levant.[70]

Most interesting is the possibility that Levantine settlements could provide not only models for cities and city-states, but for the citizen state now associated with Greek democracy, what Aristotle called a "partnership of citizens in a constitution."[71]

Aegean city-states were still ruled for the most part in the eighth century BCE by monarchs.[72] The grand warrior burials that had marked out community leaders were fading away, however. More of the community received simple communal burial rites, and money was increasingly spent on communal institutions instead of private tombs and houses.[73]

We first see positive evidence for popular participation in government at Sparta, a small and strange community made up of five neighboring villages in a green valley of the central Peloponnese. In later centuries at least girls were educated at Sparta, women could own property, and the notion of citizenship was reinforced by the way in which all citizen men or "peers" (*homoioi*), including the king, ate at common tables rather than with their families, consuming a notoriously frugal diet.[74] We don't know when these customs started, but seventh-century Sparta already had a council of elders and a public assembly that held regular meetings in addition to its two kings.[75] While assembly members could voice an opinion, sovereignty still rested above them.[76]

This looks similar to older Levantine monarchies. Even in the Late Bronze Age there is plenty of evidence for councils, assemblies, and other collective civic bodies at Tyre, Byblos, Arwad, and elsewhere.[77] Letters to Amarna reveal that they could represent the citizens—the "sons" of the city—as well as the city itself as a legal entity, could oppose their kings, and could act independently of them as well.[78] They could also represent the city abroad: when a local king is unavailable, both city elders and a larger citizen body send letters to the Egyptian king.[79]

Similar arrangements still seem to be in place when a treaty was made around 675 BCE between the Assyrian king Esarhaddon on the one hand, and on the other Baal I of Tyre and "all Tyrians, young and old." The Hebrew prophet Ezekiel mentions elders of Byblos in the sixth century, and in the fourth century we hear again of councils and assemblies.[80]

And Levantine migrants had already gone farther in the west: according to later Greek commentary Carthage was governed "from the first" not by kings but by chief magistrates known as *basileis,* as well as a council of elders and an assembly.[81] How much real power ordinary citizens had as individuals or as an institution is another question, but one that applies equally to any Aegean polity for at least another two centuries.

Levantine links weren't the only ones that mattered to Greek speakers in the early first millennium BCE. They must have had a great deal of cultural exchange with Anatolians as well, the product of centuries of cohabitation going back to the Bronze Age when mainland Greek pottery became popular in Anatolian ports and Millawanda allied with

Ahhiyawa. By the early first millennium there were Greek-speaking communities in western Anatolia itself as well as on nearby islands. We don't know their real origins, and tales told by later Greek authors of a migration across the Aegean around the end of the Bronze Age are impossible to verify, but from at least the sixth century BCE they saw themselves as distinct from the indigenous inhabitants of the same lands.[82]

We have no detailed sense of relations in earlier eras, precisely because people were living side by side. We do however find occasional echoes of cultural convergence in later Greek writing from the region: the poet Alcaeus, for instance, writing on Lesbos around 600 BCE, mentions an ancient ruler of the island called "Myrsilos," one word used for "king" in the Luwian language of southern Anatolia. This suggests that the term had been borrowed from local Luwian speakers long enough ago for its origin to be forgotten.[83]

It is much easier to see the links between the Aegean, the Levant, and their overseas foundations that framed and fostered the institutions that distinguish Classical Greece in many minds today, from the alphabet to the colony to the citizen state. They too though are part of a bigger story and a much longer east–west axis across the Mediterranean in the shadow of greater power.

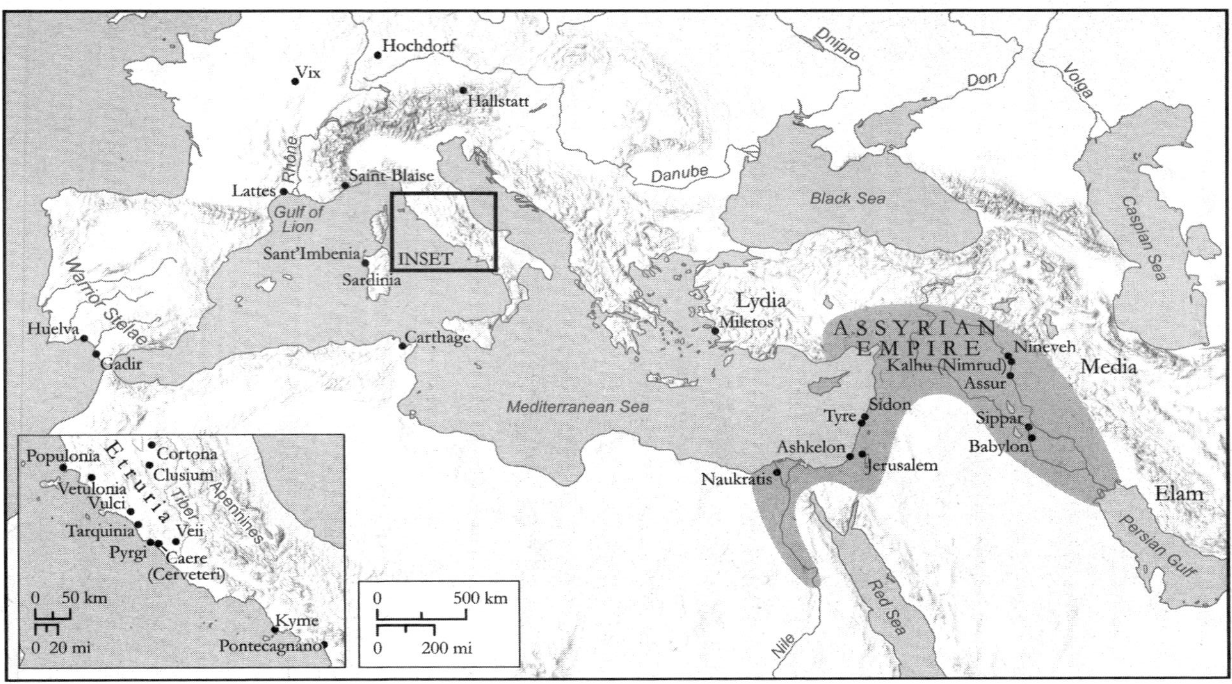

The Assyrian Mediterranean in the seventh century BCE

CHAPTER ELEVEN

The Assyrian Mediterranean

TARSHISH, C. 670 BCE

The kings of Assyria had their own problems at the end of the Bronze Age, and for centuries they took little sustained interest in lands far to their west. In the early ninth century BCE Ashurnasirpal II did reach the Mediterranean, and he did well out of it:

> I cleansed my weapons in the Great Sea and made sacrifices to the gods. I received the tribute from the kings of the sea coast, from the lands of the people of Tyre, Sidon, Byblos, Mahallatu, Maizu, Kaizu, Amurru, and Arwad, which is in the sea, consisting of silver, gold, tin, bronze, a large bronze bowl, linen garments with multicolored trimmings, a large female monkey, a small female monkey, ebony, boxwood, and ivory from *nahirus*, which are sea creatures. They [the kings, not the sea creatures] clasped my feet.[1]

They certainly tried their best. In 879 BCE, as ships of Tarshish began to travel west on a regular basis, the kings of Tyre and Sidon made a harder journey east, 600 kilometers overland for the opening of the palace at Ashurnasirpal's new capital of Kalhu (Nimrud). Again, it was worth it: the Assyrian king carefully records that he welcomed 69,574 guests, had them bathed and then offered them 17,300 sheep and cattle, 10,000 jugs of beer, and 10,000 skins of wine.[2]

Occasional Assyrian visits to the Levant continued for more than a century. Levantine ports paid tribute again to Ashurnasirpal's son Shalmaneser III (r. 854–829), who arrived with an army three times the size of his father's and left a statue of himself on the coast, and then to Adad-Nirari III (r. 810–783).[3] These attentions provide more context for contemporary Levantine interest in the precious metals of the far west: local kings surely encouraged their merchants in ventures that provided appropriate gifts as required, and in the meantime allowed these monarchs to imitate on a smaller scale the marvels of Assyrian court life.

By the middle of the eighth century, however, Assyria was getting more aggressive. A thousand years after the quasi-democratic city-state revealed in the archive of Karum Kanesh, hyper-strong kings now took responsibility for protecting the world from cosmic disorder—which included the existence of lands outside their power. They tackled this anomaly by building a territorial empire from Iran to Anatolia, the largest yet seen in western Asia.[4]

Assyrian kings had the help of a huge army that specialized in chariotry, siege warfare, and the battering ram. The soldiers were the state: every male citizen was liable to serve in the annual campaigns, which were often led by the king himself, and all state officials had military rank and title. Prudent monarchs from the ninth century on ensured that many of the leading officers in the army and state bureaucracy were also eunuchs—the "men of the head," those closest to the king, as opposed to the "men of the beard," an older governing class of urban noblemen.[5] In return for the singular devotion of these castrated servants—who had no prospects outside his household—the king fed and clothed them, and paid for all their expenses, including their funerals.

A new road system consolidated expansion: empires don't need to hold the whole of their territory in constant and expensive occupation if they control the routes through it. This network also carried state communications that connected the king, his governors, and his ambassadors at vassal courts in what was in effect a postal service, separating message from messenger for the first time.[6] Couriers rode standard daily stages in and out of road stations equipped with accommodation, always traveling with a pair of mules in case one went lame en route.*

It wasn't only soldiers and couriers on the move: once new land was conquered, Assyrian imperial policy revolved around mass relocation.[7] A total of 157 separate forced resettlements around Assyrian lands are recorded between the ninth and seventh centuries BCE, involving well over a million individuals, and that cannot be the full account. This strategy allowed the Great King to bring labor and skill into new areas at the same time as he cut his subjects' local ties and made them dependent on himself alone. It also reinforced an ideology of Assyrian empire as a single people under one ruler—a people the king was increasingly determined to extend westward.

Tiglath-Pileser III finally subdued the Levant in the 730s BCE, incorporating most of its cities and kingdoms into the Assyrian provincial system.[8] Tyre itself remained semi-autonomous, although in 701 BCE, Sennacherib confiscated its mainland territories, imposed a king and deported parts of the population to his new capital of Nineveh.[9]**

*The Assyrians were the first to realize the full potential of the hardy and sure-footed mule, the offspring of a female horse and a male donkey. These barren but long-lived animals were considered so valuable by the Assyrian army that when one was loaned out around 670 BCE, it was guaranteed at more than thirty times the value of a human slave (Karen Radner, "An imperial communication network: the state correspondence of the Neo-Assyrian empire," in Karen Radner, ed., *State Correspondence in the Ancient World: From New Kingdom Egypt to the Roman Empire,* Oxford: Oxford University Press, 2014, 73–4). By using them in relays the Assyrian state could move messages as fast as any system managed before the Ottomans introduced the telegraph to the region in 1865.

**They would at least have had something to look at: Nineveh has been identified as the most plausible candidate not only for the Hanging Gardens misidentified since the Roman period with Babylon, but for a so-called Archimedes' screw, which delivered water up to their thirsty terraces, 500 years before Sicilian Archimedes was born (Stephanie Dalley, *The Mystery of the Hanging Garden of Babylon: An Elusive World Wonder Traced,* Oxford: Oxford University Press, 2013).

Tyre's continued freedom as a rare "client kingdom" in a vast Assyrian territory was key to the commercial success of what the seventh-century Hebrew prophet Isaiah calls this "city of revelry, the old, old city, whose feet have taken her to settle in far-off lands . . . whose merchants are princes, whose traders are renowned in the earth."[10] The Sidonians were less fortunate: after a revolt against Esarhaddon in the 670s their king lost his head, the city was destroyed, and Assyria replaced the population. Sidon became its first directly controlled port on the Upper Sea, "Esarhaddon's Harbor."[11]

In an inscription he erected at Nineveh around 670 BCE, Esarhaddon makes a bigger claim, professing to have reduced to tribute all of the kings "in the middle of the sea," from Cyprus to "Tarsisi."[12] Some scholars interpret Tarsisi here as the city of Tarsos in southern Anatolia, but as this is otherwise a list of regions it is more likely to be Tarshish, making this a claim to sovereignty over the whole Mediterranean.

It is in reality unlikely that Esarhaddon received regular tribute from anywhere west of the Levant. Indeed he had probably barely heard of these places: when Assyrians refer to peoples of the Mediterranean in this period, they often just call them all "Hittites."[13] Assyrian kings were only really interested in the Mediterranean as the source of precious metals that arrived in Levantine ports, above all Tyre.

We know that some of the return cargoes consisted of wine: two eighth-century BCE shipwrecks discovered in 1997 by a nuclear submarine sixty kilometers off the coast of the Gaza Strip contained large numbers of Levantine wine amphoras, with 385 still visible in the top layers of one wreck, 396 on the other. Each amphora carried around eighteen liters, and they are the first known wine containers lined with resin to guard against seepage.[14] The location means that the ships must have been heading west from the port of Ashkelon; fourteen or fifteen meters long and one-third as wide, they are a real-life glimpse of ships of Tarshish.

What survives of these journeys west for the most part however is a tidal wave of luxury goods, remarkable objects made from rare materials or with rare skill. Wealthy householders across southern Europe in this era ate feasts cooked in great bronze cauldrons decorated with the heads of bulls, lions, and griffins and served from intricately decorated metal bowls; adorned themselves with jewelry made of silver, gold, and electrum; and embellished their horses and furniture with delicate ivory plaques.[15] All this is often subsumed in museums under a vague "Phoenician" label, following the Greek literary tradition that associates luxury and wealth above all with the Levant. In reality it is the product of Cypriot, Egyptian, and Assyrian workshops too.[16]

The quantity, quality, and simple beauty of these ancient artifacts can be overwhelming. But as we stand in front of a glass cabinet glittering with ivory and metalwork, jewels, and glazed ceramic, dazzled and a bit confused, we should see too the ghostly reflections of the meetings in which people acquired these goods, and those in which they showed them off as emblems of their wealth and taste.

Trade was only one way these luxury crafts reached new homes, and perhaps not the most common. We get a glimpse of the possibilities in the Homeric epics, where such items are primarily associated with hospitality, diplomacy, and competition: At the funeral games for his beloved friend Patroclus, for instance, Achilles offers as a prize a large silver bowl that had been made in Sidon and taken by "Phoenician" sailors to the island of Lemnos as a present to the royal house, from where Patroclus had acquired it as ransom for a Trojan prisoner of war.[17]

None of this was anonymous: in a world before container ships and online shopping, even the simplest commercial transactions involved a meeting of minds, and people learned from one another as well. Just as striking as the imported artwork is the boom in artistic development in the western Mediterranean that responded to it.[18] Migrant artisans and the locals they trained were soon producing work so similar that it can be impossible to tell apart. Local artists also integrated techniques and themes from farther east into their own traditions: sphinxes and griffins, sirens and lotus flowers, gods and heroes begin to appear on local styles of pottery in the Iberian mountains as well as the Aegean islands.

It's easy to understand why scholars of the ancient Mediterranean have traditionally labeled the century or so from around 750 to 650 BCE "the orientalizing period." But although things changed dramatically in many western communities, the ways they changed were still shaped by local ideas and traditions. Levantine travelers did not "orientalize" the societies of the western Mediterranean; local people collaborated with them to "occidentalize" new symbols, technologies, and ideas to suit their own interests. Just as Levantine migration had taken different forms in the Mediterranean, so did local reactions to ongoing contact.

Let's start in southwest Iberia, where the adoption of new technologies coincides with dramatic social and cultural transformation. Huelva itself was becoming a large and wealthy city in the eighth century BCE. People began to build ashlar walls like those of Tyre and to replace circular huts made of wattle and daub with square houses constructed in mud brick with masonry foundations, although they did not adopt the layout of Levantine homes around an internal court.[19]

Local grandees were now buried in sumptuous tombs filled with imports and imitations of goods from Cyprus, Egypt, and western Asia: silver, bronze, and alabaster vessels, mirrors, ivory caskets, and incense burners. Two opulent seventh-century graves even contain chariots. At the same time, we see very poor burials for the first time as well. All this suggests that old kin-based social structures were disintegrating in response to new economic opportunities—opportunities that clan leaders were in a better position to exploit for personal benefit than others.[20]

The changes went well beyond Huelva, right across the deep valleys that divide southern Iberia from east to west. Their slopes had long housed villages where people lived on cattle raising, mining, and small-scale metalworking, trading with one another along rivers and mountain paths.[21] Now iron smelting arrived, and goldsmiths started to work with new alloys that allowed better temperature control and to experiment with hollow work, filigree, and granulation. Some Iberian potters adopted the fast wheel and hotter, larger kilns to produce thinner and more colorful pottery on a commercial scale.[22] As in Huelva, square-built houses with drystone foundations begin to replace older oval structures from the middle of the eighth century BCE, and by the early seventh Levantine-style walls appear inland.[23]

The adoption of new technologies may not signify much beyond a good eye for an opportunity, but we can see people changing their ideas about how to live as well. In particular, people across Tarshish began to pour libations of oil and wine for the dead, gifts to the gods of the underworld, and to make wine in quantity.[24]

Wine itself wasn't a Levantine invention: grapes were first cultivated to make an alcoholic drink in the southern Caucasus in the fifth millennium BCE, and they were pressed in what is now northern Greece by the fourth.[25] It had however become a Levantine specialty during the Bronze Age, exported in great "Canaanite" clay jars. In the western Mediterranean by contrast beer was the standard alcoholic drink, although wild grapes were sometimes pressed to make a basic wine.

This all changed when Levantine traders and settlers brought their own wine to sell and cuttings from their own vines too, which could be crossed with local grapes to produce new varieties.[26] They also knew how to produce wine of quality: what soils work best, what slopes and what care and intervention growing vines need to mature at their best before you can even begin to turn the grapes into an alcoholic drink. We could compare the introduction of Italian coffee-making techniques, machines, and cups to northern Europe and America in the late twentieth century, which transformed not only the quality but the whole experience of coffee drinking: where people do it, with whom, and how much more it costs. In a similar fashion, drinking wine gave wealthy locals a way to distinguish themselves from the rest of society with a more expensive, exotic, and technically demanding beverage.

We can trace changing local ideas and ideals over this period in a long-lived indigenous artistic tradition. Around 140 "warrior stelae," or menhirs, have so far come to light in southwest Iberia, stone markers 150 to 180 centimeters high and covered in carvings of items that date from the thirteenth to seventh centuries BCE.[27] Many of them were found out of context, looted, or recycled, but where their original locations are known they cluster near paths and settlements, sometimes in cemeteries but never clearly associated with a specific grave.

They must have memorialized heroes and ancestors, and earlier examples appear to embody an individual, adorned with a standard set of weapons found all along the Atlantic coast in the Late Bronze Age: a spear, a sword, a helmet, and a shield with a V-notched boss. The design of these menhirs suggests that they originally lay on or even under the ground, mimicking a body or burial. Around the end of the millennium however, going by the style of the armor depicted, exotic luxuries begin to appear on these markers just as they do in the material record: Mediterranean combs and dress pins; Cypriot lyres; even chariots. Human figures appear as well: if these represent the deceased, then the whole conception of the stone has changed. And in even later examples carvers leave the bottom third of the slabs undecorated so that they could be stuck upright in earth, making monuments that look more like the stone stelae set up in Levantine settlements around the Mediterranean.

Finally Phoenician letters reached Tarshish: when the first writing in Iberia appears in the seventh century BCE, it is based once again on the Tyrian script.[28] As with Greek, the inventor or inventors of this script recycled signs for sounds they didn't need to use for ones they did. In this case however they went further, adding syllables as well as vowels, and new signs of their own. Some examples of this writing are found close to Gadir, but most come from indigenous areas, including almost one hundred gravestones clustered in the Portuguese Algarve.

As we don't know the language the new letters were used to write, they are impossible to read. We know what we are missing all the same: the geographer Strabo claimed in the first century CE that the "Turdetani"—the name used at that time for the people of Tarshish—are "considered the wisest of the Iberians; they use writing, they possess ancient treatises and poetry, and they have laws in verse 6,000 years old."[29]

We see a different reaction on the island of Sardinia. The local population there had embraced new technologies since Levantine sailors had arrived in the late ninth century BCE at Sant'Imbenia, an indigenous village with a natural deep harbor near copper mines on the northwest coast. They brought with them transport amphoras full of oil and wine to swap for the local copper. Local potters quickly spliced the design together with Sardinian pottery styles to produce the earliest amphoras made in the western Mediterranean, which then carried Sardinian products to new ports.

These Sardinian transport containers were a great success: eighth-century Carthaginians imported them in greater numbers than amphoras from anywhere else, and adapted the new design to make their own versions.[30] Some examples excavated at Huelva meanwhile have traces of grape seeds in the bottom, so it seems that Sardinians were now making wine for export as well as for domestic consumption—although the Levantine alphabetic writing on another suggests that the newcomers were in charge of shipping and distribution, at least on this route.[31]

These islanders were on the other hand relatively uninterested in the luxury arts and crafts that Levantine sailors brought west. They kept the traditions of the Levant at a distance, too, and pre-existing cultural norms remained paramount.[32] Rather than building towns, the islanders continued to live in the old tower houses or "nuraghi," which expanded into multi-towered structures or even large, fortified settlements with tens of thousands of inhabitants.[33] Once again, increasing social complexity may well be in part a reaction to new contacts, but although the island boasts some of the earliest Phoenician inscriptions in the western Mediterranean, Sardinians themselves appear to have avoided writing of any kind. They also eschewed the unusual religious practices that Levantine settlers observed in the new tophets on the island, which may themselves help to explain why neighbors preferred to keep their cultural distance.

The story is different again in another western region that saw little Levantine settlement at all. Like most of Europe in this era, central Italy had no "Dark Age." It did have rich agricultural land, while the mountains to the north were full of copper and iron. Settlements of more than a thousand inhabitants had existed in the region since the late second millennium BCE, but it was in the early first millennium BCE that people who had been scattered throughout the landscape in farms and small villages came together on flat plateaus in communities of up to 200 hectares.[34] By the eighth century fortifications appear and cemeteries had moved outside some of these sites.

The greatest glories are found in Etruria, a triangle of land north of the Tiber, south of the Arno, and west of the Apennines. The farmers and metalworkers who lived here were called "Tyrsenoi" and "Tyrrhenoi" by Greek authors, and later by Romans "Etrusci." Modern scholars often call them "the Etruscans," but I deliberately use the less familiar geographical adjective "Etrurian," as there's no evidence that these people saw themselves as a single ethnic community. They called themselves simply *rasna,* "people" or citizens of individual cities, which also meant "soldiers": if you could not afford the weapons and armor for military service you had no political rights, and later Greek historians call these Etrurians *penestai,* the "poor."[35]

As with the "Phoenician" ports, the cities of Etruria had no strong political links to one another either. What marked them off as a distinctive group to their neighbors, deserving of a distinctive name, was their language. Etruscan, a term I reserve in this book for the language, was not only very different from other Italian tongues, it was not even Indo-European.[36] It seems likely to be a holdout—like modern Basque dialects—from the languages brought into Europe by early farmers in the sixth millennium BCE that had largely by now been displaced by Indo-European tongues adopted across the continent millennia later.*

This unusual tongue aroused great curiosity about its speakers' origins. Herodotus reports in the fifth century BCE a suggestion that the "Tyrrhenians" were originally from the wealthy Anatolian mining kingdom of Lydia that had come to prominence in the early seventh century.[37] One problem with this theory is that the Etruscan language is nothing like Lydian, which is for a start Indo-European. Another is the evidence from aDNA (ancient DNA) that the people of ancient Etruria have the same genetic profile as their central Italian neighbors.[38] Instead—like the biblical tales of the king of Tyre and the queen of

*Etruscan has only one known relation: Raetic, spoken in the Alps in the second half of the first millennium BCE, which may be a daughter language.

Sheba, or the Greek legends of Kadmos and Thasos—this story seems to have been invented by Lydians themselves in the sixth century BCE as a way to weave their own history together with a famous and noble people, in this case one to the west.[39]

Three hundred years earlier, the richer tombs that begin to appear in ninth-century Etruria first suggest the emergence of a distinct upper class. Their occupants were often buried in classic Mediterranean "warrior" style with weapons and armor, but there was an occasional local twist: in some cases the ashes were placed in urns shaped like the huts in which these people had lived.[40]

The earliest Levantine goods to arrive on Italian soil in the ninth century BCE must have come through Sardinian ports, but from the early eighth century Levantine traders were regular visitors to Etruria themselves, in search of local metals and produce, and perhaps also connections with the trade route that still ran from Italy up to Denmark.[41] As usual, they brought wine with them and, as usual, it went down well. Some domesticated vines are already found in Italy during the Bronze Age but the evidence for viticulture before the eighth century BCE is slight.[42] In the seventh century, however, Etrurians started to make wine amphoras for their own product.[43]

The wealthy acquired distinctive eastern vessels to drink the wine as well: bronze bowls with very pronounced ribs to catch the sediment. These were also popular in eighth-century Assyria but rare in the coastal cities of the Levant and elsewhere in the western Mediterranean, suggesting a carefully curated trading strategy on the part of Levantine merchants to target local tastes.[44] Artisans meanwhile borrowed subjects and techniques from the visitors, as humans, animals, and mythical monsters came to dominate the local artistic repertoire, and black-glazed bucchero pottery produced on a fast wheel imitated the sheen of eastern metalwork.[45]

With new people came new relations with the gods, as in the Aegean. Religious activity in Etruria had traditionally revolved around sacred huts, offerings pits, and occasional ritual killing, in this case of adults as well as children.[46] Around 650 BCE however, a house for gods was constructed in a sanctuary at Tarquinia using Levantine technologies: the

Egyptian cubit and ashlar architecture.[47] It still doesn't look much like temples elsewhere: it is a big stone hut divided into two rooms with an altar inside.

Etrurians began to treat their dead differently too. By the late eighth century BCE burials in pits and trenches gave way to stone-built underground chamber tombs, some covered with large mounds reaching fifty meters across.[48] They were filled with exotic goods acquired from and through the Levant, from bronze cauldrons to ostrich eggs. At Tarquinia a woman was buried with gold and bronze work, Egyptian figurines, glazed ceramics, and a scarab with the cartouche of the pharaoh Bakenranef, who ruled briefly around 720 BCE. One early-seventh-century grave at Pontecagnano in southern Campania, a community with close links to Etruria, exaggerates these eastern connections to the point of absurdity with a nonsensical hieroglyphic inscription carved on the rim of a silver drinking cup.[49]

In other cases these tombs suggest quite specific knowledge of Levantine culture. Extensive banqueting equipment is often found inside, signaling the adoption of funerary feasting.[50] And some of the richest seventh-century burials also contain scepters, thrones, and chariots, all traditional signs of political and military authority farther east: the inscription on the tenth-century sarcophagus of King Ahirom at Byblos, for instance, had threatened dreadful punishment if any king, governor, or general attacked Byblos and uncovered the coffin: "may the scepter of his judgment be broken, may the throne of his kingship be overturned, and may peace depart from Byblos!"[51]

We should not however assume that the same goods meant the same things in different contexts. Scepters, thrones, and even chariots are found in women's tombs in Italy as well as men's. That doesn't necessarily mean that these women were driving chariots in battle, and they are buried with equipment for spinning and weaving too. Instead, in Etruria these special items may symbolize individual women's power in other contexts, or the military power of the household that they literally reproduced.[52]

Some wealthy men and women continued to be buried in "houses" too: the most elaborate aristocratic tombs in Etruria have multiple rooms with space for dining and other rituals, plastered and decorated like domestic interiors, with shields and bowls lining the walls.[53] The upper classes may have embraced the social power of Levantine luxury goods and royal symbols in fashions much closer to that of Tarshish than Sardinia, but they adapted them in different ways to support their own power bases in a different society.

Over the course of the seventh century BCE Etrurian merchants themselves developed new links in new directions. Some went south: Bucchero pottery and Etruscan inscriptions appear in seventh-century Carthage. We can see the prestige attached to this particular connection in a set of inscriptions written on three gold sheets around 600 BCE and nailed up in a sanctuary dedicated to the Etrurian goddess Uni at Pyrgi, the main port for Caere.[54] Two contain Etruscan texts, one of which is translated on the third into Phoenician, skillfully written by a practiced scribe in a style typical of contemporary Carthage rather than the Levant. It records the dedication of "a holy place" by Thefarie Velianas, the king of Caere, "to the lady Ashtart . . . since Ashtart asked him for it"—that is, for the "holy place" or temple.

Thefarie Velianas is acting here as much in the religious tradition of Carthage as in his own.[55] Such arrangements are found across western Asia from the third millennium BCE, as when God asks King David to build him a temple at Jerusalem. Furthermore, the close relationship implied in the inscription between the king and the goddess as well as the exchange of favors between them are both standard features of Phoenician-language dedications, as illustrated in the Carthage tophet.

Other Etrurian connections went west: in the seventh century BCE wine production became a mass-market phenomenon in Italy, and as the cities of Etruria grew larger and more powerful, their ships carried wine in increasing quantities west to settlements along the Gulf of Lion, along with their trademark glossy black jugs and cups to serve it.[56] The people of what is now southern France were already fond of feasting, and the addition of wine to the festivities offered the upper classes a convenient way to distinguish themselves from the rest of society: it transports and stores well, and its relatively high alcohol content compensates for the effort involved in moving it from one place to another.[57]

For Etrurian merchants the attractions of this trade included the metals, salt, and wool with which Gaul was richly supplied. They may have included slaves as well, bought or kidnapped inland and then traded into the Mediterranean: the young serving staff and musicians depicted in the fresco paintings of lavish feasts found in Etruria—some with blond or red hair—are unlikely to represent the host's own children.[58]

The Rhône Valley also offered a highway north into central Gaul where wealthy metalworking communities emerged on hilltops and riverbanks across continental Europe from Burgundy to the Carpathians in the seventh century BCE. This phenomenon is now labeled Hallstatt after the Austrian village where one of the first such sites was excavated but other important examples include Hochdorf and Vix. Their leaders were buried in monumental funerary mounds with weapons, four-wheeled wagons, and exotic goods from all directions: Baltic amber, African ivory, Athenian cups and bowls, acquired in exchange for gold, leather, skins, and furs.[59]

Finally, Etrurian traders were developing new relationships to the east as well. Aegean pots had begun to arrive in central Italy in the eighth century, and by the seventh there is good evidence for trade between Etruria and Corinth.[60] Greek-speaking traders and businessmen were now arriving in Italy in significant numbers and in the second half of the century Greek elements begin to appear in personal names as well, suggesting a degree of intermarriage.[61] And as in other parts of the Mediterranean, contact with new people prompted Etrurians to write their language down for the first time. In this case however they borrowed not the Tyrian alphabet but its Greek daughter, discarding letters such as *b* and *d* for which the Etruscan language had no use.

There was an ancient story about the origins of the Etruscan alphabet that captures real relationships in an era of migration. It concerns an eighth- or seventh-century Corinthian merchant named Demaratos who sailed regularly between his hometown and the cities of Etruria before trouble at home sent him into political exile in Tarquinia, where he married a local noblewoman and introduced Greek letters.[62]

This is of course a legend, but it gets the location at least of transmission right: the earliest Etruscan inscriptions are indeed found at Tarquinia and date from the late eighth century BCE. By the middle of the seventh century other cities in Etruria had adopted this new alphabet, and after various experiments the direction of writing was standardized around 600 BCE as right to left.[63]*

By the later seventh century, settlements in Etruria were finally beginning to look more like other cities around the Mediterranean, with earthen walls and marked-off sanctuaries. Square-built houses on stone foundations with pottery roof tiles replaced thatched oval huts.[64]

Social norms remained rather different. In particular, women always had a larger public role in Etruria than in Greece or the Levant. Paintings show them wearing outdoor cloaks and sturdy shoes, and attending athletics games, while later inscriptions often give people's mothers' names as well as their fathers'.[65] Sculpture from at least the early sixth century depicts scenes of companionable marriage as well, as men and women relax together at feasts on couches festooned with comfortable cushions.[66]

This is more unusual than it may sound. Reclining on couches to eat and drink was originally an Assyrian practice, where, it seems, men reclined while women sat upright.[67] By contrast, upper-class Levantine men gathered alone to recline on couches and eat and drink at the *marzeah*. Greek images of reclining at the *symposion* found from the late seventh century onward also exclude respectable women, and appear to exclude food as well, separating eating from drinking. Farther west, images of the Italian *symposium* in this era depict food and wine, men and women, with both reclining on couches. The same Assyrian fashions are adapted differently across the Mediterranean to local tastes.[68]

. . .

*Etruscan inscriptions tell us less about their authors than we might like. We know that legends and religious lore were written down on scrolls that later Roman authors called the "Etruscan Disciplines," but they are now lost. The inscriptions that remain include some ritual texts and property contracts, but most are just names, which do not help much in the reconstruction of a language: the basic rules of Etruscan grammar are now well understood, but the vocabulary is still often baffling.

Many people in ancient times spent their whole lives in small worlds revolving around farm and family, traveling no farther than a local festival, shrine, or market. Others, though, lived on the road—or more often on the sea—learning one another's languages, settling in one another's lands and cities, and adapting one another's gods and social customs.

They told one another stories as well, living cultural counterparts to the gleaming objects that now fill museum cabinets. Together, they created an overlapping set of legends, gods, and heroes all across the Mediterranean, and then used them to tell more local tales.

To see best how this worked we can return to the Homeric poems, first written down at the height of this occidentalizing period. This time though we are interested not in the traces to be found there of earlier Aegean traditions, but in their connections with stories told in other places about different people.

CHAPTER TWELVE

He Who Saw the Deep

LEGENDARY JOURNEYS IN MYTHICAL TIME

Despite its title the *Iliad* is not really a story about "Ilios," the Greek name for Troy. Nor is it about the Trojan War: it deals neither with the origins of the conflict nor in any detail with its end. Instead, the poem focuses almost exclusively on the events of a few weeks in the tenth and final year of the siege of the Anatolian citadel, and for most of that time on conflicts within the Greek camp. Furthermore, the relationship at the heart of the emotional drama is not between Helen, queen of Sparta, and her Trojan lover Paris—the affair over which the expedition had been launched—but between two Greek warriors, the hero Achilles and his beloved boyhood companion Patroclus.

This is the story of the *Iliad.* Achilles is leader of the Myrmidon contingent in the Achaean alliance against Troy. He falls out with the overall mission commander Agamemnon over a local woman named Briseis, whom Achilles has enslaved for sexual services after killing her family. When Agamemnon takes Briseis for himself instead, Achilles refuses to continue fighting and retires to his tent to sulk. Patroclus replaces him in the front line and is slain by the Trojan champion Hector with the help of the god Apollo. Distraught, Achilles kills Hector in a personal grudge match.

The version of the *Iliad* that has survived down to our own day was finalized around 700 BCE: while it mentions temples and cult statues, which first appeared in Greece in the late eighth century, there are no signs of later cultural innovations or artistic developments.[1] The obvious explanation for this halt to the process of oral recomposition is that the adoption of the alphabet meant that this version of the story was finally written down. And while we have already seen that elements in this "standard" version go back to stories told in the Bronze Age Aegean, others relate to traditions from farther east.[2]

In particular, the work is full of echoes of another poem with a relationship between men at its core: the devoted friendship between Gilgamesh, the legendary king of Uruk, and his companion the wild man Enkidu.[3] This pair were first immortalized in Sumerian poems of the third millennium BCE, and then in Akkadian works of the second; the latter were finally compiled around 1100 BCE into a "Standard Babylonian" version of the tale, which became in the first millennium BCE a classic work of Mesopotamian literature, like Homer for Greek speakers, or Shakespeare to Anglophones today.

This poem is usually now called *Gilgamesh,* but like other Akkadian poems it was known to its original readers by its first words, "He who saw the deep" (*Sha naqba imuru*). It relates the adventures of Gilgamesh and Enkidu, a creature created by the gods to challenge the king's arrogance who becomes his companion instead. The pair travel together to the Cedar Forest (probably Mount Lebanon) and slaughter its monstrous guardian Humbaba, but then unwisely kill the Bull of Heaven sent by the goddess Ishtar to destroy Gilgamesh for spurning her advances. The gods decide that Enkidu must pay the ultimate price, leaving Gilgamesh to journey on alone in search of immortality.

The actual plots of *Gilgamesh* and the *Iliad* are completely different: Gilgamesh and Enkidu fight not foreign princes but gods and monsters, as well as each other. But like Achilles and Patroclus these heroes set out on a journey together and engage in heroic combats with mighty opponents. As in the *Iliad,* Enkidu dies at the whim of the gods, leaving Gilgamesh bereft. As in the *Iliad,* the men are not explicitly portrayed as lovers in a physical sense: all four of our heroes have sexual relationships with women, but in both works it is clear that they love each other beyond all others. And at the end of their respective poems we leave both Gilgamesh and Achilles tragic, lonely kings. Men who had hoped to live forever face up to death.

Some of the parallels between Gilgamesh and Achilles might be expected of any self-respecting hero: both can talk directly to gods, and both are themselves semi-divine. Others seem less likely to be coincidental: both of their mothers lament the risks they take, for instance, and the language used of them mourning their lost partner is very similar indeed. Achilles is compared to a grieving lion who has discovered that its cubs have been stolen by a hunter, while Gilgamesh is described as "like a lioness deprived of its cubs, pacing to and fro."[4] They are so distressed, in fact, that neither of them will let the corpse go before it begins to decompose: Achilles is concerned about flies laying eggs in Patroclus' body so that worms cause his flesh to rot, while Gilgamesh admits, "I did not surrender his body for burial until a maggot dropped from his nostril."[5]

The story of Gilgamesh also has distinct similarities with that of Homer's other flawed hero, Odysseus, the king of the island of Ithaca off the west coast of Greece whose slow and eventful journey home around the Mediterranean provides the focus of the *Odyssey*.[6] Both attack a giant monster—Gilgamesh, Humbaba; Odysseus, the one-eyed giant Cyclops—and both eventually return from their long travels to rule their old kingdoms. Again, such achievements are perhaps only to be expected of great men, but both also get directions for journeys to visit wise men in the underworld from a woman who lives in a remote outpost herself: Gilgamesh from the alewife Siduri, Odysseus from the enchantress Circe.

The Homeric epics have other parallels too. In the Egyptian "Tale of the Shipwrecked Sailor," dating from around the eighteenth century BCE, a retainer describes to his master how he set out on a voyage down the Red Sea in a crew of 120, but after losing his ship and crewmates in a storm he was washed onto a fantastical island. There he lived on fish and birds until he was found and protected by a giant human-headed serpent god with a meter-long beard, who introduces himself as the king of Punt, and eventually sends the man home safe with a huge cargo of gifts including incense, eye paint, and giraffe tails.

In the *Odyssey,* written down about a thousand years later, the Spartan king Menelaus tells Odysseus' son Telemachus of his own adventure on a voyage from Egypt. As in the Egyptian tale, Menelaus is marooned on a desert island where he and his men eat fish and birds before he encounters Proteus, the mythical Old Man of the Sea, who turns into a variety of animals including a snake, and tells him how to return safely home.[7]

The Greek texts also echo literary tradition in the Levant: not only is Homer's general depiction of fractious and flirtatious gods close in tone to the Ugaritic Baal Cycle, but versions of the mysterious Ugaritic phrase "the word of the tree and the whisper of the stone" turn up twice in the Homeric corpus. Meanwhile Homer's metalworking god Hephaistos finds his own parallel in the Ugaritic god of craft, Kothar-wa-Hasis—both work with a bellow and tongs, both build houses, and both make special weapons for the hero at his mother's request.[8]

Finally, the Homeric poems echo texts preserved in the archives of Hattusa: Homer's descriptions of both Dawn and the Sun rising up from the waters of the Ocean find parallels in Hittite cosmology, for instance, where a solar deity rises from the sea.[9] Anatolian literature might even have provided the Trojan setting: one tablet records a fragment of Luwian song beginning "when they come from steep Wilusa"—Ilios.[10]

Other Anatolian tales find their way into the work of an early-seventh-century Boeotian poet named Hesiod, who composed a cosmological poem in epic hexameter, the *Theogony,* recounting the creation of the world and the story of how successive generations of gods overthrew their predecessors. As he tells the story, Ouranos ("Sky") keeps his children imprisoned in the womb of their mother Gaia ("Earth") through continuous intercourse until brave young Kronos castrates him with a sickle, severing heaven from earth. The offcuts land in the sea and give birth to Aphrodite. Learning from his father's error, Kronos himself then eats his own children as soon as they are born, until one day their mother serves him a stone instead of a baby. The surviving child is the storm deity Zeus, who grows up to defeat his father, liberate his siblings, and become king of the gods.

The idea of a succession of divine generations starting with a sky god in which a god of storms or winds emerges victorious is found in both Mesopotamian and Hittite legends, but this story has particular parallels with a myth preserved in Hittite archives about the god Kumarbi.[11] In this tale Kumarbi bites off and swallows the genitals of his father the sky god Anu, and as a result gives birth to various children. He attempts to eat one but eats a stone instead. The storm god Tessub is born from his body and overthrows him. This is not the same story, but it is built from similar ingredients.[12]

There is no doubt then that the earliest works of Greek literature preserve traces of encounters with a bigger world of song in other languages. When these happened is a more difficult question. Most of the recognizable Egyptian, Anatolian, and Levantine parallels are found in much earlier texts. Some may already have arrived in the Aegean during the Bronze Age, when Ahhiyawa was briefly part of the big world of the Brother Kings. But this could also be a trick of the light: we have far more evidence for writing in general in these areas from the Bronze Age than from the early first millennium.

This is partly because large and bureaucratic empires produce and preserve a lot more writing than the smaller states more typical of the later period. It is also partly because so many Bronze Age cities were destroyed by fire, which literally baked their stories into the clay tablets on which they were written. They couldn't then be soaked for a few hours and reused, even if anyone had stayed around to do so. The main problem however is the widespread switch at the turn of the millennium from writing cuneiform script on clay tablets to alphabetic writing in Aramaic or Phoenician on papyrus, leather, and (wooden) wax tablets. This was disastrous from the point of view of conservation, especially in rainy regions like the Levant.

The same stories continued to be told, and where people continued to write on clay we continue to find them: much of our knowledge of

Bronze Age Mesopotamian literature comes from the library built by Esarhaddon's son Ashurbanipal, whose reign saw the height of Assyrian power east of the Euphrates, including a decade or so of rule over Egypt.[13]

Whenever they encountered these stories, it is unlikely that many Greek bards could read cuneiform, hieroglyphic, or even alphabetic texts in Semitic languages, and there is no evidence that any were translated into written Greek. The tales must have spread through speech and song in places where people spoke more than one language. Much of this was surely in the hands of professionals, traveling singers who met in foreign courts and competed at festivals and games. But stories would have been told among merchants too, within mixed marriages and mixed households, and shared among slaves and nurses, teachers, pupils, and friends. In a fragment of a play by the fifth-century Athenian tragedian Euripides, the heroine tells a story of the creation of heaven, earth, and the human race, and explains that she heard it from her mother.[14]

Such conversations could have happened in all sorts of places, and no doubt did. Plenty of Greek speakers lived in western Anatolia, tradition always associated Homer with this coast, and by around 700 BCE inter-city festivals were held there that could have attracted a wide range of participants.[15] A century later local Greek poets were adopting contemporary Anatolian techniques into their own poetry, and there is no reason to think that such borrowings were new.[16] Farther east, Cilicia presented further opportunities, and Cyprus would have been particularly fertile territory for the exchange of tales, an island of commerce and court culture where both Phoenician and Greek were spoken during the Iron Age, and which had its own syllabic script for writing Greek.[17]

Contemporary Levantine cities must have had their own storytelling traditions as well. If they were ever written down they are now lost, but one clue to their existence is a later account of a "Phoenician" myth written down in Greek in the Roman era by a Byblian author called Philo, which has a number of parallels with texts written on Ugaritic tablets unavailable to Philo himself, suggesting a shared regional mythscape.[18] The Levantine courts were meeting places for foreigners too, as reflected in the tenth-century Tale of Wenamun when King Zakerbaal of Byblos sends the hero an Egyptian singer called Tanetne to cheer him up; we should imagine that before and after this errand she sang to his own household and other visitors.[19] In the end though the mechanics of transmission, and even the specific parallels, are less interesting than the result: a shared world of big ideas about humans, gods, and storytelling across the eastern Mediterranean.

All the same, it is important to note that this was of no interest to the people who told these stories and listened to them: neither Homer nor ancient Greek scholars who commented on him ever mention the parallels with other traditions laid out here.[20] And the phenomenon itself should not be exaggerated: such borrowings contribute only a fraction of the content and meaning of these poems, which are in many ways dramatically different from the literature of Egypt and western Asia.[21]

And at the same time the Homeric epics played a part in creating a single, mutually comprehensible "Greek" language out of a number of different local dialects.[22] They helped to create a common culture as well, as they collected local folktales and cult myths from different areas of the Greek-speaking Aegean and combined them into single stories that invented a communal past for their Greek readers.[23] As the Athenian chronicler of the Peloponnesian Wars Thucydides points out in the fifth century, before the Trojan War there is no indication of any common action in Hellas.[24] Like the Israelite Exodus from Egypt in the Hebrew Bible, the *Iliad* is a story about a joint expedition in the distant past that brought a people together as a community, told in a language they share. The *Odyssey* then defines a distinct shared world from which its heroes have sailed, and to which they attempt with varying success to return.

This is not yet however civilizational thinking: a shared heritage is not the same as an exclusive one, and these Greek songs defined an open community. Trojans appear to worship the same gods and speak the same language as Greeks in the poems—or at least bilingualism is so common that language never gets in the way—and they are presented not only as very similar in culture to the Achaeans, but in at least one case as guest friends: the Greek hero Diomedes and the Trojan ally Glaukos recognize a close bond on the battlefield through the friendship of their grandfathers.[25]

In a changing world Greek speakers themselves were making ever more links with an even greater variety of people. They also constantly adapted and expanded their own myths to incorporate the novel people and places they encountered farther west, explaining the origins of unfamiliar societies in terms of heroes and ancestors they already knew, making relatives of new friends. The people of Etruria, for instance, do not appear in Homer's *Odyssey*, but by the early seventh century BCE Hesiod describes Odysseus himself as the founder of various Italian peoples through the three sons he fathered on the witch Circe, including men who "ruled over the famous Etruscans [*Tyrsenoi*], very far away, in a recess of the Holy Islands."[26]

As usual we know more about Greeks than about anyone else, but they were not the only storytellers in the Mediterranean, and people farther west also incorporated foreign stories into local worlds. Etruria, for instance, had plenty of legends of its own, preserved for us by Greek and Roman writers as well as by local artists. These are tales of men like the prophet Tages, born of the earth with the face of a child and the figure of an old man, who taught his people the secrets of divination by reading the livers and other internal organs of sacrificed animals.[27]

In the seventh century however Aegean legends and heroes start to appear, both on Aegean-style pottery and in local artwork. This curiosity was not indiscriminate: Etruscan speakers were particularly interested in maritime scenes and one of their favorite heroes was Odysseus.[28] These entangled ideas promoted creativity but they must have led to confusion at times. Let's imagine a trader from Greece—Corinth, perhaps—arriving in the Etrurian port of Caere around 675 BCE. He already has contacts in the city, and naturally they invite him to a party.

It's not exactly what he's used to: the focus is more on food and feasting than on the drinking or drinking games of Aegean *symposia,* where men entertained one another with alcohol, music, and sex workers. More surprising, women are reclining on the couches—and they are not paid entertainers, but wives, daughters, even friends, taking as lively a part in the conversation as the men.

Our merchant's eyes drift to something more familiar: a sturdy bowl full of wine sitting at the center of the low table. The decoration is exuberant: checkerboard patterns, free-form stars, bands of paint on the inside, and two dramatic scenes painted front and back—a battle at sea on one side, and on the other the episode from the *Odyssey* in which Odysseus and his shipmates blind the Cyclops who had imprisoned the crew and was snacking his way through them.

At first glance, the bowl looks like a Greek original, perhaps a souvenir of an earlier merchant's visit. It is a little crude, with an unruly spider squatting under one handle, but it is signed by its painter in Greek letters: "Aristonothos made this." This is also the first real clue that something is wrong—or at least rather odd: Aristo-nothos translates into Greek as "Best [or Noble] Bastard"—unsurprisingly a very rare name. Then there is the Cyclops Polyphemos himself, depicted on this vase not as a giant, as in Homer's story, but as the same size as his Greek assailants.[29]

Our friend turns to his hosts for an explanation, but it takes him a little time to understand their version of the story. His Phoenician is better than his Etruscan in any case, but as the assembled company discuss the scene they talk not of "Odysseus" but of a local hero called "Utuse," who helps the people of Etruria carve out their own space in a shared world of Mediterranean myth that is also shared with traditions farther east. Perhaps they already saw Utuse as an ancestor of their own: we have positive evidence from the fourth century that he was also honored in Etruria as a founder figure—not of an Etruscan people, however, as Hesiod had suggested, but of a single city. This version of the story has Odysseus come home to Ithaca to discover that his wife Penelope has been unfaithful. He leaves her to return to Italy, where he founds the city of Cortona and where he lives the rest of his life.[30]

. . .

Etrurians weren't the only westerners in the first millennium BCE to tailor foreign stories to suit themselves. On Sardinia people remix Levantine rather than Greek myth to make a local founder figure called Babi the son of "Makaris" or Melqart.[31] And in Tarshish a myth of origins preserved in Latin by the Roman historian Pompeius Trogus draws on ideas from both the Aegean and western Asia.

Gargoris, the first king of the "Kouretes," lived in the forests of Tartessos (a later Greek term for Tarshish). He was also the first man to collect honey, but he was principally remembered for repeatedly trying to kill his daughter's illegitimate son. On his orders the child was successively exposed, trampled by cows, thrown to savage dogs, and then cast into the sea; in every case he was saved by kindly animals. Eventually Gargoris relented and with some admiration appointed the boy his successor. Habis proved an excellent king, who "united a barbarous people with laws," stopped them from eating foraged food and taught them how to plow with oxen and grow grain. He banned his people from carrying out "servile duties" and settled them in seven cities.[32]

The names Gargoris and Habis are otherwise unknown, and there is no reason to doubt that this is a local story.[33] Just as the tale told by the people of Gadir about the foundation of their city treated the land in which the settlers arrived as empty, this one makes no mention of external factors in local cultural development at all, let alone of foreign visitors and settlers. It still finds parallels in other traditions.[34]

Habis himself is a lawgiver, a figure who frequently appears in Levantine tales—Moses is the most obvious example—as well as in legends of Greek cities: one Lykourgos, for instance, supposedly introduced the Spartan constitution. Habis also however invents civilization itself, building on Gargoris' exploitation of the produce of the natural world to introduce agriculture and the city. Greek legends tend to ascribe inventions to the gods—Hephaistos, for example, is the first blacksmith. To have a mortal man as a "first inventor" is a distinctive characteristic instead of Levantine myth: in the Hebrew Bible Cain and Abel were the first shepherd and farmer, and Noah the first vintner, while in the second century CE Philo of Byblos reports an ancient local origin myth in which mortal men introduce hunting, cattle raising, villages, justice, and salt.[35]

We don't know for sure when people in Tarshish started to tell the story of the Forest Kings, but when they did they were drawing on the mythical traditions of cultures far to the east, familiar to them through centuries of conversation with merchants and migrants, as a Mediterranean mythscape slowly came together. It transcended any individual society, but helped them all position themselves in an ever wider world.

By the middle of the seventh century BCE ships of Tarshish were a rarer sight, and Tyre itself was on the way out: Ashurbanipal had finally incorporated much of its territory into the Assyrian provincial system and crippled its trade with commercial restrictions. The supply of "oriental" goods in the western Mediterranean came to a halt; the fashion for imitations dried up too.

Assyria's own fall was even faster. In the confused aftermath of Ashurbanipal's death in 631 BCE, the Levantine cities broke away, and a local official in Babylon named Nabopolassar led a successful rebellion to free his city from its Assyrian overlords. By 616 he and his allies were strong enough to invade Assyria itself, sacking the old capital of Assur in 614, and Nineveh in 612. Nabopolassar killed King Ashur-etil-ilani, Ashurbanipal's successor, burned down the palaces, deported the population, and inherited most of what was left of the empire.

Nabopolassar's son and successor Nebuchadnezzar (r. 604–562 BCE) recaptured the Levantine cities and continued the strategy of forced resettlement in response to local revolts. He most famously sent people of Judah to Babylonia in three separate episodes between 597 and 582, with one uprising in 587 also prompting the Babylonians to sack Jerusalem and destroy Solomon's temple.

At the same time, Nebuchadnezzar tightened the imperial noose around Tyre, with increased demands for cedar and other kinds of tribute, trade blockades, and intermittent military campaigns; this put a final end to the city as a Mediterranean trading center.[36] We get a taste of neighborly schadenfreude in the Book of Ezekiel, written from the perspective of a sixth-century BCE Hebrew prophet in Babylonian exile himself at the time:

> When your merchandise went out on the seas,
> you satisfied many nations;
> with your great wealth and your wares
> you enriched the kings of the earth.
>
> Now you are shattered by the sea
> in the depths of the waters;
> your wares and all your company
> have gone down with you. . . .
>
> The merchants among the nations scoff at you;
> you have come to a horrible end
> and will be no more.[37]

CHAPTER THIRTEEN

The Bitter River

MILETOS, C. 600 BCE

The first surviving map of the world was etched around 600 BCE into a clay tablet rediscovered at Sippar in Iraq in the late nineteenth century.[1] It is a tiny little thing, just eight centimeters across and twelve up. The map itself is oriented to the north and it depicts the world as a disk of land centered on Babylon and surrounded by a circular sea labeled *marratu:* the salty or bitter river. The city of Babylon itself is a rectangle stamped across the upper part of the central island and bisected like the land itself by the Euphrates River. Around the city, circles denote other regions and cities in western Asia including Assyria and Elam; most are placed in approximately correct positions in relation to Babylon.

This Babylonian map is still a work of the imagination. Across the "bitter river" extend triangular islands, originally as many as eight; the one farthest north is captioned "place where the sun is not seen." Notes about these "regions" on the back of the tablet describe one as the home of fast-moving cattle with horns, another as a place that winged birds cannot reach. Further fragmentary commentary above the map itself alludes to ruined cities, ruined gods, scorpion men, serpents, and dragons, all apparently associated with these lands across the river. It also includes the names of Sargon, king of Mesopotamian Akkad in the

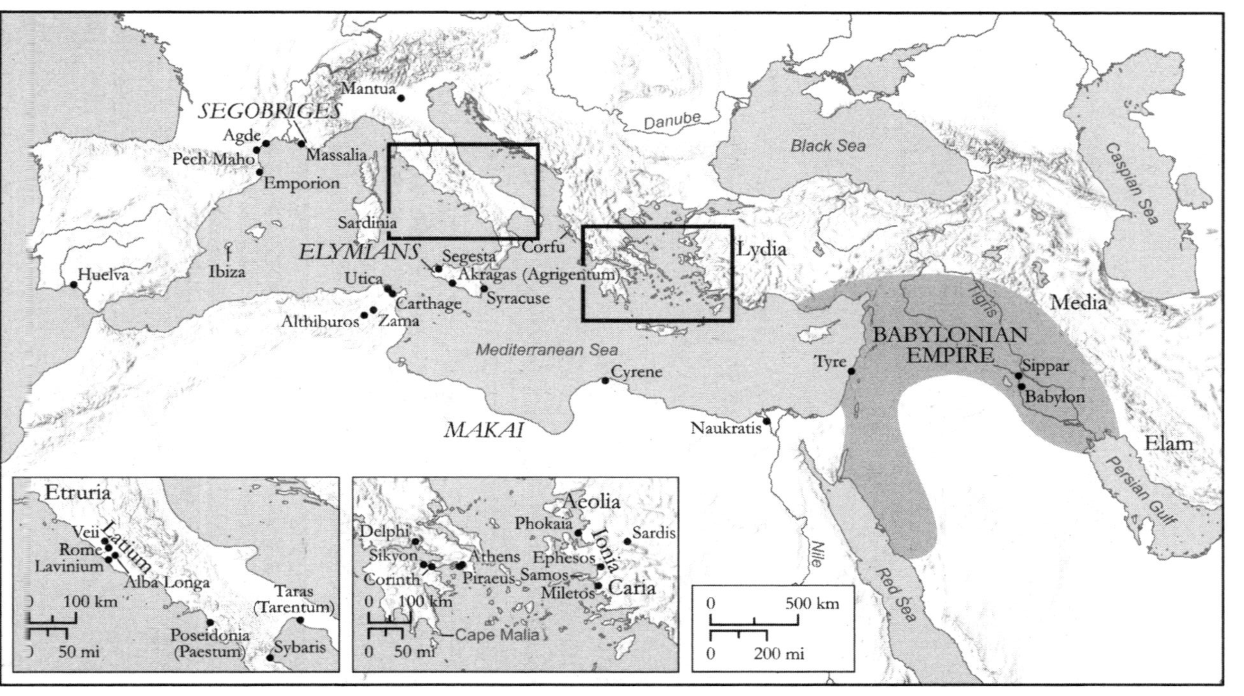

Babylon and the Mediterranean, c. 550 BCE

third millennium BCE, and Utnapishtim, who survived the great flood in *Gilgamesh.* It isn't clear how they fit in, but their presence adds to the sense of distance, across both time and space. The mapmaker puts themself—and by implication the viewer—at the center of a world that gets stranger the farther you roam.

Babylon was, to be fair, the largest city in the world at the time, with eighteen kilometers of ramparts and a population of 150,000 or more.[2] Between a vigorous policy of deportation from subject lands and the positive attractions of a thriving economy, new residents arrived regularly from Elam, Egypt, the Levant, and Anatolia. The city's bankers offered credit and mortgages, its trading houses dealt across the empire and, in the decades that followed the fall of Assyria, imperial profits and the labor of deportees allowed Babylonian kings to build on a magnificent scale.[3]

Nabopolassar himself restored the ancient ziggurat Etemenanki ("Link between Heaven and Earth"), which ascended in seven stepped stories from a base ninety-one meters square to a sanctuary of the city's god Marduk. According to the inscription he deposited in the building's foundations, Nabopolassar and his son got directly involved in the work:

> I bowed [my] neck to the god Marduk, my lord, rolled up [my] garment, the ceremonial attire of royal majesty, and carried mud bricks and mud on my head. I had baskets made from gold and silver, and [then], alongside my workmen, I made Nebuchadnezzar—[my] first-born child, the beloved of my heart—carry mud that was mixed with wine, oil, and crushed aromatics.[4]

They found time to build for themselves too: Nabopolassar's royal palace had 250 rooms arranged in blocks around five great courtyards, with the throne room at the very center. When Nebuchadnezzar succeeded to the throne he extended these cramped quarters.

Babylon was still a great center of science as well, where scholars studied the heavens as well as the earth. For more than a millennium they had been recording natural events—solar eclipses, earthquakes, lunar haloes, and even thunder—which they saw as omens. In the late seventh century BCE a new system of nightly celestial observations began, with scholars recording the positions of the heavenly bodies in a long series of "Astronomical Diaries" along with the events they predicted, from the level of the Euphrates to the outcomes of battles.[5] As a result of their meticulous recordkeeping, Babylonian astronomers could predict lunar and solar eclipses, as well as the rising and setting of planets, which they called *bibbu,* or "wandering sheep," as opposed to the fenced-in sheep of the constellations.[6]

All this was of interest to Greek speakers farther west, not on the Greek mainland, but in the cities of western Anatolia, which had much closer connections to Babylon. Like the Assyrians before them, Babylonians called all Greek speakers "Yawnaya," a word borrowed from the Greek term "Ionian" used of themselves by communities on the central Anatolian coast and nearby islands like Chios and Samos.[7] Looking west, these wealthy, sophisticated cities dominated Mesopotamian perspectives.*

Seated proudly at the forefront of these eastern Aegean ports was Miletos, the terminus of the overland route from Mesopotamia through Anatolia, where merchants ferrying goods overland from the Euphrates and Greek-speaking mercenaries traveling to serve Babylonian kings met traders beating the Anatolian coast between the Mediterranean and the Black Sea.[8] Although it now wallows ten kilometers inland because of erosion, silting, and sea-level change, in its heyday Miletos was at the center of a huge network of trade and information.

It is no surprise then that this was where the first Greek-speaking scientists appeared, nor that their interests coincide with those of their counterparts farther east: Thales (c. 625–545), a merchant of reportedly Phoenician origins who had also studied in Egypt and became famous for predicting a solar eclipse in 585 BCE, and his pupil Anaximander (c. 610–545), who is credited with making the first Greek "geographical map."[9]

*Looking from the opposite direction, Romans similarly called all Greeks "Graeci," originally the name of a small community on the northwestern Greek mainland—which is why people who call themselves "Hellenes" are now known as Greeks in many languages.

No copies of this map survive, but there are good reasons to believe that, like the Babylonian map, it depicted an inhabited disk in the middle of an encircling ocean. For one thing, Herodotus later complains that all the existing maps of the world depicted "Ocean flowing round an earth as circular as if it had been traced by compasses."[10] For another, we are told that Anaximander himself believed that the earth was a flat disk shaped like the drum of a column, three times as wide as it was deep, with a slightly concave surface, presumably to keep the water in.[11] The most obvious design for his map would simply extend the Babylonian model to include the Mediterranean, displacing the encircling ocean beyond the Pillars of Hercules and placing the Aegean, rather than Babylon, in the upper center of the map. Like our anonymous Babylonian mapmaker, Anaximander would then put himself at the heart of his world.

There is still considerable debate over the extent to which the "pre-Socratic" scholars of western Anatolia took Babylonian science as a model. But there is no doubt that as new powers emerged from the shadow of Assyrian empire and Tyrian commerce, and the old east–west axis across the Mediterranean broke down, port cities across the Mediterranean sea looked for new inspiration in all directions.

Anatolia itself provided the most convenient models for the Greek speakers living on its western coast, especially in their nearest neighbor there, the kingdom of Lydia, which had first come to prominence under a man called Gyges (r. 680–645). Herodotus tells us that he had been a bodyguard to the previous king, Candaules, who was in love with his own wife. So keen was he for others to appreciate her physical perfection that he forced Gyges to hide in their bedroom to watch her undress. Having completed the task unwillingly, Gyges attempted to sneak out, but the unnamed woman saw him. Understandably furious at this invasion of her privacy, she gave him a simple choice: kill the king and take his place, or kill himself. Gyges chose the former, and ruled wisely and well for many years, building up the glittering city of Sardis on a hot and dusty inland plain and minting the world's first coinage.[12]

In reality Gyges probably came to power in a coup, and the nature of his reign inspired contemporary Greek authors to find a new word for it: borrowing a Luwian term for "king," they called him a *tyrannos,* a word used in Greek to mean a ruler who attains office without inheriting it or being elected to it.[13] Little opprobrium attached to the term, at least at first; on the contrary, wealthy Greek speakers were fascinated by Lydian luxuries from perfumes to chariots, turbans to lyres. These shared tastes now drew together a self-consciously superior class to whom international culture was more valuable than citizenship in a *polis.*[14]

In some cases curiosity extended to the wider community: a choral "dance of the Lydian Maidens" was celebrated at Ephesos. It was also at Ephesos that Greek speakers first adopted the Lydian technology of dividing metal ingots for convenience into small disks or coins.[15] First minted in Lydia around 650 BCE, probably at Sardis itself, coinage spread quickly across the Aegean and beyond, reaching the central Mediterranean in the sixth century, and Iberia by the fifth.[16] Some Greek cities went further in their emulation of Lydian political technologies: in Corinth a general named Kypselos seized power in the mid-seventh century to become the first Greek *tyrannos.*

Other ambitious men staged coups at Sikyon, Athens, and Samos, where Polykrates (r. c. 550–522) mimicked on a smaller scale the court of a grand west Asian king.[17] As well as recruiting talented poets from the rest of the Greek-speaking world, he imported technology from farther east to build a splendid aqueduct, employing for long sections a tunneling technique first found in ninth-century Assyria by which regular vertical shafts are dug down from the surface, and then joined up with short sections of underground gallery. This breaks the work down into manageable sections, while the shafts provide ventilation and routes for removing the excavated earth; later they can be used for maintenance.[18*]

*The same technology reached Etruria around the same time, where it was used to construct networks of drainage channels known as *cuniculi* that diverted streams or drained valleys, some more than five kilometers long (Tom Rasmussen, "Urbanization in Etruria," in Robin Osborne and Barry Cunliffe, eds., *Mediterranean Urbanization 800–600 BC*, Oxford: Oxford University Press, 2005, 84–5).

Links with Egypt become more visible in this period as well. Surviving donations at the Samian sanctuary of Hera reveal the extent of contact: they include hippo teeth, antelope horns, and the skull of a Nile crocodile. Some gifts seem to have come from Egyptian women, including bronze mirrors inscribed to the Egyptian goddess Mut.[19] Polykrates himself was a formal guest-friend of Pharaoh Amasis (r. 570–526), who sent gifts to a variety of Greek sanctuaries, including statues of himself, and is said to have married a Greek woman called Ladice from Cyrene on the coast of modern Libya.[20]

Amasis also employed Greek-speaking mercenaries, who had served for hire in Egypt since at least the beginning of the sixth century.[21] And he supported foreign merchants: around 570 BCE he gave the river port of Naukratis in the Nile Delta to traders from nine different Aegean cities—all but one on the Anatolian coast or nearby islands—who agreed to collect import taxes there for the Egyptian government.[22]

The site of Naukratis is about eighty kilometers up the western, more navigable, branch of the Nile, and archaeologists there have documented copious imports from the Aegean, Levant, and Egypt itself.[23] We hear from literary accounts of human imports too: one story with a relatively happy ending concerns Rhodopis, a woman from Thrace who was enslaved and then taken to Naukratis by a man from Samos, was freed by another Greek, made a fortune as a courtesan, and dedicated a tenth of her wealth to Apollo at Delphi in the form of iron roasting spits, each large enough for an entire ox.[24]

There is no doubt that control of Naukratis was a great boon to sailors already operating at the intersection of routes from Egypt, Mesopotamia, the Aegean, and the Steppe. But the pharaoh's gift may have had a larger legacy, as the traders at Naukratis began to make dedications to "the gods of the Greeks" in a sanctuary known—perhaps first by their Egyptian hosts—as the "Helleneion."[25]

This is the first time in history we hear of "Greeks," and for the most part people from Greek-speaking cities continued to identify themselves by their city, district, or father instead. But it is not the only sign of a notion of collective "Hellenic" identity emerging in the sixth century: literary accounts suggest that it was in this era that a set of fictive ancestral figures associated with the Ionian, Dorian, and Aeolic dialects of Greek—Ion, Dorus, and Aeolus—acquired a new ancestor called Hellen.[26] As Greek speakers traveled farther around the Mediterranean, they began to see one another as more like themselves.

Increasing engagement with overseas culture also offered opportunities to assert a new sense of cultural autonomy. We can see this in the marble sculptures of naked men erected in sanctuaries and cemeteries across the Aegean from the late seventh century BCE, the first large-scale male figures carved by Aegean sculptors. These beardless kouroi, or "youths" as they are known to art historians, stride forward, their arms by their sides with fists clenched. Their long coiled hair cascades down their shoulders.

As the ancients noted themselves, they owe a great deal to the sculptural traditions of ancient Egypt, in their style, proportions, and technique, as well as in their large, almond-shaped eyes and tight-lipped smiles.[27] They even carry a rolled-up handkerchief in their hand, just like the Egyptian statues. In this sense the kouroi allowed the wealthy across the Aegean to underline their own status and difference from the rest of society by emphasizing overseas contacts.

These youths do not faithfully reproduce their Egyptian model, however. Some of the changes are practical: because the kouroi are smaller than the Egyptian sculptures, they could be made freestanding without a supporting pillar at their back. Their nakedness however marks a real cultural distinction from their predecessors, and might well have been distasteful to an Egyptian viewer. Herodotus tells us that it was considered shameful by Lydians and other foreigners for a man to be seen naked at all.[28]

Nudity was a new fashion even among Greeks. In the Homeric epics, nakedness is shameful, and athletes gird their loins.[29] In seventh- and sixth-century Greek art, however, men are regularly depicted naked, even in entirely unrealistic situations like funerals. In reality public nudity seems to have been limited to sporting contests, and even there it was a recent invention: writing in the late fifth century Thucydides notes that Greeks used to wear loincloths for athletics, and that foreigners still do.[30] There were limits to the enthusiasm: at the same time as they stripped young men, Aegean artists transformed Levantine figurines of naked women, often sculpted in ivory, into stone statues of clothed *korai* or "girls."[31]

Farther west the trading vacuum left by the decline of Tyre brought new opportunities to ambitious cities in the central Mediterranean. Ports like Tarentum in southern Italy and Syracuse and Agrigentum on Sicily rose above the rest in the sixth century to build commercial empires in their own sectors of the sea.[32] The biggest winner though was Carthage, where trade brought enormous wealth and sophisticated tastes: the dead were now buried with sphinxes, scarabs, amulets, and figurines of Egyptian gods.[33]

The African city had some links inland. A little Carthaginian pottery reaches the indigenous settlement of Althiburos, more than 200 kilometers away in the Tunisian Tell, all related one way or another to the drinking of wine: fragments of clay wine jars, cups, and mortars to grind up spices to add to the drink. More surprising, the people of Althiburos build a large water cistern in this era in exactly the same style as one excavated at Carthage.[34] And the inscriptions that begin to be carved on the tophet markers at Carthage in the sixth century contain numerous Libyan as well as Semitic names.[35]

For the most part however Carthaginians looked out to sea. The shape and fabric of the amphoras found in excavations at Carthage suggest that the largest proportion of the city's long-distance overseas trade in this era was with Greek communities from southern Italy and Sicily to the Aegean.[36] But a major factor in Carthage's success was its fierce defense of its own interests and markets farther west.

Rule over the island of Ibiza from around 650 BCE gave the city control of northern and southern routes to the Strait of Gibraltar.[37] It then aggressively policed new settlement attempts by Greek speakers in the western Mediterranean, building up strategic alliances with others who had an interest in maintaining the status quo: with Elymians and Segestans in western Sicily; with Makai and other "Libyans" in Africa itself; and with Etrurians in the Sardinian Sea.[38]

In one case only did Carthage fail decisively to prevent a foreign foundation, when sailors from Phokaia in western Anatolia arrived around 600 BCE in the Gulf of Lion and established the city of Massalia (modern Marseille). This was much farther west than Greek speakers had ever settled before. The Carthaginians mounted an attack as the new settlement was being built, but suffered an unusual and humiliating defeat.[39] After that the two cities settled into an uneasy truce that lasted centuries, Carthage always the larger and more powerful, but Massalia a constant threat, as they split the western sea between their interests.

According to Massalia's own foundation legend, Phokaian sailors had spotted a promising harbor at the mouth of the Rhône on earlier trips west and a mission set out to explore the possibilities under the command of two men, Protis and Simos. They arrived in the area during a festival given by Nannos, king of the Segobriges who dominated southwestern Gaul, and were made welcome. The event was the betrothal of the king's daughter Glyptis to a man she would choose by tradition from among her suitors by offering him water. Eschewing the local talent, she gave her water to Protis, and Massalia was their wedding present.[40]

The story reflects the realities of migration in this era in its focus on relations with the Gaulish hamlets that already littered the hills and valleys inland, a world of farmers and stockbreeders. Newcomers had to establish themselves within a busy landscape and get along with their neighbors, or they wouldn't last long. And in this case, Protis and Simos would have needed local help just to get into the harbor: as you sail northwest up the coast toward Marseille itself the westerlies constantly threaten to push you into dangerous shallows on the shoreline. A string of offshore islands ending in the notorious Île d'If offers some protection, but in the end you have to trust in your sails and sense of the local seascape to round the final headland before proceeding with great caution through the rocks at the entrance to the harbor.

It is worth it. What is now Marseille's Vieux Port follows the contours of one of the "calanques" that interrupt the coastline of modern Provence, steep flooded valleys reaching far inland. It creates an excellent natural harbor with a narrow entrance to a long, protected basin, a deep-water port that offered a convenient berth to traders and travelers in larger ships.[41] To the east the land rises sharply; the new town of Massalia spread instead across an undulating promontory to the west that backs onto a broader bay framing small islands and blue sea.

In this magical landscape the settlers built temples on the breezy heights to homeland gods, from where they could stroll down past their new houses to a sheltered marketplace just above the port. Close relations with communities inland are reflected in the architectural techniques used to build the city, including the use of load-bearing posts and mud-brick walls, as well as the large quantities of local handmade pottery that arrive there.[42] In return the pottery wheel and the controlled draft kiln arrived on the coast of France along with olives and vines.[43]

Massalia's economic role in its early years was more as a market and a maritime facility than as a center of production itself. The new settlement imported wine from Etruria—90 percent of the transport amphoras found there in the first half of the sixth century were made in Etruria—and hosted resident Etrurian traders too.[44] Around 550 BCE, however, the Massaliots began to produce their own wine for sale to local communities, and by the end of the sixth century Massaliot merchants had edged the Etrurians out of the market in southern Gaul.[45]

By now they were carving out their own maritime trading zone around the Gulf of Lion to mirror that of Carthage. A generation or two after the foundation of Massalia, a group from the city settled at the Iberian trading post of Emporion on the other side of the Pyrenees. It was a stop on the way to the metals of southern Iberia, and a place where they could meet and trade with the Etruscan- and Phoenician-speaking merchants who had gotten there first.[46]

Perhaps it was even Massaliot traders who scratched the Greek writing on sixth-century pots at Huelva, including dedications to Aegean gods, which suggests that a small merchant community of Greek speakers had finally established itself on the Atlantic coast. If so, they witnessed the end of an era: Huelva was abandoned during the sixth century, along with other old Iberian centers and some of the Levantine settlements on the southern coast. Tarshish fell victim to the decline in the east–west metal trade, a drop in the value of silver across the Mediterranean and a major earthquake and tsunami that geomorphological surveys have revealed hit the Atlantic coast of Iberia some time in the sixth century.[47] This marked the definitive collapse of both poles of the old east–west trade and crowned the new powers of the central Mediterranean, above all Massalia and Carthage.

All this activity in western seas must have been watched with interest from one central Italian town. It was not yet a big player in these dramas, but it provides a vivid example of the mixed communities that formed in western ports in this era, importing ideas along with goods from all directions, and creating cultural entanglements that would continue to inspire this city as it conquered half the world.

People had been living on the hills that became Rome since the mid-second millennium BCE: this is the last place that you can ford the Tiber, the waterway that connects much of central Italy to the sea, and divided Etruria to the north from Latium to the south.[48] By the eighth century villages had grown up on the different heights, already covering between them an area of 150–200 hectares, a size to rival Etrurian Caere or Tarquinia.[49] In the seventh century they came together, draining and paving the swampy central valley between them to create a forum where people could gather from the heights to market, worship, gossip, and debate.[50] Thatched huts and mud-brick buildings gave way across the settlement to stone houses with terra-cotta roof tiles.

The nascent Romans spoke the Latin language of Latium, but to write it down they borrowed the Etruscan alphabet along with the Etrurian counting system. Ancients used a variety of methods to write numbers down: Greek, for instance, recycles letters of the alphabet. Etrurian cities by contrast used a tally method, making a single stroke (I) for one, crossing it to make ten (X), and then cutting that in half to produce a Λ for five. The Romans turned that symbol upside down and added some more characters to represent larger numbers: L=50, C=100, M=1,000. Like the people of Etruria before them, though, they continued to place a single numeral before a larger one to indicate subtraction, so that XI represented the number eleven (ten added to one), but IX the number nine (one taken from ten).[51] Other technologies Romans imported from Etruria include divination by the entrails of sacrificed animals, itself probably borrowed from Assyria, by thunder and lightning, by androgynous births, and by talking cows.[52]

Rome attracted an increasing number of merchants from overseas as well. Traders gathered at a natural stopping point on the river just below the modern Tiber Island that became known as the Forum Boarium ("Cow Market"). They brought their gods with them. Although we are later told that an Ara Maxima ("Great Altar") was established in the Cow Market in the seventh century BCE to a god called "Herakles" in Greek, imported into Latin as "Hercules," the fact that women and dogs were banned from the precinct suggests that the cult was originally associated primarily with Tyrian Melqart, whose sanctuaries elsewhere in the Mediterranean had similar regulations.[53] Roman merchants meanwhile traditionally swore contracts by Etrurian "Hercle," who was worshipped as a god in central Italy—again more like Melqart than Herakles, who was at most semi-divine.[54]

Aegean cultural models are present too. When the first stone temple in Rome was built in the Cow Market in the early sixth century BCE, at the foot of the Capitoline Hill, it was also the first temple in central Italy known to be raised on a high podium with a staircase at the front and a *cella* or inner sanctuary, features already found in sanctuaries in the Greek-speaking Mediterranean, at Syracuse, Athens, and Corfu.[55]

We don't know which god or gods lived inside this temple, but a terra-cotta sculpture added to the complex in the later sixth century depicts a suitably flexible divine couple: Hercules, who is also Herakles, Hercle, and Melqart; and Minerva, who is also Athena, Ashtart, and Menrva.[56] They probably stood on the roof of the temple in the Etrurian style, but both sculptures wear distinctively Greek clothing, and the scene itself seems to come from a Greek myth in which Athena leads Herakles to Mount Olympus.[57]

Religion was more conservative in the civic center. Toward the end of the sixth century BCE the Romans built an enormous new temple high on the Capitoline Hill overlooking the forum, which confirms their ambitions within the larger cultural world that commerce had brought up the Tiber.[58] It was by far the largest in Italy, and approached the size of temples in the Aegean and on Sicily that were the largest in the Mediterranean at the time. The design however follows local Italian traditions, and the story went that the temple's cult statue and architectural decorations were made by a master coroplast—a sculptor in terra-cotta—called Vulca from the Etruscan-speaking city of Veii about fifteen kilometers up the Tiber.[59]

The new temple reflected Etrurian ideas about the gods as well. It is easy to imagine that Romans simply worshipped Greek deities under different names, especially given a modern tradition of calling Greek gods by Roman names. But the Capitolium was dedicated to three Roman gods called Jupiter, Juno, and Minerva, based on the traditional Etrurian triad of Tinia, Uni, and their daughter Menrva. This arrangement is quite different from the individuals and couples worshipped in contemporary Greek and western Asian cities.

Rome had grown fast over the previous century, acquiring walls built of great square tufa blocks that encompassed the seven hills and more than 350 hectares of land.[60] It was now the largest settlement in central Italy, and across the Italian peninsula only the wealthy Greek-speaking ports of Tarentum and Sybaris on the south coast were larger.[61] It was still however a relatively small player in the western Mediterranean when compared to the great harbors of Syracuse and Agrigentum on Sicily, or to Massalia and Carthage themselves.

Today however ancient Carthage is much less familiar than Rome, while Massalia is positively obscure. The trouble is, their timing was all wrong. Nineteenth-century scholars decided, in the spirit of civilizational thinking, that ancient history happened first in the Greek Aegean and then moved west for a second act in Roman Italy. The traditional high points of each of these "civilizations" in the fifth century BCE and the first century CE respectively coincide with their imperial apogee as well as an outpouring of literary texts on topics—and in languages—easy to teach in the schoolroom.*

Earlier powers in the western Mediterranean that do not fit into this neat binary scheme have been brushed under the carpet of the canon, along with ancient peoples beyond the Mediterranean to north and south. Even the great empires to the east are usually acknowledged only as backstory to the real business. They too however have stories of their own, and they had a strong impact on the Classical world.

*At my own university the core ancient history courses were established in 1872 to cover Archaic and Classical Greece on the one hand, and late Republican and early Imperial Rome on the other, ending with the death of Trajan. The only significant change since then has been to move the end of the core Roman history course back to 54 CE. This is admittedly an extreme case.

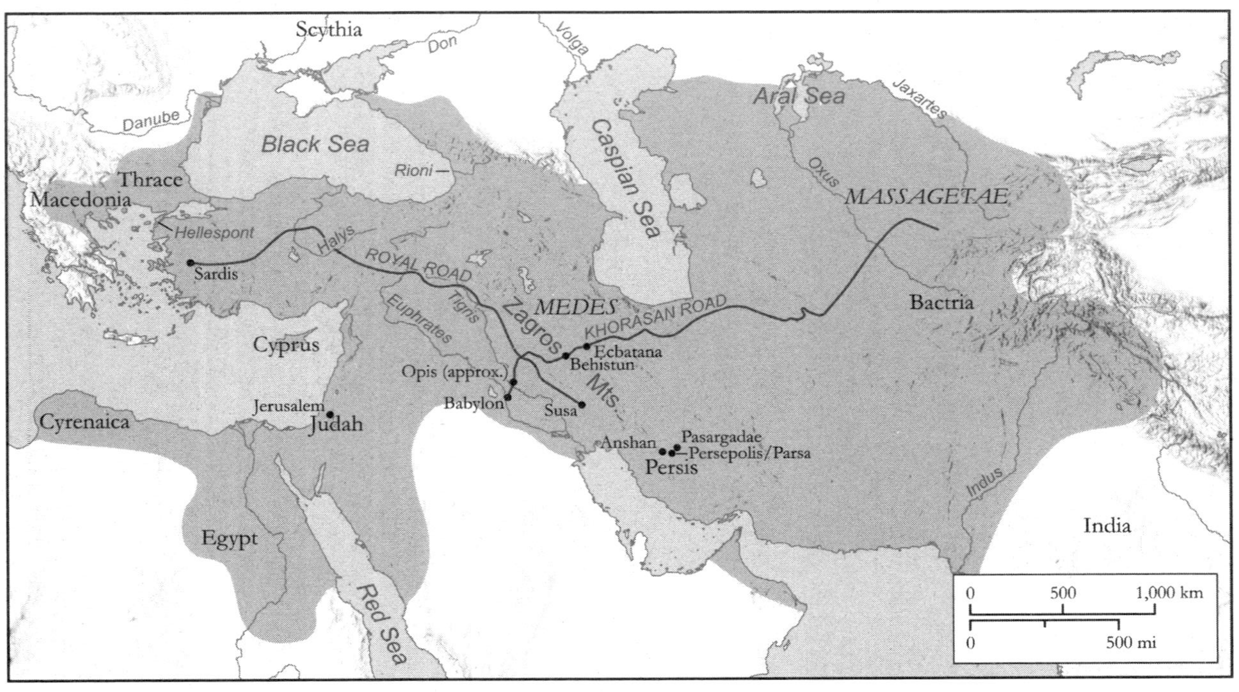

The Persian Empire under Darius I, c. 500 BCE

CHAPTER FOURTEEN

The King of Kings

BABYLON, 539 BCE

It is October 29, 539 BCE.

You are Cyrus, king of Anshan.

Your barge docks at the city's river harbor, and your troops are there to meet you. They have swapped their tunics and trousers for draped and patterned ceremonial robes, and their gleaming daggers and spears are unused: they took the city nineteen days ago without a fight. They lead you past palm plantations and orchards to a bridge over the moat that surrounds the inner rampart. Here the soldiers pause to draw up. It is autumn, but still warm, and for a moment everything is quiet. The air smells of ripe fruit, flavored by the herbs and spices grown over the wall in the palace gardens.

At your signal, the march begins. As you'll later tell it, your men surround you "innumerable like the water of a river," and you'll say you have another companion too: Marduk, the patron god of this city, who has selected you to replace its king. They guide you down the road toward the gate, between high walls carved with close-to-life-size lions striding toward you, sixty on each side. They are made of baked, glazed bricks molded into shape, with shaggy yellow manes and mouths red and roaring. These animals are sacred to Ishtar, goddess of love and war, and straight ahead is the gateway called "Ishtar repels her enemies." Built by Nebuchadnezzar to be an object of wonder to all people, it is twenty-five meters high, and the ground slopes up to it from both directions.[1] The sun glints off bricks painted in yellow and deep blue, and more painted animals: alternating rows of bulls and magic dragons, protecting the city from forces stronger even than you.

Then you are inside the gate itself. The temperature drops, the light fades, and the crashing footfall of the soldiers fills your head. Out the other side the sun is blinding, but as your eyes adjust you finally see the city, and the crowd, and the shouting begins in many tongues.

Straight ahead are white mud-brick houses as far as you can see, their cool inner courtyards hidden by windowless walls. To the right stretches the long façade of the royal palace. The crenellations of forty temples break up the skyline. Rising above them all is an enormous stepped pyramid. It has inspired some in the multitude around you to imagine a city called Babel, where in their pride and ambition the sons of man built a tower to reach the heavens, prompting God to punish the human race by confusing their single language into many, and scattering them across the world.

There will be time to explore the city later. Now princes and governors line up to kiss your feet. Finally your proclamation is read out. "I am Cyrus, king of the world, mighty king, king of Babylon."[2]

The Persian empire came from nowhere, a line of minor kings from the highlands of south-central Iran.[3] Anshan had been part of the Elamite kingdom before it was finally conquered by Assyria in 639 BCE. A few decades later, in the wake of the Assyrian collapse, new Persian lords established themselves there. They ruled quietly, locally, and as far as possible in the style of their Elamite predecessors.

When Cyrus came to power in Anshan around 560 BCE he changed his family's fortunes. Babylonian records report that by 550 he had defeated the neighboring Medes and taken control of their capital at Ecbatana, as well as the mountainous lands south of the Caspian Sea and the Khorasan Road, which ran east from Babylon through the Zagros range to central Asia.[4] Around the same time he took the lowland Elamite capital of Susa.

Up in Anatolia, a Lydian king was watching with concern. Gyges' great-great-grandson Croesus (r. 560–546) had recently subjected his Greek-speaking neighbors to the west to tribute; according to Herodotus, he now appealed to the oracle of Apollo at Delphi for advice on whether to attack Cyrus too. If he did so, said the priestess who spoke for the god, he would destroy a great empire.

Emboldened, Croesus marched his men across the River Halys. Cyrus' troops beat him back to his capital of Sardis, sacked the city in 546 and annexed his kingdom—which had been, at least to Croesus, a great empire. The Persians then put down attempted revolts by the Greek-speaking cities on the coast, reduced them to tribute again and accepted the submission of the eastern Aegean islands to boot.[5]

Next came the biggest prize of all. After Nebuchadnezzar died in 562 BCE, Babylon had endured a series of short reigns by weak kings. The last was Nabonidus, who came to the throne in 555 but chose to rule from his Arabian territories, and preferred the moon god Sin to Babylon's own Marduk. The writing was on the wall, and Cyrus' troops entered the city unopposed in 539; the fact that the Persians had just sacked the nearby city of Opis and prudently killed all of its inhabitants may have been factored into the Babylonians' decision to open their gates.[6]

Cyrus himself arrived just over a fortnight later. His own account of these events is preserved in a bulging clay tablet known as the "Cyrus Cylinder" that was buried in the foundations of Marduk's main temple at Babylon, the Esagil ("House Whose Top Is High"), to commemorate rebuilding work carried out by Cyrus. In fluent Babylonian Akkadian, the text presents Cyrus as a savior who poses no threat to the city or its gods. He has been selected by Marduk himself to undo the acts of Nabonidus, which were bad for the gods and bad for the city, and to bring order to the kingdom. He was, he tells us, greeted by the people of Babylon "with shining faces."[7]

Cyrus' empire was on a different scale from those that came before. Assyria and then Babylon had laid claim in effect to the Fertile Crescent, to which the Persians now added Anatolia, the southern Steppe and the lands east of the Tigris for thousands of kilometers into central Asia as far as the River Jaxartes (Syr Darya) and the coast of the Aral Sea. At its height the Persian empire covered well over 5 million square kilometers, larger even than Rome's later territory at its greatest extent.[8]

To govern this vast realm Cyrus usually retained the local administrative arrangements put in place by his predecessors, overlaid with a new tapestry of provinces or "satrapies," governed by officials he called satraps.* The nub of subjection to Persia was the delivery of annual tribute and soldiers as required.[9] Only Persia itself was exempted from the former requirement, but Cyrus showed respect to those who played by his rules, allowing the people of Judah to return home from Babylon and rebuild their temple.

The Persian king found some of his fiercest opponents in the far north of his new realm among the "Saka," a generic label for the semi-nomadic shepherds, riders, and warriors who had controlled trade and travel across much of the Steppe since at least the ninth century BCE. These Scythians, as Greek authors called them, produced metal weapons and ornaments with fantastical animal themes, sold livestock, furs, skins, and slaves to settlements around the Black Sea, and buried their dead—humans and horses—under enormous mounds or "kurgans."

The Greek historian Ktesias, who lived at the Persian court around 400 BCE, tells of a campaign in which Cyrus captured a king of the Saka called Amorges, but then had to release him after being defeated by his wife at the head of an army of 300,000 men and 200,000 women.[10] Herodotus even reports that Cyrus himself died east of the Jaxartes in 530 BCE fighting a Scythian group called the Massagetae who were ruled by a woman named Tomyris.[11]

These stories of warrior women on the Steppe were long dismissed by scholars who lumped them together with legends of Amazons who lived in belligerent female bands and removed their own right breasts

*Herodotus' description of the Persian postal service, inherited from the Assyrians but now run on horsepower, became the motto of the United States Postal Service: "Neither snow nor rain nor heat nor gloom of night stays these couriers from the swift completion of their appointed rounds": Cf. Herodotus 8.98, with Xenophon, *Cyropedia* 8.6.17–18.

in order more easily to draw a bow.[12] There was no room in civilizational thinking for cultures run aggressively and successfully by women. In recent decades, however, more than one hundred women's graves containing axes, swords, and occasionally armor have come to light in Russia and Ukraine.[13] Many can be dated by pottery to the mid-first millennium BCE. These women may even have inspired the tales of Amazons.

Whether or not Cyrus really died at the hands of Massagetae male or female—reports do vary—there is no doubt that he was buried at Pasargadae in the Persian heartland, where his simple cenotaph still sits high up on a stepped platform on the outskirts of the royal city he built there around a palace and audience hall with an irrigated pleasure garden. His son Cambyses then added Cyprus and Egypt to the Persian portfolio, and accepted the submission of Egypt's African neighbors as well as the Greek-speaking settlements of Cyrenaica in what is now eastern Libya before dying in Egypt in 522.

What happened next is less clear, as we only have the survivor's story. This was recovered in 1836 by a British officer named Henry Rawlinson helping to train the shah's army, who managed to climb a sheer rock face in western Iran overhanging the Khorasan Road between Babylon and Ecbatana. On it was carved a huge relief sculpture of the Persian king Darius towering over ten prisoners, surrounded by lengthy inscriptions in the local Persian language, Elamite and Babylonian Akkadian. Rawlinson made an accurate copy of much of the text and then returned to Behistun in 1847 with planks and ropes to reach the rest. Conveniently, he already knew modern Persian (Farsi) and what there was to know of the ancient language, and he managed to decipher the inscription, the earliest historical narrative surviving from antiquity.

In it Darius tells his own version of how he won the throne. Cambyses, he says, had secretly arranged to have his own brother Bardiya killed before he died himself. Back in Babylon, a usurper named Gaumata seized the throne by pretending to be Bardiya. Darius bravely confronted this pretender in a remote Median fortress, and with the help of six other nobles killed him. Darius then took the throne himself and restored order to Persia.

Darius' account does not withstand investigation. It is true that a

Bardiya ruled as king in Persia, presumably after the death of Cambyses: his name is used to date Babylonian documents from spring to autumn 522.[14] But there is no reason to suppose that he was not the real Bardiya, succeeding as normal to his brother's throne: Darius left no evidence to identify the man he had killed. And the revolts that the Behistun inscription describes erupting across Cyrus' great empire and even in Persia itself suggest that there was considerable discontent with this turn of events. In just over a year, Darius tells us, he put down nine rebellions in nineteen battles.[15]

Understandably enough, the Behistun inscriptions also emphasize the legitimacy of Darius' own royal descent, claiming that both he and Cyrus were members of a larger clan descended from one Achaemenes. This ancestor had not been mentioned by previous kings, but Darius was able to put that right: as he completed Cyrus' building projects at Pasargadae, he forged inscriptions there declaring, "I am Cyrus, the king, the Achaemenid."[16] In case any doubt remained, Darius married all the surviving women of Cyrus' family: two daughters and a granddaughter.[17]

At the same time, Darius rejected Cyrus' policy of borrowing the royal titulature of older Mesopotamian empires, resurrecting instead a title used only very rarely in the past: he was the Xsayathiya Xsayathiyanam, "the King of Kings." He also makes what may be the first explicit claim in world literature to an ethnic identity related to a specific place and bloodline, calling himself "an Aryan of Aryan stock."[18] He calls the Persian language in which he writes "Aryan" as well.[19]

This isn't the first time people talk about "Aryans." In the late second-millennium Indian *Rig Veda,* however, the word had meant something like "noble." It was these texts that prompted nineteenth-century scholars to reimagine the Aryans as a primal group of aristocratic Indo-European speakers who had emigrated in the distant past from somewhere in central Asia into Europe, India, and Iran.[20]

This idea was then reimagined again in the twentieth century, in combination with the old notion of a "barbarian" contribution to indigenous European culture, as a genetic link between at least some Europeans and an ancient white master race of "Aryans" with a homeland in

Scandinavia or Germany.[21] Despite these fantasies, the idea that Aryans were white is entirely modern, and the ancient Indian and Iranian texts that name them never link them to Europe at all.

Darius does use Aryans for his own form of proto-nationalist myth-making: for him the term delineates a distinctively Iranian cultural and linguistic group that included both Persians and Medes, but sets them apart from the Elamites alongside whom they lived and from their imperial subjects as well. This has obvious parallels with modern civilizational thinking and linguistic nationalism, and it did good work for him: he needed to appeal to a group identity that could include both him and his royal predecessors, while distinguishing them strongly as rulers from the ruled. He was replacing real kinship as the basis of monarchy with an imagined version that was under his own rhetorical control.

Similar rhetoric survives in Darius' art. A few kilometers to the south of Pasargadae he built his own ceremonial center, which Greek authors called Persepolis. It is a remarkable complex, with reception rooms, courtyards, and private quarters sprawling across a single great platform. The buildings themselves are supported by vast numbers of columns and are covered in relief sculpture. The largest structure of all was at the summit of the citadel: the Apadana or Audience Hall, seventy-six meters by seventy-six and twenty meters high, with a hundred columns holding up the roof. Bands of sculpture on the central staircase depict a long procession of Persia's subjects bringing their tribute to the king. Again foreshadowing aspects of later civilizational thinking, groups from different places are carefully distinguished from one another by culture—in this case their clothing—as well as by their gifts.[22]

Herodotus later reports a Persian saying that Cyrus was a father, Cambyses a slavemaster, and Darius a shopkeeper.[23] Darius was not however averse to military action. He continued to put down revolts and relocate rebels, in one case moving prisoners of war from Greek Cyrenaica to a village in remote Bactria, now Afghanistan. Farther east again he annexed the Indus Valley. To the west he installed a client king on the island of Samos and then crossed the Hellespont between Asia and Europe in 513. He conquered Thrace (modern Bulgaria); accepted the submission of Macedonia, a timber-trading kingdom north of ancient Greece; and advanced his border to the Danube, which gained him access to the valuable metals of the southern Balkans and continental Europe.[24] He nonetheless stopped short of mainland Greece.

This wasn't due to unfamiliarity with Greek speakers in general. They had been part of the Persian world since Cyrus had incorporated the cities of coastal Anatolia into his empire in the 540s and acquired the services of their fleets, and some came to Persia itself.[25] Greek stonemasons are singled out for mention in inscriptions commemorating Darius' building projects at Susa and Persepolis, and graffiti found at a quarry at Persepolis include two Greek names, Pytharchos and Nikon, while study of the stonework itself reveals that some of the workmen used distinctively Aegean tools and techniques.[26] Greek laborers, including women, are mentioned in administrative records.[27] At least one administrative tablet from Persepolis was written in the Greek language and script, and another was written by a scribe with a Greek name, "Dahiwukka"—that is, Deiokes.[28]

Some even got close to the king. Later Greek authors praised a sculptor from Ionian Phokaia called Telephanes who worked for both Darius and his son Xerxes, and reported that Darius' own physician was a Greek called Democedes, originally from Italy, who had arrived in Susa as a Persian prisoner from the island of Samos. Even when they came from Italy, however, to the Persians they were all "Yauna," Ionian, as they had been "Yawnaya" to the Assyrians and Babylonians before them. The Greek-speaking cities of Ionia, full of merchants and scholars, still dominated the landscape. By contrast, Persians took little interest in the relatively poor and unremarkable towns of the southern Balkans.

The first story of diplomatic contact between the Persian empire and western Aegean powers is dubious. Herodotus claims that an ambassador from Sparta, the leading city-state in mainland Greece in the sixth century BCE, appeared before Cyrus at Sardis in the 540s to protest against his conquest of the Greek-speaking communities of Anatolia, proclaiming—rather too late—that the Spartans would not allow him to harm a single Greek city.[29] This encounter sounds like a subsequent invention to distract from Sparta's failure to send military aid to fellow Hellenes in time, but one part rings true: Cyrus has no idea who the Spartans are.

Herodotus provides a more plausible report of ambassadors from Athens arriving at Sardis in the last decade of the sixth century, to request an alliance with the Persians to protect them from continuing Spartan interference in their political affairs.[30]

By now Athens was a serious challenger to Sparta within mainland Greece. Its port of Piraeus had overtaken Corinth as a trading hub: as boats got larger, hauling them—or their cargo—across the isthmus became less attractive, and the longer trip around Cape Malea less intimidating. Most Greek vases produced for export were now made in Athens, even if the craftsmen themselves were often immigrants: some of the most famous names signed by sixth-century Greek vase painters are Phrygian, Lydian, and Egyptian.[31]

Once again, however, the Persian satrap has no idea who these ambassadors are. When he is informed, he explains that Darius would be happy to make an alliance with the Athenians, if they will give him earth and water—the traditional tokens of submission to the King of Kings. The envoys aren't sure about this, but decide to accept the offer, and although Herodotus says that they were "severely blamed" for this when they got home, there is no indication that the alliance was repudiated.

All the same, the next time Athenians arrived in Sardis, they were armed.

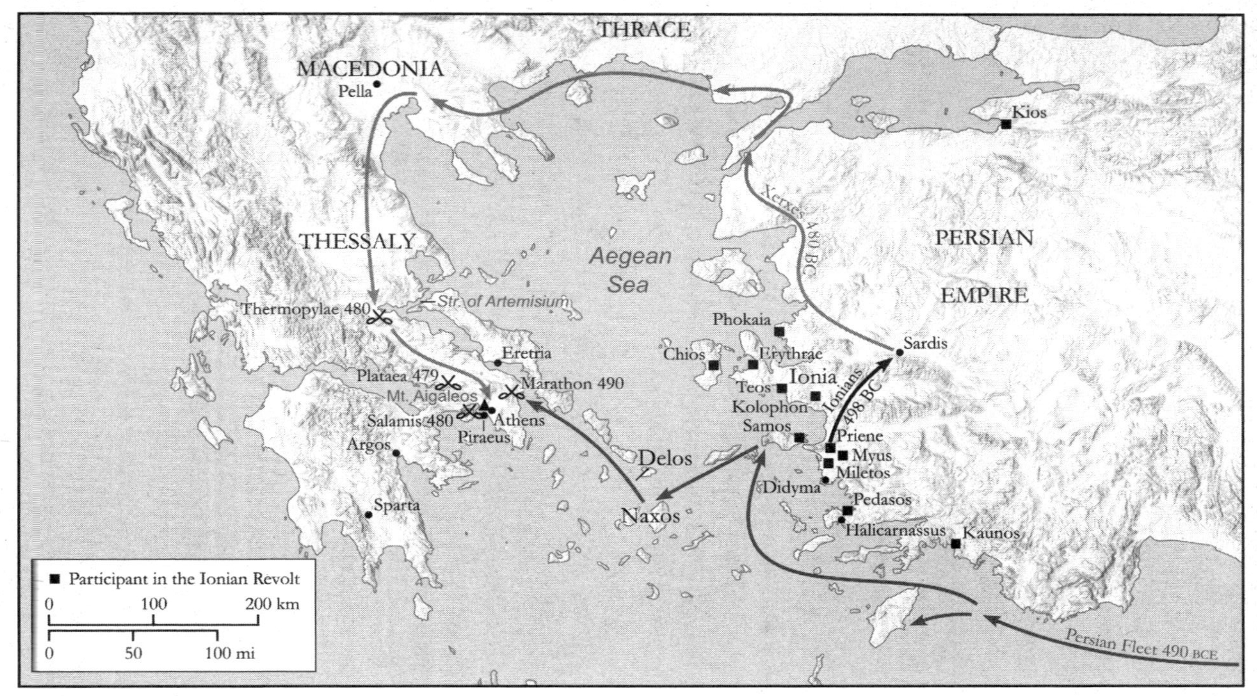

Persian campaigns in the Aegean in the early fifth century BCE

CHAPTER FIFTEEN

The Persian Version

MOUNT AIGALEOS, 480 BCE

The Persian Wars have long held a special place in ideas of Western history: we have already seen the nineteenth-century British philosopher John Stuart Mill call the Athenian victory at the Battle of Marathon in 490 BCE more important for English history than the Battle of Hastings. Nowadays more people embrace a Greek defeat: the Battle of Thermopylae, in which 300 Spartans confronted the Persian army in a hopeless last stand. The futile bravery of the Greeks is encapsulated in the response the Spartan king is supposed to have made to the Persian king's demand that his men surrender their weapons: *Molon labe*—"Come and take them."[1] (He did.)

This slogan is now associated with neo-fascist activism, featuring on flags carried in the attack on the U.S. Capitol on January 6, 2021, where some rioters wore replica Spartan helmets to evoke the idea of resistance to totalitarianism.[2] This is nothing new: an idea of the Spartans as unusually ascetic, rigorous, and martial appealed to German Nazis, who used reports of the Spartan education system as a model for the Hitler Youth.[3]

Modern appropriations of the Spartan stand against Persia are not however limited to the far right. There is a lot of singing in the Irish diaspora, and one of the favorites is "A Nation Once Again." Originally written in the 1840s by Thomas Osborne Davis, it was re-recorded by the Wolfe Tones in 1972, the year of the Bloody Sunday massacre in Derry. The first verse is especially stirring: "When boyhood's fire was in my blood / I read of ancient freemen, / Of Greece and Rome who bravely stood / Three hundred men and three men; / And then I prayed I yet might see / Our fetters rent in twain, / And Ireland long a province be / A Nation once again."

These "ancient freemen" were soldiers who fought for the honor of their native land: the 300 Spartans who fought at Thermopylae, and three Romans who held off an attack by Etrurian Clusium in the late sixth century long enough for the bridge on which they fought to be destroyed, cutting their city off and so saving it. It was a profoundly sad song, especially in 1972.

Greek victories over Persia at Salamis and Plataea are still remembered today; defeats have been quietly forgotten, along with the fact that the Persians sacked Athens not once but twice. The war with Persia has become a tipping point in European history, when Greek courage, democracy, and freedom saved the day, and saved civilization.

From the Persian perspective things look rather different. What are now called the "Persian Wars" of 490 and 480–479 BCE were punishment expeditions against a few rogue states in their western borderlands, little known and soon forgotten. The Great Kings did not aim to conquer Greece, nor did they target Greeks as a whole; indeed most Greek speakers allied with them. And these wars were, in the end, a success for Persia—qualified at the time, but later confirmed.

The story of the Persian campaigns in the southern Balkans starts in the Ionian Greek city of Miletos, whose tyrant Aristagoras was a Persian puppet. In 499 BCE he rounded up fellow Persian clients in western Anatolia and on Cyprus in a rebellion against their overlords. This was not an act of principle but one of desperation: Aristagoras had secured Persian support for an attack on the island of Naxos and then bungled the mission. His only hope of survival now was to get out of Persian clutches.

He appealed for aid to Sparta and Athens. The Spartan king refused to supply aid against such a powerful foe, but as Herodotus tells the story the Athenian assembly was more easily persuaded to send support: twenty ships that were, as he puts it, "the beginning of evils for Greeks and barbarians."[4] They were joined by five ships from the Euboean city of Eretria, which was under an existing obligation to Miletos. Thus reinforced, the Ionian rebels marched on Sardis, the seat of the local Persian satrap, and destroyed its shrines and temples.

This was an act of hubris and blasphemy that the Great King could not ignore. Over the next few years his generals defeated the Ionian rebels, destroyed their fleet, and reconquered their cities. As instigator of the revolt, Miletos itself was captured, the city's great sanctuary at Didyma razed, and much of the population either killed or deported to the Persian Gulf.[5]

Darius then moved against Ionia's allies farther west. First he isolated them, sending messengers to states throughout Greece and the Aegean in 491 requesting earth and water—in effect, submission. Most agreed, with the exception of Athens and Sparta. There the messengers were not only rebuffed but killed: the Athenians threw them into a pit, the Spartans into a well. If they wanted earth and water, they were told, they could find them there.[6] Like destroying the temples at Sardis, these were serious offenses against interstate norms.

The Persian fleet then sailed across the Aegean for the first time. Persian troops besieged Eretria, took the city, destroyed its temples, and deported the population. Moving on to Attica, they anchored at Marathon, intending to head inland toward Athens to complete their revenge. When they came ashore, however, they were trapped in marshland by a surprise attack and lost the ensuing battle. Taking stock of this unexpected development, they decided to quit while they were still ahead.

The victory at Marathon crowned Athens' reputation within Greece as a rising power, but it was a relatively minor blow to Persian pride.[7] When Darius died in 486, he could still claim as his tributary subjects Ionia, Thrace, and the "petasos-wearing Ionians"—the Macedonians, who wore flattish broad-brimmed hats that were memorably funny to outsiders.[8] The mission against Athens was not abandoned but put on hold.

In 481 Darius' son Xerxes decided to complete it. He again sent messengers to Greek cities demanding earth and water. Most of northern and central Greece either capitulated or agreed to remain neutral, as did most of the islands. Even Greek communities in Sicily and southern Italy submitted, as well as some of Sparta's enemies in the Peloponnese.[9] Understandably enough the ambassadors didn't even approach Sparta and Athens this time around, and they formed the core of an anti-Persian alliance of southern Greek cities and islands.[10]

The Persian army gathered at Sardis in 480. According to Herodotus, "although in name the King's expedition was directed against Athens, it was sent against the whole of Greece."[11] This interpretation suits the central theme of Herodotus' own work, the conflict between Greeks and Persians, but it seems unlikely as a reading of Xerxes' motives: Aegean cities were poor compared with those of the eastern Mediterranean and had no significant raw materials to offer the Persians that they could not obtain more easily elsewhere. Persian kings had always been more interested in Thrace and the Danube region, which were not only rich in metals but offered links through to new revenue sources to the north and west. Contemporary voices meanwhile support Xerxes' version, even by Herodotus' own report: in 479, he says, a Spartan ambassador accused Athens of starting the war with Persia without consultation with other Greeks, and complained that a war over Athens alone had ended up involving the whole of Greece.[12]

Much of it was involved on the Persian side. Xerxes' fleet included more than 200 ships from the Greek-speaking cities in western Anatolia, and Persian troops marched down toward Athens through the territory of Greek allies, who provided supplies and logistical support.[13] At the narrow pass of Thermopylae between the mountains and the sea they easily defeated a small and underprepared group of opponents led by the Spartan king Leonidas, who had badly misjudged the relative strength of the two forces; once the Persians had circumvented his blockade by way of a well-known local bypass most of his Greek soldiers had already fled, outnumbered and outflanked.

A few men did remain behind with Leonidas: the figure of 300 Spartans comes from Herodotus, but reports vary on the size and composition of this group. They did so to avoid the dishonor of retreat, Herodotus tells us, and to reserve for Spartan citizens the glory even of certain death.[14]

For all its lasting fame, however, their stand made no difference to the course of the war: in the aftermath of this Spartan defeat the Athenians abandoned their own naval engagement with Persian ships in the Strait of Artemisium, and evacuated their city without a fight.[15] The Persians seized the Athenian acropolis and destroyed its temples, finally completing their revenge for the attack on Sardis almost twenty years earlier.

It is unclear why Xerxes then pursued a naval battle as well; perhaps he still aimed to secure an explicit and humiliating surrender from the Athenians, or perhaps he just wanted to share some of the glory with his navy, which had so far participated only in skirmishing. It was in any case a mistake as bad as that of the Spartans at Thermopylae: the Persian fleet was trapped by the Athenians and their allies in the narrow and unfamiliar Strait of Salamis, and lost decisively. Xerxes himself saw it happen, watching the action from a throne placed on the slope of Mount Aigaleos, a mainland peak opposite the island of Salamis itself.

At this point the King of Kings lost interest in the proceedings and returned to Persia, leaving forces in northern Greece to offer the Athenians an alliance, in return for which the Persians would rebuild the Athenian temples.[16] The Athenians refused, and so the Persians occupied Athens again in 479 and destroyed whatever they had missed the first time around.[17] Still the Athenians declined to submit, and again the Persians lost a battle, this time on land at Plataea.

The Persians cut their losses and headed for home. Xerxes had made his point on the Acropolis, the Greek states posed no real threat to him, and war in the Aegean had proved more trouble than it was worth. Despite the failure to cow the Athenians into symbolic submission, the ashes of Athens itself meant that the mission as advertised had been a success. Then, as after other minor defeats on distant borders in Scythia, Kush, and the Indus Valley, the Persians simply moved on.

. . .

It would be interesting to know what Xerxes made of his brief visit to Athens. He brought back with him to Susa an odd souvenir: a statue group from the Athenian marketplace of two aristocrats, Harmodius and Aristogeiton, who had killed a member of the city's ruling dynasty in 514.[18]

The sculpture was quickly replaced: this pair were local heroes, celebrated in local culture, art, and drinking songs as "Tyrannicides" who had brought equality to Athens, and their descendants were awarded free meals at state expense.[19] This was a convenient fiction: as all later accounts admit, the man they slew was not the tyrant himself but his brother, and the tyrants of Athens were eventually overthrown several years later by a Spartan king, a useful thing for Athenians to forget. It was only in 507 that they had finally decided to adopt a democratic constitution. The murder itself furthermore was not a political gesture but a crime of passion: the victim had pursued the younger of the pair and then insulted him, enraging the older man, his lover.[20]

For many modern viewers, this is the most interesting aspect of the artwork: a public celebration of love between men at the heart of the ancient city. It does not however mean what it might today. Like the nudity of the two men, it encapsulates one of the many aspects of ancient Greek life distinctly at odds with modern ideals of Western Civilization. As in all known human societies, sexual relations between men were common in Athens (and no doubt between women as well, were we to have the evidence). What was unusual was the specific cultural ideal involved: the institution of "pederasty" found in Athens and several other Greek city-states, which involved sexual relationships between older and younger males. They ended when the latter became adults: for a grown man to "submit" to another was incompatible with citizen status and virtue. And they had no bearing on the same men's "heterosexual" activities: the older men were already married; the younger men would be.

It is not clear how young these younger men really were, or exactly what they did with their older companions, despite the imaginative efforts scholars have applied to these questions.[21] Nor is it clear whether such relationships happened much outside the aristocracy: the elaborate gift-giving and courting rituals between men depicted on Athenian vases would have required considerable time and money. What we do know is that although modern Western ideas about human sexuality often assume that people have a consistent "sexual orientation" toward one or more genders, Athenians conceptualized sexual behavior and even desire very differently, with reference instead to age, status, and stages of life. As is so often the case, antiquity provides a robust challenge to the notion of "human nature"—a good reason in itself to study Greek history.

Herodotus later claims that Persians learned from Greeks "how to have sex with boys," although they also took many wives and still more concubines.[22] But Xerxes was probably more interested in the political importance of the sculpture as a symbol of the Athenian democracy, still less than thirty years old at the time, and another institution that operated very differently in ancient Athens from the way it functions in the modern West. Like pederasty and public nudity, democracy was a distinctive local practice that worked to distinguish some Greek-speaking communities in a sea in which they were relatively small but unusually adaptable fish.

Athens was in fact something of a latecomer to democratic politics. As we have seen, various institutions of popular government had long existed in western Asia, and the power, or *kratos*, of the people, or *demos*, had been growing in cities throughout the Aegean for some time. In the seventh century BCE the *demos* had been at best one civic actor among others, and not the most authoritative, but by the mid-sixth the island of Chios had a "council of the people" that could judge appeals, and Herodotus describes the institution of popular government at Cyrene and Samos decades before the same thing happened at Athens.[23]

Democracy was familiar to Persians as well, and sometimes useful. In the aftermath of the Ionian revolt, the Persian general Mardonius had replaced the rebellious Greek tyrants of the Ionian cities with democracies—suggesting, among other things, considerable Persian faith in popular support for their own hegemony.[24] Democratic government even in Persia itself was not unthinkable, at least to Greek authors: in his account of Darius' coup, Herodotus reports a debate among the Persian nobles over what form of government they should adopt. There the case for democracy is not only made but almost wins the day. This conversation is very unlikely to have taken place—but Herodotus considers the scenario plausible, or thinks that his audience might.

Herodotus' account of this debate also gives us a useful sense of what "democracy" actually meant, if not to sixth-century Persians then at least to fifth-century Greeks—and how little it has in common with what is usually called democracy today: "When the people rules . . . offices are held by lot, office holders are held to account, and all resolutions are put to the commons."[25] The basic principles of ancient democracy were that every free male citizen had a direct say in government; could be called *by chance* to serve in government, whatever his class, views, or experience; and would then be held to account.

About 600 of Athens' 700 officials were chosen by lottery rather than election, with the remainder mostly military posts—the one group of officials it is hard to imagine electing today. Selection for office by lottery was more straightforwardly democratic than any form of election in the sense that it gave more power to more people. It also brought a wider range of experiences and opinions into public office; it made the whole community responsible for interpreting and enforcing its communal values; and in combination with short terms of office—usually a year—it meant that many more people got to know how the systems that governed them really worked. It was worth doing so: public officials had to answer at the end of their term to teams of public accountants and assessors: in Athens, ten each.

Communal decision-making was at the heart of the system. People did not elect councilors or parliamentarians to decide matters for them, but every political decision was put to universal discussion among citizen men, who gathered on the Pnyx Hill for a day at a time for this purpose. This can be explained in practical terms: even Athens was still a relatively small city. Assemblies of citizens who could all see and even hear one another were possible in a way they would not be in most modern cities, let alone states. But it gave the citizenry a huge amount of information about the decisions that faced their city, as well as a real stake in them, and Athens went further than most Greek city-states by paying men to attend the assembly and vote.

This aspect of democracy has not completely disappeared: modern versions tend to rely instead on representation, but referenda and other forms of mass decision-making are still relatively common at a local or regional level. They can still have dramatic effects even—perhaps especially—where they are used rarely. By contrast the wide spread use of the lot is alien to most modern political cultures, surviving only for jury service, and even there heavily policed. And the idea that elected officials should answer for their actions in office at the end of their term would send most aspiring politicians down a different career path.[26]

There is much to be said for Athenian democracy—and for introducing some of its principles to politics today. Pay for participation promoted equality of access to political decision-making. The lottery undermined cynical populism. And rigorous exit-audit provided a partial obstacle at least to corruption and malpractice.

Politics remained a time-consuming game that was much easier for the wealthy to play. But there were limits to the power of individuals within this system, just as there were limits to the power of the majority. The lottery stood in the way of political careers, and public audit in the way of exploiting them. And if that wasn't enough there was always ostracism, another attractive if short-lived Athenian political institution from which modern democratic states have shied away.

For several decades from the year 488/7 or so, Athenians took an annual vote to determine whether to exile a member of their own community—which is to say, an unpopular politician.[27] If it passed, then with no further discussion or debate each man simply voted for his preferred candidate by scratching their name on a sherd (*ostrakon*) of pottery. People had to care: According to differing sources, either a quorum of 6,000 votes were required for a valid process, or 6,000 votes were needed against a single person. In any case, the "winner" had ten days to prepare to leave the city for ten years.[28] After that, he was free to return and resume life as if nothing had happened. We only know for certain of about a dozen ostracisms over the seventy years that they occurred—some allies of the old tyrants, some of Sparta, others simply prominent politicians, but there may have been many more.*

One thing that does link modern and ancient forms of democracy is their reliance on exclusion. Equal privileges only work if everyone is sharing the work—or, more often, getting other people to do it for them. The creation of strong and institutionalized equality among citizens—or members of any exclusive club—depends on keeping a large proportion of the population outside that citizen body. Athenian citizenship was restricted in 451 BCE to the children of two native-born Athenians, and this community of free citizens was built on enslaved labor acquired through trade and war from regions including Thrace, central Anatolia, the Black Sea, and the Levant.[29] These Athenians had no say in their own lives, let alone civic business, and they were required to provide not only agricultural and domestic but also sexual services to their owners.[30]

Whether or not this disturbed him, Xerxes might well have been shocked by what he heard of the plight of Athenian women. Upper-class and royal Persian women conducted extensive business dealings, owned large amounts of property as well as estates, and seem to have traveled relatively freely.[31] Queen Artemisia of Herodotus' own Halicarnassus led a Persian naval contingent at the Battle of Salamis, commanding her own five ships and advising the King of Kings.[32] Women outside the aristocracy assumed positions of responsibility and authority in the imperial building programs. Documents from Persepolis reveal a vast army of free laborers working at the site, men, women, and children, all paid in rations according to their level of qualification for the work. The best paid of all were the female heads of work groups from different local villages: every month they got fifty quarts of grain, thirty quarts of wine, and half a sheep.[33]

*Syracuse on Sicily adopted a version of ostracism in the 450s, with no quorum and a "sentence" of five years. It is known as petalism, because the names were written on olive leaves (*petala*), not pieces of pottery (Diodorus 11.87).

Athenian women by contrast were unable to work, travel, or engage in any significant financial transactions without permission of a male "guardian." This was usually their father or husband, sometimes another relative, even a son.[34] They could not inherit property except to hold it for their male relatives. When they had to leave the home they traditionally covered their heads and in some circumstances at least they wore veils.[35]

Much of the silence and seclusion that surrounded women was the result of social rather than legal requirements, admittedly, and compliance no doubt varied by family and individual. All women visited relatives and graves, and attended weddings and festivals, while poorer women worked the fields and markets. But in the words of a speech Thucydides gives the great Athenian general Pericles, the greatest glory for a woman was to be least talked about among men, whether for good or bad.[36]

Whatever Xerxes took from his sojourn in Attica, Athenians learned an important lesson about the attractions of empire. In 478 they exploited their surprise victories over Persia to corral more than 300 other cities all over the Aegean into an alliance under Athenian leadership to take revenge on the departed Persians and to defend Greek freedom.[37] Scholars now call this the "Delian League," because the members paid their contributions to a shared fund held on the island of Delos, though there is little indication in ancient sources of a league-like structure, and there was no doubt about who was in charge: Ionian cities that signed up simply swapped tribute to Persia for tribute to this alliance, apparently set at the same rate.[38]

In 454 even the treasury was removed to Athens, where annual inscriptions record the monies now paid to the city by each of its "allies."[39] Regulations drawn up by Athens around the same time for Ionian Erythrae show that the members of that town's council had to declare obedience not to the group as a whole, but to the council and people of Athens.[40]

The material benefits to Athens can still be seen in the great temple on the Acropolis dedicated to the city's goddess Athena Parthenos—the Virgin—which was built between 447 and 438 BCE over the ruins of the Persian sack, and at least in part from imperial tribute.[41] More a secure depot for the "donations" of Athens' subjects than a place of religious worship, the Parthenon lacked an altar, and its doors were secured by grilles.[42] The frieze that ran around the inner wall of the temple before it was stripped by Lord Elgin depicts preparations for the Panathenaic Procession, a ritual for which Athens' imperial subjects in the Aegean came to the city to offer gifts to the goddess. It is not surprising that the sculpture and design echo those of the great Apadana built a few decades earlier by Darius at Persepolis, with its procession of subjects bringing tribute to the king.[43]

The alliance's military achievements are more questionable. The Athenians continued to goad the Persians whenever possible, securing the removal of Persian garrisons from Thrace and winning a prized victory at the Eurymedon river in Pamphylia in 469 or 466. In 460 however the Persians got their revenge when the Athenian fleet supported an Egyptian revolt against Xerxes' son Artaxerxes. The rebels took Memphis and killed the satrap, but Persian troops recovered the city, destroyed fifty Athenian ships and stranded 200 more by rechanneling the water in which they lay. The Persian general magnanimously allowed the Athenian sailors to return home—but only, to their shame, by land.

Soon Athenians had a new enemy to distract them: around 450 BCE paintings in a stoa (covered walkway) in the city's marketplace paired the Battle of Marathon between Athens and Persia with the Battle of Oenoe between Athens and Sparta. And over the following decades, as tensions continued to rise between the two Greek states, both began to court the Persian king.[44]

The Peloponnesian War between these rival cities began in 431 BCE and would last almost three decades. In 423 Darius II of Persia confirmed an alliance with Athens; in 411 he switched his favor to Sparta after the Athenians rashly decided to back a Persian rebel satrap in western Anatolia.[45] Sparta's eventual victory in 404 was built on Persian cash.

Athens lost its empire, and Sparta formally conceded the cities of Ionia to Persian authority in the "King's Peace" of 387, which ended a second round of fighting between Athens, Sparta, and their allies. This treaty was negotiated at Susa and guaranteed by Artaxerxes II. The Persian Wars may have been a draw, but the Peloponnesian War was won by the King of Kings.

CHAPTER SIXTEEN

Continental Thinking

ATHENS, C. 450 BCE

Ionian Greek scholars invented the continents. We don't know whether the map Anaximander made around 550 BCE already marked them, but when his fellow Milesian Hekataios wrote *Journey Around the World* in the later sixth century—in fact a journey around the Mediterranean and the Black Sea—it came in two parts, one on "Europe" and the other on "Asia."[1]

The names themselves weren't new to Greek. As far back as Bronze Age Linear B the term "Aswiai" had designated the rebellious lands of Assuwa, a coalition formed in the fifteenth century BCE by a number of western Anatolian cities, and the term continues to refer to western Anatolia in early alphabetic writing.[2] And even later Greek authors still sometimes use "Europe" to describe a similarly limited region on the other side of the Hellespont.[3] But now geographers at Miletos repurposed and expanded these regional labels to fill the whole world known to them.

Greek authors learned a lot about these continents from foreign explorations. The first great adventure was the work of Necho II of Egypt (r. 610–595), who established that Africa was surrounded by sea by sending Phoenician sailors to circumnavigate the continent from the

Red Sea to the Pillars of Hercules.[4] A century later, "the greater part of Asia was discovered by Darius" when the Persian king sent an Ionian sea captain called Scylax down the Indus, famous for its crocodiles. His mission was to find out where it met the sea, and from there he found a route west around Arabia.

The motivations of these kings were not scholarly: once Scylax had reported back, Darius subdued the Indians and opened a maritime route from southern Asia to the Red Sea.[5] Exploration aided commerce too: Herodotus credits Carthaginians with providing information about maritime trade on the Atlantic coast of Africa, and it must have been Egyptian merchants who told him about a trans-Saharan trade route leading west from Egyptian Thebes.[6]

Herodotus could still identify a major gap in geographical knowledge when he was writing in the late fifth century BCE: "when it comes to Europe, no one is sure if it is surrounded by water to the east and north or not." He also reports uncertainty over the continent's eastern boundary: some scholars place it at the River Don, others at the River Rioni.[7]* And over a thousand years after amber and tin started to arrive in Greek-speaking lands Herodotus still knew almost nothing about their origins. "I myself do not believe reports of a river the barbarians call Eridanus flowing into a northern sea, from where amber is said to come, nor do I know anything about tin-islands. . . . This only we know, that our tin and amber come from the most distant parts."[8]

Much else remained controversial about the new continents, including their size and number. Herodotus adds to his complaints about earlier cartographers that "they make Asia the same size as Europe," which they did by including Africa (to them "Libya") in Asia.[9] By the time he was writing, people had begun to talk of three continents rather than two, though they still suffered from considerable foreshortening: China

*Modern geographers have long wrestled with the definition of Europe's eastern frontier as well: western Russia always fell within Europe, including the traditional capital of Moscow, the eighteenth-century city of St. Petersburg, and the White Sea port of Archangel, but it wasn't until around 1850 that maps and atlases converged on the now conventional boundary tracing the Ural and Caucasus Mountains through the Caspian Sea.

was on no one's horizon yet. He himself had little time for the concept at all: "I cannot guess for what reason the earth, which is one, has three names."[10]

He's right, of course: Europe and Africa were historically attached by land to Asia—a lot of land in the case of Europe, rather less in the case of Africa. He bows to pragmatism nonetheless—"whatever; I will use the customary names for them"—and I have done the same in this book, but we should remember that the continents were from the beginning products of human imagination, not of the natural world.[11] Moreover, their modern symbolism in terms of culture, contrast, and confrontation is first associated with Persians: Greeks may have invented the continents, but it seems most likely that Persians invented continental thinking.

Early Ionian geographers used continents of Europe and Asia as a neutral, organizational device, but in the fifth century we catch an occasional glimpse of symbolic meaning attached to them in Greek—and to the distinctions among them we still live with today. One comes from a poem dedicated by the Athenians to commemorate a success over Persian forces on Cyprus, probably in 449 BCE. These verses, which were famous enough to survive in later quotations, call this victory the greatest deed "since the sea divided Europe from Asia," and claim furthermore that "Asia groaned greatly" over the losses of Persians on land and Phoenicians at sea.[12]

It is unsurprising that such sentiments were rare: neither the idea that the border between Asia and Europe really *mattered* nor the association of "all Asia" with the Persians and their allies made good sense from the perspective of Persia's Athenian enemies, whose own empire included Greek-speaking cities in both Europe and Asia. An identification between Asia and the Persian interest makes a lot more sense if it came from fifth-century Persians themselves, uninterested in holding territory in distant Europe but keen to justify their claim to western Anatolia.[13]

Herodotus provides the best evidence that this was in fact the case in the opening chapters of his *Histories* of the Persian Wars, which deal with the origins of the conflict. He begins with the causes not as he sees them himself but as "Persian chroniclers" explained them, with a series of kidnappings and counter-kidnappings of women that all involved an unwarranted incursion from one continent into the other.[14]

First, Phoenician merchants seize the Greek princess Io from Argos and take her to Egypt (part of Asia, of course, in the earliest understanding of continents); then Greek sailors (not riding bulls) steal Europa from Phoenician Tyre; more Greeks (Jason and the Argonauts) take a princess called Medea from Colchis in the Black Sea; and finally the Trojan prince Alexander (also known as Paris) abducts Helen of Sparta, and the Greeks invade Asia en masse.

The whole story is told from the Persian perspective: "From that time forth, the Persians regarded the Greek people as their foes. For the Persians claim as their own Asia and the barbarian peoples who live there, but Europe and the Greeks they hold to be separate." This is the earliest known version of a binary polarity setting Europe against Asia, and that, concludes Herodotus, "is how the Persians say it happened."[15]

There's no particular reason to doubt him. Herodotus grew up as a subject of the Persian empire in Carian Halicarnassus, a city ruled by Artemisia, one of Xerxes' closest advisers. Men of Halicarnassus fought alongside other Yauna on the Persian side against Greece.[16] He was familiar with Persian histories like the story Darius tells on the Behistun inscription and he would have known the Persian version of the roots of this war too.

The ingredients of his stories still came from the Greek tradition: legends of Io and Europa, Medea and Troy, and the basic notion of continents. And this "continental thinking" was no part of public discourse in Persia itself. Persian intellectuals at the court at Susa would have had little interest in categorizing the far-off western fragments of their world, and there is no mention of Europe or Asia in the great royal inscriptions that list the Persian king's subjects. There is however plenty of evidence that Persian strategists informed themselves about the art, literature, and ideas of those subject peoples, in order to manage their own image in their foreign territories.[17]

We have already encountered the example of the Cyrus Cylinder at Babylon, which presented Cyrus' conquest in traditional Babylonian terms and language, and Herodotus himself describes Persian interest in Greek myths about the Trojan War, at least for the purposes of propaganda.[18] He tells us that when Xerxes was on his way to Athens with his army he stopped at Troy, on the plain bordering the Hellespont, to sacrifice a thousand cattle to Athena "Ilias"—of Troy. The Persian wise men who accompanied him offered libations to the heroes of Homer's ancient conflict. The number of animals involved suggests considerable forward planning: Xerxes is sending a message to Homer's Greek readers about the revenge he plans for the ancient city.

Once in Greece itself, a similar tactic allowed the Persians to appeal to kinship to secure the neutrality of Argos, by equating the mythical Argive prince Perseus with an imaginary ancestor of their own called "Perses."[19] Inventing an exclusive ethnic identity for Persians as "Aryan" may have been useful to Darius at home, but outside the Persian realm Xerxes found it just as useful and entirely acceptable to claim shared blood with a Greek city.

Herodotus' "Persian chroniclers"—perhaps scholars based at Sardis—would have been working in a long tradition when they borrowed these and other useful Greek legends to weaponize the new continents invented by their Ionian subjects. And the continental thinking that they pioneered, as passed down by Herodotus, still informs ideas about the world today.

On the Greek mainland, meanwhile, the Persian Wars brought a new sense of isolation and insecurity, along with a narrowing of horizons and of the imagination. Greek identity itself took a more oppositional character than before. The hints of a collective "Hellenicity" that began to appear in the sixth century BCE had been based above all on a shared language. These early ideas emphasized similarities and relationships between Greek speakers rather than their differences from others. In the fifth century, however, Greeks began to distinguish themselves more strongly from non-Greeks—or, as they now called them, "barbarians."[20]

Originally the word "barbarian" seems simply to have meant "people who don't speak Greek," but it was increasingly used to designate them as primitive, stupid, or slavish.[21] It was applied with particular enthusiasm to Persians, whose wealth, decadence, and above all despotism are a new and conspicuous theme in fifth-century Athenian literature and art, often contrasted with Greek courage, rationality, and freedom. In Aeschylus' *Persians,* for instance, a tragedy produced in 472 BCE and set at the court in Susa, the queen mother dreams that her son tries to yoke a Greek woman and a Persian woman to his carriage; the latter accepts the bridle, but the former struggles violently and tosses Xerxes to the ground.[22]

Persia's "Phoenician" allies took a reputational hit as well: Thucydides describes them as "barbarians" for the first time at the end of the fifth century, and Herodotus tells us that Phoenicians were still to be found in his own day among the great families of Classical Athens, including the clan to which both Harmodius and Aristogeiton belonged. In the intensely patriotic generations that followed the Persian Wars, however, they tried to cover this up.[23]

Greek authors still understood the fundamental differences between people as cultural rather than natural: "barbarians," after all, were people who didn't speak Greek. But for a few decades at least, Greeks didn't only see the Persians and their allies as different from themselves, they saw them as worse. They also focused more on each other: this was an era of "panhellenism" at least among a subset of Hellenes, much encouraged by Athens. The imperial Athenian alliance was overseen by officials called Hellenotamiai, the "treasurers of the Greeks."[24] And around the outside of the Parthenon mythical battles were depicted between Greeks, their gods, and various barbarians: giants, centaurs, Amazons, and Trojans, all metaphors for a panhellenic defeat of the Persians.

Open hostility faded however with fading memories of the Acropolis on fire, as imperialism turned Athens into a hub of maritime power and commercial traffic in the Mediterranean alongside Carthage, Massalia, and Syracuse. For a taste of the imports that arrive in the city in this era we have a mock-epic catalogue preserved from the works of the fifth-century comic playwright Hermippos: silphium and oxhides from

Cyrene, mackerel from the Hellespont, pork and cheese from Syracuse, sails and papyrus rope from Egypt, frankincense from Syria, cypress wood from Crete, ivory from Africa, slaves from Phrygia, dates and wheat from Phoenicia, and cushions and rugs from Carthage.[25]

This is presumably exaggerated, but not too much, because that wouldn't be funny. There is plenty of archaeological evidence too for fifth-century trade between Levantine ports and the Aegean, and even between Athens and Persia: good-quality Attic pottery reaches Babylon and Susa, Greek coins are found at Persepolis and other Persian sites, and gold Persian darics and silver sigloi are found in Athens.[26]

At the same time, Athenians remained transfixed by Persian culture as a symbol of refined taste.[27] Fashionable Athenians had long been drinking out of Persian-style tankards and horns, but after Xerxes' campaign against them they began to use striped and fluted Persian drinking bowls to pour libations for the gods, and they adopted Persian dress, above all sleeves, which were a great novelty in Greece.[28]

Persian-style clothes were prized by the gods as well: records kept at the sanctuary of Artemis at Brauron in Attica show that Athenian girls dedicated sleeved tunics as part of female initiation rites that also saw them dress as bears and perform a special bear dance in honor of the goddess, who was fond of bears. In 435 BCE even the Athenian general Pericles built an enormous Odeon or music theater in the middle of Athens in a distinctively "multi-columned" Persian style—so much so that it was said to have been a deliberate imitation of King Xerxes' tent.[29]

It wasn't only Persian culture that was welcomed into the city. New gods arrived in this era from both Asia and Europe: Phrygian Sabazios and Bendis from Thrace were formally admitted to Athens in exactly the same manner as the goat god Pan and the healing deity Asklepios from the Peloponnese; Plato sets his *Republic* during the inaugural festival of Bendis at the Athenian port of Piraeus.[30]

And while human barbarians may have been seen as different in Athens, they were now embraced as well. We hear of Thracians, Phrygians, Egyptians, and Scythians in the city, but by the fourth century Levantines made up the biggest percentage of immigrants living there, and the Athenians passed a decree exempting Sidonian traders from the standard "alien" tax in the city.[31] These newcomers included Zeno, the founder of Stoicism, a merchant from Kition (Larnaca) on Cyprus, nicknamed the "little Phoenician" and whose tomb was eventually built at public expense.[32] Other Phoenician-speaking philosophers arrived from Carthage, Sidon, and Tyre.[33]

In time Greek authors came around to continental thinking too, by combining it with another geographical notion reported first in Persia, "environmental determinism," or the idea that climate and other physical factors have a decisive effect on people's physical, emotional, and intellectual abilities.

Just as he begins his work with the Persian boundary between Europe and Asia, Herodotus concludes it with King Cyrus' observation that "soft lands breed soft men"; for this reason, Herodotus says, the Persians chose "to live in a wretched land and rule rather than cultivate the plains enslaved to others."[34] Cyrus was comparing lands within Asia, but as with the Persian treatment of Greek continents, Greek treatments do not simply parrot the old Persian idea but do more with it. The result is a new version of continental thinking reliant on a mutual exchange of ideas across the border of Europe and Asia that undercuts its original core message of an important boundary between them.[35]

An early example comes in an anonymous medical text written around 400 BCE called *Airs, Waters, Places,* which has much to say about the differences between Europe and Asia, and how they produce different human populations.[36] Our author explains that in Asia the temperature is relatively stable and the climate mild, so things grow well and everything is both beautiful and large, including the people. They are also gentle and affectionate, but they lack courage and endurance, enterprise and high spirits.[37] In Europe, however, while the changing seasons lead to a greater variety in both terrain and people, the latter are in general tougher, courageous, and more warlike—as well as wild, unsociable, and passionate.[38]

It is not surprising that ancient Greek texts present parallels with nineteenth-century ways of thought in western Europe: they inspired many of them. Still, this is not yet civilizational thinking in the full modern sense. Our anonymous author does differentiate Europe from Asia, as did Herodotus' Persian chroniclers. In an echo of Darius' organization of his subjects into culture groups on the Apadana at Persepolis he also associates the two continents with different cultures. And like King Cyrus he adds an explanation for this cultural difference based on local factors—principally climate—rather than contact with other people and places. His claim is not however that Asians or Europeans *naturally* behave in any particular way: it is that the environment of Asia and Europe encourages particular behaviors, and this is true, he insists, both of those born in these lands and of visitors.[39]*

Nor is Europe ranked above Asia on this theory, or treated as a focus of identity. Even for Greek writers who accepted the new continental system with more grace than Herodotus, Greece itself often stood outside the model, between Asia and Europe and better than both. We see this most clearly in the claim made by the philosopher Aristotle in the fourth century BCE that Greece occupies an admirable middle ground between Europe and Asia, and its inhabitants therefore avoid the character defects brought on by the undesirable climate of either:

> Those who live in a cold climate and in Europe are full of spirit, but wanting in intelligence and skill; and therefore they retain comparative freedom, but have no political organization, and are incapable of ruling over others. Whereas the natives of Asia are intelligent and inventive, but they are wanting in spirit, and therefore they are always in a state of subjection and slavery. But the Hellenic stock, which is situated between them, is likewise intermediate in character, being high-spirited and also intelligent.[40]

*Environmental determinism helped Greeks understand differences in skin color in a relatively neutral way as well: a lack of sunlight made northerners curiously pale, while "Ethiopian" literally means "burnt-face." They found themselves, as often, in the middle: Greek vases that contrast the faces of Africans and Greeks use not black and white but black and brown skin tones respectively (Sarah F. Derbew, *Untangling Blackness in Greek Antiquity*, Cambridge: Cambridge University Press, 2022, 29–50). White skin was a characteristic of women, who stayed out of the sun, and of northern barbarians, who didn't get enough of it. An ancient Greek man would probably have been offended to be described as white, with its implications of effeminacy and northern provincialism.

This means that Italians could be as bad as Persians, if not worse. The fourth-century Greek author Theopompus decries decadence among "all the barbarians living in the west": Italian men and women, he claims, both remove their hair with pitch or by shaving, and there are even businesses that provide this service. This is again not a natural character flaw, but one introduced by the environment: even Greeks in Italy, he reports, have learned this habit from their new neighbors.[41]

This self-positioning outside the continental system helps to explain the lack of Greek interest in the modern notion of "east versus west." In purely practical terms, the early Ionian Greek geographers divided the world between the European north and the Asian south. So did later environmental determinism: differences in latitude are always more striking than those in longitude, and Aristotle himself began a practice that would last for millennia among cartographers of dividing the world primarily not into continents but into five zones or "climes" from north to south.[42]

Attitudes changed again as Greek cities came under the control of a new foreign power. Philip II, the warlord who ruled Macedon, ascended to the throne in the 350s BCE. Over the next two decades he extended his rule south, ruthlessly playing different Greek states and politicians off against one another until he had conquered them all. It was, he insisted, for their own good, and enough of them were prepared to go along with this analysis for a new league of Greek states to unite under Philip's leadership.

Philip may seem a strange standard bearer for hellenism, given Macedon's old alliance with Persia.[43] Links between Persian and Macedonian nobility had remained warm, to the extent that Philip's son Alexander tried to marry the daughter of the Carian satrap Pixodaros.[44] The Athenian politician Isocrates nonetheless begged him in 339 to lead the Greeks against Persia: it was a shame, he said, "to let Asia thrive more than Europe, and the barbarians prosper more than the Greeks."[45]

Isocrates not only resurrects here the Persian distinction between Asia and Europe more than a century after the Athenians first to our knowledge made use of it, but he goes further: he now associates Greece with Europe as well as Persia with Asia, and suggests for the first time that just as Greeks are superior to barbarians, Europe is superior to Asia.[46]

Not everyone agreed. For Isocrates' Athenian contemporary the orator Demosthenes, Philip himself was "not only not Greek, nor related to the Greeks, but not even a barbarian from any place that can be named with honor, but a pestilent knave from Macedonia, from where you can't even buy a decent slave."[47] Nonetheless, in 337 the Macedonian king announced that the Hellenic League's next project would be a war of revenge on Persia for its attacks on Greek cities and temples during the Persian Wars 150 years earlier: the exact inverse of the justification the Persians had used for their own invasion of Greece, and an argument that turned continental thinking decisively against its first inventors.[48]

Within a year however Philip had been assassinated, and it was his son Alexander III, the Great, who would lead the Greeks east on a mission that collapsed the distinction between Asia and Europe completely.

CHAPTER SEVENTEEN

Of Elephants and Kings

SUSA, 324 BCE

The great mound of Troy had been Xerxes' last stop before he crossed to Europe in 480 BCE, and 146 years later it was Alexander's first stop in Asia. Alexander sacrificed to Athena and poured a libation to the heroes—just as Xerxes and his entourage had done, a model he must have had in mind. Alexander's own heroes were on the other side: when someone offered to show him the lyre played by his namesake the Trojan prince Alexander, so the story went, he was interested only in the lyre of Achilles.[1]

Alexander was about twenty years old in 334 BCE, but already he was an experienced general and formidable soldier, and had been king for two years. His visit to Troy fits in with the branding of the mission he had inherited from his father: to avenge the Persian invasion of Greece.

He next expelled the Persian garrisons from the Greek-speaking cities of Ionia, and then swept through Anatolia to defeat the Persian king Darius III in person at the Battle of Issus in 333. The king offered Alexander a peace deal that would have given him much of Anatolia.[2] Alexander's negative response is preserved in a letter reportedly sent to Darius but certainly intended for consumption on his own side. It articulates the rhetoric of revenge he had inherited, but suggests that his

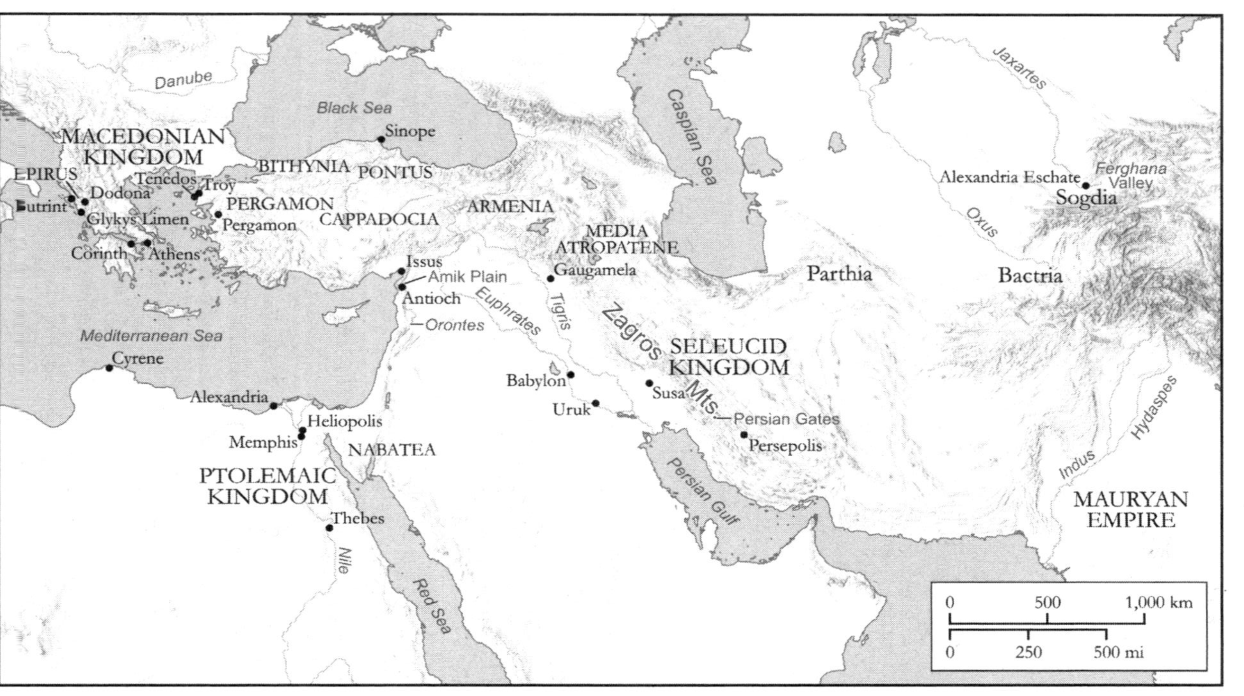

The Kingdoms of Alexander's Successors in 281 BCE

own ambitions already went further. "I have invaded Asia to take revenge on Persians for aggressions you began," he begins, but he ends with an order: "when you send to me in future, send to me as King of Asia."[3]

Darius' empire fell fast. In 332 Alexander took the Levantine ports and appointed his own satraps to replace the Persian officials. He himself continued to Egypt, where he founded a new city on the Mediterranean that he called Alexandria. Turning east he defeated Darius again in October 331 at Gaugamela in what is now northern Iraq, and his own troops now proclaimed him king of Asia.[4] He was still king of Macedon as well, and leader of the Greeks: Alexander had transcontinental ambitions, and his campaigns would bring European, Asian, and African people, culture, and ideas into unprecedented contact.

Gaugamela was also where Alexander's troops got their first sight of elephants.[5] There don't seem to have been many in the Persian ranks—perhaps fifteen—but the soldiers may well have been familiar with Greek tales of India that described this animal as the only creature impervious to the poisonous bite of the human-headed serpent-tailed lion called a manticore. It must have been a shock to discover that at least one of the two really existed.[6]

Alexander marched on to Babylon, where he met no resistance, entering the city to a ceremonial welcome like that given to Cyrus two centuries earlier. Like Cyrus he ordered the restoration of temples and sanctuaries, including the ziggurat.[7]* And in another example of his eagerness to learn from Persian tactics, he established his own stable of elephants from the veterans he had inherited.[8]

Elephants would soon become a familiar sight farther west. They are

*This came to nothing, or worse. The ziggurat was already in ruins after Xerxes had it partially destroyed 160 years earlier in response to a Babylonian revolt. Now it was fully dismantled but it was never reconstructed, and it disappeared from history for more than two millennia, its mud bricks quarried for local building. Archaeologists finally located the famous monument again in 1901 when they realized that a strange square pond surrounding an island was in fact filling the foundation trenches of the great tower (Andrew George, "The truth about Etemenanki, the ziggurat of Babylon," in Irving L. Finkel and Michael J. Seymour, eds., *Babylon: Myth and Reality*, London: British Museum Press, 2008, 128–9).

emblematic of the appropriation of local technologies that allowed Macedonian generals to control large portions of Asia and Africa as well as Balkan Europe, learning from their predecessors and neighbors how to rule new realms and engaging with a vast array of new languages, cultures, and ideas.

In January 330 Alexander's army forced the pass in the Zagros Mountains known as the Persian Gates and finally reached Persepolis, its extraordinary pillared assembly rooms marking the center of the Persian world. According to the later Sicilian historian Diodorus it was "the wealthiest city under the sun."[9] Alexander's troops plundered the town with their commander's permission, killing every man they found. Then they turned to the palace itself, to drag away its women and its gold. Job done, they feasted in halls Xerxes had built, and then set them on fire.

Darius himself retreated to the desert east of modern Tehran with Alexander in close pursuit. Hiding in an oxcart, he was finally stabbed by his own men and left to die.[10] Alexander pushed on to confront rebels and rivals on the northeast frontier, where he married a Bactrian princess called Roxane. He horrified his more conservative Macedonian companions by encouraging foreign practices at court, including prostration before the king.[11] He also adopted a new style of mixed Perso-Macedonian dress. Its signature was a diadem or ornamental headband that would remain a symbol of Macedonian royal power for centuries.[12]

In an echo of Assyrian, Babylonian, and Persian resettlement programs Alexander launched a program of involuntary integration between his own forces and the local population, settling his veterans in new towns in central Asia. As far north as modern Tajikistan, for instance, Alexandria Eschate or "Farthest Away" was built in twenty days on the banks of the Jaxartes to replace a Persian border post called Cyropolis, "Cyrus Town." It housed Alexander's troops, both Greeks and Macedonians, as well as local refugees from nearby towns he had destroyed.[13]

Alexander then turned south toward India. In 326 he crossed the Indus and then the Hydaspes, where he defeated the Indian king Poros and a large corps of battle elephants.[14] Poros had placed the animals in the front line as a shield for his infantry, and rode the largest himself. After some initial confusion the Macedonians worked out how to wound the elephants with javelins, and the poor creatures ran amok among their own ranks.[15] At the end of the battle Alexander captured eighty beasts alive.[16]

The conquest of India seemed in sight, but it would not be easy: reports of the Nanda kingdom on the Ganges river mentioned 200,000 infantry and 3,000 to 6,000 war elephants.[17] Still, ancient commentators reassure us, Alexander was not daunted; it was his troops who decided that they had had enough. Their arms, armor, clothing, and even their horses' hooves were wearing thin, and it had been raining for almost three months. In the face of potential mutiny, Alexander magnanimously agreed to march back west.[18]

Returning to the relative familiarity of Mesopotamia, he added his new elephant herd, augmented by diplomatic gifts along the way, to the royal stables.[19] The animals were deployed in Babylon during his lifetime for ceremonial rather than military purposes, but they represented something more: the control of local culture in the interests of universal royal power.

Similarly, Alexander organized a mass wedding of his generals to Persian noblewomen at Susa in 324.[20] He took the opportunity himself to marry Darius' eldest daughter as well as one of his nieces, underlining his claim to the old king's possessions and to the resources of conquered lands. This event privileged the Persian nobility within Alexander's empire at the same time as it confirmed where status and power really lay: it wasn't Greco-Macedonian women marrying Iranian men.

The later Greek historian Plutarch nonetheless described the king's strategy in romantic terms. Alexander, he explained, "brought men from everywhere into a single body, mixing as if in a loving cup their lives and traits and marriages and social practices. He commanded them all to think of the inhabited world as their fatherland, of the army camp as their fortress and guard, of all good men as their relatives, and only of evil men as foreigners."[21]

This interpretation makes Alexander an early adopter of a new philosophical fashion. "Cosmopolitanism" or the doctrine of world citizenship rejected the assumption that you owe greater allegiance to some people than to others just because you live under the same political authority as them, and rejected the fifth-century distinction between Greeks and barbarians. As Plutarch summarizes the thesis advanced by Zeno of Kition in the early third century BCE, "we should live not divided into cities and districts [demes] by separate rules of justice, but we should regard all men as fellow demesmen and fellow citizens."[22] This call to universalist rather than communitarian politics has inspired European philosophers ever since although, or perhaps because, it still involves a fundamentally Greek idea of citizenship itself.[23]

Cosmopolitanism was supposedly first articulated as an intellectual attitude in the mid-fourth century by Diogenes the Cynic (c. 390–323), a popular public intellectual in exile from the western Anatolian city of Sinope who then lived in a large jar in the marketplace at Athens, mocking the abstract philosophers of the day and masturbating. Alexander had in fact met Diogenes in 336 in Corinth, where the latter now lived in a barrel. Starstruck, the young prince asked what he could do for the great thinker. Replied Diogenes, "Stand a little out of my sun."[24]

Diogenes' credentials as the first cosmopolitan philosopher are questionable. His claim to be a "citizen of the world" is reported without context, and may simply have been a rejection of the city-based system that had (perhaps understandably) rejected him.[25] It is equally unlikely that Alexander's own actions were based on high-flown philosophical ideas about the unity of humankind, let alone about justice.[26] For him as for many since, cosmopolitanism was more of a convenient lifestyle choice than a political ideal, one that appropriated foreign customs, symbols, and resources for personal benefit.[27] Even today it takes unusual privilege to live like this, and enjoying the products and practices of other cultures is a by-product of power. As Alexander knew, being a citizen of the world works best for those who rule it.

· · ·

Alexander died in 323, a month short of his thirty-third birthday, probably of alcohol poisoning. He left behind an empire on both sides of the Hellespont, an illegitimate child named Herakles, and by Roxane an unborn son. More than two decades of conflict followed as his old generals fought over his kingdom and the remains of his army. These included the elephant corps, augmented when one of Alexander's old generals assassinated Poros around 315 BCE and brought 120 more of his animals back home.[28]

A shifting mosaic of smaller "Hellenistic" kingdoms emerged out of Alexander's old realm. They imposed the Greek language as a condition of access to power and brought aspects of Mediterranean culture as far as India, in a remarkable example of cultural entanglement that endured for over a millennium.[29] At the same time, one of the most interesting things about these Greco-Macedonian kingdoms is how much art, science, and empire owed to Asia and Africa.

The details of the wars between Alexander's generals are convoluted, but the overall situation is summarized with admirable clarity in a prophecy recorded in the Book of Daniel, set in the sixth century BCE but composed in the second:

> A mighty king will arise, who will rule with great power and do as he pleases. After he has arisen, his empire will be broken up and parceled out toward the four winds of heaven. It will not go to his descendants, nor will it have the power he exercised, because his empire will be uprooted and given to others. The king of the South will become strong, but one of his commanders will become even stronger than he and will rule his own kingdom with great power.[30]

The king of the South was Ptolemy, one of Alexander's longest-serving and most trusted commanders. He was a historian as well, and although his chronicle of Alexander's expedition is now lost it served as one of the principal sources for the surviving accounts. After Alexander's death, Ptolemy staked an early claim to his old friend's legacy by seizing his body as it passed through Syria on its way home to Macedon. He buried the king instead at Memphis in Egypt where he established his first power base, before moving both corpse and capital to

Alexandria. He also founded his own new city, Ptolemais, as a southern capital, reducing the ancient Egyptian cities of Memphis and Thebes to heritage status.

Ptolemy ruled in Egypt first as satrap, adopting the Persian terminology, but in 305 he took the grander title of king: not king of Egypt, of Asia, or even of Macedon, but simply "king." Under the shadow of Alexander's mausoleum his family endured longest of Alexander's "Successor" dynasties, and their realm came to encompass not only Egypt but also Cyrenaica, Cyprus, Cilicia, the Aegean islands, and considerable portions of the Levantine coast.

Alexandria was the Ptolemies' showcase, filled with gardens and colonnades, baths and gymnasia, monuments and elegant houses, all whipped by the fresh sea breeze.[31] The city became a great trading center, connecting the ports of east Africa and the Red Sea to the Mediterranean.[32] It attracted sailors in search of ivory and gold, spices and silk.

The new kings themselves encouraged trade with the introduction of coinage to Egypt. They reopened a shipping canal from the Red Sea to the Egyptian Delta begun by the Egyptian pharaoh Necho and first completed by the Persian king Darius I, pre-empting the Suez Canal of the 1860s by more than 2,300 years.[33] They also built a great lighthouse to guide ships into port, the first known in the world and one of the standard entries on the lists of Seven Wonders of the World that began to appear in the second century BCE. It stood more than a hundred meters high and ancient and medieval sources describe a rectangular base, an octagonal midsection and a cylindrical top, the whole capped by a statue.[34] It survived into the fourteenth century CE.

People came to Alexandria for culture as well as commerce. It was probably Ptolemy II (r. 284–246 BCE) who founded a grand Mousaion in the city, a House of the Muses. Although this is the root of our word "museum," the original was more like a research center than a gallery, a laboratory for science and art with a hall, a refectory, and a population of scholars.[35]

We don't know whether any teaching went on there, but the building may also have housed the famous Library of Alexandria, where one list of works ran to 120 volumes, suggesting that the institution could have held up to 100,000 scrolls.[36] Because the library often acquired multiple manuscripts of the same works, it became a center for textual editing where definitive texts of Greek masterpieces were established, beginning with the Homeric epics.

It was run by a succession of famous librarians, noted scholars like Aristarchus of Samos (c. 310–230 BCE), who argued that the sun and not the earth was at the center of the solar system—a suggestion that was largely ignored.[37] Astronomy was still a subject of great interest at Alexandria, and one that depended on the city's connections to the east as well as on a long Egyptian astronomical tradition.

By the fifth century BCE Babylonian astronomers had identified "the way of the moon": the belt running around the heavens through which the sun, moon, and planets travel. Building on the city's proud mathematical heritage, they split this circle into twelve regions of thirty "degrees." Each corresponded to one month, and was named after one of the constellations it contained. They could also make charts ("horoscopes") of the position of heavenly bodies at any particular moment, in order more accurately to read the messages sent to them in the stars by the gods about the future. This included the future of individuals based on the arrangements of the heavens at their birth: astronomy was still the handmaiden of what is now called astrology.[38]

Later reports traced the introduction to Greek thought of the way of the moon to a fifth-century scholar named Kleostratos from Tenedos, an island off the Anatolian coast. By the beginning of the second century it had reached Alexandria.[39] Greek scholars called it the *zodiakos kyklos* or "cycle of little animals," and several of the signs of the zodiac still maintain their original Babylonian identities today: Taurus is the Babylonian Bull of Heaven, Gemini the Great Twins, Cancer the Crab. By the Hellenistic period Greek scholars had borrowed the names of planets as well as stars from Babylon: the Star of Ishtar became the Star of Aphrodite (Roman Venus); the Star of Nabu became the Star of Hermes (Roman Mercury).[40]

Another illustrious librarian was Eratosthenes (276–194 BCE), who came from Libyan Cyrene. He was a polymath who wrote on astronomy, poetry, history, mathematics, and music, dated the sack of Troy precisely to 1184 BCE, eventually went blind, and then starved himself to death. He is best known now as a geographer. Greek scholars had been aware since at least the fifth century BCE that the earth was not flat but spherical: this explained the way that stars change as you travel north or south, and why the tops of the buildings come over the horizon first when you sail into port.[41] Eratosthenes was however the first to devise a reliable method to determine its size.[42]

Other Alexandrian scientists brought about extraordinary advances in mathematics—it was there that Euclid worked out the principles of geometry—and in mechanics, as witnessed in the gearing of the automaton that took part in a great procession staged in the city by Ptolemy II. A wagon pulled by sixty men carried an "image" of a woman called Nysa, twice life size and dressed in a yellow cloak. Nysa stood up, poured milk from a gold libation cup, and sat back down again, all without anyone touching her.[43]

Alexandria's Jewish scholars meanwhile undertook the immense project of translating the Bible from Hebrew into Greek. This "Septuagint" became the basis of later translations into Latin and through them the early translations into modern languages.[44] Its Latin name, literally "the seventy," came from a later legend that Ptolemy II had invited seventy-two Jewish scholars to write down the Torah in Greek. Working from memory rather than a text, they produced versions that matched exactly. In reality, the Septuagint translation was a Jewish initiative to save their sacred texts as knowledge of the Hebrew language within their community faded.[45]

In the modern era this extraordinary city disappeared. Between new building, earthquakes, subsidence, and erosion, ancient Alexandria was considered a lost cause. But underwater excavations in the harbor over the last three decades have revealed the Ptolemies' royal palace, temples, and port structures, as well as elements very likely to belong to the lighthouse.[46] The divers also discovered more surprising remains: older Egyptian statuary from Heliopolis near modern Cairo, as well as six enormous statues of Ptolemaic monarchs in the guise of Egyptian pharaohs and their wives.[47]

The Ptolemies described themselves as Macedonian, but like Alexander they presented themselves even to their compatriots in hybrid form. Language and custom were flexible in the service of empire. Ptolemy V, who came to the throne in 202 BCE, may have been the first to be formally crowned as pharaoh by the high priest of Ptah at Memphis, but his predecessors were already depicted as pharaohs in local temples in traditional Egyptian dress, and they took on the rights and responsibilities of Egyptian kings.[48]

They also emulated pharaonic practice in the custom of brother–sister marriage, first adopted by Ptolemy II, who married his sister Arsinoe and acquired the sobriquet Philadelphus or "sister-loving." The custom of brother–sister marriage was maintained down to the last Ptolemaic monarch, the notorious Cleopatra: as a young queen she married not one but two of her brothers, both of whom would have been aged around ten at the time.

The size of the Greco-Macedonian population in Egypt was still relatively small, around 15 percent of the total, and the regime's success rested in part on pre-existing Persian infrastructure, including the postal service.[49] Outside Alexandria the Ptolemies pursued a policy of relocation and colocation. Greco-Macedonian immigrants were settled throughout Egypt in farming colonies that combined Egyptian irrigation technology, Macedonian drainage expertise, and new Mediterranean crops: durum wheat, olives, and vines did well, as did pigs, though an attempt to introduce Greek cabbages to the Egyptian desert was unsuccessful.[50] They lived alongside Egyptian settlers, intermarrying and even dancing together.[51]

As the prophet Daniel noted, Ptolemy was not the only "Successor" to make a success of it. The king of the North was Seleucus, a more junior officer in Alexander's army who became satrap of Babylon a few years after his death, but fled the city in 316 under attack by a Macedonian rival. Ptolemy gave him sanctuary in Egypt, and he returned the favor by commanding Ptolemy's fleet against their mutual Macedonian foes.

In 312 he set off east again to reconquer Babylon, and he counted the years of his reign from then, introducing a new "Seleucid Era," which remained in use in Syria and central Asia into late medieval times, and among Yemenite Jews into the twentieth century.[52] Seleucus called himself "commander" (*strategos*) of Asia at first, then like Ptolemy in 305 he took the title of king. He spent the next twenty-five years earning his epithet of Nikator, "Conqueror," annexing most of Anatolia and crossing the Indus to create a vast Seleucid empire.

Seleucus established colonies across his realm, but the greatest was the coastal city of Antioch on the east bank of the Orontes. As with Alexandria in Egypt, Antioch gave Seleucus a new capital to counterbalance traditional centers of power. It also provided a Mediterranean port that controlled inland trade routes up the river and through the Amik Plain between two mountain ranges. Seleucus settled Macedonian and Cretan colonists in the new town, which became the main seat of the Seleucid kings in the second century BCE. Under Rome it was the biggest city in the Levant, and one of the largest in the Mediterranean, although always alarmingly vulnerable to earthquakes.[53]

The fundamental point of any empire is to turn a profit, and then deliver it safely to the imperial center. In the Seleucid realm, vast distances, difficult terrain, and hundreds of languages made this particularly tricky. Like the Ptolemies, Seleucus knew that in order to rule successfully they had to incorporate local leaders, languages, and customs into the world they were creating. His own wife, Apame, was from Sogdia in central Asia, making the Seleucid kings that succeeded him half Sogdian.

They recycled the old Persian satrapy and taxation systems, as well as the use of multiple capitals, and they relied as had the Persians before them on the collaboration of local priests, power brokers, and political leaders. The Seleucids also continued the Persian policy of using local languages for local administration: in both Babylon and Uruk people were still writing in Akkadian cuneiform, and sometimes still in Sumerian, until close to the end of the first millennium BCE.[54]

Seleucus himself recruited local troops into his imperial army, including another contingent of elephants from India where the Mauryan king Chandragupta had overthrown the Nanda and extended his own empire far to the south, encompassing about half of modern India.

Chandragupta made a peace treaty with Seleucus in 304/3 BCE, swapping territory to the east of modern Kandahar for 500 war elephants from the 9,000 that he himself deployed.[55]

Access to this new supply of elephants gave the Seleucids a major advantage in an endemic conflict with the Ptolemies over the boundaries between their territories. One way or another the Ptolemies had gotten their hands on a good number of Poros' herd, but over the years the surviving animals died of old age. In response the Ptolemies set up an elaborate, expensive, and dangerous program of elephant hunting along the coast of east Africa, the fruits of which were borne back to Egypt on specially built large, low boats called *elephantegoi* or elephant carriers.[56] It must have included extensive consultation with specialists from east Africa itself or from India on how to capture, tame, and care for the animals.

Despite the efforts involved, however, the results were patchy: Seleucid elephants prevailed in a battle in 217 BCE not only because of their larger number (102 against 73) but, we are told, because they were themselves larger.[57] Ptolemy's animals were not then the massive African bush elephant, which is considerably bigger than its Asian colleague, and even less tractable. In fact, these immense beasts were never to our knowledge used in Mediterranean warfare, and they may not even have been known to the Ptolemies. Instead, their captives were probably African forest elephants, a smaller species still found in dwindling numbers in west Africa and the Congo basin.[58]

Although both the Ptolemies and Seleucids eventually had to source new supplies of the beasts that had come to symbolize Macedonian empire, Poros' old herd had one last hurrah in the army of a Hellenistic king far to the west. Epirus was one of a host of small states that grew up alongside the larger realms of Alexander's successors in this era. It was a high, rainy region of mountains and valleys, walled hilltop forts, and grazing land between Macedonia and the Adriatic, occupying a region now split between Greece and Albania.

This forbidding landscape had long welcomed visitors: harbors at Butrint and Glykys Limen had been in use since the Bronze Age, as had the sanctuary of Zeus at Dodona, whose oracle was second only in reputation by Homer's time to Delphi. In the early third century BCE a new temple was built at the site and a huge new theater looked out across a plain to the great low bulk of Mount Tomaros, capped for much of the year by snow.

This was the work of a king called Pyrrhus, second cousin to Alexander the Great. He was also the first king to cross the Adriatic with troops, in 281 BCE, taking with him 28,000 men and twenty war elephants as he went to the aid of his allies at the Greek port of Tarentum in southern Italy, which was under attack. As so often is the case, it isn't entirely clear how he had gotten hold of the elephants, but it was from a king of Macedon in possession of animals from Poros' original herd.[59] Over five decades they trudged slowly from India to Italy, witnesses to an ever-increasing flow of ideas in all directions across languages, histories, and continents. They ended their lives in the hands of westerners who would destroy the entangled world Alexander and his generals had created.

CHAPTER EIGHTEEN

Clouds in the West

ZAMA, 202 BCE

The so-called Punic Wars had a long legacy: even in the modern period Europeans were still invested in the differences between Carthage and Rome, and in an ancient imperial clash they could read as contemporary fable.* Rome was seen as an empire of the land, based on territorial conquest and a citizen army; Carthage as an empire of the sea, run on commerce and colonies and reliant on mercenaries for military force.[1] As the Scottish philosopher Adam Ferguson put it in 1767, the Romans were "destined to acquire wealth by conquest, and by the spoil of provinces," while the Carthaginians were "intent on the returns of merchandise, and the produce of commercial settlements."[2]

As early as the seventeenth century English politicians used this contrast to symbolize their own differences from their great rival, the Dutch Republic. The English wanted to be "another Rome in the west," as the poet Milton noted skeptically in 1660, and it was useful for them to

*The use of the word "Punic" to mean western Phoenician or more specifically Carthaginian is a modern convention. It is taken from the Latin terms *poenus* and *punicus,* but those were originally just transliterations of the Greek word *phoinix,* as Latin for a long time lacked aspirated consonants (Jonathan R. W. Prag, "Poenus plane est—but who were the 'Punickes'?," *Papers of the British School at Rome* 74 [2006]).

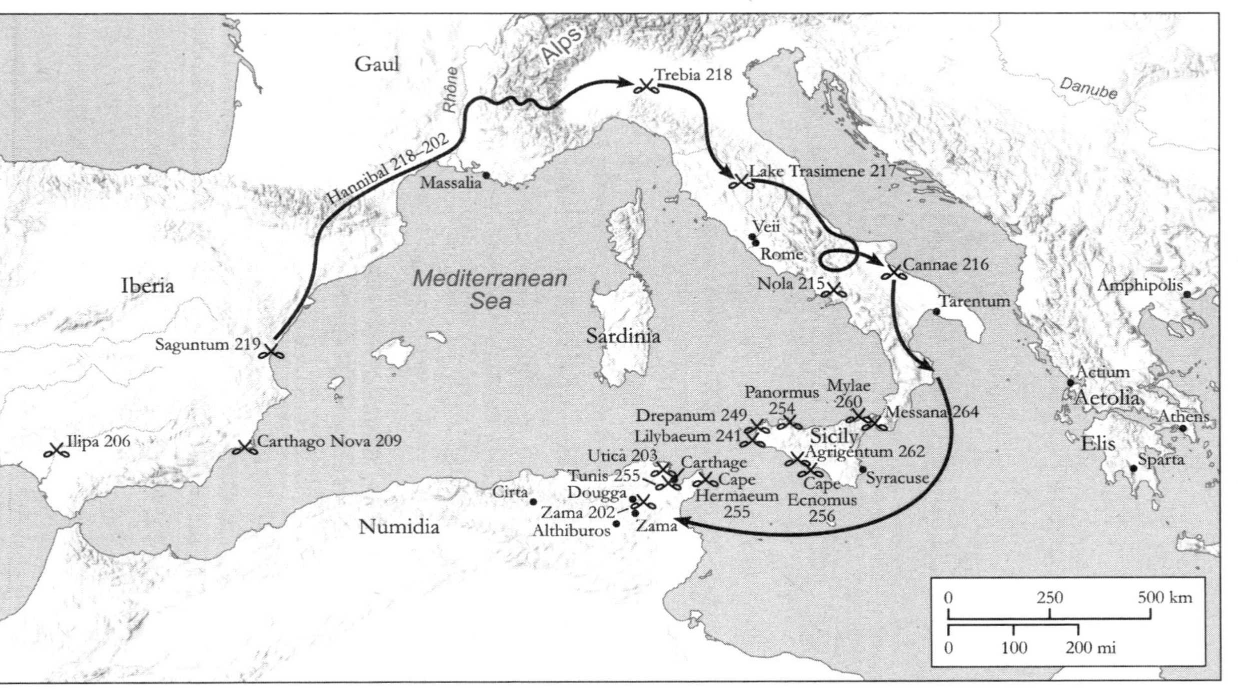

The wars between Carthage and Rome in the third century BCE

align the Dutch by contrast with the Carthaginians, notorious treaty breakers hungry for profit. The Anglo-Dutch conflicts of 1652–74 became new Punic Wars, and in 1673 the Earl of Shaftesbury borrowed the Roman hawk Cato the Elder's constant refrain to declare to parliament, *Delenda est Carthago,* "Carthage must be destroyed."[3] For Dutch writers, by contrast, it was England that was the "New Carthage."[4]

All this would have surprised authors writing during the Punic Wars themselves. From their perspective, the two cities looked very similar: not so much chalk and cheese as Oxford and Cambridge. Our best eyes on the era are those of the Peloponnesian statesman Polybius, who spent almost two decades as a political prisoner in Rome in the middle of the second century BCE. As a foreign dignitary he was well treated, and he used the time to write an account of the meteoric rise of Rome for his shell-shocked fellow Greeks. In it he regularly draws parallels between Rome and Carthage: both cities were unusually well governed, for instance, because their constitutions combined aspects of monarchy, aristocracy, and democracy, so that all decisions were made by the people best placed to make them.[5]

Polybius also remarks of the Romans themselves that they are unusually willing to substitute their own customs for better practice from elsewhere.[6] This had been going on for some time.

A treaty agreed between Rome and Carthage in the late sixth century BCE illustrates the relative strengths of these cities at the time. It is preserved for us in a later Greek translation of an archaic Latin document found in the Roman archives.[7] The original must itself have been a translation from Phoenician, as the format is quite unlike other early Roman (and Greek) alliances: it was probably one of a series Carthage struck with different cities.[8] It is traditionally dated to the year 509 BCE, in which the Romans deposed their kings and established a republic, a good moment for the Carthaginians to clarify relations.

In this treaty Carthage recognizes Roman control of parts of Latium, but lists much larger domains of its own in which Romans have restricted trading rights: Sardinia, western Sicily, and the African coast in both directions.[9] There is no doubt which is the greater power, but over the following centuries the Romans learned a lot from their new ally.

For one thing, Carthaginian models may have played a larger role in the emergence of Roman republican institutions than is usually acknowledged.[10] The two consuls who were now elected at Rome each year as joint chief officers of state, for instance, echo the two annual magistrates who ruled Carthage, who were also elected by a citizen assembly. In some contexts the Roman consuls are even called "judges"—a direct translation of the word used at Carthage, *shofetim*.[11] Perhaps this is just a coincidence, but another example has a whiff of a cover-up.

Roman law was written down for the first time in the mid-fifth century, on twelve bronze tables. Later Roman historians claimed that the project involved an embassy to Athens to find out how such things were done. The problem is that the scraps that survive of the "Twelve Tables" in quotations bear no resemblance to Greek law, or for that matter to later Roman law either.[12]

Instead, they are surprisingly close in form and approach to west Asian law codes like those of Hammurabi and the Hebrew Bible. Rather than establishing general principles, the clauses of the Twelve Tables take the form "If someone does X, their punishment shall be Y"—"If he has broken a bone of a free man, 300, if of a slave 150 asses [bronze coins, not donkeys] are to be the penalty."[13] Compare a provision from the Eshnunna code, written in eighteenth-century BCE Babylonia: "If [a man] breaks [another man's] leg, he shall pay half a mina of silver."[14]

Some scholars have argued that such models could still have reached Rome via Greece instead of Carthage.[15] But there is no evidence at all for such "textbooks" of law in Greece, let alone in this format, while any law code at Carthage would naturally have followed west Asian norms, just like their treaties.

In 348 BCE Carthage renewed its alliance with Rome.[16] The text of this treaty reveals that the two aristocratic republics were still very unequal partners: the Romans now agreed to avoid Africa and Sardinia entirely, as well as much of Iberia, restricting their trading activities to the city of Carthage and Carthage's province in Sicily.

This is no surprise. Carthage itself was still the largest city in the western Mediterranean, with a circuit wall more than thirty kilometers long.[17] Housing now covered the plain between the Byrsa Hill and the sea, and German excavations there in the late twentieth century give us a good idea of how wealthy Carthaginians lived, in houses of 300 to 600 square meters provided with wells, cisterns, latrines, and bathrooms, and laid out on a new grid pattern aligned with the coast.

Business in the city was booming. Ships from the Aegean brought fine wine and pottery to Carthage's merchant harbor, while amphoras full of salted fish returned to Athens and Corinth.[18] Carthaginian traders settled in overseas ports and a Greek community grew up at Carthage itself. The Carthaginians still policed access to their own sea. A Greek geographer reports in the mid-fourth century BCE that the Carthaginians controlled ports from Gibraltar to Cyrenaica, and in the early third Eratosthenes of Alexandria claimed that they "drowned any foreigners who sailed past on their way to Sardinia or the Pillars."[19]

We can now see high levels of travel and migration around this Carthaginian world in studies of aDNA from Iron Age Sardinia—a historically isolated population—which have identified considerable evidence for immigration of people of eastern Mediterranean and north African descent: six burials between the eighth and fifth centuries BCE sampled at the inland site of Villamar, for instance, all turned out to have significant (20–35 percent) north African heritage.[20] This went both ways. Little aDNA from Carthage itself has yet been studied, although one man of western European heritage was buried on the Byrsa Hill in the late sixth century. But out of twelve burials investigated at the town of Kerkouane farther east along the African coast and dating to a century or two either side of 500 BCE, five appear to have had local origins, while seven were genetically more similar to people in Sicily and central Italy.[21]

Rome however was expanding fast, and it was beginning to catch up. In 396 BCE the city had defeated the Tiber port of Veii fifteen kilometers to the north, an event that marked the beginning of the end for the city-states of Etruria. Over the course of the fourth century Romans conquered central Italy from Etruria to Campania, and established military and civilian colonies up and down the peninsula. They built the first roads in western Europe to transport troops across Italy, although they were a boon to trade as well.[22]

At first Carthage seems to have welcomed Rome's growing power as a counterbalance to the ambitions of old Greek ports in southern Italy like Tarentum. But soon Rome had Tarentum itself in its sights: in 282 it provoked a naval confrontation and then declared war. This was when the Tarentines sent for help across the Adriatic.

Pyrrhus won two victories in quick succession, but he was on unfamiliar ground and his forces diminished fast, while the Romans could call down endless reserves from their Italian subjects. "If we win one more battle against the Romans," Pyrrhus is supposed to have complained, "we will be utterly destroyed."[23] Instead he returned to Greece, leaving his elephants behind to star in a Roman triumph.[24]

Carthage was a good ally to Rome in the same war, providing naval transport for Roman troops, destroying Pyrrhus' supplies and intercepting his fleet.[25] By now, Polybius reports, the Carthaginians possessed an African territory, many parts of Iberia, all the islands in the Sardinian and Tyrrhenian seas, and almost all of Sicily west of Syracuse.[26] And as a result of their victory the Romans meanwhile took control of the whole Italian peninsula south of modern Pisa.

All that stood between the two cities now was the port of Messana (now Messina), on the Sicilian Strait, which was in the hands of a small band of Italian mercenaries at war with the king of neighboring Syracuse. These Italians appealed first to Carthage and then to Rome for help. Both powers agreed to come to their aid, and hostilities between them seem to have broken out by mistake when the mercenaries ejected a Carthaginian garrison to make way for Roman troops. This prompted Carthage to join Syracuse instead against Messina—and, by extension, against Rome.

By 262 the Romans had reduced Syracuse to submission, which left them free to concentrate on Carthage, in what came to be known as the First Punic War. At first the Carthaginian fleet seemed unbeatable. In time, however, the tide began to turn. Polybius' explanation for this may not be reliable, but it is revealing of Rome's reputation for cultural and technological appropriation. In 261, the Greek historian tells us, the

Romans captured one of the Carthaginian quinqueremes, huge galleys with many banks of oars much larger and more powerful than their own old-fashioned triremes. They then used it as a model to build a new and more effective Roman fleet, updating the design whenever they caught new Carthaginian ships, until twenty years later the loss of a sea battle off Sicily forced the Carthaginians to sue for peace.[27]

Rome had learned other lessons from Carthage too, as we see in the treaty that ended the war. It was drafted at Rome this time, but it was still modeled on the old treaties proposed by Carthage in traditional west Asian terms. The first pact between the cities in 509 BCE had begun, "There shall be friendship between the Romans and the allies of the Romans and the Carthaginians and the allies of the Carthaginians on these terms . . ." while the 241 treaty draft starts, "There shall be friendship between the Carthaginians and Romans on the following terms . . ."[28]

In the text of this later treaty Carthage agrees to pay Rome a large sum in war reparations and to give up western Sicily, which then became Rome's own first overseas province. Four years later Rome exploited a revolt against Carthage in Sardinia to seize that island as well.[29]

The Romans also borrowed old strategies to rule their new provinces. Instead of simply demanding obedience and collaboration from nominal "allies" in western Sicily, as they had in Italy, they began to collect the same taxes as Carthage had before them. In return Sicilians were allowed to keep their own land and govern their own cities, saving Romans the job. When they defeated King Hieron of Syracuse in 215, bringing the entire island of Sicily into their possession, the Romans once again maintained the existing taxation regime, charging their new subjects a tithe of their crops, before apparently transplanting Hieron's tax system to Sardinia, another crucial breadbasket for the capital where a tithe could efficiently deliver the grain Rome required.[30]

By then a second Punic War had broken out over an Iberian city under siege from a young Carthaginian commander called Hannibal.[31] In 218 BCE Hannibal took the war to Italy with a remarkable march east over the Alps.[32] He even brought a troop of elephants through a high pass, animals that Carthage seems to have recruited to its army after the encounter with Pyrrhus. They were probably sourced from now extinct north African populations in the Atlas Mountains, similar in size to forest elephants. With the support of Rome's disaffected Italian subjects Hannibal then efficiently defeated the Romans four times in a row as he marched south.

Rome meanwhile concentrated its fire on the Carthaginian commanders left in Iberia, employing local mercenaries there in the Carthaginian tradition.[33] By 206 BCE they had driven the Carthaginians out of the Iberian peninsula. Rome inherited the Carthaginian mines, and with them the peninsula's gold, silver, copper, tin, and iron, and established new Carthaginian-style provinces.

The theater of war shifted to Africa, where both sides recruited the cavalry of rival local kingdoms to their cause. Although Greek and Roman authors call these north Africans "Numidians," from the word for nomad, they were in fact settled farmers who had built fortified villages like Althiburos on narrow spurs of land as early as the tenth or ninth centuries BCE. They dwelled in many cases in towns of significant size, like Zama, Thugga, and Cirta, and they were led by talented, ambitious men.[34]

The struggle came to a head in 202 BCE on a battlefield near Numidian Zama, now in central Tunisia. Hannibal had returned to Africa, and he commanded eighty elephants. By now however the Romans had learned these animals' ways. They scared the elephants with trumpets, prompting some of the beasts to turn in panic on their own troops and others to stampede toward their Roman tormentors who simply opened up corridors in their ranks to let them through.

Fighting on home turf, the Carthaginians still had the strongest infantry—almost twice as many men—but Rome's Numidian ally Massinissa commanded a cavalry force that easily overcame the Carthaginian horse. It then turned around to attack Hannibal's flanks and rear, routing the Carthaginian army completely. The final death toll is supposed to have been 1,500 on the Roman side and 20,000 on the Carthaginian, with almost as many prisoners taken too.

Rome demanded enormous reparations from Carthage: 10,000 silver talents (260,000 kilos), to be paid over fifty years.[35] The fine was designed to cripple the African city for two generations. The Carthaginians were allowed to keep a small local territory in Africa, but had to hand much of their land over to Massinissa. They also had to give up all but ten of their war vessels and to watch them being burned at sea. From now on they were forbidden to make war without Roman consent, even in their own defense.

The Romans themselves had developed a taste for conquest, and Polybius credits his fellow Greeks with the gift of foresight in this regard. In 217 BCE a peace conference was held to end a war between the current king of Macedon, Philip V, who still controlled most of Greece, and the rebel Greek states of Aetolia, Elis, and Sparta. Imagining this event decades later, Polybius gives the Aetolian ambassador a speech full of foreboding as he begs the Greeks to band together against external threats, which now come from a new direction: "If you allow the clouds now gathering in the west to settle on Greece, I fear greatly that we shall find the power to make truces and wars and all the other games we play with each other taken entirely away from us."[36]

The stakes were higher than anyone realized at the time, and for reasons outside their control. The Battle of Zama took place near the beginning of what is now often called the "Roman Climate Optimum," or, more informally, the "Roman Warm Period." From circa 250 BCE to circa 150 CE the Mediterranean and neighboring lands enjoyed unusually warm and stable weather, with reliable rainfall and temperatures similar to those recorded for the period 1880–1960 CE.[37]

We have learned a great deal about the ancient climate in recent years, a side effect of greater scientific interest in climate change in general.[38] Of course we don't have for antiquity the absolute measurements of temperature, rainfall, and so on that exist for the modern era. We can however use so-called proxy data from sources such as ice cores, lake sediment, and tree rings. We know what these proxies look like in periods for which we also have hard data, and that gives us the information we need to interpret them when they are all we have.

In this case the main evidence for climate change comes from a reduction in the number of "cosmogenic" isotopes like carbon-14. These are formed in the atmosphere by cosmic rays from outside the solar system and then deposited in trees and ice. The more solar activity (such as sunspots), the less energy there is in cosmic rays. So smaller deposits of the related isotopes reveal periods of higher solar activity and the warmer weather that comes with it. At the same time trees from northern Europe and the Alps up to 2,400 years old record in wide rings a warm and wet "plateau" in this era. This doesn't of course explain Rome's triumph over Carthage or indeed Greece—but it does help us to understand why the Roman empire then prospered for so long.

Until now, few Greeks had taken any notice of the Romans, a lack of interest that was not reciprocated. Looking back in the first century BCE the Roman poet Horace famously claimed that "captive Greece captured her savage conqueror, and introduced the arts to rustic Latium," but the turn to Greek culture at Rome happened some time before the Roman conquest of Greece itself.[39] It was the product not of Greek but of Punic wars: it can't be a coincidence that Romans began to watch Greek-style plays at their religious festivals and funerary games in 240 BCE, the year after their first victory against Carthage.[40]

Before this, Roman audiences had preferred improvised shows based on mime, farce, and striptease to the scripted tragedy and comedy pioneered in fifth-century Athens. Now however their new status as a Mediterranean power prompted a quest for new cultural cues that itself produced the first Latin literature, in the form of translations from Greek epic and drama, and the first history of Rome, written in Greek by a senator named Fabius Pictor.[41]

Roman culture benefited from foreign wars in multiple ways. Senators may have enjoyed showing off their linguistic skills, but many of those who wrote in Latin were enslaved. The first Latin playwright was Livius Andronicus, who also translated the *Odyssey* from Greek, and was said to have been captured from Tarentum. The Latin "Livius" would have been his Roman master's name. The Greek "Andronicus" might have been his own, although Romans often gave their slaves

Greek names no matter where they were from, revealing what Romans really thought of contemporary Greeks.

Sometimes nicknames pointed to other origins: one comic playwright writing in the early second century BCE was known as Terentius Afer, "the African." According to his later biographer Suetonius, he was born at Carthage before being enslaved at Rome to one Terentius, who had him educated like a free person (presumably in both Greek and Latin) before giving him his freedom because of his talent and beauty.[42] The man we now call Terence may have paid dearly for the privilege.

Rome's cultural turn to the east involved art and architecture too. Third-century Italian temples look increasingly similar to Greek ones, and the same is true of the gods themselves: this is when the familiar Greek "pantheon" or family of gods finally arrives in Rome, a concept in itself quite alien to central Italian traditions, and a number of old Roman gods acquire the distinctive characteristics of Greek counterparts.[43] These new notions weren't universally popular. Cicero could still imagine a Roman statesman in the 70s BCE urging his peers to reject the use of Greek myths about the gods and their origins because they are distorting traditional Roman religion.[44]

Their gods did not protect Greeks from Rome's imperial ambition. Three years after the Aetolian ambassador's speech Roman forces crossed the Adriatic to confront Philip himself after discovering evidence of an alliance between Carthage and Macedon. Almost a decade followed of ill-tempered skirmishing in which the Greek cities and leagues nervously picked sides. It was only after the Second Punic War ended, however, that the Romans could turn their full attention to matters farther east. In 197 BCE they decisively defeated Macedon with technology borrowed from their own Iberian mercenaries, in particular the double-edged "Spanish sword," which was useful for thrusting as well as cutting in close combat.[45]

The Roman conquest of western Asia was as swift as Alexander's. The Seleucid kingdom was already weakened by the loss of territory to the east: in the mid-third century the governor of Bactria had declared independence, and his counterpart in Parthia soon followed suit. It could not cope with a new threat from the west as well. In 191 BCE Rome declared war on King Antiochus, cowing him into an unequal peace three years later, and forcing him to yield his territory west of the Taurus Mountains to Rome's allies.

It wasn't enough. In 168 BCE the Roman general Aemilius Paullus defeated the popular new Macedonian king Perseus at the Battle of Pydna, and his kingdom was then split into four new "republics"; two decades later both Greece and Macedon would become Roman provinces in the old Carthaginian tradition. Paullus celebrated his victory with great games "in the Greek style" at the old Macedonian city of Amphipolis, with musical and theatrical performances as well as athletics and equestrian events. The Greeks were—Romans said—amazed by the sophistication of the staging.[46]

Paullus also deported about a thousand prominent Greeks to Italy, including Polybius. On the way home he sacked Epirus on suspicion of sympathy with Macedon and took 150,000 slaves.[47] Back at Rome the profits of empire meant that the government could abolish domestic taxation, and ensure future access to enslaved labor by establishing a "free port" on the island of Delos in 166 BCE. Strabo tells us that 10,000 captives a day could pass through the island's slave market, the largest in the eastern Mediterranean, giving rise to a saying: "Sail in, merchant, and unload: everything has been sold."[48]

It wasn't only people that Roman commanders brought back from overseas campaigns.[49] Artworks came too—painting, sculpture, even architectural fragments—and foreign technology. One shipwreck of the second century BCE off a small Greek island on the sailing route west contains the small box of bronze gears and axles now known as the "Antikythera mechanism." It has dials and instructions (in Greek) on the outside, and when operated by a crank handle it shows the motions of the sun, moon, and five planets, as well as a variety of calendars, solar, lunar, and astronomical, Mesopotamian, Egyptian and Greek, including the four-year cycle of the Olympic Games.[50]

Rome now controlled the eastern Mediterranean, with the Seleucid kingdom rendered weak and compliant, and the Ptolemies watching uneasily from Alexandria. Back west the stage was set for the final confrontation. The Carthaginians had come back strong from their defeat at Zama. After just ten years they offered to pay back the whole of the fifty-year fine: the Romans refused, and they must have been appalled.[51] No matter: the Carthaginians had other things to spend their money on, including a huge new port for the city's fleet with sheds for 170 ships.

Housing reached the top of the Byrsa Hill for the first time in this period as well: the roads there were still unpaved, and the drainage rudimentary, but these were smart homes, with rooms opening off a small central courtyard and in some cases featuring hip baths. In the wealthier quarters down by the sea wall, houses were enlarged and knocked together to make enormous compounds over a thousand square meters in size with peristyles, columns, and stucco decoration. By the 150s Carthage had a population of a quarter or even half a million people, and Polybius tells us that it was said to be the richest city in the world.[52]

When Carthage finally finished paying off its fine, however, the Romans had no further use for the city. Just a year later in 150 BCE a concrete pretext for action appeared. The frustrated Carthaginians had gone to the defense of one of their towns, which was under yet another Numidian attack. Massinissa won the battle, and then massacred the Carthaginian troops who surrendered, but it was the Carthaginians who were blamed for breaking their treaty with Rome. Perhaps they believed that with the full discharge of the indemnity they were also released from its conditions. In any case, they were surprised by news of incoming Roman warships and immediately sued for peace.[53]

The Romans now offered the Carthaginians an impossible choice: move sixteen kilometers inland from the sea, or fight to the death. They chose the latter, murdered the politicians who had argued for appeasement, freed their slaves to fight and turned the entire city, even the temples, into a giant weapons factory. Women were said to have donated their hair for catapult rope. The city held out for almost three years before the Romans sent out a new general to break their resistance.

Scipio Aemilianus was underage and inexperienced, but he quickly proved his worth, cutting Carthaginian supply lines on the land side, and building a mole across the entrance to the harbor to isolate the city from the sea. The harbor then provided a route into the city for the final assault in the spring of 146 BCE.[54]

There were three streets leading up to the top of the Byrsa Hill, where most of the city's inhabitants had taken refuge. They were closely packed with housing up to six stories high. As the Carthaginians rained down missiles from above, the Romans methodically seized the buildings and made their way onto the roofs, laying plank bridges between them so that they could fight their way up the hill over the houses themselves as well as at ground level. They killed everyone in their path, hurling the bodies into the streets below, and when they reached the top they set fire to the buildings there.

Cleaning parties constantly cleared the debris from the soldiers' path with mattocks and boat hooks, sweeping the burning bodies dead and alive into mass graves and ditches, ignoring the cries of their victims. The later historian Appian of Alexandria says that some of them were thrown in headfirst, and that their legs still writhed for a long time. Those who fell feet first had their skulls crushed by the Roman cavalry rushing overhead. Scipio had to rotate his men to keep them fresh, and so that the horror of what they were doing did not drive them mad, rendering them useless for further shifts.

After six days the elders of the city surrendered, and 50,000 people left for slavery, many in Rome itself.[55] Carthage was completely destroyed. Scipio brought his old friend and tutor Polybius with him to witness the city's last stand, and Polybius tells us that the Roman general wept at the sight of Carthage burning—not for Carthage itself, but because he feared that Rome would one day meet the same fate.[56] Although the story that the Romans salted the site was invented in the nineteenth century, the marks of fire are still visible on the stumps of the houses preserved under the massive foundations of the later Roman city.[57]

The land around Carthage became Rome's first province in Africa, where the Romans once again borrowed the existing Carthaginian tax system.[58] The rest of Carthage's territory went to African cities that had defected to Rome, and to the kings of Numidia, who also inherited Carthage's library. The Romans kept back one work by the agricultural writer Mago, to be translated into Latin by a team headed by a bilingual senator: they knew they still had things to learn from their old enemy.[59] As Rome confronted Carthage, conquered Greece, and built an empire on the ideas and traditions of their new subjects, they took the strategies of imperial appropriation that we have already seen in Persia and the Hellenistic kingdoms to new heights.

The modern scholars who refought the Punic Wars were wrong. Carthage and Rome were not as different as they thought. Both were imperial powers on land and sea with extensive commercial interests. They were sibling rivals, and like siblings the younger learned from the older. Doing so opened up ever larger horizons of power, until Rome copied Carthage to death.

Over time the English themselves embraced the maritime example set by the Dutch United Provinces, until they had outstripped their neighbors across the North Sea. Eighteenth-century Britons now presented themselves as Carthaginians, ruling the waves by skill and trade, and their new enemy France as an old-fashioned territorial empire in the Roman style, outfoxed by the masters of the sea. French views on "perfidious Albion" were naturally different: as the parliamentarian Paul Gauran put it in 1798, "*Que Carthage soit détruite.*"[60]

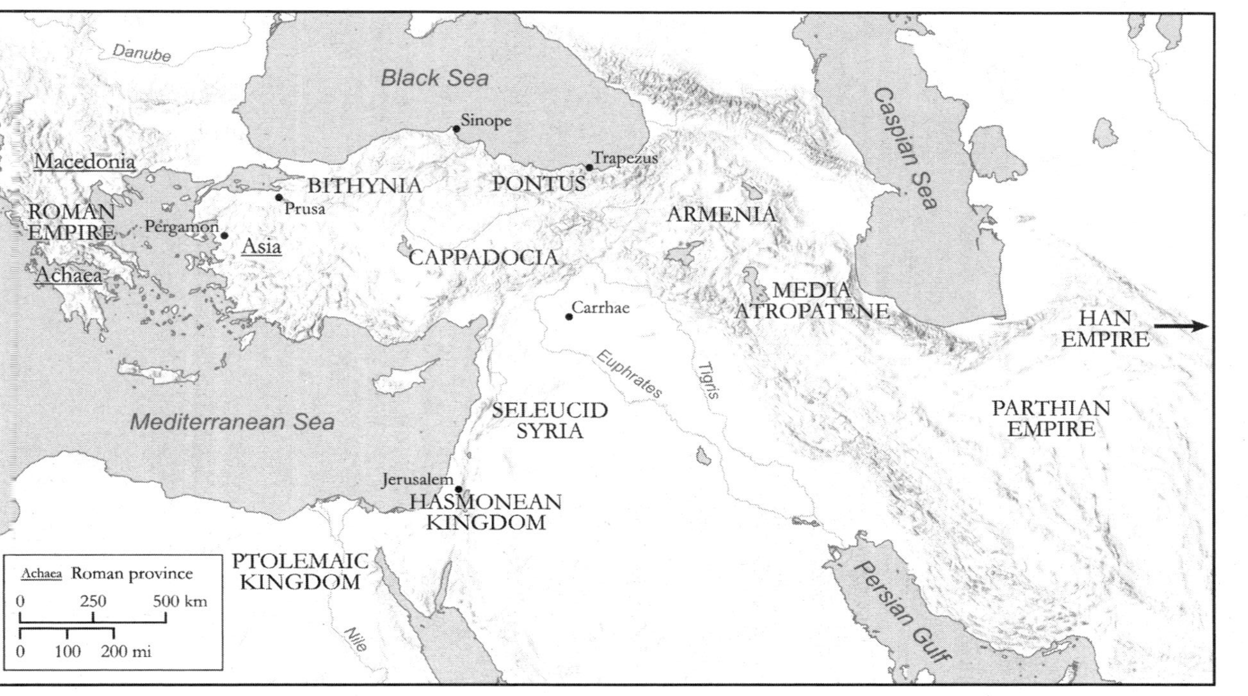

The world between Parthia and Rome in the first century BCE

CHAPTER NINETEEN

Fighting for Freedom

CRIMEA, 67 BCE

In 1770 a new opera premiered in Milan. It was about Mithridates VI, Rome's most dangerous enemy after the destruction of Carthage. *Mitridate, re di Ponto* starts at the end of the story. Mitridate is an old man. He has been on the throne of the kingdom of Pontus on the Black Sea in what is now northeastern Turkey for almost sixty years, and he has just suffered a comprehensive defeat at Roman hands. His two sons are waiting for him at the Crimean port of Nymphaion, as is his fiancée Aspasia, with whom both sons are in love. They take the news of their father's suspected death as an opportunity to make their cases to her. Farnace, a Roman sympathizer, is more forceful. Sifare, loyal to his father at least when it came to the war, is more successful.

Then unexpected trouble arrives: Mitridate himself, with Ismene, a princess from nearby Parthia that he has brought as a bride for Farnace—who refuses her. Ismene loves Farnace, Farnace loves Aspasia, Aspasia loves Sifare who loves her back, but feels it his duty to his father that they part. When Mitridate discovers the extent of his sons' personal and political betrayals he condemns all concerned to death. These emotional complications are however put on hold when Roman troops besiege the town. Mitridate returns to battle, joined by Sifare and eventually by Farnace too; after another defeat he forgives his family, blesses the marriage of Aspasia and Sifare, witnesses Farnace's agreement to marry Ismene, and commits suicide. The survivors join in song to declare their determination to fight Rome for freedom.

The opera is rarely performed these days. It's long—four hours or so—and the arias are tough. Three of the seven roles were written for castrati. The music can be stunning though, and the Austrian composer can be forgiven for demanding a lot from his performers and his audience: Mozart was fourteen years old when he wrote his second full-length opera in the grand Italian style.

At the time Mithridates' reign was a popular subject for performances of all kinds. Mozart's Italian opera was only one of eighteen composed on the topic, and it was adapted from a French play by Jean Racine that had been performed at Versailles in 1674 for Louis XIV. The Sun King was a great admirer of the Pontic monarch.[1]

That Mithridates of Pontus and his neighbors in Bithynia, Cappadocia, and Armenia are no longer household names is due not only to the narrow focus of "ancient" history today on the Greco-Roman world, but also to the sources we have for these kings. Their stories do not survive in the works of the canonical Classical authors that have formed the basis since the late eighteenth century of a curriculum designed to teach wealthy young men (for the most part) how to read and write "good" Greek and Latin prose.[2] Instead, we owe them to longer, later, messier, and often much funnier works of history and biography that were widely read in translation for centuries before the invention of classics consigned them to the margins.

Greek and Roman authors had wider horizons than many of their modern students, and these stories illuminate the world in which Rome now operated as it extended its territorial empire beyond the Mediterranean, first to the east and then to the west. They also highlight the disadvantages of an increasingly connected world, especially for the less powerful, which is visible above all in the level of resistance to Roman conquest in the first century BCE.

. . .

On a map the kingdom of Pontus looks seriously remote, located on the southern fringes of the Black Sea and made up for the most part of mountains. Look a little closer, though, and you begin to see the rich fields and pastureland, the Greek trading posts on the coast, the mines in the mountains producing iron, copper, silver, alum, and salt. And then of course there is the sea itself, a whirlpool of contacts from the earliest human times between mountains and steppe, fishers and farmers.

Pontus emerged from the embers of the Persian empire in the aftermath of Alexander's conquests. As Seleucid power in the region later declined, the kingdom grew slowly but surely under kings called Mithridates, which in Old Persian meant "Sent by Mithra," the Iranian sun god.[3]

Mithridates V (r. 152/1–120 BCE) was the first to ally with Rome, dispatching ships and troops to aid the offensive against Carthage in the 140s and then sending support against rebels in Greece in the 130s.[4] In 120 BCE he was assassinated by poison, his mother took over as regent, and his eldest son went into hiding.[5] The young man returned about five years later to claim his throne as Mithridates VI, and he quickly extended his writ around the northern shores of the Black Sea as far as the Bosphorus Strait.

This Mithridates embraced the complexities of his realm, and was said to have spoken all twenty-two of his subjects' languages.[6] He also constructed a complex personal legend, tracing his descent from the Achaemenid monarchs Cyrus and Darius as well as from Alexander the Great.[7] He wore the clothes of a Persian king, but modeled his coin portrait on Alexander's and dated his reign according to a "Bosphoran Era" that had started in 297 BCE.

His kingdom was sandwiched between Rome and its only real rival for world power. Parthia had been a remote northeastern region of the Persian and then Seleucid empires, east of the Caspian Sea in what is now northern Iran. This was a harsh land of snow-capped mountains, hot plains, and thick forest. As the Seleucids lost control of their eastern provinces in the mid-third century BCE, a warlord named Arsaces conquered the satrapy of Parthia and declared himself king. He quickly expanded his new territory to the west, defeating the Seleucid king himself in battle and declaring a new "Arsacid Era" in Parthia, on the model of the existing Seleucid Era but beginning in 247 BCE.[8]

As Rome squeezed the Seleucids from the west in the second century, so Parthia did the same from the east. The Arsacids took control of Media and the Iranian Plateau south of the Caspian Sea, and in the early 130s they acquired Babylonia as well. They built a new capital at Ctesiphon, an old Seleucid army camp on the Tigris, where they liked to spend the winter.

We know very little about Parthians from their own point of view. There are no Parthian books, inscriptions, or archives; only their coinage remains, found as far away as India and Russia.[9] Greek and Roman authors tell us that they specialized in riding and breeding horses, so much so, claims one Roman historian, that free Parthian men never walked anywhere.[10] Others note that their heavily armed cavalry, the "cataphracts," were covered like their horses in armor, while the party trick of their lightly armed riders was the "Parthian shot"—shooting backward from horseback while in apparent flight.[11]

For the first time however we also have a Chinese source, a record of the first mission sent west by the Han dynasty that had ruled China since the late third century. Emperor Wu (r. 140–87 BCE) had strategic motives for this expedition. To the north of his realm in what is now Mongolia, semi-nomadic people called the Xiongnu had created an empire of shepherds and farmers. They had been mounting successful campaigns against China for decades, reducing it at times to a vassal and forcing the Han to pay an annual tribute.[12] In addition to building defensive walls across vast distances—a Chinese specialty since the seventh century BCE—Wu needed allies among the Steppe peoples to create a buffer against them.

That was the commission he gave the diplomat Zhang Qian in 138 BCE: to seek support from the Yuezhi, who had themselves been displaced west by the Xiongnu to the Ferghana Valley in modern Tajikistan.[13] This involved a long journey along the flat Gansu "corridor" that leads west out of China for 800 kilometers, and then around the Taklamakan Desert. The expedition almost ended in disaster right at the start when the Xiongnu captured Zhang Qian and held him hostage for ten years. He managed to get away, with a Xiongnu wife and son, and carried on until he reached the Yuezhi but he was unsuccessful in his diplomatic mission: the Xiongnu had used the skull of the last Yuezhi king as a drinking cup, and his son was less interested in revenge than in a peaceful life.

When Zhang Qian returned to China around 126 BCE, via another period in Xiongnu custody, he was able to report in detail on the routes west through the Tarim Basin and the peoples he had heard of beyond. He describes Parthia (Anxi in Chinese) as a large and populous farming country with hundreds of walled cities, whose traders regularly go long distances beyond their borders by cart or boat. "The coins of the country are made of silver and bear the face of the king. When the king dies, the currency is immediately changed and new coins issued with the face of his successor. The people keep records by writing horizontally on strips of leather."[14]

Wu followed up by occupying the Gansu corridor and sending a formal delegation to Parthia to request friendship. The Parthian king gave these Chinese ambassadors a grand welcome on his eastern frontier, accompanied by 20,000 cavalry, and sent them home with gifts for the emperor of ostrich eggs and conjurers. These exchanges led to a lucrative trading relationship between the two great Asian empires, with Chinese goods exchanged above all for Parthian horses.

By the 90s BCE the Parthians controlled Armenia, an old Persian satrapy that had broken away in 321 BCE to form an independent kingdom. They installed a puppet king there called Tigranes. This brought the Parthian sphere cheek to cheek with the kingdom of Pontus.

The first Roman to engage with the kings of both Parthia and Pontus, around 95 BCE, was a general called Sulla. His main business in the area lay with Mithridates of Pontus, and in persuading him to withdraw his increasing interest in the monarchy of Cappadocia to the south of his realm in the interests of the incumbent, an ally of Rome.[15] The king of Parthia—another Mithridates, an unhelpfully popular name in the region—took the opportunity to send an envoy to the Roman commander to make an alliance. Sulla offended the Parthians by sitting between their ambassador and the Roman client king of Cappadocia. This accorded the two men equal respect, and assumed more for Sulla himself. As a reward for enduring this humiliation the Parthian envoy was executed on his return home.[16]

Parthia still seems to have honored its side of the bargain, with the king refusing to get involved in subsequent Roman altercations with Pontus: it may be that the Romans were doing him a favor by keeping the other Mithridates distracted.[17] The king of Pontus meanwhile planned for war.[18] First he deposed the Roman client who ruled the Black Sea kingdom of Bithynia to his west, before setting his sights on the new Roman province of "Asia": the old kingdom of the Attalids based at Pergamon in western Anatolia, bequeathed to Rome by the dynasty's last king in 133 BCE.*

This generous gift had given Rome lucrative trade routes running east across Anatolia as well as the riches of the Attalid treasury and new subjects to tax. Rome farmed these taxes at arm's length, through businessmen who bid for contracts from the Roman senate, competing to offer the highest returns. It was a recipe for exploitation, and Asia quickly became Rome's most lucrative province.[19] It also attracted settlers from Italy and Rome itself—think Algeria under French occupation. They included not only the wealthy tax collectors and bankers who oversaw the transfer of Anatolian resources into Roman hands, but merchants, shopkeepers, lawyers, and of course slave traders.

A generation later the local population, including the Greek-speaking inhabitants of the old Ionian cities, were impoverished and angry. When Mithridates sought allies against Rome they not only defected to him en masse but eagerly obeyed his command to kill all the Romans and other Italians resident in the province.[20] Their bodies were to remain unburied and their goods to be split between the killers and King Mithridates.[21]

On a single day in the spring of 88 BCE Rome's Anatolian subjects

*Like the small province of "Africa" established around Carthage thirteen years earlier, the name betrays the way in which the primary meaning of these continental labels was still limited in the Roman imagination to small regions on their Mediterranean borders.

slaughtered every Roman or Italian man, woman, and child they could find, offering clemency to their slaves if they betrayed or killed their masters. It wasn't just the individuals they resented but the institutional power they represented: the killers tore down Roman statues and inscriptions too.

Credible ancient reports tell us that 80,000 people lost their lives. The sudden cutoff of the repayments they owed to bankers and investors in Rome itself caused a credit crunch in the capital that was still proverbial a generation later.[22] Mithridates swept through Anatolia and occupied the ancient city of Pergamon itself, before continuing west to Roman Greece where his troops were welcomed into Athens. The Roman fleet in the Black Sea, which was manned by Greeks, went over to him too.[23]

In 87 BCE five Roman legions arrived in Greece with Mithridates' old acquaintance Sulla at their head. They besieged and recaptured Athens, cutting down sacred groves in the city and seizing temple treasures, before defeating Mithridates' troops in central Greece. Sulla then followed the king back to Asia and in 85 forced him to agree to peace terms. These were surprisingly generous: Sulla was keen to conclude the business quickly as he was embroiled in a civil war with other Roman commanders at the time. In return for surrendering his most recent conquests in Anatolia and Greece and providing Sulla with money and supplies, Mithridates retained his original territory, obtained immunity for his supporters, and was recognized as a Roman ally.

Skirmishing still continued between Pontus and Rome over the next two decades, and in the end it took the greatest general of the late Roman Republic to defeat the king. An awkward man in civilian life, Gnaeus Pompeius—Pompey the Great—was a phenomenon in battle, on land or at sea. Now in 67 BCE he pushed Mithridates back into the Crimean redoubt memorialized in *Mitridate, re di Ponto.*

The internal intrigue Mozart depicted accorded with the facts, but there was in reality no final reconciliation. The king killed Xiphares (Sifare) not because he loved his father's fiancée but because his mother had surrendered a key fortress to the Romans, and Pharnaces (Farnace) led the armed revolt that ended his father's reign and life. After decades of taking small doses of poison to build up his immunity, Mithridates failed in his attempt to commit suicide. Instead he required a Gallic bodyguard to run him through with a sword.[24]

Pompey meanwhile put the last Seleucid king out of his misery, captured Jerusalem, and annexed Syria for Rome. In Anatolia he twinned Pontus and Bithynia as a single Roman province, and farther east, where direct rule was still more trouble than it was worth, he relieved Tigranes of the Armenian empire he had quietly extended to the Mediterranean, leaving him a rump kingdom as the reward for alliance with Rome.[25] This decision brought Roman forces face-to-face for the first time with the king of Parthia, who moved in to occupy part of the old Armenian territory. Pompey expelled him, making a show of force east of the Euphrates, but the two sides carefully avoided direct engagement.[26]

After Pompey returned from the east, however, another general sought glory there. Marcus Crassus was the richest man in Rome, fond of flattery and less famous for his military valor or experience than for his invention of a for-profit fire brigade: if your house was on fire, Crassus' men would put it out—but only if you agreed to sell it to him first.[27] Crassus and Pompey had served as consuls together in 70 BCE and did so again in 55. They despised each other with a mutual loathing that was restrained only by their alliance with a third man, Julius Caesar, in an unofficial triumvirate that controlled Roman politics in the 50s BCE.

When Crassus was made governor of Syria after his second consulship, he saw an opportunity to go one better than his great rival and defeat a greater eastern kingdom than Pontus. Without permission from the senate, or any provocation from Parthia itself, Crassus led Roman legions across the Euphrates against the stellar Parthian horsemen. The campaign was a disaster: despite commanding far greater numbers, Crassus was trapped at Carrhae near modern Urfa in southern Turkey in 53 BCE. He lost the Roman standards, or military banners, along with 20,000 men. Another 10,000 were sold into Parthian slavery, where they remained for more than thirty years.

Crassus himself was among the dead. According to one legend the Parthians filled his greedy mouth with gold; in another account the Parthian king presented his head to the king of Armenia at a banquet.[28] Either way, the Parthians and Armenians cemented a new anti-Roman alliance in the east, while back at Rome the death of Crassus pitted Caesar and Pompey against each other in a struggle that would end the republic.

Unlike Crassus, who came from a wealthy but "plebeian" or non-aristocratic Roman background, or Pompey, who had grown up in the Italian Marches in a family new to Roman politics, Julius Caesar was one of the few remaining "patrician" Romans, who traced their lineage back to the city's first senators. His political career was assured by his family background, but high office less so—especially as he was notoriously bad with money, good at making enemies, and morally suspect after a widely rumored affair with the king of Bithynia.

He was however the only man who could persuade Pompey and Crassus to work together, and with their joint support he was elected consul for 59 BCE. Predictably enough Caesar antagonized his co-consul, who retired to his house to "watch for omens"—making all state business carried out in his absence illegal. Caesar continued to conduct it nonetheless. He came to regret this bold disregard for religious law when his consular term ended, and his political immunity with it.

Now he faced prosecution as a private citizen that could end his career. Instead, his friends arranged for him to leave town for a command over Rome's holdings north of the Alps.

By this time the Romans had destroyed their competitors in an east–west strip from the Euphrates to the Atlantic, but most of northern Europe still lay beyond their power and even knowledge. Caesar's new province, the first in Gaul, had emerged only in the late second century BCE in a typical example of Roman alliance turned annexation.

Until then, the main power in this region was Massalia. Reports of the city from this era do not match most people's idea of an ancient Greek city-state.[29] It was run by a council of 600 wealthy men appointed for life. To be eligible you needed to have had Massaliot citizenship for three generations, and you needed to have children. Civic laws were austere: theater in bad taste was banned, and the sword that had been used to execute criminals since the foundation of the city was kept in use for centuries despite its rust. By contrast, suicide by hemlock was free on justified application to the 600. The Massaliots were also notoriously suspicious of foreigners, who according to the same authors had to give up their weapons on arrival in the city.

They were still curious about their world. The first surviving account of the Atlantic coast of Europe describes the voyages of the Massaliot Pytheas, who sailed up the coast of France in the fourth century BCE as far as Britain, and then claims to have circumnavigated the island.[30] We should believe him: he reports plausible measurements of the relative height of the sun on the isles of Man and Lewis. He also describes reaching an amber-trading island off Jutland (Heligoland?) and an island called Thule six days' journey north of Britain, probably Iceland.[31] One day farther north was a frozen ocean, in which he said "there was not land per se nor sea nor air, but a sort of mixture of all three of the consistency of a jellyfish": a phenomenon that is in fact encountered in the Arctic Circle when freezing fog descends on sludgy ice.[32]

Massalia had supported Rome's cause during the Second Punic War and become an important trading partner. Under attack from the local Salluvii in 125, it made sense for the Massaliots to appeal to Rome for help. As usual, however, the Romans outstayed their welcome, founding a settler colony at Narbo (Narbonne), building a road to connect Italy to their holdings in Iberia and appropriating the whole coastal strip around it, the region still called Provence.

It was only as Roman interest in this area increased that the local Gauls began to write their own language down in the Greek alphabet.[33*] By the early first century CE the city of Massalia was in the words of the

*The names Keltoi and Galatai, used more or less interchangeably in Greek sources for continental Europeans, are external labels: we do not know what, if anything, these people called themselves. They are at least ancient labels; by contrast the modern usage of the term "Celt" to refer to the indigenous population of Ireland and Britain has no ancient source at all, going back instead to a decision made in the early eighteenth century by the Welsh linguistics scholar Edward Lhuyd to call the related languages of those islands and Brittany "Celtic."

Greek geographer Strabo "a school for the barbarians," where Gauls and even Romans went to study Greek literature and law.[34] Greek was now a language not of foreign power in the region but of potential resistance to it.

Farther north, free or "Hairy" Gaul was of interest to Romans largely as a source of enslaved labor. The wealthy Hallstatt graves had disappeared in the fifth century BCE, along with the settlements around them. New communities that emerged in central regions in the second century BCE began to build fortified settlements located near major roads or rivers and mines. These oppida, as Caesar called them, didn't look quite like the towns of the Mediterranean, or rival them for size, but they performed the same functions: they had workshops, mints, government institutions, sanctuaries, and markets.[35]

The Italian wine amphoras that pile up in these settlements from the later second century BCE reveal the extent of trade with Roman merchants farther south.[36]* Diodorus tells us that the Gauls were so fond of wine—which they were unable to grow in their cold climate—that the Italian merchants who now supplied it by boat and wagon could get a slave for every jar.[37] By contrast, Gaul north of the Massif Central becomes emptier in this era from an archaeological perspective, probably because so many of its people were being kidnapped and sold south to the markets of the Roman province.[38]

Farther east were people Caesar calls Germans, quarrelsome and land hungry. It was to get away from these difficult neighbors that in 58 BCE a large group called the Helvetii decided to leave their homeland in a mountainous region north of Lake Geneva to find a new home in free Gaul to the west. To strengthen their resolve they burned their twelve towns and 400 villages before they set off. Unfortunately for the Helvetii, the new governor of the Roman province that lay on their fastest route west objected to their plan.

Caesar continued to object even when the Helvetii changed their

*The archaeological evidence for the cargoes suggests that the Gallic preference was for red wine and that, although Italians preferred white, Italian businessmen were happy to cater to this demand (Elizabeth B. Fentress, "The Domitii Ahenobarbi and tribal slaving in Gaul," in Mirco Modolo et al., eds., *Una lezione di archeologia globale: studi in onore di Daniele Manacorda,* Bari: Edipuglia, 2019, 152).

route to avoid Roman territory, gathering useful accusations of plunder and destruction from nearby Roman allies that gave him an excuse to pursue them anyway. Like Crassus in Syria, he sought no senatorial authorization for the extension of his mission beyond the Roman border. Instead, he raised legions on his own initiative and with his own funds. After several brutal military encounters, he forced the Helvetii back to their destroyed homes as Roman subjects. More than 350,000 Helvetians had set out west. Just 110,000 returned.[39]

This was the first act in what became Caesar's private mission to conquer free Gaul, and it set the pattern for the next eight years as he extended the Roman empire to the North Sea. The story is preserved in the annual reports Caesar himself made to Rome. "Gaul, if you take all of it into account, is divided into three regions," he begins, and the campaigns he describes can be divided into three phases. In the first three years he conquered central France, the Belgian lowlands, and the peoples on the shores of the Atlantic. From 55 to 53 BCE he turned his attention to groups across the Rhine and the Channel, with even more ferocity but less success.* This gave the Gauls space to regroup and launch a series of rebellions that took Caesar three more years to suppress.

According to his own reports, Caesar acts only in response to credible threats to the Roman province or Rome's allies. He makes no attempt however to hide the brutality involved: military conscription for all male citizens made Romans unsentimental about human life. He describes with relish mass slaughter, destruction, deportation, and enslavement. In Belgium, he tells us, all but 500 of the 60,000 Nervii were killed in battle.[40] When he captured the capital of the Aduatuci, he sold the entire population of 53,000 as slaves in a single lot.[41] When some Germans came to ask him for a truce, he imprisoned them, stormed their camp, killed everyone who resisted, and then sent his cavalry out to kill the fleeing women and children. Some 300,000 died, and on news of the victory, the senate voted sacrifices of thanksgiving.[42]

*Caesar's campaigns in Britain in 55 and 54 BCE did yield booty and prisoners, and Caesar reported back to Rome on the peculiar inhabitants of the island who wore mustaches, tattooed themselves with woad, kept geese as pets, and practiced wife swapping (Caesar, *Gallic War* 4.33, 5.12–14).

Appian of Alexandria plausibly reports that Caesar fought more than 4 million Gauls, killed 1 million and took as many prisoner to sell into slavery.[43] For a long time however archaeologists found little sign of Caesar's activities on the ground. Perhaps the vast numbers of casualties were exaggerated, it was thought; perhaps the social effects were overblown. But recent work has produced gruesome confirmation of Caesar's own account.[44] Huge quantities of human remains have been recovered from battlefields in Belgium and Germany. Vast numbers of lead sling bullets litter the site of the Aduatuci fort of Thuin in Belgium, which was then completely deserted for more than 200 years. And pollen analysis has revealed a significant increase in woodlands from the mid-first century BCE in the region formerly occupied by the Eburones, suggesting a significant decrease in human activity.

Caesar made a large personal profit from the wars in Gaul, enough to keep his soldiers and his colleagues in Rome in line, and to fund building projects in the city that kept him in the public eye throughout the long absence that his legal troubles enforced.[45] At the end of the decade, however, with Crassus dead and Pompey estranged, Caesar's opponents in the senate declared him an enemy of the state.[46] If he was to save himself his only option was to cross the Rubicon, which marked the barrier between his province and Italy proper: a stream north of Rimini so unobtrusive that no one is now quite sure which one it actually is. And in January 49 BCE, that is what his army did.

Pompey headed the senatorial army that opposed him in a war that raged across the Roman empire. Caesar defeated Pompey's forces in Italy and Spain, and then Pompey himself in Greece in 48 BCE. Pompey thought of asking the Parthian king for help, but settled instead on an appeal to the ruler of Egypt, the thirteen year-old Ptolemy XIII. It was the wrong call. He was killed at an Egyptian harbor on the orders of the royal house, and his head was delivered to Caesar when he arrived three days later.

Caesar remained in Alexandria to arbitrate between the competing claims to the throne of Ptolemy himself and his twenty-one-year-old sister-wife Cleopatra. In the conflict between the pair the library suffered significant fire damage, the young king drowned in the Nile, and the queen allegedly had herself delivered to the Roman general through enemy lines wrapped in a sack.[47] However that may be, Caesar did not dispute paternity of her son Caesarion. He was born shortly before Caesar himself finally left the Egyptian capital for the Black Sea, where Mithridates' son Pharnaces was taking advantage of the general chaos to harvest territory from local Roman allies. It took Caesar five days to undo Pharnaces' patient work, a lightning campaign he later commemorated at Rome with the slogan *Veni, vidi, vici:* I came, I saw, I conquered.[48]

Caesar went on to defeat the remnants of Pompey's army and allies in Africa and Spain, where he showed that his brutal tactics were not reserved for barbarians: he built a siege wall out of the bodies and weapons of defeated Pompeians, topped by the heads of the enemy stuck on sword points.[49]

With no opponents left standing, Caesar was awarded a ten-year dictatorship to rule the Roman state—a standard resort in a state of emergency, but an office normally limited to a maximum of six months. He was good at it too, putting the Roman economy back on track with a combination of rent control, debt relief, public works, and settlement programs abroad that provided land and a living for veterans and the poor. He even found time to reorganize the calendar in 46 BCE, replacing the existing 355-day year, which was close to lunar cycles but constantly fell behind the seasons, with a 365-day one closer to the solar year, and adding leap years to bring it closer still.*

As ever, Caesar pushed his luck too far. In February of 44 BCE he accepted a dictatorship for life, and divine honors too, including a priest

*After some immediate rejigging to sort out how best to count leap years, this system worked well for a millennium and a half. It gained only one day every 128 years, because the solar year is not in fact 365.23 but 365.2425 days long. It was only in 1582 that Pope Gregory finally changed the rules, with Easter falling a worrying ten days "late": the Gregorian calendar misses out leap years that fall in years divisible by 100, but not 400—so the year 2000 was a leap year, but 2100 will not be. Protestant countries stuck with Caesar's system for a long time—Britain only changed over in 1752, Sweden in 1753—and the Julian calendar is still used in much of the Orthodox Church, as well as by a number of communities in the Maghreb.

to manage his own cult.[50] Worst of all, he refused to recognize the equal dignity of Roman senators, choosing to remain seated as they approached. On the ides of March—the 15th of the month—a large group of them stabbed him to death.

Julius Caesar's assassins may have hoped for a return to collective senatorial rule, but instead they got thirteen more years of civil war, as the dictator's seventeen-year-old great-nephew Octavian fought for power with Caesar's henchman Mark Antony, a brilliant general and enthusiastic sybarite, whose emulation of his old friend and mentor encompassed a liaison with the queen of Egypt lasting over a decade that produced several children and a formidable military alliance.

Cleopatra kept Egypt independent of Rome for more than two decades, but in 31 BCE Octavian finally defeated the queen and her lover at the naval battle of Actium. The following year Cleopatra and Antony committed suicide, and Octavian annexed Egypt as a Roman province, making the Mediterranean a Roman pond.

Octavian's attempts to extend Roman power up the Nile were defeated by a one-eyed queen of Kush (Roman Nubia), and the eastern border remained the Euphrates.* In Europe, however, he extended Roman control over the whole of the Iberian peninsula and took the northern border to the Danube. Instead of returning Rome to its republican roots, Caesar's assassins had ushered it into an even bigger world.

*Strabo, who had traveled in Egypt, calls her "Kandake," but this is a generic local title for the mother of the heir to the throne (Strabo 17.1.54; cf. Dio 54.5.4; Acts 8:26–40). She was probably the queen known from Kushite inscriptions as Amanirenas, the first woman to be called *qore*, or monarch. After Augustus' failed campaign, female monarchs ruled at the Kushite capital of Meroë for at least another generation (*EAH*, "Kings of Kush").

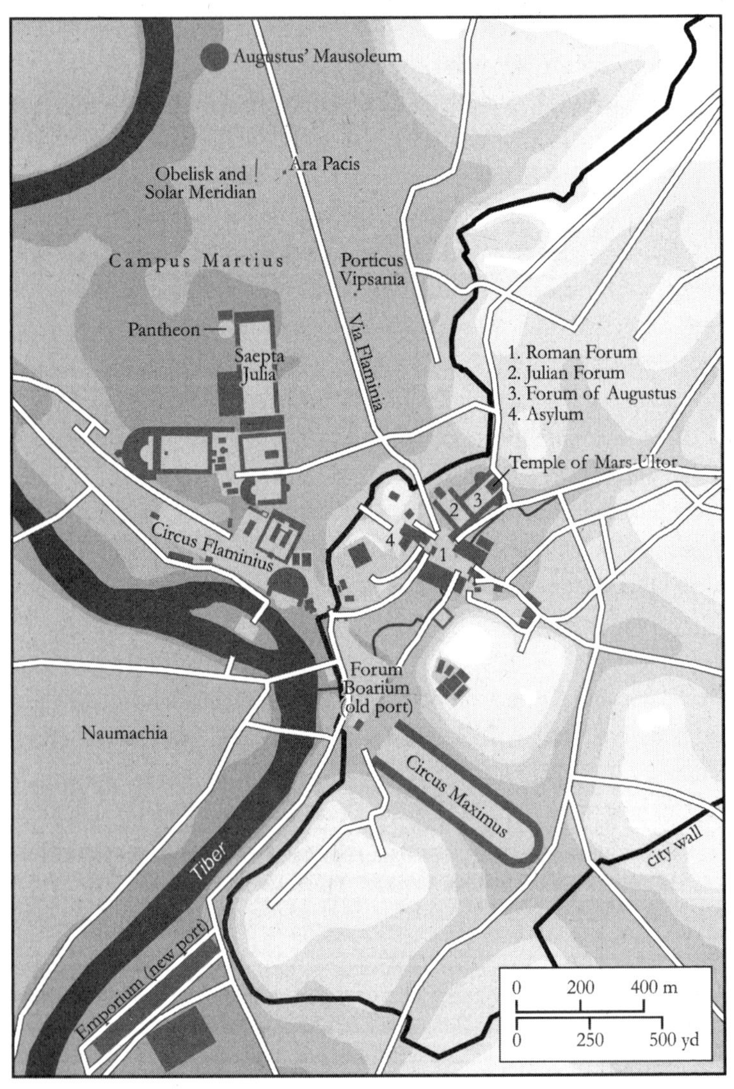

The city of Rome in 2 BCE

CHAPTER TWENTY

Rome, Open City

FORUM OF AUGUSTUS, 2 BCE

For a decade after Actium, Octavian consolidated his unelected and unofficial position as ruler of Rome. Rather like Muammar Gaddafi in Libya, his authority was largely informal. Over time, he resigned from or rejected all the grand offices of state, retaining only the political powers of a "tribune of the plebs"—a symbolic gesture, but one that also allowed him to propose and veto legislation in the name of the Roman people while the cogs of the old republic continued to grind.[1]

He was known by a variety of titles, but most often as the *princeps,* or "first man."* In 27 BCE he accepted a new name from the senate: Augustus, "the consecrated one," which would become what Romans called their rulers for centuries.[2] Another possibility that the senators consid-

*The Roman "emperor" is a modern invention, with misleading connotations of formal power. It is confusing too, giving us two different "Roman empires," one the actual empire built up during the Roman republican period, the other a shorthand for the period of monarchic government that followed it. In antiquity Augustus and his successors never used the military honorific *imperator* ("commander") to describe their political position, and the label *augustus* focused attention on the charisma of the individual, not the people he ruled. Strictly speaking I should refer throughout the rest of this book to the Roman "augustus," if to do so would not distract unnecessarily from the story I want to tell.

ered and discarded was "Romulus," after the city's legendary founder and first king. Kings were traditionally unpopular at Rome, and that one was a fratricide as well, but he still had his uses in Rome's unusually inclusive civic ideology.

A local story tracing the origins of Rome to twins called Romulus and Remus existed by the third century BCE.[3] According to the detailed version given by the historian Livy writing under Augustus, the boys were born to a princess of the Latin town of Alba Longa who had been condemned to life as a virgin priestess when her uncle usurped her father's throne.[4] Despite this precaution she became pregnant, on her own account by the god Mars. After the birth, her uncle had the infants left to drown at a spot where seven hills surrounded a crossing of the Tiber. There they were discovered by a she-wolf, who suckled them until they were found by the king's shepherd.

He and his wife raised the boys as herdsmen, but when Remus was jailed on a charge of cattle rustling he was recognized by his grandfather, the deposed king of Alba Longa. The truth out, the twins killed the usurper and reinstalled the rightful king before leaving to found their own settlement where they had once been left to die. They quarreled over the right to name and govern the new city, however, and in the fight Remus was killed.

Once he had eliminated his brother and built the walls of his city, Romulus still needed citizens. He created what Livy calls a sanctuary or "asylum" between the two peaks of the Capitoline Hill, where Michelangelo later designed the grand piazza between the wings of the Capitoline Museums.[5] There arrived a "great mob" from neighboring peoples, slave and free, and eager for "new things"—rarely a righteous impulse in the eyes of Roman authors—"and this was the first step on the way to greatness."[6]

The sequel is less uplifting. Romulus may have peopled his city with men, but to produce a new generation he needed women as well, and he acquired them by violence and deception.[7] His Sabine neighbors feared the growing city, and refused to allow intermarriage with the rabble he had gathered on the hills of Rome, so he invited them to a lavish festival. When they arrived with their families, the Romans seized the young women and took them home as wives.

The Sabines tried to rescue the girls of course, but despite his pastoral background Romulus proved an excellent general. After defeating his neighbors he generously allowed them to unite their communities with his own. Rome was the center of government, and the difference between this arrangement and straightforward subjection may have been as hard to define at the time as it is now.

According to this legend Rome was from the start a city built on the twin strengths of immigration and imperial conquest. And this fitted in with another popular story about the foundation of Rome that had appeared even earlier, locating Rome in the expanding imaginary world of the Trojan War and ascribing its foundation to Aeneas, prince of Troy.[8]

Long before the time of Augustus these two stories had merged together.[9] We can see one result in Rome's greatest epic, the *Aeneid*, written like Livy's work in the 20s BCE by Publius Vergilius Maro (Vergil), a poet from Mantua (Mantova) in what was then "Gaul this side of the Alps." The poem concentrates on the adventures of Aeneas, who in Vergil's tale escapes the sack of Troy with his son and his followers, sails the western Mediterranean looking for a new home and after abortive stops in Africa and Sicily eventually arrives on the shores of Italy. There he defeats one local king, marries the daughter of another, and founds a new city for his people to live in. He names it Lavinium after his new wife, and his son then founds Alba Longa, making Trojan Aeneas an ancestor of the local heroes Romulus and Remus.

Such stories tell us nothing about Rome's real beginnings, but they do reveal that later writers saw the city's origins as mixed, and Roman society as not only open to but dependent upon outsiders.[10] In the case of Aeneas the outsider is the founder. In the case of Romulus, it is the rest of the population.

These stories also help to explain the nature of Roman identity. Being "Roman" was never an ethnic concept, but one based on citizenship, which could be earned by service to the state—or, for the enslaved, to its citizens.[11] This approach was very different from that taken in fifth-century Athens, for instance, where outsiders were unwelcome in the citizen body. One relevant difference is that real power was always restricted at Rome to a much smaller political class.

They helped to justify Roman empire too: if Romans came from anywhere, everywhere belonged to Rome. Taking the story further, and in line with the standard ancient model for historical change, Livy underlines the early city's cultural debts to Etruria: Romulus adopted his twelve attendants or "lictors" from "Etruscan" practice, as well as the "curule chair" later occupied by senior Roman magistrates, and the purple-bordered toga.[12] Etruria was of course by Livy's time under Roman control.

Finally they helped to justify the emperor himself. Augustus was especially proud of his own family's purported descent from Aeneas and his mother the goddess Venus, putting portraits of them on his coinage. His relationship to Romulus was less clear—it depended on which of Aeneas' sons founded Alba Longa, and even Vergil wasn't sure—and perhaps that was useful too, but the masks of both men were carried as ancestors in his funeral procession.[13]

In the final decades of the first century BCE the *princeps* built this double Trojan and Latin heritage into a new public gathering place he constructed to the north of the city's old republican center. Two series of statues ran along the walls of this "Augustan" forum, one celebrating Augustus' own Julian family, beginning with Aeneas, the other Rome's political heroes—its *summi viri* or greatest men—beginning with Romulus.[14] At the heart of the complex was a temple to Mars Ultor—the Avenger, in this case of Julius Caesar—with Augustus' own name running across the architrave, looming above inscriptions listing the names of the peoples he had defeated.

The temple's star attraction was a display of the Roman standards that Crassus had lost to Parthia at Carrhae.[15] Despite the militaristic context in which they were displayed, these banners had been retrieved by diplomacy, not by force. When the Parthian prince Phraates was kidnapped by one of the king's rivals and taken to Rome, Augustus swapped him for more than a hundred Roman standards lost to Parthia over the previous decades and the remaining Roman prisoners from Carrhae.

Most of these men returned to Rome with the standards in 19 BCE, although after thirty-three years some could not be found, and others are said to have committed suicide rather than go home.[16] The return of the prisoners and the standards was treated nonetheless as a great victory at Rome, with a commemorative arch erected in the old republican forum and more Roman coins issued to mark the occasion than for any military campaign of Augustus' reign.[17]

The Parthians are almost forgotten today, but for Augustus that wasn't an option: as the contemporary historian Pompeius Trogus put it, they "divided the world with the Romans."[18]

They could however be appropriated for Roman messages, and in the temple of Mars Ultor itself the standards returned by Parthia stood alongside those recovered from Dalmatia, Spain, and Gaul in the Roman conquest of those lands. The display incorporated Rome's unsuccessful eastern campaigns into the story of those that built its empire, and reveals Augustus' own skill as a storyteller. And we can get more of a sense of this from a great festival Augustus held across the city to inaugurate his new forum and temple in 2 BCE, showcasing his capital at the height of its power and glory.[19]

It's hard to imagine ancient Rome. The constant sound of the building works, the poverty, the filth, the disease, and the slaves—all that makes sense. But then there are the hot colors covering every marble surface, the smell of the laundries running on human urine, the constant bloody sacrifices to petty squabbling gods, and the wider theater of slaughter. Let's try, all the same, walking south for the festivities along the Via Flaminia, the modern Corso, into an imperial metropolis teeming with foreign art and ideas, a city full of other places.

To our right is what is now the *centro storico* or "historic center" of the city, a warren of streets and churches, unexpected squares, and unlikely flavors of ice cream. In 2 BCE, however, the Campus Martius ("Field of Mars") was a park outside Rome's walls, open grassland for the most part and rather swampy in the middle. Since troops on active service were not allowed into the city itself, it had traditionally served as a training ground and camp for the army, which is why it was named after the god of war.[20] There is a great sense of space then as we approach the city, the wind blowing warm across the grass, carrying the sounds of the holiday. There are also signs of changing times and expanding horizons.

The first attraction on the meadow to our right is the family tomb Augustus had built in 28 BCE, a great mound on the bank of the Tiber covered in trees and topped with a bronze statue of the *princeps* himself.[21] At eighty-nine meters across, it is on a completely different scale from the earlier burials that line the roads leading toward the city proper, where corpses, like soldiers, were not permitted. The tomb's isolation in the landscape, surrounded by gardens and paths, increases the impression of bulk. It will be another sixteen years before it welcomes Augustus himself, but it already contains the bones of his sister, his nephew, his stepson, and his son-in-law: close association with the emperor was a dangerous business.

Contemporaries nicknamed the monument the "Mausoleum," after the dynastic tomb of the Carian king Mausolus at Halicarnassus, in western Anatolia.[22] That tomb was square-sided however, whereas this one is round, and a closer association for many local viewers would have been the now ancient funerary mounds built outside Etrurian cities. Augustus himself may have had a third model in mind: the little we know about Alexander's tomb at Alexandria suggests that it too was a tumulus.[23] We also know that Augustus visited this monument after his victory at Actium, daring to touch the body itself and reportedly knocking off a piece of the nose. He was careful by contrast to avoid associations with the newly defeated Ptolemies, reportedly refusing the opportunity to view their tombs with the words "I came to see a king, not corpses."[24]

Farther along the road to the right is a clearer symbol of Egypt: an obelisk that dominates the view across to the Tiber.* Originally erected

*This was one of the first two obelisks brought to Rome from Egypt, both from the Heliopolis temple. It stood in its original location into the medieval period. The pedestal was then rediscovered in the sixteenth century by a barber digging a latrine, and several fragments of the shaft were excavated in 1748. It was restored with granite from the shaft of the column of Antoninus Pius and in 1792 it was re-erected in Piazza di Monte Citorio where it still stands, in front of the Italian parliament and not far from

at Egyptian Heliopolis in the reign of Pharaoh Psammetichus II (595–589 BCE), this thirty-meter pillar of red granite was removed to Rome in 10 BCE.[25] It operated in its new home as a symbol of Augustus' conquest not only of the despised Ptolemies but of the ancient Egyptian people they had ruled before him.

For Romans as for Greeks, Egypt symbolized the height of culture and the depth of time, but a new fascination with Egyptian culture and religion in this era was part and parcel of Roman rule over Egypt.[26] To ensure that the point wasn't missed, an inscription on the obelisk's new base announced that it was a gift from Augustus to the sun, "now that Egypt has been brought under the power of the Roman people." The deity was carefully chosen: Romans knew that in Egypt obelisks were traditionally dedications to the sun god as well as symbols of monarchical rule.[27] Cultural cosmopolitanism was closely linked, as ever, to imperial power.

Augustus put the obelisk to work as the pointer or "gnomon" of a giant solar meridian—a line running north of an object that casts a shadow—laid out in bronze on travertine paving.[28] The length of its shadow at noon tracked the length of the day from the winter solstice, when it was farthest away from the obelisk itself, into the summer solstice and back out again. If we walk over to have a closer look, we will see that the meridian strip marks out the individual days, labels the months (in Greek) with the appropriate sign of the zodiac—Virgo, Leo, Taurus, more learning from conquered foes—and gives notes on the seasons too: "trade winds end," "summer begins."[29]

Finally, as we turn back toward the Via Flaminia we would notice that the obelisk stands on an axis with the entrance to an elegant rectangular marble enclosure backing onto the road.* This is the Altar of Peace, vowed to Augustus by the senate in 13 BCE to celebrate his return

its original position. The other Heliopolis obelisk was first erected in the Circus Maximus, with the same inscription, but it was moved by Pope Sixtus V to Piazza del Popolo in 1589, where it is guarded by four magnificent lions.

*Fragments of the altar began to emerge in the sixteenth century and it was fully excavated by Mussolini's fascist government in the late 1930s and re-erected on the bank of the Tiber. It was given a new building in 2006, designed by Richard Meier.

from the provinces of Iberia and Gaul, and dedicated a year after the obelisk itself.[30] Its design is based on the small Egyptian "chapels" traditionally erected at temple sites along the Nile, which also have their entrance and exit on either side of a central structure that you have to walk around; at least one stood on an axis with an obelisk.[31] These buildings would have been more familiar to ancient Roman architects than to modern scholars of Classical art, especially after an extensive reconstruction program Augustus had carried out on Egyptian temple complexes. It is no accident either that the Altar of Peace resembles older pharaonic chapels more closely than examples erected by the Ptolemies.[32] Augustus has not only conquered Egypt but rescued it.

Continuing down the road we pass a new portico on our left. Here we can see not just Egypt, but the Roman empire as a whole. The Porticus Vipsania was finished in 7 or 6 BCE after the death of its commissioner Marcus Agrippa, Augustus' closest aide and confidant. His sister Vipsania began to build it, but Augustus himself finished it off and displayed inside it what the polymathic scholar Pliny the Elder, who died in the eruption of Vesuvius in 79 CE, calls the *orbis terrarum,* the known world.[33]

It is generally assumed that this was a map, although no ancient source quite says that: it could also have been a list of places arranged as an itinerary, a common approach to geographical description in the Roman period. Either way, it was not always reliable: Pliny tells us that Agrippa miscalculated the size of the Iberian province of Baetica. This comment reveals more than a typo: if Agrippa's "map" somehow marked the Roman provinces, it showed the world not only as it was understood at Rome, but as Rome ruled it. Like the old British maps that colored the empire red, it reassured its viewers of Roman power.

Leaving the portico we face a choice of entertainments that bring other lands to Rome. We could carry on south to the Circus Maximus, where Augustus has organized a beast hunt with 260 lions brought over from Africa. Or we could head across the river to a new amphitheater built especially to hold sea battles, where 3,000 gladiators in Greek and Persian costume are reenacting the Battle of Salamis.[34] The Persians stand in of course for Parthians.

Instead, though, we turn off to the right, past a great hall built by Julius Caesar where we can hear the screams and roars of the crowd watching gladiators. We thread our way through the buildings that now cover the southern Campus Martius, from small temples commemorating victories in the First Punic War to huge stone theaters erected in more recent years. Finally we emerge into the Flaminian Circus, an open area on the banks of the river that was normally used for chariot and horse racing. Today though it has been flooded for a crocodile hunt, with thirty-six of the animals ferried in from Egypt, along with the specialists from Dendera on the Upper Nile who captured and then cared for them until they met their bloody end.[35*]

The crocodiles aren't the only foreigners we'll see today. As in the Assyrian empire a millennium before, the extension of Roman power brought with it the movement of people, both voluntary and enforced, and plenty of them moved to Rome itself.[36] Some had no choice in the matter: out of a total population of around a million people in the Augustan city, perhaps 300,000 were enslaved.[37] There were however no restrictions, to our knowledge, on migration to the city, and in the 40s CE the philosopher Seneca claimed that the majority of the population were migrants; he himself came from Córdoba (ancient Corduba) in Spain.[38]

Overall, a genome study of 127 individuals buried at twenty-nine different sites in and around Rome in the first to third centuries CE shows a very substantial shift in ancestry toward the eastern Mediterranean and western Asia.[39] This fits in with other evidence: by the Augustan period, for instance, there were several thousand Jews in Rome, some of them originally taken prisoner in Roman campaigns in the Levant.[40] Within a few decades they were joined by members of a new Jewish sect

*The exploitation of African animals for public entertainment at Rome remained popular: in one notorious display under the next emperor, Tiberius, twelve elephants were trained to dance in a troupe and then dressed for a formal dinner, which they took reclining on vast low couches and cushions to eat off gold and silver plates (Aelian, *On Animals* 2.11).

focused on a young preacher called Jesus the Christ (the Greek term for the Hebrew "Messiah," the "anointed one") who had amassed a large following in the Roman province of Judea before he was executed for treason. Jesus' followers believed that he had been resurrected after his death and that he was the Son of God. They began to distance themselves from other Jewish traditions and to recruit among gentiles as well, forming small religious communities in cities throughout the Roman empire and beyond.

Elsewhere in Italy, Roman soldiers wrote graffiti in Arabic at Pompeii in the 70s CE, and mitochondrial DNA analysis has revealed that a man and a woman with maternal ancestry in east Asia were buried at a rural estate near Gravina in Puglia in the Roman imperial period. At the same time the study of the oxygen and strontium isotopes in their teeth reveals that they were both born in southern Italy, and the man at least on the estate itself.[41]

We shouldn't exaggerate mobility in the Roman empire. People who moved generally moved relatively short distances. Women almost never moved any significant distance alone. People moved back and forth as well: seasonal migration would have been a significant phenomenon within Italy, especially during the summers and when major building projects attracted laborers to Rome and other big cities.[42] At the same time, migration was not limited to the metropolis or even to Italy. It brought people from all over the empire and beyond to destinations as far as distant Britain.[43*]

. . .

*Animals moved with empire as well. Domestic cats finally crossed the Alps with the Roman conquest of Gaul, although even in Italy no cats have been found among those killed at Pompeii by the eruption of Vesuvius in 79 CE, and unlike with dogs, not a single cat's name is preserved from antiquity. They only became popular companions in the medieval period (Claudio Ottoni et al., "The palaeogenetics of cat dispersal in the ancient world," *Nature Ecology & Evolution* 1, no. 7 [2017]; Iain M. Ferris, *Cave Canem: Animals in Roman Civilization,* Stroud: Amberley Publishing, 2018). Camels got as far north as Belgium and even Greenwich under Roman imperial rule, presumably imported by the army for transportation, although they are also found in civic and domestic contexts in Rome's European provinces (Fabienne Pigière and Denis Henrotay, "Camels in the northern provinces of the Roman empire," *Journal of Archaeological Science* 39, no. 5 [2012]).

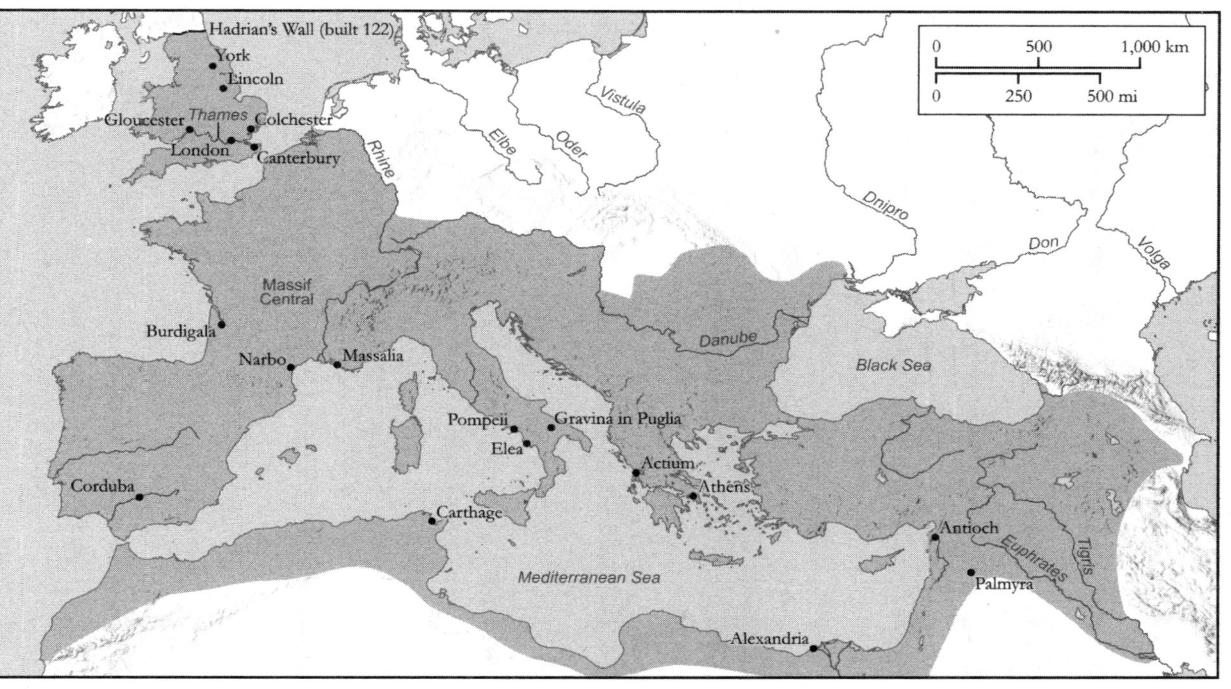

The Roman Empire under Trajan in 117 CE

When Augustus died in 14 CE he left a memorandum advising his fellow Romans to maintain the empire within its present borders.[44] For the most part his stepson Tiberius and his great-grandson Caligula followed this advice, content to enjoy the fruits of the empire as it stood, and to garrison the frontiers. The next major expansion came under Rome's fourth emperor, Caligula's uncle Claudius, who succeeded to the Roman throne in 41 CE.

Claudius presided over the administrative annexation of the old Roman client states of Mauretania, Lycia, and Thrace as full provinces, but for reputational reasons he needed a military victory too, and for that he now looked north to Britain. In 43 CE his army invaded southern England.[45] Four Roman legions made short work of the Catuvellauni who controlled much of the southeast of England from Camulodunum (modern Colchester). Suetonius reports that Claudius received the submission of the south of the island "without battle or blood" in a few days and then immediately returned to Rome for what the historian implies was an ill-deserved triumph.[46] Over the following decades the army worked its way farther into the island, reaching the Scottish borders in the 70s.[47]

Between 2010 and 2014 a treasure trove of new evidence emerged for the commercial settlement of London, founded by traders on uninhabited land at the head of the Thames estuary around 50 CE.[48] In the second century London would become the capital of the Roman province, but these documents, found during rescue excavations before the construction of a new European headquarters for Bloomberg, date from the later first century CE, when London was still an informal—but apparently very lively—port, well placed for travel farther upriver as well as across to the Rhine Delta. The new settlement was centered on two low hills on either side of the River Walbrook, a tributary of the Thames that brought fresh water into the heart of the city.[49]

A total of 409 wax tablets were recovered—or rather, the folding tablets were recovered into which blackened wax was once poured. The message was then written into the wax with a stylus, revealing the pale wood behind; once it had served its purpose the wax was warmed up and smoothed over, ready for a new text. The wax itself has disappeared in the long centuries these documents have been buried. But the marks made in the wood below often survive and they can be read under raking light—unless too many messages were written on top of the others, producing an incomprehensible grid of slanting lines. Latin cursive handwriting is hard to read anyway, but texts written on about eighty of the tablets can be deciphered.[50]

These include the first known occurrence of the name "Londinium" itself, an alphabet written out by someone practicing their writing, legal contracts, and letters. Most of the letters concern business and finance and many are written by, or about, slaves or freedmen—perhaps acting on behalf of their current or former owners. The addressees include merchants, brewers, coopers, and veterans, but no women. A typical example is addressed on the outer side: "You will give this to Titus," and on the inside we can read the advice of an anonymous well-wisher, or busybody: "they are boasting through the whole of the market that you have lent them money. Therefore I ask you in your own interest not to appear shabby . . . you will not thus favor your own affairs . . ."[51]

The names found on the letters suggest that this community contained a substantial number of migrants who had come over from the continent to exploit the new commercial possibilities offered by Roman occupation. We find one letter addressed to Luguseluus, a Celtic name otherwise found only in Gaul, who is the son of Junius, a Latin name adopted enthusiastically in Gaul and Noricum. Another is sent to one Martialis who has taken a Latin name himself, but whose father has the Celtic name Ambicuus, again attested only in Gaul.[52]

More direct evidence for Gauls in London comes from a writing tablet dating to around 100 CE that records the sale of a woman from northern Gaul to a man called Vegetus for 600 denarii. This is a fairly standard price, equivalent to two years' salary for a legionary soldier; what is more interesting is that Vegetus is the slave of a slave belonging to the emperor himself. The document specifies that the unfortunate woman was handed over in a healthy condition and has no history of running away.[53]

London remained a commercial center as it became a political one, and later tombstones commemorate merchants from Antioch and Athens, and a "sailor" (*moritix*) from Gaul.[54] Migration occurred at all levels of society: lead isotopes preserved in the teeth of a very wealthy woman buried at Spitalfields may have come from the city of Rome itself.[55] Studies of oxygen isotopes, which preserve the composition of the water that people drank as children, suggest that nineteen out of twenty-two people buried in a Southwark cemetery between the second and fourth centuries CE came from a Mediterranean-like climate.[56] Analysis of the carbon and nitrogen isotopes meanwhile, which reflect recent diet, show that the same individuals had all been resident in London for years. This proportion of immigrants is unusual even in a British context, and they may have gathered in this district south of the river.

Similar results come from York, founded in the 70s CE as a military base on the main road through to the forts on the border farther north. It became Rome's northern capital in Britain from around 200 CE, by which time it had a temple to the Egyptian god Serapis, built by a Roman military official.[57] Recent investigations have shown that burials from the second and third centuries CE include a man with Levantine genetic affinities, closest to Palestine, Jordan, and Syria, and from the later fourth century a woman known as "Ivory Bangle Lady" who died at the age of eighteen to twenty-three. She was celebrated for her rich grave goods and exotic jewelry long before analysis of the oxygen isotope ratio preserved in her tooth enamel showed that she grew up drinking water a long way from York, and almost certainly outside Britain.[58]

We hear of Roman officials and administrators living in Britain too, men like Quintus Lollius Urbicus, the governor of the province from 139 to 142 CE, who was born in Algeria and died there too. Most of all, of course, there were soldiers: the Roman army was an engine of social and literal mobility.

Augustus had overseen a profound reorganization of Rome's military structures that turned a citizen militia into a professional standing army with standard pay, conditions, and a sixteen-year term. It was open both to Roman citizens, who made up its legions, and to noncitizen "auxiliaries," who served in separate units but could expect Roman citizenship on discharge from long service, and perhaps some land in a veteran colony as well.

Soldiers served in a single legion or unit throughout their military career, often one stationed a long way from home, and there was a deliberate policy of posting auxiliary units far from their points of origin. Soldiers from north of the Danube served as far away as Egypt and Syria, on the Parthian frontier; others made it a condition of enlistment that they not be deployed beyond the Alps.[59]

Three Roman citizen legions were permanently stationed in Britain, along with about seventy-five auxiliary units, and three Roman colonies were established for veteran soldiers on the sites of old forts as the army moved north, at Colchester, Gloucester, and Lincoln.[60] Inscriptions at Britain's northern border forts record cohorts from modern France, Basque-speaking Spain, and the Balkan mountains, as well as a detachment of archers from Syria and a unit of Mauretanians.[61]

Over time Roman regiments began to recruit locally as well, while soldiers from overseas often retired where they had served, and married local women. These were men like Barates, who came to Britain from Palmyra in Syria as an auxiliary soldier or a camp follower. In the late second century CE he commissioned a gravestone at the fort of Arbeia (now South Shields near Newcastle) for his wife, a British woman known as Regina—"Queen"—whom he had owned, freed, and then married.[62] The tombstone has a standard Latin epitaph—"Barates a Palmyrene [made this] for the *Di Manes* [spirits] of Regina, freedwoman and wife, by birth a Catuvellaunian, thirty years of age"—but it also has a postscript in Palmyrene Aramaic, "Regina, freedwoman of Barate, alas." Where he found a sculptor who could carve these words is an interesting question, but not an impossible one in an era that brought Chinese silk to London and Indian pepper to northern border forts.[63]

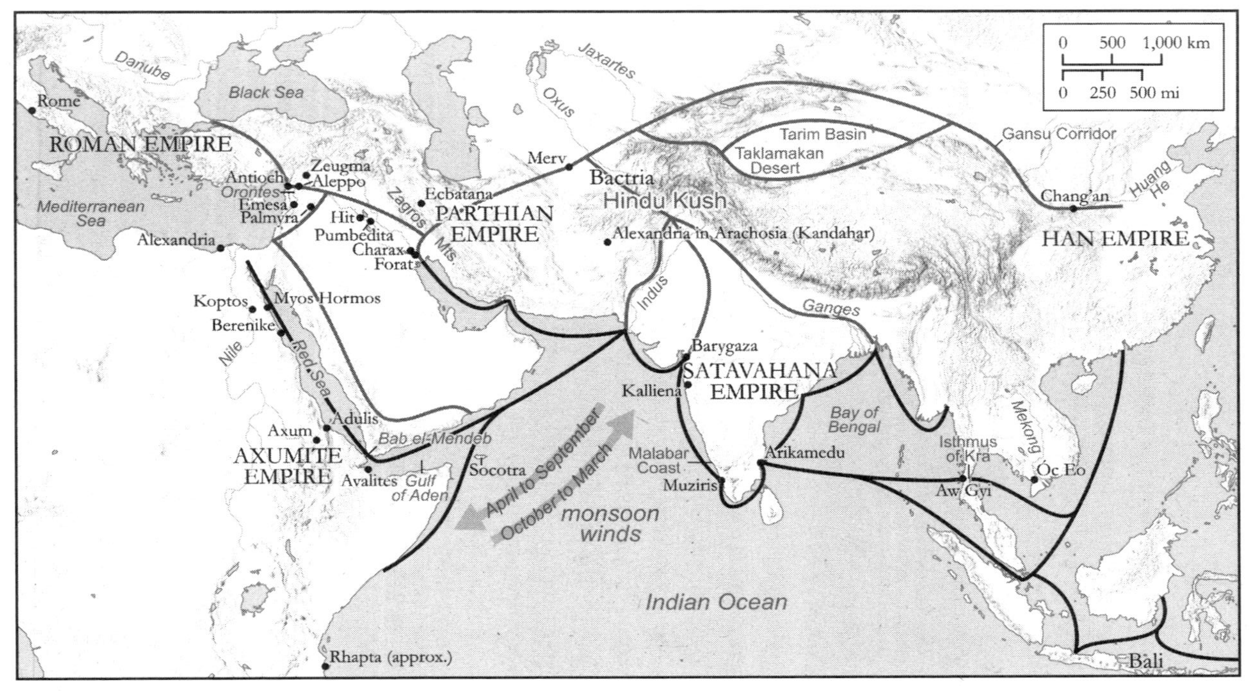

Routes between China and the Mediterranean in the second century CE

CHAPTER TWENTY-ONE

Trade Winds

PALMYRA, C. 200 CE

Barates himself died in England at the age of sixty-eight: his tombstone was found in 1911, reused in paving at the Roman fort of Corbridge.[1] Perhaps he got to go home again first, a final chance to see Palmyra after decades on the far edge of the Roman empire, and one last season in the sun.

It would have been a long journey from Hadrian's Wall, around three months if Barates set out toward the end of the summer. First would come the bumpy ride from his fort to the sea, then a series of ferries along the east coast of England, into the Channel and down the west coast of Gaul. If his boat sailed into the great Gironde estuary and down to the river port of Burdigala (modern Bordeaux) he could have shaved a week or two off the journey at some extra expense by cutting down the Roman road to Narbo on the Mediterranean in a shared wagon. Alternatively he could simply have continued south by sea around the Iberian peninsula and through the Pillars of Hercules. From any Mediterranean port he would have found ships heading on toward the great Syrian emporium of Antioch.

As the seas got choppy and the weather wet, it would have been a relief to arrive on dry land again, perhaps sometime in November.

From Antioch, Barates would have headed south by cart up the valley of the Orontes behind the coastal mountains to the old Arab citadel of Emesa (modern Homs). From there the road descends east into an increasingly rugged landscape, the grass becoming scrub, the air thick with dust. The going isn't too bad though with baggage and rations strapped to a mule, and after three or four days Barates would have been climbing the last steep range of rocky hills.

As he started down the other side the oasis would have spread out slowly before him, with the great flat desert beyond. Palmyra itself emerges last from the gray sands, tucked into the shallow embrace of the hills on which he stood. Walking down past the funerary towers of his ancestors, Barates would finally have reached flat ground and the column-lined street leading through the center of the town.

After the warm dusty silence of the desert, the Great Colonnade is all action and noise, winding through the city for more than a kilometer with plenty to restore a weary traveler. Stallkeepers offer food, medications, a change of clothes; women call out their own prices, on the right a marketplace jostles with customs collectors trying to keep order, and then comes a grand theater built in the Mediterranean style. Donkeys and camels crowd the thoroughfare, unpaved for their convenience.

The people dress for the sand and heat, the men in trousers and short tunics, the women in long robes. They are all made in light, costly, brightly patterned fabrics that keep out the heat, falling in sumptuous gathers and folds caught up with chunky belts and topped with heavy jewelry made of precious stones. On every column stand bronze statues labeled with the names of the local cameleering gentry both in Greek and in Barates' own Palmyrene Aramaic. He must have known some of these men, some of these families. After months of travel across the Roman empire, he was back in the middle of the world.

The Silk Roads—*die Seidenstrasse*—were invented in 1877 by Baron Ferdinand von Richthofen, a German geographer who compiled a geological survey of China with a view to the establishment of German colonies and infrastructure projects there, including a rail link to Europe.[2]* Ancient trade routes across central Asia were clearly of interest, and the "Silk Road" that interested him most was one that had been described around 100 CE by the Tyrian geographer Marinos, the first scholar to attempt to locate places by latitude and longitude.** Marinos himself got his information on this route from agents of a Macedonian merchant called Maes Titianus who were apparently the first commercial travelers to make a journey all the way from the Euphrates to China, in the first century CE. It led from somewhere called the "Stone Tower," probably a trading station in the Pamir Mountains, to Sera, "the metropolis of the Seres," or the Chinese. They reported a journey of seven months that was afflicted by bad storms.[3]

Richthofen combined Greek reports like this with information gleaned from Chinese historical sources and the latest geological studies to provide new information—and ammunition—for his railway project. The Chinese government opposed such foreign interventions, but it was severely weakened by the Opium Wars it had fought from 1839 to 1860 in an unsuccessful attempt to block British imports of the addictive drug to China.

In 1897 the Germans annexed the eastern naval base of Qingdao, where they established the brewery that still produces Tsingtao beer. But it was the Russians who got the concession to build a trans-Manchurian railway in 1897–1902, creating a useful shortcut across China from Siberian Chita to Vladivostok on the Pacific coast of Russia far to the north of the route Marinos had described.***

*Richthofen's nephew was the First World War flying ace and Snoopy's nemesis the Red Baron.

**Marinos established the first prime meridian for longitude, at the "Fortunate Isles," probably the Canary or Cape Verde Islands and in any case comfortably west of the Atlantic coast (since no one thought measurements farther west would be required). The Canaries were still being used as the prime meridian by Gerardus Mercator in 1541, but by the eighteenth century most European countries had established their own, usually at their capitals. In 1884 delegates from twenty-five nations to the International Meridian Conference in Washington, D.C., selected Greenwich as the shared standard—and the boundary, strictly speaking, between the eastern and western hemispheres. Marinos measured latitude north and south of the island of Rhodes, but it was Ptolemy of Alexandria's calculation of parallels from the equator that became standard.

***The better known trans-Mongolian route dates from the late 1940s.

Richthofen's dream of retracing that ancient path through central Asia wasn't dead: in the 1930s his Swedish student Sven Hedin popularized the use of the term "Silk Road" to describe Marinos' route, and issued a plea to the current Chinese government to revive it as part of a "motor road" from Shanghai to Hamburg and Boulogne that "should unite two oceans, the Pacific and the Atlantic; two continents; two races, the yellow and the white; two cultures, the Chinese and the Western."[4] The project again went nowhere, but the idea of the Silk Road as a synecdoche for commercial and cultural relations between East and West was born.

Richthofen's "Silk Road" was however based on a misunderstanding: there is no suggestion in ancient sources that Marinos was recording a regular overland trade route. Indeed, there is every indication that his informants' journey across central Asia was extremely unusual: these Macedonian merchants were of interest to Marinos precisely because they could provide him with unique information on routes and distances in the far east of Asia.

Overland routes across Asia did exist, encouraged by the unification of large parts of India and China in the third century BCE under the Mauryan and Qin empires respectively.[5] They were highways of empire, however, not trade, and they rarely joined up.[6]

At the western end travel between the Parthian and Roman empires was frequently disrupted by friction on the border between them, where local nomadic populations had taken advantage of the collapse of Seleucid power in the late first millennium BCE to take control of the Euphrates Valley.[7] The ancient trade route along the Euphrates from the Mediterranean to the Gulf was now both dangerous and expensive for commercial travelers, subject to taxation by multiple small fiefdoms along the way.

Farther east, roads had crossed Parthian lands since the time of the Achaemenid kings, but again they were not primarily commercial. A Greek work known as *The Parthian Stations* written around the Augustan era by one Isidorus of Charax on the Persian Gulf describes an overland route from Zeugma—the nearest crossing point on the Euphrates to the Mediterranean port of Antioch—through the Zagros Mountains to Ecbatana, and on to the oasis of Merv in what is now Turkmenistan.[8] It is a spare text, listing the travel times between towns, villages, and Parthian imperial stations, with occasional comments on sites of local interest: an island in the Euphrates served as a treasury for the Parthian king Phraates who under enemy attack "cut the throats of his concubines."[9]

It doesn't mention trade at all, and instead of continuing east from Merv to the Tarim Basin and China, like the journey Marinos described, the route cuts south through what is now Afghanistan to Alexandria in Arachosia (modern Kandahar) in the flatlands south of the Hindu Kush. This marked the edge of the Parthian empire near the border not of China but of India.[10]

Turning south made sense: overland travel east of Merv was again dangerous, through regions controlled by displaced Yuezhi and Scythians, and then through the half-subdued oases of the Taklamakan Desert in the Tarim Basin, the "Western Regions" (*Xiyu*) that only came fully under Chinese control in the 90s CE. Although records, receipts, and cargo manifests preserved at Chinese garrisons and customs posts in the area regularly note the arrival of caravans carrying tribute and diplomatic delegations, they rarely mention commercial travelers.[11]

All this helps to explain the lack of even indirect commercial contact between Rome and China in the first millennium BCE. Romans writing under Augustus still mention only the coarser silk produced by worms farmed on the Aegean island of Cos, and both Vergil in the 20s BCE and Seneca around 40 CE state confidently that silk grows on trees.[12]

The first Roman contact with China, according to later reports, was when Chinese envoys came to Rome to pay their respects to Augustus himself.[13] There is no mention of this mission in Chinese records, and they were probably in fact curious merchants. They came in any case with Indians "who live beneath the sun itself," and they would all have come by sea: the real Silk Roads of the early first millennium CE were across the Indian Ocean, faster and cheaper than the overland journey, with Indian and Egyptian ports mediating trade between China and points west.

These maritime routes weren't new: trade between China and India had increased with growing prosperity and political integration in both places from the third century BCE.[14] All it took to integrate the Red Sea into these networks was an understanding of the monsoon winds that blow ships southwest across the Indian Ocean between April and October, before reversing direction in the winter. Armed with this knowledge, the journey from the Red Sea to India and back could be completed well within a year.

The Ptolemaic kings knew of these trade winds by the second century BCE, and they laid out caravan routes across the eastern desert from the Nile to new ports in the southern half of the Red Sea, which could be reached by sail without fighting the counter winds farther north. Square stone markers signaled the way, and road stations with dug wells and cisterns provided regular watering points.[15]

The Ptolemies' main interest however was in dominance of the Red Sea and trade with the coasts of east Africa, where they found elephants, ivory, monkeys, and spices, and of Arabia for perfumes. Private interests were involved in this trade too, some operating at long distances: a papyrus dating from the mid-second century BCE records a loan arranged by an Italian called Gnaois for a venture to the "Spice-Bearing Land," which in other texts means the region of modern Somalia. It is to be undertaken by a consortium of merchants from Egypt, southern Greece, Elea in Italy, Carthage, and Massalia, and the loan has to be repaid within ninety days of their docking at a Red Sea port.[16]

The archaeological evidence suggests that contacts with India were limited in the Ptolemaic period and initially operated through the ports of southern Arabia. By the first century BCE however fragments of heavy Greek amphoras begin to appear in Indian ports, and direct trade expanded after the Roman annexation of Egypt: Strabo reports (perhaps with some friendly exaggeration) that when he visited Egypt in the 20s BCE, 120 ships a year left the Egyptian port of Myos Hormos (Mussel Harbor) on the Red Sea for India, "although under the Ptolemaic kings, very few braved the voyage."[17] Increasing trade through the Red Sea also helped the Roman authorities undermine the caravan routes through Arabia.[18]

Excavations at Myos Hormos confirm the large-scale import of precious stones, spices, and textiles on maritime routes from India and Sri

Lanka, as well as mung beans, rice, and bamboo.[19] They also unearthed fragments of ships and rigging made from Indian teak and cloth: ships were sailing in both directions.[20] Conversely, archaeologists working at the port of Arikamedu in modern Tamil Nadu on the east coast of India have revealed a first-century BCE fishing village filling up over two centuries with Mediterranean pottery. There are amphoras once full of wine from Greece and Italy, olive oil, and grain. Thousands of Roman coins begin to be found in India. And Tamil poets remark on the large ships of the "Yavana"—from the Persian term "Yauna" for Greeks, but a word used in this period for westerners in general—that exchange gold and wine for pepper at Muziris near the southern tip of India in modern Kerala.[21]

As early as the 20s BCE the poet Propertius draws attention to the Indian gemstones in young women's hair, but trading activity along these routes was at its height in the first half of the first century CE between the reigns of Augustus and Nero.[22] We know that Indian spices like ginger, cumin, and turmeric were used in the Mediterranean not only for food, but also for perfume, incense, cosmetics, and medication; pepper was mixed into an ointment and used as a treatment for eye disorders.[23]

It is only after Augustus' death that we finally begin to hear of Chinese silk arriving in Rome. The cost, light weight, and quasi-transparent effect made it both popular and scandalous, and early in the reign of Tiberius the senate passed a decree banning men from "defiling" themselves with Chinese garments.[24] Whether or not this worked, the eruption of Vesuvius in 79 CE preserved Pompeian wall paintings full of women—and goddesses—in beautiful, translucent silk dresses.

Trade through Egypt into the Mediterranean was conducted under Roman regulation.[25] Cargo traveled in caravans along the eastern desert routes under seal and armed guard, stopping at fortified road stations along the way, to Koptos on the Nile where it was stored in government warehouses before traveling downriver to Alexandria, where the imperial authorities charged a 25 percent tax in kind on both imports and exports.

This could be very lucrative indeed: a cargo list preserved on papyrus for the *Hermapollon,* a second-century CE vessel carrying nard (an essential oil), ivory, and clothing from Kerala to an Egyptian Red Sea port, values the goods at almost 7 million sesterces after tax—about the price of a high-class country estate back in Italy. If every load was this valuable, the port taxes from a hundred ships arriving every year—a conservative estimate—would raise around 230 million sesterces: a third of the estimated annual cost of the Roman army to the state. Unfortunately, unless more papyri appear we have no way of knowing how typical this list really is.[26]

For observers like the philosopher Dio Chrysostom, from Prusa in Bithynia, the Red Sea trade meant that Alexandria itself "lies at the crossroads of the whole world, as it were, and of even the remotest peoples."[27] He made this point to the people of Alexandria in a speech delivered in their own theater around 100 CE, in which he also denounced them for paying too much attention to entertainments and too little to serious matters such as philosophy. He pointed out that they should be especially ashamed of such behavior because it took place "in the presence of all humankind. For I myself see among you [in the theater] not only Greeks and Italians and from neighboring lands Syrians, Libyans, and Cilicians, and from more distant regions Ethiopians and Arabs, but even Bactrians, Scythians, Persians, and a few Indians."[28]

We get the best sense of this Indian Ocean world from a remarkable document called the *Periplus of the Red Sea*—to ancient authors the "Red Sea" usually included not only the narrow gulf between Africa and Arabia but the Indian Ocean too. Preserved in a tenth-century manuscript kept in the university library at Heidelberg, it appears to be a compilation of reports from the first and early second centuries CE to create a gazetteer of all the trading ports that can be reached from Myos Hormos.[29]

The work presents itself as a guide to help merchants design their own itineraries, out and back, or triangular. It works its way around the coast in both directions from this starting point, first tracking down the east African coast as far as modern Tanzania—the last stop is Rhapta, modern Dar es Salaam—then heading up and around the Red Sea itself, through the Bab el Mandeb, along the southern Arabian coast and across to India. It describes every harbor en route, noting who controls the port and its trade and what the locals are prepared to buy and sell. It also provides tidbits on local history and customs, and is especially interested in marine life, detailing the different snakes peculiar to each port that come out to meet the ships.

We read for instance of a bay in modern Eritrea where merchants can find natural obsidian as well as a market for glass ornaments, brass, and copper items to be cut up for local purposes. The locals will also buy a limited quantity of wine from Italy and the Levant, as well as Egyptian garments, as long as they are unused.[30] By contrast, at Avalites farther down the coast there is a market for secondhand clothing, as long as it is clean, while the king himself will purchase silverware, goldware, and cloaks of a modest price. The *Periplus* also lists the Indian items that can be sold in this harbor: iron, steel, and cotton, and various specialized garments. Traders in African ports along the Gulf of Aden, meanwhile, will buy Indian foodstuffs: rice, ghee, sesame oil, and cane sugar.[31]

The best month to depart from Egypt for these African ports, the *Periplus* advises, is July.[32] This exploits northerly winds heading down the Red Sea, and then allows the ship to travel back through the Gulf of Aden with the early northeast monsoon in October and catch the first of the winter southerlies in the Red Sea, a relatively brief trip. The summer months are also the best time to head straight to India, hopping on to the southwest monsoon winds and arriving in September.[33] The work assumes that most traders will sail straight across to the Indian coast from the Gulf of Aden, bypassing the old Persian Gulf ports.

It also arms them with useful information: the port of Kalliena on the west coast of India, for instance, is the center of a trade dispute between local peoples, so if ships arrive in the area by mistake then migrant Scythians who live a little farther north give them a military escort to their own chief port of Barygaza (Bharuch in modern Gujarat).[34] There things look up: merchants will buy wine, preferably Italian (though Syrian or Arabian will do), copper, tin, and lead, and multicolored girdles, while the king is partial to silverware, female concubines, enslaved musicians, and "expensive clothing with no adornment."[35]

The *Periplus* describes a great many other ports around the coast of India, and several inland cities and regions too, but beyond the Bay of Bengal all is rumor and imagination. Near the Ganges is Gold Island (Burma?), the region farthest east of the inhabited world, which supplies the finest tortoiseshell in the Indian Ocean. Beyond that to the north there is a great city called Thina (China) that supplies silk floss, yarn, and cloth, which are then carried overland to ports: via Bactria to Barygaza or via the Ganges River to the Malabar coast. Egyptian merchants buy Chinese silk at these Indian ports, our author notes, because journeys to Thina are difficult, and journeys from it rare.[36]

Another sense of Roman horizons in the early first millennium CE comes from a Roman itinerary map preserved in a thirteenth-century manuscript now known as the "Peutinger Table." This takes the form of a long, thin east–west strip that lays out the roads and waterways that link the Atlantic coast with the farthest known regions to the east. It places a "temple of Augustus" at Muziris on the southwest coast of India, which marks the eastern end of the map's Roman world, and effectively ends at the Bay of Bengal, although the place name China or "Sera Maior" is written at an apparently randomly chosen spot along the far eastern coast.[37]

By the time the *Periplus* was compiled, land or sea were no longer mutually exclusive options for difficult journeys east. During the first century CE entrepreneurs from the ancient oasis city of Palmyra opened up a new hybrid route from the Mediterranean that involved traveling overland as far as the Persian Gulf and then on to India by sea. They did so by providing an alternative to the dangerous and expensive northern route between the Mediterranean coast and the Euphrates via Aleppo: a shortcut through their own oasis to the Gulf, from where it was a relatively short voyage to Indian ports.[38] This cut journey times from India to the Mediterranean by up to three months by avoiding the long detour around Arabia, up the Red Sea, and across Egypt's eastern desert.

The Palmyrenes had two trump cards. One was the camel. Palmyra stood on the border of the true desert, at a transition point between tracks west over rocky hills toward the Mediterranean coast that could only be traveled by donkey and mule, and routes east across the desert to the lower Euphrates that were suited to the one-humped dromedary, which has large, soft feet that are useless among rocks or in rain but ideal for sand and gravel. The other was local connections among the pastoralists who controlled the Syrian desert and had until now deterred attempts to travel through it. The leading families of Palmyra had roots in these clans, and by diplomacy, bribery, intimidation, or a combination of all three they were able to secure safe passage for merchants and cargo.

The details of these arrangements can be reconstructed from thirty or so inscriptions erected at Palmyra itself and at pit stops on the route east that record the gratitude of the merchants to those who made their journeys possible. Palmyrene traders hired local caravan leaders who came equipped with camels, wranglers, guides, and tents to transport their goods to river ports like Hit, far enough south on the Euphrates to avoid the worst currents and rapids. This seven-day trek across the desert was the route still used by the Ottoman postal service in 1850.[39]

The camels could then be left to graze in the pastures of what is now southern Iraq while the cargo was loaded onto rafts made of inflated skins to travel down to the port of Forat near modern Basra on the Gulf. There it was transferred again to ships sailing east. To avoid a difficult journey upstream on the return leg, camels picked the goods up from Charax, much closer to the sea, and set off on a monthlong trek back to Palmyra.[40]

These caravans would have been annual affairs, timed to coincide with the trade winds as well as with the seasonal movements of the desert herders who must have supplied the guides. By the second and third centuries some Palmyrene traders were traveling on with their goods into the Indian Ocean: they are found in southern Arabia, on the island of Socotra off the coast of Yemen, on the Nile and even at Rome.[41]

Palmyra itself meanwhile grew from a desert pit stop to a caravan city.[42] Pliny the Elder could already describe it in the later first century CE as fertile, well watered, and surrounded by sand, "a city removed as it were by nature from the world, with its own fate between the two great empires of the Romans and the Parthians."[43] Although it was incorporated into the Roman province of Syria at some point in the first century CE, Palmyra was the only city in Roman western Asia to issue its own coinage with neither the name nor the image of the Roman emperor, and its citizens maintained strong links to the Parthian empire as well: in the second century CE a Palmyrene was acting for a Parthian prince as satrap of Bahrain.[44]

It never looked much like a Roman city. Its unorthodox art and spectacular architecture marked a borderland between worlds and bore witness to the importance of traffic between them. Its citizens wrote inscriptions in Palmyrene and Greek; they used the Seleucid dating system; they kept a Babylonian religious calendar. They buried their dead in stone towers, their mummies wrapped in colorful Chinese silk, often decorated with Chinese characters.[45]

By the second century CE the new Palmyra route was hugely popular. The Red Sea route continued too, however: it was longer but easier, involving much less travel overland. The two routes were not in any case in direct competition, but operated together for more than two centuries on quite different seasonal schedules.[46]

A ship that left India for the Gulf on the November monsoon wind would arrive in January, an ideal time to complete the arrival formalities and organize the monthlong journey north across the desert to Palmyra to coincide with the season in which desert dwellers moved their flocks north. If they reached Palmyra in March, the goods could be in Antioch or other Syrian ports by April or May, ready for the sailing season to open on the Mediterranean.

An Indian ship bound for the Red Sea, by contrast, could leave a little later in the season, perhaps in December or January, in order to arrive at an Egyptian port before the end of the Red Sea southerlies in April. The cargo then sat at Koptos awaiting the late summer floods that allowed larger boats to carry it north along the shallow river. They would finally arrive at Alexandria in August or September, before the sea closed again for the winter. This dual system ensured a regular, resilient supply of Indian Ocean goods to the Roman empire as long as ships could sail the sea.

This Indian Ocean trading system linked far-distant ports. Glass beads from the Mediterranean are found at the port of Aw Gyi in southern Myanmar in the Roman imperial period.[47] And a variety of Mediterranean objects appear at sites in southern Thailand: fragments of glass, cameos, intaglios (precious seal stones that could be used as signet rings). There are also pendants with medallions made from molds of Roman coins minted under Antoninus Pius (r. 138–161 CE) and other emperors.[48] Similar medallions have been found at the port of Oc Eo in Vietnam along with contemporary Mediterranean-style jewelry and a Chinese mirror: they must have been portaged across the Malay peninsula at the isthmus of Kra.[49] Roman goods even got to Indonesia: three tiny beads made from natron glass in Roman Egypt have been identified at a port in northern Bali in a context indicating the first century CE or an even earlier date, along with the same kind of "Rouletted Ware" pottery produced in India that is found at Myos Hormos and other Egyptian Red Sea ports.[50]

On the other side of the ocean east African kingdoms prospered on maritime links as well. We first read in the *Periplus* of Axum, a city high in the uplands of modern Ethiopia south of Kush. It is a week's journey inland from the port of Adulis in the southern Red Sea, we are told, where merchants exchanged Axumite ivory and tortoiseshell, rhino horn, obsidian, and gold for glass, bronze, and Mediterranean amphoras filled with wine and olive oil.[51] The *Periplus* doesn't say much about the city itself, but reports that King Zoskales, although possessive and greedy, is "in other respects a fine person and well versed in reading and writing Greek."[52]

The king of Axum was also ambitious, imposing tribute in head of cattle on other rulers in the region; his city grew, and by the third century he ruled an empire composed of territories in both east Africa and Arabia on the opposite coast, riding high on the Indian Ocean trade.[53] As Axumite exports reached Egypt and India, Mediterranean glass and wine jars appear in significant numbers at Axum itself.[54] Palaces, temples, and fine houses are built there too, and the world's tallest obelisks, giant spindly towers up to thirty-three meters high carved out of granite in the form of multi-story buildings with false doors at the bottom and windows all the way up. Around 270 CE Axum became the only ancient state south of the Sahara to issue coinage, on Roman weight standards, but inscribed in Greek and the local script of Geʿez.*

Over the centuries Roman knowledge of southeast Asia improved, but ideas about China and the Chinese were always very vague. There are regular references to the Seres, or "Silk People," but no evidence at all for a notion that they controlled an empire comparable in terms of size and population to Rome's own.[55] Chinese ideas about Rome were hazy too. The only lengthy Chinese account of the Roman empire (which they called Dà Qín or Great Qin) is found in the *Hou Hanshu*—the "Book of the Later Han," a historical chronicle of the first two centuries CE compiled in the fifth century CE from contemporary documents.** It describes a farming people, tall and honest, who "all shave their heads, but wear embroidered clothes." Rome itself has five palaces with columns made of glass that the king circulates between, one a day. These kings, it adds, are not permanent, but are selected for their merit, and unceremoniously demoted in the case of calamity, such as bad weather.[56]

The *Hou Hanshu* description of the "Western Regions" also highlights the continuing dangers of the overland route west through Parthia to the Persian Gulf, where there are fierce tigers and lions on the road that kill travelers: "If the party does not include over 100 men furnished with arms, they are invariably devoured." It also reports that

*Geʿez is an "abugida" writing system in which vowels are attached to consonants to denote syllables. It derives from a south Arabian script that broke off from the linear Levantine alphabet in the eleventh century BCE and was written from left to right. It is still used to write some Ethiopic and Eritrean languages, and it is the liturgical language of the Ethiopian Orthodox Church.

**The Chinese term for the Roman empire is taken from the name of the Qín dynasty who unified the country in the third century BCE; Chinese sources explain this through the similarity of the two peoples (*Hou Hanshu* 88, with D. D. Leslie and K.H.J. Gardiner, *The Roman Empire in Chinese Sources*, Rome: Bardi, 1996, 232).

in 97 CE a Chinese envoy, sent for the first time to the Roman empire, traveled safely overland as far as the Gulf, but then turned back when local sailors told him that if he was unlucky with the winds his ship might take two years to get to Dà Qín via the Red Sea.[57] Perhaps these alarming stories were official legends: according to the same source the Parthians blocked envoys from the Roman "king" from reaching China because they wanted to control the trade in silk.

Some people did make the journey in the other direction: the Chinese emperor An (r. 107–125 CE) receives an embassy from somewhere to the south (perhaps Burma) bringing him men from the Roman empire who perform magic tricks, eat fire, and can juggle many balls at once. The actual number of balls varies in different versions of this story from ten to a thousand.[58] Finally a Roman embassy was sent to China in 166 CE by Marcus Aurelius (r. 161–180 CE; Andun in Chinese), the first official contact described in Chinese sources. These envoys arrived by sea, bearing gifts of elephant tusks, rhinoceros horn, and turtle shell they had picked up on the way, which were considered a bit disappointing given earlier reports of Roman wealth and power.[59]

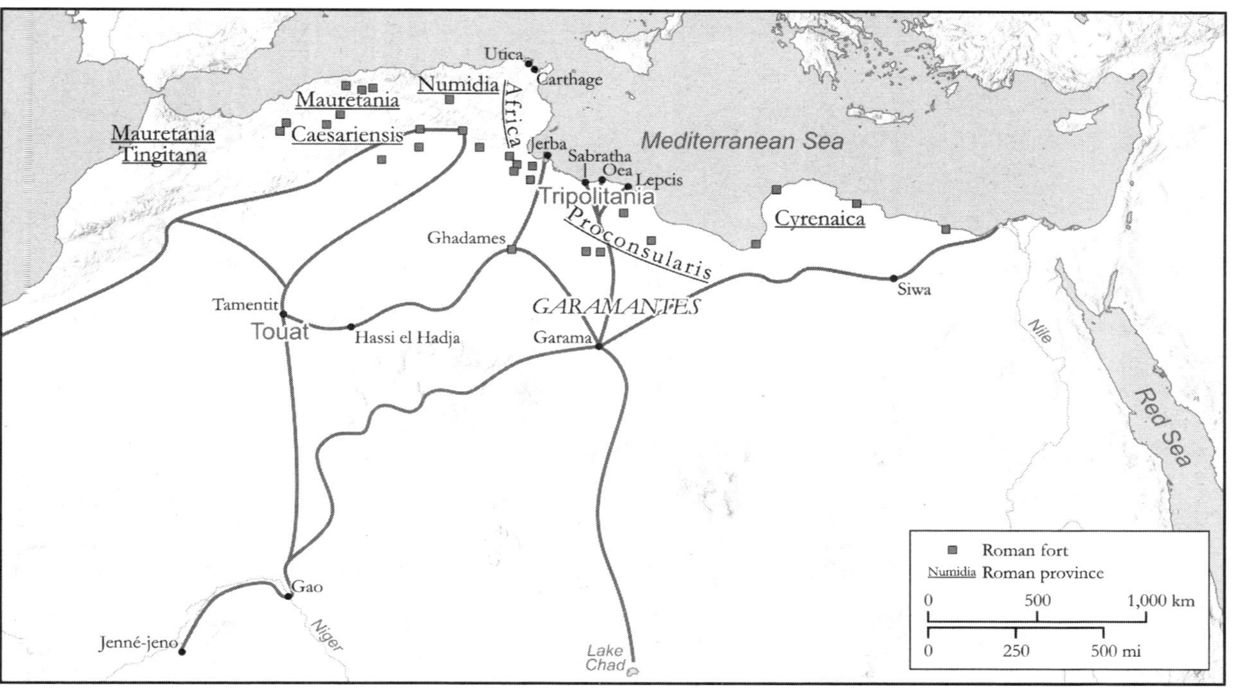

Northern Africa and the Sahara in the third century CE

CHAPTER TWENTY-TWO

Salt Roads

LEPCIS, 202 CE

The idea that "all roads lead to Rome" is a modern one, though people have long thought that many of them can. The French theologian Alan of Lille said in 1175 that "a thousand roads over the centuries lead to Rome men who wish to seek the Lord with all their heart," and by the time Chaucer was writing in the late fourteenth century the notion that "diverse pathes leden the folke the right wey to Rome" had become proverbial: he uses the phrase to make the point that the same scientific truths are found in multiple languages and traditions.[1]

What is striking in the ancient context is how few roads did in fact lead to Rome. The capital city was often far removed from the hubs and routes of its empire, and for that matter from the minds of its inhabitants. Roman empire reached its greatest extent in the early second century CE under the Iberian-born Trajan (r. 98–117 CE), the first emperor to come from the provinces. In 106 he seized the Nabataean kingdom in Arabia; in 107 he conquered Dacia across the Danube in modern Romania; and in 114–16 he annexed Armenia and subjugated Mesopotamia. Yet there is almost no mention of Rome in the *Periplus of the Red Sea,* and the ships that sail the trade routes from Egypt to Arabia, India, and east Africa are referred to throughout as "Hellenic." Agriculture and industry meanwhile were increasingly centered on north Africa, in fertile provinces that lay between the sea and the Sahara, home to another powerful state entangled with Rome by slavery and salt.

It's easy to imagine deserts as empty spaces, vast lonely seas of sand. In fact, they are more like real seas: forbidding to the uninitiated and the ill-equipped, but faster to cross than other terrain, with fewer obstructions. There are helpful oasis "islands," and a lack of fixed roads makes it easy to disappear. As a home to herders, smugglers, oilmen, and political radicals the Sahara has always been busy, but in antiquity it was home to a great trading kingdom based in what is now the southern Libyan Fazzan.

We first meet the Garamantes in the fifth century BCE, when Herodotus calls them "a very mighty people" on the trans-Saharan trade route leading west from Egyptian Thebes: a chain of freshwater oases ten days distant from each other, with date palms and enormous salt deposits extracted from the beds of dried-up prehistoric lakes.[2] His understanding of the route itself is vague: he thinks it leads ultimately to the Pillars of Hercules, although in fact it can be traced to the Niger Bend, where the archaeological remains of trading cities date back to this period.[3]

According to Herodotus, the Garamantes live in an oasis thirty days' travel from the Nile, where they farm crops and salt, herd cows that graze backward because of the awkward shape of their horns, and hunt "cave-dwelling Ethiopians" in chariots pulled by four horses.[4] Decades of archaeological fieldwork in the Libyan desert have overturned the impression Herodotus gives here of a relatively primitive community, but at least one detail seems to have been true: horse-drawn chariots are depicted in numerous rock carvings in the central Sahara, perhaps by their terrified victims.[5]

The origins of the Garamantian state lie in climate change, but its prosperity depended on the liberal importation of ideas and technologies along trade routes.[6] A period of desertification at the beginning of the first millennium BCE encouraged Saharan herders to invest in new irrigation systems for agriculture. First they began to dig *shaduf* wells, a simple and robust system for raising water to ground level found in western Asia from the third millennium BCE and in Egypt from the second. This allowed the early Garamantes to farm the wheat, barley, vines, dates, and figs that they acquired along the same routes, no doubt along with horses and the know-how to build chariots.[7]

The next step was to adapt the old Assyrian shaft-and-gallery tunneling technology to bring water from underground lakes to lower-lying settlements and farmland through tunnels up to four or five kilometers long.[8]* These "foggaras" were already found in arid environments in western Asia, and they now allowed the Garamantes to farm the central desert, where daytime temperatures can reach 131 degrees Fahrenheit and average annual rainfall—if it rains at all—is little more than a centimeter.

By the fourth century BCE the Garamantes were moving down from hill forts to villages and then towns in the valleys, suggesting confidence in their own ability to control and defend the region. They founded Garama, which would remain their capital for almost a thousand years, and made themselves a crossroads in the desert. Tracks led east to the Nile, west to the Niger, south to Lake Chad, and north to the "Lotus-Eaters" who lived on or near the island of Jerba, a caravan journey of thirty days.

There is a persistent myth that significant trans-Saharan trade only started in the medieval period, but small amounts of Carthaginian pottery begin to appear at Garama as early as the third century BCE, and pottery made in the Roman empire has been found at more than 200 Saharan sites, starting in earnest in the late first century CE.[9] By now the

*It is easy to spot foggaras on aerial photographs because the earth dug out of each access shaft was simply deposited around the top of the hole, leaving long lines of what look like giant molehills across the Saharan landscape. The assumption was however that the technology arrived during the Roman or Islamic era, until work in 1999–2001 to match individual channels to specific sites and settlements revealed that some were dug much earlier; their appearance means that ironworking must have reached the Sahara too, since foggaras could not be excavated by hand or stone. It was only later that this technology traveled north across the Roman frontier reaching Lambaesis, where the Roman legion was based (Andrew Wilson, "The spread of foggara-based irrigation in the ancient Sahara," in David J. Mattingly et al., eds., *The Libyan Desert: Natural Resources and Cultural Heritage*, London: Society for Libyan Studies, 2006).

Garamantes had created a powerful, urbanized kingdom with an economy based on oasis agriculture, long-distance commerce and workshops that churned out worked glass, carnelian, and wool for the caravans.

New technologies continued to arrive from both sides of the Sahara: summer crops like pearl millet, sorghum, and cotton from the south; from the north, Mediterranean-style rotary hand querns to grind wheat, the wine press, warp-weighted looms, mud-brick and ashlar masonry. Garama itself acquired stone-built houses, Ionian and Corinthian columns, and a temple with a colonnaded court. Someone even imported specialized tiles from Roman Tripolitania on the Libyan coast to build a Roman-style bathhouse.[10]

Although we have nothing like the *Periplus of the Red Sea* to guide us in the desert, we can guess how these north–south routes worked. For one thing, they were increasingly traveled by camel. The dromedary was in use as a pack animal in the Sahara by the second century CE at the latest, introduced from north Arabia via Sinai and Egypt. By the fourth century CE it had reached Senegal, along with donkeys and chickens.[11]

Different breeds of dromedary may have been used for different stages of the journey too: in more recent times it was standard to move cargo across at a convenient central oasis from a beast with smaller, harder feet suited to the rocky southern Sahara—the animals now associated with the Touareg—to one with broader, splayed toes for the sandy northern stretches. And as in nineteenth-century accounts, the caravans probably traveled in winter, and broke into smaller groups a day or two apart so as not to overtax oases' water resources.[12]

When it comes to reconstructing the cargo they carried, the archaeological evidence preserves as usual the shadow of ancient trade: the containers, and the small and durable items added to the consignment to make a little more profit. It misses the bulk of commerce in organics: animals, foodstuffs, textiles, and human beings.[13] But the key is to abandon the notion of *trans*-Saharan trade as the norm.

The Garamantes were far more than just middlemen, and the basic pattern they masterminded involved exchanges within as well as across the desert, in at least three different stages.[14] Triangular trade is more familiar from the early modern Atlantic, where goods manufactured in Europe—weapons, wine, and cloth—were exchanged for captive humans in west Africa, who were then transported to the Caribbean to be sold for the brutal work of producing the cotton, sugar, and tobacco that then traveled back to Europe. But something similar was already happening in the ancient Sahara.

We know most about cargo that traveled from the Mediterranean coast down to the desert, because the pottery in which it arrived survives: amphoras designed to carry wine, oil, and salted fish. No such pots are found south of the desert, but aerial photographs of Garamantian territory show ancient salt beds gridded into pans. They also reveal traces of the foggaras that delivered water to dissolve the sodium chloride out of the more complex natural deposits, and the hearths on which the Garamantes evaporated the resulting brine back into a dry and portable substance.[15]

Unlike pepper, salt is essential for life: the body needs it for a variety of physical functions. It can also be used to preserve food, which is especially important in regions where ice is impossible to manufacture; its role as a seasoning is just a bonus. In west Africa there are very few natural deposits of salt, and we know from medieval Arab travelers that huge salt blocks strapped to the sides of camels were cut up into pieces there and used for trade like gold and silver.[16]

There is much less evidence for what came back north.[17] All we hear of reaching Rome are carnelian stones or "carbuncles" mined in the Sahara, which Roman authors call both "Garamantian" and "Carthaginian" stones, indicating the route they took from the desert to the Mediterranean.[18] They couldn't have supported a trade route alone.

In the medieval period the west African gold mines would be the major driver of trans-Saharan trade, but very little gold has turned up at Garamantian sites.[19] Wild animals aren't the answer either. The bones of one unfortunate giraffe were found at Garama, but it is hard to imagine that African animals were regularly transported across the desert for weeks at a time: those destined for the Roman games would have been hunted farther north or transported by sea.[20]

The only plausible solution is human labor.[21]* The direct evidence for an ancient Saharan slave trade is admittedly limited and late: only in the fourth century CE does a Latin geographer say explicitly that Mauretania in the far west exported textiles and slaves.[22] For more than a millennium before that, however, vase paintings and figurines of Black Africans are made across the Mediterranean.[23] Some have definite indications of slavery, such as shackles; others are engaged in menial tasks, like cleaning a boot. Many are children, which fits in with reports that the prisoners brought north across the Sahara to slave markets in the nineteenth century CE were often children, relatively docile and cheaper to feed, even if they could carry a little less.[24]

By the mid-second century CE the Roman empire would have required a quarter to half a million new slaves a year to refresh a total enslaved population of around 10 million.[25] The conquest of much of Europe had sharpened the issue: slaving was not permitted in the Roman provinces. All the same, we should not assume that these Garamantian slave routes always led to Rome, or even across the Mediterranean.

Many of the prisoners could have been put to work in the Fazzan itself, where the needs of the Garamantian state were considerably greater than those of medieval and early modern Saharan populations, who had no comparable agricultural kingdoms.[26] Quite apart from farming and workshop production, there were hundreds of foggaras to dig and maintain: hard, unpleasant, and dangerous work, and it is difficult to imagine that there were many volunteers. Then there was also plenty of demand for labor in the Roman provinces of north Africa itself as they became the driving force of the Roman imperial economy.

. . .

*Slavery was still at the heart of Saharan trade in the nineteenth and twentieth centuries, which remained triangular: salt was taken south from the desert oases to trade for human prisoners and gold dust, which were then exchanged on the Mediterranean coast for manufactured goods, which came back down to the desert (Andrew Wilson, "Saharan trade in the Roman period: short-, medium- and long-distance trade networks," *Azania* 47, no. 4 [2012], 413).

An Egyptian stone relief made around 2475 BCE portrays a substantial seagoing sailing ship. Its tall, heavy mast is stowed, it has oars for steering and additional propulsion, and supporting trusses add rigidity. Some of the men on board have the long hair and beards associated with Levantines in Egyptian art: this is a Byblos ship.

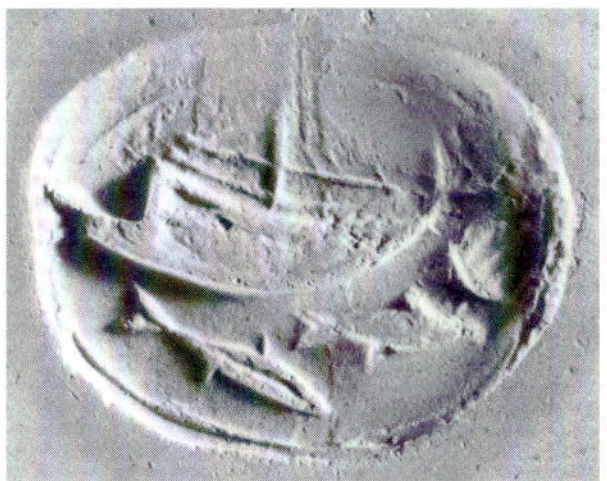

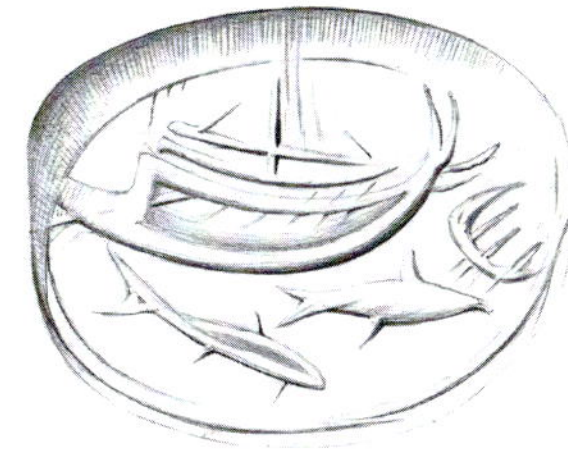

An impression of the tiny sealstone, just 1.8 cm across, that carries the first known depiction of a sailing vessel from Crete. It was buried with its owner in a cemetery in the south of the island around 2000 BCE.

A bronze disk, 32 cm in diameter, found by treasure hunters near Nebra in Saxony in 1999 and dated by a variety of methods to around 1600 BCE. The sun, moon, and stars are picked out in gold, and the golden arc at the bottom could be the boat that carries the sun in Scandinavian rock carvings. One of two thick gold strips later added to frame the scene also survives. Isotope analyses suggest that the copper came from the Alps but the tin and early gold from Cornwall, on the same routes and rivers that brought amber to Mycenae.

A detail of the "flotilla" frieze reveals a variety of boats: one has a mast for a sail, but most are propelled by paddle alone, and some are highly decorated for the occasion. Surrounded by frolicking dolphins, the people on board are enjoying the ride across the waters that define their horizons.

A detail from the narrower riverscape on the east wall, a natural world of Nilotic plants and fantastic animals juxtaposed with the human dramas on the walls to either side.

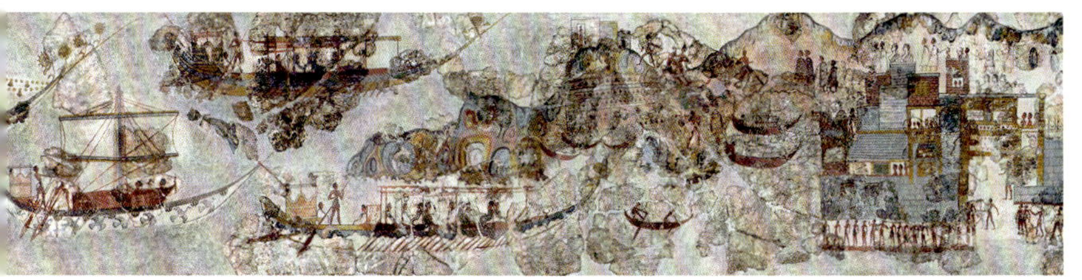

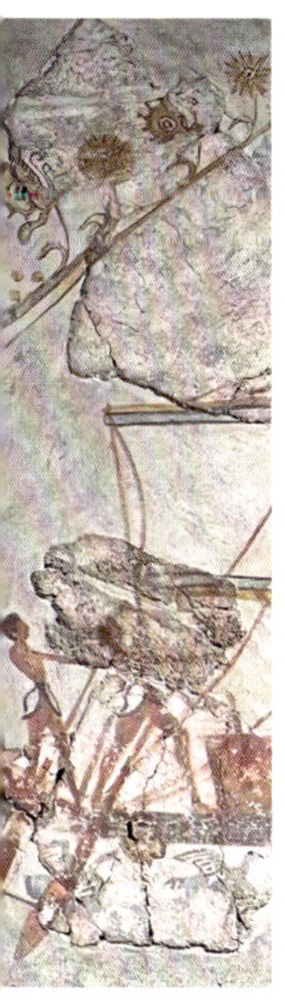

Above: A frieze running along the top of the south wall of a room on the first floor of the "West House" at Theran Akrotiri, an Aegean port devastated by a volcano in the sixteenth century BCE. It depicts a cheerful procession of boats between two towns, perhaps celebrating a local festival. Although the scene may be set on Thera itself, it recalls Cretan painting, and the artist also utilizes Egyptian artistic conventions, stacking the houses vertically to convey visual depth.

Below: Details from the frieze that runs along the same room's north wall depict men drowning at sea, perhaps in a battle, while soldiers march on shore, sporting the oxhide shields, boar's-tusk helmets, and long spears popular on the Greek mainland. Danger and threat pervade the painting, in stark contrast to the flotilla scene opposite: these are two different sides of Aegean life.

One of four gold signet rings buried with the "Griffin Warrior" in a shaft grave at Pylos c. 1500 BCE. 4.5 centimeters across, the bezel depicts five ornately dressed women similar to those in Cretan art. They are standing or dancing on a beach on either side of an inlet leading to a small shrine flanked by trees.

Part of the list of "all the difficult lands north of Asia" carved on the base of a statue of Amenhotep III at his mortuary temple around 1350 BCE. It reveals detailed knowledge of the Aegean: here on the left side the labels for places including Mycenae, Nauplion, and Kythera are carved under the Egyptian king's great foot.

A clay tablet from Ugarit carved with the local cuneiform alphabet about 1400 BCE, perhaps for teaching purposes. The script may be unusual, but the order is familiar: aleph, bet, gimel . . .

This stone monument, 1.3 m in length, was found at Solana de Cabañas in the Spanish province of Extremadura. It was carved in the early first millennium BCE in a long-standing local tradition of "Warrior Stelae," but it also underlines the long-distance contacts that brought central European V-notched shield design south to Iberia, along with Atlantic swords and spears in this era. At the same time, Mediterranean mirrors, clothespins, and chariots traveled west.

This gilded silver bowl found in the Bernardini tomb at Praeneste in central Italy dates to the seventh century BCE, when similar bowls are found elsewhere in Italy, on Cyprus, and in Assyria, part of a shared landscape of cultural tastes and ideas that now stretched across the Mediterranean. The decoration is an amalgam of Egyptian and Assyrian imagery, and the outer ring tells a story as you turn it clockwise: a man leaves a city in a chariot to go hunting, catches his prey, makes an offering, but is then attacked by an ape-like figure. He kills the creature with the help of a winged deity, and returns home.

A wine-mixing bowl found in a seventh-century tomb at Caere in Etruria reveals local interest in Aegean storytelling traditions. Made by a man called Aristonothos, the pot depicts Odysseus and his shipmates blinding the Cyclops—but here the one-eyed monster is not a giant, as in Homer's version, and Odysseus himself may already be the Etrurian hero Utuse.

Central Italians were interested in Carthaginian ideas as well. These gold tablets nailed up in a sanctuary at Pyrgi, Caere's principal harbor, record in Carthaginian Phoenician (left) and Etruscan (middle and right) the dedication of a shrine to the goddess Uni by the local king, Thefarie Velianas. The texts do not directly translate each other: in Phoenician Uni becomes Levantine Ashtart, and the king's title is left out of the Etruscan version, presumably because Etruscan speakers already knew who he was. The event is also dated by different religious calendars in the two languages.

The custom of reclining to feast spread west from Assyria from the eighth century BCE. There it was a distinctively male practice: in this stone relief (above) of a scene set in Ashurbanipal's palace garden and dating to around 645 BCE the king relaxes on a couch while the queen sits enthroned, fanned by women with fly whisks. Their sumptuous retreat is shaded by trees, from one of which hangs the head of King Teumman of Elam. When reclining reached Etruria women adopted it as well, as on this sixth-century terra-cotta sarcophagus (below) from a cemetery in Caere. Farther west there is no evidence for reclining at all.

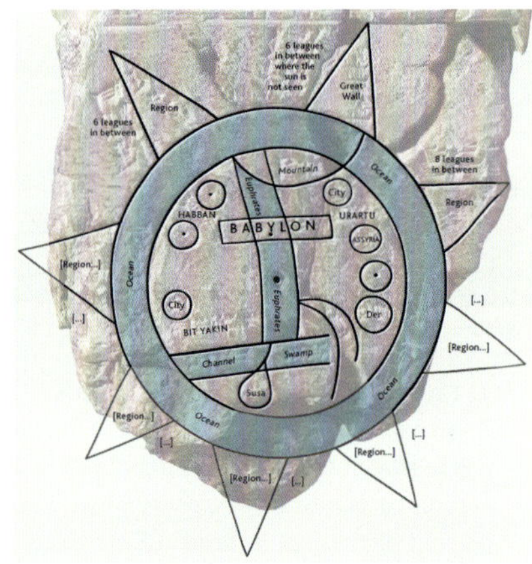

The first surviving map of the world, carved on a clay tablet in the seventh century BCE, is the product of Babylonian scholarship. The inhabited world is contained within a circular ocean and centered on Babylon itself, with "the Euphrates cutting through the city from north to south. Beyond the "bitter river" are eight islands full of strange animals and sights. At least one of the places named—the Kassite homeland of Habban—is incorrectly placed west of Babylon, but this schematic account of western Asia is otherwise strikingly accurate.

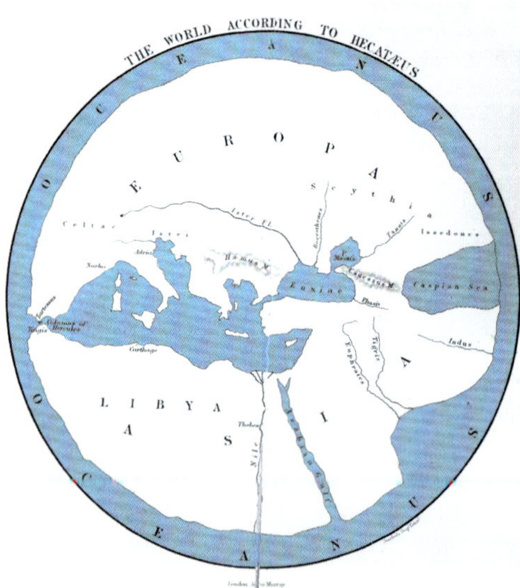

Babylonian geography may well have inspired the first attempts by Greek speakers to make sense of the world. Scholars based at the trading city of Miletus in western Anatolia began to make maps in the sixth century BCE that depicted the known world floating in the middle of an ocean. It probably had Miletus at its center. None survive, but as this modern reconstruction based on literary descriptions shows they also divided the lands they knew into two continents of Europe, to the north, and Asia, to the south. A continent of Africa was only identified in the fifth century BCE.

Babylon's Ishtar Gate was built in baked brick by Nebuchadnezzar II in the early sixth century BCE. Blue and yellow glaze highlighted animals molded in relief, including *mushushu,* creatures sacred to Marduk with the head of a snake, eagles' talons on their back legs, and the body and front paws of a lion.

Darius I had this monument carved on Mount Behistun, high above the road from Babylon to Ecbatana. 15 × 25 meters in size, it commemorates his acquisition of the Persian throne in 522 BCE and his defeat of the revolts that then broke out throughout the empire. A relief sculpture of Darius himself and the bound rebel kings is surrounded by lengthy inscriptions describing his achievements in Elamite, Babylonian Akkadian, and Old Persian, a language now written down for the first time.

Parthian kings reveal flexible cultural affiliations on their coinage. In the later third century BCE the first monarch Arsaces I wears a long, soft headdress with earflaps in a local style (top left). His coins had Greek legends, however, and they were minted on the Athenian weight standard. Mithridates I, who extended the Parthian realm in the mid-second century, has a bare head and diadem in the style of his Greek-speaking Seleucid neighbors (top right), and the Greek legends on his coins declare him a "Philhellene." By the time Mithridates II came to the Parthian throne in 124 BCE the Seleucid kingdom was in decline, and he wears a tiara covered in jewels that has no Mediterranean models (bottom left). By contrast, Mithridates VI of Pontus (r. 120–63 BCE) returned to the iconography of Alexander the Great, wearing his hair in long waves with a forelock and a diadem (bottom right). Rising Roman power had made references to Greek culture a symbol of resistance.

The circular tomb Augustus built for himself and his family just outside the city of Rome in 28 BCE; it was quickly pressed into service.

The tomb of Regina, a British freedwoman who died around the age of thirty in the late second century CE at the Roman fort of Arbeia (South Shields) on Hadrian's Wall. Her Palmyrene husband Barates commissioned this monument depicting her spinning wool in northern European clothing—a tunic over a longer skirt—above both Latin and Palmyrene inscriptions.

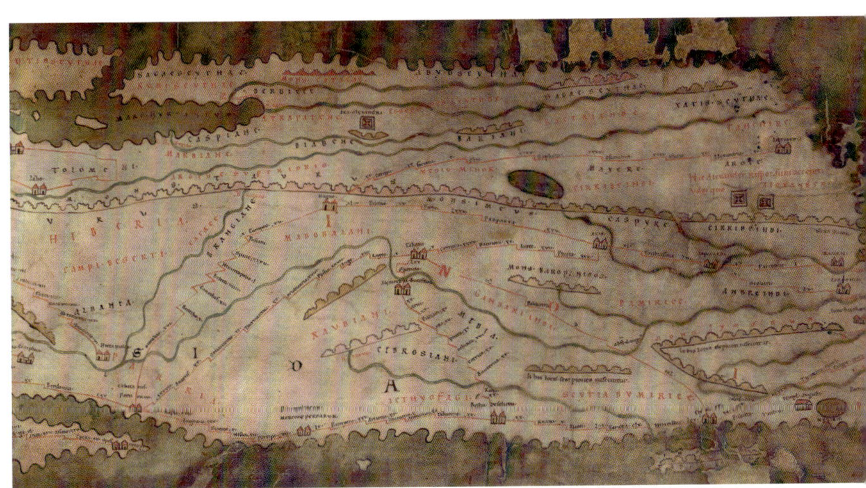

The Peutinger table is a medieval copy of a Roman map of the road network that linked the known world in the early first millennium CE. Long and narrow—6.75 m × 33 cm—it looks not down on the landscape, like a modern map, but along the routes through it: a perspective that has made a comeback in the twenty-first century. This far eastern section depicts Asia from Oman to the Pacific, including the southern Indian port of Muziris, the inland region "where elephants are born," and a vague reference to *Sera Maior* or Great Silk—China.

A view west across the oasis city of Palmyra to the mountains beyond. In the foreground is the temple complex of Bel, a colonnaded Levantine-style courtyard 200 meters along each side (above). From a distance the rectangular temple itself with its peristyle of columns could be a Mediterranean monument. From closer up it looks very different. Its Corinthian columns were crowned with Mesopotamian-style crow-foot merlons and a roof terrace. The walls had windows, the main entrance was in one of the long sides, and the interior had shrines at both ends. It now lies in ruins (below), blown up by Islamic State in August 2015 along with the temple of Baal Shamin, the great arches, part of the theater, and the funerary towers where Palmyra's merchant princes had slept in peace for almost 2,000 years.

A poorly preserved fresco painted at the Ummayad ruler Walid II's desert retreat in the early eighth century CE depicts the "Kings of the World" of the early seventh century, before their power was eclipsed by that of the Islamic caliphate. They stand in two rows of three, and labels in Greek and Arabic survive for the Roman Caesar, the Visigothic Roderic, the Sasanian Khosrow, and the Axumite Negus. The monarchs are distinguished from each other by their headgear, a variety of hats, helmets, and turbans that reveal knowledge of their own self-presentation at home.

The Lewis Chessmen, carved in Scandinavia from walrus ivory and whales' teeth, arrived on Scotland's Western Isles around 1150 CE. Although the game of chess came to Europe from India via the Islamic world, these pieces are indebted to Scandinavian artistic styles. And despite the name they are not all men: as in other medieval European chess sets, the Arabic "vizier" or minister has become the queen we see here.

Invisible from the exterior of the Norman king Roger II of Sicily's royal palace, his "Palatine" Chapel is dazzling. Once your eyes have recovered from the onslaught of light, color, and gold, you begin to see the different elements: the columns of the nave, looted from local Roman buildings; golden mosaics like those of Constantinople; Greek and Latin inscriptions. Above them the gilded, painted wooden ceiling is carved in a Fatimid *muqarnas* or honeycomb pattern that includes Arabic inscriptions and Christian crosses. The different traditions bleed into each other across the landscape of the chapel, finished in 1143 CE.

The west façade of St. Mark's basilica in Venice drew on Islamic models in the thirteenth century CE: the outer doors sit below delicate ogee arches pierced with stone openwork, elements appropriated from Egypt and the Levant, as well as mosaics in the eastern Christian style, while in the upper register composite arches combine the double curve of the ogee with the rounded arches of Christian tradition.

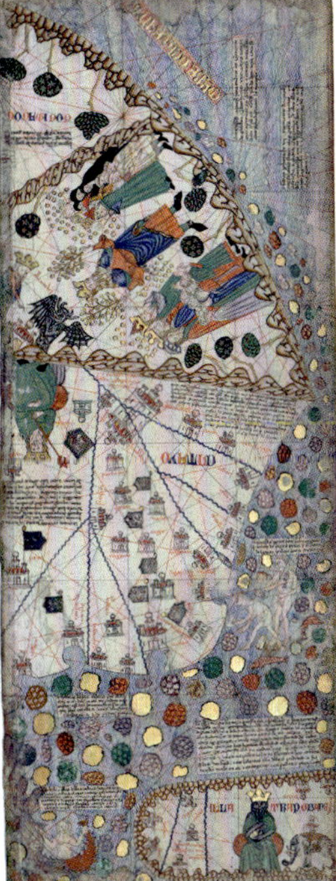

The *Catalan Atlas,* made by Jewish mapmakers on Mallorca for the Infante of Aragon, gives a snapshot of the world as it looked from the western Mediterranean in 1375 CE. It showcases new knowledge: unlike on the Roman Peutinger table, China is full of people and cities, and the long legend (center left) is a detailed description of the double-walled city of Khanbaliq (Beijing). This is decades out of date, however, as it is taken from Marco Polo—as is the information about the "Great Khan" Kubilai, depicted at the center of these sheets and dead now for more than eighty years. The sense that east Asians live in an eternal present is underlined by the portrait just above of Alexander the Great.

Only Europe lacks vivid illustrations in the *Catalan Atlas.* Instead the map highlights the power of contemporary Christian kingdoms: even still-Islamic Granada is marked with a cross, while Ireland is stamped with a large English flag. In Africa meanwhile Mansa Musa of Mali, who died around forty years earlier, hands a nugget of gold to a north African trader riding a camel from a Saharan camp. Off the Atlantic coast are the Azores, Madeira, and the Canaries, islands that would soon become pit stops on routes west to the Americas.

Within its bright blue cobalt rim this tin-glazed earthenware bowl depicts a ship sailing before the wind under the arms of imperial Portugal. The vessel is a caravel, light, fast, and good at beating to windward, with triangular lateen sails carried on two or three masts. The preferred choice of Iberian merchants and Atlantic explorers, this boat must belong to a Christian merchant. The bowl itself was long assumed to be the product of Christian artists working at Valencia who had borrowed the techniques of tin glaze and decoration with gold luster from Islamic traditions, but recent analyses of the clay show that it was actually made in Islamic Málaga around 1425 CE.

Mehmed II conquered Constantinople in 1453 CE and made the new capital of his Ottoman Empire a great center of culture and trade. This portrait was painted a few months before the Sultan's death in 1481 by Gentile Bellini, who had been sent from Venice to serve as resident artist at Mehmed's court.

The Roman territories in northwest Africa were the product of two great conquests: the first of Carthage in 146 BCE, the second of Pompey a century later, along with the local Roman governor and their Numidian allies. When Caesar prevailed in the civil war, he dramatically enlarged Rome's African provinces by annexing Numidia. He also increased Rome's stake in the region by settling large numbers of veterans in its fertile farmlands and refounding Carthage itself as a Roman colony.

The last major revolt occurred during the reign of Tiberius, led by a Numidian clan leader called Tacfarinas.[27] Tacfarinas exploited classic guerrilla tactics along with his knowledge of the local terrain to keep Roman armies busy for seven campaigning seasons until they finally cornered him in 24 CE, and slaughtered him along with his family. After that, just one Roman legion out of twenty-eight was stationed in Africa, in addition to auxiliary troops—no more in total than 25,000 men and perhaps considerably fewer.

These soldiers were charged with securing the southern frontier, managing movements across it—from long-distance camel caravans to locals moving animals between pastures, seeking farmwork in the province or trading with the Roman camp itself—and extracting as much tax as possible along the way.[28] This border region would have supplied many of the wild animals, skins, and ivory destined for Mediterranean markets and arenas: leopards, ostriches, and elephants lived on both sides of the Roman frontier until they were hunted to extinction in late antiquity.[29]

Farther north, increasing prosperity depended on grain exports: in the late republic much of Rome's grain had come from Sicily and Sardinia, but ever-expanding demand from the city and army called increasingly on the reliable harvests of Egypt and the fertile farmland of the northwest African provinces. It had deep roots in the region all the same.[30] Roman-era farming was based on ancient techniques of land and water management with proven value in the dry local soils: the people of Althiburos were already farming wheat, barley, millet, lentils, peas, and beans before the foundation of Carthage. Now however the institutions of an empire added further capital, coercion, and rewards as well.

Most important in this respect was the *annona*, a Roman state agency that managed the distribution of grain to the army and to Rome itself: one half of the "bread and circuses" that according to the acerbic Roman poet Juvenal now placated a people who used to wield real power.[31] Some of the *annona*'s African grain came from imperial estates, but much was obtained as in-kind taxes, which gave the Roman authorities good reason to encourage the creativity and ingenuity of local farmers and entrepreneurs.

State representatives could also purchase additional supply if it was available, giving private landowners their own incentives to invest capital and resources in cash crops. The roads and bridges the Roman army built for their own convenience and that of Rome's tax collectors further aided the transportation of all these goods to markets and ports.

Archaeological surveys have revealed how farming expanded in northern Africa in this era, peaking from the second to fourth centuries CE, and how the rural population grew with it. Even in the dry and dusty fringes of the Sahara south of modern Tripoli a British survey between 1979 and 1989 to investigate mysterious traces of ancient agricultural activity found that farmers with entirely indigenous names had successfully dammed local wadis (seasonal rivers and streams) to trap the little rainwater available, and manufactured a local landscape of cash crops: orchards growing fruit, olives, almonds, and pistachios.[32]

African oil came to dominate the Mediterranean supply, as we can see in Rome at the new, larger river port established by the Tiber at modern Testaccio in the second or first century BCE. There "Monte Testaccio" is a pottery "mountain" made entirely out of amphora fragments: unlike wine amphoras, oil containers could not be recycled and so they were simply emptied and smashed. In the first and second centuries the vast majority of the amphoras in this dump come from Spain, where the Guadalquivir valley supplied most of Rome's oil and a lot of grain too, but higher up the mound are increasing quantities of north African amphoras.

When the *annona* expanded in the third century to handle olive oil and wine as well as grain, the African provinces were in pole position to profit. Over time, Italian pottery workshops too succumbed to the greater efficiency of African factories, with glossy orange "African Red

Slip" plates, bowls, and cooking pots filling up Mediterranean ports and Garamantian settlements from the second century CE.

North of the Mediterranean things looked different. Even before Trajan's death in 117 CE revolts were under way in the east, and the empire began to shrink again. The next emperor, Hadrian (r. 117–138 CE) put an end to further imperial expansion, even building a wall across Britain to mark the boundary of Roman control and taxation.*

By now the Roman imperial economy depended heavily on African agriculture, manufacturing, and trade, much of which was in the hands of Africans themselves. At the same time, local landowners attained great power and status in Rome: by the 180s CE nearly a third of Roman senators were of African origin.[33]

These were men like Septimius Severus, who was born in 145 CE in the commercial port of Lepcis on the coast of modern Libya. As an ambitious young man Severus sought a political career at Rome, where two of his cousins had already served as consul, and he worked his own way up to that office in 190 CE. In 191 he became governor of Upper Pannonia (modern Austria and Hungary), a European frontier province that gave him control of a healthy proportion of the Roman army. In 192 the emperor Commodus was assassinated; two more were killed the following year, and Severus claimed the throne with the support of the sixteen legions now stationed on the Danube and the Rhine; the senate prudently agreed with him. Rome may have ruled Africa for centuries, but by the end of the second century CE an African ruled Rome.

Severus spent most of his reign on frontier campaigns, including the annexation of two new provinces out of Parthian territory beyond the Euphrates. In 202, however, he made a trip home to the city of his birth, like Palmyra a trading center on the edge of the Roman empire that participated in more than one world.[34]

The city had been entrenched in a Roman province for well over two

*The Antonine Wall built farther north in 142 CE between the Firth of Forth and the Firth of Clyde in modern Scotland held for less than a decade.

centuries but it still proudly advertised its own identity as an ancient colony of Tyre.[35] Phoenician was still the local language at all levels of society; it was said that when Severus' own sister came to visit him in Rome, her Latin was such an embarrassment to him that he sent her home again.[36] Lepcis represented in miniature the ancient Maghreb as a whole in this era, poised between networks of the desert and the sea, at the economic heart of the Roman imperial project but keeping Rome itself at something of a distance.[37]

When he disembarked at the city's great harbor, recently renovated at his own expense, Septimius Severus must have been proud of what he saw: not only the gleaming marble of the new quay, but the bustle and hum of a commercial port. The winds and currents made Lepcis a reliable stop on routes west to Italy even from the northeast Mediterranean, and it got a lot of traffic.[38] He could have watched customs officials interviewing skippers and annotating their records, stevedores loading thousands of amphoras of grain and oil onto hulking cargo ships and driving prisoners into them as well.

Just a few minutes' walk in the salt air would then have brought him and his entourage to the flagstone paving of the ancient city's central piazza, where two temples to local gods flanked a larger one to Rome and Augustus built in the reign of Tiberius, adorned with statues of that emperor's family and inscriptions in Phoenician as well as Latin.

As they processed south down the main street the imperial party could have seen more Phoenician inscriptions before passing under an arch dedicated to the emperor Trajan. Over to the right loomed the curved walls of a theater built in the Italian style; a little farther away was the Alexandrian merchants' temple to the Hellenistic Egyptian god Serapis.

Where the road now finished, a grand new four-way arch awaited, built by the city for their favorite son in a fashionably baroque style, but still designed on the Punic cubit, not the Roman foot. The fine coating of sand on its paving gave a taste of the desert beyond, the start of a caravan route south via Ghadames to Garama and the Saharan world.

. . .

Severus died at York in 211 while attempting to conquer Scotland. The imperial throne did not revert to Europeans: he was succeeded by his half-African, half-Syrian son, nicknamed Caracalla for the distinctive hooded cloak or *caracallis* that he liked to wear. A year later the young man extended Roman citizenship to the entire freeborn male population of the Roman provinces, marking the moment at which an empire spread across three continents swallowed up the ancient Roman state.

Caracalla was murdered by one of his bodyguards in 217, and was replaced by another African, Macrinus, a Berber from modern Algeria. He himself was deposed after just over a year in a plot led by Caracalla's aunt Julia Maesa, in favor of her Syrian grandson Elagabalus, who became emperor at the age of fourteen. The young man brought with him to Rome the Syrian sun god Elagabal, a large black meteorite, to replace Jupiter at the head of the Roman pantheon. This was not his only outrage against local taste: he was said to have married several men and a Vestal Virgin, eaten parrots, and fed them to pet lions too. He was assassinated by soldiers in a latrine at the age of eighteen and thrown into the Tiber.[39]

Rome's center of gravity had by now shifted far from Italy, and from the European provinces, where the economy was in freefall. The problems were in part environmental, relating to the end of the Roman Warm Period that had started three centuries earlier. They were compounded by previously unknown diseases that traveled along trade routes.[40] Simultaneous outbreaks of an early form of smallpox seem to have occurred in Rome and China in the mid-second century CE, possibly killing the emperors Marcus Aurelius and Lucius Verus at the western end and hastening the demise of the Han dynasty at the other. A century later the "Plague of Cyprian"—perhaps Ebola—spread from Ethiopia to Egypt and from there to the whole of the Roman empire.

Both prices and inflation rose sharply from the later second century, and silver production declined: there were fewer people to mine it, and far fewer who could afford to buy it. We can trace this process in cores taken from the Greenland ice, which preserve a record of declining lead pollution produced by the silver industry farther south.[41] We can also see it in the Roman money supply itself: in 50 CE the silver coinage had been 97 percent pure, in 250 it was 40 percent, and in 270 only 4 percent.[42]

Cities declined, construction stopped, there were uprisings in the countryside and the rising cost of transport encouraged the localization of trade in all but luxury goods. Taxes and rents were increasingly paid in kind rather than in cash. Only the provinces of northern Africa, along with Egypt the wealthiest in the empire, were largely untouched by the troubles.[43]

Eventually the army took full control of the Roman imperial machine, appointing and dispatching emperors according to their military prowess or pliability, in what has been called the "Crisis of the Third Century": Rome had more than twenty-five rulers in fewer than fifty years from 235 CE. Some never saw Rome itself.

CHAPTER TWENTY-THREE

The Rise of the Barbarians

AQUITAINE, 418 CE

To understand the vulnerability of the Roman empire, we have to think of it not as a collection of lands but as a series of coasts. By the end of the first century BCE Rome controlled the edges of the Mediterranean, and by the second century CE the shores of the Black and Red seas, but that was as far as it easily went. Attempts to secure territory farther inland tended quickly to collapse or required a vast military presence to maintain. The issue was only in part the cost of travel and transportation overland and the difficulty of monitoring the hills and forest country. The real problem lay with the border, and the free land on the other side.

Europe had always been especially hard to hold. Of the twenty-five Roman legions in existence at the end of Augustus' reign, eighteen were stationed in Europe. This is where resistance to the Roman presence was always greatest and the frontiers most vulnerable, requiring a massive, permanent military presence. In a sense the Romans reaped the consequences of their own success. Contact with the Roman empire had dramatic effects.

The "Germans" that Caesar encountered across the Rhine in the 50s BCE—a label Romans put on peoples living as far to the east as modern

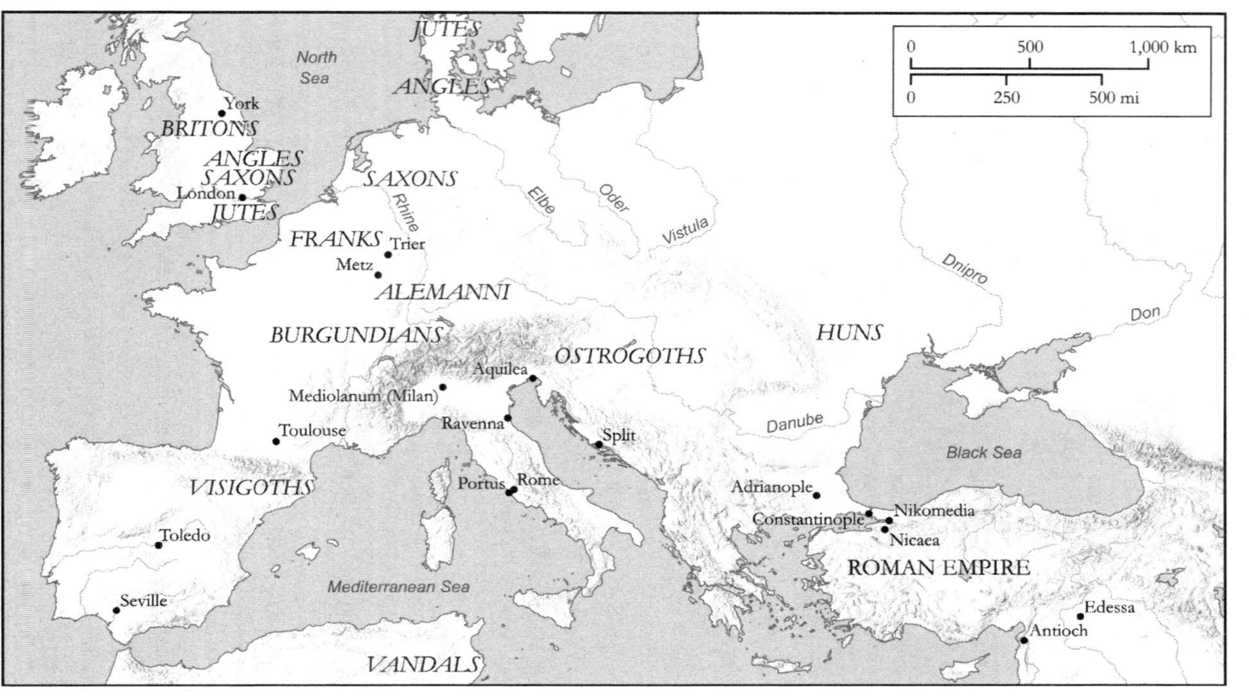

Europe in the fifth century CE

Slovakia—had, he reported, an egalitarian society based on kinship and clans, ruled by a tribal council, with tribal land redistributed on an annual basis.[1] This romantic idea of primitive German liberty, reinforced by Tacitus in his ethnographic work *Germania,* has fueled modern civilizational thinking since Guizot traced the origins of European civilization in 1828 to the Romans, the Church, and the German barbarians.[2] It wasn't new even then: in 1748 the French *philosophe* Montesquieu suggested that the admirable political liberties of the English were rooted among the Germans who threw off the Roman yoke: "this fine system was found in the forests."[3]

If it was ever true, however, then once Caesar himself established a border at the river and war gave way to trade, diplomacy, and mercenary service, society on the other side changed fast. Gifts and payments from Roman merchants and officials allowed some people to impose their authority over their neighbors. Tacitus reports that by the early first century CE Roman merchants had already settled in the court of a powerful German king who ruled the Marcomanni in the region of modern Bohemia.[4]

He was an exception in this era, but across the lands north of the border archaeology reveals the emergence of a wealthy warrior class. Where hamlets of just a few households had been common, larger settlements often gathered around one house much bigger than the rest. In time Roman-style villas were built well beyond the Rhine. Farther north again, huge quantities of Roman weapons are found in Scandinavia, and the Danish runes that first appear in the second century CE were loosely based on an Italian script.[5]

At the height of Roman power in the second century, a heavily militarized frontier ran from the Black Sea to the North Sea, picked up in Britain by Hadrian's Wall. The increasingly centralized and stratified societies beyond were too much trouble to subdue fully, but easy enough to repel as necessary, and the heavy concentration of Roman legions in Europe ensured that they were not yet a threat to compare with the Parthians in the east. In the third century, however, bigger confederations came together north of the border. From west to east they included the Franks, the Alamanni, the Vandals, and the Goths, whose heartland was north of the Black Sea. Roman reporters make no real distinctions between them when it comes to their lack of culture and mindless belligerence.

As Romans battled the economy, the weather, and one another, the northerners began to launch raids across the border as far as Iberia, Attica, and even Rome. In 251 a Roman emperor died during a battle against Goths south of the border in Moesia. Parts of the Danube frontier were conceded permanently to peoples beyond, and by 275 the Roman army had to withdraw across the Danube from Dacia.

In the end however the "fall" of the western Roman empire was due not to assault by armed hordes crossing the border, but to the slow eradication of the border itself, as the people on either side became increasingly integrated, those to the south grew alienated from Roman power, and those to the north gained the upper hand. At the same time, a new east–west division within the Roman empire itself paved the way for the rise of a new imperial capital on the border between Europe and Asia.[6]

As northerners moved back and forth across the borders of the Roman empire, they offered the rural Roman peasantry a new perspective on their own situation. Modern arguments about whether historical empires were simply "good" or "bad" for their subjects miss the point: empire is always good for some and bad for others, in both the conquered and conquering societies. It is just the proportions that differ. Some people—and communities—did very well out of the Roman occupation. The success of Roman government relied for centuries on the cooperation and collaboration of local people, especially those who were already powerful and wealthy, and the Romans took care to keep them that way.

For others, however, the Roman empire looked very different. Rome's subjects paid taxes to fund their own occupation and saw little benefit from it: Roman roads and aqueducts were built for Roman forts, mines, and colonies, not for the native population. Now they could see an alternative as well, a less institutional form of government that made fewer demands on small landholders. As early as the 250s Bishop Gregory "the Wonder Worker" chastised his congregation in Pontus on the Black Sea for defecting to the Goths, murdering their neighbors, and directing the barbarians to the houses most worth plundering.[7]

Farther east meanwhile the Parthian empire had finally collapsed in the 220s, brought down in a revolt led by a client king based in the old Persian heartland. The Romans soon found out that Ardashir's new Sasanian dynasty posed a greater threat, as his family constructed a third great "Iranian empire," as they called it, and ruled it for more than 400 years.[8] In 260 Shapur I (r. 240–270 CE) defeated the Roman emperor Valerian at the Battle of Edessa, seized thirty-seven Roman cities in Syria, Cilicia, and Cappadocia, and sold 70,000 Roman soldiers into slavery. Various stories circulated about Valerian's own fate: on one account he was used for a time as the emperor's footstool for mounting his horse, and then skinned, dyed, stuffed, and put on display in a temple to scare Roman ambassadors.[9]

Roman territory began to break away in chunks. In 260 the governor of Lower Germany established a "Gallic empire" out of the provinces of Gaul, Germany, Britain, and Spain, which lasted for almost fifteen years and was only reabsorbed in 274. In 270 the self-titled Queen Zenobia, widow of a powerful Palmyrene warlord who had ruled the oasis kingdom in Rome's name, launched a brief but stunningly successful campaign of expansion, reaching Antioch in the north and the borders of Egypt in the south. In 273 the new Roman emperor Aurelian took revenge. He sacked Palmyra, destroyed its trading networks and reduced it to a minor Roman military outpost.

Rome's first effective ruler in half a century was Diocletian, who came to power in 284 with little respect for Roman tradition. He designed a new palace at Split in modern Croatia on Persian principles, employed large numbers of eunuchs at his court, and encouraged his subjects to call him *dominus*, and *deus* too. Lord and God.[10] They may have been more impressed by the Sasanian embassy that arrived during his reign accompanied by thirteen elephants, six charioteers, and 250 horses.[11]

Diocletian was at the same time a natural populist, obstructing and persecuting religious minorities, including Christians. He knew how to save the Roman empire as well, moving the administration out of the city and closer to the front, dividing the territory in two to face different threats to east and west, and dividing the leadership between four "tetrarchs." Two Augustuses would rule together for a fixed term, one more senior based in the east at Nikomedia—Diocletian appointed himself to this onerous position—and the other his junior at Milan in the west, with two Caesars based at Trier and Antioch as their deputies and presumptive heirs.

The most powerful military commanders in the empire were now working with rather than against one another, and the junior parties were incentivized by the hope of smooth promotion through the new structure. The Roman military response along the frontiers grew stronger, and the barbarians were temporarily subdued; south of the border they were increasingly incorporated into Roman structures. In 305 Diocletian and his co-Augustus retired alive, as planned, in favor of their Caesars—only to witness civil wars break out again between them, their new deputies, and a variety of pretenders.

Seven years later, the city of Rome is braced for invasion from the north. A warrior is on his way, a man born in what is now Serbia, the son of a local soldier and his Bithynian wife or concubine. He already controls Britain and Gaul, and his soldiers have proclaimed him ruler of the Roman west at the urging of a German king. Now he is marching south at the head of a great army made up in large part of barbarians, supported by a foreign god. His ultimate goal is to overthrow Diocletian's constitution.

Constantine was the son of the western Augustus and had expected to succeed his father when he died in 306. Frustrated by the refusal of the senior Augustus to recognize him as more than Caesar, he turned to his father's ally Crocus, king of the Alamanni.[12] Led by this barbarian his troops acclaimed the young commander Augustus at York, and he arrived on the outskirts of Rome in 312. Prompted by a vision of a cross of light—or so he later said—he bade his soldiers add Christian symbols to their standards, and at the Milvian Bridge over the Tiber he defeated his principal rival for power in the west.

In 324 Constantine also defeated the eastern Augustus Licinius to take sole control of the whole of the empire, temporarily reuniting its two halves. He regularly fought barbarians on the northern front, polishing his military reputation as a champion of Rome, but he recruited widely among them as well, especially among the Franks. He wasn't the only one: in his decisive battle against Licinius, Franks fought for Constantine, and Goths for his rival.[13]

Like Diocletian, Constantine took his style from the east: from his reign onward Rome's rulers replaced their laurel wreaths with diadems in the tradition of the old Hellenistic kings and the contemporary Sasanian court.[14] He also propelled to power an Asian deity, the Christian God, working with his eastern counterpart to guarantee freedom of religious worship across the empire.[15]

This put an end to the persecution of Christians, at least by pagans. In 325 Constantine convened the first conference of Christian bishops, the Council of Nicaea. It established a common framework for determining the date of Easter, and declared that the followers of an Alexandrian priest named Arius were heretics: they took the superficially plausible view that Jesus the son must have been born after God his father, and could not therefore partake of exactly the same substance.

Constantine returned to Rome just twice, in 315 and 326. This was not unusual by now: most Roman rulers saw little or nothing of the original capital, choosing to live and fight closer to the borders, where military action was now relentless. Rome received only five imperial visits in the whole of the fourth century.[16]

Constantine however went further, founding a second capital far to the east at the Greek-speaking town of Byzantium on the border of Europe and Asia and filling it with grand monuments and churches.* The new city was called Constantinople, but it was dedicated in 330 as Nova

*Since the sixteenth century scholars have called the eastern Roman empire "Byzantium," after the ancient city on the Bosphorus rebranded as Constantinople. The term is redolent of the exotic and baroque, and it is unnecessary: however alien it looks to modern eyes, the administration at Constantinople saw itself and was seen by others as Roman. Renaming it reinforces the notion of Rome as essentially western, and suggests that a "Rome" farther east must be hiding something entirely new.

Roma: New Rome. It symbolized the increasing importance to the Roman state of its lucrative eastern territories over the west and Rome itself.

Constantine was finally baptized when he was close to death. He was given a Christian funeral, and Christianity became fashionable in the higher echelons of Roman society, as churches were built in towns small and large across the empire. Christian missionaries crossed the northern border too, people like Ulfilas ("Little Wolf") who had grown up among Goths after his family had been taken prisoner in a raid on Anatolia and now preached them the gospel.

Ulfilas also invented an alphabet in which to write the Gothic language out of a combination of Greek and Latin letters and Nordic runes. This allowed him to translate the Bible for the benefit of his hosts, although he left out the Book of Kings on the grounds that Goths needed no encouragement when it came to aggressive expansion.[17] Like many of the missionaries who converted barbarians to Christianity in the fourth century, however, Ulfilas was of the Arian persuasion, and the Goths remained heretics in the eyes of Nicene Christians until well into the sixth century CE.

Only one fourth-century Augustus, Julian "the Apostate" (r. 361–363 CE) rejected the new religion, restored and reopened the pagan temples, and ostentatiously practiced animal sacrifice at least twice a day. Otherwise, the Roman state moved over the fourth century from persecuting Christianity to enforcing it. In 380 the Augustus Theodosius outlawed the traditional pagan rituals and sacrifices, and issued an edict that all peoples subject to Rome should profess the Christian religion.

During the fourth century the eastern provinces of the Roman empire pulled decisively ahead in both prosperity and prestige.[18] The western empire meanwhile was falling to pieces. And as the new internal division between east and west established itself, that between north and south of the border lost much of its meaning.

Northerners moved into Roman cities in large numbers in the fourth century and many signed up to the Roman army too, in return for a good wage as well as land, farming equipment, and tax exemptions on discharge, cleverly extended to cover the new recruit's parents as well.[19] Not everyone came voluntarily: there was an extensive trade in Goths, and when a Roman aristocrat named Symmachus brought a group of barbarian prisoners to Rome to fight in games arranged for his son, twenty-nine died by strangulation in a suicide pact.[20]

The real trouble started in the 350s, when central Asian nomads that the Romans called Huns began to move in on Gothic lands around the Black Sea.[21] In the 370s large groups of displaced Goths sought permission to cross into the Roman empire and asked for a place to live there. In return they offered hostages and service in the Roman legion. At first these arrangements suited the Roman authorities, but relations between the new arrivals and their hosts soon broke down: in the most notorious episode in 376 tens of thousands of Goths crossed the Danube into holding camps where Ammianus Marcellinus reports that corrupt border troops supplied the starving families with dogmeat in exchange for their own children.[22]

Two years later large groups of frustrated Gothic soldiers united in arms at Adrianople, destroyed two-thirds of a Roman legion, and killed the Augustus Valens. A contemporary historian described it as the worst Roman defeat since Hannibal's victory at Cannae in 216 BCE.[23] Valens' successor Theodosius took the hint and settled the Goths south of the border as allied forces, but the Roman empire now had to take more notice of the Steppe.

At the same time, discontent within the empire grew. Reforms to the Roman fiscal system from the mid-fourth century tied peasants to the place they were registered for tax, along with their descendants, and then even to the specific estates on which they worked. This ensured that landlords had a permanent source of labor and rent at no ongoing cost, and their tenants had no escape route. Tax evasion by the wealthy became a significant problem as well: one late-fourth-century law designed to curb it explicitly notes that the failure of the rich to pay their share adds to the burdens of the poor.[24] The world of the peasant farmer grew smaller and more wretched. Sporadic revolts that had broken out within the northern provinces from the late third century now mutated into continuous guerrilla warfare against local Roman administrators.

By now a barbarian had risen to the top of the Roman imperial administration: Flavius Stilicho, the son of a Vandal. Stilicho had become the head of Theodosius' household and negotiated a treaty with Shapur III in 383 that partitioned Armenia and brought peace to the eastern frontier; around the same time he married Theodosius' niece Serena. When Theodosius died in 395 he left the empire to his sons, the east to Arcadius in Constantinople and the west to the ten-year-old Honorius, with Stilicho as regent and overall commander, at least in the west. Honorius had to content himself with anti-barbarian gesture politics, including banning trousers and boots from the streets of Rome.[25]

It is characteristic of the times that Stilicho's own biggest headache was another barbarian. Alaric was a Goth who had pursued a career in the Roman administration interspersed with fitful marauding around Roman territory with a large and loyal group of supporters. In 401 they invaded Italy—probably the proximate cause of the shift of the western capital to the Adriatic port of Ravenna in the Po Delta the following year—and met with several defeats at Stilicho's hands before the Vandal changed tack and involved Alaric in a murky plot against Arcadius. Amid suspicion of treason Stilicho was murdered by the regime in 408, Alaric besieged Rome, and when negotiations with Honorius failed in 410 he sacked the city for three days.

That was all there was to it: when the food ran out, he and his men left quietly, and Alaric himself died shortly afterward. The Iberian Christian Paulus Orosius reported a few years later that a visitor to the city would scarcely have known that anything had happened.[26] But the symbolic value of the first sack of Rome in 800 years was immense, and other Christian commentators made much of it, ensuring its continued notoriety to this day: "the city was captured that captured the whole of the world," whimpered the ascetic Jerome from his library at Bethlehem, "the brightest light of all the lands has been extinguished."[27]

In fact, Rome simply continued its gentle decline as its great coastal harbor at Portus silted up. Constantinople was increasingly seen as the sole capital of the Roman empire, and it became the center of the

Roman world. New walls built in 413 added a third to the city's size, as the population of Rome itself began to plummet, dropping from around 600,000 at the time of Alaric's sack to fewer than 100,000 in the sixth century CE.[28]

Perhaps it was the increasingly stark distinction between the two halves of the empire that suggested to the great African bishop Augustine of Hippo (now Annaba in Algeria) a new way to divide the world as a whole. In *City of God,* written in the early fifth century, he explains that the world can be divided either into three unequal continents or into two more equal parts: the Oriens (Asia) and the Occidens (which would include both Europe and Africa).[29]

This was a new way of thinking about "east and west," and the one on which the modern concepts ultimately depend. References in Greco-Latin literature tended to treat the pair not as separate spheres but as two ends of a spectrum: the path of the sun and the axis of the Mediterranean Sea, the natural orientation of ancient thought.[30] But Augustine's binary formulation had as yet no theological or symbolic content, and the terms Occidens and Oriens themselves still refer to the rising and setting sun: a natural not a cultural phenomenon.

Italy meanwhile faced invasion by Huns who had followed the Goths into central Europe under a new leader named Attila, established themselves on the Hungarian Plain, and bullied the Roman emperor into paying them tribute.[31] In 452 Attila took Aquileia and Milan and threatened Rome, but he died of malaria the following year.

Scholars have agreed since the sixth century that the final "fall of Rome" to the barbarians should be dated to 476 CE, and that it was a catastrophe.[32] It has become a landmark in the traditional story of Western Civilization, marking the end of its first phase, and the beginning of a dark and dangerous period of medieval history before the hardy scholars of the Italian Renaissance shone a torch back through the gloom.

This is again, however, civilizational myth-making. The Roman state didn't fall in 476. Things were changing in the western Roman provinces, leading to different ways of life and government. But the Roman empire itself had already been based for a century at Constantinople, and it survived there until 1453.

What happened in 476 was an exchange of power between men with northern roots that left Constantinople formally in charge. Odoacer was a Hunnic officer in the Roman army when he deposed the last western Augustus, Romulus, whose own family came from Pannonia. He took control of Italy in the name of the eastern Augustus, himself an Isaurian chieftain called Zeno who had served in his predecessor's bodyguard and married his daughter. Odoacer ruled from Ravenna as "king," but his gold coinage depicted Zeno, with his own portrait relegated to the silver. The consuls he appointed were approved by the Roman senate.

Thirteen years later Zeno authorized Odoacer's overthrow by Theodoric, the Arian king of a group of eastern (or "Ostro-") Goths who had established their own kingdom in Zeno's Balkan territory in the fourth century. Theodoric replenished the treasury by raising taxes, and repaired aqueducts and baths across Italy.[33] His Ravenna was a city of high, hybrid culture and many faiths: Arian Goths built their own churches alongside those of the mainstream Nicene Christians (who included Theodoric's own mother), and when locals burned down the Jewish synagogue the Gothic authorities forced them to rebuild it.[34] The barbarians continued a tradition of mosaic art begun by the Roman imperial family, but they brought their own touches to it. The portrait of Christ in Theodoric's baptistery portrays him in the Arian style as an unbearded young man, not the mature adult of the Nicene tradition.

Theodoric still ruled in Zeno's name, and he ruled for thirty-three years with the tolerance, if not enthusiasm, of the regime at Constantinople. He was always careful to acknowledge the greater authority even in his own "Roman Republic" of the Roman emperor, his edicts often followed Roman legal precedent, and, as in Constantinople, eunuchs guarded his private quarters.[35]

Meanwhile, the old western provinces had become independent kingdoms. There was no single moment of change, a year when you would have known that you were no longer, really, in the Roman empire. But

Rome's successors transformed a world empire based in central Italy into a mosaic of territories with kings that claimed sole power over their subjects, at least when it came to war and the law.

It started with a series of agreements that allowed barbarian leaders to establish their own domains in Roman Iberia and Gaul. In 418 Honorius settled Alaric's old followers on attractive new lands on the Garonne Valley with easy access to the Mediterranean. In return they agreed to defend the region on Rome's behalf against other invaders. These "Visi-" or western Goths established what was in effect an independent state in Aquitaine, centered on Tolosa (Toulouse), and over time they expanded south into Iberia.[36]

Not all such arrangements were made by mutual agreement. In 429 a group of Vandals entered Africa accompanied by Alans from the Black Sea region, and they began to annex Roman land. Ten years later the Vandal king Geiseric captured Carthage and then the rest of Roman Africa, taking control of Rome's wealthy African territory, farms, and factories and halting vital grain supplies to Italy a century after the founding of Constantinople had diverted Egyptian grain from the peninsula.[37]

Roman soldiers had left Britain in the first decade of the fifth century, meanwhile, amid a complex series of usurpations and a final revolt.[38] By the mid-fifth century new settlers were arriving from modern Denmark and Germany: Jutes, Angles, and Saxons. Some were initially invited as mercenaries by local kings, but they quickly began to establish their own chiefdoms in the east and center of the country, bringing their language, religion, crops, and crafts with them. Saxon-style houses with sunken floors appear in the ruined Roman cities of Canterbury and Colchester, while the city of London was abandoned completely.

The genetic data suggests that the newcomers arrived in significant numbers, both men and women, that migration along these routes continued into the eighth century and that there was a significant level of interaction with the existing British population over ensuing generations, while burials suggest little social or economic stratification between the two groups.[39] Only in the far west of the island did vestiges of Roman culture and language remain, and of Christianity.

Finally in the 480s Clovis, king of the Salian Franks, united all the petty Frankish kingdoms to the north of the Gothic kingdom and took control of the last remnants of the Roman empire in Gaul. His family, the Merovingians, were to rule the Franks for the best part of 300 years.

Across western Europe these new administrations were forces for stability and calm after a period of great disorder, and then during one of increasing isolation. From the fifth century onward the trans-Mediterranean economy withered away, maritime traffic decreased dramatically, factories were abandoned, and the standard of living dropped across the old Roman west: houses became huts, pottery was now handmade, farms appeared in cities.

We might see some of this in terms of simplification rather than collapse. People no longer needed surplus cash to support Roman taxation and the Roman army. Conversely, opportunities for trade or mercenary service with the Romans dried up. But climate change was a serious factor as well.[40]

As the Roman Warm Period receded, the weather became less predictable. Analyses of alluvial deposits in the Rhône Valley suggest a dramatic increase in rainfall from the late fourth century, and there is evidence for the advance of Alpine glaciers from the late third: Europe was becoming much wetter and colder in this era, and peasant farmers in particular will have suffered badly. In this light, the regionalization of the late antique west starts to look less like passive decline than a sensible, forward-thinking reaction to an unpleasant turn of events.

The barbarians maintained continuities with the Roman past. The Visigoths used Latin for their bureaucracy—because they employed the same scribes—and their cities were centers of Latin learning: in the early seventh century the superstar Iberian bishop Isidore of Seville put together an encyclopedia under Visigothic patronage that remained one of the most popular books in Europe right up to the sixteenth century.[41]

They brought their own ideas and values to the old Roman provinces as well. One was a belief in the abilities of women. Inheritance customs in these new kingdoms distributed a landholder's property among his children on his death, male and female, and women could manage their own property. Fortunate women could amass ample resources, and in post-Roman Britain women sometimes attended public assemblies.[42] Resourceful women privileged by birth or marriage could sometimes even seize the reins of power, and one woman who made more than most of these new opportunities was the Visigothic princess Brunhilda, queen of the Franks—and an inspiration for Richard Wagner's Valkyrie.[43]

The Visigoths had abandoned Toulouse in 507 under pressure from the Franks, and Brunhilda was born in their new capital of Toledo in the early 540s CE. She was educated well and married to a Frankish king, Sigebert I, who ruled from Metz. Her troubled path to power began when her sister Galswintha married his brother Chilperic, another Frankish king with territories to the west. This caused great dismay to Chilperic's mistress Fredegund, and soon enough to Chilperic himself as well, when his new wife banned his courtesans.

One way or another Galswintha was strangled, and Chilperic married Fredegund. Brunhilda made a lifelong enemy of the new queen, and their brother-husbands went to war. When Sigebert got the upper hand, he too was killed, with a poisoned dagger, and Brunhilda was imprisoned. She won her freedom in unorthodox fashion by marrying her nephew, Chilperic's son by an earlier marriage, whereupon Chilperic had his unruly offspring tonsured and packed off to a monastery.

Brunhilda seized her dead husband's Frankish throne in 578, supposedly on behalf of her eight-year-old son: women in these kingdoms still could not rule in their own right. She imposed an effective if authoritarian regime of infrastructural, financial, and military reorganization, and joined her own kingdom to that of the Burgundians next door. She retired briefly in 583 when her son became an adult at the age of thirteen, but more in theory than practice. When the Roman emperor Maurice wrote to the young king from Constantinople in 584 it was Brunhilda who replied to thank him, and to explain that she had counseled her son on his response.[44]

Brunhilda's son died in 595, and Brunhilda herself returned to the throne, now in the names of two grandsons. Fredegund died two years later, but Brunhilda's troubles were not over. One of the grandsons married a woman who had served Brunhilda as a slave, and in 599 she persuaded her new husband to exile her old mistress from his court. Brunhilda set her other grandson to war against his brother, engaging a series of lovers in plots to fan dissent between them, and murdering any nobles who opposed her as well as a bishop who had the temerity to question her chastity.

Finally, with both grandsons dead—one of dysentery, the other probably by Brunhilda's own hand—she took the throne a third time in 613 as regent for her great-grandson. Betrayed on the battlefield by her own resentful dukes, she was captured and brought to trial in front of Fredegund's son Clothar for the murder of ten kings. Contemporary chronicles record that she was found guilty by acclamation, led through the army on a camel and then tied to wild horses and torn apart.

Brunhilda's life isn't typical of early medieval Europe, even for a woman of royal birth, but it showcases many of its innovations: educated women, rival and related courts, and an important role for public opinion too. It also shows how slowly some things change: the institution of slavery was still a natural part of life to these Christian men and women. But Christians across Europe and beyond were about to get an almighty shock.

CHAPTER TWENTY-FOUR

Kings of the World

QUSAYR ʿAMRA, C. 730 CE

By the early eighth century an Islamic state stretched from the borders of China to the shores of the Atlantic. Its rulers lived in Damascus, but they also built retreats outside the city to get away from the bustle, the noise, and the constant demands from their own bureaucrats. These square stone castles were not on the coast or in the countryside, but nestled in corners of the desert. They were places of quiet contemplation and conspicuous consumption. The addition of a bathhouse provided a pleasant diversion for the resident lord, and signaled to his guests his unfettered access to water even in the driest of landscapes, a precious natural resource that also nourished his elaborate gardens and the crops grown on-site for the kitchen.

The bathhouse is all that remains of Qusayr ("Little Castle") ʿAmra in modern Jordan, a collection of domes and vaults rising out of the gray, pebbly sand of the desert steppe, now surrounded by scrubby gorse.[1] According to an inscription discovered during conservation work in 2012, Walid II built his desert home there when he was still crown prince, some time between 723 and 743 CE.[2]

It is not an imposing building, and its stone walls are roughly cut. Walid saved his money for the interiors, painting the little edifice

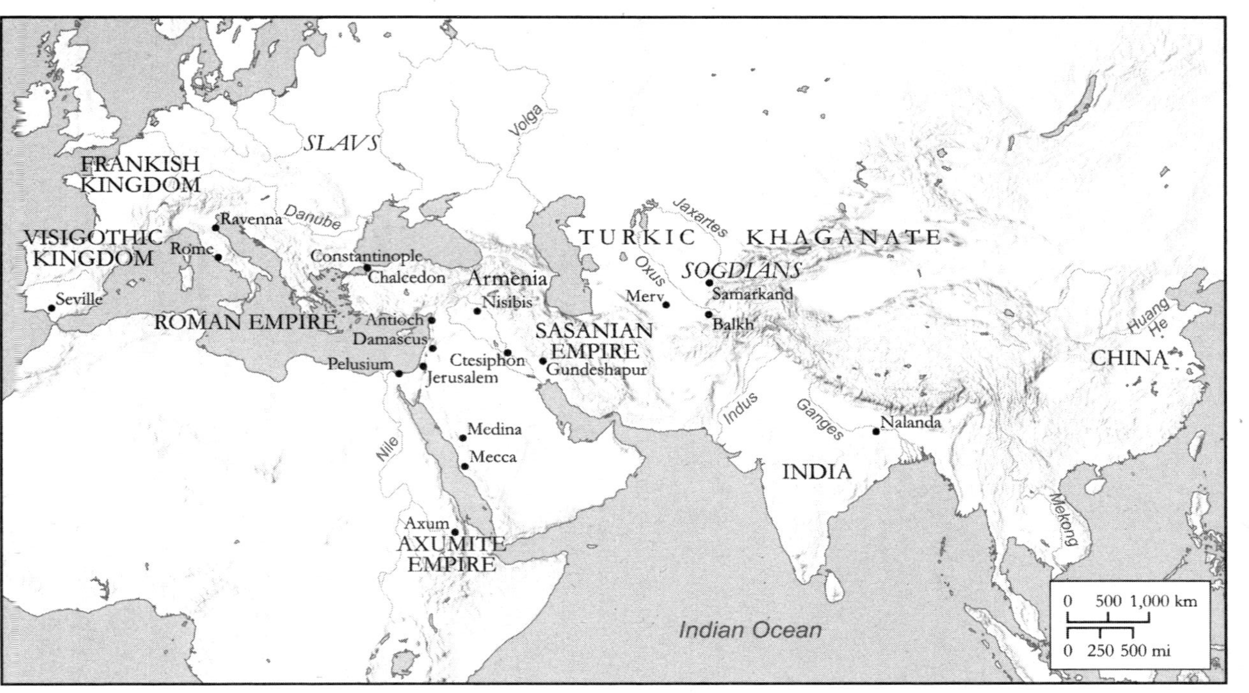

The Kings of the World, c. 560 CE

throughout with vivid scenes of hunting, drinking, naked women, and animal musicians. Islamic divines may have disapproved of figurative art as too close to idol worship, and may have frowned upon many of the matters depicted as well. This was however a private building, and Walid himself was a notorious libertine and poet.[3]

One particular vignette is painted in an inner corner of the audience hall, the first room you enter, and blessedly cool and dim. It depicts six kings standing together under an arcade, making gestures of supplication toward an image of Walid and his family on the adjoining wall. Labels in both Greek and Arabic survive for four of them: the Roman emperor (*kaisar/qaysar*), the Visigothic king (*rodoricos/ludhriq*), the Sasanian shah (*chosrois/kisra*), and the negus (*nego/najashi*) of Axum—all men whose kingdoms had now been overshadowed or eclipsed by the Islamic Caliphate.*

The six foreign rulers are depicted as young and pale, and their faces have a pudding-like quality that contrasts with paintings throughout the bathhouse of the bearded prince who built it engaging in manly activities. But this is not simply a caricature, or the glorification of conquest: the men retain their own dignity, which makes their submission to Walid the more impressive. It is instead a claim to the legacy of kings who by ancient tradition ruled the world. It would also have reminded Walid's visitors of the immense, powerful, and interconnected world of the sixth and seventh centuries CE that his family had inherited.

The concept of the "Kings of the World" was borrowed from Iranian court tradition. The cast varies, giving us a number of candidates for the two kings at Qusayr ʿAmra whose names can no longer be read. As early as the third century CE the Mesopotamian prophet Mani described the four great kingdoms of the world as "the land of Babylon and Persia," the Romans, the Axumites, and "Silis"—perhaps China.[4] At the

*"Negus" in Ethiopic languages simply means king, while the Roman and Persian labels are taken from the legendary early monarchs Caesar and Cyrus. The name of the last Visigothic king, Roderic, is also treated as generic because he was the one Muslims had met as they conquered his kingdom.

sixth-century Sasanian palace at Ctesiphon three empty thrones stood below that of the shah for the use of the kings of China, Rome, and the Turks.[5] A story preserved in a medieval Persian source about "Kings of the World" who came to visit Shah Khosrow II in the seventh century lists the rulers of China, Rome, India, and the Turks.[6]

Sasanian geographical traditions meanwhile present Iran as the center of the world, surrounded by six other regions or states. This list also varies, but it often includes India, Arabia, China, and Turkic central Asia as well as Black Africa (al-Sudan), north Africa including Spain, and Rome (Rum).[7]

The place of Sasanian Iran at the heart of these political and geographical systems was not just patriotism. It reflects the leading role taken by the Sasanian dynasty in interregional commerce since the mid-first millennium CE, pulling together new trade routes from China and India to their own lands and the Mediterranean beyond.[8]

Conquests on their eastern flank had given early Sasanian kings control of central Asian trading cities like Merv, as well as Balkh and Samarkand, in modern Afghanistan and Uzbekistan respectively. Before this, merchants coming from China usually headed south from these cities toward the Indian Ocean to reach destinations farther west, but now they could continue overland across Sasanian territory.

Further expansion gave the Sasanians northern Indian ports as well, and with them control of the old, fast routes to the Gulf. As a result, from the fourth century on, almost all Indian trade with the Mediterranean passed through the Gulf rather than the Red Sea, and the Sasanian kings rerouted the riverine portion of that journey from the Euphrates on the border with Rome to the Tigris well within their own territory.

The Sasanians couldn't manage all this alone. The system also relied on the Sogdians of eastern Iran who operated central Asian land routes out of cities between the Oxus (Amu Darya) and the Jaxartes (Syr Darya) from the late fourth century CE. The Sasanian kings now offered them services in their own lands and cities and security against bandits and pirates there, in return for hefty import and export taxes. These lucrative arrangements encouraged Sogdian merchants to branch out into banking in Chinese cities and arranging long-distance credit across central Asia.

The Sogdians also acted as a bridge between Persia and the semi-nomadic empires of the Eurasian Steppe, first the Huns who harassed the late Roman west, and then a new federation of Altaic-speaking Turks who emerged in Mongolia. By the mid-sixth century CE they had built a large, militarized but still mobile state across the Steppe from the Caspian to Bactria, ruled by a khagan (khan of khans).[9] Over time these Turks came to dominate Sogdiana, offering its merchants capital investment and safe passage through the eastern Steppe in return for profit sharing and a warm welcome in Sogdian trading cities, usefully stable bases for an empire on the move.

The new trade routes brought to Sasanian cities silk, pearls, perfumes, spices, and wild animals from all over central Asia and the Indian Ocean. Iranian factories produced elegant silverware and elaborate garments made of silk, wool, and pearls that became popular in both the Chinese and the Roman empires. As in all periods, however, most goods were still transported and sold locally, with only the lightest, most compact, and valuable cargo sent long distances: precious weapons, silver, and above all silk. Very little except silk traveled all the way from China to the Mediterranean, and while many Sasanian coins dating from the fifth to eighth centuries are found in Chinese tombs, there are only a very few Roman ones. Useless for commerce in China, they were apparently used as ornaments.[10]

The sixth century saw the high-water mark of Persian court culture. Traditions like hunting and banqueting were given new life: court musicians and singers reworked ancient Persian stories and legends, and hunting and military training developed into the sport of jousting, dueling on horseback with lances.[11] Architects developed dramatic new techniques: the catenary arches at Ctesiphon were only surpassed in the twentieth century by the Gateway Arch at St. Louis, Missouri.[12]

The greatest shah was Khosrow I Anushirvan ("the Immortal Soul," r. 531–579 CE), who strengthened the Persian economy by centralizing tax collection and then subsidized infrastructure and irrigation projects throughout his vast land. He married a Turkic princess, and invited scholars and scientists from all over the known world to his court, including philosophers from Athens who found a welcoming home there for a time. Meanwhile Christians and Indian Buddhists rose to high office in the Persian administration, and Khosrow also imported books from China and games from India, including polo and chess.[13]

A Persian work of this era, *On the Explanation of Chess and Backgammon,* explains the invention of these games as a story of competition between the rulers of Persia and India. The Indians invent the game of chess and send a set made of emerald and ruby pieces to Iran, with a challenge to work out the rules or pay tribute. A Persian wise man called Wuzirgmir solves the problem in three days and explains the game to the Indian ambassador: the Indian king, he says, "has designed this chess like a battle."[14] The king is at the center, the rooks on the flanks, the vizier (later a queen in European versions of the game) is the "Commander of the Warriors," the elephant (who became a bishop) is the "Commander of the Bodyguards," the horse is the "Commander of the Cavalry," and the pawn is the foot soldier at the front of the battle. Wuzirgmir then beat the Indian envoy at the game three times, before inventing the game of backgammon and sending it back to India, where the best minds in India could not work out how to play it.

Other Kings of the World were growing frustrated by their position on the outer edges of world trade, and found common ground. In the fourth century the kings of Axum had embraced Christianity around the same time as the rulers of Rome, and made it the state religion before them.[15] Churches had replaced obelisks in Axumite cites, including the church of Maryam Tsion in Axum itself, which still stands today and according to local legend contains the Ark of the Covenant.

By the early sixth century Axumite merchants found it impossible to source Chinese silk at Indian ports because Sasanian traders, with their head start on the monsoon winds from the Gulf, had cleared the markets out.[16] Rome had a similar problem: since the early fifth century

Persia had only allowed high-value trade across the Roman border to operate through markets like Nisibis that it controlled and taxed.[17]

In the early sixth century Axum allied with Rome in an attempt to bypass the Gulf trading network by seizing southern Arabia, then ruled with Persian backing by a Jewish king known as Yusuf Dhu Nuwas. Accusations that Dhu Nuwas was persecuting Christians gave the Axumites an excuse to conquer and occupy his kingdom and his Red Sea ports with the support of a Roman fleet sent by Justin I, an Illyrian peasant who had risen to the imperial throne in 518.[18]

Soon afterward, Justin was succeeded by his nephew Justinian, the greatest Roman ruler of this era (r. 527–565 CE). The new emperor recaptured Africa, Italy, and southern Spain. In Constantinople itself he built the church of Hagia Sophia in 537, which had the highest dome in the world until Michelangelo designed the new St. Peter's in Rome in the 1540s, and still has the largest in diameter.[19] His political refinements finally abolished the old republican institution of the consulship; not coincidentally even senators were required to kiss his boots.[20] He codified Roman law into the system that became the *Corpus Iuris Civilis* of the middle ages and undergirds the modern civil law of most of Europe.* And it was Justinian who arranged for Chinese silkworm eggs to be stolen in a hollow stick so that the Romans could establish a silk industry of their own.[21]

He kept peace with Sasanian Iran, more or less, by paying for it. Justinian negotiated an "infinite" treaty with Khosrow in 532 in exchange for 11,000 pounds of gold, which did not stop Khosrow invading the Roman empire again in 540, sacking Antioch and taking a symbolic dip in the Mediterranean.[22] Further treaties followed, and further Roman payments, in 545, 551, and 561, by which time the price of peace had gone up to 30,000 pounds of gold.[23]

Rome and Iran faced bigger problems in this era than each other. One was still the weather. After a period of unusually low volcanic ac-

*Justinian's law code was also one of the last great Roman documents originally written in Latin, as Greek supplanted the Italian tongue in the imperial bureaucracy. It is known as the Justinianic Codex, the *codex* or "book" having superseded the papyrus roll in the fourth century CE.

tivity during the Roman Warm Period, ash from at least one massive eruption in El Salvador in the late 530s caused an "aerosol veil" to form across much of Europe, western Asia, and north Africa. It blocked solar radiation and warmth.[24] According to an eyewitness report, "the sun shone without brightness, like the moon, for the whole year."[25] A "Late Antique Little Ice Age" began as temperatures dropped about 4 degrees Fahrenheit, making 536–45 the coldest decade in 2,000 years.[26]

Then in 541 a new sickness appeared in the Nile Delta. It caused fever, vomiting, and swelling buboes in the armpits or groin. Analysis of microbial aDNA in sixth-century Bavarian graves has now definitively identified this pandemic as bubonic plague, caused by *Yersinia pestis,* the same bacterium as the Black Death in the fourteenth century and the "Steamship Plague" of the early twentieth.[27]

Isolated instances of plague are found in an area from Siberia to the Baltic Sea as far back as 3000 BCE.[28] But severe outbreaks are very unusual. They happen only when the conditions are exactly right for the bacterium to thrive in a suitable carrier (fleas are often blamed, but any arthropod will do) that can itself find a convenient host (including rats, gerbils, and camels) from which it can launch an assault on humans.[29*]

Now for the first time the pace of trade and transportation across a shared world allowed the disease to cross over to humans in large numbers, traversing Asia in flea-ridden furs and on donkeys covered in ticks, or crossing the Indian Ocean on ships full of rodents feasting on stocks of grain.[30] The plague was first reported at the Delta port of Pelusium, and it seems likely that it first arrived via the Indian Ocean and the Red Sea. Maritime commerce could provide the food, transportation, rodent hosts, and human victims on which *Yersinia pestis* thrived.

In 542 plague devastated Constantinople. At its height more than 10,000 people died every day in the city, according to an eyewitness report, and the living were insufficient to bury the dead. It also dealt a

*Plague spreads by insect bites or abrasions (causing bubonic plague), by ingestion (gastrointestinal plague), or directly from other humans by inhalation (pneumonic plague). Each mode of transmission triggers a different set of immune responses depending on the tissue first encountered.

severe blow to Roman imperial taxation, and almost killed Justinian himself.[31]

Contemporary authors report that by 543 it had reached Armenia, Rome, and Gaul, and by 544 Ireland. Scientific investigations in one sixth-century cemetery in rural Cambridgeshire found that more than 40 percent of the individuals whose remains could be analyzed had died of plague.[32] An outbreak is reported in the late 540s in Axum, and a second in the late 550s hit Persian Mesopotamia.[33] It kept coming back until the middle of the eighth century.

As the initial waves receded, Rome and Persia continued to conduct trade wars by proxy and stealth. After the Persians themselves had acquired silk-making technology and then refused Turks and Sogdians permission to trade in their territory, the Turkic khagan, with Sogdian help, made a formal alliance with Justinian's nephew Justin II (r. 565–578 CE) in the late 560s. This gave Roman merchants a northern route to China that bypassed Persia, and it gave Roman politicians a glimpse of a very different world: when a Roman embassy arrived at the court of a minor western Turkic prince in 575 or 576 its members were commanded to slash their faces with daggers as a mark of respect for the ruler's father, who had recently died, and then witnessed the ritual killing of four Hunnic prisoners sent as messengers to the dead khagan.[34]

The alliance didn't last long: by the 580s the Turkic khaganate was preoccupied by internal wars, and in the end it broke up into western and eastern empires.[35] In 570 meanwhile Sasanian troops reconquered Axumite southern Arabia, breaking the east African kingdom's control of the Red Sea and blocking Roman routes to the Mediterranean.

These blows to Roman trade relations came on top of the loss of most of Italy to Lombards (Lango-Bards, or long-beards) who crossed the Alps from Pannonia in 568. They met little resistance: Justin II was fighting regular bouts of insanity and now he was in direct conflict again with Iran. Their conquests meant that Constantinople now possessed only the provincial capital of Ravenna and the city of Rome in northern Italy, as well as a road corridor across the Apennines between them.[36]

In the end Rome and Persia were each other's downfall.[37] In the early years of the seventh century the army of Khosrow II (r. 590–628 CE) seized Roman Antioch, Damascus, and Jerusalem, and removed the Holy Cross to Ctesiphon. By 615 they had reached Chalcedon opposite Constantinople itself, and by 619 they had conquered Egypt. This was a significant loss to the Roman empire not only in terms of territory and access to the southern seas, but also because as part of the Indian Ocean weather system the Nile Valley offered respite when Mediterranean harvests failed.[38]

A counter-offensive through Armenia, in alliance again with Turks, retrieved Rome's Levantine territories and in 628 threatened Ctesiphon itself, until Khosrow II destroyed the bridges into the capital. He was then murdered in a coup by his son, and a succession of short-lived rulers mounted the Sasanian throne, including two of his daughters: Azarmidukht for four months, and Puran for a year (630–631), during which she returned the Holy Cross to Jerusalem.[39] Meanwhile in 629 the Visigoths took the last remaining Roman province in Spain.

A year later, a charismatic merchant rode into the great trading center of Mecca in western Arabia and destroyed the pagan idols in its great holy court or Kaaba. Muhammad had begun to hear messages from God in around 610 CE, revealing to him the verses of the Quran. He gathered followers or "Companions" around him, acting as their prophet, general, and lawgiver, and preaching the virtues of monotheism and submission (*islam*) to God.[40] Now they captured Mecca, made it the capital of their new religion, and quickly extended their authority over much of Arabia.

The subsequent Arab conquest of the Persian empire and much of Rome's as well was unexpected. Up to now the peoples of Arabia had attracted little attention, quietly and effectively running their trade routes over land and sea. But after Muhammad died in 632, he was succeeded over the next three decades by four of his Companions, who were elected in turn as *kaliph* (representative) and presided efficiently over a massive expansion of Islamic territory into richer lands: this was economic, not religious, imperialism.

Abu Bakr (r. 632–634 CE) completed the unification of Arabia. With raiding no longer an option in home territory, Caliph Umar (r. 634–644 CE) took the Levant, including Jerusalem, from the Roman emperor. The Muslims ("those who submit") took over the existing administration, but imposed their own taxation regime on war booty, the wealthy, and non-Muslims. Christians, Jews, and Zoroastrians were allocated to a special category of dhimmi, or "protected person," who paid a poll tax in return for political and religious toleration.[41]

The new rulers did not care for the most part what religion their subjects practiced, as long as they paid their taxes; indeed, there was no benefit to the Caliphate in conversion, since non-Muslims paid more taxes. Christians, Jews, and Muslims all worshipped the same God of Abraham, as far as Muslims were concerned, and Jews were now allowed to live in Jerusalem for the first time since the Roman destruction of the Second Temple in 70 CE.

New Christian churches were built in cities and the countryside in the Levant into the late eighth century. Mosques themselves were often built within churches, and Muslims shared this space with Christians. Intermarriage was permitted for Muslim men, and it was common in the new territories. New wives were not required to convert, but their children were brought up as Muslims in the Arabic language, which replaced Greek as the language of administration in the Levant around 700.

By 642 Islamic forces had secured Egypt as well, giving them control of both sides of the Red Sea. They dredged the old canal from the Nile through the Eastern Desert to the Red Sea, and restarted regular grain shipping from Egypt, no longer through Alexandria toward Constantinople but from the new Islamic city of Fustat (what is now Old Cairo) east to Mecca and Medina.[42]

Under Caliph Uthman (r. 644–656 CE) Arab troops captured Cyprus, seized the African coast as far as modern Tripoli, and conquered the whole of the Sasanian realm up to the Afghan border. The last shah was killed, perhaps by a courtier, and the crown prince fled to the Tang court, which employed his descendants for generations in the Chinese imperial administration. Just as they had in the Roman Levant, the new rulers appropriated Persian administrative structures and administrators.[43] They also embraced the silk-trading routes, building their own relations with the Tang dynasty.

Uthman's successor Ali (r. 656–61 CE) was overthrown by Muawiyyah, the governor of Syria, who made Damascus the new capital, and restricted the Caliphate to his own family. For a century under these Ummayads the Levant was at the center of the world again, and had the buildings to prove it: not only elegant desert castles but enormous public architecture that drew on earlier Christian models.

In the holy city of Jerusalem, Caliph Abd al-Malik built the Dome of the Rock in 691–92 beside Al-Aqsa ("the Farthest") Mosque already erected by Caliph Umar. The inscriptions already included quotations from the Quran, as well as direct appeals to the Christian population, advising them for instance (in Arabic) "not to say three; refrain, it is better for you; God is only one God."[44] At the same time the design owes a great deal to fifth- and sixth-century Syrian churches with its columns, wooden roof and dome, marble panels, and glass mosaic; it must have involved local construction workers and craftsmen.[45]

New societies are always entangled with the worlds around them in both space and time, and Iran continued to inspire the Ummayad caliphs. Rulers like Walid II adopted Sasanian court traditions and sat on Sasanian-style couch thrones, the cushions reportedly sometimes piled so high that the prince was almost invisible. His uncle Caliph Hisham ordered an Arabic translation of the biographies of the twenty-seven Sasanian shahs, including the two women.[46]

The Islamic conquest of northwestern Africa (in Arabic, al-Maghrib, a name that has stuck ever since) was not a planned campaign but an opportunistic set of adventures. It exploited the unpopularity of the Roman government in Africa and the strength of Berber rebels in the region, many of whom threw their lot in with the newcomers. In 670 the new city of Kairouan in what is now Tunisia became the capital of an Islamic province of Ifriqiya.

In 697 a new offensive finally delivered Carthage, the last outpost of Roman territory in Africa. Like the Romans before them the victors razed the port. They then built the new city of Tunis inland to replace it, pushed through to Morocco and charged Tariq ibn Ziyad, a Berber freedman of the governor of Ifriqiya, with holding their new far western lands. He did so and more: in 711 Tariq and his largely Berber army crossed the Strait of Gibraltar (Jebel, or mountain, of Tariq) and defeated the Visigothic king Roderic on the banks of the Guadalete River.

The Ummayads had reached the western ocean, and in 718 they attempted to complete the conquest of the Roman empire too by taking Constantinople. The siege failed, and an equilibrium was reached. By the time Walid II built his castle a few years later the Caliphate had replaced Persia at the center of the world, the remaining kings were subservient, and New Rome was surrounded.

Viking routes around Europe, c. 800 CE

CHAPTER TWENTY-FIVE

The Father of Europe

BETWEEN POITIERS AND TOURS, 732 CE

Far to the west, the Caliphate was still making gains.[1] By 718 Islamic troops had crossed the Pyrenees to occupy the old Visigothic lands in what is now the south of France. In the 720s they marched up the Rhône Valley to Burgundy, where they threatened the Duchy of Aquitaine, now a dependency of the king of the Franks. In 732 a high-ranking Frankish nobleman defeated them north of Poitiers in a victory that gave him the name Charles Martel, "the Hammer" in Old French. It also helped propel him to power over the Franks as prince and duke in 737. It had less effect on the Muslim soldiers who remained in southern France for four more years, finding willing Christian allies among the Franks' enemies.

A report of the Battle of Poitiers composed by an anonymous Iberian Christian in 754 describes Charles Martel's forces in Latin as *Europeenses.*[2] This is odd: use of the terms "Europe" and "European" was rare in this era. After the Persian Wars continents had been left for the most part to the geographers. As late as the first century BCE some Roman geographers were still unsure whether Europe and Africa were separate continents.[3] And in an empire that stretched across them all the concept was largely irrelevant.

They remained for the most part geographical curiosities in the early medieval period rather than ideological weapons, and to the extent that anyone took an interest, Europe was considered secondary to the lands of the Bible. One of the twenty books of the Iberian bishop Isidore's seventh-century encyclopedia was dedicated to "the earth and its regions," and it starts in the east, where the sun rises, and with the continent of Asia, strongly associated with the roots of Christianity.[4]

The odd exception to a general rule would be of little interest were it not for an additional curiosity: the difference the Iberian chronicler marks between his Europeans and their opponents. This is not simply geographical, but religious: he makes the other army not Africans or Asians but "Saracens." Originally a Greco-Latin term for Arab peoples, and especially the mobile populations of the desert, "Saracen" was widely used by now to mean Muslims of all kinds. The connotations of primitive, peripheral nomadism helped differentiate Muslims from the Christians, who worshipped the same God.[5]

In some eyes at least, these Christians could now be associated with the continent of Europe. The term "Europe" itself became more fashionable at court under Charles Martel's successors, and it continued to be linked by some with the Christian faith. It still did not however have wide appeal: the idea of a distinctively Christian Europe faced overwhelming evidence to the contrary from all directions. Christians shared the continent with Muslims, Jews, and pagans, and within it they were themselves increasingly divided as the world as a whole started coming back together.

The streets of Córdoba in Islamic Iberia wind down to the mosque on the banks of the Guadalquivir, or Wadi al-Kabir ("Great River"), which connects the new capital to the sea. These narrow, busy alleys open out at the bottom of the slope to reveal the full length of the sacred enclosure. Behind a decorated doorway in the middle of its wall a courtyard is filled with the sound of fountains and the scent of orange trees. Beyond it, open archways lead into the mosque itself, where heavy, sweet waves of incense waft through the fresh interior.

The building is huge but not high. A grid of marble columns organizes the space of the prayer hall, with supporting arches striped in red and white stone. On the eastern wall, intricate stucco designs frame a keyhole archway with sacred inscriptions picked out in gold on black stone. It leads into a small glittering domed space in front of the mihrab pointing to Mecca, where shafts of sunlight highlight words proclaiming the greatness of God.

The mosque of Córdoba still stands intact today except for bricked-up archways and the incongruous insertion into the interior of a sixteenth-century Christian cathedral, its nave blocking the light and long perspectives of the prayer hall, its profile poking high into the city skyline above the massive presence of the original edifice. When the mosque was built in 756 CE, it was the glory of a new state.

In 750 the governor of Iraq had toppled the Ummayad caliph in Damascus to found a new dynasty of his own, the Abbasids, based in a new city at Baghdad. One Ummayad prince named Abd al-Rahman escaped to take shelter among his mother's Berber people in northern Africa, and in 755 he took advantage of internal conflict within the Islamic government of Iberia to cross the Strait of Gibraltar and claim the region for himself and his family. He fought his way to Córdoba, where he established his capital, his mosque, and an Ummayad "Emirate" of al-Andalus. Over the following decades this incorporated most of Iberia from the Pyrenees to the Algarve (al-Gharb, "the land of the setting sun"), save a few small Christian and Muslim kingdoms that carved out independent enclaves in the north.

The Ummayad regime pursued for the most part a policy of religious toleration that modern scholars have called *convivencia.* Al-Andalus had churches and synagogues as well as mosques and, as in the Levant, Jews and Christians were in general left to practice their rites as they wished. We shouldn't be too romantic about this: the policy ensured a healthy return from taxes on non-Muslims, and it kept them at a reassuring distance from the Islamic religious and social community.[6] No new churches were built in Iberia, the ringing of bells was forbidden, and blasphemy against Islam was rewarded with decapitation. As in the east there was little pressure on anyone to convert, but intermarriage did its work, as did the attractions of taking a full part in the benefits of empire. With no extensive program of settlement, therefore, most Muslims in al-Andalus were of local descent.[7]

All this made for lively exchange, especially in the arts. Arabic secular poetry thrived in Iberia, lively and experimental, mixing genres and registers, and often using colloquial forms of Arabic and other languages. The ninth-century Córdoban poet Paul Alvarus wrote with disapproval that his fellow Christians "love to read the poems and romances of the Arabs," claiming that for every one who could write basic Latin there were a thousand with elegant Arabic.[8]

European lands to the north meanwhile were increasingly preoccupied by a split within the Christian Church. The two great Christian bishoprics in Europe had been at odds since the sixth century over matters great and small: the Roman Church required bishops and priests to observe at least nominal sexual continence, for instance, whereas priests in the Eastern Church based at Constantinople were allowed to have sex.

This was in large part a struggle for male status. As Rome itself had become increasingly irrelevant to the Roman state over the course of the fourth century, the local ecclesiastical authorities carved out a new role for the city within the new Roman religion. Church councils from 381 onward repeatedly confirmed the bishop of Rome as senior to the bishop of Constantinople, a situation never likely to conduce to harmony between the two. The rivalry only sharpened when the seventh-century Islamic conquests of western Asia, Egypt, and much of northern Africa isolated Rome and Constantinople from the other sees.

Rome was in formal terms by now a duchy of the Roman empire's Italian province, ruled by a dux under the authority of the provincial capital at Ravenna, but eighth-century bishops of Rome had more power in the city. Already often called "popes," they looked not to Constantinople but to their western neighbors for protection against local threats, above all from the Lombards, who seized Ravenna in 751.

In 754 a pope crowned Charles Martel's son Pepin "King of the

Franks," marking his "Carolingians" final defeat of the old Merovingian dynasty. Two years later Pepin defeated a Lombard advance on Rome's territory. He then "donated" the old duchy of Rome to the popes, marking the origin of the Papal States: Rome the city was now formally free of the Roman empire, and over the next century the Franco-papish alliance went from strength to strength.*

Pepin's son Charles became king of the Franks at the age of twenty in 768. More usually known as Karolus Magnus or Charlemagne, he expanded his father's realm, defeating the Lombards in northern Italy in 774, and moving on to occupy southern France. In 778 he entered Iberia at the invitation of the pro-Abbasid Muslim governor of Barcelona, where he began to establish the "Spanish March" in modern Catalonia as a border zone between his own kingdom and the Ummayad Emirate of al-Andalus. He then turned east to conquer large swaths of central Europe.

His vast conquests mean that Charlemagne is now often celebrated as a founder figure for a modern and self-consciously Christian Europe. His efforts united a realm that maps reasonably closely onto the original core of Christian nations that made up the European Economic Community—France, West Germany, Italy, Belgium, Luxembourg, and the Netherlands—and one of the main buildings housing the European Union institutions in Brussels is named after him.** This isn't entirely new either: contemporary supporters and courtiers also liked to equate Charlemagne's realm in vague terms with "Europe"—a usefully larger term than "Gaul"—and to describe his realm as a "Christian Empire."[9]

Charlemagne himself had different reference points. Despite his enduring partnership with the popes, his strategy was dictated not by re-

*This was not the end of the Roman empire's western holdings: Constantinople retained considerable territories in the south of Italy into the eleventh century, as well as the Venetian Lagoon.

**He is also claimed as a national founder figure by both Germany and France, where a sword identified as his was used to crown French kings from 1271 up to the coronation of Napoleon Bonaparte in 1804. Now held in the Louvre, "La Joyeuse" has been much restored over the years but the oldest parts date no earlier than the tenth century.

ligion but by his own interests, whether these were best served by alliance with Muslim rulers in Spain or by the enforced Christianization of Saxony.[10] And the idea of Europe was less important to him than that of Rome. He called his new capital at Aachen Roma Ventura, "Future Rome," borrowed architectural designs from Italy, Constantinople, Jerusalem, and Antioch and looted building materials directly from Ravenna and Rome itself.[11]

In 799 Pope Leo III was overthrown by enemies in Rome, having been accused of perjury and adultery. He fled to Charlemagne, who reinstated him by threat of force, underlining the Frankish king's own power in western Europe and over the western Church.[12] A poem written about their meeting shortly after the event, the so-called Paderborn Epic, appears to describe Charlemagne in the spirit of the times as the *pater . . . Europae*—"father of Europe."[13]

Charlemagne arrived in Rome the following year to show his support for Pope Leo. On Christmas Day 800 he attended mass at Old St. Peter's, a rectangular slab of a building built by Constantine almost 500 years before to house 4,000 Christians at prayer. Now Charlemagne processed through the huge door of the church and up the nave toward a mosaic of Constantine and St. Peter himself presenting a model of the church to Christ. As he knelt at the altar—and surely as prearranged—the pope walked up behind him, placed a crown on his head and anointed his feet. From then on Charlemagne called himself "Most Serene Augustus, crowned by God, Great and Pacific Emperor ruling the Roman Empire and also by God's grace King of the Franks and the Lombards."[14*]

The explanation given at the time for the creation of a new "Roman Empire" uniting Frankish and Italian lands as a rival to the existing one in Constantinople was simple misogyny.[15] Three years earlier imperial power at Constantinople had passed to a woman, an Athenian aristocrat named Irene. She was the widow of the previous Roman emperor, Leo IV, and now regent to their son Constantine VI. On Leo's death she

*While *imperator* was still a fundamentally military title, it now also carried the modern connotations of imperial rule.

immediately put down a coup, and went on to summon two Church councils and restore the veneration of icons, which had been punished severely during her husband's reign.

Irene also dealt with an Islamic invasion of Anatolia, paying for peace in a series of unequal treaties, and oversaw a more successful campaign in the Balkans. She proved herself an able diplomat as well, even betrothing the young king at the age of about ten to one of Charlemagne's daughters, although the match was broken off before they married. From 792 she and her son became formal co-rulers, but Irene tired of Constantine's restless urge to reign alone; her supporters gouged his eyes out and imprisoned him, and from 797 she commanded the empire as "queen" (*basilissa*).[16] The problem was, the pope insisted, that women could not rule. From this perspective the throne of the entire Roman realm was vacant and available.

The "Holy Roman Empire," as Charlemagne's creation came to be called, lasted more than a millennium and was only dissolved during the Napoleonic Wars in 1806. Back in the real Roman empire, things moved on: Irene was exiled to Lesbos after a revolt in 802, and the throne was filled once again by a man.

It wasn't all blood and battle. Charlemagne's reign saw an outpouring of art, architecture, and literature in western continental Europe. This was the fruit of economic prosperity as the weather began to improve again after the Alpine glaciers had reached their maximum extent around 700 CE, and industrial activity picked up: higher levels of lead and copper found in Greenland ice cores reveal a sharp upward spike in lead and silver mining in the later eighth century.[17]

Medieval geographers meanwhile continued to juggle two hemispheres, three continents, four "quarters" and five or more "climes." As a result, European maps were of three distinctly different types. In the Greek tradition there were simplified versions of a map designed in the second century CE by Ptolemy of Alexandria, who set out the principles as well as the information—mostly sets of coordinates—needed to represent the known world: a tricky business, because it involved translating the surface features of a sphere onto a flat surface.* These maps were traditionally oriented to the north and divided north to south into climes, of which Ptolemy himself had identified as many as eleven.

Christian ideas by contrast produced "T–O" maps showing a trinity of continents separated by lines that formed a "T" within an "O," the circle of God's creation. These were oriented to the east with Paradise at the top and Jerusalem in the center. Also known as *mappae mundi*—"maps of the world"—they made the whole world at least potentially Christian, dividing it into the three realms peopled according to medieval Christian tradition by the three sons of Noah.[18]

Finally, there were itinerary maps of smaller regions for the use of travelers, laid out in linear form in less elaborate variations on the approach taken by the Roman "Peutinger Table." These are equally imaginative, simplifying reality to emphasize the relationships between individual sites like the map of the London Underground. All three genres in their different ways militated against the idea of a binary divide between Europe and Asia, or indeed between "east" and "west," and none associated Europe in particular with Christendom—*Christianitas*—or the Christian faith.

Charlemagne himself continued to cultivate friendly relations with Constantinople, lesser Christian rulers in the west, and the various Islamic powers of his day.[19] He exchanged regular gifts with al-Andalus; embassies from the Aghlabids who ruled Ifriqiya (modern Tunisia and Tripolitania) as nominal vassals of the Abbasids brought him a lion and a bear; and in 802 the Abbasid caliph himself sent a mechanical brass clock and an elephant.[20] The animal's name, the Royal Frankish Annals carefully note, was "Abul Abaz"—Abu al-Abbas—and he caused great

*The idea that people in the Middle Ages thought the earth was flat is a myth, apparently created by the nineteenth-century American novelist Washington Irving (Jeffrey Burton Russell, *Inventing the Flat Earth: Columbus and Modern Historians,* New York: Praeger, 1991, 51–7). Drawing the spherical earth as a disk in both Christian and Islamic mapmaking traditions was simply a practical convention, and before the discovery of the Americas cartographers saw no need to depict more than one hemisphere, believing the other to be covered by sea.

excitement throughout northern Europe, living until 810. Apparently unaware that he was being treated as a subordinate ruler, Charlemagne sent back to Baghdad some dogs—unusually swift and fierce, apparently, but they must have been a disappointment.[21]

Diplomacy with al-Andalus continued after Charlemagne's death in 814, although it was strained when the Ummayad emir supported rebels against Charlemagne's grandson Charles the Bald in 847 and invaded Carolingian territory himself in 852 and 856. In the 860s however envoys from the "king of the Saracens" brought the Carolingian king "many gifts, such as camels carrying couches and tents, and various kinds of cloth and many perfumes."[22]

Charles was honored not only by the gifts, but also by the beasts that carried them: although camels had been a relatively common sight in Roman and Visigothic Iberia, no remains have been found from al-Andalus before the tenth century and they were rare until the twelfth, when camel-breeding Sanhaja Berbers arrived with the Almoravids from Morocco.[23] Carolingian Europe may not have been at the center of the world, but its ruling class at least was not isolated from it.

Ambitious and aspiring courtiers continued to use the language of Europe, and the equation of the Carolingian empire with the continent continued after Charlemagne's death, as Muslims occupied more of southern Europe.[24] Andalusian pirates conquered Crete in the 820s, and the north African Aghlabid dynasty slowly annexed Sicily, one of the last outposts of the eastern Roman empire west of the Adriatic.[25] They captured Palermo in 830, made it the capital of a new Emirate of Sicily in 831, and took the last significant Roman holdout of Taormina in 902. In 870 the Aghlabids also annexed Malta, from 847 to 871 a small independent Islamic emirate held the Italian city of Bari, and the Emirate of Fraxinet (Saint-Tropez) controlled much of Provence from 888 to 973.* By now however new boats were appearing in the Mediter-

*As ever, new people brought new technologies and ideas. Sicily in particular saw a revolution in urban planning and in water-management systems based on the North African foggara, which allowed the introduction of thirsty crops like oranges and lemons to the island (Giusy Lofrano et al., "Water collection and distribution systems in the Palermo Plain during the middle ages," *Water* 5 [2013]).

ranean, launched far to the north. Their pagan crews undermined still further any association between Christendom and Europe.

The Scandinavians were established masters of maritime travel. Shipping on the North Sea had reached a low point in the sixth century, but by the seventh the weather was already getting better and connections had picked up again, sometimes across very long distances.[26] Scandinavian ships sailed in increasing numbers to take advantage of markets on the Frisian and British coasts. They dealt with migrant Angles, Saxons, and Jutes who still shared a cultural world with the lands in modern northern Germany and Denmark they had left behind: the Old English epic *Beowulf*, written some time before 1000 CE, is set entirely in Scandinavia.

We can see the results in a cemetery at Sutton Hoo in East Anglia, where seventeen or eighteen mound burials contain the earthly remains of one of the groups of continental adventurers now well established in eastern and central Britain. They were dug high on a hill above the River Deben just a few kilometers from the Suffolk coast.

One of these burials was excavated intact in 1939 after Tudor grave robbers missed it by a whisker; the best candidate for its occupant is Raedwald of the Wuffinga dynasty, king of East Anglia from circa 599 to 624. He is buried in a chamber set inside a twenty-seven-meter wooden boat that the mourners must have dragged up the steep slope. The acidic soil has now eaten it away, like the body inside, but the vessel is recognizable by its surviving iron rivets. The grave also contains drinking horns taken from the aurochs that still patrolled Scandinavia and central Europe, a beautiful silver bucket from Constantinople engraved with a lion hunt, a Coptic bowl from Egypt, and metalwork decorated with garnets from India or Sri Lanka. Even the bitumen used to waterproof the ship must have been imported from Asia. Through the North Sea, the rulers of these small English kingdoms were already part of a very large world to the east.

In the eighth century however Scandinavian shipbuilders perfected a new longship design, "clinker-built" with overlapping planks and a keel, giving the vessels strength, speed, and stability.[27] They had shallow hulls, so that they could travel by sail and oar far up rivers, and they were light enough to be carried or dragged by the crew onto a beach or even from one body of water to another.

The new ships were useful for trading and raiding alike, and we call those who sailed on them "vikings," from the old Norse *víkingr,* which referred to expeditioners and buccaneers of all kinds and origins.[28] Their Christian neighbors called them "northmen," pagans and heathens: although the English had converted in the seventh century, Christianity reached Denmark only in the tenth and came later still to Norway and Sweden.

Introducing these vikings to history in the eighth century CE gives too great an impression of rupture. What changed now was not the routes, or even the personnel, but the methods by which they acquired their goods.[29] Reports of attacks by northmen on the coast of Britain and Ireland begin to appear in the late eighth century, starting in Dorset in 789. In 793 the *Anglo-Saxon Chronicle,* a compilation of reports from the Roman Conquest up to the twelfth century, reports that "the heathen" (*hæthenra*) destroyed the Abbey of Lindisfarne off the coast of Northumbria "by looting and slaughter." The locals had known that trouble was coming: not only were there "immense flashes of lightning" over the region but "fiery dragons were seen flying in the air."[30]

Some of these northmen carried on. Attacks on the Irish coast began a few years later, and in 799 the first Scandinavian attack on Frankish territory is documented on the island of Noirmoutier in the Loire region. These sailing expeditions were not sent by any state: this was a world of small chiefdoms ruled by big men with long halls. It was only in the tenth century that substantial kingdoms began to emerge in Denmark and Sweden.

Six separate viking campaigns are recorded against al-Andalus to the south, until expeditions in the 860s headed through the Strait of Gibraltar into the Mediterranean. As in Christian Europe, the vikings are seen in Islamic sources primarily as pagans. The standard Arab term for them was *majus,* a word that originally referred to Persian priests called *magi* but had become a general term for people who did not practice a "religion of the book."

Soon some vikings stopped going home at all. In 841 a group founded a settlement at Dublin on the Irish coast. In England a large military force arrived in East Anglia in 865, captured York in 866, and went on to defeat a series of Old English–speaking kings. They suffered occasional defeats themselves: a mass grave found in Derbyshire and dated by radiocarbon to the late ninth century houses more than 250 skeletons of unusually tall men, many with trauma injuries. Analysis of the strontium isotopes from these individuals' teeth tells us more: they are not local but could in most cases have grown up in Scandinavia.[31]

Many of the Scandinavian warriors settled down to farm the countryside, pushing their English-speaking cousins' kingdoms west, which in turn drove Celtic speakers into Britain's far western peninsulas. In 878 Alfred, the king of the West Saxons, finally blocked the northmen's progress across England and made a truce with Guthrum, the new king of East Anglia. It split the land between Alfred's own realm and the "Danelaw," a huge swath of territory from Chester in the northwest to London in the southeast. The newcomers shared not only geographical roots and a related language with their Old English neighbors, but a northern tradition of popular participation in government based on an assembly of the free male population known as "the Thing."*

In the east of England viking place names are still common: a -by is a settlement; a -thorp is a dependent settlement; a -thwaite is a meadow or clearing.[32] The legacy of the Danelaw is still clearly identifiable in wider English language and culture as well: the days of the week are named after Norse gods, and all sorts of English words are of Scandinavian origin, including "ill," "sky," and "window."

Other northmen settled on the Orkney, Shetland, and Faroe islands. Around 870 they founded the first permanent settlements on Iceland, where as kings gained ground in Scandinavia itself a "republic of farmers" emerged.** Its members gathered at an annual "Althingi" founded

*The more abstract modern use of the word is an expansion of this original meaning.

**The relative isolation of the island means that the modern Icelandic language is far closer to the Old Norse written and spoken by these wanderers than are the languages of their homelands, which are no longer intelligible to a native Icelandic speaker. This means that modern Icelanders can also read the Old Norse sagas, family stories of island life passed down for generations before they were committed to writing in the thirteenth and fourteenth centuries.

in 930 that is now the world's longest-surviving parliament. According to later storytellers it was also the venue, around 1000 CE, of the islanders' decision to convert to Christianity.[33] Meanwhile Scandinavian seafarers led by a Christian convert called Rollo carved out a duchy of "Normandy" in northern France in the early tenth century.

Other vikings sailed in a different direction. Genetic studies now confirm that while people from western Scandinavia tended to head west, from Norway to the Orkneys, Ireland, Man, and Iceland, and from Denmark to Britain, the proto Swedish lands produced Baltic voyagers who built a Scandinavian trade network stretching through the Gulf of Finland and down the eastern European river system.[34]

Some of these ships traveled down the Dnipro and through the Black Sea to Constantinople. By 880 they had founded a commercial capital at modern Kyiv, where they were known as "Rus," the word that gives modern Russia its name. Others sailed down the Volga and crossed the Caspian Sea en route to Baghdad, looking for precious metals from the vast Abbasid realm as "silver fever" developed in Scandinavia itself.[35] They supplied in return furs, weapons, and enslaved human prisoners.

Vikings were not only mobile themselves but agents of mobility. Many of the slaves they traded east were captured from among the Sclavenians, people of central Europe first mentioned by sixth-century Greek authors—to the extent that variations on the word "sclavus" replaced *servus* from the ninth century as the standard Latin term for unfree human laborers. Women in particular were targeted for sex trafficking, men by contrast often simply killed.[36]

Farther west meanwhile aDNA analyses have revealed that two occupants of graves on Orkney that look entirely Scandinavian in cultural terms are genetically much more closely related to Irish and Scottish populations, and that a significant proportion of the settlers on Iceland, especially the women, were from Scotland and Ireland too; we don't know of course how many volunteered.[37] Farther south, an Irish chronicle describes how vikings brought Black ("blue") men from Morocco to Ireland in the ninth century and claims that they stayed there for a long time.[38]

By now the Scandinavian trading circuit reached across the top of the known world from Ireland to Baghdad and beyond. Indian garnets and African ivory reached Scandinavia along with metalwork from the Roman empire.[39] It is not at all uncommon to find silver dirhams issued by the Abbasid Caliphate—the equivalent in ancient Eurasia of the modern dollar, euro, or yen in terms of stability and exchangeability—in ninth-century Britain, along with the occasional cowrie shell from the Indian Ocean.[40]

Charlemagne's dynasty fell in 888 when the absence of a legitimate heir to the imperial title created a power vacuum, and the major European power of the tenth century was the Saxon Ottonian dynasty. Their realm was about half the size of Charlemagne's, and half as complex, though the language of "Europe" continued alongside a growing sense of a Latin Christian culture within it.[41]

Marriages still took place with the court at Constantinople, and with Muslim courts as well: almost all the tenth-century emirs of al-Andalus had blond hair and blue eyes because their mothers came from northern Spain or Gaul. Abd al-Rahman III resorted to dyeing his beard black to emphasize his Arab heritage. "Saracens" continued to send the Holy Roman Emperor presents too, including lions, camels, apes, and ostriches, animals that breathless contemporaries report had never before been seen.[42]

Not all diplomatic exchanges went smoothly: a series of ill-tempered embassies to and from the court of Abd al-Rahman III in the 950s saw Muslim diplomats kept hostage in the Saxon empire for three years. But religion was a secondary consideration to rulers in the Holy Roman Empire, al-Andalus, and the rising Scandinavian kingdoms, as western Europe became ever more involved in bigger worlds to south and north. These worlds revolved, like viking trade, around Baghdad.

CHAPTER TWENTY-SIX

The Translation Movement

THE HOUSE OF WISDOM, C. 830 CE

In the eighth century CE the Abbasids undertook to collect the wisdom of the world in their new capital at Baghdad.[1] This project started with the second Abbasid caliph, al-Mansur ("the Conqueror," r. 754–74), who commissioned Arabic translations of important scientific texts from Persian, Sanskrit, Greek, and Syriac (a late form of Aramaic), and came into its own under al-Ma'mun ("the Trusted One," r. 813–33). The operation was lavishly funded by the caliph himself, as well as by members of his household, courtiers, merchants, bankers, and military leaders. It reflects the prosperity of the era, as the Abbasids created a powerful centralized government based on a land tax, which as conversion became more common they pragmatically extended to Muslims as well as non-Muslims.[2]

The most important thing to understand about what is often now called the "Translation Movement" is that it wasn't primarily about translation. It was part of a wider commitment by Islamic scholars and political leaders to scientific investigation that also saw caliphs commission new works of science, geography, poetry, history, and medi-

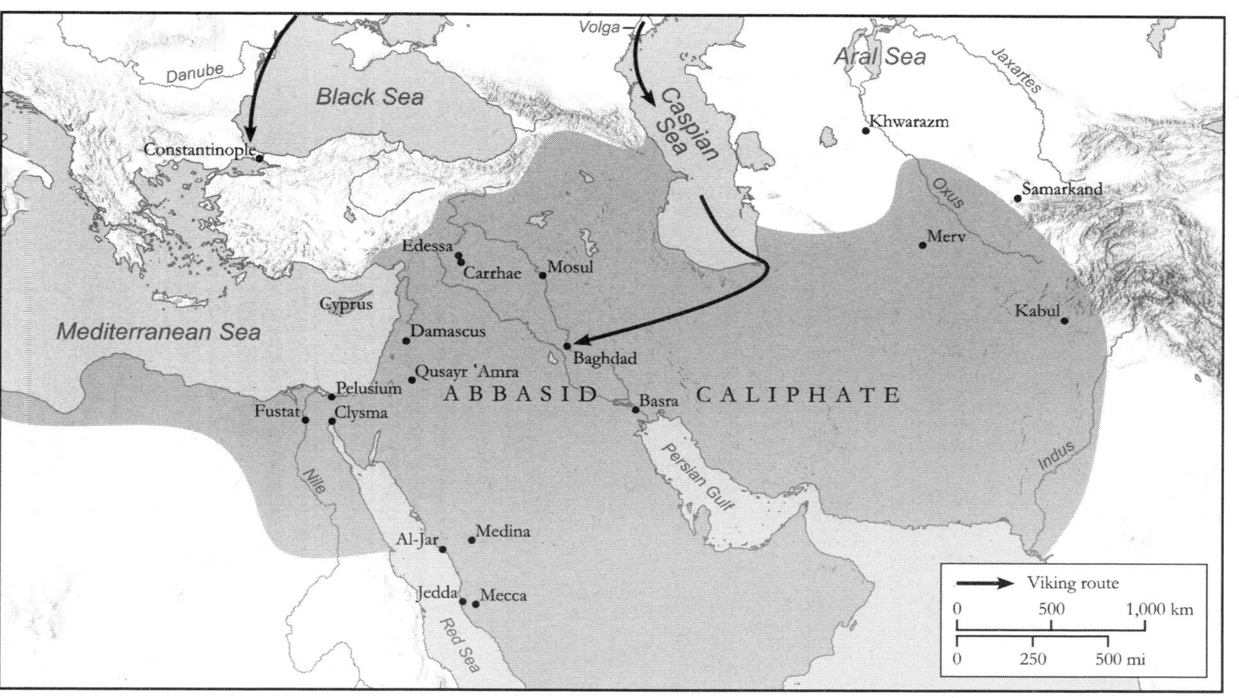

The Abbasid Caliphate, c. 850 CE

cine. It is well known that classic works of Greek science and philosophy were translated into Arabic before they were translated into other European languages—including Latin. What is less well known is that the point of translating foreign works was not to preserve them but to build on them. As links around the Mediterranean continued to increase, that Arabic scholarship began to reach western Europe, and to change the way people there thought.

Back in Baghdad, as so often happened, cultural change began from the outside—and in this case with the collection and comparison of foreign knowledge. The fundamental model and first material for the Abbasid translation project came from Iran, where sixth-century Sasanian shahs had commissioned Persian translations of important Indian and Greek works. Living Iranians were an inspiration too. Sasanian intellectual traditions had weathered the Arab conquest, and Persian remained a major Iranian language, but Persian scholars had already started to translate classic works of their own literature into Arabic. This ensured their preservation, and advertised the history and high culture of Iranian lands.[3] Sasanian intellectuals also maintained useful links with scientific traditions farther east, above all with Indian mathematicians, the most advanced in the ancient world, and they had already translated important works from Sanskrit into their own language.[4]

The benefits for the Abbasid caliphs of engaging with Iranian traditions were not purely intellectual. It helped them establish roots for themselves in the old Sasanian territory of Mesopotamia that they now occupied; in a similar spirit they built Baghdad itself in 762 in the circular form characteristic of Sasanian cities. Incorporating the work of Greek thinkers into the Arabic canon was by contrast a declaration of cultural hegemony over the rump Roman empire at Constantinople, where older learning had been set aside in favor of Christian genres from sermons to saints' lives, and where ancient science and philosophy now moldered in archives and monasteries.[5]

More immediately, the project took inspiration from the contemporary intellectual culture of western Asia, revitalized by the unification under Islam of regions once subject to either Persia or Rome.[6] Intellectual centers from Christian Edessa and Mosul to Zoroastrian Merv and resolutely pagan Carrhae were now not only in touch with one another but freed from the religious orthodoxy imposed by their old masters: theological disputes among foreigners were of little interest to the caliphs. This world produced well-traveled intellectuals expert in topics from military strategy to astrology, and comfortable in Greek, Syriac, Middle Persian (Pahlavi), and now Arabic as well.

The final key component came from farther east. Paper had been invented in China in the second century BCE and by the second century CE it is found in the trading oases of the Tarim Basin. It was first used as wrapping, but people soon realized that like leather and wood it made a useful surface for inked text. The craft of papermaking reached the Abbasid world in the eighth century, and the first paper mill was built in Baghdad in the 790s.[7] As paper was much cheaper to produce than papyrus, it finally made writing in great quantity a practical prospect.[8]

In the early ninth century scientific scholarship in Baghdad coalesced around a library called the "House of Wisdom" (Bayt al-Hikma), and the translation efforts were put on a more organized footing.[9] The translators were paid a monthly salary, and the translations themselves often passed through several stages.[10] Persian scholars translated into Arabic works that had already been translated from other languages into their own, and since there was comparatively little direct Greco-Arabic bilingualism, Arabic translations of Greek works were often made from Syriac versions.[11] Translation from Greek was therefore largely in the hands of Levantine Christians, already used to working across different languages including Greek and Syriac as well as Arabic.[12]

We have a useful guide to the foreign works considered worthy of investigation in the form of a later encyclopedia entitled *Keys of the Sciences* written in the tenth century CE by Abu Abdullah Muhammad al-Khwarizmi, a scholar from the central Asian oasis of Khwarazm, south of the Aral Sea. He divided the work into two books: one describes "Islamic religious law and Arabic sciences," defined as law, theology, grammar, secretaryship, poetry, and history; the other is devoted to "the sciences of foreigners such as the Greeks and other nations": philosophy, logic, law, medicine, arithmetic, geometry, astronomy/astrology, music, mechanics, and alchemy.[13]

The Greek philosophers translated into Arabic ranged from Plato and Euclid writing in the fourth century BCE to the third-century CE Egyptian-born philosopher Plotinus. Arabic scholars took a particular interest in the work of Aristotle, as well as in Greek commentaries on it. More practical Greek texts also found their way into the collection, on topics from engineering to military tactics to falconry. Popular literature included books of fables, "wisdom sayings," and letters supposedly exchanged between famous historical figures. Classical poetry, drama, and history were of less interest: even Homer only appears in quotations found in scientific authors.[14]

This was in part because the scholars involved knew how difficult it was to translate poetry well.[15] Even translating scientific vocabulary relies on a shared way of seeing the world that was hard for intellectuals working centuries later to capture. They managed it with varying degrees of success, especially when it came to the more abstract, philosophical texts. Some translations incorporate a great deal of interpretation: the "gods" become "the god" and one rendering of Plotinus' work equates his idea of a "first principle" with Allah himself.[16] But new manuscripts were acquired whenever possible to check against existing texts and new translations were issued where clear improvements could be made.[17] Scholars also thought hard about the methodology and challenges of translation: a Nestorian Christian doctor from Basra who worked in Greek, Syriac, Persian, and Arabic called Hunayn ibn Ishaq argued strongly for the principle that translations should be fluent and relatively free, rather than rigorous but unreadable word-for-word renditions.[18]

Some of the Greek texts were acquired through personal request, even from the caliph himself.[19] Other manuscripts were found on investigative missions, or indeed rescued: a tenth-century compendium of literature written in Baghdad reports that camel-loads of old works were discovered in a pagan Greek temple that had been locked since the arrival of Christianity, getting worn and gnawed at by pests.[20]

Some works still proved elusive: Hunayn ibn Ishaq reports a quest for a work by the Roman doctor Galen (129–216 CE) who mapped the four "humors" (blood, phlegm, black bile, and yellow bile) onto personality types. After searching in vain through northern Mesopotamia, Syria, Palestine, and Egypt, he eventually finds "about half of it, in disorder and incomplete, in Damascus."[21]

The legacy of the Translation Movement is not in the translations themselves. The notion that the Arabs "preserved" ancient Greek learning that would otherwise have been lost is largely a myth.

Most ancient science was indeed lost to western Europe for almost a millennium: such works were usually written in Greek, even by Romans, and they disappeared with the knowledge of that language. Only a few Latin translations of Greek works had ever been made: Plato's *Timaeus* and various works of Aristotle, as well as practical works like Ptolemy of Alexandria's *Handy Tables*, containing the basic information needed to calculate the positions of the sun, moon, and planets, as well as the times at which they rise and set, and to predict eclipses.

For the most part however the original texts survived as well, kept and copied in the libraries, archives, and monasteries of the eastern Roman empire. Modern versions of ancient Greek texts are naturally based on those. The Arabic translations are still useful, as they were often made from earlier and more accurate Greek manuscripts. And there are a few Greek works that survive only in Arabic translation, but they are curiosities rather than canonical texts: examples include a guide to estate management written in the first century CE by a Roman author now known as Bryson, and a second-century CE treatise on physiognomy by the sophist Polemon.

The real legacy of the Arabic translations is the impetus they gave to further thought. As the Syriac patriarch Barhebraeus summed it up in the thirteenth century CE:

> there arose among [the Arabs] philosophers, mathematicians, and physicians, who surpassed all the ancients in subtlety of understanding. While they built on no foundations other than those of the Greeks, they constructed greater scientific edifices by means of a more elegant style and more studious researches, with the result that, although they had received the wisdom from us through translators . . . now we find it necessary to seek wisdom from them.[22]

His story is too neat: Greek texts were far from the only inspiration for Arabic science. But as western European monks and nuns laboriously copied Latin manuscripts in candlelit monasteries, the manipulation, criticism, and sometimes outright rejection of foreign works by intellectuals working in the Islamic world catalyzed a scientific revolution.[23]

Ninth-century scholarship based on "foreign sciences" had already advanced well past translation. Arabic medical writers, for instance, drew on Greek sources, and especially those of Galen, but they were also inspired by Indian texts on Ayurvedic medicine translated into Persian and then Arabic.[24] Islamic astronomy combined Babylonian, Persian, and Indian scientific traditions with Greek works and Greek inventions like the astrolabe, an astronomical calculator first developed at Alexandria in the third or fourth century CE. The various dials built into this "star taker" could be turned to measure altitude and latitude from the position of celestial objects and to establish the time and direction. This was especially useful for making five daily prayers at specific times and facing in a specific direction.

In a microcosm of the Translation Movement itself, the astrolabe was the subject of a sixth-century Greek treatise, a seventh century Syriac one, and then one written in Arabic by "Albatenius" (al-Battani) around 920. The first known examples of an actual astrolabe constructed in the Islamic world come in the eighth century CE, and Arabic scholars added additional elements to the device: angular scales and circles indicating azimuths, or arcs measured along the horizon. In the ninth century Caliph al-Ma'mun himself established observatories at Baghdad and Damascus to test and update the information received in the Greek, Persian, and Indian astronomical traditions.[25*]

Study of the heavens was closely linked to study of the earth, and cartography was another great interest among Abbasid scholars. Their ideas about mapping were based above all on those of Ptolemy of Alexandria. In the early ninth century another scholar from Khwarazm, Muhammad ibn Musa al-Khwarizmi (c. 780–850), who worked at the House of Wisdom, wrote a work on "the depiction of the earth" (*Surat al-ard*). It corrected Ptolemy's coordinates and reworked his geography, recognizing, for instance, that the Indian Ocean was not landlocked but continued into the Pacific.

Indian mathematics meanwhile bequeathed to western Eurasia the numerals that are now called "Arabic." Even in Arabic, however, which is otherwise written from right to left, these numerals are still written left to right as they once were in Sanskrit. They were a development out of the ancient Babylonians' counting system, which combined a tally method like that used in Etruria and Rome with the concept of "positional notation," using different columns for numbers of different powers. Because the basic Babylonian unit of counting and measurement was sixty, you could count up to fifty-nine in each column, but to make this easier there was a "sub-base" of ten. Babylonian scholars counted wedges in groups of one to nine, with differently angled wedges marking tens, and then collected them together in each column in up to six groups.

Tally systems work for recording numbers and performing basic arithmetic, but they are difficult to manipulate. From the third century BCE Indian scholars developed a more flexible approach that used a new set of stand-alone numerals in combination with positional notation. Rejecting base-sixty, which is unwieldy for the calculations required by advanced math, geometry, and astronomy, Indian mathematicians used base-ten alone. So two vertical lines in their decimal positional nota-

*Al-Ma'mun also oversaw the first known archaeological excavation in Egypt in 832, opening up the tomb chamber of the Great Pyramid of Khufu—which had unfortunately already been robbed.

tion meant eleven and not, as on the Babylonian system, sixty-one—or, in Roman numerals, two.

The next step forward came when Indian mathematicians invented the concept of zero.[26] Positional notation always needed a placeholder to indicate the absence of a number in a column; otherwise "11" and "101" would look the same. Babylonian scribes simply left a space, but by the third or fourth century CE Indian works use dots.[27] Over time a hole appeared within the dot. But it was only in 628 CE that a scholar called Brahmagupta began to treat this hollow dot as an independent number that could be used for calculation as well as recording: multiplying any number by zero, for instance, produces the answer zero.

Brahmagupta also gave rules for solving quadratic equations, calculating square roots, and working with negative numbers. This had practical uses, not least for calculating debts. He set down for the first time the now familiar principles that subtracting a negative number is equivalent to adding a positive number, and that multiplying a negative and a positive number will always produce a negative number.

While some aspects of Islamic mathematics were always heavily reliant on Greek scholarship—geometry would be one example—the arrival of Indian scholarship and numerals in the Arabic-speaking world transformed computational mathematics. Like the ancient Greeks, early Arabic writings used the alphabet, dividing the twenty-seven letters of the old Levantine abjad into three groups representing 1–9, 10–90, and 100–900. But the House of Wisdom's al-Khwarizmi championed the use of Indian numerals instead, as well as the positional-decimal system that came with them.* Around 825 CE he wrote a work explaining how to perform basic calculations with the new numerals, and he also used them to develop the art of advanced arithmetic now known as "algebra" from the title of his classic work on how to solve linear and quadratic equations, *The Handbook of Calculation by Restoration* ("al-

*The numerals now used in modern Arabic look different because they were "ossified" by the printing press at a different time from those used in European alphabets (John Crossley, "Old-fashioned versus newfangled: reading and writing numbers," *Studies in Medieval and Renaissance History* 10 [2013], 84).

Jabr," moving a term from one side of the equation to another) *and Balancing* ("al-Muqabalah," adding the same term to both sides).*

Around the year 900 a lawyer and music scholar named Abu Nasr al-Farabi wrote *Enumeration of the Sciences,* laying out various areas of contemporary study. Instead of distinguishing between Arabic and foreign sciences, al-Farabi took a different approach. Al-Farabi divides the sum of human knowledge into five parts:

1. Linguistics: grammar, rhetoric, and poetry
2. Logic
3. Mathematics: arithmetic, geometry, mathematical astronomy, music, the transportation of loads, mechanics, and optics
4. Physics and metaphysics
5. Politics: jurisprudence (*fiqh*) and theology[28]

The first thing to notice here is that the "Arabic" and "Greek" sciences have already been integrated into a single project. The second is that the mathematical sciences have already expanded beyond the old "Greek" categories to include new work on topics like optics and mechanics. The third is that the first three categories map onto the educational syllabus followed in western Europe since the sixth century.

Schooling in medieval Europe was based on the "seven liberal arts." After children had learned to read, write, and do basic math, this syllabus divided the disciplines deemed worthy of study into a lower "trivium" of the arts of language—(Latin) grammar, logic (including dialectic), and rhetoric—and a higher "quadrivium" of the arts of calculation: arithmetic, geometry, astronomy, and music. There was also plenty of Bible study and Christian training, and a fair amount of Latin literature.

*Al-Khwarizmi's own name has given mathematics the word "algorithm" for the set of rules used in calculation.

This curriculum was first championed in the early fifth century CE by the north African scholar Martianus Capella, a native of Madaura in modern Algeria and not to our knowledge a Christian. Martianus wrote a long didactic prose poem called *The Marriage of Mercury* (the god of profit) *and Philologia* (the love of learning), in which the wedding presents include seven enslaved women who represent the seven arts of dialectic argument, rhetoric, grammar, geometry, arithmetic, astronomy, and musical harmonics.

The model was popularized above all under the Visigoths by Isidore of Seville, and further encouraged by Charlemagne, who ordered all monasteries and cathedrals to sponsor free schooling out of ancient Latin textbooks for boys with academic talent.[29] In al-Farabi's syllabus, categories 1 and 2 map onto the trivium, 3 to the quadrivium, while the fourth and fifth relate to the more specialized education increasingly needed in both the Islamic and Christian worlds to enter the professions.

Greater contact between Islamic and Christian intellectual traditions was encouraged by the growth in trade through the Indian Ocean. This was itself fueled by the Chinese economy, which had begun to overtake Rome's from around 600 CE in what has been called the "First Great Divergence."[30] By the middle of the eighth century Buddhist monks in China had invented the art of printing, and in the ninth Chinese chemists developed gunpowder. By the early tenth century gunpowder was used to ignite flamethrowers, arrows, rockets, and catapult bombs.[31]

On the other side of the Indian Ocean commercial connections continued through the Red Sea and into the Mediterranean, where shipping had reached its lowest point in the eighth century, but soon began to recover. We already get hints of revival in a late-eighth-century Psalter or book of psalms found in 2006 by a man digging for peat in a bog in Ireland's County Tipperary. It was written in an Irish monastery on animal skin or parchment, but its cover was stiffened with papyrus from Islamic Egypt or the Levant.[32]

By 885 CE the Persian geographer Ibn Khordadbeh explains the trading operations of a Jewish merchant house based in Baghdad: "they speak Arabic, Persian, Greek, Frankish, Andalusian, and Slavic, and they travel from the east to the west and from the west to the east, both by land and sea."[33] He details the way in which merchants carry slaves, brocade, beaver skins, furs, sable, and swords from the ports of Francia (Firanja) across the Mediterranean (the "western sea"), dock at Pelusium in the Egyptian Delta and then carry their merchandise to the port of Clysma on the Red Sea. From there they sail to al-Jar and Jedda on the "eastern sea" and on to al-Sind (in modern Pakistan), al-Hind (India), and finally al-Sin (China). They make the return journey with musk, aloeswood, camphor, cinnamon, and other local specialties.

This is when Arabic science began to cross over into Christian Europe, above all in Catalonia, a borderland of Christian kingdoms. Here fashionable monastics could acquaint themselves with scientific developments in Córdoba, acquiring for example Latin accounts of Arabic astronomy as well as guides to the construction of the astrolabe.[34] It wasn't just the Greek texts that scholars were after; it was the scientific advances Arab scholars had built on them—and much else. From about 975 CE Latin manuscripts written in Spain begin to use Indian numerals.[35] Indian chess, which had reached Islamic Iberia by the ninth century, is found in Catalonia by the tenth and the north Atlantic islands by the twelfth.[36]

The weather was improving too, and the economy with it. A "Medieval Climate Anomaly" from the tenth to thirteenth centuries—in Europe, at least, a warm period—meant that European agriculture took off and the population increased.[37] Towns throughout the continent grew in number and size, and larger kingdoms rose again in southern Italy, Germany, and France. All this helped to fuel long-distance trade in luxury goods, some of it handled by Jewish merchant houses based in Islamic cities like Egyptian Fustat, where an immense repository or *geniza* preserves the records of the Jewish community from late antiquity into the modern era, from Bibles to business accounts, divorce decrees, and shopping lists.

This *geniza* reveals networks of contact and commerce through the Mediterranean and Red Sea that reached from Morocco and Marseille to Valencia and India, where communities of Jews had lived in Kerala since Roman times.[38] Most of this trade was in basic goods of real economic importance—cloth, for example, and its raw materials—and this is what tied together the richer, Muslim-ruled regions of the Mediterranean. The luxury trade by contrast was relatively small-scale, but this was how the rest of the world first reached Christian Europe.

Trade and translation now linked the known world across its southern regions, connecting with the viking network that stretched across the north from Ireland to Iraq to form a great circle around continental Europe, and commercial opportunities attracted Jewish and Muslim communities to France, England, and Germany.[39]

At the same time, the Islamic world was undergoing its own process of regionalization. In 929 the Emirate of Córdoba briefly became a self-declared full Caliphate, before breaking up in the early eleventh century into smaller Islamic states known as *taifas.* Around the same time a new Fatimid dynasty established itself in Tunisia, took most of Sicily from the Aghlabids, and then expanded its African territory west to the Atlantic coast. These same Fatimids then occupied Egypt in 969, where they established themselves as rivals to the Abbasids in Baghdad. They took control of the lucrative Red Sea trade routes, abandoning northwest Africa along the way to their old Almoravid governors.

The world of the northmen meanwhile was expanding west, as vikings established a colony on Greenland around 980 to exchange walrus hides, fat, and ivory for European iron; earlier settlers had already made short work of a population of walruses native to Iceland.[40] Greenland was also a staging post for journeys to the coast of North America, no doubt in search of the timber that they had already razed on Iceland and that Greenland lacked entirely.

Stories of these adventures are preserved in the *Greenland Saga,* written down in Old Norse in the thirteenth century. It describes how Erik the Red was outlawed from Iceland for fighting and founded the first colony on Greenland, how another sailor blown off course on his way to the new colony discovered lands still farther west, and how Erik's son Leif led an expedition there that identified a "Land of Flat Stones," a "Land of Forests," and a "Land of Vines."[41] A number of voyages of exploration followed, but attempts to establish a permanent settlement in North America were thwarted by poor relations with the indigenous population, not helped when the visitors conducted a small massacre.

Women play a large part in these ventures. Erik's daughter Freydis has most of the members of her own expedition to America killed, decapitating the womenfolk herself. His daughter-in-law Gudrid Thorbjarnardóttir comes to Greenland from Iceland at around the age of fifteen, by seventeen is on to her second marriage to an Icelandic trader and travels with him to Vinland, where they spend three years. There she has a baby called Snorri and meets Americans, before the couple return to Iceland to farm. She made a pilgrimage to Rome in middle age, before dying in Iceland a nun.

These stories appear to preserve a great deal of genealogical information relating to real Icelandic families, and while the details of individuals' adventures and interrelationships are no doubt much embellished, they describe a plausibly harsh world of constant travel, danger, and ingenuity on the western edge of the world. The basic outlines of the migrations they describe also match the archaeological remains in Iceland, Greenland, and Canada, and the settlement in North America was discovered in the 1960s at L'Anse aux Meadows on what is now Newfoundland: a small village with houses, workshops, and a boat shed built out of wood and turf in the same style as on Iceland and Greenland. Its timber cottages have recently been dated precisely by tree rings: the wood was cut with metal tools (previously unknown in the region) in 1021 CE.[42]

This little community lasted only a decade or so, but Icelandic vikings were the first to see a truly new world to the west, and the first to exploit its resources for the ever-more-entangled societies and economies of Afro-Eurasia.

CHAPTER TWENTY-SEVEN

The Sign of the Cross

CLERMONT, 1095 CE

On July 16, 1054, the pope in Rome excommunicated the patriarch of Constantinople, who excommunicated him right back.* The Great (and final) Schism of this era between what now became Roman Catholicism and Eastern Orthodoxy arose over a variety of matters from the use of unleavened bread for communion to the wording of the creed, but it continued to reflect the fundamental disagreement over whether the patriarch should subordinate himself to the pope.**

Western or "Latin" Christians found other battles to fight, as Christian kings set about what nineteenth-century historians called the "Reconquista" of Iberia. It was in reality a conquest: these monarchs had little to do with the Visigoths, and the process did not preclude strategic alliances with local Muslim powers. In 1085 Alfonso of Catholic Castile and León took the *taifa* of Toledo, provoking the remaining Islamic states of Iberia into reuniting under the rule of the north African Al

*The decrees of excommunication were lifted in 1965 by Pope Paul VI and Patriarch Athenagoras I.

**The word "creed" comes from *credo,* "I believe," the first word in Latin of the confession of Christian faith.

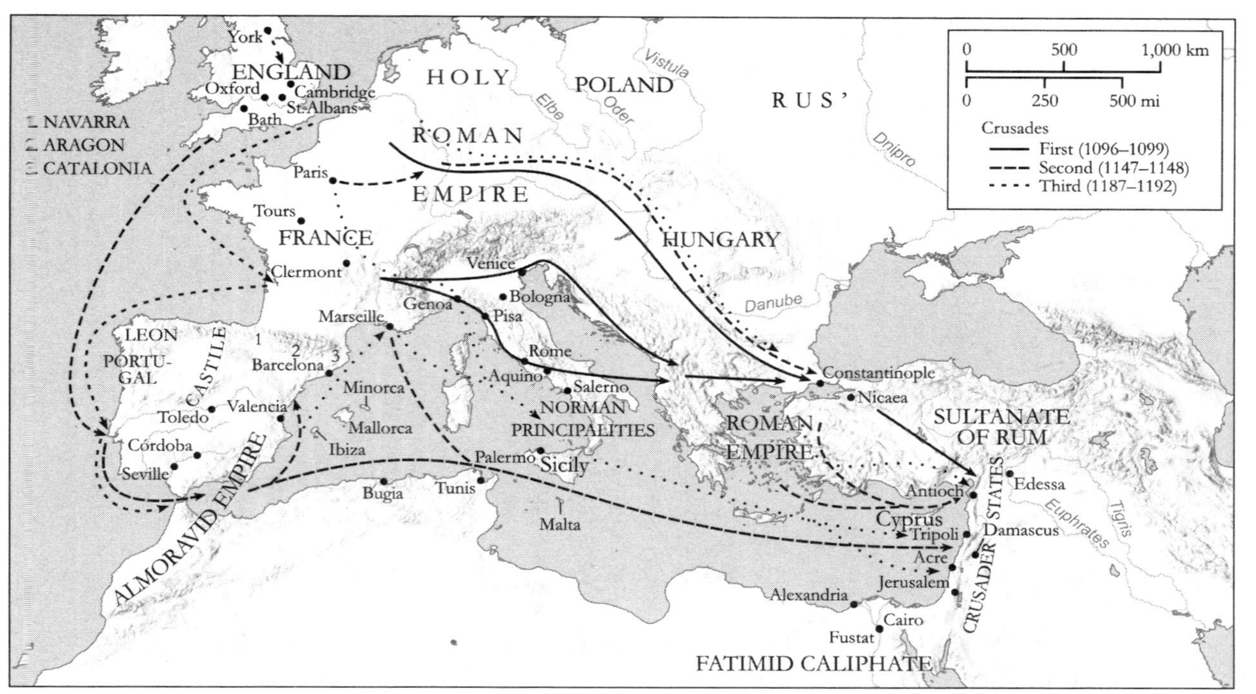

The world of the Crusaders in the twelfth century CE

moravids. Norman knights were also making inroads in the Islamic Mediterranean: in 1072 Robert Guiscard and his brother Roger took Palermo, in 1091 they subjected Malta to tribute, and Roger ruled Sicily as "Great Count" for another ten years.[1]

Religion was not always—perhaps not even often—what mattered most in these wars: in 1066 Rollo's great-great-great-grandson William had conquered Christian England, for instance, and in 1071 Norman soldiers of fortune seized the last eastern Roman city in southern Italy. As Christian territory in Europe increased, however, by conquest and conversion, so Christianity created an increasingly shared culture across these lands. Popes began to enforce a shared liturgy and other cultic practices on their growing flock: Gregory VII (r. 1073–85) insisted for instance that Sardinian priests shave their beards, according to "the custom of the holy Roman church," on pain of losing their property, and refused permission to Bohemian Christians to use their own vernacular rites.[2]

Eastern Christians meanwhile had problems. A group of Seljuk Turks from the central Asian oasis of Khwarazm had converted to Islam and conquered Iran and Iraq in the mid-eleventh century. In 1071 they defeated the eastern Roman emperor Romanos IV and in the twenty-five years that followed, Turkish forces occupied a third of the eastern Roman empire, including the great cities of Antioch and Nicaea, the latter just ninety kilometers southeast of Constantinople itself. Schism or no, the Roman emperor Alexios I asked the pope at Rome for help.

Urban II (r. 1088–9) had challenges of his own at the time, including a rival pope *in situ* at Rome with the support of the Holy Roman Emperor, consigning Urban himself to effective exile in northern Italy and France. The opportunity to assert moral as well as military leadership within the Church was too good to pass up. He convoked a Church council at Clermont in 1095 where he urged Christians to take action, and in 1096 the first pilgrim soldiers from France and Germany set out.

The First Crusade was fought in the name of Christianity, "against the enemies of the Christian name," but those enemies were vaguely construed: on their way to Anatolia expedition members massacred large numbers of Jews in the Rhineland.[3] When they reached the shores of Asia the city of Nicaea surrendered to Alexios, and the Crusaders themselves marched on across Anatolia to capture Antioch in 1098. Then they carried the fight south to Jerusalem, took the city in July 1099 and massacred both the Jewish and the Muslim populations.

The Crusaders did not return Jerusalem to Christian Constantinople, from which Muhammad's followers had captured it almost 500 years before. Instead, a Frankish duke called Godfrey of Bouillon established a Christian kingdom of his own there, under the aegis of the pope at Rome. Other Latin noblemen did the same at Antioch, Edessa, and Tripoli, carving a series of freebooter kingdoms out of the Levant, or Outremer—"Beyond the Sea"—where hundreds of European soldiers stayed for good.

This was a classic case of mission creep: it is unclear whether the pope mentioned the Holy Land at all in his sermon at Clermont, and he certainly didn't suggest settlement there.[4] Nor did Holy War heal the Great Schism; indeed the arrival of "Latin" Christians in the Levant exacerbated tensions between the eastern and western Church. It was still something to celebrate. In the words of Fulcher of Chartres, chaplain to Baldwin of Boulogne, who served as king of Jerusalem from 1100 CE: "in our time God has transferred the West into the East. For we who were Occidentals are now made Orientals . . . why would someone who has found the East like this return to the West?"[5]

This rare evocation of East and West in the service of ideology depends of course on Augustine's old geographical division of the world into the Asian Oriens and the Afro-European Occidens. Now, however, the distinction has become meaningful—not as a mark of separate civilizations, as today, but as something to overcome. Christendom was still a universal ambition, and the resurgent confidence in that idea is reflected in stories that now began to emerge of Prester John, a fictional Christian king of a faraway Asian realm beyond the Muslim world.[6]

However much the Crusades may look like Holy War between opposing cultures, the Crusader era provides a very different perspective from that of modern civilizational thinking, the idea that separate and enduring cultures map onto different geographical regions: this is a world where culture has no natural location. At the same time contact, even between enemies, leads to entanglement, and the expansion of

Christian rule in all directions led paradoxically to closer economic and cultural encounters over the twelfth century between Christians, Muslims, and Jews at all social levels.

Sea routes around the Mediterranean became denser and more complex as ships from Christian ports ferried warriors and pilgrims to and from the newly accessible Holy Land, and brought back from Islamic Egypt silk and spices, linen and paper. Words that entered Romance languages from Arabic in this era reflect the commercial nature of the connections involved: *douane/dogana*, tariff, traffic, risk, bazaar, check.[7]

The Crusades were especially good for the "maritime republics" that had emerged in ports like Pisa, Genoa, and Venice, the last transformed by the fall of Ravenna from a minor local port into the principal trading harbor on the Adriatic.* These mini-states legislated not through a small group of lords but through larger citizen assemblies and magistrates who were either elected or selected by lot, and before the Crusades they already imported goods from Muslim Tunisia, Sicily, and al-Andalus. Pisa had built its late-eleventh-century cathedral on the profits of sacking Islamic cities on Mediterranean islands, but raiding segued easily into trading.[8]

At the same time as supporting Latin knights with their fleets they now made commercial treaties with eastern Christian and Muslim ports around the Mediterranean. The archbishop of Pisa became the Latin patriarch of Jerusalem in 1100, but Pisa itself concluded treaties with Constantinople in 1101, Cairo in 1154, and Tunis in 1157.[9] We can see the importance of trade with the Arab world in the name of the early-twelfth-century dockyard that produced the fleet of Venice, the Arsenale, from the Arabic *dar al-sina* or "house of industry."[10] In Genoa the same Arabic phrase becomes *darsena.***

*Settlement on the central islands that make up the modern city of Venice had begun in earnest in the later eighth century, and in 811 the ducal seat moved from Malamocco on the Lido that shields the lagoon from the sea to Venice itself, where the doge built his palace and consecrated the chapel of San Marco in 832.

**The use of "arsenal" to mean a weapons store is a later, English development.

Half-hearted attempts by popes to impose boycotts on trade in slaves and war materials (timber and iron) with Muslim powers were routinely ignored: they also sold exemptions to Christian traders, which their Muslim partners were often happy to cover.[11] Italian merchants with cloths and silks from Islamic ports then traveled across the Alps to do business with merchants from equally busy North Sea harbors bringing woolens and furs from Rus'.[12]

Meanwhile, a new breed of Tuscan bankers built on the expertise in commercial finance developed by Jewish merchants in Cairo and Alexandria. Other technologies came west too, from glassmaking to glazed pottery.[13] And tastes converged in a literal sense, as traders and Crusaders returned to Europe with a new appreciation for sugar, a Sanskrit word that reached European languages through Arabic. This reflected the earlier role of the Caliphate in bringing Indian sugarcane west to its own territories and above all to Egypt, which dominated the sugar trade until the late middle ages.[14]

Increasing prosperity and new routes to the wealth and wisdom of Islamic cities also fostered the transformation of European artistic and intellectual culture that is often called the "Twelfth-Century Renaissance." Works of Greek medicine, science, and philosophy finally began filtering back into western Europe, some of them directly from the libraries of Constantinople and Antioch, but most in Arabic versions.[15] There was new interest in Islamic scholarship itself as well, and a concerted search began for Arabic texts to translate into Latin in the expanding borderlands of Christian Europe. No one had yet invented Classical roots for a European civilization, and the marvels of medieval science were fostered by Arabic commentaries, criticism, and new ideas.

As Latin Christian rulers worked their way south through the Iberian peninsula, the multilingual and multi-confessional kingdoms of Catholic Iberia were the main gateway for Latin Christian scholars to Islamic letters and learning. *Sirr al-asrar* ("The secret of secrets"), for instance, an Arabic work of political advice written as a fictional letter from Aristotle to his pupil Alexander the Great, was first translated into Latin as the *Secretum Secretorum* around 1120 CE for the queen of the new kingdom of Portugal. It became one of the most widely read texts in western Europe from the thirteenth to the sixteenth centuries, surviving in hundreds of manuscripts in languages from Provençal to Anglo-Norman to Dutch.[16]

The most important meeting place however was Toledo, already a famous city of learning before it surrendered to Alfonso VI of Castile and León in 1085.[17] High on top of a hill, Toledo had been the home of the astronomer al-Zarqali (1029–1100), who corrected Ptolemy of Alexandria's calculation of the length of the Mediterranean, and Said al-Andalusi (1029–70), a local *qadi* or judge whose book on the "Categories of communities" (*Tabaqat al-'umam*) described the contributions to science of the Indians, Persians, Chaldeans, Egyptians, Greeks, Romans, Arabs east and west, and Jews.

Not only did the new Catholic authorities tolerate the city's large Muslim and Jewish populations, but Alfonso called himself "the king of the two religions."[18] Many Muslims and Jews chose to remain in the city, alongside an even older population of "Mozarab" Christians who had remained faithful to the Visigothic liturgy rather than the Latin rite practiced in the Catholic kingdoms farther north; predictably enough the pope now enforced the latter on them.[19] The city also attracted Mozarabs and Jews from what was left of Islamic Iberia, especially after the conservative and puritanical Almohad dynasty overthrew their fellow Berber Almoravids in Morocco in 1147, and by 1172 had taken al-Andalus from them as well.

Now Christians keen to access Arabic works started to arrive in Toledo too, and some stayed to study with Arabic scholars. A Frankish quarter grew up next to the cathedral, and the city became a center for the translation of Arabic science and philosophy into Latin. Since Latin was the one language the peoples of Toledo didn't already speak, translations were again often made in a two-step process: first by locals from formal Arabic into their own Arabic or Romance dialect, and then into Latin by the foreigners.

Central to this work was a scholar named Gerard from Italian Cremona who arrived in Toledo around 1140. He came in search of Ptolemy's work on mathematical astronomy, known in Greek as *He megale syntaxis,* "The great treatise," and in English as the *Almagest,* taken from the Arabic title, which transliterated the Greek for "the greatest." One proof of the enduring importance of Arabic scholarship in Europe is that even though a slightly earlier translation made directly from a Greek manuscript was also available, Gerard's 1175 translation from Arabic became the most popular version of the work for centuries.[20]

Gerard himself was so impressed by the breadth of Muslim, Jewish, Indian, and Greek scholarship he found in the city that he stayed for the rest of his life, becoming a canon of the cathedral. He learned Arabic, and in the end he translated more than seventy scholarly works from Arabic to Latin by a laborious word-for-word method that made for accuracy, if tough reading. They included books by Aristotle, Euclid, and Galen, as well as al-Khwarizmi, al-Farabi, and Ibn Sina (Avicenna), a tenth-century Persian scholar from the central Asian trading city of Bukhara who became one of the most influential thinkers of the medieval period on philosophy, astronomy, and above all medicine.

Other Christian scholars of this era were more itinerant: men like Adelard of Bath (c. 1080–1150), who studied at Tours and traveled in Italy and Sicily.[21] He composed philosophical works of his own, but he is best remembered for his many translations from Arabic works of philosophy, astronomy, alchemy, and mathematics. A devotee of Indo-Arabic numerals, he may have been the first translator of al-Khwarizmi's ninth-century work on arithmetic, now lost in Arabic and preserved only in the twelfth-century Latin versions, which brought the new numbers to the attention of scholars and merchants across Europe.

They were admittedly a hard sell. Latin notaries used them in commercial contracts with Muslim trading partners, Mediterranean merchants employed them for calculation, and northern European scholars began to see the point of counting "nothing" or even negative numbers. But ready-reckoner tables made basic arithmetic with Roman numerals relatively easy, while the new symbols were difficult to write: one early-twelfth-century manuscript of al-Khwarizmi now held in the Cambridge University Library leaves spaces for some of the Indo-Arabic numerals, presumably with the intention of filling them in later, or getting someone else to do so. Even when they were written they were carefully marked off in boxes or with points to distinguish, for instance, .6. from b.[22]

It wasn't only in Iberia that Christian kings funded cosmopolitan, multi-confessional courts in an era of crusading and "reconquest." Roger II inherited the countship of Sicily in 1104 at the age of nine. A Roman Catholic educated by Greek and Arab scholars, he took the title of king of Sicily in 1130. Over the course of his fifty-year reign he conquered most of southern Italy and temporarily ruled the coastal regions of Ifriqiya, taking land from Christian and Muslim adversaries with equal enthusiasm.

Roger's administration borrowed a great deal from the traditions of contemporary Arabic powers, and he used an honorific Arabic title borrowed not from the earlier Sicilian Emirate, but from Fatimid Egypt.[23] His courtiers in Palermo spoke Arabic, Greek, Latin, and French, and they practiced Christianity in eastern and western forms as well as Islam.

Although the new king made Sicily another center for Latin translation from both Greek and Arabic, different literary genres continued to be written on the island in the different languages traditional to them: Greek was for liturgy, Latin for history, and Arabic for poetry.[24] Arabic was still the principal language of science as well, and Roger invited Arabic-speaking philosophers, doctors, mathematicians, and poets to his court.

His star resident scholar was a north African geographer named Muhammad al-Idrisi. Born at Ceuta in Morocco around 1100, al-Idrisi studied in Córdoba and began to travel the Mediterranean and Atlantic as a teenager, reaching the coast of England.[25] By 1138 he had joined Roger's court in Palermo, where he was commissioned to make a scientific map of the world. What emerged was very different from the simple zonal diagrams, fabulous T–O maps, and schematic itineraries found until now in the Christian tradition.

As he tells the tale himself, for over fifteen years al-Idrisi and a team of researchers studied the work of ten distinguished Arabic geographers as well as an Arabic translation of Ptolemy of Alexandria's Greek geography and a fifth-century *History* written in Latin by the Christian scholar Paulus Orosius.[26] They discussed the problems of cartography with experts in the field—a rather disappointing exercise, apparently—carried out new fieldwork, and interviewed travelers, summoning all those known to have useful knowledge of foreign lands. Al-Idrisi was proud of the scientific methodology they used: "When their accounts agreed with each other and corroborated each other, he recorded what was most reliable and most trustworthy. When they varied among each other, he put their information aside and disregarded it."

Having recalculated all the relevant coordinates and distances according to the best available information—which was understandably still better for western Europe and the Islamic world than for China and southeast Asia—al-Idrisi oversaw the production of a new map of the known world. It was oriented to the south and organized around seven climes or climate zones, depicting "their nations and regions, their coastlines and seashores, their bays, seas, rivers, and the mouths of rivers, the populated regions and the unpopulated, and the well-traveled internal roads of each nation and those between nations with the distance figured and recorded in miles, as well as the best-known anchorages."

The map was first drawn on paper with compasses, and then transcribed onto a huge disk of pure silver. At Roger's direction, al-Idrisi produced a companion commentary entitled *Amusements for Those Who Long to Traverse the Horizon* (*Nuzhat al-mushtaq fi ikhtiraq al-afaq*), but usually called the Book of Roger.[27] The work divided each of the seven climes into ten sections from west to east, and contained a written description and individual map for each of the seventy regions.

Beginning with the Canary Islands in the far southwest, it described the lands, seas, and mountains; the crops, buildings, employments and industries, imports and exports; and the reported marvels and the condition of the people: "their appearance, their nature, their faith, their clothing and ornaments, their languages." Finally, the book included a drawing of the circular silver map of the world.

Al-Idrisi's world was still fundamentally the same one known to

Ptolemy of Alexandria. It stretched from the Canaries east to Korea and the equator north to the Arctic, beyond which were regions held to be too hot or too cold for human habitation.[28] There is much here though that is new: we hear about the cities of Sudan and Ghana and the sources of the Nile, and get far more detail than in earlier accounts of eastern Europe and the Baltic. Sicily itself receives a great deal of attention, but al-Idrisi also has kind words for Toledo, where he had spent his student days.

Not all his information is reliable: his Norwegians for instance have no necks and live inside trees. All the same, the Book of Roger was by far the most sophisticated work of both cartography and human geography to date, building on mathematical Islamic mapping that was itself based on an Alexandrian Greek tradition to create an Arabic product in honor of a Norman king.

The work was completed in 1154, shortly before Roger died. Al-Idrisi carried on working in Palermo for his son William I, but in a failed revolt in 1160 the barons of Sicily burned the palace archives, including the silver map and a Latin translation of the Book of Roger that al-Idrisi had overseen. The original work was first printed in an abridged form in Rome in 1592—one of the earliest printed books in Arabic—but it was only translated into Latin again in the seventeenth century; its legacy is not as a model for later European cartography but as a testimony to the intercultural world of twelfth-century southern Europe.

Roger's strategy in the prosperous and culturally rich island of Sicily was very different from the approach Norman knights had adopted in England, where William the Conqueror introduced French language and customs, and made Latin rather than Old English the language of administration. It was also different from the strategies adopted in the independent lordships established by Latin knights in the Levant.[29]

Daily life and survival required these petty kings to make treaties and compromises with their new neighbors, both Muslim and Christian: plenty of Christians were still living in the region when the Crusaders arrived, as conversion had only become popular in the previous century.[30] Local custom had its uses too: Christians used Arabic to keep customs records in Acre in 1184.[31] But these were still places of coexistence, not of easy or equal cultural interchange, and they demanded clear statements of Christian identity: the trophy Church of the Holy Sepulchre at Jerusalem, originally built in the fourth century CE to replace a Roman temple, was renovated in the first half of the twelfth with a bell tower in the Romanesque European style.

Crusading itself was going badly. A second campaign in 1147–50 was a disaster: the Seljuk Turks defeated the kings of France and Germany in separate battles, and even these monarchs' combined forces failed to take Damascus in 1158. A new threat then appeared in the Kurdish warrior Salah al-Din Yusuf ibn Ayyub, better known to Latins as Saladin. Having taken over Fatimid Egypt in 1171, Saladin captured Jerusalem in 1187. The city's Frankish rulers fled to the coast, reestablishing their principality at Acre, and three European kings—Philip II of France, Richard I (the Lionheart) of England, and Frederick I Barbarossa of Germany, Italy, and the Holy Roman Empire—set out on what became known as the Third Crusade (1189–92). It ended in stalemate, and Barbarossa drowned in a Cilician river.

Latin knights increasingly focused instead on using the ideology of religious war to sanitize lands closer to home. As well as continuing the conquest of Islamic Iberia, they brought Roman Christianity with violence to the pagan Baltic from the 1140s and to Gaelic Ireland in the 1170s.[32] Settlers from the traditional strongholds of Christendom were tempted to newly Christian territories with land and low rents, especially in Iberia and eastern Europe.[33]

An ever more homogeneous Latin Christian way of life developed across much of Europe as well in this period. Local cults of holy men and women with local names, often centered on the site of their relics, succumbed to a few shared superstar saints, such as Mary, Peter, and John, whose names now appear in churches all over the continent.[34] Independent monasteries yielded to centralized networks with standardized structures and practices: the Burgundian Cistercians opened more than 500 houses in the twelfth century from Spain to Ireland to Norway.[35]

This trend toward cultural isolation in Europe is acknowledged around 1170 in the work of the Old French poet Chrétien de Troyes, whose Arthurian romances celebrate the social practices known as chivalry, from the French *chevalerie* or "cavalry": courtesy, generosity, and worldly accomplishments.[36]* He notes in the prologue to his romantic tale of the knight Cligès who falls in love with his uncle's wife that "our books teach us . . . that Greece first had renown in chivalry and knowledge. Then came chivalry to Rome, and the whole of knowledge, which has now come into France. God grant that she may stay there."[37] Here, as in modern civilizational thinking, a culture can change its name and even within limits its location, but not its nature. Chrétien's own views may have been more subtle: he goes on to make numerous references throughout the text to cities of Arab learning.[38]

In real life, the persecution of European Jews that had begun in earnest during the First Crusade led to their expulsion from Paris in 1182 and the massacre of the entire community at York in 1190.[39] The Crusades themselves provided opportunities to correct Christian heresy: Richard I captured Orthodox Cyprus on his way east, and the Fourth Crusade (1202–4) sacked Orthodox Constantinople itself, with widespread looting, and with the help of Venice. They imposed Latin rites and bishops on this Orthodox territory, while the rulers of a rump Roman empire based themselves at Nicaea. Unorthodox Catholics were targeted as well: in southern France the Albigensian Crusade of 1209 attempted to expunge the Cathar heresy that there were two Gods, one good and one bad, a project that led to the establishment in the 1240s of the Holy Inquisition.

As Latin Christendom was increasingly confined to Europe, it became increasingly powerful there, and increasingly intolerant of differ-

Key components of both crusading and chivalry have eastern parallels. In Sunni Islam groups of holy warriors ('ayyarun*) are found as early as the ninth century, battling opponents both Christian and Islamic. And an Islamic *futuwwa* movement developed a code of conduct very similar to that of European chivalry, extolling bravery, purity, self sacrifice, the defense of the weak, and the upholding of justice (D. G. Tor, *Violent Order: Religious Warfare, Chivalry, and the 'Ayyār Phenomenon in the Medieval Islamic World*, Würzburg: Ergon in Kommission, 2007, 243–51; *BEI*, 'Ayyār).

ence. In 1215 the pope convoked a general Church Council—"Lateran IV"—that established clear and common criteria, beyond baptism, for membership of the Christian community: Christians should confess their sins to a priest at least once a year and take the Eucharist at least at Easter.[40] It also barred Jews from public office and ordered that Jews and Muslims be distinguished from Christians by their dress; in 1218 Jews in England were legally obliged to wear a special badge.

All this was part of a new focus in Europe from the twelfth century onward on heresy as a distinct problem, and a turn to persecution as a regular practice that soon became a habit—targeting not only dissenters, Muslims, and Jews but vagrants, sodomites, prostitutes, and the poor.[41] This process has parallels with the military campaigns of Roman Catholic conquest in Ireland, Iberia, and the Baltic of the same era, but it had little to do with Latin knights and not as much with the Roman Church itself as one might think. Secular authorities were at least as enthusiastic as bishops in the pursuit of heretics and other antisocials, and the profits that came from seizing their property. And at the same time organized processes of inquisition and punishment provided work, status, and authority for an army of educated bureaucrats—men who were increasingly the product of the new "universities" that were beginning to appear in European cities.

Institutions of higher learning were already familiar farther east. In China an Imperial Academy ("the Grand School") had existed in Changan since 124 BCE, with a lecture hall, halls of residence, and even a student prison. By the mid-second century CE it had 30,000 students, and it would play a central role in preparing students for the Imperial Civil Service examinations introduced in 598 CE, which were set until 1905.[42] Yeshivas or Jewish academies existed as well, with the most famous established at Pumbedita, near Falluja, in the third century CE. In India the Nalanda Buddhist monastery offered religious and secular education from the early fifth century including philosophy, logic, and medicine to thousands of students: a Chinese visitor in the seventh century reported that one of its three library buildings was nine stories high.[43]

In the later fifth century an academy was established in the Sasanian city of Gundeshapur by "Nestorians" whose ideology had diverged from mainstream Christianity as they refused to compromise their belief in the double nature, both human and divine, of Christ.[44] After being declared heretics at Church councils, they fled to the Sasanian empire and set up a school based on ancient educational institutions at Egyptian Alexandria and Syrian Antioch. By Khosrow I's time it specialized in medical teaching in the Greek, Persian, and Zoroastrian traditions, by local as well as Nestorian scholars.[45]

In the eleventh century madrasas or "places of study," especially the study of Islamic law, multiplied across the Muslim world. Founded and funded by individuals, they offered accommodation and prayer halls as well as teaching, for which students would receive an *ijaza* certifying them to teach what they had learned to their own students.[46] Centers of specialist training began to emerge in Europe as well, with a famous medical school at Salerno in Italy attracting students and scholars from far afield. A Muslim trader and doctor from Carthage known as Constantine the African (c. 1020–87) was said to have translated many important Arabic works on medicine into Latin for the first time there, before becoming a monk.[47]

Some time in the twelfth century, however, something quite new happened, when students studying Roman law in Bologna formed a guild or *universitas,* like those of tradesmen or lawyers, to manage the provision of training by the individual masters settled in the city. Further such experiments soon followed at Paris, Oxford, and Cambridge, where a university was established in 1209 by a faction of scholars from Oxford.

Unlike the University of Bologna, these later institutions covered a wide range of subjects: Paris had faculties of arts, theology, medicine, and canon (Church) law.[48] They were led by guilds not of students but of the masters who taught them, who established the syllabus, arranged the teaching, and held examinations by which students could qualify to teach the same subjects themselves (whether or not they really meant to).

These universities had no buildings at first and rented teaching and event space, often from churches. They still attracted students from all over Europe, and over time they gained charters from authorities including the Holy Roman Emperor and the pope that awarded them special privileges and protections in return for the prestige and direct economic benefit they brought.

New universities opened for business over the thirteenth century in France, Italy, Spain, and Portugal.[49]* Students enrolled at the age of fourteen or fifteen under a specific master, and usually had to qualify first in the *studium generale* or liberal arts, a course that built significantly on the old trivium and quadrivium. Then they could take a higher degree, usually in medicine, law, or theology. The *studium generale* took around five years, and a higher degree perhaps another five, although over time both expanded: a full course of studies to the highest level at Oxford in the fourteenth century lasted around seventeen years. Completion, even of the *studium generale,* was rare.[50]

Over time the syllabus also focused increasingly on theological, scientific, and philosophical training at the expense of the "lower" arts. Al-Farabi's description of an ideal scholarly curriculum was soon available in multiple Latin translations, and by the early thirteenth century its reading list of appropriate Greek and Arabic authorities was being incorporated into the standard European syllabus.[51]

Students read the new Muslim and Jewish scholarship alongside advanced ancient Greek works, all translated from Arabic into Latin—works like Ibn al-Haytham's *Optics,* al-Khwarizmi's *Algebra,* Euclid's *Elements of Mathematics,* Ptolemy of Alexandria's *Almagest,* and Ibn Sina's *Canon of Medicine,* itself an integration of Greco-Roman and Islamic ideas that remained an important textbook on medicine from India to England until the nineteenth century.[52] Aristotle became particularly popular in the thirteenth century, alongside his Arabic commentators, men like the twelfth-century Muslim Córdoban scholar Ibn Rushd (1126–98), known north of the Pyrenees as Averroës.

*In England the masters of Oxford and Cambridge held tight to their privileges, forcing graduates of the two universities to swear an oath not to lecture outside them (William Whyte, "The medieval university monopoly," *History Today* [March 7, 2018]). Scotland had no such qualms, acquiring five universities between the establishment of St. Andrews in 1413 and 1582, when Edinburgh University was founded. The third university established in England was London, in 1828.

The institution of the university has distinct parallels with the madrasa, in its corporate nature outside the direct control of either city or church, in the principle of studying under a specific master and in the introduction of a "license to teach." Furthermore, students were taught through lectures and formal oral disputation, which required them to first clarify and then attempt to resolve two contradictory arguments: an approach dubbed "scholasticism" that became the hallmark of the medieval university. Disputation was however already widely used in Islamic education, part of a dialectical approach to the advancement of knowledge in both traditions ultimately rooted in Aristotelian logic.[53]

The intellectual world of thirteenth-century western Europe is symbolized above all by the work of an Italian monk from Aquino named Thomas who studied at the University of Paris in the 1240s and went on to write works of philosophy and theology inspired by Ibn Rushd and his Jewish contemporary Moses ben Maimon, better known to Christian scholars as Maimonides. Thomas Aquinas drew on ancient Greek ideas, later Arabic commentary, and the principles of his own theological tradition—just as the scholars of Baghdad, Cairo, and Córdoba had done before him.

Popes declared two more Crusades to the east, in 1217–21 and 1228–9, but by the middle of the century the Latin Christian presence in the Levant was confined to the coast and a few heavily defended castles like Krak des Chevaliers up in the hills of western Syria. In Europe itself, however, an order of "Teutonic" knights originally established at Acre launched a "Prussian Crusade" in 1230 against the remaining pagans of the Baltic, and farther west the conquest of al-Andalus proceeded apace, under the direction of ever larger Christian kingdoms.

In 1229 the Crown of Aragon in eastern Iberia took the island of Mallorca, which had been in Muslim hands since 902; in 1238 its forces captured Valencia, and they then proceeded to occupy Sicily, Minorca, Ibiza, part of Sardinia, and southern Italy up to Naples. Farther west Córdoba fell to the kingdom of Castile in 1236, followed by Seville in 1248. The following year the far western kingdom of Portugal took the Algarve. Across their new holdings the conquerors took over the agricultural industries, learning how to produce Seville oranges, bananas, rice, and sugar.[54]

Some Christian kings continued to resist cultural isolationism, up to a point. In Sicily the death of Roger's grandson William II in 1189 led, after a war and German conquest, to the accession in 1198 of his three-year-old German cousin Frederick, son of Roger's daughter Constance and Frederick Barbarossa's son Henry VI of Hohenstaufen.[55] Crowned Holy Roman Emperor himself in 1220, Frederick II ruled a realm that stretched from Sicily north to Germany.

He spoke six languages and was excommunicated a total of three times by two different popes. He nonetheless departed on the Sixth Crusade in 1228, and his command of Arabic made him the most successful Catholic diplomat of the era. He even negotiated the temporary return of Jerusalem to Christian hands in 1229, although the Crusader kingdom continued to be ruled from Acre.

Frederick's wide connections brought him access to one crucial currency of medieval diplomacy that also reveals the extent of commercial networks in this era: exotic animals. He was especially fond of hunting with cheetahs, which he obtained from Tunisia and sometimes gifted to other European monarchs; this sport was popular in Indian courts and probably originated in Persia.[56] A work he wrote on falconry in the early 1240s includes a drawing of a bird he owned that was finally identified in 2018 as a yellow-crested or sulfur-crested cockatoo, imported from Indonesia or even farther away two centuries earlier than the next known example found in Europe. It came to Frederick from the "Sultan of Babylon"—the standard name at the time for the Fatimid caliph in Cairo, al-Malik al-Kamil, a regular correspondent of Frederick's, who had perhaps imported the bird from China. He also sent Frederick a gyrfalcon, an Arctic bird captured in Iceland.[57]

Like Roger before him, Frederick collected scholars too. He continued to commission Latin translations from Arabic, including translations of Ibn Rushd, and he supported Leonardo Fibonacci, a champion of the Indo-Arabic numbers that were still used only sparingly in western Europe. The son of a Pisan merchant who had taken a job at a trading post in the north African port of Bugia in 1192, Leonardo received an excellent education there in mathematics, and went on to study in Egypt, Syria, Greece, Sicily, and Provence before publishing his own textbook in 1202 on "the method of the Indians." This *Liber Abaci* ("Book of Calculation") explained how to use Indo-Arabic numbers for everyday purposes, to convert between weights, measures, and currencies, and to calculate interest, as well as how to perform more abstract mathematical operations.*

At the same time, the production of literary Arabic on Sicily ceased during Frederick's reign, and that in Greek diminished, as Frederick looked beyond the great cultural traditions of the past to promote the local vernacular language.[58] The first Sicilian poets wrote under his patronage a century before Dante began to compose in Tuscan. They introduced a new focus on romance and a new sonnet form, and their inspiration was not Arabic, Greek, or Latin literary culture, but new poetry in French, German, and Occitan that had been emerging to the north over the previous century.[59]

Frederick was also responsible for the return of the idea of the West to European mental horizons.[60] He had been Holy Roman Emperor for two decades when a pagan people rode into central Europe. In 1241 Mongols reached Poland, Hungary, and Austria, and threatened the borders of Germany. Matthew Paris, a Benedictine monk based at the Abbey of St. Alban, described their "very large heads, by no means proportionate to their bodies" and how "they feed on raw flesh, and even on human beings . . . impious and inexorable men."[61] He also preserves a long letter from Frederick to the Christian kings of western Europe asking them to unite with him against these new enemies.

The Mongols, Frederick warns, "are now purposing to enter the boundaries of Germany, which is the gate, as it were, to Christendom . . . intending the destruction of the whole of the West [*toti occidenti excidium*] and of ruining and uprooting the faith and name of Christ. . . . But we hope in our Lord Jesus Christ . . . that these also . . .

*It continued to be an uphill struggle: although the new system was used to number the beams in Salisbury Cathedral in 1224, and Tuscan bankers began to take a genuine interest in the fourteenth century, Roman numerals were still used a great deal in 1500.

after experiencing the strength of the West, . . . be thrust back to their own Tartarus"—the ancient equivalent of hell.[62]

This appeal reverses Fulcher's celebratory imagery of 141 years before: far from a constraint for Christians to overcome, "the West" is now a symbolic Christian space worth fighting for. Frederick sets up no explicit dichotomy between *East* and West. In fact he specifies that the Mongols have emerged "from the regions of the south" and first marched "toward the northern parts."[63] We are still a long way from modern civilizational thinking, but it is now becoming possible to carve off Christian Europe from the world.

The notion of the West disappeared again as the threat receded, when the death of the Mongol ruler prompted his troops to return home. It had never been serious: occasional incursions into Europe were just border raids on the edge of a vast Mongol empire that already stretched from the Pacific to the Black Sea. Instead, they heralded unprecedented levels of contact and exchange between Europe and the rest of the known world.

CHAPTER TWENTY-EIGHT

Kalila wa-Dimna

KARAKORAM, 1254 CE

In 1254 a Flemish missionary called William of Rubruck arrived on a great plain in central Mongolia where the tents and towers of Karakoram rose above the sandy scrub. William was not the first Christian friar to visit Mongolia: the pope had sent several Dominicans and Franciscans in the 1240s to acquire information about the Mongols and to investigate potential alliances with them against Muslim powers. But he is the only one to have left a detailed description of the Mongol capital itself, in a report written for his patron, King Louis IX of France.[1]

Although Karakoram was just a couple of decades old, William reports that it was already a walled city with separate Muslim and Chinese quarters, the former associated in particular with traders, the latter with craftsmen. The population worshipped at twelve "idol temples" (Buddhist and Daoist shrines), two mosques, and a Nestorian Christian church.[2] William meets people from Russia, Georgia, Armenia, and Hungary, and he befriends a Parisian silversmith named Guillaume Bucher who had been taken prisoner in Belgrade. The city isn't much to his liking all the same: he complains about the food, the drunkenness, and the Mongolian emperor's increasingly direct attempts to persuade him to go home.

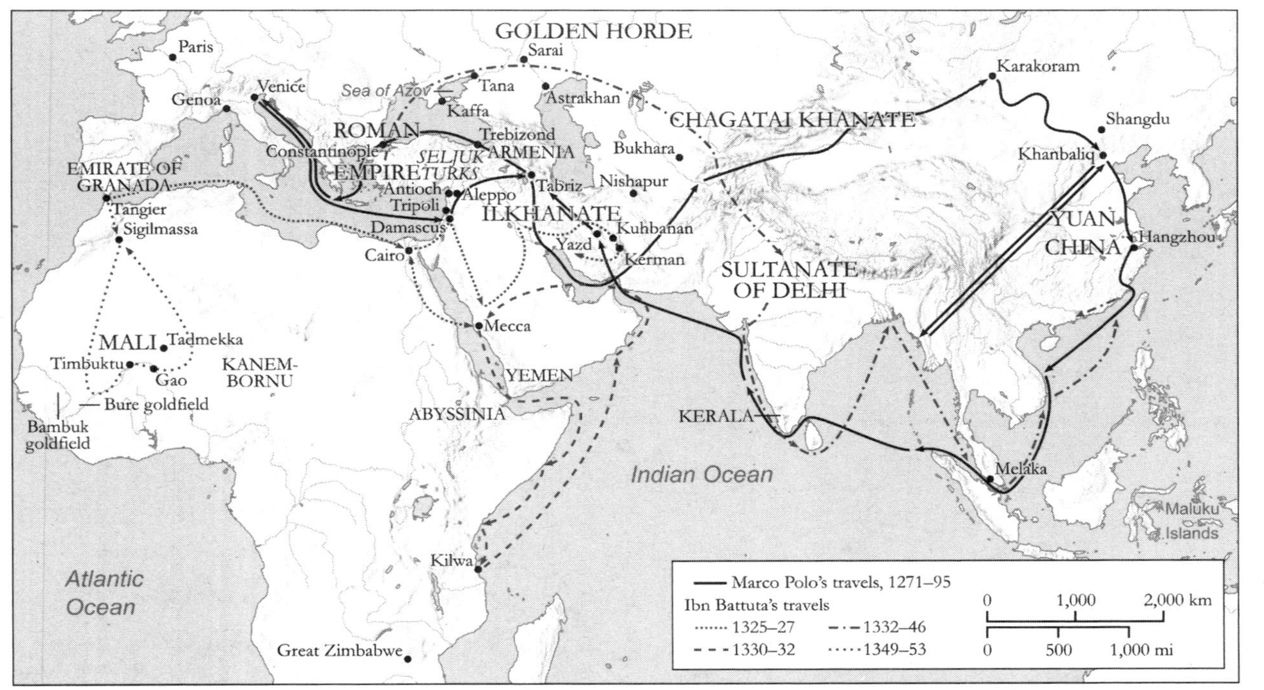

A connected world, c. 1300 CE

Möngke Khagan himself had a great palace at Karakoram, where he received visitors for parties, and where Bucher had that very year designed a silver tree with performing automata in the branches: four golden serpents and a trumpet angel. When the khagan ordered another round, a servant hidden in the mechanism blew through a pipe to make the angel raise his trumpet and sound it, while others poured drinks into four pipes that issued from the mouths of the serpents into silver basins at the base of the tree: wine, mare's milk, honey mead, and rice ale, to be conveyed by servants to the waiting guests.[3]

Möngke followed the traditional shamanic religion of his forefathers, but his was a tolerant regime. Buddhism had reached the far east of Asia from India along trade routes by the first century CE, and by the sixth century communities of Nestorian missionaries had arrived via India and Iran as well.[4] Möngke's own mother was a Christian, and he completed a Buddhist temple and built a stupa for the city.[5] He maintained good relations with religious leaders of all stripes, taking an interest in their activities and granting them tax breaks, and he took advantage of William's visit to organize a public debate among Christians, Muslims, and a Buddhist.

William finds the occasion typically trying. For one thing, he gets caught up in disagreements with Nestorian Christians who also wish to speak for their supposedly shared faith but then support the Buddhist's arguments before getting distracted by an attempt to convert an elderly Uighur priest. For another, the Muslims present enthusiastically agree with William on all points. Finally the Nestorians and Muslims fall to singing while the despairing Buddhist retreats into silent meditation, and "after that everyone drank heavily."[6]

The debate captures the power of contact, travel, and migration to channel ideas across vast distances, and to open up spaces for discovery, learning, and change—even if they don't always lead to appreciable progress on the Enlightenment model of civilization. And there was more and more of it. Building on new levels of conquest, war, and wealth, the century from 1250 to 1350 CE saw movement across a larger canvas than ever before. It created an economic ecosystem across three continents where curious observers from Europe were learning fast.

. . .

The Mongolian empire was the singular creation of a single man called Temüjin (c. 1160–1227).[7] After the death of his father, a Mongol clan leader, Temüjin was abandoned in the desert with his mother and siblings as a relative assumed leadership of the clan and led it away. It was a character-building experience, and he rejoined society as a storied warrior and built up a federation of allies. In 1206 the assembled Mongol leaders of eastern central Asia acknowledged him as Chinggis (Genghis) Khan: Oceanic ("Universal") Ruler.

Temüjin did his best to live up to the new title. First he conquered the northern edge of China, where siege engineers defected to him with catapults and crossbows.[8] Then he led his troops west through central Asia. He was a brilliant military leader and a born showman, with a taste for scorched earth: enraged by the killing of his son-in-law during a siege of the old Seljuk capital of Nishapur in northern Iran, he ordered the massacre of every single inhabitant of the city, down to the cats and dogs, and had their skulls piled up in giant pyramids around the city.[9]

By the time Temüjin died in 1227, his Mongol empire reached from the Pacific Ocean to the Caspian Sea. His sons, his grandsons, and one of his daughters-in-law enlarged it further, overthrowing the Jin dynasty in northwest China in 1231–4—where the Mongols first acquired fire lances, smoke bombs, and gunpowder—conquering southern Russia and capturing Kyiv in 1240.[10] The limits of Mongol territory were largely dictated by the land, and in particular the availability of pasture: this army was almost entirely made up of cavalry and commanded half the horses in the world, with several replacements available to each soldier.[11]

All the same, when Temüjin's grandson Möngke came to the throne in 1251 he inherited the largest continuous land empire the world has ever known. His own generals conquered Korea, Iran, and Kashmir. His brother Hulagu finally destroyed what remained of the Abbasid Caliphate in 1258, took Aleppo and Damascus, and reached the Mediterranean coast, where the Latin knight Bohemond VI, Crusader prince of Antioch, submitted in 1260.[12]

Once the blood had been washed away, business took over. Conquest and commerce made Mongol courts very rich, and the guarantees they could offer of safe overland travel across the whole of central and eastern Asia, along with the subsidies and tax breaks they awarded to merchant associations, gave the overland trade in luxury goods across the known world a significant boost.

On the other side of that world, west African kings were making their own fortunes from the Bambuk and Bure goldfields on the Senegal and Niger rivers, which they controlled through vassal kingdoms in the forests of what are now Ghana and Ivory Coast.[13] As early as the seventh century Arabic sources report on the abundance and accessibility of west African gold, as well as its unusual quality: with purity levels of 98 to 99 percent, there was no need to refine it further. It wasn't easy to get at though. A drop in the groundwater table from the fourth century CE had destroyed the irrigation systems that the Garamantes relied on and the Saharan trade they managed with it, and in the fifth century migrants from the south caused severe disruption in the borderlands of Roman and Vandal power. A few routes from Egypt and southern Tunisia survived into the seventh century, but then these too petered out, and it was only under the Fatimids in the tenth century that trans-Saharan trade took off again.[14]

According to al-Idrisi's Book of Roger, twelfth-century merchants carried wool, copper, and beads, and they exchanged them for gold and prisoners captured farther south.[15] They crossed the desert from entrepôts in the southern Maghreb to places like Timbuktu and Gao in modern Mali, multilingual cities on the southern edge of the Sahara, where plentiful archaeological evidence attests to Mediterranean and even Indian Ocean trade: cowrie shells traveled via the Red Sea and Egypt to western Africa in vast numbers, as well as a single sherd of Chinese porcelain found at Tadmekka in Mali.[16] This form of fine pottery, first invented in China in the first millennium CE, was much appreciated around the Indian Ocean for its quasi-transparent delicacy.[17]

These traders got no farther south: local kings were keen to conceal the location of the goldfields. But these same kings embraced the Islamic merchants, and from the eleventh century they began to convert to Islam themselves.[18] A shared religion is a good basis for the trust required for successful commerce.

In the thirteenth century a new empire of Mali incorporated other west African cities and kingdoms from the Atlantic into central Africa.[19] A lengthy report written by Ibn Fadlallah al-ʿUmari, a contemporary Syrian bureaucrat working in Cairo, tells us that Mali's greatest ruler, or *mansa,* was called Musa, and that his reign began in 1312 when his predecessor abdicated to explore the Atlantic, set out with 2,000 ships, and was never seen again.[20]

Mansa Musa was a devout Muslim who, some claim, was the richest man who ever lived.[21] He was also famous for his generosity and culture, and like Möngke Khagan he was interested in religious traditions. He built mosques and madrasas in cities across his realm, with the madrasas of Timbuktu in particular accumulating hundreds of thousands of manuscripts.

In 1324 Mansa Musa became an international celebrity when he made a pilgrimage to Mecca, traveling through the Sahara and Egypt. According to one later Egyptian historian, his retinue ran to 60,000 people, including 14,000 enslaved women and a hundred camels, each loaded with pure gold.[22] Al-ʿUmari reports that people were still talking about him in Cairo twelve years later, and no wonder. He had distributed so much gold that the market collapsed along with the Egyptian economy. Musa himself had to borrow money for his journey home.

The Mongol khagan and the *mansa* of Mali ran the engine rooms at opposite ends of an interconnected set of economic zones that encompassed the east–west span of the whole world known to its inhabitants, from the Pacific to the Atlantic coasts, with trade operating between them on a much greater scale than ever before.[23]

This system revolved around the Indian Ocean, where the quantity and value of maritime commerce dwarfed overland ventures in central Asia and the Sahara. It linked eastern Asia, where Hangzhou in China was the largest city on earth, to India, the Gulf, Cairo—the largest city in Mediterranean lands—and east African powers like the gold-rich kingdom ruled from Great Zimbabwe, where walls eleven meters high enclosed a city whose 10,000 or so inhabitants imported glass beads from Persia and porcelain from China.[24] When a German explorer came across the remarkable structures of this city in 1871, he could not believe that Africans had built it and suggested instead that it was the work of the queen of Sheba.[25]

Europe was still on the edge of the network, but European silver and wool were much in demand, and European merchants continued to thrive on their overseas connections.[26] Venetian and then Genoese traders established direct links with Mongol agents across the Black Sea, giving them access to goods like "cloth of gold," brocade woven from silk and golden yarn that had been invented in western Asia but had since become a Mongol specialty.[27] For the most part, however, their trading interests operated through Islamic ports.

From northern African harbors came the gold that now covered European paintings, as well as ivory and "grains of paradise," a seed of a plant related to ginger that was extremely popular in France. Enslaved humans came too: 3,000 to 5,000 African slaves are estimated to have arrived in Europe each year in the medieval period.[28] From Egypt came alum, Indian pepper, and ever-more-exotic spices like the cloves, nutmeg, and mace found only in the Indonesian Maluku Islands east of India through the Strait of Malacca.[29] The lightest and most expensive wares now traveled all the way from one end of this world to the other—Chinese porcelain even arrived in England—and new technologies made their way into Europe along the same routes: almost all the elements of the mid-fourteenth-century European mechanical clock can be found earlier in the Arabic-speaking world.[30]

As the goods and capital, technology, and ideas flowing across Africa and Asia lapped up on European shores, so did stories. Arabic fables were hugely popular in medieval Europe, along with an Arabic storytelling device called the "frame tale," which collects a number of short stories, often loosely related at best, within a larger narrative. Like many of the stories themselves, this format originated in India and made its way to the Islamic world via Persia.

One of the advantages of the frame tale is that individual stories within it can be added, removed, and altered; this also means that it is impossible to establish a definitive edition of the overall collection in any language, and the best were translated into many. Some scholars describe them not as texts but as "text networks," and like the routes of trade, faith, and diplomacy they connected a vast world from the Pacific to the Atlantic.[31]

The most famous example in Europe today is the *Thousand and One Nights,* a collection of ancient Indian and Persian stories set within a brutal Persian frame tale: each night a great sultan marries a virgin and then kills her in the morning, until his own vizier's daughter Scheherazade volunteers for the position and starts to tell him a series of stories, each interrupted in the middle at dawn. Desperate to hear the end of the tales, the sultan keeps postponing her fate until she finishes her last story and he confesses his love. They live happily ever after, though he was probably happier than she was.

This frame tale had been translated into Arabic by the ninth century, but the collection as a whole arrived in Europe only in the eighteenth century.[32]* Instead, the classic frame tale known to medieval Europe was *Kalila and Dimna,* which originates in an Indian collection of the early first millennium CE called the *Panchatantra* ("Five Treatises"), a set of animal fables told to three princes by a sage.[33] In the sixth century CE the Sasanian shah Khosrow I had had these stories translated from Sanskrit into Middle Persian by his learned physician Burzoe, who added more fables of his own. That version was then translated into Arabic by Ibn al-Muqaffaʿ, and further expanded in eighth-century

*Over the centuries hundreds more tales were added to the Arabic version, and older ones updated with references to guns, tobacco, and coffee. When Antoine Galland translated a fourteenth- or fifteenth-century Arabic manuscript into French as *Les mille et une nuits* in 1704, he himself added other details and even stories of uncertain origin, including the tales of Aladdin and Ali Baba. Some were told to him by a Maronite Arab in Paris called Hanna Diyab. These additional stories were later translated back into Arabic versions (Robert Irwin, *The Arabian Nights: A Companion,* London: Allen Lane, 1994, 16–17). The first, anonymous, English translation appeared a few years after Galland's as *The Arabian Nights' Entertainments,* before Sir Richard Burton published a version based on a wider range of manuscripts in the 1880s.

Baghdad as part of the wider Translation Movement.* The result was the first work of Arabic prose fiction, and a classic of the "mirror for princes" genre, in which a ruler receives advice from a wise counselor.[34] It is also the earliest version of the collection to survive.

In the Arabic *Kalila wa-Dimna,* a wise man called Bidpai counsels a tyrannical and self-indulgent Indian king with a series of educational fables. The first introduces a pair of jackals called Kalila and Dimna, brothers who serve at the court of a lion king. The ambitious Dimna becomes jealous of the king's friendship with a bull named Schanzabeh. Against Kalila's advice, he persuades the lion that Schanzabeh is plotting against him and should be killed, while persuading the bull that the lion intends to eat him. As a result the lion kills the bull and is badly wounded himself: an illustration of the danger of allowing a dishonest confidant to come between friends.

Within the different stories Bidpai tells, the animals tell one another stories as well. Dimna tries to persuade Kalila that he can get the better of the bull despite his meager size with a story of a crow whose chicks were being eaten by a serpent: instead of trying to claw out the animal's eyes, which might have been dangerous, the bird stole a human's jewelry and threw it into the snake's burrow, whereupon the human killed the snake in order to retrieve the jewelry. Even within that story, the crow is herself persuaded to this course of action by another wily jackal who tells her how a crab was able to use brute force to prevent a heron eating him. Many of the animals featured nonetheless meet sticky ends, including Kalila and Dimna themselves.

Kalila wa-Dimna was translated into Greek in the early twelfth century, but it became known in western Europe through the Arabic tradition. In 1251, for instance, it was one of the texts selected by Alfonso X "the Wise" of Christian Castile for translation from Arabic into the local vernacular to raise the status of Castilian as a literary language,

*The story of this series of translations is told in another venerable medieval text, Ferdowsi's late-tenth-century Persian poem *Shahnameh,* or "Book of Kings," ending with the retranslation of the Arabic work into contemporary Persian as a verse epic that is still celebrated in its own right today.

along with works on astronomy, optics, clockmaking, magic, and veterinary science, and the rules of chess and backgammon.[35]

Calila e Digna became popular in the Iberian peninsula and the queen of France commissioned a translation from Castilian into Latin for French readers around 1300, but the most popular bridge to a European readership was a different Latin translation made in Italy around the same time by John of Capua, working from a Hebrew translation of the Arabic.[36] As these stories made their way across languages and cultures the shape and content of the collection shifted. Over time the Brahmin adviser to Indian royalty in the Sanskrit story became in Sasanian Persia a philosopher, in Islamic Baghdad an ascetic, and in the Latin version a hermit, while European translations often add biblical stories to the mix.[37]

It is easy to think of European literature in terms of new vernacular traditions that accord with narratives of emerging national self-identification, and center the Christian faith.[38] The *chansons de geste,* for instance, poems sung in French from the twelfth to fourteenth centuries that relate the great deeds of Frankish Christian kings, often celebrate conflicts between Christians and "Saracens" too.[39] *The Song of Roland* (c. 1100), often seen as the foundational work of French literature, concerns a minor action during Charlemagne's campaigns in Iberia, when the Frankish king was betrayed on his way back across the Pyrenees by the Christian rulers of the kingdom of Pamplona to their Muslim allies and kinsmen, who attacked and defeated his rearguard at the Pass of Roncesvalles. It elevates this battle to an epochal encounter in a Holy War with a tragic hero in Charlemagne's own fictional nephew, who in the face of certain death at the hands of Saracens literally blows his own brains out by blowing too hard on an oliphant horn as he calls for revenge.

The Song of Roland however survives in just ten manuscripts and fragments, while *Kalila wa-Dimna* has a good claim to being the most widely distributed and translated work of world literature apart from the Bible. Hundreds of manuscripts are preserved, and by the nineteenth century the text had been translated into more than forty different languages, from Mongolian to Javanese to Icelandic to Berber

Tashelhit.[40] The stories that people were really reading in medieval Europe were mobile, multicultural tales told across creeds and cultures through serial translations.

Sharing is not the same as caring, and prejudice against people of other creeds and, increasingly, colors was still rife.[41] Opportunities to conquer non-Christians within Europe were becoming exhausted, although mopping-up operations included the conquest of Wales in the 1280s; at the same time expulsions of Jews became common in France after 1250, as well as in Germany (Bavaria in 1276), Italy (Naples in 1288), and England in 1290—one year before the last Franks were expelled from the Holy Land. Preserving the cultural purity of Christendom became increasingly important in Europe as it became increasingly irrelevant elsewhere.

After Möngke's death in 1259 the Mongol empire fractured into four provinces ruled by Temüjin's descendants: the original Grand Khanate based in Mongolia; Chagatay in central Asia; the Golden Horde on the northern Steppe, which controlled Kyiv and the Volga River; and the Ilkhanate of Persia and Mesopotamia, where Hulagu brought together Chinese, Arab, and Persian scientists at the most advanced astronomical observatory in the world at Maragheh in northwestern Iran.

One by one the Khanates all converted to Islam, with one exception: the Grand Khanate inherited by another of Möngke's brothers, Khubilai. In the 1270s Khubilai Khan defeated the Song dynasty to take the whole of China, where he established a Yuan dynasty and set up new capitals, first at Shangdu ("Xanadu"), then farther south at Khanbaliq (Beijing). His court became a magnet for astronomers, doctors, scholars, and one family of Venetian merchants.

Venice itself in the later thirteenth century was a very wealthy port, with a population of perhaps 100,000.[42] It was also full of signs of contact with a bigger world to the east. By the 1250s new palaces for merchants and noble families as well as the expansion of churches like San Marco took inspiration from Egypt, a major trading partner, and the Levant.[43] Unlike in Jerusalem and Acre, Sicily, or Spain, however, this hybrid style was the product not of different people living in the same place, but of Venetian interests in lots of different places.

It was still more sea than city. Without the network of permanent stone bridges that connects a hundred or more islands today people moved for the most part by water. We know surprisingly little about the urban layout—the first map of Venice dates to the mid-fourteenth century.[44] But the only connection between the eastern and western halves of the city was a pontoon at the Rialto, site of the city's main marketplace. It charged pedestrians a toll and could separate to allow shipping to pass along the Grand Canal, which was much wider then than it is today.[45]

Close by was the house of the Polo merchant family. Niccolò and Maffeo Polo first traveled to China in 1260, four years before the first raised wooden drawbridge was built at the Rialto. They had set out on a commercial mission from Constantinople across the Black Sea to the Crimean peninsula, and traveled on with a caravan to the chief city of the Golden Horde, Sarai. There they were cut off by warfare, and decided to continue east. They crossed the desert to the great trading center of Bukhara in Chagatay where they met an envoy from Hulagu who persuaded them to accompany him on his journey to Khubilai, for "the great lord of the Tartars has never seen a Latin and has a great desire and will to do so."[46]

Khubilai Khan was indeed delighted to meet the merchants, asking them many questions about European politics, culture, and religion, which they were able to answer in full since—unlike William of Rubruck a decade earlier—they had learned Mongolian. In fact, he was so pleased that he sent the Polos back to ask the pope for up to one hundred well-educated Christian missionaries.[47]

The brothers dutifully returned to the Mediterranean, a journey of three years, and found that things had changed. In 1261 the Crusaders had lost Constantinople, and in Italy the pope was dead, and there was a delay in electing a new one. The only people they could persuade to accompany them back to China were two Dominican friars who took fright at an encounter with Egyptian troops in Armenia and turned back.

The Polos carried on to Shangdu with only Niccolò's seventeen-year-old son Marco to show for their efforts. It was enough: the family spent another seventeen years at Khubilai's court, where, according to Marco's later account, they "held honor above all other barons," before finally returning across the Indian Ocean to western Asia and then Europe in 1295.[48]

Three years later Marco was imprisoned in Genoa in obscure circumstances, and made friends in jail with a noted Pisan writer who specialized in Arthurian romance. A collaboration was born: Rustichello used the stories Marco told him to compose a new work in the Franco-Italian vernacular used across much of western Europe at the time entitled *Le devisement du monde*, or *The Description of the World*.[49]

From the opening lines Rustichello assumes that his readership is interested in the whole of the world: "Lords, emperor and kings, dukes and marquises, counts, knights, and townsfolk, and all of you who wish to know the diverse peoples of men and the diversities of the diverse regions of the world, take this book and have it read."[50] These are also the opening lines of Rustichello's earlier romance *Méliadus:* apparently he considered them likely to sell books. In this case at least he was right: around 150 manuscripts of the work exist in five different European languages, and it remained hugely popular for centuries. Almost 200 years later Christopher Columbus brought a copy with him on his journeys to the Americas.[51]

Le devisement du monde is not a straightforward travel narrative in the style of William of Rubruck. Only the first nineteen out of 233 chapters describe the Polo family's own adventures. The next 180 are a gazetteer loosely structured around a series of itineraries through Asia and India, and along the coast from Japan to east Africa.

Marco gives brief sketches of places along the way with particular attention to who rules them and their religion, recent history, and economy. There are also discussions of food, dress, traditions, distinctive flora and fauna, lengthy digressions on local marvels and miracles, and useful notes on unusual customs: in the Chinese province of Jiandu, for instance, it is considered helpful with the gods to offer foreigners the company of your wife, leaving the marital home yourself for up to three days to afford appropriate privacy.[52] And there is advice on the journey itself: it is seven days, Marco explains, from Yazd to Kerman, with only three places to stay en route; on the other hand you ride through lovely woods and see "some very beautiful wild donkeys." On the road between Kerman and Kuhbanan, by contrast, the salty water will give you "an exceedingly bad case of the runs."[53]

As well as informing Europeans of worlds far away, the work also draws on a multitude of literary styles from across the medieval world.[54] The individual descriptions recall the Book of Roger. The unpredictable order in which places are discussed, as the text follows multiple routes from the same starting point or jumps between faraway sites, echoes another Islamic genre, the "book of routes and kingdoms" (as in the ninth-century work of Khordadbeh). The end of the work then shifts tone again to describe the civil wars of the era within and between the western Khanates of Persia and the Golden Horde in a series of vignettes that have reminded scholars of French romances and *chansons de geste.*

Marco himself plays little part in the text. Although the foreign missions that he undertook for Khubilai Khan must be the source of much of his information, it is a surprise to come across him from time to time, sent somewhere new or escaping from bandits. He may not have visited all the places described.[55] But he paints a picture of a world full of men like him, Latin merchants in Trebizond on the Black Sea, at Iranian Tabriz, and in the Persian Gulf, riding through lands devastated by recent warfare and maneuvering around Nestorians, Zoroastrians, Saracens, and triumphant Mongols.

After his release from jail, Marco Polo returned to Venice, married, and embraced the family business. As far as we know he never left the Veneto again. But messengers continued to travel between Europe and the Mongolian khans. The Ilkhanate was in regular contact with the Roman emperor at Constantinople, the pope at Rome, and the kings of France and England. Franciscans built a residence or *fondaco,* from the Arabic *funduq,* for Catholic merchants at Quanzhou on the Chinese coast, most of them from Genoa. And in 1307 Pope Clement V established a Catholic archdiocese in Khanbaliq, naming as archbishop a Franciscan friar called John from Monte Corvino in Italy who had already built two churches in the city.[56]

John lived in what is now Beijing for more than thirty years, teaching children (some purchased slaves) Greek and Latin, preaching in Chinese, translating the New Testament and the Psalms into the old Uighur language used by the local Mongols, and arguing with Nestorians. He had traversed a world more connected than at any previous point in its history. But it contained the seeds of its own destruction, and it had given Europeans the means to destroy another: siege engines, gunpowder, the sternpost rudder and the compass, which had been used on Chinese ships since the eleventh century.[57]

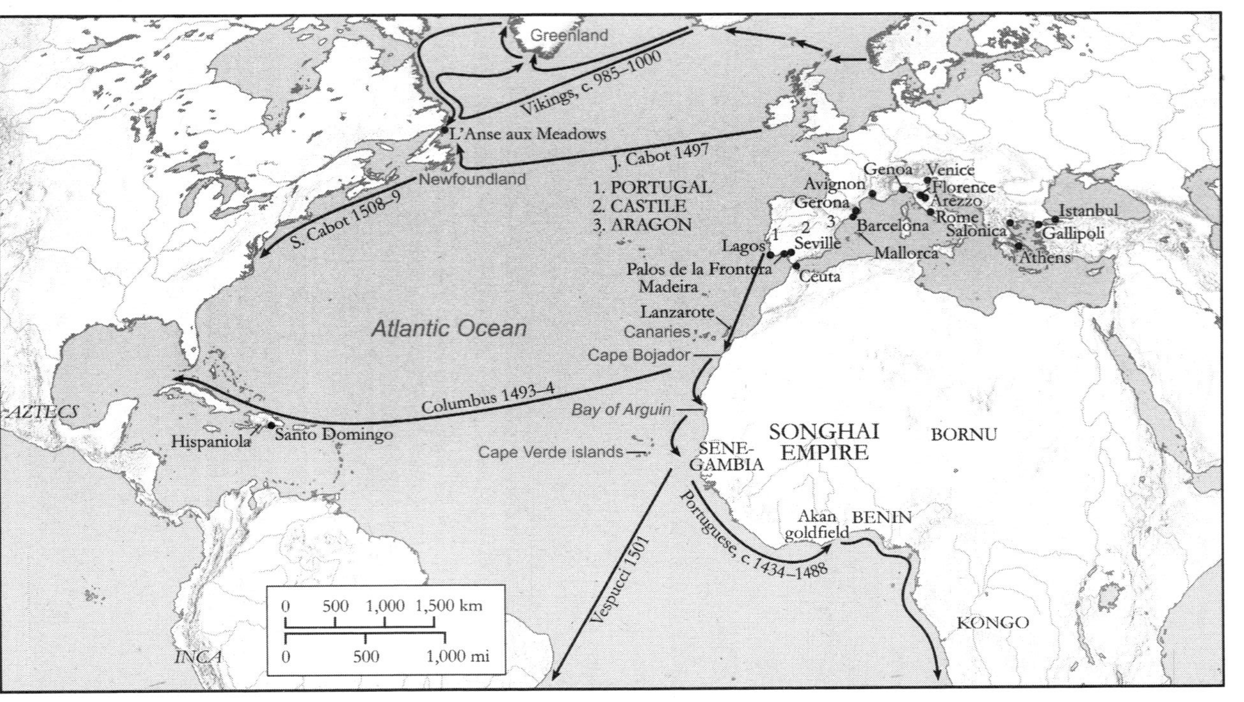

The Atlantic West, c. 1500 CE

CHAPTER TWENTY-NINE

The Land of Darkness

ALEPPO, 1349

A generation after Marco Polo came home, another man traveled the same world from end to end and left us one last look at it. Ibn Battuta set out from his hometown of Tangier in Morocco on pilgrimage to Mecca in 1325, and then kept going—for 75,000 miles, and twenty-nine years.[1] Relying on his legal training as currency, he traveled through Iraq and Iran, down the coast of east Africa as far as Tanzania and up through the Black Sea and the Golden Horde to Astrakhan. From there he continued overland to India and across the South China Sea to Hangzhou. Finally he returned home via Sumatra and Syria, and the sultan of Morocco hired a secretary to take down his reminiscences.[2]

The world Ibn Battuta describes is still dominated by the Muslim religion—which is why he can pay his way on his travels as a *qadi,* judge, in Islamic courts.[3] When he travels through the Golden Horde he describes Özbeg Khan as "one of the seven kings who are the great and mighty kings of the world," listing alongside him the sultan of Morocco, the sultan of Egypt and Syria, the sultan of the Two Iraqs (the Ilkhanate), the sultan of the land of Turkistan and the land beyond the River Oxus (Chagatay), the sultan of (northern) India—a Turkic ruler based in Delhi—and the sultan of China.[4] Leaving aside Ibn Battuta's polite nod to his own king, a minor figure on the world stage, six kings still rule the world, four of them now Mongol and all but one—the emperor of China—a Muslim.

By contrast, Ibn Battuta travels in Europe only three times, and only on its very edges. There is a three-week trip through the "lands of the Greeks" on the borderlands of the Black Sea with a large caravan escorting the Roman emperor's daughter, now the khatun of Astrakhan, on a visit home to Constantinople from the Golden Horde. There is a brief stop on Sardinia where he mentions the wonderful harbor and bazaars but is worried about being taken prisoner by the island's Christian inhabitants. Finally there is a journey to Islamic Granada to fight for Gibraltar, under siege from Alfonso XI of Castile, where Ibn Battuta meets men from India, Samarkand, and Konya in central Anatolia.

Ibn Battuta is a prime witness to the way in which war, marriage, and commerce enmeshed people and culture around the edges of Europe in the mid-fourteenth century. But the world he journeyed through was falling apart behind him. The Ilkhanate disintegrated in the 1330s; the Chagatay Khanate was overthrown in the 1340s; and the Golden Horde would fracture from the 1350s on. The Yuan dynasty meanwhile had been in decline since the death of Khubilai, and in 1368 it would yield to the Chinese Ming.

The other end of the old Afro-Asiatic economic system was in trouble too. Back in Morocco in the 1350s Ibn Battuta journeyed south to Mali though Sijilmassa, a traditional gateway to the Sahara and the riches of west Africa beyond, where he stayed with a jurist called al-Bushri whose brother he had met in China. He then describes a dangerous, thirsty journey across the desert in which one of his company was lost, or perhaps dispatched by a fellow traveler, and the party encountered a crocodile "looking like a little boat."[5] Worse was to come: when he arrives in Mali about fifteen years after Mansa Musa's death in 1337 he finds the empire in steep decline and is disappointed to be gifted bread, beef, and yogurt by the current monarch instead of the clothing and money he expected. He returns to Morocco via Timbuktu, and admires there the graves of a famous poet from Granada and a great Alexandrian trader: one gets the impression that such visitors were less frequent by this time.[6]

By then however something else was very wrong. In 1348 Ibn Battuta had encountered a terrible sickness in Damascus that was killing 2,400 people every day. When he returned home to Morocco he found that it had killed his mother. By the time he reached al-Andalus in 1350 Alfonso XI had just died from the same cause.[7]

The Syrian geographer and historian Ibn al-Wardi encountered the same sickness in Aleppo in 1349 and described its origins as he understood them. "It began in the land of darkness"—the regions ruled by the Golden Horde. "It has been current for fifteen years. China was not preserved from it nor could the strongest fortress hinder it. The plague afflicted the Indians in India. It weighed upon the Sind. It seized with its hand and ensnared even the lands of the Uzbeks . . . it gnawed away at Crimea."[8] It also killed Ibn al-Wardi.

Genetic studies in 2011 confirmed that this sickness—long known as the "Black Death" from the blotches that appeared on its victims' skin—was again plague.[9] After centuries dormant, *Yersinia pestis* had reemerged sometime in the thirteenth century, not in fact in the "land of darkness" but far to the east in the Tian Shan, the mountains between China and Kyrgyzstan, where a resident marmot population had long harbored a reservoir of the ancient disease.[10]

We don't know exactly what caused plague to break out again, and to break into four new variants as well, but climate change was probably involved. The end of the Medieval Climate Anomaly brought cooler temperatures to much of Eurasia from the later thirteenth century.* This was the result of a variety of factors: more volcanic eruptions, less

*This also helps to explain the demise of viking settlement on Greenland around 1440, rendered unviable by a cooling climate, increasing pack ice, changing European tastes for African elephant ivory rather than the walrus and narwhal product, and Inuit and Inupiat immigration (Andrew Dugmore et al., "Cultural adaptation, compounding vulnerabilities and conjunctures in Norse Greenland," *PNAS* 109, no. 10 [2012]). The old theory that the colony fell victim to systemic inbreeding is ruled out by recent analyses of their remains (Ashot Margaryan et al., "Population genomics of the Viking world," *Nature* 585, no. 7825 [2020], 392).

solar activity, and changes in atmospheric currents and the rotational axis of the earth.[11] Disturbances in the weather would have led to fluctuations in rodent populations, from the unfortunate Tian Shan marmots to gerbils on the overland routes through central Asia, to the rats resident on grain ships. Warm and wet conditions first encouraged unusual growth in numbers and with it an increasing payload of plague-carrying passengers, then colder weather brought a swift decline, forcing fleas to seek new mammalian hosts.[12]

Globalization played its part too, as plague traveled once again with traders and diplomats, missionaries, and soldiers who had stitched together a century of unprecedented prosperity, mobility, and connectivity. It is now becoming clear that this outbreak of plague reached China, where descriptions of early Mongolian raids in the region also report a strange and serious new illness, as well as southern Africa, where it may well have caused the collapse of trading cities like Great Zimbabwe.[13]

One sturdy variant traveled west in the 1340s toward the Caucasus and the Levant. According to a contemporary Italian historian, plague reached Europe when an infected Mongol army unit threw their corpses into the besieged Genoese city of Kaffa on the Crimean peninsula before the traders there fled back to Italy.[14] The sieges of Kaffa in fact predated by more than a year the outbreak of plague in Europe in 1347, and more likely culprits can be found in grain ships sailing west from Tana (near Rostov-on-Don) on the Sea of Azov.[15]

The Black Death killed more than 100 million people between 1346 and 1353, and it kept coming back.[16] Between 40 and 60 percent of the people living in Europe, western Asia, and north Africa died. Population levels took 200 years to recover. Coming on top of climate change, the effects on trade, industry, and agriculture were dramatic, and for at least a couple of generations dire.[17]

Long-distance trade did not come to a standstill in the second half of the fourteenth century, especially at the upper end of the market, but it certainly diminished.[18] Some economies were worse affected than others. In Egypt population decline brought about the collapse of the labor-intensive artificial irrigation system of canals and dykes, and this benefited European interests: sugar now came from Sicily instead.[19]

Even in Europe, though, things were very difficult. Loss was great, lives were hard, and horizons narrowed. The connected world of commerce and culture that had for millennia characterized the Mediterranean and drawn western Europeans into larger networks of world trade and diplomacy fell away for a century or more, and increasing value was placed on the persecution and exclusion of the socially and culturally undesirable.

When plague arrived in Catalonia in the spring of 1348, for instance, twenty Jews were killed in the port of Barcelona, eighteen at Cervera and 300 at Tàrrega.[20] Jews were then expelled from the whole of Hungary in 1360, from the whole of Austria in 1420, and they were massacred on Mallorca in 1435. The Christian conquest of pagan Europe was completed meanwhile with the conversion of the Grand Duke of Lithuania in 1386, when he became king of Poland as well. Separation and distance become a central thread not just of European but of western European politics, religion, and ideas, alongside an ever stronger sense of shared Christian identity.*

Some turned in despair to the past. The roots of what nineteenth-century scholars would label the "Renaissance" lie in the Italian *studia humanitatis*. Humanism was a new educational curriculum that emphasized literary and historical studies over the science, medicine, and law prized in medieval universities and adopted ancient pagans as models and guides.[21]

One of its early champions was Francesco Petrarca, the obsessive scholar, collector, and poet from Arezzo in Tuscany to whom we owe the first glimmerings of a notion of an era of "darkness" between the

*Foreigners could still be received graciously, as long as they were not Jewish or Muslim. In a curious incident in the summer of 1366, Edward III of England welcomed to his court the son of the king of "Inde"—a catchall term in this era for east and south Asia that sometimes included Ethiopia as well and evoked the hazy specter of Prester John. Edward housed the man in London at his own expense until the visitor was unmasked as a fraud named John Balbat and transferred to prison (W. M. Ormrod, "John Mandeville, Edward III, and the king of Inde," *Chaucer Review* 46, no. 3 [2012], 336–8).

glories of the Classical world and their Italian rebirth.[22] This reversed the standard Christian metaphor of the light of Christ that had finally illuminated a path out of the errors of pagan antiquity. In the middle of the fourteenth century it's easy to understand why even a staunch Catholic like Petrarch might look for hope elsewhere. His son Giovanni died of the plague in 1361, at the age of twenty-four.

Petrarch was also unusually keen both on the language of "Europe" and on the notion of local roots to cultural tradition.[23] For him and his fellow humanists in the fourteenth century antiquity meant the art and letters of ancient Rome, not the Greek science that had captivated earlier scholars via Arabic and then Latin translations.[24] It was only in the following century that Greek literary manuscripts preserved in eastern Mediterranean cities began to arrive in western Europe in any number, and were finally translated by the few scholars who knew the language. Other ancient traditions from Egypt to Etruria also attracted attention in this era, but without the ability to read the languages scholars were unable to get much beyond antiquarian fascination. And the Christian humanists ignored entirely the literature and learning of the Islamic world.

Human studies spread quickly, and they have assumed great importance in retrospect with the success of the idea that the "humanities" can and should constitute an education in themselves.[25] They were not however the only scholarly pursuits in fourteenth- and fifteenth-century Europe. Interest in medieval Islamic science persisted at least for a while, as demonstrated by the discovery in 2018 of a fifteenth-century manuscript containing part of a translation of Ibn Sina's medical work into Irish.[26]

Older world literature continued to be popular too: a large number of manuscripts of *Kalila wa-Dimna* survive from fifteenth-century Europe, while John of Capua's Latin version was translated into German in 1470 and into Castilian Spanish (again) in 1483. Even in Tuscany we can see the continuing inspiration of the old text networks in the work of Petrarch's friend Giovanni Boccaccio, whose *Decameron* is an Arabic-style frame tale of the 1350s that borrows liberally from Arabic stories. In it a group of ten young people—seven women and three men—

retreat from plague-ridden Florence to a countryside villa to tell one another stories: ten a night, making one hundred in all.

Some adapt individual tales from the *Thousand and One Nights* collection that were already in circulation in Europe.[27] "The *qadi* who had a baby" inspires "The man who thinks he is pregnant." "The simpleton husband," in which a woman convinces her husband that climbing a particular tree produces sexual hallucinations by disporting herself with her lover in front of him when he climbs up to check, becomes the "Story of Lydia and Pyrrhus"—although Boccaccio tones down the gender politics by giving the woman's lover a larger part in devising the plot.[28*]

The Decameron is also notable for its warm depiction of Muslims and interreligious relations: there are two flattering portraits of the scourge of the Crusader kingdoms Saladin, and in "The tale of Gerbino" William II of Sicily and his vassal the king of Tunis deal fairly and honorably with each other as William's grandson and the Saracen's daughter plot to marry in a tale of star-crossed love and incompetent piracy.[29]

Like the text networks themselves, however, these were now stories from the past. The same is true of *The Book of Sir John Mandeville,* a spoof travelogue originally written in the 1360s in French and translated into Middle English around 1400.[30] It now survives in around 300 manuscripts in ten languages, suggesting that it was more popular even than Marco Polo's *Description of the World.*[31] Sir John is an English knight from St. Albans who has traveled abroad for thirty-four years. He has visited Jerusalem, served in the Chinese khan's army, and met Prester John. He has also met other strange people and animals, like the little lambs that grow inside fruit on trees somewhere beyond China.[32] Anachronisms abound: Sir John visits the pope in Rome in the 1360s when—as readers would have known—the Holy Father had in reality been based at Avignon since 1309.[33] They are a feature, not a bug: this is

*"The tale of the simpleton husband" gets another outing in Chaucer's *Canterbury Tales* (c. 1400), related and reimagined by the Merchant. As in the Arabic version the heroine is credited with the plot to deceive her husband, though this is not in the Merchant's view to her credit, and absurdly in this case it is the lovers who climb into the pear tree for their revels.

a nostalgic look back at a larger and more entangled world that was already fading into myth.

We could say the same of the way the Catholic rulers of Castile, now the largest kingdom in Iberia, built and rebuilt Islamic palaces or "Alcázars" (from the Arabic *al-qasr,* the castle, itself derived from Latin *castrum*). They paid fulsome tribute to the Islamic traditions of the peninsula, down to walls covered in the same Arabic inscriptions proclaiming the greatness of Allah that could be found at the Alhambra palace of still-Islamic Granada. Such messages had, however, lost their power farther north, where the new kings used Christian craftsmen and added Gothic and Romanesque elements to the local traditions. This spectacular blended style was later labeled "Mudéjar" after the derogatory term for the "tamed" Muslims who remained in the new Christian kingdoms.

Despite this nostalgia for the pre-Reconquista culture, Europeans in general took little interest at this point in contemporary learning from beyond the Mediterranean, from advances in infinite-series calculus by fourteenth-century mathematicians in Kerala to the great work of universal history begun by the north African polymath Ibn Khaldun in 1377.[34] Nor did they exploit new inventions. Coffee was first brewed in Yemen around 1400 by boiling beans from the Ethiopian "arabica" plant, but although both coffee and coffeehouses spread quickly around the Muslim world, the drink arrived in Christian ports only around 1600, and the first coffeehouse opened in Venice in 1615.[35*]

As Latin Christendom expanded within the continent and lost its territories beyond, a monoculture was emerging—and not from ancient roots, but out of ethnic cleansing and imperial conquest.

. . .

*Tea only just beat coffee to Europe, arriving on sixteenth-century merchant ships, although it is already found in China in the first millennium BCE (Jianrong Jiang et al., "The analysis and identification of charred suspected tea remains unearthed from Warring State period tomb," *Scientific Reports* 11, no. 1 [2021]). It was an even later arrival in India, brought by British settlers in the nineteenth century in order to compete with the Chinese market.

We can see a new vision of the world in 1375, when Jewish cartographers working on the island of Mallorca produced a painted parchment map of the world, probably as a present from the duke of Girona to the king of France.[36] It marks a departure from the old T–O maps depicting a trinity of continents with Jerusalem at the center, which were now looking distinctly old-fashioned: the Crusades were over, the knights had come home, and the idea that the whole world was or ever could be Christian must have seemed increasingly naive.

Instead, the "Catalan Atlas" builds on a new and more practical genre of portolan charts produced in response to advances in navigation. Drawn up from around 1300 CE, these were not intended for general interest or education. They were functional tools to aid navigators that made little sense outside a ship's cabin. They usually depict specific regions in and around the Mediterranean or, like the old itinerary maps, specific routes. Their standard orientation to north reflects the widespread adoption of the magnetic compass, and their seas are covered in overlapping wind rose or "rhumb" lines, routes of constant bearing fanning out from fixed points to aid navigation with a compass. They show few features inland, but the coasts are drawn in great detail, with bays, capes, and shallows marked. The ports are all labeled, and their political allegiances denoted with flags, or shields with coats of arms, and sometimes crescents to denote Muslim powers—useful information for sailors that also organizes the world in terms of religion.[37]

Like the portolan charts, the Catalan Atlas is rectangular, oriented to the north with an arrow on the first known compass rose—and covered in rhumb lines, giving a pleasing sense of the state of the art. Larger ports are labeled in red, the rest in black. Flags, domes, crescents, and crosses organize cities inland as well as on the coast into political and religious tribes. This is not however a working document: instead, it tells stories aimed at an audience more interested in strange lands, exotic animals, and big personalities than practical navigation. And it draws not just on portolan charts but on Greco-Roman writings, the Bible, and the travels of Marco Polo and "John Mandeville."

The Catalan Atlas makes you the traveler: the captions and illustrations are designed to be read from the edges of the map, so you have to move around the whole world to fully understand it. As you do so, you can trace the late medieval Afro-Asian trading system in portraits and descriptions of its presiding figures from Mansa Musa and Khubilai Khan to the "Sultan of Babylon" in Cairo and Janibeg, the ruler of the Golden Horde.

You can admire traders crossing the Sahara and riding the Silk Roads with their animal companions and read notes on their customary itineraries. Note the biblical figures, too, including the Three Wise Men, and fantastical Christians like Prester John, and note how they jostle alongside descriptions of Islamic pilgrimage routes. This is not a Christian map in the old tradition: although Jerusalem still falls very close to the center of the map, handsomely illustrated by the Church of the Holy Sepulchre, no caption or striking portrait draws your attention to it.

You would soon notice something strange as well. Looking down from the top edge of the map you can see that as on the other continents European cities are marked with flags and religious buildings, in most cases topped with crosses—even in Islamic Granada, perhaps a suggestion that the Nasrid Emirate based there was in effect a vassal of the kingdom of Castile ("Chastel" in this Catalan Atlas). But Europe lacks the vivid illustrations and information that fill up the spaces of Africa and Asia, except on the edge of the map, at the fragile edges of the Christian world: Norway, Ireland, and some offshore islands have lengthy captions. The island of Ireland is also stamped with a large English flag, reflecting the Anglo-Norman conquest two centuries before.

The Catalan Atlas encapsulates the connectivity that had characterized the world in which these mapmakers grew up, but it also reflects the new world in which they are working: it depicts Europe in clearer detail and treats it quite differently from other continents. It does not construct a straightforward hierarchy, but it does create a strong distinction between "us" Europeans, who need no illustration, and the rest of the world: "them," the people we are looking at. Theirs is a world without history, where the past exists all at once, for the present entertainment of western European observers: the information given for Asia and Africa is out-of-date, by decades or even millennia.

. . .

In reality Europe was still not wholly Christian, and at one end was getting less so. The Emirate of Granada remained entrenched in southern Iberia, while in the east a small Turkish beylic founded in northwestern Anatolia in the thirteenth century by "Ottomans," named after their second ruler, Osman (r. 1280–1323), had expanded in 1354 to encompass the Gallipoli Peninsula on the European side of the Dardanelles. By the 1380s they were in control of most of the Balkans.

A threat appeared on the horizon with the Turko-Mongol nomad emperor Timur ("the Lame," or Tamerlane) who led the Chagatay Khanate from 1370 and came close to repeating Chinggis Khan's imperial successes: he conquered Iran, Iraq, Armenia, Georgia, and the Golden Horde, and captured both Delhi and Damascus.[38] Timur trounced the Ottomans in 1402, but after his death in 1405 their fortunes revived and they themselves pushed farther into the Balkans, taking Salonica (Thessaloniki) in 1430.[39]*

The fall of Constantinople to Sultan Mehmed II in 1453 was in its own right then a minor event: the Roman "empire" based there was by then tiny, and the Turks continued to rule it much as before, allowing Christians and Jews to worship freely. After 2,000 years, this final fall of Rome was still a blow to Christian Europe, and governments across the continent reacted with shock, dismay, and calls for military action.[40] All the same, on this occasion only Rome, Venice, and Genoa had sent troops before the Turks took the city, when it might actually have helped.

Sentimental fantasies of the world beyond Europe stuck in a timeless if colorful past could not compete with the hard intelligence that the sultan's army numbered more than 200,000 men, far larger than any contemporary European force.[41] It was easier to explain the defeat of Constantinople as God's punishment for heresy and schism: the eastern Romans had never been real Christians anyway.[42] This attitude could also excuse Mehmed II's conquest of Athens five years later, to the extent that anyone noticed it, the capture of the "Morea," or Pelopon-

*The Chagatay Khanate left a hefty legacy: in the sixteenth century a Chagatay Mongol called Babur founded the Mughal empire, which ruled in India from the seventeenth to the nineteenth centuries.

nese, the only remaining Christian-ruled region in mainland Greece, and in 1461 the fall of Trebizond, the last Christian territory in Asia.[43]

Military skirmishing continued in the 1460s and 1470s, especially with Venice, but the wealth of Mehmed's court at Constantinople attracted diplomats and kings from across the known world. These were men like the king of Bornu in eastern Nigeria, an important clearing house for gold heading north toward the Sahara: the king had collaborated with Cairo and Abyssinia in the fourteenth century, but now he allied with Constantinople, where demand for gold and slaves was rising fast.[44]

European merchants, artists, and scholars also crowded into the city, which was already becoming known as Istanbul.* There they vied for the favor of the sultan, who was by all accounts a talented linguist as well as a learned and discriminating patron. The poet Giovanni Maria Filelfo was commissioned by an Italian merchant to write a prose poem for Mehmed in 1470; in 1479 Gentile Bellini spent time in Istanbul on loan from a reconciled Venetian senate and painted a highly sympathetic portrait of the sultan in the Italian style.[45]

As this new Islamic empire ripped through Europe's insubstantial eastern border, however, interest in the idea of "Europe" itself increased, along with its Christian connotations. The central machinery of Christianity was now restricted to the continent of Europe, and the fall of Orthodox Constantinople removed another obstacle to Christian unity in that sphere.[46] Although "Christendom" remained a far more popular term, and "Europe" would not become commonplace for hundreds of years, it is invoked more frequently in the fifteenth century, especially in the aftermath of the fall of Constantinople. It was encouraged in particular by Pope Pius II (r. 1458–64), who championed the adjective "European" as well as Europe's Christian associations.[47]

. . .

*The Turkish colloquial name for Istanbul (often to Europeans Stamboul) comes from the Greek phrase *eis ten polin* —"in the City"—and originally referred to the area within the walls. On its coinage and in other formal contexts Istanbul intermittently retained the formal name of "Kostantiniyye" into the nineteenth century. The name Istanbul was only formally adopted in 1930.

At the same time, western Europeans were turning increasingly to a new horizon, taking with them a new ideology of difference and, for the first time, of superiority.

The Catalan Atlas reveals the beginnings of this Atlantic world. Off the west coast of Africa are the "Fortunate Islands" or Canaries. The legend on the map mentions the islands' attractions: honey, milk, and lots of goats. It omits the fact that there are humans too, the Guanches, who had come originally from the north African coast. They had been largely out of contact for a thousand years when a Genoese sea captain in Portuguese service named Lancelotto Malocello arrived on one of the islands in 1312 and stayed for twenty years: Europeans called it Lanzarote in his honor.[48]

Below these islands is a small boat with a caption explaining that it is the ship of Jaume Ferrer, who sailed south from Portugal in 1346 "for the River of Gold." Since reports of west Africa's great wealth first arrived in Europe, explorers had yearned to find Musa's gold, hidden for centuries from outside eyes. Caravans continued to operate across the Sahara, and new inland kingdoms arose to the south, like the Songhai empire, which supplanted Mali in the fourteenth century.* But in the fifteenth century Portuguese attention turned to maritime routes and to extending Portuguese interests along the Atlantic coast.

In 1415 King João I of Portugal besieged and captured Ceuta in Morocco. In 1419 Portuguese sailors discovered an uninhabited island just to the north of the Canaries that they named Ilha da Madeira—"Island of Wood"—because it was covered in forest that they immediately exploited for lumber; by the 1430s they were growing wheat on its increasingly bare soils.[49] In 1434 explorers rounded the tricky cape at Bojador and in the 1440s traders reached the Senegal River and then Cape

*In 1447 a trader for a Genoan bank called Antonio Malfante made it by land as far as the oasis of Touat in what is now the Algerian desert, writing back to his employers to describe a thriving market city where Muslim traders charged 100 percent commission on transactions and Jewish middlemen a commission on top. When he inquired about the location of the actual goldfields, however, his local informer told him that he had been searching for them himself for fourteen years (François-Xavier Fauvelle, *The Golden Rhinoceros: Histories of the African Middle Ages*, trans. Troy Tice, Princeton: Princeton University Press, 2018, 222–31).

Verde, sparking interest in the nearby islands, which were colonized from the 1450s.

In the 1470s Portuguese sailors reached the Gold Coast, and in 1482 they built a castle at Elmina in modern Ghana. They militarized the region, bringing with them cannon, muskets, and trained musketeers, and arming local rulers.[50] Inland meanwhile extraction ramped up: in the 1480s we hear of mining to a depth of almost seventy meters in the Akan goldfields on the Volta River—the richest of all the west African sources, opened in the fourteenth or fifteenth century in response to increasing demand.[51] In the 1490s João II of Portugal was known in Italy as *il Re d'Oro,* the King of Gold.[52]

Gold was not the only goal. Portuguese agents began kidnapping humans in raids from 1441; in 1444, a total of 235 Africans were captured in the Bay of Arguin off Mauretania and taken to the port of Lagos in Portugal, where the first slave market in modern Europe was established.[53] By the mid-fifteenth century a Venetian trader reports that the Portuguese were shipping a thousand slaves a year from their Arguin fort.[54]

Slaves were acquired through trading as well as raiding, and not all were acquired for Europe: in the 1460s the Portuguese turned Madeira from a wheat field into a sugar plantation, with labor provided for the most part by indigenous people from the Canaries and African slaves. The brutality of the work lay not only in the harvesting and processing of the sugar, a temperamental crop that needs to be harvested as cane at exactly the right time, with considerable difficulty, and then processed within forty-eight hours before it begins to rot, but also in digging irrigation channels across the whole island.[55]

The maritime kingdoms of Iberia were settling meanwhile into something recognizable on a modern map: the Spanish Crowns of Castile and Aragon were united by marriage in 1479, leaving only Portugal and Granada alongside them. In the Canaries the Guanches resisted wholesale conquest with some success, but when they were passed from Portugal to Spain in a 1479 treaty they could not withstand a renewed assault conducted by means of firearms, cannon, and above all disease.[56] In 1400 the indigenous population of the Canaries stood at around 80,000. By 1496 they had been wiped out, and these islands too were turned over to sugar production.

European trade east was increasingly important again as well. Murano glass beads made in Venice are found in Alaska in contexts dated by radiocarbon to the mid-fifteenth century, before European ships had crossed the Atlantic, suggesting they arrived through the Bering Strait.[57] Pressure increased to find an alternative passage to the Indian Ocean that bypassed the ports of the eastern Mediterranean. In 1483 Portuguese navigators got to Kongo, and in 1488 Bartolomeu Dias rounded the Cape of Good Hope, 2,000 years after Levantine sailors did so in the opposite direction. Ten years later Vasco da Gama reached India.

Another captain meanwhile dreamed up a different route to India, this time heading west. Funded in this case by the new Spanish Crown, Christopher Columbus set sail from Palos de la Frontera on August 3, 1492, made land on the island of Hispaniola and came back in March of the following year declaring that he had reached the Indies. In fact he had reached the Caribbean, and he returned four times over the next decade. In 1493 the first Spanish colony was established at Santo Domingo (now the capital of the Dominican Republic). In 1500 the first Portuguese ships arrived in Brazil. And the first west African slaves arrived in the Americas with their Spanish owners in 1502.

The devastating spread of smallpox and measles from Europe across the Americas in the sixteenth century made the job of conquest easier. It had taken the Spanish 150 years to exterminate the Guanches; the population of Taínos and Caribs on the island of Hispaniola, estimated at hundreds of thousands when Columbus arrived there in 1492, had dwindled by 1546 to a couple of hundred.[58]

The original Americans also died from forced labor on the land or in the mines, especially after the *encomienda* system established in Spanish territories in 1503 allotted indigenous workers to colonists on pain of death and in return for the benefit of Catholicism.[59] Meanwhile the inland kingdoms of west Africa went into precipitous decline as gold now traveled straight from the mines to European trading posts on the coast, and as commerce in captive African labor found new markets in the transatlantic slave trade.[60]

. . .

The new Atlantic West was, like all that came before it, the product of long contact with other peoples, ideas, and networks that had drawn Europeans into a wider world. The same connections had supplied the technologies Europeans now used to find new subjects and keep them at a distance. At the same time, conquest, conversion, and settlement followed patterns established over centuries already in Europe itself, as did the underlying Latin Christian ideology of cultural distance and superiority.

Christianization continued at home as well as overseas. In 1492 the recently united kingdom of Aragon and Castile finally succeeded in running the Islamic Emirate of Granada out of western Europe. King Muhammad XII (Boabdil) surrendered to King Ferdinand and Queen Isabella on condition that their Muslim subjects would have freedom of religion, but according to a decree passed in the same year, the Jews of Spain and Spanish dominions were forced to convert, leave, or die. In 1502 the same decree was extended to all Muslims under the Crown of Castile. Portugal meanwhile expelled its Muslims in 1497, and forcibly converted its Jews. The rest came before the West, and to construct a new culture they had to be removed.

CHAPTER THIRTY

A New World

The "Age of Exploration," when western Europe first became the crossroads of world commerce linking new Atlantic routes to the Americas and India, is often celebrated as an important moment of connection between the world and the West. It is seen as a period of contact and convergence between civilizations that had developed until then in separate spheres.[1] And there's no doubt that the entanglement of cultures and economies intensified dramatically over the following centuries, as new ships crossed new seas to create the first truly global era.[2]

But I have argued throughout this book that exchange between people from different places and cultures is a much older story—indeed, that without it there wouldn't be much of a story at all. Conversation, commerce, and theft, sex, war, and enslavement had for millennia been engines of change, and they all helped create what we now call the West.

Now something different was going on. European nations created new distinctions between cultures with the removal of Jews, Muslims, and other "undesirables" from their own lands. And as the range of sail increased in the fifteenth century, so did sailors' distance from the people they encountered overseas. In this sense the connected world I have sketched out now came to an end, as the maritime kingdoms of western Europe and their settler colonies forged a new world together that did not include the people they displaced.

. . .

The isolation of the West was for a long time work in progress, and the idea of a distinct Western civilization was still centuries away. Western Europeans settled all along the new ocean-going trade routes, establishing colonies around the Indian Ocean as well as in South America and the Caribbean. European artists and diplomats continued to flock to Istanbul, where strategic alliances with the Sublime Porte provided the only balance in the sixteenth-century Mediterranean to the hegemony of Charles V, who was at once Holy Roman Emperor, king of Spain, king of Naples, and lord of the Netherlands.[3] Ambassadors from the great west African kingdoms of Senegambia, Benin, and Kongo arrived at Portuguese and Spanish courts in both Europe and the Americas, as well as at the Vatican.[4]

Fascination among the European intelligentsia with contemporary Turkish power, Arab traditions, Chinese society, or Native American thought was not always predicated on Western superiority.[5] And fascination with the foreign past continued: the first English translation of *Kalila wa-Dimna* was published in 1570 by Sir Thomas North, whose translations of Plutarch inspired several of Shakespeare's plays. As an editor put it in 1888, it was "the English version of an Italian adaptation of a Spanish translation of a Latin version of a Hebrew translation of an Arabic adaptation of the Pehlevi version of the Indian original."[6]

The breadth of European interest in ancient history well into the eighteenth century can be seen in the title alone of Charles Rollin's *Ancient History of the Egyptians, Carthaginians, Assyrians, Babylonians, Medes and Persians, Macedonians, and Grecians,* published in French in twelve volumes between 1730 and 1738.* It became one of the international bestsellers of the Enlightenment as well as a popular school text, and it was translated not only into English but also into Italian, Greek, Spanish, Portuguese, Italian, and Bengali.[7]

*A completist, Rollin followed up with a *History of Rome,* which he began at the age of seventy-seven. He finished five out of a projected nine volumes before his death, aged eighty, in 1741.

Furthermore, the fact of the new Atlantic world did not yet dictate a way of understanding it: as "the" West, in opposition to "an" East. We have seen intermittent glimpses in this book of confrontation between Europe and Asia, of distinction between East and West, and of geography- and culture-based notions of community. We've seen the idea of Europe itself slowly gain some traction, and we've seen increasing prejudice and persecution against European Muslims, Jews, and pagans for centuries.

These seeds of civilizational thinking continued to germinate: the increasing popularity of the language of "Europe" in the sixteenth and seventeenth centuries reflects continued fear of the Turkish empire to the east and new distaste for the "savages" encountered farther west.[8] By 1748 Montesquieu could contrast the "genius for liberty" in Europe's states with despotic Asia's "spirit of servitude."[9]

But it was only in the nineteenth century that scholars mapped shared cultures onto specific geographies that emerged and developed in isolation from each other. This is when they fused ideas of Europe, East, and West, reinforced them with notions of civilizations and racial hierarchy, and invented "Western Civilization."

The question we now face is not whether Western Civilization is bad or good, but whether civilizational thinking helps explain much of anything at all. Understanding societies in terms of lonely trees and isolated islands is 200 years out-of-date and it is demonstrably, historically wrong. It is time to find new ways to organize our common world.

ACKNOWLEDGMENTS

My first thanks go to my agents. The original idea for *How the World Made the West* emerged out of discussions with Catherine Clarke at Felicity Bryan Associates, and she has masterminded its transformation into this book. Zoë Pagnamenta at Calligraph Lit has looked after me in the United States for almost as long, and they have both guided the whole enterprise with wisdom, generosity, and good humor. I'm grateful too to Catherine's colleagues for their welcome into the FBA family.

I've been lucky with my editors as well. Right at the outset Michael Fishwick at Bloomsbury made me believe in my own project, Alexis Kirschbaum then championed it through growing pains, and Jasmine Horsey shaped the book it became with great patience and skill. In New York Sara Bershtel at Metropolitan taught me to write for readers, and to try harder for her, while in the later stages Mark Warren at Random House got my own voice onto the page. All the while Christoph Selzer at Klett-Cotta has provided warm encouragement. I'm also very grateful to Molly Turpin, Monica Brown, Ada Yonenaka, Samuel Wetzler, Rachel Parker, Michael Hoakand, Zora O'Neill, and Jane Farnol and Astor Indexers for seeing the U.S. edition through to publication. Jo Carlill sourced the images, and Mike Athanson drew the wonderful maps.

I owe a great deal to institutions, and above all to my colleagues at Oxford University, the Faculty of Classics there, and the Bodleian Library. Thanks for strategic support as well as supportive friendship to Constanze Güthenke, Neil McLynn, Hayley Merchant, Teresa Morgan, Jonathan Prag, and Tobias Reinhardt. At Worcester College my particular gratitude goes to my colleagues in Classics: Scott Scullion, Peta Fowler, Michail Peramatzis, Dominic Dalglish, Alex Wilson, and Lewis Webb. In 2019–20 I was lucky enough to be awarded a fellowship at the Cullman Center for Scholars and Writers, and I'm grateful to Lauren Goldenberg, Paul Delaverdac, Salvatore Scibona, and my fellow fellows for a community that carried over into the COVID times and kept me going in person and alone. Special thanks for particular help with the book to Eric Sanderson, Justin Smith, Bill Goldstein, Sally Rooney, and Ken Chen, and the staff in the Maps Division of the New York Public Library, one of the two most admirable institutions I know. The other is the NHS, which saved my eyesight as I began work on this project.

Many friends, colleagues, and internet acquaintances have helped me write this book, one way or another: my thanks to Daniel Ackerman, Usaama al-Azami, Pascal Arnaud, Laura Ashe, Arthur Asseraf, Jonathan Bate, Mary Beard, Richard Bellamy, Imed Ben Jerbania, Seth Bernard, Ed Bispham, Alastair Blanshard, Glen Bowersock, Cyprian Broodbank, Paula Byrne, Ben Cartlidge, Eric Cline, Surekha Davies, Flint Dibble, Jaś Elsner, Merve Emre, Lisa Fentress, Ann Fielding, Peter Frankopan, Liz Frood, Elena Giusti, Penny Goodman, Anthony Grafton, Lucy Grig, Katherine Harloe, Louise Hitchcock, Joe Howley, Gregory Hutchinson, Katherine Ibbett, Panagiotis Iossif, Maya Jasanoff, Anna Judson, Georgy Kantor, Gavin Kelly, Borja Legarra Herrero, Maria Rosaria Luberto, Irad Malkin, Vito Messina, Lisa Mignone, Rana Mitter, Neville Morley, Theo Nash, Lucia Nixon, Carlos Noreña, Vladimir Olivero, Hussein Omar, Richard Ovenden, Emanuele Papi, Dan-el Padilla Peralta, Michael Pollak, Tanya Pollard, Colin Quinn, Sailakshmi Ramgopal, Eleanor Robson, James Romm, Greg Rowe, Miri Rubin, Katherine Schofield, Jeremy Simmons, Jai Singh, Barnaby Taylor, Rob Tempio, Philip Thibodeau, Angela Trentacoste, Andrew Wallace-Hadrill, William Whyte, Andrew Wilson, Greg Woolf, and Liv Yarrow. I am also particularly grateful to Alex Wilson and David Lambert for checking my facts and footnotes, though I alone bear responsibility for the errors that no doubt remain.

Special thanks to those who commented on one or more chapters: Aneurin Ellis-Evans, Senta German, Olivier Hekster, Susan Hitch, Adrian Kelly, Conrad Leyser, Tzveta Manolova, Dimitri Nakassis, Charlotte Potts, Seth Sanders, Peter Sarris, Peter Thonemann, John Watts, Chris Wickham, and Selena Wisnom. Very special thanks to Raj Patel, who read and commented in detail on the entire manuscript. He has made the book immeasurably better.

Chris Brooke has read more drafts than I can remember and helped in more ways than I can count: this book is a conversation with him. Much of it was in the end written in my study at home in Oxford in conversation with our cat Ptolemy, no less inspiring for being somewhat one-sided. Thanks to the rest of my family as well for their encouragement and patience with me: to Richard, Christine, Jim, Biddy, and to Henry, still so much missed; to Sarah, Paddy, Nicole, Caroline, Mike, and Nick; and to my godmother Jacky.

Thanks above all to my teacher, supervisor, and dear friend Erich Gruen, and to his vision of human history in full: this book is dedicated to him with all my love.

NOTES

Abbreviations

BEI *Brill's Encyclopedia of Islam* (online database)
BNJ *Brill's New Jacoby* (online database)
EAH *Encyclopedia of Ancient History* (online database)
IG *Inscriptiones Graecae* (1860–)
MGH *Monumenta Germaniae Historica* (1826–)
OCD *Oxford Classical Dictionary* (online database)

Introduction

1 Catullus 11:11.

2 This tradition is based ultimately on Genesis 10; cf. 1 Chronicles 1 and Jubilees 8–9.

3 Tamara Griggs, "Universal history from Counter-Reformation to Enlightenment," *Modern Intellectual History* 4, no. 2 (2007), 221. Not everyone signed up: the European encounter with native Americans also brought into vogue a theory of "polygenesis," which held that the full range of human types now known were too physically different to share the same ultimate ancestors (Justin E. H. Smith, *Nature, Human Nature, and Human Difference*, Princeton: Princeton University Press, 2015, 92–113).

4 Jean Starobinski, "Le mot civilisation," *Le temps de la réflexion* 4 (1983), 13, tracing the first usage in this sense to the Marquis de Mirabeau in 1759. The noun came from an adjective *civilisé*—meaning polished or refined—which had been in use in France since the sixteenth century. See on the details Michael Sonenscher, "Barbarism and civilization," in Richard Whatmore and Brian Young, eds., *A Companion to Intellectual History*, Chichester: Wiley Blackwell, 2015, with Katherine Blouin's essay at https://everydayorientalism.wordpress.com/2018/02/23/civilization-whats-up-with-that.

5 See in particular Adam Ferguson's *Essay on the History of Civil Society* (1767) for use of the noun throughout, and for the explication of "stadial theory" the Lectures on Jurisprudence that Adam Smith delivered between 1762 and 1766.

6 John Stuart Mill, "Civilization," *London and Westminster Review* no. 1 (April 1836), reprinted at John Stuart Mill, *Essays on Politics and Society, Part I*, ed. John M. Robson, Toronto: University of Toronto Press, 1977, 120.

7 Ibid., 120–1.

8 Imperial ideologies: Uday Singh Mehta, *Liberalism and Empire: A Study in Nineteenth-Century British Liberal Thought*, Chicago: University of Chicago Press, 1999; Jennifer Pitts, *A Turn to Empire: The Rise of Imperial Liberalism in Britain and France*, Princeton: Princeton University Press, 2005; Duncan Bell, "Empire and imperialism," in Gareth Stedman Jones and Gregory Claeys, eds., *The*

Cambridge History of Nineteenth-Century Political Thought, Cambridge: Cambridge University Press, 2011, 867–75, with Duncan Bell, "John Stuart Mill on Colonies," *Political Theory* 38, no. 1 (2010).

9 On the East India Company, the private contractor that ran British imperial interests in India until the late nineteenth century, see William Dalrymple, *The Anarchy: The Relentless Rise of the East India Company,* London: Bloomsbury, 2019. Mill himself never set foot in India.

10 John Stuart Mill, *On Liberty,* reprinted at John Stuart Mill, *Essays on Politics and Society, Part I,* 224.

11 François Guizot, *General History of Civilization in Europe,* New York: D. Appleton, 1896, 4 (Lecture 1).

12 Ibid., 26 (Lecture 2).

13 Ibid., 1 (Lecture 1), 32–3 (Lecture 2).

14 John Stuart Mill, "Grote's History of Greece [I]," *Edinburgh Review* 74 (October 1846), reprinted at John Stuart Mill, *Essays on Philosophy and the Classics,* ed. John M. Robson, Toronto: University of Toronto Press, 1978, 273.

15 See Karuna Mantena, *Alibis of Empire: Henry Maine and the Ends of Liberal Imperialism,* Princeton: Princeton University Press, 2010, for the abandonment of liberal universalism and the mission of civilization in this era.

16 Although the idea that the human race is divided into different types by color and other physical characteristics became widely popular only in the nineteenth century, it went back to the work of eighteenth-century scholars. The Swedish botanist Carl Linnaeus' *Systema Naturae (A General System of Nature)* first published in 1735, classified all natural organisms into three "kingdoms" of plants, animals and minerals, which were then divided up into classes, orders, genera, and species. Linnaeus did not formally divide the human "genus" into different "species," but he did list different "varieties" of human with differing physical characteristics, based above all on skin color.

17 Georgios Varouxakis, "When did Britain join the occident? On the origins of the idea of 'the West' in English," *History of European Ideas* 46, no. 5 (2020), tracing usage of "the West" to the late eighteenth century and pointing out that the term was imported into English from continental Europe, and appears even later in the United States.

18 Jasper M. Trautsch, "The invention of the 'West,'" *Bulletin of the German Historical Institute* 53 (Fall 2013), 91–5; Varouxakis, "When did Britain join the occident?," 569–72.

19 Edward A. Freeman, *The History of Sicily from the Earliest Times,* Oxford: Clarendon Press, 1891, 1:10–11.

20 The earliest examples of the phrase are found in the 1840s: Varouxakis, "When did Britain join the occident?," 571.

21 John Clarke Stobart, *The Grandeur That Was Rome: A Survey of Roman Culture and Civilization,* London: Sidgwick & Jackson, 1912, 1. On the viability of the notion of western civilization itself see David Graeber's essay at https://theanarchistlibrary.org/library/david-graeber-there-never-was-a-west.

22 Trautsch, "The invention of the 'West,'" 96–9, and note 2.

23 The classic example is Arnold Toynbee's *A Study of History,* 12 vols., London: Oxford University Press, 1934–61, a comparison of twenty-one world civilizations. These projects were often prompted by concerns about Western civilization and

its prospects, from the German writer Oswald Spengler's *Der Untergang des Abendlandes,* Vienna: Braumüller, 1918–22, trans. into English by Charles F. Atkinson as *The Decline of the West,* New York: Alfred A. Knopf, 1926–8, to the American historian William McNeill's *The Rise of the West,* Chicago: University of Chicago Press, 1963. McNeill did make the case for communication and diffusion between civilizations throughout history, but he focused on the diffusion of ideas from "civilizations" to "aliens," and his book culminates in an extended study of the importance of Western influence over other civilizations after 1500. Will Durant's *The Story of Civilization,* New York: Simon & Schuster, 1935–75, is in fact the story of Western Civilization. There are interesting recent works that connect the cultural history of East and West, but these too tend to focus on later periods, or on intellectual constructions (e.g., Jack Goody, *The Theft of History,* Cambridge: Cambridge University Press, 2006). One exception is a wonderful short book by Jerry H. Bentley on *Old World Encounters: Cross-Cultural Contacts and Exchanges in Pre-Modern Times,* New York: Oxford University Press, 1993, a truly global history that covers a similar timeframe to my own, told from a more limited, Western perspective.

24 Fernand Braudel, *A History of Civilizations,* trans. Richard Mayne, London: Penguin, 1995, 22.

25 Ibid., 29, 12, 35.

26 Samuel P. Huntington, *The Clash of Civilizations and the Remaking of World Order,* New York: Simon & Schuster, 1996, 40, 21. Huntington's definition of a civilization is "the highest cultural grouping of people and the broadest level of cultural identity people have short of that which distinguishes humans from other species" (43).

27 https://www.ramsaycentre.org/studying-western-civilisation/ba-degrees. Similar approaches can be seen at conservative U.S. liberal arts colleges like Hillsdale College in southern Michigan, where the core syllabus invites prospective students to "explore the ways in which modern man is indebted to the Greco-Roman culture and the Judeo-Christian tradition": https://www.hillsdale.edu/academics/classical-liberal-arts-core.

28 The Pharos Project regularly documents this phenomenon: http://pages.vassar.edu/pharos/white-nationalism-white-supremacy; see for these examples http://pages.vassar.edu/pharos/2018/06/15/spqr-and-white-nationalism and https://pages.vassar.edu/pharos/2017/11/17/scholars-respond-to-spartan-helmets, with https://pharos.vassarspaces.net/2021/06/04/richard-spencer-who-we-are-white-identity-greco-roman-antiquity and https://eidolon.pub/this-is-not-sparta-392a9ccddf26.

29 David Reich, *Who We Are and How We Got Here: Ancient DNA and the New Science of the Human Past,* New York: Pantheon Books, 2018; Adam Rutherford, *How to Argue with a Racist: History, Science, Race and Reality,* London: Weidenfeld & Nicolson, 2020.

30 Reich, *Who We Are and How We Got Here,* 81.

31 I am grateful to Eric Sanderson for this suggestion.

32 There has been a gratifying increase in discussions of these links in both academic and popular writing over the last few years. To take just a few illustrative examples in academic publishing, in 2018 the journal *Past & Present* published a special edition, "The Global Middle Ages"; in 2019 Tamar Hodos edited the new *Routledge*

Handbook of Archaeology and Globalization, London: Routledge; and Cambridge University Press launched a new academic journal, *Global Antiquities*, in 2020, and in 2021 a new monograph series, Antiquity in Global Context. All this builds on earlier synthetic works like Toby C. Wilkinson, Susan Sherratt, and John Bennet, eds., *Interweaving Worlds: Systemic Interactions in Eurasia, 7th to the 1st Millennia BC*, Oxford: Oxbow, 2011. Meanwhile scholars have published major works on particular—often very large—periods and places: on the Mediterranean, Peregrine Horden and Nicholas Purcell's *The Corrupting Sea: A Study of Mediterranean History*, Oxford: Blackwell, 2000 (as well as their later work, *The Boundless Sea: Writing Mediterranean History*, Abingdon: Routledge, 2020) and Cyprian Broodbank's *The Making of the Middle Sea: A History of the Mediterranean from the Beginning to the Emergence of the Classical World*, London: Thames & Hudson, 2013; on the Indian Ocean world, Philippe Beaujard's *Les mondes de l'océan Indien*, Paris: Armand Colin, 2012 (trans. into English as *The Worlds of the Indian Ocean: A Global History*, Cambridge: Cambridge University Press, 2019); on central Asia, Peter Frankopan's *The Silk Roads: A New History of the World*, London: Bloomsbury, 2015; and on the Eurasian Steppe, Barry Cunliffe's *By Steppe, Desert, and Ocean: The Birth of Eurasia*, Oxford: Oxford University Press, 2015. For even bigger perspectives, see Eivind Heldaas Seland's *Antikkens globale verden*, Kristiansand: Portal, 2008 (trans. into English as *A Global History of the Ancient World: Asia, Europe, and Africa Before Islam*, London: Routledge, 2022) and Michael Scott's *Ancient Worlds: An Epic History of East and West*, London: Hutchinson, 2016.

33 *Ex oriente lux*: Wolfgang Helbig, *Das homerische Epos aus den Denkmälern erläutert: archäologische Untersuchungen*, Leipzig: Teubner, 1884; Wolfgang Helbig, "Sur la question mycénienne," *Mémoires de l'Institut National de France* 35, no. 2 (1896); Oscar Montelius, *Der Orient und Europa: Einfluss der orientalischen Cultur auf Europa bis zur Mitte des letzten Jahrtausends v. Chr.*, Stockholm, 1899; Oscar Montelius, *Die älteren Kulturperioden im Orient und in Europa*, Stockholm, 1903.

34 Michael Baxandall, *Patterns of Intention: On the Historical Explanation of Pictures*, New Haven: Yale University Press, 1985, 58–62.

35 The term Levant, from the Italian *levante*, the "rising" sun, has a checkered history in the modern period, but I use it here as a relatively neutral and usefully vague term for the lands between the Euphrates and the Mediterranean (see Thomas Scheffler, "'Fertile Crescent,' 'Orient,' 'Middle East': the changing mental maps of southwest Asia," *European Review of History* 10 [2003], for alternatives). Farther north, the name Anatolia for the peninsula occupied by modern Turkey also comes from a term meaning "sunrise," the ancient Greek *anatole*.

1. A Single Sail

1 Byblos and its harbor: Honor Frost, "Byblos and the sea," in Claude Doumet-Serhal, ed., *Decade: A Decade of Archaeology and History in Lebanon*, Beirut: The Lebanese British Friends of the National Museum, 2004; Marwan Kilani, "Byblos in the Late Bronze Age: Interactions between the Levantine and Egyptian Worlds," DPhil. thesis, University of Oxford, 2017, 19–21, 55–8. Tower Temple: Honor Frost,

"Marine prospection at Byblos," *Baal: Bulletin d'archéologie et d'architecture libanaises* 3 (1998–9), 253–8.

2 The name of Shu-ilisu, a translator of the "Meluhha-language" spoken in the Indus Valley, is preserved on a tiny cylinder seal found in Mesopotamia and dating from c. 2300 BCE: Louvre Museum AO 22310.

3 Guy S. Jacobs et al., "Multiple deeply divergent Denisovan ancestries in Papuans," *Cell* 177, no. 4 (2019); Lu Chen et al., "Identifying and interpreting apparent Neanderthal ancestry in African individuals," *Cell* 180, no. 4 (2020).

4 Festivals at Göbekli Tepe in southern Anatolia: Oliver Dietrich et al., "The role of cult and feasting in the emergence of Neolithic communities: new evidence from Göbekli Tepe, southeastern Turkey," *Antiquity* 86, no. 333 (2012). Celebrations and trade at the "mammoth houses" of southern Russia and Ukraine: most recently David Graeber and David Wengrow, *The Dawn of Everything: A New History of Humanity*, London: Allen Lane, 2021, 90–1.

5 Trevor Watkins, "Supra-regional networks in the Neolithic of southwest Asia," *Journal of World Prehistory* 21, no. 2 (2008), 155–7.

6 Peter J. Richerson, Robert Boyd and Robert L. Bettinger, "Was agriculture impossible during the Pleistocene but mandatory during the Holocene? A climate change hypothesis," *American Antiquity* 66, no. 3 (2001); Trevor Watkins, "New light on Neolithic revolution in southwest Asia," *Antiquity* 84, no. 325 (2010). A millennium or two later a similar but separate agricultural initiative began in the river valleys of eastern China.

7 Greg Woolf, *The Life and Death of Ancient Cities*, Oxford: Oxford University Press, 2020, 44.

8 Barry W. Cunliffe, *By Steppe, Desert, and Ocean: The Birth of Eurasia*, Oxford: Oxford University Press, 2015, 98; Volker Heyd, "Kossinna's smile," *Antiquity* 91, no. 356 (2017), 42–3.

9 Marc Van de Mieroop, *A History of the Ancient Near East, ca. 3000–323 BC*, 3rd ed., Chichester: Wiley Blackwell, 2016, 24–6. The city of Tell Brak emerged more or less simultaneously in a wet-farming region to the north, reaching a similar size by the end of the fourth millennium (Woolf, *The Life and Death of Ancient Cities*, 68–9).

10 Lorenz Rahmstorf, "The concept of weighing during the Bronze Age in the Aegean, the Near East and Europe," in Iain Morley and Colin Renfrew, eds., *The Archaeology of Measurement: Comprehending Heaven, Earth, and Time in Ancient Societies*, Cambridge: Cambridge University Press, 2010; Lorenz Rahmstorf, "Re-integrating 'diffusion': the spread of innovation among the Neolithic and Bronze Age societies of Europe and the Near East," in Toby C. Wilkinson, Susan Sherratt, and John Bennet, eds., *Interweaving Worlds: Systemic Interactions in Eurasia, 7th to the 1st Millennia BC*, Oxford: Oxbow, 2011.

11 Robert K. Englund, "Accounting in Proto-Cuneiform," in Karen Radner and Eleanor Robson, eds., *The Oxford Handbook of Cuneiform Culture*, Oxford: Oxford University Press, 2011.

12 For other approaches that reach similar conclusions, see James C. Scott, *Against the Grain: A Deep History of the Earliest States*, New Haven: Yale University Press, 2017, and Graeber and Wengrow, *The Dawn of Everything*.

13 David Wengrow, *What Makes Civilization? The Ancient Near East and the Future of the West*, Oxford: Oxford University Press, 2010, 93; Cyprian Broodbank, *The*

Making of the Middle Sea: A History of the Mediterranean from the Beginning to the Emergence of the Classical World, London: Thames & Hudson, 2013, 336–7, noting that tin and tin-bronze appear in Mesopotamia and Anatolia from c. 3000 BCE, and in much larger quantities from c. 2500 BCE.

14 Elamite sources of tin in Afghanistan and Luristan: Daniel T. Potts, *The Archaeology of Elam: Formation and Transformation of an Ancient Iranian State,* 2nd ed., New York: Cambridge University Press, 2016, 158. There are considerable quantities of tin in mountains in Bohemia and some in the Taurus range of western Anatolia, but there is as yet no good evidence for significant exploitation of these sources during the Bronze Age (Broodbank, *The Making of the Middle Sea,* 337).

15 Cunliffe, *By Steppe, Desert, and Ocean,* 99–100. It is as yet unclear whether the very first wheels were made on the Steppe proper or in neighboring regions of what is now called eastern Europe: although the bulk of the evidence comes from farther east, a wheeled vehicle is depicted on a pot found in Poland dating to 3500–3350 BCE, and the earliest surviving wooden wheel in the world, carbon-dated to c. 3150 BCE, was excavated in Slovenia in 2002.

16 Johnny Baldi and Valentine Roux, "The innovation of the potter's wheel: a comparative perspective between Mesopotamia and the southern Levant," *Levant* 48, no. 3 (2016), with a discussion of the evidence for an early and brief appearance of potters' wheels in the southern Levant in the fifth millennium BCE.

17 Birgitta Kimura et al., "Ancient DNA from Nubian and Somali wild ass provides insights into donkey ancestry and domestication," *Proceedings of the Royal Society B: Biological Sciences,* no. 1702 (2011); Birgitta Kimura et al., "Donkey domestication," *African Archaeological Review* 30, no. 1 (2013); Evelyn Todd et al., "The genomic history and global expansion of domestic donkeys," *Science* 377, no. 6611 (2022).

18 Broodbank, *The Making of the Middle Sea,* 289.

19 Peter Mitchell, *The Donkey in Human History: An Archaeological Perspective,* Oxford: Oxford University Press, 2018, 24.

20 David Fabre, *Seafaring in Ancient Egypt,* London: Periplus, 2004, 89.

21 Neil Brodie, "The donkey: an appropriate technology for Early Bronze Age land transport and traction," in Neil Brodie, ed., *Horizon: A Colloquium on the Prehistory of the Cyclades,* Cambridge: McDonald Institute for Archaeological Research, 2008, 299; Mitchell, *The Donkey in Human History,* 76.

22 James Henry Breasted, *Ancient Records of Egypt: Historical Documents from the Earliest Times to the Persian Conquest,* Volume 1, Chicago: University of Chicago Press, 1906, nos. 65–6, 146–8; James B. Pritchard, *Ancient Near Eastern Texts Relating to the Old Testament,* Princeton: Princeton University Press, 3rd ed., 1969, 227; Ezra Marcus, "Early seafaring and maritime activity in the southern Levant from prehistory through the third millennium BCE," in Edwin C. M. van den Brink and Thomas E. Levy, eds., *Egypt and the Levant,* London: Leicester University Press, 2002, 408.

23 Steve Vinson, *Egyptian Boats and Ships,* Princes Risborough: Shire, 1994, 17; Nicole Boivin and Dorian Q. Fuller, "Shell middens, ships and seeds: exploring coastal subsistence, maritime trade and the dispersal of domesticates in and around the ancient Arabian peninsula," *Journal of World Prehistory* 22, no. 2 (2009); Cyprian Broodbank, "'Ships a-sail from over the rim of the sea': voyaging,

sailing and the making of Mediterranean societies c. 3500–500 BC," in Atholl Anderson, James H. Barrett, and Katherine V. Boyle, eds., *The Global Origins of Seafaring*, Cambridge: McDonald Institute for Archaeological Research, 2010, 254–5; Broodbank, *The Making of the Middle Sea*, 290; Philippe Beaujard, *The Worlds of the Indian Ocean: A Global History*, Cambridge: Cambridge University Press, 2019, 50. It is possible that sailing technology was in fact invented in the Persian Gulf and traveled by word of mouth in the other direction, but Broodbank notes that the single suggested depiction of a sailing ship at a Gulf site in the sixth or fifth millennium BCE is uncertain ("'Ships a-sail from over the rim of the sea,'" 254–5). It is also worth noting an example of the independent invention of sail in the Pacific, perhaps even earlier than on the Nile or in the Gulf, as there are examples of writing in central America and probably China too in later periods.

24 In another blow to the progressivist assumptions of eighteenth-century civilizational thinking, there are no signs in the Indus Valley of temples or royal palaces, of armies or grand individual burials; these cities were probably ruled by corporate bodies rather than kings: Jonathan Mark Kenoyer, "The Indus civilization," in Colin Renfrew and Paul Bahn, eds., *The Cambridge World Prehistory*, Cambridge: Cambridge University Press, 2014. Cf. Adam S. Green, "Killing the priest-king: addressing egalitarianism in the Indus civilization," *Journal of Archaeological Research* 29, no. 2 (2021) for an argument for political egalitarianism in these cities, and the thoughtful discussion at Graeber and Wengrow, *The Dawn of Everything*, 313–21.

25 Byblos ships: Shelley Wachsmann, *Seagoing Ships and Seamanship in the Bronze Age Levant*, College Station: Texas A&M University Press, 1998, 12–19; Marcus, "Early seafaring and maritime activity in the southern Levant," 408; Fabre, *Seafaring in Ancient Egypt*, 92, noting reservations.

26 Ulrich Hartung et al., *Umm el-Qaab II: Importkeramik aus dem Friedhof U in Abydos (Umm el-Qaab) und die Beziehungen Ägyptens zu Vorderasien im 4. Jahrtausend v. Chr.*, Mainz am Rhein: P. von Zabern, 2001, 313–16; Broodbank, *The Making of the Middle Sea*, 287–8.

27 Broodbank, "'Ships a-sail from over the rim of the sea,'" 251; Broodbank, *The Making of the Middle Sea*, 301–3.

28 Broodbank, "'Ships a-sail from over the rim of the sea,'" 254.

29 Marcus, "Early seafaring and maritime activity in the southern Levant," 404.

30 Broodbank, "'Ships a-sail from over the rim of the sea,'" 254; Broodbank, *The Making of the Middle Sea*, 290.

31 Cunliffe, *By Steppe, Desert, and Ocean*, 98; Heyd, "Kossinna's smile," 351.

32 Brodie, "The donkey," 301–2.

2. The Palace of Minos

1 5,000 people: Cyprian Broodbank, *The Making of the Middle Sea: A History of the Mediterranean from the Beginning to the Emergence of the Classical World*, London: Thames & Hudson, 2013, 570.

2 For a detailed description of the palace in its heyday, see John C. McEnroe, *Architecture of Minoan Crete: Constructing Identity in the Aegean Bronze Age*,

Austin: University of Texas Press, 2010, 69–79. My description here reflects the later phases of the complex, which is to say its archaeological remains.

3 *CMS* [*Corpus der Minoischen und Mykenischen Siegel*] II 1 287 (MMIA–MMIB: c. 2100–1900 BCE); for a slightly later example cf. *CMS* II 2 261 (MMIB–MMII). See also Shelley Wachsmann, *Seagoing Ships and Seamanship in the Bronze Age Levant,* College Station: Texas A&M University Press, 1998, 83–122, esp. 99; Cyprian Broodbank, *An Island Archaeology of the Early Cyclades,* Cambridge: Cambridge University Press, 2000, 342; Cyprian Broodbank, "'Ships a-sail from over the rim of the sea': voyaging, sailing and the making of Mediterranean societies c. 3500–500 BC," in Atholl Anderson, James H. Barrett and Katherine V. Boyle, eds., *The Global Origins of Seafaring,* Cambridge: McDonald Institute for Archaeological Research, 2010, 255–6.

4 The main sources are late (Apollodorus 3.1.1; Diodorus Siculus 5.78), but the story was already well known by the fifth century BCE when Herodotus provides a rationalized version (1.2.1; cf. Apollodorus 2.5.7 on a mention in Akousilaos of Argos, c. 500 BCE).

5 Homer, *Iliad* 14.315–28, and these are only the ones he confesses to his wife.

6 Sarpedon and the Termilae: Herodotus 1.173, with 7:92. Minos' reign: Herodotus 1.171, 3.122; Thucydides 1.4.1, 8:7; Diodorus Siculus 4.79.1, 5.78.3. Pasiphaë: Diodorus Siculus 4.77. Theseus: Apollodorus 3.1, 15; Plutarch, *Theseus* 15–20. Some ancient authors add more siblings.

7 My claim here is somewhat different from Martin Bernal's in *Black Athena* (3 vols., New Brunswick: Rutgers University Press, 1987–2006), where he argues for the validity of an "ancient model" that saw the roots of Greek culture in Egypt and the Levant. As we shall see, there's a lot to be said for that—if not quite everything Bernal said—but the "ancient model" that interests me here is a larger and more abstract notion of the causation of cultural change through human interaction.

8 Herodotus 4.45.

9 John K. Papadopoulos, "Inventing the Minoans: archaeology, modernity and the quest for European identity," *Journal of Mediterranean Archaeology* 18, no. 1 (2005), 96.

10 Ibid., 98.

11 See for instance Richard Chandler, *Travels in Asia Minor: Or, an Account of a Tour Made at the Expense of the Society of Dilettanti,* Dublin: R. Marchbank, 1775.

12 J. A. MacGillivray, *Minotaur: Sir Arthur Evans and the Archaeology of the Minoan Myth,* New York: Hill & Wang, 2000.

13 Arthur J. Evans, *Through Bosnia and the Herzegovina on Foot During the Insurrection, August and September 1875,* London: Longmans, Green, 1876, 308.

14 Papadopoulos, "Inventing the Minoans," 96.

15 Arthur J. Evans, "The 'Eastern Question' in anthropology," *Report of the Sixty-Sixth Meeting of the British Association for the Advancement of Science* (1896), 922.

16 J. Lesley Fitton, *The Discovery of the Greek Bronze Age,* London: British Museum Press, 1995, 76.

17 Arthur J. Evans, *The Palace of Minos: A Comparative Account of the Successive Stages of the Early Cretan Civilization as Illustrated by the Discoveries at Knossos,* vol. I, London: Macmillan, 1921, 1.

18 Ilse Schoep, "Building the labyrinth: Arthur Evans and the construction of Minoan civilization," *American Journal of Archaeology* 122, no. 1 (2018). Evans did

not in fact invent the term "Minoan" as he claimed, but borrowed it from Karl Hoeck's *Kreta* (1823), not the only example in German scholarship of the 1820s. It was however used in that earlier era with a primarily chronological rather than cultural meaning: Nektarios Karadimas and Nicoletta Momigliano, "On the term 'Minoan' before Evans's work in Crete (1894)," *Studi Micenei ed Egeo Anatolici* 46, no. 2 (2004).

19 Evans, *The Palace of Minos,* vol. I, 24, with Papadopoulos, "Inventing the Minoans," 94.

20 Papadopoulos, "Inventing the Minoans," 106–10.

21 Joan Evans, *Time and Chance: The Story of Arthur Evans and His Forebears,* London: Longmans, Green, 1943, 370.

22 Evans, *The Palace of Minos,* vol. I, 15–19.

23 V. Gordon Childe, *The Dawn of European Civilization,* London: Kegan Paul, Trench, Trubner & Co., 1925, 29.

24 Peter Tomkins and Ilse Schoep, "Crete," in Eric H. Cline, ed., *The Oxford Handbook of the Bronze Age Aegean,* New York: Oxford University Press, 2012, 69.

25 Broodbank, *An Island Archaeology of the Early Cyclades,* esp. 92–106.

26 Two weeks: ibid., 105.

27 Analysis of lead isotopes has shown that silver and copper found throughout the Aegean in this era come from the mines at Lavrion on the southern tip of Attica in mainland Greece: Jack L. Davis, "Minoan Crete and the Aegean islands," in Cynthia W. Shelmerdine, ed., *The Cambridge Companion to the Aegean Bronze Age,* Cambridge: Cambridge University Press, 2008, 201; Noel Gale, Maria Kayafa and Zofia Stos-Gale, "Further evidence for bronze age production of copper from ores in the Lavrion ore district, Attica, Greece," in *Archaeometallurgy in Europe II,* Milan: AIM, 2009.

28 On Troy and its contacts in this period (Troy II), see Andrew Sherratt, "What would a Bronze Age world system look like? Relations between temperate Europe and the Mediterranean in later prehistory," *Journal of European Archaeology* 1 (1993), 22–3, and Naoíse Mac Sweeney, *Troy: Myth, City, Icon,* London: Bloomsbury Academic, 2018, 40–3. For a recent study suggesting that silver from the Cyclades may even have reached Egypt in this period, see Karin Sowada et al., "Analyses of Queen Hetepheres' bracelets from her celebrated tomb in Gia reveals new information on silver, metallurgy and trade in Old Kingdom Egypt, c. 2600 BC," *Journal of Archaeological Science: Reports* 49 (2023).

29 Broodbank, *The Making of the Middle Sea,* 332–3, 335–7, also noting that true bronze has a lower casting temperature.

30 Wheel and stamp seals: ibid., 336. For the donkey see ibid., 326–7; Peter Mitchell, *The Donkey in Human History: An Archaeological Perspective,* Oxford: Oxford University Press, 2018, 111, and Neil Brodie, "The donkey: an appropriate technology for Early Bronze Age land transport and traction," in Neil Brodie, ed., *Horizon: A Colloquium on the Prehistory of the Cyclades,* Cambridge: McDonald Institute for Archaeological Research, 2008, which notes the coincidence of the appearance of bronze in Anatolia and the Aegean and the arrival of the donkey, who could carry copper and tin overland.

31 Andrew Bevan, *Stone Vessels and Values in the Bronze Age Mediterranean,* New York: Cambridge University Press, 2007, 93–4, for the connections between Crete and the Cyclades in the third millennium, and their decline in its final centuries.

32 The name comes from the Italian town of Faenza, later a production center for a similar material.

33 Sturt W. Manning, "Formation of the palaces," in Shelmerdine, ed., *The Cambridge Companion to the Aegean Bronze Age,* 115; Broodbank, *The Making of the Middle Sea,* 336. Heavier Egyptian stone vessels of pre-Dynastic and Old Kingdom date found out of archaeological context on Crete may have been antiques brought to the island in a later period, perhaps even as a result of tomb robbing: Bevan, *Stone Vessels and Values in the Bronze Age Mediterranean,* 95.

34 Susan Sherratt, "A globalizing Bronze and Iron Age Mediterranean," in Tamar Hodos, ed., *The Routledge Handbook of Archaeology and Globalization,* London: Routledge, 2017, 604; Jorrit M. Kelder, Sara E. Cole, and Eric H. Cline, "Memphis, Minos and Mycenae: Bronze Age contact between Egypt and the Aegean," in Jeffrey Spier, Timothy Potts, and Sara E. Cole, eds., *Beyond the Nile: Egypt and the Classical World,* Los Angeles: Getty Publications, 2018, 10.

35 Borja Legarra Herrero, "About the distribution of metal objects in prepalatial Crete," *Papers from the Institute of Archaeology* 15 (2004), 33–4; Borja Legarra Herrero, "New kid on the block: the nature of the first systemic contacts between Crete and the eastern Mediterranean around 2000 BC," in Toby C. Wilkinson, Susan Sherratt, and John Bennet, eds., *Interweaving Worlds: Systemic Interactions in Eurasia, 7th to the 1st Millennia BC,* Oxford: Oxbow, 2011; Noel H. Gale and Zofia Anna Stos-Gale, "Cross-cultural Minoan networks and the development of metallurgy in Bronze Age Crete," in Susan La Niece, Duncan R. Hook, and Paul T. Craddock, eds., *Metals and Mines: Studies in Archaeometallurgy,* London: Archetype, 2007.

36 Wheel: Carl Knappett, "Tradition and innovation in pottery forming technology: wheel-throwing at Middle Minoan Knossos," *Annual of the British School at Athens* 94 (1999). Mouse: Thomas Cucchi et al., "Tracking the Near Eastern origins and European dispersal of the western house mouse," *Scientific Reports* 10, no. 1 (2020).

37 Cretan scripts: Helène Whittaker, "The function and meaning of writing in the prehistoric Aegean: some reflections on the social and symbolic significance of writing from a material perspective," in Ruth D. Whitehouse and Kathryn E. Piquette, eds., *Writing as Material Practice: Substance, Surface and Medium,* London: Ubiquity Press, 2013. The so-called "Archanes" signs now appear to be an early form of Cretan Hieroglyphic: Silvia Ferrara, "Another beginning's end: secondary script formation in the Aegean and the eastern Mediterranean," in Philippa Steele, ed., *Understanding Relations Between Scripts: The Aegean Writing Systems,* Oxford: Oxbow, 2017, 15.

38 Tomkins and Schoep, "Crete," 71.

39 By contrast, the sealing system that started to be used a century or so later to secure access to island stores and storehouses follows Egyptian models quite closely, at least at first, before branching out into local variations: Judith Weingarten, "The sealing structures of Minoan Crete: MMII Phaistos to the destruction of the palace of Knossos: Part I: the evidence until the LMIB destruction," *Oxford Journal of Archaeology* 5, no. 3 (1986), 280.

40 Broodbank, *An Island Archaeology of the Early Cyclades,* 347–50. The weather didn't help either, with a drought that gripped much of Europe and western Asia around 2200 BCE, romantically known to scientists as the 4.2k BP ("Before

Present") Climactic Event; the most recent research however suggests that it had limited and variable effects: Calian J. Hazell, Matthew J. Pound, and Emma P. Hocking, "High-resolution Bronze Age palaeoenvironmental change in the eastern Mediterranean: exploring the links between climate and societies," *Palynology* 46, no. 4 (2022).

41 Bronze: Legarra Herrero, "About the distribution of metal objects in prepalatial Crete," 32.

42 Barry Molloy, "Swords and swordsmanship in the Aegean Bronze Age," *American Journal of Archaeology* 114, no. 3 (2010).

43 Tomkins and Schoep, "Crete."

44 Keith Branigan, "Aspects of Minoan urbanism," in Keith Branigan, ed., *Urbanism in the Aegean Bronze Age*, Sheffield: Sheffield Academic Press, 2002; Todd Whitelaw, "The urbanization of prehistoric Crete: settlement perspectives on Minoan state formation," in Ilse Schoep, Peter Tomkins, and Jan M. Driessen, eds., *Back to the Beginning: Reassessing Social and Political Complexity on Crete during the Early and Middle Bronze Age*, Oxford: Oxbow, 2011, 146.

45 For differences between Cretan and Levantine architecture, see Branigan, "Aspects of Minoan urbanism," 43–5, and Ilse Schoep, "Architecture and power: the origins of Minoan palatial architecture," in Joachim Bretschneider, Jan M. Driessen, and Karel van Lerberghe, eds., *Power and Architecture: Monumental Public Architecture in the Bronze Age Near East and Aegean*, Leuven: Peeters, 2007.

46 Jan Driessen, Ilse Schoep, and Robert Laffineur, eds., *Monuments of Minos: Rethinking the Minoan Palaces*, Liège: Université de Liège, 2002: see chapters by Betancourt, Driessen, and Hamilakis; Ilse Schoep, "The Minoan 'palace-temple' reconsidered: a critical assessment of the spatial concentration of political, religious and economic power in Bronze Age Crete," *Journal of Mediterranean Archaeology* 23, no. 2 (2011).

47 Ilse Schoep and Peter Tomkins, "Back to the beginning for the Early and Middle Bronze Age on Crete," in Schoep, Tomkins, and Driessen, eds., *Back to the Beginning*, 8–10.

48 Tomkins and Schoep, "Crete," 118.

49 *ARMT* [*Archives Royales de Mari, Textes*] 23, no. 556, lines 28–31, trans. Eric H. Cline, in *Sailing the Wine-Dark Sea: International Trade and the Late Bronze Age Aegean*, Oxford: Tempus Reparatum, 1994, cat. D2.

50 Shoes: *ARMT* 21, no. 342, lines 5–12, trans. Cline, *Sailing the Wine-Dark Sea*, cat. D7. Other Cretan goods mentioned in the Mari archives: Cline, *Sailing the Wine-Dark Sea*, cat. D3-6, 8-12.

51 Mari parallels: Robert B. Koehl, "The Near Eastern contribution to Aegean wall painting and vice versa," in Joan Aruz, Sarah B. Graff, and Yelena Rakic, eds., *Cultures in Contact: From Mesopotamia to the Mediterranean in the Second Millennium* B.C., New York: Metropolitan Museum of Art, 2013. Tell el-Burak: Jens Kamlah and Hélène S. Sader, eds., *Tell el-Burak I: The Middle Bronze Age*, Wiesbaden: Harrassowitz, 2019, 381–4. Dating: Felix Höflmayer et al., "New evidence for Middle Bronze Age chronology and synchronisms in the Levant: radiocarbon dates from Tell el-Burak, Tell el-Dab'a, and Tel Ifshar compared," *Bulletin of the American Schools of Oriental Research* 375 (2016).

52 Eric H. Cline, Assaf Yasur-Landau, and Nurith Goshen, "New fragments of Aegean-style painted plaster from Tel Kabri, Israel," *American Journal of Archaeol-*

ogy 115, no. 2 (2011); Eric H. Cline and Assaf Yasur-Landau, "Aegeans in Israel: Minoan frescoes at Tel Kabri," *Biblical Archaeology Review* 39, no. 4 (2013); *EAH*, "Minoanizing paintings in the eastern Mediterranean"; Constance von Rüden, "Reconsidering the Alalakh frescoes within their Levantine context," in K. Aslıhan Yener and Tara Ingman, eds., *Alalakh and Its Neighbors*, Leuven: Peeters, 2020.

53 Carlo Zaccagnini, "Patterns of mobility among ancient Near Eastern craftsmen," *Journal of Near Eastern Studies* 42, no. 4 (1983), 247–9; Jack M. Sasson, "Texts, trade, and travelers," in Joan Aruz, Kim Benzel, and Jean Evans, eds., *Beyond Babylon: Art, Trade, and Diplomacy in the Second Millennium* B.C., New York: Metropolitan Museum of Art, 2008.

54 Amélie Kuhrt, *The Ancient Near East: c. 3000–330* B.C., London: Routledge, 1995, 102.

55 John Bennet, "Minoan Crete: a world of objects, a world of places," in Yannis Galanakis, ed., *The Aegean World: A Companion Guide to the Cycladic, Minoan and Mycenaean Collections in the Ashmolean Museum, University of Oxford*, Oxford: Ashmolean Museum, 2013, 114.

56 Claus Wilcke, "Mesopotamia: early dynastic and Sargonic periods," in Raymond Westbrook, ed., *A History of Ancient Near Eastern Law*, Leiden: Brill, 2003.

57 Electronic Text Corpus of Sumerian Literature 2:4.2:03 (Shulgi C), line 37. I am grateful to Eleanor Robson for pointing this out to me.

58 Klaas R. Veenhof, "Ancient Assur: the city, its traders, and its commercial network," *Journal of the Economic and Social History of the Orient* 53 (2010); Gojko Barjamovic, *A Historical Geography of Anatolia in the Old Assyrian Colony Period*, Copenhagen: Museum Tusculanum Press, 2011.

59 Veenhof, "Ancient Assur," 52–3, 63–70; Marc Van de Mieroop, "Democracy and the rule of law, the assembly, and the first law code," in Harriet Crawford, ed., *The Sumerian World*, London: Routledge, 2013, 280.

60 http://cdli.ox.ac.uk/wiki/doku.php?id=list_of_old_assyrian_limmu_officials.

61 Eva von Dassow, "The public and the state in the ancient Near East," in Gernot Wilhelm, ed., *Organization, Representation, and Symbols of Power in the Ancient Near East*, Winona Lake: Eisenbrauns, 2012, with the other workshop papers on "The public and the state" collected in the same venue; Marc Van de Mieroop, "Popular participation in the political life of the ancient Near East," in Claudia Horst, ed., *Der Alte Orient und die Entstehung der Athenischen Demokratie*, Wiesbaden: Harrassowitz, 2020.

62 Classic discussion at Thorkild Jacobsen, "Primitive democracy in ancient Mesopotamia," *Journal of Near Eastern Studies* 2, no. 3 (1943), 165–6.

63 Jeremy A. Black et al., *The Literature of Ancient Sumer*, Oxford: Oxford University Press, 2004, 283.

64 Veenhof, "Ancient Assur," 52–3; Daniel E. Fleming, *Democracy's Ancient Ancestors: Mari and Early Collective Governance*, Cambridge: Cambridge University Press, 2004, esp. 196–7 and 211–16. See Dassow, "The public and the state in the ancient Near East," 173, on the evidence elsewhere in contemporary western Asia for "republican" forms of government and for the *limum*, and for extra-state actors see Seth L. Sanders, "From people to public in the Iron Age Levant," in Wilhelm, ed., *Organization, Representation, and Symbols of Power in the Ancient Near East*, 193–7.

65 Andrea Seri, *Local Power in Old Babylonian Mesopotamia*, London: Equinox

Publishing, 2005, with Stephanie Dalley's review in *American Journal of Archaeology* 11, no. 4 (2007); Dassow, "The public and the state in the ancient Near East," 181–3.

66 Eleanor Robson, *Mathematics in Ancient Iraq: A Social History,* Princeton: Princeton University Press, 2008, 85–124, exploring the educational and social contexts of Old Babylonian mathematics.

67 Kerma: *EAH,* "Kerma"; Charles Bonnet, *The Black Kingdom of the Nile,* Cambridge, Mass.: Harvard University Press, 2019. Kush/Nubia: Geoff Emberling and Bruce Williams, eds., *The Oxford Handbook of Ancient Nubia,* Oxford: Oxford University Press, 2021.

68 Richard B. Parkinson, *The Tale of Sinuhe and Other Ancient Egyptian Poems, 1940–1640* BC, Oxford: Clarendon Press, 1997, collects and translates these works with useful notes.

69 As translated at ibid., 173.

70 Cyprian Broodbank, "Minoanisation," *Proceedings of the Cambridge Philological Society,* no. 50 (2004), 62; Davis, "Minoan Crete and the Aegean Islands," 202; Nicoletta Momigliano, "Minoans at Iasos?," in Colin F. Macdonald, Erik Hallager, and Wolf-Dietrich Niemeier, eds., *The Minoans in the Central, Eastern and Northern Aegean—New Evidence,* Athens: Danish Institute in Athens, 2009; Wolf-Dietrich Niemeier, "'Minoanisation' versus 'Minoan thalassocrassy'—an introduction," in Macdonald, Hallager, and Niemeier, eds., *The Minoans in the Central, Eastern and Northern Aegean—New Evidence,* 15–16; Theodore M. S. Nash, "Cultures of writing: rethinking the 'spread' and 'development' of writing systems in the Bronze Age Mediterranean," in Philip J. Boyes, Philippa Steele, and Natalia Elvira Astoreca, eds., *The Social and Cultural Contexts of Historic Writing Practices,* Oxford: Oxbow, 2021, 214.

3. The Amber Routes

1 James Clinton Wright, "Early Mycenaean Greece," in Cynthia W. Shelmerdine, ed., *The Cambridge Companion to the Aegean Bronze Age,* Cambridge: Cambridge University Press, 2008, 234; Sofia Voutsaki, "From the kinship economy to the palatial economy: the Argolid in the 2nd millennium BC," in Daniel J. Pullen, ed., *Political Economies in the Aegean Bronze Age,* Oxford: Oxbow, 2010, 87–93.

2 David A. Traill, *Schliemann of Troy: Treasure and Deceit,* London: John Murray, 1995, provides a lively account of Schliemann's adventures.

3 Pausanias 2.16.5–7.

4 Elizabeth B. French, *Mycenae: Agamemnon's Capital,* Stroud: Tempus, 2002, 20.

5 Lena Papazoglou-Manioudaki et al., "Mycenae revisited part 3: the human remains from Grave Circle A at Mycenae. Behind the masks: a study of the bones of Shaft Graves I–V," *Annual of the British School at Athens* 105 (2010), 218.

6 For a convenient summary of the graves and their contents, see Giampaolo Graziadio, "The process of social stratification at Mycenae in the Shaft Grave Period: a comparative examination of the evidence," *American Journal of Archaeology* 95, no. 3 (1991). A sixth grave came to light a year after Schliemann's initial excavations.

7 Pottery technology: Ina Berg, "The potter's wheel in Mycenaean Greece: a

re-assessment," in Giampaolo Graziadio et al., eds., *Φιλική Συναυλία: Studies in Mediterranean Archaeology for Mario Benzi,* Oxford: Archaeopress, 2013. Swords: Wolf-Dietrich Niemeier, "'Minoanisation' versus 'Minoan thalassocrassy'—an introduction," in Colin F. Macdonald, Erik Hallager, and Wolf-Dietrich Niemeier, eds., *The Minoans in the Central, Eastern and Northern Aegean—New Evidence,* Athens: Danish Institute in Athens, 2009, 16.

8 Bridle gear: Kristian Kristiansen and Thomas B. Larsson, *The Rise of Bronze Age Society: Travels, Transmissions and Transformations,* Cambridge: Cambridge University Press, 2005, fig. 79; the shaft graves also contain west Asian versions of the same technology.

9 Joseph Maran, "Bright as the sun: the appropriation of amber objects in Mycenaean Greece," in Hans Peter Hahn and Hadas Weis, eds., *Mobility, Meaning and the Transformations of Things,* Oxford: Oxbow, 2013, 147.

10 Carpathians: Andrew Sherratt, "What would a Bronze Age world system look like? Relations between temperate Europe and the Mediterranean in later prehistory," *Journal of European Archaeology* 1 (1993); Klára Pusztainé Fischl et al., "Transformations in the Carpathian Basin around 1600 BC," in Harald Meller et al., eds., *1600—Cultural Change in the Shadow of the Thera-Eruption?,* Halle: Landesmuseum für Vorgeschichte, 2013; Helle Vandkilde, "Breakthrough of the Nordic Bronze Age: transcultural warriorhood and a Carpathian crossroad in the sixteenth century BC," *European Journal of Archaeology* 17, no. 4 (2014).

11 Colin P. Quinn and Horia Ciugudean, "Settlement placement and socio-economic priorities: dynamic landscapes in Bronze Age Transylvania," *Journal of Archaeological Science: Reports* (2018), 937.

12 Sherratt, "What would a Bronze Age world system look like?," 26; John M. O'Shea, "A river runs through it: landscape and the evolution of Bronze Age networks in the Carpathian Basin," *Journal of World Prehistory* 24 (2011), 166. Deforestation: Maren Gumnior and Astrid Stobbe, "First palynological results from lowland sites in the Romanian Banat and their implications for settlement and land use dynamics in the southeastern Carpathian Basin," *Quaternary International* 583 (2021).

13 Xinyi Liu, Harriet V. Hunt, and Martin K. Jones, "River valleys and foothills: changing archaeological perceptions of North China's earliest farms," *Antiquity* 83, no. 319 (2009); Martin Jones et al., "Food globalization in prehistory," *World Archaeology* 43, no. 4 (2011).

14 Cyprian Broodbank, *The Making of the Middle Sea: A History of the Mediterranean from the Beginning to the Emergence of the Classical World,* London: Thames & Hudson, 2013, 326; Pablo Librado et al., "The origins and spread of domestic horses from the western Eurasian steppes," *Nature* 598, no. 7882 (2021).

15 P. F. Kuznetsov, "The emergence of Bronze Age chariots in eastern Europe," *Antiquity* 80, no. 309 (2006); Barry W. Cunliffe, *By Steppe, Desert, and Ocean: The Birth of Eurasia,* Oxford: Oxford University Press, 2015, 137.

16 Sherratt, "What would a Bronze Age world system look like?," 2; Kristiansen and Larsson, *The Rise of Bronze Age Society,* 181–2; Kristian Kristiansen, "Bridging India and Scandinavia: institutional transmission and elite conquest during the Bronze Age," in Toby C. Wilkinson, Susan Sherratt, and John Bennet, eds., *Interweaving Worlds: Systemic Interactions in Eurasia, 7th to the 1st Millennia BC,* Oxford: Oxbow, 2011, 255. Chronology: David W. Anthony, *The Horse, the Wheel,*

and Language: How Bronze-Age Riders from the Eurasian Steppes Shaped the Modern World, Princeton: Princeton University Press, 2007, 402–3. Steppe horses had arrived in Mesopotamia in the late third millennium, and chariots replaced clumsier wheeled battle carts there in the eighteenth century BCE, but in more hierarchical societies they had less work to do; they were new pieces in existing games. See Anthony, *The Horse, the Wheel, and Language,* 412–18, with Kristiansen, "Bridging India and Scandinavia," 245.

17 Kristiansen, "Bridging India and Scandinavia," 255.

18 Santul Mare: John M. O'Shea and Amy Nicodemus, "'. . . the nearest run thing . . .': the genesis and collapse of a Bronze Age polity in the Maros Valley of southeastern Europe," in Attila Gyucha, ed., *Coming Together: Comparative Approaches to Population Aggregation and Early Urbanization,* Albany: State University of New York Press, 2019, 71.

19 Sherratt, "What would a Bronze Age world system look like?," 26; Wolfgang David, "Gold and bone artifacts as evidence of mutual contact between the Aegean, the Carpathian Basin and southern Germany in the second millennium BC," in Ioanna Galanaki et al., eds., *Between the Aegean and Baltic Seas: Prehistory Across Borders,* Aegaeum 27, Liège: Université de Liège, 2007; Fischl et al., "Transformations in the Carpathian Basin around 1600 BC," 363; Vandkilde, "Breakthrough of the Nordic Bronze Age," 605.

20 Vandkilde, "Breakthrough of the Nordic Bronze Age"; Lene Melheim et al., "Moving metals III: possible origins for copper in Bronze Age Denmark based on lead isotopes and geochemistry," *Journal of Archaeological Science* 96 (2018), 90–2.

21 Martin Furholt, "Mobility and social change: understanding the European Neolithic period after the archaeogenetic revolution," *Journal of Archaeological Research* 29, no. 4 (2021), 484.

22 Andrew Sherratt, "Warriors and traders: Bronze Age chiefdoms in central Europe," in Barry Cunliffe, ed., *Origins: The Roots of European Civilization,* London: BBC Books, 1987, 63; Sherratt, "What would a Bronze Age world system look like?," 29; Vandkilde, "Breakthrough of the Nordic Bronze Age," 614, 619.

23 O'Shea, "A river runs through it," 169. The route goes west along the Mureş River, south down the Tisza and Morava past Belgrade and then, with a short portage near Skopje, into the Varder.

24 Michail Vavelidis and Stelios Andreou, "Gold and gold working in Late Bronze Age northern Greece," *Naturwissenschaften* 95, no. 4 (2007), discuss evidence for gold-working in the northern Aegean in a later period, from the fourteenth century BCE.

25 Jorrit M. Kelder, "A thousand black ships: maritime trade, diplomatic relations, and the rise of Mycenae," in Rolf Strootman, Floris van den Eijnde, and Roy van Wijk, eds., *Empires of the Sea: Maritime Power Networks in World History,* Leiden: Brill, 2019, 41.

26 Robert Drews, *Militarism and the Indo-Europeanizing of Europe,* London: Routledge, 2017, 146–7.

27 Vandkilde, "Breakthrough of the Nordic Bronze Age," 604.

28 Andrew Sherratt and Susan Sherratt, "From luxuries to commodities: the nature of Bronze Age trading systems," in Noel H. Gale, ed., *Bronze Age Trade in the Mediterranean,* Jonsered, Sweden: Åström, 1991, 356.

29 Christian Heitz, "Burying the palaces? Ideologies in the Shaft Grave period,"

revised master's thesis published at https://archiv.ub.uni-heidelberg.de/propylaeumdok/volltexte/2008/89, Heidelberg University, 2008, 23. See Oliver Dickinson, "What conclusions might be drawn from the archaeology of Mycenaean civilization about political structure in the Aegean?," in Jorrit M. Kelder and Willemijn J. I. Waal, eds., *From "LUGAL.GAL" to "Wanax": Kingship and Political Organisation in the Late Bronze Age Aegean,* Leiden: Sidestone Press, 2019, 36, for a summary of early mainland links with Crete.

30 Similar funerary assemblages: Oliver Dickinson, "Invasion, migration and the Shaft Graves," *Bulletin of the Institute of Classical Studies* 43 (1999), 106–7. Horse gear: David, "Gold and bone artifacts," 412. Similar if less wealthy shaft graves, without decorated markers, are found at nearby Lerna and Argos as well as in Laconia farther to the south; the earliest of all are probably on the island of Aegina.

31 Andrea Vianello, *Late Bronze Age Mycenaean and Italic Products in the West Mediterranean: A Social and Economic Analysis,* Oxford: British Archaeological Reports, 2005; Reinhard Jung, "The time around 1600 B.C. in southern Italy: new powers, new contacts and new conflicts," in Meller et al., eds., *1600—Cultural Change in the Shadow of the Thera-Eruption?.*

32 Broodbank, *The Making of the Middle Sea,* 443, especially for the route; Jung, "The time around 1600 B.C. in southern Italy"; Michael L. Galaty, Helena Tomas, and William A. Parkinson, "Bronze Age European elites: from the Aegean to the Adriatic and back again," in A. Bernard Knapp and Peter van Dommelen, eds., *The Cambridge Prehistory of the Bronze and Iron Age Mediterranean,* Cambridge: Cambridge University Press, 2015.

33 Emma Blake, "The Mycenaeans in Italy: a minimalist position," *Papers of the British School at Rome* 76 (2008), 8; Broodbank, *The Making of the Middle Sea,* 443.

34 On links with Scandinavia in particular: Johan Ling et al., "Moving metals II: provenancing Scandinavian Bronze Age artifacts by lead isotope and elemental analyses," *Journal of Archaeological Science* 41 (2014); Melheim et al., "Moving metals III"; Johan Ling et al., "Moving metals IV: swords, metal sources and trade networks in Bronze Age Europe," *Journal of Archaeological Science: Reports* 26 (2019). Britain and Ireland: C.F.E. Pare, *Metals Make the World Go Round: The Supply and Circulation of Metals in Bronze Age Europe,* Oxford: Oxbow, 2000, 20–2.

35 Fischl et al., "Transformations in the Carpathian Basin around 1600 BC." The Transylvanian plateau with its wealth of local resources was less badly affected than other parts of the region: Colin P. Quinn et al., "Rethinking time, culture and socioeconomic organization in Bronze Age Transylvania," *Antiquity* 94, no. 373 (2020).

36 Maran, "Bright as the sun," 148.

37 Anthony Harding, "Trade and exchange," in Harry Fokkens and Anthony Harding, eds., *The Oxford Handbook of the European Bronze Age,* Oxford: Oxford University Press, 2013, 376; Sabine Gerloff, "Von Troja an die Saale, von Wessex nach Mykene: Chronologie, Fernverbindungen und Zinnrouten der Frühbronzezeit Mittel- und Westeuropas," in Harald Meller and François Bertemes, eds., *Der Griff nach den Sternen. Wie Europas Eliten zu Macht und Reichtum kamen,* Halle: Landesamt für Denkmalpflege und Archäologie Sachsen-Anhalt, 2010, with fig. 34.

38 Overland transport of metals in Europe: Andrew Sherratt, "Why Wessex? the Avon route and river transport in later British prehistory," *Oxford Journal of Archaeology* 15, no. 2 (1996). Cypriot copper in Sweden: Ling et al., "Moving metals II," 124–5; Ling et al., "Moving metals IV," 19–20.
39 Van de Mieroop, *A History of the Ancient Near East, ca. 3000–323* BC, 130–1.
40 Maran, "Bright as the sun."
41 Joseph Maran, "Lost in translation: the emergence of Mycenaean culture as a phenomenon of glocalization," in Wilkinson, Sherratt, and Bennet, eds., *Interweaving Worlds,* 289; Maran, "Bright as the sun," 149, 159.
42 Christos Tsountas and James Irving Manatt, *The Mycenaean Age: A Study of the Monuments and Culture of Pre-Homeric Greece,* London: Macmillan, 1897, 10–11.
43 Sofia Voutsaki, "The Hellenization of the prehistoric past: the search for Greek identity in the work of Christos Tsountas," in Sofia Voutsaki and Paul Cartledge, eds., *Ancient Monuments and Modern Identities: A History of Archaeology in 19th & 20th Century Greece,* London: Routledge, 2017.
44 Tsountas and Manatt, *The Mycenaean Age,* 359–60. I am grateful to Dimitri Nakassis for discussion of these passages.

4. The Erupting Sea

1 Louise A. Hitchcock, "Entangled threads: who owned the West House at Akrotiri," *Journal of Prehistoric Religion* 25 (2016).
2 Dating of eruption to June/July by weevils and other pests found in storage jars in this West House, suggesting that it occurred shortly after harvest: Eva Panagiotakopulu et al., "Ancient pests: the season of the Santorini Minoan volcanic eruption and a date from insect chitin," *Naturwissenschaften* 100, no. 7 (2013). The island of Santorini already encircled a substantial, shallow caldera, which was about to become larger: Dávid Karátson et al., "Toward reconstruction of the lost Late Bronze Age intra-caldera island of Santorini, Greece," *Scientific Reports* 8 (2018); Dávid Karátson et al., "Constraining the landscape of Late Bronze Age Santorini prior to the Minoan eruption: insights from volcanological, geomorphological and archaeological findings," *Journal of Volcanology and Geothermal Research* 401 (2020).
3 Eruption: Walter L. Friedrich and Jan Heinemeier, "The Minoan eruption of Santorini radiocarbon dated to 1613 ± 13 BC," in David A. Warburton, ed., *Time's Up! Dating the Minoan Eruption of Santorini,* Athens: Danish Institute at Athens, 2009; Floyd W. McCoy, "The eruption within the debate about the date," in Warburton, ed., *Time's Up!;* Walter L. Friedrich and Nikolaos Sigalas, "The effects of the Minoan eruption," in Warburton, ed., *Time's Up!*. Size: Hendrik J. Bruins, Johannes van der Plicht and J. Alexander MacGillivray, "The Minoan Santorini eruption and tsunami deposits in Palaikastro (Crete): dating by geology, archaeology, C-14, and Egyptian chronology," *Radiocarbon* 51, no. 2 (2009), 399.
4 Tsunami: Hendrik J. Bruins et al., "Geoarchaeological tsunami deposits at Palaikastro (Crete) and the Late Minoan IA eruption of Santorini," *Journal of Archaeological Science* 35, no. 1 (2008).
5 Spread of tephra (ash and pumice): Jan Driessen and Colin F. MacDonald, "The eruption of the Santorini volcano and its effects on Minoan Crete," *Geological*

Society Special Publication 171, no. 1 (2000), 83; McCoy, "The eruption within the debate about the date," 84–5, with fig. 6.

6 Ahmose Tempest Stela recto 6–10 = verso 7–12, as interpreted at Robert K. Ritner and Nadine Moeller, "The Ahmose 'Tempest Stela,' Thera and comparative chronology," *Journal of Near Eastern Studies* 73, no. 1 (2014), 5–10, with Christopher Bronk Ramsey et al., "Radiocarbon-based chronology for dynastic Egypt," *Science* 328 (2010), and Hendrik J. Bruins, "Dating Pharaonic Egypt," *Science* 328 (2010), on the compatibility of the dating.

7 Christos Doumas, *Thera: Pompeii of the Ancient Aegean,* London: Thames & Hudson, 1983, 140, 149; Hendrik J. Bruins and Johannes van der Plicht, "The Exodus enigma," *Nature* 382, no. 6588 (1996), 213–14; Walter L. Friedrich, *Fire in the Sea: The Santorini Volcano, Natural History and the Legend of Atlantis,* Cambridge: Cambridge University Press, 2000, 147–57.

8 Spyridon Marinatos, "The volcanic destruction of Minoan Crete," *Antiquity* 13, no. 52 (1939); quotation at 438–9.

9 Charlotte L. Pearson et al., "Annual radiocarbon record indicates 16th century BCE date for the Thera eruption," *Science Advances* 4, no. 8 (2018); Charlotte Pearson et al., "Securing timelines in the ancient Mediterranean using multiproxy annual tree-ring data," *PNAS* 117, no. 31 (2020); Charlotte Pearson et al., "Geochemical ice-core constraints on the timing and climatic impact of Aniakchak II (1628 BCE) and Thera (Minoan) volcanic eruptions," *PNAS Nexus* 1, no. 2 (2022); Jonny McAneney and Mike Baillie, "Absolute tree-ring dates for the Late Bronze Age eruptions of Aniakchak and Thera in light of a proposed revision of ice-core chronologies," *Antiquity* 93, no. 367 (2019). For a different way of arriving at a mid-sixteenth-century date, see Yael Ehrlich, Lior Regev, and Elisabetta Boaretto, "Discovery of annual growth in a modern olive branch based on carbon isotopes and implications for the Bronze Age volcanic eruption of Santorini," *Scientific Reports* 11, no. 1 (2021). Arguing for an earlier date, in the Second Intermediate Period: Sturt W. Manning, "Second Intermediate Period date for the Thera (Santorini) eruption and historical implications," *PLOS ONE* 17, no. 9 (2022).

10 Limited effects of tephra: McCoy, "The eruption within the debate about the date," 84–5; Jeffrey S. Soles, "The impact of the Minoan eruption of Santorini on Mochlos, a small Minoan town on the north coast of Crete," in Warburton, ed., *Time's Up!;* cf. Jan Driessen, "The Santorini eruption: an archaeological investigation of its distal impacts on Minoan Crete," *Quaternary International* 499 (2019), 197–9. Limited effects of tsunami waves: Dale Dominey-Howes, "A re-analysis of the Late Bronze Age eruption and tsunami of Santorini, Greece, and the implications for the volcano–tsunami hazard," *Journal of Volcanology and Geothermal Research* 130, no. 1 (2004); Philip P. Betancourt, "Evidence from Pseira for the Santorini eruption," in Warburton, ed., *Time's Up!;* Bruins et al., "Geoarchaeological tsunami deposits at Palaikastro (Crete) and the Late Minoan IA eruption of Santorini"; Bruins, van der Plicht, and MacGillivray, "The Minoan Santorini eruption and tsunami deposits in Palaikastro (Crete)"; Driessen, "The Santorini eruption," 196.

11 Cyprian Broodbank, *The Making of the Middle Sea: A History of the Mediterranean from the Beginning to the Emergence of the Classical World,* London: Thames & Hudson, 2013, 416; Driessen, "The Santorini eruption," 200.

12 For another version, Carl W. Blegen, "Preclassical Greece," in *Studies in the Arts and Architecture,* Philadelphia: University of Pennsylvania Press, 1941, 9.

13 Yannis Galanakis, "Arthur Evans and the quest for the 'origins of Mycenaean culture,'" in Yannis Galanakis, Toby C. Wilkinson, and John Bennet, eds., *ΑΘΥΡΜΑΤΑ: Critical Essays on the Archaeology of the Eastern Mediterranean in Honour of E. Susan Sherratt,* Oxford: Archaeopress, 2014, 92 n. 25.

14 Arthur J. Evans, "The Minoan and Mycenaean element in Hellenic life," *Journal of Hellenic Studies* 32 (1912), 282. See also Arthur J. Evans, *The Palace of Minos: A Comparative Account of the Successive Stages of the Early Cretan Civilization as Illustrated by the Discoveries at Knossos,* vol. IV, 2, London: Macmillan, 1935, 755; Alan J. B. Wace, "Foreword," in Michael Ventris and John Chadwick, *Documents in Mycenaean Greek,* Cambridge: Cambridge University Press, 1956, xxii.

15 Alan J. B. Wace and Carl W. Blegen, "The pre-Mycenaean pottery of the mainland," *Annual of the British School at Athens* 22 (1918); Carl W. Blegen, "The coming of the Greeks: II. The geographical distribution of prehistoric remains in Greece," *American Journal of Archaeology* 32 (1928); Carl W. Blegen and Alan J. B. Wace, "Pottery as evidence for trade and colonization in the Aegean Bronze Age," *Klio* 32 (1939), esp. 140; Wace, "Foreword." Debate: Yannis Galanakis, "'Islanders v. mainlanders,' 'the Mycenae wars,' & other short stories," in Natalia Vogeikoff-Brogan, Vasiliki Florou, and Jack L. Davis, eds., *Carl W. Blegen: Personal and Archaeological Narratives,* Atlanta: Lockwood Press, 2015. Race: Wace, "Foreword," xx. Stock: Blegen, "The coming of the Greeks: II. The geographical distribution of prehistoric remains in Greece," 154.

16 Blegen, "Preclassical Greece," 11, 14, based on a 1940 lecture. Dimitri Nakassis discusses this passage at https://englianos.wordpress.com/2017/03/14/looking-back-with-blegen.

17 Iosif Lazaridis et al., "A genetic probe into the ancient and medieval history of southern Europe and west Asia," *Science* 377, no. 6609 (2022). People in different areas have particular connections with neighboring regions, as you'd expect: A woman buried at Zakros on Crete sometime before 1700 BCE has substantial Levantine ancestry, for instance, while many (but not all) of the remains studied from the Greek mainland inherit a minor genetic component—less than 10 percent—from the Steppe, revealing in diluted form the southern extension of migrations west from that region in the third millennium that have been reported by multiple aDNA studies in recent years (e.g. Morten E. Allentoft et al., "Population genomics of Bronze Age Eurasia," *Nature* 522, no. 7555 [2015], and Wolfgang Haak et al., "Massive migration from the steppe was a source for Indo-European languages in Europe," *Nature* 522, no. 7555 [2015], with Volker Heyd, "Kossinna's smile," *Antiquity* 91, no. 356 [2017], 351; Susanne E. Hakenbeck, "Genetics, archaeology and the far right: an unholy Trinity," *World Archaeology* 51, no. 4 [2019]; Martin Furholt, "Mobility and social change: understanding the European Neolithic period after the archaeogenetic revolution," *Journal of Archaeological Research* 29, no. 4 [2021], 484).

18 Crete: Barry P. C. Molloy, "Martial Minoans? War as social process, practice and event in Bronze Age Crete," *Annual of the British School at Athens* 107 (2012). For mainlanders as relatively non-militaristic, Oliver Dickinson, "How warlike were the Mycenaeans, in reality?," in Galanakis, Wilkinson, and Bennet, eds., *ΑΘΥΡΜΑΤΑ: Critical Essays on the Archaeology of the Eastern Mediterranean in Honour of E. Susan Sherratt.*

19 Doumas, *Thera: Pompeii of the Ancient Aegean,* 119; Christos Doumas, "Akrotiri,"

in Eric H. Cline, ed., *The Oxford Handbook of the Bronze Age Aegean*, New York: Oxford University Press, 2012, 757.

20 Lyvia Morgan, *The Miniature Wall Paintings of Thera: A Study in Aegean Culture and Iconography*, Cambridge: Cambridge University Press, 1988; Lyvia Morgan, "New discoveries and new ideas in Aegean wall painting," *British School at Athens Studies* 13 (2005); Sarah P. Morris, "A tale of two cities: the miniature frescoes from Thera and the origins of Greek poetry," *American Journal of Archaeology* 93, no. 4 (1989); Christos Doumas, *The Wall-Paintings of Thera*, Athens: The Thera Foundation, 1992.

21 Morgan, *The Miniature Wall Paintings of Thera*, 109–15.

22 J. T. Hooker, "The Mycenae siege rhyton and the question of Egyptian influence," *American Journal of Archaeology* 71, no. 3 (1967).

23 Morgan, *The Miniature Wall Paintings of Thera*, 146–50; Morris, "A tale of two cities," 529. This is not the only house at Akrotiri whose walls provide a window on a larger world and demonstrate familiarity with the people who inhabit it: an intriguing fragment of wall painting from the north of the site depicts the head of a brown-skinned, black-haired man with a large gold earring.

24 Penelope A. Mountjoy, "Knossos and the Cyclades in Late Minoan IB," in Gerald Cadogan, Eleni Hatzaki, and Adonis Vasilakis, eds., *Knossos: Palace, City, State*, London: British School at Athens, 2004; Penelope A. Mountjoy, "The Cyclades during the Mycenaean period," in Neil Brodie et al., eds., *Horizon: A Colloquium on the Prehistory of the Cyclades*, Cambridge: McDonald Institute for Archaeological Research, 2008, 470.

25 Carl Knappett, Ray Rivers, and Tim Evans, "The Theran eruption and Minoan palatial collapse: new interpretations gained from modelling the maritime network," *Antiquity* 85, no. 329 (2011).

26 Cyprian Broodbank, "Minoanisation," *Proceedings of the Cambridge Philological Society* 50 (2004), 50, 71; Christopher Mee, "Mycenaean Greece, the Aegean and beyond," in Cynthia W. Shelmerdine, ed., *The Cambridge Companion to the Aegean Bronze Age*, Cambridge: Cambridge University Press, 2008, 372–3; Knappett, Rivers, and Evans, "The Theran eruption and Minoan palatial collapse," 1015.

27 Penelope A. Mountjoy and Matthew J. Ponting, "The Minoan thalassocracy reconsidered: provenance studies of LH IIA/LM IB pottery from Phylakopi, Ay. Irini and Athens," *Annual of the British School at Athens* 95 (2000); Mountjoy, "Knossos and the Cyclades in Late Minoan IB"; Mountjoy, "The Cyclades during the Mycenaean period"; Carl Knappett, "From network connectivity to human mobility: models for Minoanization," *Journal of Archaeological Method and Theory* 25, no. 4 (2018).

28 Knappett, Rivers, and Evans, "The Theran eruption and Minoan palatial collapse."

29 Daniel Berger et al., "Isotope systematics and chemical composition of tin ingots from Mochlos (Crete) and other Late Bronze Age sites in the eastern Mediterranean Sea: an ultimate key to tin provenance?," *PLOS ONE* 14, no. 6 (2019).

30 Early bull grappling: Lena Papazoglou-Manioudaki, "Rhyta, figures and figurines in the shape of bull in prehistoric Greece," in Sappho Athanassopoulou and Yannis Tzedakis, eds., *The Bull in the Mediterranean World: Myth and Cults*, Athens: Hellenic Ministry of Culture, 2003. Bull leaping: Dominique Collon, "Bull-leaping in Syria," *Ägypten und Levante* 4 (1994), 81–5; İbrahim Tunç Sipahi, "New evidence from Anatolia regarding bull leaping scenes in the art of the

Aegean and the Near East," *Anatolica* 27 (2001); Joan Aruz, "Bull leaping," in Joan Aruz, Kim Benzel, and Jean M. Evans, eds., *Beyond Babylon: Art, Trade, and Diplomacy in the Second Millennium* B.C., New York: Metropolitan Museum of Art, 2008.

31 Shelley Wachsmann, *Aegeans in the Theban Tombs*, Leuven: Peeters, 1987; Diamantis Panagiotopoulos, "Foreigners in Egypt in the time of Hatshepsut and Thutmose III," in Eric H. Cline and David O'Connor, eds., *Thutmose III: A New Biography*, Ann Arbor: University of Michigan Press, 2006. Clothing: Paul Rehak, "Aegean breechcloths, kilts, and the Keftiu paintings," *American Journal of Archaeology* 100, no. 1 (1996); Paul Rehak, "Aegean natives in the Theban tomb paintings: the Keftiu revisited," in Eric H. Cline and Diane Harris-Cline, eds., *The Aegean and the Orient in the Second Millennium*, Liège: Université de Liège, 1998, 42–5.

32 Translation adapted from Eric H. Cline, *Sailing the Wine-Dark Sea: International Trade and the Late Bronze Age Aegean*, Oxford: Tempus Reparatum, 1994, 109–10: cat. A12. For more on the definition and use of the term "Keftiu," see Uroš Matić, "'Minoans,' *kftjw* and the 'islands in the middle of w3d wr' beyond ethnicity," *Ägypten und Levante* 24 (2014).

33 Panagiotopoulos, "Foreigners in Egypt in the time of Hatshepsut and Thutmose III," 392–6. Cretans appear at other tombs occupied by Thutmose's officials as well.

34 Cline, *Sailing the Wine-Dark Sea*, 110: cat. A13 (Papyrus British Museum 10056), A14 (Annals of Thutmose III, 34th year).

35 For a full catalog of references to "Keftiu," see ibid., 32, 108–14.

36 Cyprian Broodbank and Giulio Lucarini, "The dynamics of Mediterranean Africa, ca. 9600–1000 BC: an interpretative synthesis of knowns and unknowns," *Journal of Mediterranean Archaeology* 32, no. 2 (2019), 238. Cf. Broodbank, "Minoanisation," 48.

37 Cline, *Sailing the Wine-Dark Sea*, 110: cat. A.15 (Annals of Thutmose III, 42nd year).

38 Oliver Dickinson, "What conclusions might be drawn from the archaeology of Mycenaean civilization about political structure in the Aegean?," in Jorrit M. Kelder and Willemijn J. I. Waal, eds., *From "LUGAL.GAL" to "Wanax": Kingship and Political Organisation in the Late Bronze Age Aegean*, Leiden: Sidestone Press, 2019, 36.

39 Jack L. Davis and Sharon R. Stocker, "The lord of the gold rings: the Griffin Warrior of Pylos," *Hesperia* 85, no. 4 (2016); Sharon R. Stocker and Jack L. Davis, "The combat agate from the grave of the Griffin Warrior at Pylos," *Hesperia* 86, no. 4 (2017); Jack L. Davis and Sharon R. Stocker, "The gold necklace from the grave of the Griffin Warrior at Pylos," *Hesperia* 87, no. 4 (2018); and see griffinwarrior.org. For two tholos tombs of the same era discovered in 2018, see http://www.griffinwarrior.org/tholos-tombs.

40 M. L. West, *The East Face of Helicon: West Asiatic Elements in Early Poetry and Myth*, Oxford: Clarendon Press, 1997, 10.

41 Davis and Stocker, "The lord of the gold rings," 628 n. 5, on the differences between the Pylos tomb and Argolid construction; 634 on the armor.

42 Cost ratio of land to water transport: Chris Wickham, *The Donkey and the Boat: Reinterpreting the Mediterranean Economy, 950–1180*, Oxford: Oxford University Press, 2023, 14.

43 Driessen, "The Santorini eruption," 197; John Bennet, "Minoan Crete: a world of

objects, a world of places," in Yannis Galanakis, ed., *The Aegean World: A Companion Guide to the Cycladic, Minoan and Mycenaean Collections in the Ashmolean Museum, University of Oxford,* Oxford: Ashmolean Museum, 2013, 116.

44 Jan Driessen and Ophélie Mouthuy, "The LMII–IIIA2 kingdom of Knossos as reflected by its Linear B archives," in Ana Lucia D'Agata et al., eds., *One State, Many Worlds: Crete in the Late Minoan II–IIIa2 Early Period,* Rome: Quasar, 2022.

45 Ester Salgarella, *Aegean Linear Script(s): Rethinking the Relationship Between Linear A and Linear B,* Cambridge: Cambridge University Press, 2020; Theodore M. S. Nash, "Cultures of writing: rethinking the 'spread' and 'development' of writing systems in the Bronze Age Mediterranean," in Philip J. Boyes, Philippa Steele and Natalia Elvira Astoreca, eds., *The Social and Cultural Contexts of Historic Writing Practices,* Oxford: Oxbow, 2021.

46 See for instance John G. Younger and Paul Rehak, "Minoan culture: religion, burial customs, and administration," in Shelmerdine, ed., *The Cambridge Companion to the Aegean Bronze Age,* 182; Eric H. Cline, *1177 B.C.: The Year Civilization Collapsed,* Princeton: Princeton University Press, 2014, 20; Malcolm Wiener, "The Mycenaean conquest of Minoan Crete," in Colin F. Macdonald, Eleni Hatzaki, and Stelios Andreou, eds., *The Great Islands: Studies of Crete and Cyprus Presented to Gerald Cadogan,* Athens: Kapon Editions, 2015.

47 Jan Driessen, "Towards an archaeology of crisis: defining the long-term impact of the Bronze Age Santorini eruption," in Robin Torrence and John Grattan, eds., *Natural Disasters and Cultural Change,* London: Routledge, 2002, 252.

48 Ibid., 251.

49 Cline, *Sailing the Wine-Dark Sea,* 9.

50 Exports: Lucia Vagnetti, "Mycenaean pottery in the central Mediterranean: imports and local production in their context," in Jan Paul Crielaard, Vladimir Sissi, and Gert Jan van Wijngaarden, eds., *The Complex Past of Pottery,* Amsterdam: J. C. Gieben, 1999; Andrea Vianello, *Late Bronze Age Mycenaean and Italic Products in the West Mediterranean: A Social and Economic Analysis,* Oxford: British Archaeological Reports, 2005; Emma Blake, "The Mycenaeans in Italy: a minimalist position," *Papers of the British School at Rome* 76 (2008); Eric H. Cline, "Bronze Age interactions between the Aegean and the eastern Mediterranean revisited: mainstream, periphery, or margin?," in William A. Parkinson and Michael L. Galaty, eds., *Archaic State Interaction: The Eastern Mediterranean in the Bronze Age,* Santa Fe: School for Advanced Research Press, 2009; Reinhard Jung, "The time around 1600 B.C. in southern Italy: new powers, new contacts and new conflicts," in Harald Meller et al., eds., *1600—Cultural Change in the Shadow of the Thera-Eruption?,* 246; Broodbank, *The Making of the Middle Sea,* 444. Donkeys: Peter Mitchell, *The Donkey in Human History: An Archaeological Perspective,* Oxford: Oxford University Press, 2018, 113. Technology transfer: Blake, "The Mycenaeans in Italy," 21–4; Emma Blake, "Late Bronze Age Sardinia: acephalous cohesion," in A. Bernard Knapp and Peter van Dommelen, eds., *The Cambridge Prehistory of the Bronze and Iron Age Mediterranean,* Cambridge: Cambridge University Press, 2014, 220.

51 Blake, "Late Bronze Age Sardinia."

52 A. Bernard Knapp, Anthony Russell, and Peter van Dommelen, "Cyprus, Sardinia and Sicily: a maritime perspective on interaction, connectivity and imagination in

Mediterranean prehistory," *Cambridge Archaeological Journal* 32, no. 1 (2022), emphasizing the unreliability of current studies of the provenance of copper found on Sardinia, and the potential overstatement of Cypriot presence.

53 Jeanette Varberg, Bernard Gratuze, and Flemming Kaul, "Between Egypt, Mesopotamia and Scandinavia: Late Bronze Age glass beads found in Denmark," *Journal of Archaeological Science* 54 (2015), 172.

54 Flemming Kaul, "The Nordic razor and the Mycenaean lifestyle," *Antiquity* 87, no. 336 (2013).

55 Johan Ling and Zofia Stos-Gale, "Representations of oxhide ingots in Scandinavian rock art: the sketchbook of a Bronze Age traveler?," *Antiquity* 89, no. 343 (2015); Lene Melheim and Anette Sand-Eriksen, "Rock art and trade networks: from Scandinavia to the Italian Alps," *Open Archaeology* 6, no. 1 (2020); see also Kristian Kristiansen and Thomas B. Larsson, *The Rise of Bronze Age Society: Travels, Transmissions and Transformations*, Cambridge: Cambridge University Press, 2005, fig. 107.

56 Varberg, Gratuze, and Kaul, "Between Egypt, Mesopotamia and Scandinavia"; Jeanette Varberg et al., "Mesopotamian glass from Late Bronze Age Egypt, Romania, Germany, and Denmark," *Journal of Archaeological Science* 74 (2016); Kristian Kristiansen, "Interpreting Bronze Age trade and migration," in Carl Knappett and Evangelia Kiriatzi, eds., *Human Mobility and Technological Transfer in the Prehistoric Mediterranean*, Cambridge: Cambridge University Press, 2016, 166.

57 Qatna sculpture: Anna J. Mukherjee et al., "The Qatna lion: scientific confirmation of Baltic amber in Late Bronze Age Syria," *Antiquity* 82, no. 315 (2008). Tutankhamun's tomb: Varberg, Gratuze, and Kaul, "Between Egypt, Mesopotamia and Scandinavia," 173.

58 Broodbank, *The Making of the Middle Sea*, 441.

5. Band of Brothers

1 Frederick John Giles, *The Amarna Age: Western Asia*, Warminster: Aris & Phillips, 1997, 20–2. The rich earth of mud bricks makes excellent fertilizer.

2 J.D.S. Pendlebury, *The City of Akhenaten. Part III: The Central City and the Official Quarters. The Excavations at Tell-El-Amarna During the Seasons 1926–1927 and 1931–1936*, London: Egypt Exploration Society, 1951, 114–15, 150, pl. XIX. The correspondence is collected at J. A. Knudtzon, Erich Ebeling, and Otto Weber, *Die El-Amarna-Tafeln: mit Einleitung und Erläuterungen*, Leipzig: J. C. Hinrichs, 1915; Anson F. Rainey, *El Amarna Tablets 359–379*, Neukirchen-Vluyn: Butzon & Bercker, 1978, and translated into English in William L. Moran, *The Amarna Letters*, Baltimore: Johns Hopkins University Press, 1992 (which I use here unless otherwise specified); and Anson F. Rainey and William M. Schniedewind, *The El-Amarna Correspondence: A New Edition of the Cuneiform Letters from the Site of El-Amarna Based on Collations of All Extant Tablets*, Leiden: Brill, 2015. Further commentary: Giles, *The Amarna Age: Western Asia;* Raymond Cohen and Raymond Westbrook, *Amarna Diplomacy: The Beginnings of International Relations*, Baltimore: Johns Hopkins University Press, 2000; Trevor Bryce, *Letters of the Great Kings of the Ancient Near East: The Royal Correspondence of the Late Bronze Age*, London: Routledge, 2003.

3 Great King: e.g., EA [El Amarna] 1 (Egypt), EA 7 (Babylon), EA 16 (Assyria), EA 19 (Mittani), EA 41 (Hatti).
4 EA 8, trans. after Rainey and Schniedewind, *The El-Amarna Correspondence.*
5 EA 11.
6 EA 3, 7.
7 E.g., EA 3, 7, 34.
8 EA 26; cf. EA 27–9.
9 EA 9.
10 Augur: EA 35. Loans of specialists: Carlo Zaccagnini, "Patterns of mobility among ancient Near Eastern craftsmen," *Journal of Near Eastern Studies* 42, no. 4 (1983), 249–55.
11 EA 1–2.
12 EA 3–4.
13 EA 3.
14 EA 12.
15 EA 11.
16 Courtiers: e.g., EA 11. Merchants: EA 8 (Babylon); EA 39–40 (Cyprus).
17 EA 7.
18 EA 8.
19 Ibid.; cf. EA 39.
20 EA 3; cf. EA 28, 29, 35 for similar cases.
21 A man of Kaska: EA 1.38.; Kushite staff (presumably enslaved): EA 49.19–20.
22 Eric H. Cline, *Sailing the Wine-Dark Sea: International Trade and the Late Bronze Age Aegean,* Oxford: Tempus Reparatum, 1994, 35, 106–7; Christoph Bachhuber, "Aegean interest on the Uluburun ship," *American Journal of Archaeology* 110, no. 3 (2006), 356–7; Thomas F. Tartaron, *Maritime Networks in the Mycenaean World,* New York: Cambridge University Press, 2013, 28.
23 Tzveta Manolova, "The Levant," in Irene S. Lemos and Antonis Kotsonas, eds., *A Companion to the Archaeology of Early Greece and the Mediterranean,* Chichester: Wiley Blackwell, 2019, 1190.
24 Preference for imitations: Christopher Mee, "Mycenaean Greece, the Aegean and beyond," in Cynthia W. Shelmerdine, ed., *The Cambridge Companion to the Aegean Bronze Age,* Cambridge: Cambridge University Press, 2008, 380.
25 Oxhide ingots: Serena Sabatini, "Revisiting Late Bronze Age oxhide ingots: meanings, questions and perspectives," in Ole Christian Aslaksen, ed., *Local and Global Perspectives on Mobility in the Eastern Mediterranean,* Athens: Norwegian Institute at Athens, 2016; Serena Sabatini, "Late Bronze Age oxhide and oxhide-like ingots from areas other than the Mediterranean: problems and challenges," *Oxford Journal of Archaeology* 35, no. 1 (2016).
26 Tartaron, *Maritime Networks in the Mycenaean World,* 29; Michael L. Galaty, Helena Tomas, and William A. Parkinson, "Bronze Age European elites: from the Aegean to the Adriatic and back again," in A. Bernard Knapp and Peter van Dommelen, eds., *The Cambridge Prehistory of the Bronze and Iron Age Mediterranean,* Cambridge: Cambridge University Press, 2015, 169; Manolova, "The Levant," 1191; Artemis Georgiou and Maria Iacovou, "Cyprus," in Lemos and Kotsonas, eds., *A Companion to the Archaeology of Early Greece and the Mediterranean,* 1139. Tell Abu Hawam, which has the largest amount of Greek pottery in the Levant after Ugarit, also has forty times as much material from Cyprus: Manolova, "The

Levant," 1190. Cypro-Minoan script: Philippa M. Steele, *A Linguistic History of Ancient Cyprus: The Non-Greek Languages and Their Relations with Greek, c. 1600–300 BC*, Cambridge: Cambridge University Press, 2013, 9–98. The name "Cypro-Minoan" comes from the clear relationship between this script and Linear A.

27 Susan Sherratt, "A globalizing Bronze and Iron Age Mediterranean," in Tamar Hodos, ed., *The Routledge Handbook of Archaeology and Globalization*, London: Routledge, 2017, 605–6; Jeffrey P. Emanuel, "Seafaring and shipwreck archaeology," in Carolina López-Ruiz and Brian R. Doak, eds., *The Oxford Handbook of the Phoenician and Punic Mediterranean*, Oxford: Oxford University Press, 2019; Tzveta Manolova and Joachim Bretschneider, "An unprecedented depiction of a Syro-Canaanite oared galley on a jar sealing from Tell Tweini," in Joachim Bretschneider and Greta Jans, eds., *About Tell Tweini (Syria): Artifacts, Ecofacts and Landscape*, Leuven: Peeters, 2019, 130.

28 Latest edition of the Aegean list: Elmar Edel and Manfred Görg, *Die Ortsnamenlisten im nördlichen Säulenhof des Totentempels Amenophis' III*, Wiesbaden: Harrassowitz, 2005; see also Eric H. Cline and Steven M. Stannish, "Sailing the Great Green Sea? Amenhotep III's 'Aegean List' from Kom el-Hetan, once more," *Journal of Ancient Egyptian Interconnections* 3, no. 2 (2011), from where I take this translation.

29 Cline and Stannish, "Sailing the Great Green Sea?," 9–10.

30 Eric H. Cline, "An unpublished Amenhotep III faience plaque from Mycenae," *Journal of the American Oriental Society* 110, no. 2 (1990); Eric H. Cline, "Egyptian and Near Eastern imports at Late Bronze Age Mycenae," in Davies and Schofield, eds., *Egypt, the Aegean and the Levant;* Cemal Pulak, "The Uluburun shipwreck and Late Bronze Age trade," in Joan Aruz, Kim Benzel, and Jean M. Evans, eds., *Beyond Babylon: Art, Trade, and Diplomacy in the Second Millennium B.C.*, New York: Metropolitan Museum of Art, 2008, 300. The quantity and variety of Egyptian material found at Mycenae suggest that it was a standard point of entry to the Aegean market.

31 Uluburun wreck: Cemal Pulak, "The Uluburun shipwreck: an overview," *International Journal of Nautical Archaeology* 27 (1998); Cemal Pulak, "The cargo of the Uluburun ship and evidence for trade with the Aegean and beyond," in Larissa Bonfante and Vassos Karageorghis, eds., *Italy and Cyprus in Antiquity 1500–450 B.C.*, Nicosia: Costakis and Leto Severis Foundation, 2001; Pulak, "The Uluburun shipwreck and Late Bronze Age trade"; Bachhuber, "Aegean interest on the Uluburun ship," 347, all liberally drawn upon in the following discussion.

32 Copper sources confirmed by lead isotope analysis: Pulak, "The Uluburun shipwreck and Late Bronze Age trade," 292. Tin sources: Wayne Powell et al., "Tin from Uluburun shipwreck shows small-scale commodity exchange fueled continental tin supply across Late Bronze Age Eurasia," *Science Advances* 8, no. 48 (2022)

33 Discussion: Federico Zangani, "Amarna and Uluburun: reconsidering patterns of exchange in the Late Bronze Age," *Palestine Exploration Quarterly* 148, no. 4 (2016).

34 Cf. Pulak, "The Uluburun shipwreck and Late Bronze Age trade," 300–2.

35 M. L. West, *The East Face of Helicon: West Asiatic Elements in Early Poetry and Myth*, Oxford: Clarendon Press, 1997, 13.

36 Ibid., 31.

37 Carolina López-Ruiz, *Phoenicians and the Making of the Mediterranean*, Cambridge, Mass.: Harvard University Press, 2021, 218–25.

38 Sarah P. Morris, *Daidalos and the Origins of Greek Art*, Princeton: Princeton University Press, 1992, 108–10, noting examples of shrines at Melos, Tiryns, and Mycenae, and a model at Ugarit.

39 López-Ruiz, *Phoenicians and the Making of the Mediterranean*, 209.

40 Sacrifice and feasting: ibid., with West, *The East Face of Helicon*, 42.

41 For a survey of opinions on the precise meaning of the term, see Gary Beckman, Trevor Bryce, and Eric Cline, "Introduction: The Ahhiyawa Problem," in Gary Beckman, Trevor Bryce, and Eric Cline, eds., *The Ahhiyawa Texts*, Atlanta: Society of Biblical Literature, 2011. AhT numbering refers to the catalog in Beckman, Bryce, and Cline, eds., *The Ahhiyawa Texts.*

42 AhT 3; cf. AhT 22 for an earlier reference to the (same?) enemy "man" of Ahhiya.

43 AhT 1B A l. 23–4.

44 Mee, "Mycenaean Greece, the Aegean and beyond," 371–3.

45 Beckman, Bryce, and Cline, "Introduction: The Ahhiyawa Problem," 3; Mary R. Bachvarova, *From Hittite to Homer: The Anatolian Background of Ancient Greek Epic*, Cambridge: Cambridge University Press, 2016, 3.

46 AhT 1A §25'; see for later relations AhT 12; AhT 20.

47 Greetings: AhT 4 (Hatti to Ahhiyawa); AhT 6 (Ahhiyawa to Hatti—where the Ahhiyawan king actually only calls himself Great King). Gifts: AhT 8 §5.

48 Ian Rutherford, "Diplomatic marriage as an engine for religious change: the case of Assuwa and Ahhiyawa," in Michele Bianconi, ed., *Linguistic and Cultural Interactions Between Greece and Anatolia: In Search of the Golden Fleece*, Leiden: Brill, 2021, 167, on AhT 20 §24.

49 AhT 6.

50 Jorrit M. Kelder, "A thousand black ships: maritime trade, diplomatic relations, and the rise of Mycenae," in Rolf Strootman, Floris van den Eijnde, and Roy van Wijk, eds., *Empires of the Sea: Maritime Power Networks in World History*, Leiden: Brill, 2019. Some scholars even suggest that Mycenae ruled over the other mainland states in this era (e.g., Jorrit M. Kelder, *The Kingdom of Mycenae: A Great Kingdom in the Late Bronze Age Aegean*, Bethesda: CDL Press, 2010; Birgitta Eder and Reinhard Jung, " 'Unus pro omnibus, omnes pro uno': the Mycenaean palace system," in Jörg Weilhartner and Florian Ruppenstein, eds., *Tradition and Innovation in the Mycenaean Palatial Polities*, Vienna: Österreichischen Akademie der Wissenschaften, 2015), but others find differences in administrative practices hard to reconcile with this theory: Oliver Dickinson, "What conclusions might be drawn from the archaeology of Mycenaean civilization about political structure in the Aegean?," in Jorrit M. Kelder and Willemijn J. I. Waal, eds., From *"LUGAL.GAL" to "Wanax": Kingship and Political Organisation in the Late Bronze Age Aegean*, Leiden: Sidestone Press, 2019.

51 Nicholas G. Blackwell, "Making the Lion Gate relief at Mycenae: tool marks and foreign influence," *American Journal of Archaeology* 118, no. 3 (2014): 481–2.

52 Pausanias 2.16.5. Hittite construction techniques at Tiryns: Blackwell, "Making the Lion Gate relief at Mycenae," 477.

53 Fourteenth-century mainland palaces in Cretan style at Pylos and nearby Iklaina: Michael C. Nelson, "Pylos, block masonry and monumental architecture in the

Late Bronze Age Peloponnese," in Joachim Bretschneider, Jan Driessen, and Karel van Lerberghe, eds., *Power and Architecture: Monumental Architecture in the Bronze Age Near East and Aegean,* Leuven: Peeters, 2006; Michael B. Cosmopoulos, "State formation in Greece: Iklaina and the unification of Mycenaean Pylos," *American Journal of Archaeology* 123, no. 3 (2019).

54 Nelson, "Pylos, block masonry and monumental architecture," 148. Evidence for the position of the throne does not survive at Mycenae itself, where that side of the room has fallen into the ravine, but given the parallels at Tiryns and later Pylos it seems certain. On what actually went on in these rooms, see Jarrett L. Farmer and Michael F. Lane, "The ins and outs of the Great Megaron: symbol, performance, and elite identities around and between Mycenaean palaces," *Studi Micenei ed Egeo-Anatolici* 2 (2016).

55 Stefan Hiller, "Knossos and Pylos: a case of special relationship?," *Cretan Studies* 5 (1996), 76–7, 80; Nelson, "Pylos, block masonry and monumental architecture"; Michael C. Nelson, "The architecture of the Palace of Nestor," in Frederick A. Cooper and Diane Fortenberry, eds., *The Minnesota Pylos Project, 1990–98,* Oxford: British Archaeological Reports, 2017, 361–2.

56 Blackwell, "Making the Lion Gate relief at Mycenae."

57 It is possible that some or even all of the grave markers date to this era.

58 AhT 4; c. 1250 BCE.

59 AhT 2; late thirteenth century BCE.

6. Alphabet City

1 Amnon Altman, "The struggle among the Lebanese port-cities to control seaborne trade in the mid-fourteenth century BCE," *Ugarit-Forschungen* 45 (2014). See for instance EA [El Amarna] 55, 59, 126, 145–6.

2 Louise M. Pryke, "The many complaints to pharaoh of Rib-Addi of Byblos," *Journal of the American Oriental Society* 131, no. 3 (2011).

3 Marguerite Yon, *The City of Ugarit at Tell Ras Shamra,* Winona Lake: Eisenbrauns, 2006, is an excellent introduction to the site.

4 William W. Hallo and K. Lawson Younger, eds., *Context of Scripture,* Leiden: Brill, 2003, 1.106 361–62.

5 *Palais Royal d'Ugarit* 4, 37–52.

6 Trade: Carol Bell, "The merchants of Ugarit: oligarchs of the Late Bronze Age trade in metals?," in Demetrios Michaelides and George Papasavvas, eds., *Eastern Mediterranean Metallurgy in the Second Millennium BC,* Oxford: Oxbow, 2012, 181–2. Sardinian lead: Naama Yahalom-Mack et al., "Incised Late Bronze Age lead ingots from the southern anchorage of Caesarea," *Journal of Archaeological Science: Reports* 41 (2022). Central/western European tin: Daniel Berger et al., "Isotope systematics and chemical composition of tin ingots from Mochlos (Crete) and other Late Bronze Age sites in the eastern Mediterranean Sea: an ultimate key to tin provenance?," *PLOS ONE* 14, no. 6 (2019), with Ehud Galili, Noel Gale, and Baruch Rosen, "A Late Bronze Age shipwreck with a metal cargo from Hishuley Carmel, Israel," *International Journal of Nautical Archaeology* 42, no. 1 (2013), 18–19, for the markings.

7 Philip J. Boyes, "Negotiating imperialism and resistance in Late Bronze Age

Ugarit: the rise of alphabetic cuneiform," *Cambridge Archaeological Journal* 29, no. 2 (2019), 191–3; Yon, *The City of Ugarit,* 21.

8 Alashiya: RS [Ras Shamra] 94.2475, with Bell, "The merchants of Ugarit," 183–4. Egypt: Itamar Singer, "A political history of Ugarit," in Wilfred Watson and Nicholas Wyatt, eds., *Handbook of Ugaritic Studies,* Leiden: Brill, 1999, 708–11.

9 Juan-Pablo Vita, "The society of Ugarit," in Watson and Wyatt, eds., *Handbook of Ugaritic Studies,* 471–2; Kevin McGeough, " 'What is not in my house you must give me': agents of exchange according to the textual evidence from Ugarit," in Birgitta Eder and Regine Pruzsinszky, eds., *Policies of Exchange: Political Systems and Modes of Interaction in the Aegean and the Near East in the 2nd Millennium BCE,* Vienna: Österreichischen Akademie der Wissenschaften, 2015, 90–3.

10 Bruce Routledge and Kevin McGeough, "Just what collapsed? A network perspective on 'palatial' and 'private' trade at Ugarit," in Christoph Bachhuber and R. Gareth Roberts, eds., *Forces of Transformation: The End of the Bronze Age in the Mediterranean,* Oxford: Oxbow, 2009; Bell, "The merchants of Ugarit."

11 RS 34.124.

12 RS 16.238+254.

13 Vita, "The society of Ugarit," 463–4.

14 Ibid., 457–63.

15 Raid: RS 20.182A+B with Anson F. Rainey, "Who is a Canaanite? A review of the textual evidence," *Bulletin of the American Schools of Oriental Research,* no. 304 (1996), 5.

16 RS 17.130 and 18.003 (= *Palais Royal d'Ugarit* 4, 102–5), with Singer, "A political history of Ugarit," 660–1.

17 RS 1.002; see also RS 17.100A+B and (more fragmentary) RS 24.270A, RS 24.270B, RS 24.650B, RS 24.652G+K. Trans. at Dennis Pardee, *Ritual and Cult at Ugarit,* Atlanta: Society of Biblical Literature, 2002, no. 22. I am grateful to Seth Sanders for discussion of this text.

18 Pardee, *Ritual and Cult at Ugarit,* 78–9.

19 Paolo Merlo and Paolo Xella, "The Ugaritic cultic texts," in Watson and Wyatt, eds., *Handbook of Ugaritic Studies;* Pardee and Lewis, *Ritual and Cult at Ugarit,* 78.

20 For the significance of the ritual, see Seth L. Sanders, "What was the alphabet for? The rise of written vernaculars and the making of Israelite National Literature," *Maarav* 11, no. 1 (2004), 52–4, and Seth L. Sanders, *The Invention of Hebrew,* Urbana: University of Illinois Press, 2009, 59–60.

21 Sons of Emar: Emar 369. 1–3, edited at Daniel E. Fleming, *The Installation of Baal's High Priestess at Emar: A Window on Ancient Syrian Religion,* Atlanta: Scholars Press, 1992, 10, with Daniel E. Fleming, "A limited kingship," *Ugarit-Forschungen* 24 (1992), 60–3, 67, and Sanders, *The Invention of Hebrew,* 60.

22 Sanders, "What was the alphabet for?," 45–7. For the original insight that written vernaculars are not the norm, but replace more cosmopolitan languages at specific historical moments, see Sheldon Pollack, "Cosmopolitan and vernacular in history," *Public Culture* 12, no. 3 (2000). On writing at Ugarit see most recently Philip J. Boyes, *Script and Society: The Social Context of Writing Practices in Late Bronze Age Ugarit,* Oxford: Oxbow, 2021.

23 Orly Goldwasser, "Canaanites reading hieroglyphs: Horus is Hathor?—the invention of the alphabet in Sinai," *Ägypten und Levante* 16 (2006); Christopher

Rollston, "The emergence of alphabetic scripts," in Rebecca Hasselbach-Andee, ed., *A Companion to Ancient Near Eastern Languages*, Chichester: Wiley Blackwell, 2020, 75–6. Similar Levantine alphabetic signs appear around the same time or even a little earlier on rocks far to the south at Wadi el-Hôl in Egypt's western desert, close to Luxor (John Coleman Darnell et al., "Two early alphabetic inscriptions from the Wadi el-Ḥôl: new evidence for the origin of the alphabet from the western desert of Egypt," *Annual of the American Schools of Oriental Research* 59 [2005]).

24 "I was here": Sanders, "What was the alphabet for?," 44.

25 Goldwasser, "Canaanites reading hieroglyphs."

26 Gordon J. Hamilton, *The Origins of the West Semitic Alphabet in Egyptian Scripts*, Washington, D.C.: Catholic Biblical Association of America, 2000, with Goldwasser, "Canaanites reading hieroglyphs," 130–53. The Wadi el-Hôl inscriptions are also found in the vicinity of hieroglyphic inscriptions. Even earlier evidence for alphabetic writing has now been tentatively identified in signs inscribed on four clay cylinders buried in a tomb dating to the mid-third millennium BCE at Umm el-Marra in modern Syria. They were excavated in 2004 but the signs were only identified as "letters" in 2021: Glenn M. Schwartz, "Non-cuneiform writing at third-millennium Umm el-Marra, Syria: evidence of an early alphabetic tradition?," *Pasiphae* 13 (2021). These inscriptions are however very short and they cannot be deciphered, so it is as yet unclear whether this really is alphabetic writing. If that interpretation is confirmed in the future, it would not refute the derivation of alphabetic signs from Egyptian writing systems, it would just push it to an earlier date. I thank Seth Sanders for discussion of this point.

27 Aaron Koller, "The diffusion of the alphabet in the second millennium BCE: on the movements of scribal ideas from Egypt to the Levant, Mesopotamia, and Yemen," *Journal of Ancient Egyptian Interconnections* 20 (2018); Rollston, "The emergence of alphabetic scripts," 73, for a list.

28 Sanders, *The Invention of Hebrew*, 50.

29 Christopher Rollston, *Writing and Literacy in the World of Ancient Israel: Epigraphic Evidence from the Iron Age*, Atlanta: Society of Biblical Literature, 2010, 17.

30 Sanders, *The Invention of Hebrew*, 54.

31 Roland Robertson, "Glocalization: time-space and homogeneity-heterogeneity," in Mike Featherstone, Scott Lash, and Roland Robertson, eds., *Global Modernities*, London: Sage, 1995.

32 See Beckman in Hallo and Younger, eds., *Context of Scripture*, 1.55, p. 149.

33 Aaron Tugendhaft, *Baal and the Politics of Poetry*, London: Routledge, 2017, 30–1.

34 *KTU* [*Keilalphabetische Texte aus Ugarit*] 1.3 ii 7–8, 11–14, trans. Pardee in Hallo and Younger, *Context of Scripture*, 1.86, p. 250.

35 Sanders, *The Invention of Hebrew*, 51.

36 For what follows and more, see ibid., 51–3; Aaron Tugendhaft, "Unsettling sovereignty: politics and poetics in the Baal Cycle," *Journal of the American Oriental Society* 132, no. 3 (2012), 367–8; Tugendhaft, *Baal and the Politics of Poetry*, 63–99.

37 *KTU* 3.1.24–6, with Tugendhaft, "Unsettling sovereignty," 369; Aaron Tugendhaft, "Sovereignty and the gods: Ugaritic literature in the Hittite empire," *History of Political Thought* 38, no. 4 (2017), 593.

38 For a discussion of the Baal Cycle in relation to kingship at Ugarit see Nicholas Wyatt, "The religious role of the king at Ugarit," in K. Lawson Younger, Jr., ed., *Ugarit at Seventy-Five,* Winona Lake: Eisenbrauns, 2007.
39 *KTU* 1.114 = RS 24.258, R 22–3, trans. Nicholas Wyatt, *Religious Texts from Ugarit,* Sheffield: Sheffield Academic Press, 2002, 412.
40 *KTU* 1.14–16, trans. Pardee in Hallo and Younger, *Context of Scripture,* 1.102 333–43.
41 Gary Beckman, "Akkadian documents from Ugarit," in Paul W. Wallace and Andreas G. Orphanides, eds., *Sources for the History of Cyprus,* vol. 2: *Near Eastern and Aegean Texts from the Third to the First Millennia BCE,* Nicosia: Cyprus College, 1996, 27. Cypriot origins of tablet clay: Yuval Goren et al., "The location of Alashiya: new evidence from petrographic investigation of Alashiyan tablets from El-Amarna and Ugarit," *American Journal of Archaeology* 107, no. 2 (2003).
42 RS 20.238, trans. Beckman, "Akkadian documents from Ugarit," 27. The precise dating of this correspondence within the era of troubles is still debated. A newly published copy of a letter found in the House of Urtenu suggests that the king of Ugarit also sought help from Karkemish as enemies approached the city: Sylvie Lackenbacher and Florence Malbran-Labat, *Lettres en Akkadien de la «Maison d'Urtenu»,* Leuven: Peeters, 2016, 33–5 (no. 12).
43 RS 20.18, trans. Beckman, "Akkadian documents from Ugarit," 27.
44 Eric H. Cline, *1177 B.C.: The Year Civilization Collapsed,* Princeton: Princeton University Press, 2014, 151.

7. Regime Change

1 Ian Morris, *Archaeology as Cultural History: Words and Things in Iron Age Greece,* Oxford: Blackwell, 2000, 219.
2 Marc Van de Mieroop, *A History of the Ancient Near East, ca. 3000–323 BC,* 3rd ed., Chichester: Wiley Blackwell, 2016, 202–20.
3 Jürgen Seeher, "Die Zerstörung der Stadt Ḫattuša," in Gernot Wilhelm, ed., *Akten des IV. Internationalen Kongresses für Hethitologie, Würzburg, 4.-8. Oktober 1999,* Wiesbaden: Harrassowitz, 2001.
4 Maria Iacovou, "Cyprus during the Iron Age I period (Late Cypriot IIC–IIIA)," in Margreet L. Steiner and Ann E. Killebrew, eds., *The Oxford Handbook of the Archaeology of the Levant c. 8000–332 BCE,* Oxford: Oxford University Press, 2014, 665; Artemis Georgiou and Maria Iacovou, "Cyprus," in Irene S. Lemos and Antonis Kotsonas, eds., *A Companion to the Archaeology of Early Greece and the Mediterranean,* Chichester: Wiley Blackwell, 2019, 1142.
5 The term "Dark Ages" is first used for this era in the late nineteenth century (e.g., Chrestos Tsountas and James Irving Manatt, *The Mycenaean Age: A Study of the Monuments and Culture of Pre-Homeric Greece,* London: Macmillan, 1897, 365; "Dark Age," which becomes the preferred phrase, is first found in Gilbert Murray, *The Rise of the Greek Epic,* Oxford: Clarendon Press, 1907, 27. On this changing terminology see Antonis Kotsonas, "Politics of periodization and the archaeology of early Greece," *American Journal of Archaeology* 120, no. 2 (2016), and Sarah C. Murray, "Lights and darks: data, labeling, and language in the history of scholarship on early Greece," *Hesperia* 87, no. 1 (2018).

6 For a recent survey of current hypotheses and their weaknesses, see A. Bernard Knapp and Sturt W. Manning, "Crisis in context: the end of the Late Bronze Age in the eastern Mediterranean," *American Journal of Archaeology* 120, no. 1 (2016). Older explanations focusing on a mythical "Dorian" invasion were abandoned in the 1970s, with rare exceptions such as Robert Drews, *The Coming of the Greeks: Indo-European Conquests in the Aegean and the Near East,* Princeton: Princeton University Press, 1988, and Birgitta Eder, *Argolis, Lakonien, Messenien: vom Ende der mykenischen Palastzeit bis zur Einwanderung der Dorier,* Vienna: Österreichischen Akademie der Wissenschaften, 1998; see on this Jonathan M. Hall, *Ethnic Identity in Greek Antiquity,* Cambridge: Cambridge University Press, 1997, 4–16.

7 On the name, see R. Gareth Roberts, "Identity, choice, and the Year 8 reliefs of Ramesses III at Medinet Habu," in Christoph Bachhuber and R. Gareth Roberts, eds., *Forces of Transformation: The End of the Bronze Age in the Mediterranean,* Oxford: Oxbow, 2009; Ann E. Killebrew and Gunnar Lehmann, *The Philistines and Other "Sea Peoples" in Text and Archaeology,* Atlanta: Society of Biblical Literature, 2013, 1–5. Further discussion: Louise A. Hitchcock and Aren M. Maeir, "Yo-ho, yo-ho, a *seren*'s life for me," *World Archaeology* 46, no. 4 (2014); Louise A. Hitchcock and Aren M. Maeir, "A pirate's life for me: the maritime culture of the Sea Peoples," *Palestine Exploration Quarterly* 148, no. 4 (2016); Louise A. Hitchcock and Aren M. Maeir, "Fifteen men on a dead *seren*'s chest: yo ho ho and a krater of wine," in Atilla Batmaz et al., eds., *Context and Connection: Studies on the Archaeology of the Ancient Near East in Honour of Antonio Sagona,* Leuven: Peeters, 2017; cf. A. Bernard Knapp, *Seafaring and Seafarers in the Bronze Age Eastern Mediterranean,* Leiden: Sidestone Press, 2018, 37–41.

8 Hitchcock and Maeir, "Yo-ho, yo-ho, a *seren*'s life for me," 631.

9 Susan Lupack, "A view from outside the palace: the sanctuary and the *damos* in Mycenaean economy and society," *American Journal of Archaeology* 115, no. 2 (2011), 212–15; Dimitri Nakassis, *Individuals and Society in Mycenaean Pylos,* Leiden: Brill, 2013, 12.

10 For an up-to-date picture of palatial activity, see Cynthia W. Shelmerdine, "Mycenaean society," in Yves Duhoux and Anna Morpurgo Davies, eds., *A Companion to Linear B: Mycenaean Greek Texts and Their World,* Leuven: Peeters, 2008; Cynthia W. Shelmerdine, "The individual and the state in Mycenaean Greece," *Bulletin of the Institute of Classical Studies* 54, no. 1 (2011).

11 Earthquakes: Eric H. Cline, *1177 B.C.: The Year Civilization Collapsed,* Princeton: Princeton University Press, 2014, 140–2. Climate change: critical assessment at Knapp and Manning, "Crisis in context," but see more recently, for instance, Sturt W. Manning et al., "Severe multi-year drought coincident with Hittite collapse around 1198–1196 BC," *Nature* 614, no. 7949 (2023).

12 Structural risks: Christopher Monroe, *Scales of Fate: Trade, Tradition, and Transformation in the Eastern Mediterranean, ca. 1350–1175 BCE,* Münster: Ugarit-Verlag, 2009, 294–6. Network interdependence: Cline, *1177 B.C.*, esp. 160–3.

13 Early signs of this revolution in the modern treatment and interpretation of the Dark Age are found in Anthony M. Snodgrass, *The Dark Age of Greece: An Archaeological Survey of the Eleventh to the Eighth Centuries BC,* Edinburgh: Edinburgh University Press, 1971. See most recently on the archaeological

evidence Irene S. Lemos and Antonis Kotsonas, eds., *A Companion to the Archaeology of Early Greece and the Mediterranean,* Chichester Wiley Blackwell, 2019, and Guy D. Middleton, *Collapse and Transformation: The Late Bronze Age to Early Iron Age in the Aegean,* Oxford: Oxbow, 2020.

14 Detailed surveys: Irene Lemos, "Communities in transformation: an archaeological survey from the 12th to the 9th century BC," *Pharos* 20 (2014); Birgitta Eder and Irene S. Lemos, "From the collapse of the Mycenaean palaces to the emergence of Early Iron Age communities," in Lemos and Kotsonas, eds., *A Companion to the Archaeology of Early Greece and the Mediterranean.*

15 James C. Scott, *The Art of Not Being Governed: An Anarchist History of Upland Southeast Asia,* New Haven: Yale University Press, 2009, 220–37. Even in Classical Athens, Plato suggested that the invention of writing had caused people's memories to atrophy (*Phaedrus* 275a).

16 Dimitri Nakassis, "Time and the other Greeks," in Katherine Blouin and Ben Akrigg, eds., *The Routledge Handbook of Classics, Colonialism, and Postcolonial Theory* (forthcoming).

17 Effects of demography on trade: Sarah Murray, *The Collapse of the Mycenaean Economy: Imports, Trade, and Institutions, 1300–700 BCE,* New York: Cambridge University Press, 2017, 210–46.

18 Tzveta Manolova, "The Levant," in Lemos and Kotsonas, eds., *A Companion to the Archaeology of Early Greece and the Mediterranean,* 1202 (18 percent as opposed to 5 percent).

19 Imports to palaces: Murray, *The Collapse of the Mycenaean Economy,* 83, with 248 for the difficulties of interpretation this presents; Dimitri Nakassis, "The economy," in Lemos and Kotsonas, eds., *A Companion to the Archaeology of Early Greece and the Mediterranean,* 281–2, for the role played by the palaces in trade.

20 Robin Osborne, *Greece in the Making, 1200–479 B.C.,* 2nd ed., London: Routledge, 2009, 36–7; Murray, *The Collapse of the Mycenaean Economy,* 85–8.

21 Exports to the Levant: Manolova, "The Levant," 1190. Trade with Cyprus: Eder and Lemos, "From the collapse of the Mycenaean palaces to the emergence of Early Iron Age communities," 138.

22 Murray, *The Collapse of the Mycenaean Economy,* 92–3. Exceptions to European insulation from the crises farther east include the Po Valley, where many settlements were abandoned around 1200 and the whole valley drastically depopulated. Local explanations for this include drought, famine, disease, and the over-exploitation of the land, but it seems likely that trouble in the Aegean had some knock-on effects: Claudio Cavazzuti et al., "Mobile elites at Frattesina: flows of people in a Late Bronze Age 'port of trade' in northern Italy," *Antiquity* 93, no. 369 (2019), 625.

23 Kristian Kristiansen and Paulina Suchowska-Ducke, "Connected histories: the dynamics of Bronze Age interaction and trade 1500–1100 BC," *Proceedings of the Prehistoric Society* 81 (2015), 373–84.

24 Tollense: Tobias Uhlig et al., "Lost in combat? A scrap metal find from the Bronze Age battlefield site at Tollense," *Antiquity* 93, no. 371 (2019).

25 Kristiansen and Suchowska-Ducke, "Connected histories," 373.

26 Frank Falkenstein, "The development of burial rites from the tumulus to the Urnfield Culture in southern central Europe," in Elisabetta Borgna and Sylvie Müller Celka, eds., *Ancestral Landscapes: Burial Mounds in the Copper and Bronze*

Ages, Lyon: Maison de l'Orient et de la Méditerranée, 2012; Harry Fokkens and David Fontijn, "The Bronze Age in the Low Countries," in Harry Fokkens and Anthony Harding, eds., *The Oxford Handbook of the European Bronze Age*, Oxford: Oxford University Press, 2013, 558.

27 Andrew Sherratt, "What would a Bronze Age world system look like? Relations between temperate Europe and the Mediterranean in later prehistory," *Journal of European Archaeology* 1 (1993), 36, and fig. 10. Contribution of Aegean technologies: ibid., 34. There were exceptions: the Nordic bronze industry seems to collapse in this era, leading to a lot more recycling of metals in the far north, wear and tear on weapons, and the end of the long-distance luxury trade to Scandinavia: Kristiansen and Suchowska-Ducke, "Connected histories," 378.

28 Naue II flange-hilted swords: Kristiansen and Suchowska-Ducke, "Connected histories."

29 Florian Ruppenstein, "Cremation burials in Greece from the Late Bronze Age to the Early Iron Age: continuity or change?," in Michaela Lochner and Florian Ruppenstein, eds., *Brandbestattungen von der mittleren Donau bis zur Ägäis zwischen 1300 und 750 v. Chr.*, Vienna: Österreichischen Akademie der Wissenschaften, 2013, 187–9. Ruppenstein also notes the appearance in the Aegean in this era of a very few cemeteries where all the dead were cremated, and associates them with migrant communities, probably from the western Balkans (189–90).

30 Cargoes: Reinhard Jung, "Push and pull factors of the Sea Peoples between Italy and the Levant," in Jan Driessen, ed., *An Archaeology of Forced Migration: Crisis-Induced Mobility and the Collapse of the 13th c.* BCE *Eastern Mediterranean*, Louvain-la-Neuve: Presses universitaires de Louvain, 2018, 280–1. Cypriot imports: Murray, *The Collapse of the Mycenaean Economy*, 92–3.

31 Sigrid Deger-Jalkotzy, "Late Mycenaean warrior tombs," in Sigrid Deger-Jalkotzy and Irene S. Lemos, eds., *Ancient Greece: From the Mycenaean Palaces to the Age of Homer*, Edinburgh: Edinburgh University Press, 2006; Osborne, *Greece in the Making*, 59–62. Imported goods: Murray, *The Collapse of the Mycenaean Economy*, 258.

32 James Whitley, "Social diversity in Dark Age Greece," *Annual of the British School at Athens* 86 (1991).

33 Ibid., 350.

34 Deger-Jalkotzy, "Late Mycenaean warrior tombs," 172.

35 Susan Sherratt, "A globalizing Bronze and Iron Age Mediterranean," in Tamar Hodos, ed., *The Routledge Handbook of Archaeology and Globalization*, London: Routledge, 2017, 611.

36 Susan Sherratt and Andrew Sherratt, "The growth of the Mediterranean economy in the early first millennium BC," *World Archaeology* 24, no. 3 (1993), 362; Iacovou, "Cyprus during the Iron Age I period (Late Cypriot IIC–IIIA)," 670; Susan Sherratt, "'Reading the texts': archaeology and the Homeric question," *Antiquity* 64, no. 245 (1990), 811; Jonathan M. Hall, *A History of the Archaic Greek World, ca. 1200–479* BCE, 2nd ed., Chichester: Wiley Blackwell, 2014, 48.

37 Eder and Lemos, "From the collapse of the Mycenaean palaces to the emergence of Early Iron Age communities," 139.

38 Stefanos Gimatzidis and Bernhard Weninger, "Radiocarbon dating the Greek Protogeometric and Geometric periods: the evidence of Sindos," *PLOS ONE* 15, no. 5 (2020); Stefanos Gimatzidis, "The Greek Geometric pottery from Sidon and

its implications on Mediterranean chronology," *BAAL: Bulletin d'archéologie et d'architecture libanaise* 54–5 (2021–2).

39 The Trojan War does not provide the only examples of Bronze Age elements in later myth: for ingredients that contribute to later stories about Greek Thebes and its neighbors, myths almost as well known in antiquity as those of the Trojan War, see Emily Vermeule, "Baby Aigisthos and the Bronze Age," *Proceedings of the Cambridge Philological Society* 33 (1987).

40 Barbara Graziosi, *Homer*, Oxford: Oxford University Press, 2016, 5–14.

41 See *Odyssey* 1.153–5, 1.336–60, 22.331–7 for Phemius the palace bard on the island of Ithaka, and e.g., 8.47–108 for the blind bard Demodocus who sings for the king of the Phaeacians.

42 Ian Morris, "The use and abuse of Homer," in Douglas Cairns, ed., *Oxford Readings in Homer's* Iliad, Oxford: Oxford University Press, 2001, 58–64, on modern traditions, noting occasional counter-examples.

43 The classic works demonstrating the oral composition of the Homeric epics by comparison with the methods of twentieth-century oral poets in the Balkans are Albert Bates Lord, *The Singer of Tales*, Cambridge, Mass.: Harvard University Press, 1960, and Adam Parry, ed., *The Making of Homeric Verse: The Collected Papers of Milman Parry*, Oxford: Clarendon Press, 1971.

44 For an excellent brief summary of the evidence for the oral composition of the Homeric poems, see Graziosi, *Homer*, 15–27.

45 Johannes Haubold, "Greek epic: a Near Eastern genre?," *Proceedings of the Cambridge Philological Society* 48 (2002), 4, for the early term "song" for these poems.

46 Homer, *Iliad* 10.260–5.

47 Sherratt, " 'Reading the texts,' " 810–11, highlights the example of Hector's shield (*Iliad* 6.117)—which at *Iliad* 7.250 is described by contrast as completely round.

48 Angus M. Bowie, *Iliad, Book III*, Cambridge: Cambridge University Press, 2019, 42–3.

49 Morris, "The use and abuse of Homer," 62–3.

50 Sherratt, " 'Reading the texts,' " 810, 819.

51 Morris, *Archaeology as Cultural History*, 238–9; Ann C. Gunter, "Orientalism and orientalization in the Iron Age Mediterranean," in Brian A. Brown and Marian H. Feldman, eds., *Critical Approaches to Ancient Near Eastern Art*, Boston: De Gruyter, 2014, 85; Manolova, "The Levant," 1203. The Cypriot port of Amathous appears to have been a regular stopping point en route.

52 John K. Papadopoulos, "Phantom Euboians," *Journal of Mediterranean Archaeology* 10, no. 2 (1997), 200; Manolova, "The Levant," 1205.

53 Lefkandi Tomb 79 (c. 875–850 BCE), with Papadopoulos, "Phantom Euboians," 192; Christopher Monroe, "Marginalizing civilization: the Phoenician redefinition of power circa 1300–800 BC," in Kristian Kristiansen, Thomas Lindkvist, and Janken Myrdal, eds., *Trade and Civilisation: Economic Networks and Cultural Ties, from Prehistory to the Early Modern Era*, Cambridge: Cambridge University Press, 2018, 208; and Manolova, "The Levant," 1206.

8. I Am Not Your Servant

1 *Journey of Wenamun:* Alan H. Gardiner, *Late-Egyptian Stories,* Brussels: Édition de la Fondation égyptologique Reine Élisabeth, 1932, 61–76; trans. Miriam Lichtheim, *Ancient Egyptian Literature: A Book of Readings,* Berkeley: University of California Press, 2006, vol. 2, 224–30. Date: Benjamin Sass, "Wenamun and his Levant—1075 BC or 925 BC?," *Ägypten und Levante* 12 (2002). Recent retelling as a graphic novel: Rolf Potts, *The Misadventures of Wenamun: History's Original Literary Traveler,* Lawrence: Sensitive House, 2015. I am grateful to Elizabeth Frood for discussion of the text.

2 Wenamun ii.14.

3 Wenamun ii.80.

4 Trevor Bryce, *The World of the Neo-Hittite Kingdoms: A Political and Military History,* Oxford: Oxford University Press, 2012, esp. chapters 3 and 10. Note in particular the survival of city-states like Karkemish well into the Iron Age.

5 Aren M. Maeir, "Philistia transforming: fresh evidence from Tell eṣ-Ṣafi/Gath on the transformational trajectory of the Philistine culture," in Ann E. Killebrew and Gunnar Lehmann, eds., *The Philistines and Other "Sea Peoples" in Text and Archaeology,* Atlanta: Society of Biblical Literature, 2013, 204–5; Aren M. Maeir, Louise A. Hitchcock, and Liora Kolska Horwitz, "On the constitution and transformation of Philistine identity," *Oxford Journal of Archaeology* 32, no. 1 (2013); Guy D. Middleton, "Telling stories: the Mycenaean origins of the Philistines," *Oxford Journal of Archaeology* 34, no. 1 (2015). Contemporary Egyptian texts associate "Sea Peoples" with this region, above all the Peleset, later rendered in the Hebrew Bible as "Philistines"; for contrasting opinions on the extent of migration to the southern Levant at the end of the Bronze Age see Assaf Yasur-Landau, *The Philistines and Aegean Migration at the End of the Late Bronze Age,* New York: Cambridge University Press, 2010, and A. Bernard Knapp, *Migration Myths and the End of the Bronze Age in the Eastern Mediterranean,* Cambridge: Cambridge University Press, 2021. aDNA studies from Lebanon show an influx of individuals with southeast European/Anatolian ancestry in this era (Marc Haber et al., "A genetic history of the Near East from an aDNA time course sampling eight points in the past 4,000 years," *American Journal of Human Genetics* 107, no. 1 [2020]); for a more limited study from ancient Ashkelon see Michal Feldman et al., "Ancient DNA sheds light on the genetic origins of Early Iron Age Philistines," *Science Advances* 5, no. 7 (2019), finding that within two centuries the immigrant group is no longer detectable.

6 Marc Van de Mieroop, *A History of the Ancient Near East, ca. 3000–323 BC,* 3rd ed., Chichester: Wiley Blackwell, 2016, 217. For early clans among the Israelites as well: Mait Kõiv, "Monarchy in the Iron Age Levant and Archaic Greece: the rulers of Corinth in a comparative context," *Studia Antiqua et Archaeologica* 28, no. 1 (2022), 184.

7 Josephine Crawley Quinn, *In Search of the Phoenicians,* Princeton: Princeton University Press, 2018, 48–52. The word is also found as an adjective in Bronze Age Linear B texts, but is not applied there to people.

8 For the language and the spectrum of dialects, see W. Randall Garr, *Dialect Geography of Syria-Palestine, 1000–586 B.C.,* Philadelphia: University of Pennsylvania Press, 1985, 216–35; Maria Giulia Amadasi Guzzo and Gary A. Rendsburg,

"Phoenician/Punic and Hebrew," in Geoffrey Khan, ed., *Encyclopedia of Hebrew Language and Linguistics*, Leiden: Brill, 2013; Quinn, *In Search of the Phoenicians*, 68–73.

9 It is often claimed that our Phoenicians called themselves "Canaanites" in their own language, but there is no good evidence for this: Josephine Crawley Quinn et al., "Augustine's Canaanites," *Papers of the British School at Rome* 82 (2014); Quinn, *In Search of the Phoenicians*, 30–6.

10 Quinn, *In Search of the Phoenicians*, 38.

11 Tyre and Sidon, close neighbors, are a regular exception to this rule.

12 Claude Doumet-Serhal, *Sidon: 15 Years of Excavations*, Beirut: Lebanese British Friends of the National Museum, 2013, 108; Claude Doumet-Serhal, "Sidon," *Biblical Archaeology Review* 43, no. 4 (2017).

13 Ayelet Gilboa and Dvory Namdar, "On the beginnings of south Asian spice trade with the Mediterranean region: a review," *Radiocarbon* 57, no. 2 (2015); Ayelet Gilboa, "The southern Levantine roots of the Phoenician mercantile phenomenon," *Bulletin of the American Society of Overseas Research* 387 (2022).

14 See on this passage Edward Lipiński, *Itineraria Phoenicia*, Leuven: Peeters, 2004, 109.

15 The earliest evidence for alphabetic writing at Byblos is from the eleventh century: Christopher Rollston, "The emergence of alphabetic scripts," in Rebecca Hasselbach-Andee, ed., *A Companion to Ancient Near Eastern Languages*, Chichester: Wiley Blackwell, 2020, 76.

16 Seth L. Sanders, *The Invention of Hebrew*, Urbana: University of Illinois Press, 2009, 57, on failed cuneiform alphabets.

17 María Eugenia Aubet, "Phoenicia during the Iron Age II period," in Margreet L. Steiner and Ann E. Killebrew, eds., *The Oxford Handbook of the Archaeology of the Levant c. 8000–332 BCE*, Oxford: Oxford University Press, 2014, 709–13.

18 Tzveta Manolova, "The Levant," in Irene S. Lemos and Antonis Kotsonas, eds., *A Companion to the Archaeology of Early Greece and the Mediterranean*, Chichester: Wiley Blackwell, 2019, 1205.

19 This evidence is collected at Josephus, *Jewish Antiquities* 8.144–9; *Against Apion* 1.106–20. My own spelling of Hirom's name reflects the relevant Canaanite vowel shift, with thanks to Vladimir Olivero for discussion of its chronology.

20 Susan Sherratt and Andrew Sherratt, "The growth of the Mediterranean economy in the early first millennium BC," *World Archaeology* 24, no. 3 (1993), 362.

21 There is evidence for a combined palace–temple structure at seventh-century Philistine Ekron: Kõiv, "Monarchy in the Iron Age Levant and Archaic Greece," 186.

22 Hirom and David: 2 Samuel 5:11; 1 Chronicles 14:1. Hirom and Solomon: 1 Kings 5, 9–10; 2 Chronicles 8:17–18, 9:10, 21. These stories are retold at Josephus, *Jewish Antiquities* 8.141–3; *Against Apion* 1.108–11. The letters sent between Hirom and Solomon that Josephus claims were preserved in the Tyrian archives are suspect: Josephus, *Jewish Antiquities* 8.55–6, with Sebastian Grätz, "The literary and ideological character of the letters in Ezra 4–7," in Paola Ceccarelli et al., eds., *Letters and Communities: Studies in the Socio-Political Dimensions of Ancient Epistolography*, Oxford: Oxford University Press, 2018, 242–3.

23 Joint fleet on the Red Sea: 1 Kings 9:26–8, 10:11–12.

24 Kõiv, "Monarchy in the Iron Age Levant and Archaic Greece," 184, on the Dan Stele.

25 Francesca Stavrakopoulou, *King Manasseh and Child Sacrifice: Biblical Distortions*

of Historical Realities, Berlin: De Gruyter, 2004, 74–87, not committing to two full states in this era.

26 Daniel Pioske, "Gath of the Philistines: the resilience of a remembered past," in Daniel Pioske, ed., *Memory in a Time of Prose: Studies in Epistemology, Hebrew Scribalism, and the Biblical Past*, Oxford: Oxford University Press, 2018, 110.

27 Riches: 1 Kings 3:13. Wives: 1 Kings 11:1–3.

28 Interestingly, the fleet and crew are presented in the later version of this story given in the Book of Chronicles as being sent to Solomon by Hirom: 2 Chronicles 8:17–18.

29 1 Kings 10:1–13; 2 Chronicles 9.

30 Overview of evidence at Robert Hoyland, "Kings, kingdoms and chronology," in St. John Simpson, ed., *Queen of Sheba*, London: British Museum Press, 2002, 69.

31 Faisal Almathen et al., "Ancient and modern DNA reveal dynamics of domestication and cross-continental dispersal of the dromedary," *Proceedings of the National Academy of Sciences* 113, no. 24 (2016). The wild population had died out by the late first century BCE.

32 Eivind Heldaas Seland, "Camels, camel nomadism and the practicalities of the Palmyrene caravan trade," *ARAM Periodical* 27 (2015), 46. Camel couriers in modern times could travel unladen 145 kilometers in twenty-four hours, 48.

9. Through the Pillars

1 Fernando González de Canales, Leonardo Serrano, and Jorge Llompart, "The pre-colonial Phoenician emporium of Huelva ca. 900–770 BC," *BABESCH* 81 (2006), 13.

2 Fernando González de Canales, Leonardo Serrano, and Jorge Llompart, *El emporio fenicio precolonial de Huelva (ca. 900–770* a.C.*)*, Madrid: Biblioteca Nueva, 2004; González de Canales, Serrano, and Llompart, "The pre-colonial Phoenician emporium of Huelva"; Alfredo Mederos Martín, "La cronología de Huelva fenicia," in Ana Margarida Arruda, ed., *Fenícios e Púnicos, por terra e mar. Actas do VI Congresso Internacional de Estudos Fenícios e Púnicos*, Lisbon: Centro de Arqueologia da Universidade de Lisboa, 2013. An even earlier date in the late tenth century has been suggested by carbon-14 analysis of cattle bones found with the pottery, as well as finds from more recent excavations below the water table at a site about fifty meters away: Fernando González de Canales et al., "Archaeological finds in the deepest anthropogenic stratum at 3 Concepción Street in the City of Huelva, Spain," *Ancient West and East* 16 (2017). As the evidence stands a prudent dating of Tyrian contact with Huelva would still put it in the ninth rather than the tenth century BCE, but this may well turn out to be too conservative.

3 González de Canales, Serrano, and Llompart, "The pre-colonial Phoenician emporium of Huelva," 19–24; Christopher Monroe, "Marginalizing civilization: the Phoenician redefinition of power circa 1300–800 BC," in Kristian Kristiansen, Thomas Lindkvist, and Janken Myrdal, eds., *Trade and Civilisation: Economic Networks and Cultural Ties, from Prehistory to the Early Modern Era*, Cambridge: Cambridge University Press, 2018, 203.

4 Homer, *Odyssey* 15.415; Scholia on the *Iliad* 23.744, trans. Federico Mazza, "The Phoenicians as seen by the ancient world," in Sabatino Moscati, ed., *The Phoenicians*, Milan: Bompiani, 1988, 640.

5 Callimachus frag. 191.55; Aratus, *Phaenomena* 37–44; Ovid, *Tristia* 4.3.1–2; Diogenes Laërtius 1.23.

6 A classic statement of this view can still be found at John Boardman, *The Greeks Overseas: Their Early Colonies and Trade,* 4th ed., London: Thames & Hudson, 1999, 38; cf. John K. Papadopoulos, "Phantom Euboians," *Journal of Mediterranean Archaeology* 10, no. 2 (1997), for early skepticism.

7 Sebastián Celestino Pérez and Carolina López-Ruiz, *Tartessos and the Phoenicians in Iberia,* Oxford: Oxford University Press, 2016, 111–19, noting that Tarshish is not a Semitic name, so is presumably based on a local term.

8 Ships of Tarshish sailing to Ophir: 1 Kings 22:48. The destination of the "Ships of Tarshish" mentioned at 1 Kings 10:22, which sail every three years and return with gold, silver, ivory, apes and peacocks, may be Ophir or it may be Tarshish itself, the interpretation chosen at 2 Chronicles 9:21.

9 For this idea of early Phoenician navigation see for instance Sabatino Moscati, *I fenici e Cartagine,* Turin: Unione Tipografico-Editrice Torinese, 1972, 114.

10 José Luis López Castro, "Toponymy and Phoenician navigation routes to the far west at the beginning of colonization," *Oriens Antiquus* N.S. 1 (2019); Susan Sherratt, "From the Near East to the Far West," in Irene S. Lemos and Antonis Kotsonas, eds., *A Companion to the Archaeology of Early Greece and the Mediterranean,* Chichester: Wiley Blackwell, 2019, 200–1.

11 David Gal, Hadas Saaroni, and Deborah Cvikel, "Mappings of potential sailing mobility in the Mediterranean during antiquity," *Journal of Archaeological Method and Theory* (2022). The journey back with the prevailing winds would have been much faster.

12 Christine M. Thompson, "Sealed silver in Iron Age Cisjordan and the 'invention' of coinage," *Oxford Journal of Archaeology* 22, no. 1 (2003), 78–87.

13 Sardinia: Tzilla Eshel et al., "Lead isotopes in silver reveal earliest Phoenician quest for metals in the west Mediterranean," *PNAS* 116, no. 13 (2019). Iberia: Jonathan R. Wood, Carol Bell, and Ignacio Montero-Ruiz, "The origin of Tel Dor Hacksilver and the westward expansion of the Phoenicians in the Early Iron Age: the Cypriot connection," *Journal of Eastern Mediterranean Archaeology and Heritage Studies* 8, no. 1 (2020), 11–12.

14 Tzilla Eshel et al., "Debasement of silver throughout the Late Bronze–Iron Age transition in the southern Levant: analytical and cultural implications," *Journal of Archaeological Science* 125 (2021).

15 Iberian silver: Eshel et al., "Lead isotopes in silver."

16 Pseudo-Aristotle, *On Wonders* 135.

17 Diodorus Siculus 5.35, a story set in the Pyrenees.

18 Stereotypes of Phoenicians: Josephine Crawley Quinn, "Phoenicians and Carthaginians in Greco-Roman Literature," in Carolina López-Ruiz and Brian R. Doak, eds., *The Oxford Handbook of the Phoenician and Punic Mediterranean,* Oxford: Oxford University Press, 2019.

19 Social organization and metal-trading networks along the Atlantic coast: Kristian Kristiansen, *Europe Before History,* Cambridge: Cambridge University Press, 1998, 144–57. For a British-Irish–style bronze sword found in the Loukkos river in Morocco, see Youssef Bokbot, "The origins of urbanisation and structured political power in Morocco: indigenous phenomenon or foreign colonisation?," in Martin J. Sterry and David J. Mattingly, eds., *Urbanisation and State Formation*

in the Ancient Sahara and Beyond, Cambridge: Cambridge University Press, 2020, 481–2.

20 Cauldrons: Kristiansen, *Europe Before History*, 145. Carp's tongue swords: Jon C. Henderson, *The Atlantic Iron Age: Settlement and Identity in the First Millennium* BC, London: Routledge, 2007, 69.

21 Barry Molloy, "European Bronze Age symbols in prehistoric Greece? Reconsidering Bronze shields and spears from Delphi in their wider context," *Hesperia* 87, no. 2 (2018).

22 Eleftheria Pappa, "The western Mediterranean," in Lemos and Kotsonas, eds., *A Companion to the Archaeology of Early Greece and the Mediterranean*, 1329–32.

23 Celestino Pérez and López-Ruiz, *Tartessos and the Phoenicians in Iberia*, 158–9. Dating: Monroe, "Marginalizing civilization," 203.

24 González de Canales, Serrano, and Llompart, "The pre-colonial Phoenician emporium of Huelva," 22–4.

25 Ann Neville, *Mountains of Silver and Rivers of Gold: The Phoenicians in Iberia*, Oxford: Oxbow, 2007, 146; Celestino Pérez and López-Ruiz, *Tartessos and the Phoenicians in Iberia*, 187.

26 González de Canales, Serrano, and Llompart, "The pre-colonial Phoenician emporium of Huelva," 19–20.

27 López Castro, "Toponymy and Phoenician navigation routes." As at Huelva, the precise chronology of the pottery found is disputed and tenth-century calibrated carbon dates have been reported from Utica, La Rebanadilla on the Mediterranean coast of Spain, and Carambolo on the Atlantic: José Luis López Castro et al., "La colonización fenicia inicial en el Mediterráneo Central: nuevas excavaciones arqueológicas en Utica (Túnez)," *Trabajos de prehistoria* 73, no. 1 (2016). Monroe, "Marginalizing civilization," 203, with note 7, summarizes the current position.

28 López Castro et al., "La colonización fenicia inicial en el Mediterráneo Central"; López Castro, "Toponymy and Phoenician navigation routes." Later Greco-Roman sources consistently identify Utica as a Tyrian foundation: Pseudo-Aristotle, *On Wonders* 134; Velleius Paterculus 1.2.3; Justin 18.4.2; Pliny, *Natural History* 5.76, and Stephanus Byzantinus, Ἰτύκη. There is however no evidence for foreign settlement at this early date, and more than half of the pottery found in this deposit was locally made: like Huelva and the Sardinian ports, Utica was probably an indigenous settlement that attracted passing trade (Imed Ben Jerbania, "La céramique sarde trouvée à Utique: quelle signification?," *Rivista di Studi Fenici* 45 [2017]).

29 The channel between the two islands was built over during the Roman period, and although nothing now remains of the temple, Arabic sources record ruins at the site in the medieval period: William Edwin Mierse, "The architecture of the lost temple of Hercules Gaditanus and its Levantine associations," *American Journal of Archaeology* 108, no. 4 (2004), 515.

30 Silius Italicus 3.14–60; Philostratos, *Apollonius* 5.5; Porphry, *de Abstinentia* 1.25, Pomponius Mela 3.46.

31 Velleius Paterculus 1.2.3.

32 Strabo 3.5.5. There is no positive corroboration for the claim that Gadir was an official Tyrian settlement, although reports were later found in the Tyrian archives of formal state foundations in the mid-ninth century at Botrys north of Byblos

and the unidentified site of Auza on the African coast: Menander, *BNJ* 783 F 3 = Josephus, *Jewish Antiquities* 8.324.

33 Name: Pliny, *Natural History* 4.120; Celestino Pérez and López-Ruiz, *Tartessos and the Phoenicians in Iberia,* 146–7.

34 José María Gener Basallote et al., "Arquitectura y urbanismo de la Gadir fenicia: el yacimiento del 'Teatro Cómico' de Cádiz," in Massimo Botto, ed., *Los Fenicios en la Bahía de Cádiz. Nuevas investigaciones,* Pisa: Fabrizio Serra editore, 2014; Ana María Niveau-de-Villedary y Mariñas, "Gadir revisited: a proposal for reconstruction of the Archaic Phoenician foundation," *Vicino Oriente* 22 (2018).

35 The Egyptian royal cubit was 52.5 centimeters.

36 Claudio Ottoni et al., "The palaeogenetics of cat dispersal in the ancient world," *Nature Ecology & Evolution* 1, no. 7 (2017).

37 Gener Basallote et al., "Arquitectura y urbanismo de la Gadir fenicia," 42–3; Susan Sherratt, "A globalizing Bronze and Iron Age Mediterranean," in Tamar Hodos, ed., *The Routledge Handbook of Archaeology and Globalization,* London: Routledge, 2017, 612.

38 Iberia: Neville, *Mountains of Silver and Rivers of Gold,* 17–21; Eleftheria Pappa, *Early Iron Age Exchange in the West: Phoenicians in the Mediterranean and the Atlantic,* Leuven: Peeters, 2013, 51–65; José Luis López Castro, "The Iberian peninsula," in López-Ruiz and Doak, eds., *The Oxford Handbook of the Phoenician and Punic Mediterranean,* 589–91. On possible Levantine settlement in Morocco: Pappa, *Early Iron Age Exchange in the West,* 87–90; Alfredo Mederos Martín, "North Africa: from the Atlantic to Algeria," in López-Ruiz and Doak, eds., *The Oxford Handbook of the Phoenician and Punic Mediterranean,* 628–34. Lixus as a Tyrian settlement: Pliny, *Natural History* 19.63; cf. Pseudo-Skylax 112, describing neighboring Phoenician and local settlements; Emanuele Papi, "Punic Mauretania?," in Josephine Crawley Quinn and Nicholas C. Vella, eds., *The Punic Mediterranean,* Cambridge: Cambridge University Press, 2014; Bokbot, "The origins of urbanisation and structured political power in Morocco," esp. 480–1.

39 López Castro, "The Iberian peninsula," 590–1, with Carlos González Wagner, "Tartessos and the orientalizing elites," in María Cruz Berrocal, Leonardo García Sanjuán, and Antonio Gilman, eds., *The Prehistory of Iberia: Debating Early Social Stratification and the State,* New York: Routledge, 2013, 348, for the agricultural landscape.

40 Pappa, "The western Mediterranean," 1339.

41 Neville, *Mountains of Silver and Rivers of Gold,* 140–7.

42 The case for mine slavery in Tarshish: Francisco J. Moreno Arrastio, "Tartessos, estelas, modelos pesimistas," in Pilar Fernández Uriel, Carlos González Wagner, and Fernando López Pardo, eds., *Intercambio y comercio preclásico en el Mediterráneo,* Madrid: Centro de Estudios Fenicios y Púnicos, 2000, 62–6; see also Celestino Pérez and López-Ruiz, *Tartessos and the Phoenicians in Iberia,* 154, 189–90.

43 For the classic statement, where the only true slave societies are found in ancient Greece and Rome and the modern Americas: M. I. Finley, "Slavery," in *International Encyclopedia of the Social Sciences,* New York: Macmillian, 1968, with M. I. Finley, *Ancient Slavery and Modern Ideology,* London: Chatto & Windus, 1980, esp. 67–92. Recent challenges to this neat model include Noel Lenski and Catherine M. Cameron, *What Is a Slave Society? The Practice of Slavery in Global*

Perspective, Cambridge: Cambridge University Press, 2018, and David M. Lewis, *Greek Slave Systems in Their Eastern Mediterranean Context, c. 800–146 BC*, Oxford: Oxford University Press, 2018.

44 *EAH*, "Slavery, ancient Near East"; "Slavery, Greece."

45 *OCD*, "Slavery, Greek."

46 See Christopher Monroe, *Scales of Fate: Trade, Tradition, and Transformation in the Eastern Mediterranean, ca. 1350–1175 BCE*, Münster: Ugarit-Verlag, 2009, 294, on the prevalence of domestic slavery in Mesopotamia while major construction projects used free labor, and Peter R. Bedford, "The Neo-Assyrian empire," in Ian Morris and Walter Scheidel, eds., *The Dynamics of Ancient Empires: State Power from Assyria to Byzantium*, Oxford: Oxford University Press, 2009, 37, on the lack of evidence for institutionalized slavery in Assyria with (more tentatively) Lewis, *Greek Slave Systems in Their Eastern Mediterranean Context*, 223–4.

47 Homer: *Odyssey* 14.290–320, 15.415–84. Bible: Amos 1:9; Joel 4:6; Ezekiel 27:12–13. This evidence is discussed as part of a broader argument for a Tyrian model for Greek slavery at Martin Bernal, "Phoenician politics and Egyptian justice in ancient Greece," in David Chioni Moore, ed., *Black Athena Writes Back*, Durham: Duke University Press, 1993, 350–2.

48 Story: Timaios of Tauromenium *BNJ* 556 F 82. It is the Roman-era historian Appian of Alexandria who describes this as the story told by the Carthaginians and (presumably only later) by the Romans: *Libyka* 1. A different, Greek, story is told by Philistos of Syracuse (fourth century BCE): *BNJ* 556 F 47.

49 Menander *BNJ* 783 F1 = Josephus *Against Apion*, 1.116-127, quotation at 125.

50 Carbon dates: Roald Docter et al., "Radiocarbon dates of animal bones in the earliest levels of Carthage," in Gilda Bartoloni and Filippo Delpino, eds., *Oriente e occidente: metodi e discipline a confronto: riflessioni sulla cronologia dell'età del ferro in Italia*, Pisa: Istituti Editoriali e Poligrafici Internazionali, 2005; Roald Docter et al., "New radiocarbon dates from Carthage: bridging the gap between history and archaeology?," in Claudia Sagona, ed., *Beyond the Homeland: Markers in Phoenician Chronology*, Leuven: Peeters, 2008, 382–4, with caution urged at Francisco J. Núñez, "The lowest levels at Bir Massouda and the foundation of Carthage: a Levantine perspective," *Carthage Studies* 8 (2014). Early-eighth-century pottery: Boutheina Maraoui Telmini, "An Attic Middle Geometric plate in Euboean pendant semi-circle style," *Carthage Studies* 8 (2014); Boutheina Maraoui Telmini, "Early archaeological evidence," in Alfonsina Russo et al., eds., *Carthago: The Immortal Myth*, Milan: Electa, 2019. As elsewhere, it is possible that the earliest settlement at Carthage was not in fact a Levantine foundation: Pappa, *Early Iron Age Exchange in the West*, esp. 157–61; Adriano Orsingher, "The *Chapelle Cintas* revisited and the Tophet of Carthage between ancestors and new identities," *BABESCH* 93 (2018); Michele Guirguis, "Central North Africa and Sardinian connections (end of 9th–8th century BC): the multi-ethnic and multicultural facies of the earliest western Phoenician communities," in Savino di Lernia and Marina Gallinaro, eds., *Archaeology in Africa: Potentials and Perspectives on Laboratory & Fieldwork Research*, Florence: All'insegna del Giglio, 2019.

51 The regularized settlement, grid, and early city: Pappa, *Early Iron Age Exchange in the West*, esp. 143; Iván Fumadó Ortega, "¿Quién parte y reparte? Análisis de la disposición urbana en la Cartago fenicia," *Archivo Español de Arqueología* 86 (2013); Ivan Fumadó Ortega, "Urban houses," in Russo et al., eds., *Carthago;*

Boutheina Maraoui Telmini et al., "Defining Punic Carthage," in Quinn and Vella, eds., *The Punic Mediterranean;* Roald Docter, "Urbanism," in Russo et al., eds., *Carthago.* Grid plans at Cypriot Enkomi and Kition: Christopher Mee, "Mycenaean Greece, the Aegean and beyond," in Cynthia W. Shelmerdine, ed., *The Cambridge Companion to the Aegean Bronze Age,* Cambridge: Cambridge University Press, 2008, 376; Artemis Georgiou and Maria Iacovou, "Cyprus," in Lemos and Kotsonas, eds., *A Companion to the Archaeology of Early Greece and the Mediterranean,* 1142.

52 Pappa, *Early Iron Age Exchange in the West,* 158.

53 Roald Docter, "The topography of Archaic Carthage: preliminary results of recent excavations and some prospects," *Talanta* 34–5 (2002–2003), 121–2; Brett Kaufman et al., "Ferrous metallurgy from the Bir Massouda metallurgical precinct at Phoenician and Punic Carthage and the beginning of the North African Iron Age," *Journal of Archaeological Science* 71 (2016).

54 Hélène Bénichou-Safar, *Le tophet de Salammbô à Carthage: essai de reconstitution,* Rome: École Française de Rome, 2004, 342; Josephine Crawley Quinn, *In Search of the Phoenicians,* Princeton: Princeton University Press, 2018, 91–112.

55 Bénichou-Safar, *Le tophet de Salammbô à Carthage,* 1–2.

56 Kleitarchos, *Scholia to Plato's Republic* 337A; Paolo Xella, "Sacrifici di bambini nel mondo fenicio e punico nelle testimonianze in lingua greca e latina I," *Studi epigrafici e linguistici* 26 (2009), 63–88, for a collection.

57 For more detailed discussion see Paolo Xella et al., "Phoenician bones of contention," *Antiquity* 87 (2013).

58 JoAnn Scurlock, "The techniques of the sacrifice of animals in ancient Israel and ancient Mesopotamia: new insights through comparison, part 2," *Andrews University Seminary Studies* 44, no. 4 (2006), 17.

59 See, in addition to Kleitarchos, Pseudo-Plato, *Minos* 315 (c. fourth century BCE), making a broader point that customs differ between different peoples, as well as Ennius, *Annals* 7 (c. 200 BCE).

60 Judith Evans Grubbs, "Infant exposure and infanticide," in Judith Evans Grubbs and Tim Parkin, eds., *The Oxford Handbook of Childhood and Education in the Classical World,* Oxford: Oxford University Press, 2013.

61 Josephine Crawley Quinn, "The cultures of the tophet: identification and identity in the Phoenician diaspora," in Erich Gruen, ed., *Cultural Identity in the Ancient Mediterranean,* Los Angeles: Getty Publications, 2011.

62 Francesca Stavrakopoulou, *King Manasseh and Child Sacrifice: Biblical Distortions of Historical Realities,* Berlin: De Gruyter, 2004, 141–299; Heath D. Dewrell, *Child Sacrifice in Ancient Israel,* University Park: Penn State University Press, 2017, 4–69. Tophet: e.g., Jeremiah 32:35. Passing through fire: e.g., Leviticus 18:21.

63 2 Kings 23:10.

64 Curtius Rufus 4.3.23.

65 Quinn, *In Search of the Phoenicians,* 98–101.

66 Mozia: Lorenzo Nigro and Federica Spagnoli, *Landing on Motya,* Rome: Università di Roma La Sapienza, 2017, chapters 1–2. Sulcis: Valentina Melchiorri, "Le tofet de Sulci (S. Antioco, Sardaigne): état des études et perspectives de la recherche," *Ugarit-Forschungen* 41 (2009); Josephine Crawley Quinn, "Tophets in the 'Punic World,'" in Paolo Xella, ed., *The Tophet in the Phoenician Mediterranean,* Verona: Essedue, 2014, for further discussion.

67 Babette Bechtold, "Observations on the amphora repertoire of Middle Punic Carthage," *Carthage Studies* 2 (2008), 75; Peter van Dommelen, Carlos Gómez Bellard, and Roald Docter, *Rural Landscapes of the Punic World,* London: Equinox, 2008, 232–3.

68 Louise A. Hitchcock and Aren M. Maeir, "A pirate's life for me: the maritime culture of the Sea Peoples," *Palestine Exploration Quarterly* 148, no. 4 (2016), for a discussion and map of historical choke points.

69 A. Bernard Knapp, *Seafaring and Seafarers in the Bronze Age Eastern Mediterranean,* Leiden: Sidestone Press, 2018, 35.

70 *Odyssey* 13.264–92, 14.310–15, 15.444–527.

71 Hitchcock and Maeir, "A pirate's life for me," esp. 247–54.

10. The Invention of Greece

1 Plato: *Laws* 2.656; *Phaedrus* 274c5–d2; *Philebus* 18b6–d2. See also Isocrates, *Busiris* 28, where Pythagoras brings "the whole of philosophy" from Egypt to Greece; Aristotle, *Metaphysics* I.1, 981b23–5 and *On the Heavens,* II.12, 292a7–9; and Lea Cantor, "Thales—the 'first philosopher'? A troubled chapter in the historiography of philosophy," *British Journal for the History of Philosophy* 30, no. 5 (2022). Herodotus: 2.4, 43–64, 145–6.

2 Apollodorus 2.1.4.

3 Phoenician settlement of the Aegean as a whole: Thucydides 1.8. Specific islands: Herodotus 1.105:3; Pausanias 1.14.7; Ergias of Rhodes *BNJ* 513 F 1; Nikos Stampolidis, "The Aegean," in Carolina López-Ruiz and Brian R. Doak, eds., *The Oxford Handbook of the Phoenician and Punic Mediterranean,* Oxford: Oxford University Press, 2019, 494. On the stories of Europa and her siblings see Sarah P. Morris, *Daidalos and the Origins of Greek Art,* Princeton: Princeton University Press, 1992, 101–49. The first explicit associations of Agenor and his children with Phoenicia appear in the sixth or fifth century BCE, rather later than the characters themselves appear in Greek literature: Lynette G. Mitchell, *Panhellenism and the Barbarian in Archaic and Classical Greece,* Swansea: Classical Press of Wales, 2007, 182–4.

4 Thasos mines: Herodotus 6.47. Sanctuary: Herodotus 2.44, with Pausanias 5.25.12. (In some versions of the tale Thasos is Kadmos' nephew or friend rather than his brother.) Kadmos and Thebes: Herodotus 2.145, 5.58. For his descendants, see Herodotus 5.49–60.

5 Pausanias 7.4.1; Apollodorus 2.7.1; Apollonius of Rhodes 2.865–7. The winged leopard appears on Roman-era mosaics.

6 There is an intriguing suggestion of contact with Levantine culture on the island of Thasos in a prohibition on the sacrifice (and therefore consumption) of pigs: *IG* XII.8, 358 with Morris, *Daidalos and the Origins of Greek Art,* 145–6, and Irad Malkin, *A Small Greek World: Networks in the Ancient Mediterranean,* New York: Oxford University Press, 2011, 132–3.

7 Inscriptions: Giorgos Bourogiannis, "Instances of Semitic writing from Geometric and Archaic Greek contexts: an unintelligible way to literacy?," in Giuseppe Garbati and Tatiana Pedrazzi, eds., *Transformations and Crisis in the Mediterranean: "Identity" and Interculturality in the Levant and Phoenician West During the*

12th–8th Centuries BCE, Pisa: Fabrizio Serra, 2015. Further evidence for Levantines in the Aegean: Morris, *Daidalos and the Origins of Greek Art,* 130–8; John K. Papadopoulos, "Phantom Euboians," *Journal of Mediterranean Archaeology* 10, no. 2 (1997), 193; John K. Papadopoulos, "Phantom Euboians: a decade on," in David W. Rupp and Jonathan E. Tomlinson, eds., *Euboea and Athens: Proceedings of a Colloquium in Memory of Malcolm B. Wallace,* Athens: Canadian Institute in Greece, 2011, 115–20; Carolina López-Ruiz, *Phoenicians and the Making of the Mediterranean,* Cambridge, Mass.: Harvard University Press, 2021, 173–225.

8 Euboean imports to the Levant: Tzveta Manolova, "The Levant," in Irene S. Lemos and Antonis Kotsonas, eds., *A Companion to the Archaeology of Early Greece and the Mediterranean,* Chichester: Wiley Blackwell, 2019, 1206.

9 Italy: Catherine Morgan, "Euboians and Corinthians in the area of the Corinthian Gulf?," in Bruno d'Agostino and Michel Bats, eds., *Euboica: l'Eubea e la presenza euboica in Calcidica e in occidente,* Naples: Centre Jean Bérard, 1998; Francesco D'Andria, "Il Salento nella prima età del ferro (IX–VII sec. a.C.): insediamenti e contesti," in *Alle origini della Magna Grecia: mobilità, migrazioni, fondazioni. Atti del cinquantesimo Convegno si studi sulla Magna Grecia, Taranto 1–4 ottobre 2010,* Taranto: Istituto per la Storia e l'Archeologia della Magna Grecia, 2012. Phrygia: John K. Papadopoulos, "The early history of the Greek alphabet: new evidence from Eretria and Methone," *Antiquity* 90, no. 353 (2016), 1251. Al-Mina: Joanna Luke, *Ports of Trade, Al Mina, and Geometric Greek Pottery in the Levant,* Oxford: Archaeopress, 2003.

10 Lieve Donnellan, "'Greek colonisation' and Mediterranean networks: patterns of mobility and interaction at Pithekoussai," *Journal of Greek Archaeology* 1 (2016); Lieve Donnellan, "A networked view on 'Euboean' colonisation," in Lieve Donnellan, Valentina Nizzo, and Gert-Jan Burgers, eds., *Conceptualising Early Colonisation,* Brussels: Institut Historique Belge de Rome, 2016. Mixed population: Jonathan M. Hall, *Hellenicity: Between Ethnicity and Culture,* Chicago: University of Chicago Press, 2002, 94 (on the evidence from names); Olivia Kelley, "Beyond intermarriage: the role of the indigenous Italic population at Pithekoussai," *Oxford Journal of Archaeology* 31, no. 3 (2012); Jeremy Mark Hayne, "The Italian peninsula," in Carolina López-Ruiz and Brian R. Doak, eds., *The Oxford Handbook of the Phoenician and Punic Mediterranean,* Oxford: Oxford University Press, 2019, 510.

11 I can only briefly sketch here fragments of a vast topic much discussed by other scholars: classic works on the borrowings from western Asia in Greek culture include Walter Burkert, *The Orientalizing Revolution: Near Eastern Influence on Greek Culture in the Early Archaic Age,* Cambridge, Mass.: Harvard University Press, 1992; Walter Burkert, *Babylon, Memphis, Persepolis: Eastern Contexts of Greek Culture,* Cambridge, Mass.: Harvard University Press, 2004; M. L. West, *The East Face of Helicon: West Asiatic Elements in Early Poetry and Myth,* Oxford: Clarendon Press, 1997; and now López-Ruiz, *Phoenicians and the Making of the Mediterranean.*

12 Herodotus 5.58; for Kadmos see also Herodotus 2.49 (introduction of Dionysian rites to Greece) and 145 (grandfather of Dionysos; at 5.60 he is the great-great-grandfather of Oedipus).

13 Michael Gagarin and Paula Jean Perlman, *The Laws of Ancient Crete c. 650–400* BCE, Oxford: Oxford University Press, 2016, Eltynia 1, line 2 (c. 600–525 BCE);

M. Adak and Peter Thonemann, *Teos and Abdera: Two Cities in Peace and War,* Oxford: Oxford University Press, 2022, no. 2, lines 37–8 and no. 3, lines D19–21 (both Teos, c. 470); *IG* XII.2 96, line II.10, and 97, line 2, from Mytilene. Some Greeks thought that letters came from Egypt, or were an indigenous development: Barry B. Powell, *Homer and the Origin of the Greek Alphabet,* Cambridge: Cambridge University Press, 1991, 5–6.

14 Trans. Gagarin and Perlman, *The Laws of Ancient Crete,* Datala 1 (c. 500 BCE), with another probable example at Eleutherna 11, l. 5 (6th–5th century).

15 Karkemiš A15b §§19–20: John David Hawkins, *Corpus of Hieroglyphic Luwian Inscriptions,* vol. 1: *Inscriptions of the Iron Age,* Berlin: De Gruyter, 2012, no. II.24, trans. pp. 130–1.

16 Madadh Richey, "The alphabet and its legacy," in López-Ruiz and Doak, eds., *The Oxford Handbook of the Phoenician and Punic Mediterranean,* 243.

17 Maria Giulia Amadasi Guzzo, "The language," in López-Ruiz and Doak, eds., *The Oxford Handbook of the Phoenician and Punic Mediterranean,* 203.

18 Papadopoulos, "The early history of the Greek alphabet"; Richey, "The alphabet and its legacy," 243; Christopher Rollston, "The emergence of alphabetic scripts," in Rebecca Hasselbach-Andee, ed., *A Companion to Ancient Near Eastern Languages,* Chichester: Wiley Blackwell, 2020, 77.

19 The earliest Greek alphabet had five vowels—*a, e, i,* and *o,* which reused Phoenician letters, and *u,* an early addition. Longer forms of *a* and *o* were added by the end of the seventh century: Richey, "The alphabet and its legacy," 245. Lowercase Greek letters only appear in the later, eastern Roman empire.

20 Richey, "The alphabet and its legacy," 249. Transmission may still not have been direct: the earliest known true alphabetic inscriptions are not in Greek but in Phrygian, dating to around 800 BCE, and they recycle the same Tyrian letters for the same vowels as the Greek script. Either one alphabet derives from the other, or they were invented by people working together: Papadopoulos, "The early history of the Greek alphabet"; Giorgos Bourogiannis, "The transmission of the alphabet to the Aegean," in Łukasz Niesiołowski-Spanò and Marek Węcowski, eds., *Change, Continuity and Connectivity: Northeastern Mediterranean at the Turn of the Bronze Age and in the Early Iron Age,* Wiesbaden: Harrassowitz, 2018, 251–2. See Willemijn J. I. Waal, "On the 'Phoenician letters': the case for an early transmission of the Greek alphabet from an archaeological, epigraphic, and linguistic perspective," *Aegean Studies* 1 (2018), making the case for transmission as early as the eleventh century, which is hard to reconcile with the evidence from letter forms.

21 Anne Kenzelmann Pfyffer, Thierry Theurillat, and Samuel Verdan, "Graffiti d'époque géométrique provenant du sanctuaire d'Apollon Daphnéphoros à Erétrie," *Zeitschrift für Papyrologie und Epigraphik* 151 (2005); Papadopoulos, "The early history of the Greek alphabet," also describing more than twenty Greek inscriptions of the last three decades of the eighth century recently found in an underground room at Methone, a few kilometers west of modern Thessaloniki. They were written on drinking cups and transport jars from Eretria, Attica, the eastern Aegean islands, Tyre, and Sarepta.

22 Al-Mina: Richard Janko, "From Gabii and Gordion to Eretria and Methone: the rise of the Greek alphabet," *Bulletin of the Institute of Classical Studies* 58, no. 1 (2015), 13. Pithekoussai: Bourogiannis, "Instances of Semitic writing from

Geometric and Archaic Greek contexts"; Carolina López-Ruiz, "Greek literature and the lost legacy of Canaan," in Joan Aruz and Michael Seymour, eds., *Assyria to Iberia: Art and Culture in the Iron Age,* New York: Metropolitan Museum of Art, 2016, 317. What looks like the earliest alphabetic writing in the Mediterranean is scratched on a pot placed in a tomb at Gabii in inland Italy c. 775 BCE, but this may simply be "nonsense writing" by someone playing with Tyrian letters (Papadopoulos, "The early history of the Greek alphabet," 1250; cf. Janko, "From Gabii and Gordion to Eretria and Methone," 15–16).

23 Ian Morris, *Archaeology as Cultural History: Words and Things in Iron Age Greece,* Oxford: Blackwell, 2000, 264.

24 López-Ruiz, *Phoenicians and the Making of the Mediterranean,* 232–3.

25 Burkert, *The Orientalizing Revolution,* 30–1.

26 Janko, "From Gabii and Gordion to Eretria and Methone," 3.

27 Robin Osborne, *Greece in the Making, 1200–479 BC,* 2nd ed., London: Routledge, 2009, 62; López-Ruiz, *Phoenicians and the Making of the Mediterranean,* 187.

28 Bourogiannis, "The transmission of the alphabet to the Aegean," 245–6. A few more letters follow in a different hand, but their meaning is unclear.

29 Ibid., 246–7. The latest study of the remains suggests that at least three individuals were buried in the grave: Melania Gigante et al., "Who was buried with Nestor's Cup? Macroscopic and microscopic analyses of the cremated remains from Tomb 168 (second half of the 8th century BCE, Pithekoussai, Ischia Island, Italy)," *PLOS ONE* 16, no. 10 (2021).

30 *Iliad* 11.632–7, with Powell, *Homer and the Origin of the Greek Alphabet,* 165–6. This does not mean that written copies of the *Iliad* itself were circulating in the Bay of Naples by this date, but it suggests that some of its stories were familiar there. For an inscription on a wine cup from a similar period found at Methone see Janko, "From Gabii and Gordion to Eretria and Methone," 3; Papadopoulos, "The early history of the Greek alphabet," 1243–4.

31 Powell, *Homer and the Origin of the Greek Alphabet,* 170–80.

32 *IG* XII.3, ll. 536–40; discussion at Barry B. Powell, "Why was the Greek alphabet invented? The epigraphical evidence," *Classical Antiquity* 8, no. 2 (1989), 342–5.

33 I owe this point to Seth Sanders.

34 West, *The East Face of Helicon,* 14.

35 Burkert, *The Orientalizing Revolution,* 37. The Semitic roots of *makellon* are less certain than the other examples Burkert gives.

36 West, *The East Face of Helicon,* 23–4.

37 Tzveta Manolova and Joachim Bretschneider, "An unprecedented depiction of a Syro-Canaanite oared galley on a jar sealing from Tell Tweini," in Joachim Bretschneider and Greta Jans, eds., *About Tell Tweini (Syria): Artifacts, Ecofacts and Landscape,* Leuven: Peeters, 2019. Depictions of similar ships are already found in tenth-century contexts at Crete and Halicarnassus.

38 Hall, *Hellenicity,* 95; Richard N. Fletcher, "Opening the Mediterranean: Assyria, the Levant and the transformation of Early Iron Age trade," *Antiquity* 86, no. 331 (2012), 215; and Papadopoulos, "The early history of the Greek alphabet," 1251, on new evidence for Levantine writing and ceramics from the North Aegean.

39 Ian Morris, "The eighth-century revolution," in Kurt Raaflaub and Hans van Wees, eds., *A Companion to Archaic Greece,* Chichester: Wiley Blackwell, 2009, 67–9.

40 West, *The East Face of Helicon*, 31–2. Greek authors sometimes attributed western Asian roots to local musical innovation, even when it wasn't true: Yulia Ustinova, "Imaginary Phrygians: cognitive consonance and the assumed Phrygian origin of Greek ecstatic cults and music," *Journal of Hellenic Studies* 141 (2021).

41 Melqart-as-Herakles: Herodotus 2.44; Diodorus Siculus 20.14.1; Silius Italicus 3.32–44; Josephine Crawley Quinn, *In Search of the Phoenicians*, Princeton: Princeton University Press, 2018, 120–7; the earliest certain evidence is from the fifth century. Aphrodite "Ourania": Herodotus 1.105 (Levantine Ashkelon, via Cyprus); Pausanias 1.14.7 (Assyria), with Stephanie Budin, "A reconsideration of the Aphrodite–Ashtart syncretism," *Numen* 51, no. 2 (2004), noting that the traditional association of Ashtart with Aphrodite is not exclusive. See also Morris, *Daidalos and the Origins of Greek Art*, 79–100, on Kothar, Hephaestos, and Daidalos.

42 Burkert, *The Orientalizing Revolution*, 153 n. 3.

43 Michael Scott, *Delphi: A History of the Center of the Ancient World*, Princeton: Princeton University Press, 2014.

44 Burkert, *The Orientalizing Revolution*, 79–82.

45 Ibid., 20; López-Ruiz, *Phoenicians and the Making of the Mediterranean*, 209.

46 Burkert, *The Orientalizing Revolution*, 20; Morris, *Archaeology as Cultural History*, 236, 273–5; Charlotte R. Potts, *Religious Architecture in Latium and Etruria, c. 900–500 BC*, Oxford: Oxford University Press, 2015, 106; López-Ruiz, *Phoenicians and the Making of the Mediterranean*, 207–8.

47 Hélène Sader, "The archaeology of Phoenician cities," in López-Ruiz and Doak, eds., *The Oxford Handbook of the Phoenician and Punic Mediterranean*, 132–3.

48 West, *The East Face of Helicon*, 37.

49 Morris, *Archaeology as Cultural History*, 274.

50 Carolina López-Ruiz, *When the Gods Were Born: Greek Cosmogonies and the Near East*, Cambridge, Mass.: Harvard University Press, 2010, 35–6; Potts, *Religious Architecture in Latium and Etruria*, 115.

51 Burkert, *The Orientalizing Revolution*, 4; Morris, *Daidalos and the Origins of Greek Art*, 133; Scott, *Delphi*, 46.

52 Herodotus 1:14, with Papadopoulos, "The early history of the Greek alphabet," 1251.

53 Morris, *Archaeology as Cultural History*, 276.

54 Burkert, *The Orientalizing Revolution*, 19–21; López-Ruiz, *Phoenicians and the Making of the Mediterranean*, 218–22, with 178–203 for a recent survey of the "orientalizing" phenomenon in Greek art.

55 Sarah P. Morris and John K. Papadopoulos, "Phoenicians and the Corinthian pottery industry," in Renate Rolle, Karin Schmidt, and Roald Docter, eds., *Archäologische Studien in Kontaktzonen der antiken Welt*, Hamburg: Vandenhoeck & Ruprecht, 1998, 253.

56 López-Ruiz, *Phoenicians and the Making of the Mediterranean*, 199–201. Morris and Papadopoulos, "Phoenicians and the Corinthian pottery industry," 253, make an attractive argument for the involvement of resident Levantine entrepreneurs in production and distribution as well.

57 Strabo 8.6.20.

58 Dedications: Jonathan M. Hall, *A History of the Archaic Greek World, ca. 1200–479 BCE*, 2nd ed., Chichester: Wiley Blackwell, 2014, 297. Month: López-Ruiz, *Phoenicians and the Making of the Mediterranean*, 199–201, 141.

59 Thucydides 6.2.6, 6.3.3; Robin Osborne, "Early Greek colonization? The nature of Greek settlement in the West," in Nick Fisher and Hans van Wees, eds., *Archaic Greece: New Approaches and New Evidence,* Swansea: Classical Press of Wales, 1998; Jonathan M. Hall, "Early Greek settlement in the West: the limits of colonialism," in Kathryn Bosher, ed., *Theater Outside Athens: Drama in Greek Sicily and South Italy,* Cambridge: Cambridge University Press, 2012.

60 Morris, *Archaeology as Cultural History,* 257.

61 On similarities between Aegean and Levantine migration: Malkin, *A Small Greek World,* 149, 153.

62 The absolute dating of the urban layout at sites like Megara Hyblaea, Naxos, and Syracuse is in itself unclear (see, e.g., Hall, *A History of the Archaic Greek World,* 112–14), but the orthogonal arrangements found in these cities must postdate those of Levantine settlements in the western Mediterranean.

63 The emergence of Greek cities: Hall, *A History of the Archaic Greek World,* 68–95; Osborne, *Greece in the Making,* 66–130.

64 Hall, *A History of the Archaic Greek World,* 73–4, on the archaeological evidence, with Alcaeus frag. 426.

65 María Eugenia Aubet, "Phoenicia during the Iron Age II period," in Margreet L. Steiner and Ann E. Killebrew, eds., *The Oxford Handbook of the Archaeology of the Levant c. 8000–332 BCE,* Oxford: Oxford University Press, 2014; Sader, "The archaeology of Phoenician cities."

66 Oswyn Murray, "What is Greek about the *polis?*," in Pernille Flensted-Jensen et al., eds., *Polis and Politics: Studies in Ancient Greek History,* Copenhagen: Museum Tusculanum Press, 2000, on the modern invention of the Greek city-state, with Kostas Vlassopoulos, *Unthinking the Greek Polis: Ancient Greek History Beyond Eurocentrism,* Cambridge: Cambridge University Press, 2007. The suggestion that the Greek city-state drew inspiration from the Levant goes back to Jacob Burckhardt's *Griechische Kulturgeschichte,* Berlin: Spemann, 1898, I.61–2. More recently, see Anthony M. Snodgrass, *Archaic Greece: The Age of Experiment,* London: Dent, 1980, 32; Robert Drews, "Phoenicians, Carthage and the Spartan Eunomia," *American Journal of Philology* 100, no. 1 (1979); Martin Bernal, "Phoenician politics and Egyptian justice in ancient Greece," in David Chioni Moore, ed., *Black Athena Writes Back,* Durham: Duke University Press, 1993; and, drawing specific parallels between Levantine monarchies and Greek tyrannies, Mait Kõiv, "Monarchy in the Iron Age Levant and Archaic Greece: the rulers of Corinth in a comparative context," *Studia Antiqua et Archaeologica* 28, no. 1 (2022). Contra, to some extent: Kurt Raaflaub, "Zwischen Ost und West: Phönizische Einflüsse auf die griechische Polisbildung?," in Robert Rollinger and Christof Ulf, eds., *Griechische Archaik: Interne Entwicklungen—Externe Impulse,* Berlin: Akademie Verlag, 2004, emphasizing the distinctive role of aristocratic merchants in Levantine cities. For the effects of the experience of migration itself on the rise of the Greek city-state, Irad Malkin, "Inside and outside: colonization and the formation of the mother-city," in Bruno d'Agostino and David Ridgway, eds., *Apoikia: Scritti in onore di Giorgio Buchner,* Naples: Istituto Universitario Orientale, 1994.

67 Population of Athens: Morris, "The eighth-century revolution," 66.

68 Graham Shipley, "'The other Lakedaimonians': the dependent Perioikic *poleis* of Laconia and Messenia," in Mogens Herman Hansen, ed., *The Polis as an Urban*

Center and as a Political Community, Copenhagen: Royal Danish Academy of Science and Letters, 1997, with John K. Davies, "The 'origin of the Greek *polis*': where should we be looking?," in Lynette G. Mitchell and Peter J. Rhodes, eds., *The Development of the* Polis *in Archaic Greece*, London: Routledge, 1997.

69 Catherine Morgan, *Early Greek States Beyond the Polis*, London: Routledge, 2003; Emily Mackil, *Creating a Common Polity: Religion, Economy, and Politics in the Making of the Greek Koinon*, Berkeley: University of California Press, 2013; Hans Beck and Peter Funke, *Federalism in Greek Antiquity*, Cambridge: Cambridge University Press, 2015.

70 Deborah L. Nichols and Thomas H. Charlton, *The Archaeology of City-States: Cross-Cultural Approaches*, Washington, D.C.: Smithsonian Institution Press, 1998; Mogens Herman Hansen, *A Comparative Study of Thirty City-State Cultures: An Investigation Conducted by the Copenhagen Polis Center*, Copenhagen: Kongelige Danske Videnskabernes Selskab, 2000. In Mesopotamia, city-states go back to the fourth millennium BCE, often on a much larger scale and with powers and functions much closer to those of a modern state than those of ancient Greek towns: Marc Van de Mieroop, *The Ancient Mesopotamian City*, Oxford: Clarendon Press, 1997; Vlassopoulos, *Unthinking the Greek Polis*, 110–15, also discussing evidence for popular assemblies in contemporary Mesopotamia.

71 Aristotle, *Politics* 1276b: *koinonia politon politeias.*

72 Greek kings: Snodgrass, *Archaic Greece*, 90.

73 Greek burials: Osborne, *Greece in the Making*, 76–82. Communal institutions: Morris, *Archaeology as Cultural History*, 287–8.

74 Xenophon, *Constitutions of the Spartans* 5; Plutarch, *Life of Lykourgos* 10, 12; Ellen G. Millender, "Spartan literacy revisited," *Classical Antiquity* 20, no. 1 (2001). The *homoioi* comprised no more than a fifth of the free male population, and the whole system depended on the enslavement of much of the population of Laconia and neighboring Messenia as "helots" (Snodgrass, *Archaic Greece*, 88).

75 Tyrtaeus frag. 4, with Plutarch, *Life of Lykourgos* 6. Both the restricted councils and the larger assemblies of the west Asian tradition appear in Homer's epics around this time as well.

76 Osborne, *Greece in the Making*, 174–5, for examples. The seventh-century "Great Rhetra" giving "power" to Spartan citizens could present an exception to this rule, if we consider its "rider" giving the elders a right of veto to be a later amendment; for reasons to suppose that the two are in fact contemporary see Hall, *A History of the Archaic Greek World*, 205–11.

77 Eva von Dassow, "The public and the state in the ancient Near East," in Gernot Wilhelm, ed., *Organization, Representation, and Symbols of Power in the Ancient Near East*, Winona Lake: Eisenbrauns, 2012, 184. Emar was for a time without a king (Guy Bunnens, "Emar on the Euphrates in the 13th century B.C.," *Ancient Near Eastern Studies* 27 [1989], 29–31), until their Hittite overlords rectified the situation: Regine Pruzsinszky, "Emar, a town situated along the middle Euphrates and the transition from the Hurrian to Hittite power," in Marlies Heinz and Marian H. Feldman, eds., *Representations of Political Power in Times of Change and Dissolving Order*, Winona Lake: Eisenbrauns, 2007.

78 Opposition: EA [El Amarna] 138. Independence: EA 59, 100, 139–40. EA 136–40 show that decisions at Byblos were taken by "the town" after a revolt against the king.

79 EA 100 is written jointly by the "town" and "elders" of Irqata. See also EA 59, where the sons of Tunip rule their city and are in dispute with one another over political matters, and EA 254, where a visitor addresses a civic forum in the absence of the king. Overview of the role of elders and citizens in late second-millennium sources: H. Reviv, "On urban representative institutions and self-government in Syria-Palestine in the second half of the second millennium B.C.," *Journal of the Economic and Social History of the Orient* 12, no. 3 (1969).

80 All Tyrians: SAA II, no. 5, I.3; the text here is a reliable restoration. Elders: Ezekiel 27:9. Councils and assemblies: Arrian 2.15.6–7; Curtius 4.1.16.

81 Polybius 6.51; see also Aristotle, *Politics* 1272b–3b for a comparison between Carthage, Crete, and Sparta. The Greek translation of the Phoenician *shofet* ("judge," as in the biblical accounts of early Israel) as *basileus* has led some scholars to suggest that early Carthage was a monarchy, but a *basileus* can also be a magistrate in Greek (as in Classical Athens), and the word is used of Carthage in periods when the city cannot have been ruled by kings (e.g., Polybius 3.33.3): see further Drews, "Phoenicians, Carthage and the Spartan Eunomia," 54.

82 Osborne, *Greece in the Making*, 49–51; Naoíse Mac Sweeney, "Separating fact from fiction in the Ionian migration," *Hesperia* 86, no. 3 (2017); Naoíse Mac Sweeney, "Regional identities in the Greek world: myth and *koinon* in Ionia," *Historia* 70, no. 3 (2021), 279–81. There would be nothing surprising in Greek-speaking people exploring and settling new coasts, nor in Luwic-speaking people adding the Greek language or even over time a Greek identity to their repertoire. The presence of a large Greek-speaking community in western Anatolia only ended in 1923 with the population exchange.

83 Alexander Dale, "Alcaeus on the career of Myrsilos: Greeks, Lydians and Luwians at the east Aegean–west Anatolian interface," *Journal of Hellenic Studies* 131 (2011).

11. The Assyrian Mediterranean

1 *RIMA* [*Royal Inscriptions of Mesopotamia, Assyrian Period*] 2 A.0.101.1.iii.85–8, trans. A. Kirk Grayson, Toronto, University of Toronto Press, 1991, slightly adapted. The true identity of the sea creatures is not clear: guesses include hippopotamuses and narwhals.

2 *RIMA* 2 A.0.101.30.102–54.

3 Shalmaneser III: *RIMA* 3 A.0.102.2.26–7 for the statue; A.0.102.6.iii.24–33 for the army, with A.0.102.10.iii.14–25 and iv.10–11 for tribute from Tyre in 841 BCE (cf. A.0.102.16.134–5). Adad-Nirari III: *RIMA* 2 A.0.104.7.8–11, A.0.104.8.11.

4 On the Neo-Assyrian empire, see Marc Van de Mieroop, *A History of the Ancient Near East, ca. 3000–323 BC*, 3rd ed., Chichester: Wiley Blackwell, 2016, 246–88; Peter R. Bedford, "The Neo-Assyrian empire," in Ian Morris and Walter Scheidel, eds., *The Dynamics of Ancient Empires: State Power from Assyria to Byzantium*, Oxford: Oxford University Press, 2009; Karen Radner, "The Neo-Assyrian empire," in Michael Gehler and Robert Rollinger, eds., *Imperien und Reiche in der Weltgeschichte: Epochenübergreifende und globalhistorische Vergleiche*, Wiesbaden: Harrassowitz, 2014.

5 Radner, "The Neo-Assyrian empire," 105, 107; Karen Radner, *Ancient Assyria: A Very Short Introduction*, Oxford: Oxford University Press, 2015, 33.

6 Karen Radner, "An imperial communication network: the state correspondence of the Neo-Assyrian empire," in Karen Radner, ed., *State Correspondence in the Ancient World: From New Kingdom Egypt to the Roman Empire,* Oxford: Oxford University Press, 2014, 71–7.

7 Bustenay Oded, *Mass Deportations and Deportees in the Neo-Assyrian Empire,* Wiesbaden: Reichert, 1979, 19–22; Radner, *Ancient Assyria,* 108–10; Karen Radner, "The 'lost tribes of Israel' in the context of the resettlement program of the Assyrian empire," in Shuichi Hasegawa, Christoph Levin, and Karen Radner, eds., *The Last Days of the Kingdom of Israel,* Berlin: De Gruyter, 2019, 101–5.

8 Karen Radner, "Provinz. C. Assyrien," in Michael P. Streck, ed., *Reallexikon der Assyriologie und Vorderasiatischen Archäologie,* Berlin: De Gruyter, 2006, 62.

9 Sennacherib's vengeance on Tyre: *RINAP* [*Royal Inscriptions of the Neo-Assyrian Period*] 3.22.ii.37–60.

10 City of Revelry: Isaiah 23:7–8, trans. New International Version.

11 Radner, "Provinz. C. Assyrien," 63.

12 *RINAP* 4, Esarhaddon 60, obv. 9–11 (p. 135); for discussion and wording see Sebastián Celestino Pérez and Carolina López-Ruiz, *Tartessos and the Phoenicians in Iberia,* Oxford: Oxford University Press, 2016, 115–16.

13 "Hittites": Giovanni B. Lanfranchi, "The ideological and political impact of the Assyrian imperial expansion on the Greek world in the 8th and 7th centuries," in Sanna Aro and Robert M. Whiting, eds., *The Heirs of Assyria,* Helsinki: Neo-Assyrian Text Corpus Project, 2000, 28 n. 86.

14 Robert D. Ballard et al., "Iron Age shipwrecks in deep water off Ashkelon, Israel," *American Journal of Archaeology* 106, no. 2 (2002).

15 Ann C. Gunter, *Greek Art and the Orient,* Cambridge: Cambridge University Press, 2009; Ann C. Gunter, "Orientalism and orientalization in the Iron Age Mediterranean," in Brian A. Brown and Marian H. Feldman, eds., *Critical Approaches to Ancient Near Eastern Art,* Boston: De Gruyter, 2014; Marian H. Feldman, *Communities of Style: Portable Luxury Arts, Identity, and Collective Memory in the Iron Age Levant,* Chicago: University of Chicago Press, 2014, esp. 139–74.

16 Nicholas C. Vella, "The invention of the Phoenicians: on object definition, decontextualization, and display," in Josephine Crawley Quinn and Nicholas C. Vella, eds., *The Punic Mediterranean,* Cambridge: Cambridge University Press, 2014; Marian H. Feldman, "Levantine art in the 'orientalizing' period," in Carolina López-Ruiz and Brian R. Doak, eds., *The Oxford Handbook of the Phoenician and Punic Mediterranean,* Oxford: Oxford University Press, 2019.

17 Homer, *Iliad* 23.740–7.

18 Gunter, "Orientalism and orientalization," with Carolina López-Ruiz, *Phoenicians and the Making of the Mediterranean,* Cambridge, Mass.: Harvard University Press, 2021, for the bigger picture.

19 Ann Neville, *Mountains of Silver and Rivers of Gold: The Phoenicians in Iberia,* Oxford: Oxbow, 2007, 146.

20 Corinna Riva, "The culture of urbanization in the Mediterranean c. 800–600 BC," in Robin Osborne and Barry Cunliffe, eds., *Mediterranean Urbanization 800–600 BC,* Oxford: Oxford University Press, 2005, 223–5; Carlos González Wagner, "Tartessos and the orientalizing elites," in María Cruz Berrocal, Leonardo García Sanjuán, and Antonio Gilman, eds., *The Prehistory of Iberia: Debating Early Social Stratification and the State,* New York: Routledge, 2013, 348–50.

21 Ibid., 341.

22 Celestino Pérez and López-Ruiz, *Tartessos and the Phoenicians in Iberia,* 268–70, 281–3.

23 Riva, "The culture of urbanization in the Mediterranean," 211; Celestino Pérez and López-Ruiz, *Tartessos and the Phoenicians in Iberia,* 199–200.

24 Riva, "The culture of urbanization in the Mediterranean," 225.

25 Sean Myles et al., "Genetic structure and domestication history of the grape," *PNAS* 108, no. 9 (2011); Cyprian Broodbank, *The Making of the Middle Sea: A History of the Mediterranean from the Beginning to the Emergence of the Classical World,* London: Thames & Hudson, 2013, 222.

26 Ramon Buxó, "Botanical and archaeological dimensions of the colonial encounter," in Michael Dietler and Carolina López-Ruiz, eds., *Colonial Encounters in Ancient Iberia: Phoenician, Greek, and Indigenous Relations,* Chicago: University of Chicago Press, 2009, 157–60; Massimo Botto, "The Phoenicians and the spread of wine in the central west Mediterranean," in Sebastián Celestino Pérez and Juan Blánquez Pérez, eds., *Patrimonio cultural de la vid y el vino,* Madrid: UAM, 2013; Celestino Pérez and López-Ruiz, *Tartessos and the Phoenicians in Iberia,* 193.

27 Ibid., 159–70; Marta Díaz-Guardamino et al., "Rethinking Iberian 'warrior' stelae: a multidisciplinary investigation of Mirasiviene and its connection to Setefilla (Lorad el Río, Seville, Spain)," *Archaeological and Anthropological Sciences* 11, no. 11 (2019); Marta Díaz-Guardamino et al., "Late prehistoric stelae, persistent places and connected worlds: a multi-disciplinary review of the evidence at Almargen (Lands of Antequera, Spain)," *Cambridge Archaeological Journal* 30, no. 1 (2020).

28 Celestino Pérez and López-Ruiz, *Tartessos and the Phoenicians in Iberia,* 289–300; Coline Ruiz Darasse, "Writings in network? The case of Palaeohispanic scripts," in Philip J. Boyes and Philippa M. Steele, eds., *Understanding Relations Between Scripts II: Early Alphabets,* Oxford: Oxbow, 2019.

29 Strabo 3.1.6.

30 Roald Docter, "Archaische Transportamphoren," in H. G. Niemeyer et al., eds., *Karthago: die Ergebnisse der Hamburger Grabung under dem Decumanus Maximus,* Mainz am Rhein: Philipp von Zabern, 2007.

31 Fernando González de Canales et al., "Archaeological finds in the deepest anthropogenic stratum at 3 Concepción Street in the City of Huelva, Spain," *Ancient West and East* 16 (2017), 35.

32 Peter van Dommelen, "Ambiguous matters: colonialism and local identities in Punic Sardinia," in Claire L. Lyons and John K. Papadopoulos, eds., *The Archaeology of Colonialism: Issues and Debates,* Los Angeles: Getty Publications, 2002.

33 Emma Blake, "Late Bronze Age Sardinia: acephalous cohesion," in A. Bernard Knapp and Peter van Dommelen, eds., *The Cambridge Prehistory of the Bronze and Iron Age Mediterranean,* Cambridge: Cambridge University Press, 2014, 96–8.

34 Francesca Fulminante and Simon Stoddart, "Indigenous political dynamics and identity from a comparative perspective: Etruria and *Latium vetus,*" in Maria Emanuela Alberti and Serena Sabatini, eds., *Exchange Networks and Local Transformations,* Oxford: Oxbow, 2013.

35 *Rasna:* Dionysius of Halicarnassus 1.30.3; Denise Demetriou, *Negotiating Identity in the Ancient Mediterranean: The Archaic and Classical Greek Multiethnic Emporia,* Cambridge: Cambridge University Press, 2012, 10. *Penestai:* Dionysius of Halicarnassus 9.5.4.

36 Helmut Rix, "Etruscan," in Roger D. Woodard, ed., *The Ancient Languages of Europe*, Cambridge: Cambridge University Press, 2008.

37 Herodotus 1.94.

38 Silvia Ghirotto et al., "Origins and evolution of the Etruscans' mtDNA," *PLOS ONE* 8, no. 2 (2013); Cosimo Posth et al., "The origin and legacy of the Etruscans through a 2000-year archeogenomic time transect," *Science Advances* 7, no. 39 (2021).

39 Dominique Briquel, *L'origine lydienne des Étrusques: histoire de la doctrine dans l'antiquité*, Rome: École Française de Rome, 1991, 3–89.

40 Corinna Riva, "The orientalizing period in Etruria: sophisticated communities," in Corinna Riva and Nicholas C. Vella, eds., *Debating Orientalization: Multidisciplinary Approaches to Change in the Ancient Mediterranean*, London: Equinox, 2006, 120.

41 Jeremy Mark Hayne, "The Italian peninsula," in López-Ruiz and Doak, eds., *The Oxford Handbook of the Phoenician and Punic Mediterranean*. Trade route: Kristian Kristiansen, *Europe Before History*, Cambridge: Cambridge University Press, 1998, 161.

42 Filippo Delpino, "Viticoltura, produzione e consumo del vino nell'Etruria protostorica," in Andrea Ciacci, Paola Rendini, and Andrea Zifferero, eds., *Archeologia della vite e del vino in Toscana e nel Lazio*, Florence: All'Insegna del Giglio, 2012.

43 Philip Perkins, "Production and commercialization of Etruscan wine in the Albegna Valley," in Ciacci, Rendini, and Zifferero, eds., *Archeologia della vite e del vino in Toscana e nel Lazio*.

44 Massimo Botto, "The diffusion of Near Eastern cultures," in Alessandro Naso, ed., *Etruscology*, Berlin: De Gruyter, 2017, 606–7; Hayne, "The Italian peninsula," 513.

45 Borrowings: Anthony S. Tuck, "The Etruscan seated banquet: Villanovan ritual and Etruscan iconography," *American Journal of Archaeology* 98, no. 4 (1994); Ann C. Gunter, "The Etruscans, Greek art, and the Near East," in Sinclair Bell and Alexandra A. Carpino, eds., *A Companion to the Etruscans*, Chichester: Wiley Blackwell, 2016, 344–5 (on Neo-Hittite borrowings), with F.R.S. Ridgway, "Near-Eastern influences in Etruscan art," in Larissa Bonfante and Vassos Karageorghis, eds., *Italy and Cyprus in Antiquity 1500–450 B.C.*, Nicosia: Costakis and Leto Severis Foundation, 2001. Pottery: Riva, "The culture of urbanization in the Mediterranean," 205; Hayne, "The Italian peninsula," 514.

46 Human sacrifice: Nancy T. De Grummond, "Etruscan human sacrifice: the case of Tarquinia," in Carrie Ann Murray, ed., *Diversity of Sacrifice: Form and Function of Sacrificial Practices in the Ancient World and Beyond*, New York: State University of New York Press, 2016.

47 Charlotte R. Potts, *Religious Architecture in Latium and Etruria, c. 900–500 BC*, Oxford: Oxford University Press, 2015, 107: the *a telaio* architecture intersperses ashlars and smaller stones.

48 Corinna Riva, *The Urbanisation of Etruria: Funerary Practices and Social Change, 700–600 BC*, Cambridge: Cambridge University Press, 2010, 39–40, 58–9, 106–7, 125–54.

49 Pontecagnano tomb 928: Owain Morris, "Quid in nomine est? What's in a name: re-contextualising the princely tombs and social change in ancient Campania," in Elisa Perego and Rafael Scopacasa, eds., *Burial and Social Change in First-Millennium BC Italy*, Oxford: Oxbow, 2016, 152.

50 Riva, "The culture of urbanization in the Mediterranean," 225.

51 *Kanaanäische und Aramäische Inschriften* 1; I thank Vladimir Oliviero for discussion of the translation.

52 Riva, "The orientalizing period in Etruria," 123–4.

53 Ibid., 123.

54 Vincenzo Bellelli and Paolo Xella, eds., *Le lamine di Pyrgi,* Verona: Essedue, 2016.

55 Ola Wikander, "The religio-social message of the gold tablets from Pyrgi," *Opuscula* 1 (2008), 82.

56 Perkins, "Production and commercialization of Etruscan wine in the Albegna Valley."

57 Michael Dietler, "Consumption, agency, and cultural entanglement: theoretical implications of a Mediterranean colonial encounter," in James G. Cusick, ed., *Studies in Culture Contact: Interaction, Culture Change, and Archaeology,* Carbondale: Southern Illinois University Press, 1998, 305.

58 Daphne Nash Briggs, "Metals, salt, and slaves: economic links between Gaul and Italy from the eighth to the late sixth centuries BC," *Oxford Journal of Archaeology* 22, no. 3 (2003).

59 Karim Arafat and Catherine Morgan, "Athens, Etruria and the Heuneburg: mutual misconceptions in the study of Greek–barbarian relations," in Ian Morris, ed., *Classical Greece: Ancient Histories and Modern Archaeologies,* Cambridge: Cambridge University Press, 1994, 121–3.

60 Elena Isayev, "Tracing material endings of displacement," in Jan Driessen, ed., *An Archaeology of Forced Migration: Crisis-Induced Mobility and the Collapse of the 13th c. BCE Eastern Mediterranean,* Louvain-la-Neuve: Presses universitaires de Louvain, 2018, 85.

61 Daniele F. Maras, "Interethnic mobility and integration in pre-Roman Etruria: the contribution of onomastics," in James Clackson et al., eds., *Migration, Mobility and Language Contact in and around the Ancient Mediterranean,* Cambridge: Cambridge University Press, 2020.

62 Dionysius of Halicarnassus 3.46; Strabo 5.2.2; Tacitus, *Annals* 11.14; Polybius 6.11a.7; Isayev, "Tracing material endings of displacement," 84–5.

63 Rix, "Etruscan," 144.

64 Tom Rasmussen, "Urbanization in Etruria," in Osborne and Cunliffe, eds., *Mediterranean Urbanization,* 79–81; Riva, "The culture of urbanization in the Mediterranean," 211; Riva, "The orientalizing period in Etruria," 113.

65 Riva, "The orientalizing period in Etruria," 123.

66 Marek Węcowski, *The Rise of the Greek Aristocratic Banquet,* Oxford: Oxford University Press, 2014, 166: there is an image of a reclining banqueter on the lid of a funerary urn from Tolle that can be dated to the late seventh century BCE (Tomb no. 23), but since the individual is nude this may not reflect standard practice.

67 Mesopotamian origins: Annette Rathje, "Manners and customs in central Italy in the orientalizing period: influence from the Near East," in Tobias Fischer-Hansen, ed., *East and West: Cultural Relations in the Ancient World,* Copenhagen: Museum Tusculanum Press, 1988; Annette Rathje, "The adoption of the Homeric banquet in central Italy in the orientalizing period," in Oswyn Murray, ed., *Sympotica: A Symposium on the Symposion,* Oxford: Clarendon Press, 1990; Julian Edgeworth Reade, "The *symposion* in ancient Mesopotamia: archaeological evidence," in

Oswyn Murray and Manuela Tecusan, eds., *In Vino Veritas,* Rome: British School at Rome, 1995.

68 Albert Nijboer, "Banquet, *marzeah, symposion, and symposium* during the Iron Age: disparity and mimicry," in Franco De Angelis, ed., *Regionalism and Globalism in Antiquity,* Leuven: Peeters, 2013; Węcowski, *The Rise of the Greek Aristocratic Banquet,* 159–66. Amos 6.4–6 deplores the Levantine custom in the eighth century. In early seventh-century Cypriot imagery both men and women recline, as in Italy: Elizabeth P. Baughan, *Couched in Death: Klinai and Identity in Anatolia and Beyond,* Madison: University of Wisconsin Press, 2013, 203–4. Reclining is first unambiguously depicted in a Greek-speaking context on Corinthian kraters of the late seventh century BCE, while some images from central Italy continue to depict chairs as well as couches.

12. He Who Saw the Deep

1 Brief overview of the evidence available for dating: Barbara Graziosi, *Homer,* Oxford: Oxford University Press, 2016, 26–7.

2 See in much greater detail (and among other examples) M. L. West, *The East Face of Helicon: West Asiatic Elements in Early Poetry and Myth,* Oxford: Clarendon Press, 1997, 334–401; Bruno Currie, *Homer's Allusive Art,* Oxford: Oxford University Press, 2016; and above all Sarah P. Morris, "Homer and the Near East," in Ian Morris and Barry Powell, eds., *A New Companion to Homer,* Leiden: Brill, 1997, on which I heavily depend in this chapter.

3 See most recently Michael J. Clarke, *Achilles Beside Gilgamesh: Mortality and Wisdom in Early Epic Poetry,* Cambridge: Cambridge University Press, 2019.

4 Mothers: Homer, *Iliad* 1.413–18; *Gilgamesh* SBV [Standard Babylonian Version] III.1.22–54. Grieving: Homer, *Iliad* 18.318–23; *Gilgamesh* SBV VIII.61–2.

5 *Gilgamesh* SBV X.59–60; Homer, *Iliad* 19.23–7. The parallel is discussed at Carolina López-Ruiz, Fumi Karahashi, and Marcus Ziemann, "They who saw the deep: Achilles, Gilgamesh, and the Underworld," *Kaskal* 15 (2018), 95, with this translation from Andrew George, *The Babylonian Gilgamesh Epic,* Oxford: Oxford University Press, 2003, 278.

6 Morris, "Homer and the Near East," 620; West, *The East Face of Helicon,* 402–7.

7 Homer, *Odyssey* 4.350–575.

8 M. L. West, "The rise of the Greek epic," *Journal of Hellenic Studies* 108 (1988), 170; Sarah P. Morris, *Daidalos and the Origins of Greek Art,* Princeton: Princeton University Press, 1992, 79, 116.

9 Calvert Watkins, "The golden bowl: thoughts on the new Sappho and its Asianic background," *Classical Antiquity* 26, no. 2 (2007), 306–11.

10 Mary R. Bachvarova, *From Hittite to Homer: The Anatolian Background of Ancient Greek Epic,* Cambridge: Cambridge University Press, 2016, 21, on this fragment, and see ibid., *passim,* for possible connections between Anatolian and early Greek literature.

11 West, *The East Face of Helicon,* 276–80; Carolina López-Ruiz, *When the Gods Were Born: Greek Cosmogonies and the Near East,* Cambridge, Mass.: Harvard University Press, 2010, 87–94.

12 Ian Rutherford, "Borrowing, dialogue and rejection: intertextual interfaces in the

Late Bronze Age," in Adrian Kelly and Christopher Metcalf, eds., *Gods and Mortals in Early Greek and Near Eastern Mythology,* Cambridge: Cambridge University Press, 2021, 206–11; on the differences, see Adrian Kelly, "Sexing and gendering the Succession Myth in Hesiod and the ancient Near East," in the same volume.

13 Selena Wisnom, *The Library of Ancient Wisdom,* London: Penguin, forthcoming.

14 López-Ruiz, *When the Gods Were Born,* 35–7, with Euripides frag. 484.

15 Bachvarova, *From Hittite to Homer,* 234–6.

16 Poetry: Alexander Dale, "Alcaeus on the career of Myrsilos: Greeks, Lydians and Luwians at the east Aegean–west Anatolian interface," *Journal of Hellenic Studies* 131 (2011), 23.

17 See Bachvarova, *From Hittite to Homer,* 301–30, on the potential role of Cyprus, and Philippa Steele, *Syllabic Writing on Cyprus and Its Context,* Cambridge: Cambridge University Press, 2013, for Cypriot syllabic writing. I am grateful to Adrian Kelly for discussion of this point.

18 López-Ruiz, *When the Gods Were Born,* 94–109.

19 Wenamun ii.69.

20 Johannes Haubold, *Greece and Mesopotamia: Dialogues in Literature,* Cambridge: Cambridge University Press, 2013, 24.

21 There is lively scholarly debate over the full extent and significance of these borrowings: see, e.g., Adrian Kelly, "The Babylonian captivity of Homer: the case of the Dios," *Rheinisches Museum* 151 (2008); Christopher Metcalf, *The Gods Rich in Praise: Early Greek and Mesopotamian Religious Poetry,* Oxford: Oxford University Press, 2015, 130–227; Currie, *Homer's Allusive Art,* 147–222; and the papers collected in Adrian Kelly and Christopher Metcalf, *Gods and Mortals in Early Greek and Near Eastern Mythology,* Cambridge: Cambridge University Press, 2021.

22 Combination of dialects: Graziosi, *Homer,* 18.

23 Incorporation of cult myths and folktales: M. L. West, *The Hesiodic Catalogue of Women: Its Nature, Structure, and Origins,* Oxford: Oxford University Press, 1985, 164–71; West, "The rise of the Greek epic," 172.

24 Thucydides 1.3.

25 Homer, *Iliad* 6.213–36.

26 Hesiod, *Theogony* 1011–16, with Irad Malkin, *The Returns of Odysseus: Colonization and Ethnicity,* Berkeley: University of California Press, 1998, 180–91, for the authenticity of these lines.

27 Nancy Thomson De Grummond, *Etruscan Myth, Sacred History, and Legend,* Philadelphia: University of Pennsylvania Museum of Archaeology and Anthropology, 2006, esp. 22–7 on Tages.

28 Ingrid Krauskopf, "Myth in Etruria," in Sinclair Bell and Alexandra A. Carpino, eds., *A Companion to the Etruscans,* Chichester: Wiley Blackwell, 2016, 392.

29 Larissa Bonfante, "What role for Etruscans?," in Robert B. Koehl, ed., *Amilla: The Quest for Excellence,* Philadelphia: INSTAP Academic Press, 2013, 425.

30 Theopompus *BNJ* 115 F 354, with Irad Malkin, "A colonial middle ground: Greek, Etruscan, and local elites in the Bay of Naples," in Claire L. Lyons and John K. Papadopoulos, eds., *The Archaeology of Colonialism: Issues & Debates,* Los Angeles: Getty Publications, 2002, 170, for Greek versions of this story.

31 Josephine Crawley Quinn, *In Search of the Phoenicians,* Princeton: Princeton University Press, 2018, 126.

32 Justin 44.4.
33 A local story: Sebastián Celestino Pérez and Carolina López-Ruiz, *Tartessos and the Phoenicians in Iberia*, Oxford: Oxford University Press, 2016, 108; Andrew C. Johnston, *The Sons of Remus: Identity in Roman Gaul and Spain*, Cambridge, Mass.: Harvard University Press, 2017, 138–41.
34 Carolina López-Ruiz, "Gargoris and Habis: a Tartessic myth of ancient Iberia and the traces of Phoenician euhemerism," *Phoenix* 71, no. 3/4 (2017), with a discussion of plausible routes of transmission at 271.
35 Celestino Pérez and López-Ruiz, *Tartessos and the Phoenicians in Iberia*, 109–10.
36 For a skeptical reassessment of the fabled "thirteen-year siege" of Tyre in this era, see Helen Dixon, "Reexamining Nebuchadnezzar II's 'thirteen-year' siege of Tyre in Phoenician historiography," *Journal of Ancient History* 10, no. 2 (2022).
37 Ezekiel 27:33–6, trans. New International Version.

13. The Bitter River

1 British Museum 92687/1882,0714.509. For full text and commentary see Wayne Horowitz, "The Babylonian map of the world," *Iraq* 50 (1988). The text that accompanies the diagram says that it is a copy of an earlier document. Given the places included on the map, the original can't have been drawn up before the ninth century BCE. The text on the reverse of the tablet may not relate directly to the map: Johannes Haubold, *Greece and Mesopotamia: Dialogues in Literature*, Cambridge: Cambridge University Press, 2013, 107.
2 Imperial Babylon: Irving L. Finkel, Michael J. Seymour, and John Curtis, *Babylon: Myth and Reality*, London: British Museum, 2008; Marc Van de Mieroop, *A History of the Ancient Near East, ca. 3000–323 BC*, 3rd ed., Chichester: Wiley Blackwell, 2016, 294–307; Paul-Alain Beaulieu, *A History of Babylon, 2200 BC–AD 75*, Chichester: Wiley, 2018, 219–45; Karen Radner, *A Short History of Babylon*, London: Bloomsbury Academic, 2020, 111–38.
3 Finkel, Seymour, and Curtis, *Babylon*, 46–65.
4 Nabopolassar 6.ii.49–iii.13, trans. Frauke Weiershäuser and Jamie Novotny, *RINBE* [*Royal Inscriptions of the Neo-Babylonian Empire*] 1 (forthcoming); also available at http://oracc.museum.upenn.edu/ribo/babylon7/corpus.
5 John Steele, "The early history of the astronomical diaries," in Johannes Haubold, John M. Steele, and Kathryn Stevens, eds., *Keeping Watch in Babylon*, Leiden: Brill, 2019.
6 Eclipses: John M. Steele and Francis R. Stephenson, "Lunar eclipse times predicted by the Babylonians," *Journal for the History of Astronomy* 28, no. 2 (1997). *Bibbu:* John M. Steele, *A Brief Introduction to Astronomy in the Middle East*, London: Saqi, 2008, 21.
7 *Yawnaya.* Jonathan M. Hall, *Hellenicity: Between Ethnicity and Culture*, Chicago: University of Chicago Press, 2002, 70. The term could also be used of western Anatolians who didn't speak Greek.
8 Mercenaries: Strabo 13.2.3.
9 Strabo 1.1; Agathemerus 1.1; Diogenes Laërtius 2.1–2.
10 Herodotus 4.36. He also himself observes that the Mediterranean, Atlantic, and Indian Ocean are—unlike the Caspian Sea—"all one" (1.203).

11 Pseudo-Plutarch, *Stromateis* 2.
12 Herodotus 1.14. For Lydia, see Annick Payne and Jorit Wintjes, *Lords of Asia Minor: An Introduction to the Lydians,* Wiesbaden: Harrassowitz, 2016.
13 Archilochus frag. 19 West. On the Lydian origins of the term, Gregory Nagy, *Homer the Preclassic,* Berkeley: University of California Press, 2012, 363.
14 Ian Morris, *Archaeology as Cultural History: Words and Things in Iron Age Greece,* Oxford: Blackwell, 2000, 178–85.
15 Dance of the Lydian Maidens: Autocrates F1 Kock = Aelian, *On the Nature of Animals* 12.9, and Aristophanes, *Clouds* 599–600. Coinage at Ephesos: Michael Kerschner and Koray Konuk, "Electrum coins and their archaeological context: the case of the Artemision of Ephesus," in Peter van Alfen and Ute Wartenberg, eds., *White Gold: Studies in Early Electrum Coinage,* New York: American Numismatic Society, 2020.
16 Susan Sherratt, "From the Near East to the Far West," in Irene S. Lemos and Antonis Kotsonas, eds., *A Companion to the Archaeology of Early Greece and the Mediterranean,* Chichester: Wiley Blackwell, 2019, 188.
17 Polykrates of Samos: Herodotus 3.39; Strabo 14.1.16.
18 Andrew Wilson, "Hydraulic engineering and water supply," in John Peter Oleson, ed., *The Oxford Handbook of Engineering and Technology in the Classical World,* Oxford: Oxford University Press, 2008, 290–4.
19 Sarah P. Morris, "The view from east Greece: Miletus, Samos and Ephesus," in Corinna Riva and Nicholas C. Vella, eds., *Debating Orientalization: Multidisciplinary Approaches to Change in the Ancient Mediterranean,* London: Equinox, 2006, 72.
20 Herodotus 2.181–2, 3.47; cf. 2.159 for earlier dedications at Branchidae from Necho II.
21 Ionian mercenaries under Psamtik II in Egypt in the 590s: ML 7.
22 Herodotus 2.178.
23 Denise Demetriou, "Beyond *polis* religion: religious practices in the cosmopolitan *emporion* of Naukratis," *BABESCH* 92 (2017), 49–51.
24 Herodotus 2.134–5, with Denise Demetriou, *Negotiating Identity in the Ancient Mediterranean: The Archaic and Classical Greek Multiethnic Emporia,* Cambridge: Cambridge University Press, 2012, 105.
25 Herodotus 2.178; Irad Malkin, *A Small Greek World: Networks in the Ancient Mediterranean,* New York: Oxford University Press, 2011, 91; Demetriou, *Negotiating Identity in the Ancient Mediterranean,* 144–5; Josephine Crawley Quinn, *In Search of the Phoenicians,* Princeton: Princeton University Press, 2018, 43. Note the reservations about the location of the Helleneion expressed at Hugh Bowden, "The Greek settlement and sanctuaries at Naukratis: Herodotus and archaeology," in Mogens Herman Hansen and Kurt Raaflaub, eds., *More Studies in the Ancient Greek* Polis, Stuttgart: Franz Steiner, 1996, 24.
26 Hall, *Hellenicity,* 25–9.
27 Josephine Crawley Quinn, "Herms, kouroi and the political anatomy of Athens," *Greece and Rome* 54, no. 1 (2007), 97; Robin Osborne, *Greece in the Making, 1200–479 B.C.,* 2nd ed., London: Routledge, 2009, 197; see Carolina López-Ruiz, *Phoenicians and the Making of the Mediterranean,* Cambridge, Mass.: Harvard University Press, 2021, 214–16, for the argument that these design features might have arrived via the Levant.

28 Herodotus 1.10.3.

29 Larissa Bonfante, "Nudity as a costume in Classical art," *American Journal of Archaeology* 93, no. 4 (1989), for the chronology of nudity in Greek art.

30 Thucydides 1.6.5–6.

31 López-Ruiz, *Phoenicians and the Making of the Mediterranean,* 213–14.

32 Susan Sherratt and Andrew Sherratt, "The growth of the Mediterranean economy in the early first millennium BC," *World Archaeology* 24, no. 3 (1993), 374; Malkin, *A Small Greek World,* 158–60.

33 Carthage: Boutheina Maraoui Telmini et al., "Defining Punic Carthage," in Josephine Crawley Quinn and Nicholas C. Vella, eds., *The Punic Mediterranean,* Cambridge: Cambridge University Press, 2014, 131–3; Quinn, *In Search of the Phoenicians,* 83. Grave goods: Hélène Bénichou-Safar, *Les tombes puniques de Carthage: topographie, structures, inscriptions et rites funéraires,* Paris: Centre national de la recherche scientifique, 1982, esp. 267–8; Eleftheria Pappa, *Early Iron Age Exchange in the West: Phoenicians in the Mediterranean and the Atlantic,* Leuven: Peeters, 2013, 147.

34 Joan Sanmartí et al., "Filling gaps in the protohistory of the eastern Maghreb: the Althiburos archaeological project (El Kef, Tunisia)," *Journal of African Archaeology* 10, no. 1 (2012). For more on the intensification of trade between Carthage and inland African cities in the seventh and especially sixth centuries BCE, when even some Massaliot pottery reaches sites in the Tunisian Tell, see Stefan Ardeleanu, "Westlicher Maghreb," in Anne-Maria Wittke, ed., *Frühgeschichte der Mittelmeerkulturen: Historisch-archäologisches Handbuch,* Stuttgart: Springer, 2015, section D1.

35 Ahmed Ferjaoui, "Les femmes à Carthage à travers les documents épigraphiques," *Reppal* 11 (1999); Josephine Crawley Quinn, "The cultures of the tophet: identification and identity in the Phoenician diaspora," in Erich Gruen, ed., *Cultural Identity in the Ancient Mediterranean,* Los Angeles: Getty Publications, 2011, 398.

36 Babette Bechtold, "Observations on the amphora repertoire of Middle Punic Carthage," *Carthage Studies* 2 (2008), noting that because it is impossible to distinguish amphoras produced in Phoenician-speaking settlements on Sardinia and Sicily from those made in the region around Carthage itself in north Africa, short-distance trade (or taxation) connections around the Strait of Sicily cannot easily be traced in the archaeology.

37 Benjamí Costa, "Ibiza," in Carolina López-Ruiz and Brian R. Doak, eds., *The Oxford Handbook of the Phoenician and Punic Mediterranean,* Oxford: Oxford University Press, 2019, 572, 574–5.

38 Elymians in 580: Pausanias 10.11.3. Makai in 515: Herodotus 5.42. Segestans in 510: Herodotus 5.46. Battle of Alalia: Herodotus 1.164–7.

39 Thucydides 1.13.6 with Nino Luraghi, "Author and audience in Thucydides' 'Archaeology': some reflections," *Harvard Studies in Classical Philology* 100 (2000), 236–7

40 Justin 43.4.6–12; Athenaeus, *Dinner Party Guests* 13.576a–b = Aristotle frag. 560 Rose. See also Herodotus 1.163 for the claim that Phokaians had been the first Greeks to make long-distance voyages, reaching Iberia and even "Tartessos."

41 Daphne Nash Briggs, "Metals, salt, and slaves: economic links between Gaul and Italy from the eighth to the late sixth centuries BC," *Oxford Journal of Archaeology* 22, no. 3 (2003), 247.

42 Tamar Hodos, *The Archaeology of the Mediterranean Iron Age: A Globalising World, c. 1100–600 BCE,* Cambridge: Cambridge University Press, 2020, 82.

43 Sixth century: Michael Dietler, "The Iron Age in Mediterranean France: colonial encounters, entanglements, and transformations," *Journal of World Prehistory* 11, no. 3 (1997), 294–5.

44 Nash Briggs, "Metals, salt, and slaves," 247; Alex Mullen, *Southern Gaul and the Mediterranean: Multilingualism and Multiple Identities in the Iron Age and Roman Periods,* Cambridge: Cambridge University Press, 2013, 30.

45 Dietler, "The Iron Age in Mediterranean France," 294–5; Barry W. Cunliffe, *The Extraordinary Voyage of Pytheas the Greek,* London: Allen Lane, 2001, 12.

46 For Emporion see Strabo 3.4.8 with Demetriou, *Negotiating Identity in the Ancient Mediterranean,* 30–63; Denise Demetriou, "Interpreting cultural contact: how Greek inscriptions from Emporion challenge Roman texts and Hellenization," in Éric Gailledrat, Michael Dietler, and Rosa Plana-Mallart, eds., *The* Emporion *in the Ancient Western Mediterranean: Trade and Colonial Encounters from the Archaic to the Hellenistic Period,* Montpellier: Presses universitaires de la Méditerranée, 2018; David Garcia i Rubert and Francisco Gracia Alonso, "Phoenician trade in the northeast of the Iberian peninsula: a historiographical problem," *Oxford Journal of Archaeology* 30, no. 1 (2011); Peter van Dommelen, "Classical connections and Mediterranean practices: exploring connectivity and local interactions," in Tamar Hodos, ed., *The Routledge Handbook of Archaeology and Globalization,* London: Routledge, 2017, 624–7.

47 Sebastián Celestino Pérez and Carolina López-Ruiz, *Tartessos and the Phoenicians in Iberia,* Oxford: Oxford University Press, 2016, 202–6.

48 Guy Bradley, *Early Rome to 290 BC: The Beginnings of the City and the Rise of the Republic,* Edinburgh: Edinburgh University Press, 2020, 139; this is the latest survey history of early Rome.

49 Size of early Rome: Francesca Fulminante and Simon Stoddart, "Indigenous political dynamics and identity from a comparative perspective: Etruria and *Latium vetus,*" in Maria Emanuela Alberti and Serena Sabatini, eds., *Exchange Networks and Local Transformations,* Oxford: Oxbow, 2013, 121; Bradley, *Early Rome to 290 BC,* 145.

50 John North Hopkins, *The Genesis of Roman Architecture,* New Haven: Yale University Press, 2016, 27–34.

51 Helmut Rix, "Etruscan," in Roger D. Woodard, ed., *The Ancient Languages of Europe,* Cambridge: Cambridge University Press, 2008, 145; Daniele Maras, "Numbers & reckoning: a whole civilization founded upon divisions," in Jean MacIntosh Turfa, ed., *The Etruscan World,* London: Routledge, 2013, 487–8.

52 Nancy T. De Grummond, "Haruspicy and augury: sources and procedures," in Turfa, ed., *The Etruscan World,* 543.

53 Ara Maxima: Plutarch, *Roman Questions* 60, 90; Propertius 4.9.67–70; Pliny the Elder, *Natural History* 10.79; Solinus 1.10–11. Tyrian connection: Raymond Westbrook, "III. The nature and origins of the Twelve Tables," *Zeitschrift der Savigny-Stiftung für Rechtsgeschichte: Romanistische Abteilung* 105, no. 1 (1988), 98; Richard Miles, *Carthage Must Be Destroyed: The Rise and Fall of an Ancient Mediterranean Civilization,* London: Allen Lane, 2010, 109. On Carthaginian traders in Rome in later periods see Robert E. A. Palmer, *Rome and Carthage at Peace,* Stuttgart: Franz Steiner, 1997, 31–52.

54 Oath: Charlotte R. Potts, *Religious Architecture in Latium and Etruria, c. 900–500 BC*, Oxford: Oxford University Press, 2015, 115. Worshipped as a god: ibid., 112. Levantine model: Ingrid Krauskopf, "Myth in Etruria," in Sinclair Bell and Alexandra A. Carpino, eds., *A Companion to the Etruscans*, Chichester: Wiley Blackwell, 2016, 394–5.

55 Temple complex: Daniel P. Diffendale et al., "Sant'Omobono: an interim status quaestionis," *Journal of Roman Archaeology* 29, no. 1 (2016). Aegean models: Hopkins, *The Genesis of Roman Architecture*, 53–63.

56 A second pair are much more fragmentary, and therefore harder to identify, but may represent Dionysus and Ariadne: A. Mura Somella, "Arianna ritrovata! Un nuovo gruppo acroteriale dall'Area Sacra del Foro Boario," in Patricia Lulof and Christopher Smith, eds., *The Age of Tarquinius Superbus: Central Italy in the Late Sixth Century BC*, Leuven: Peeters, 2017, with Diffendale et al., "Sant'Omobono," 16.

57 Hopkins, *The Genesis of Roman Architecture*, 74–9.

58 Penelope Davies, "Exploring the international arena: the Tarquins' aspirations for the Temple of Jupiter Optimus Maximus," in Carol C. Mattusch et al., eds., *Common Ground: Archaeology, Art, Science and Humanities*, Oxford: Oxbow, 2006.

59 Pliny, *Natural History* 35.157.

60 Gabriele Cifani, *The Origins of the Roman Economy: From the Iron Age to the Early Republic in Mediterranean Perspective*, Cambridge: Cambridge University Press, 2021, 84. There is debate as to whether this first wall fully enclosed the city or provided intermittent fortifications: Seth G. Bernard, "Continuing the debate on Rome's earliest circuit walls," *Papers of the British School at Rome* 80 (2012); Margaret Andrews and Seth Bernard, "Urban development at Rome's Porta Esquilina and church of San Vito over the longue durée," *Journal of Roman Archaeology* 30 (2017), 248–50.

61 Gabriele Cifani, "The fortifications of Archaic Rome: social and political significance," in Rune Frederiksen et al., eds., *Focus on Fortifications*, Oxford: Oxbow, 2012, 86.

14. The King of Kings

1 Nebuchadnezzar II 2.vi.19, trans. Frauke Weiershäuser and Jamie Novotny, *RINBE* [*Royal Inscriptions of the Neo-Babylonian Empire*] 1 (forthcoming); also available at http://oracc.museum.upenn.edu/ribo/babylon7/corpus.

2 When Cyrus describes his entry into Babylon on the Cyrus Cylinder (*TUAT* [*Texte aus der Umwelt des Alten Testaments*] 1/4.407–10, trans. Amélie Kuhrt, *The Persian Empire*, London: Routledge, 2007, 70–4), he conflates aspects of that event with the peaceful fall of the city to his troops on October 12, and probably other episodes as well; I have followed his example. The events are mentioned more briefly in the near-contemporary Babylonian Chronicles compiled at the Marduk temple: Nabonidus Chronicle 14–19 (Albert Kirk Grayson, *Assyrian and Babylonian Chronicles*, Locust Valley: J. J. Augustin, 1975, no. 7; trans. Kuhrt, *The Persian Empire*, 50–3).

3 On Persia and its empire, see Pierre Briant, *From Cyrus to Alexander: A History of the Persian Empire*, trans. Peter T. Daniels, Winona Lake: Eisenbrauns, 2002; John

Curtis and Nigel Tallis, eds., *Forgotten Empire: The World of Ancient Persia,* London: British Museum Press, 2005; Maria Brosius, *The Persians: An Introduction,* London: Routledge, 2006; Matt Waters, *Ancient Persia: A Concise History of the Achaemenid Empire, 550–330 BCE,* Cambridge: Cambridge University Press, 2014; Bruno Jacobs and Robert Rollinger, eds., *A Companion to the Achaemenid Persian Empire,* Hoboken: Wiley Blackwell, 2021. I learned a lot about Persians myself from a lecture series given in 2018 by my colleague Peter Thonemann.

4 Nabonidus Chronicle II.1–4. He was technically Cyrus II, but we know very little of Cyrus I.

5 Herodotus 1.6.50–4, 92, 141, 161–9.

6 Nabonidus Chronicle III.12–16.

7 Cyrus Cylinder 18.

8 Comparative sizes of historical empires: Peter Turchin, Jonathan M. Adams, and Thomas D. Hall, "East–west orientation of historical empires and modern states," *Journal of World-Systems Research* 12, no. 2 (2006).

9 Herodotus 3.97.

10 Ktesias frag. 9.3.

11 Herodotus 1.205–6, 211–14.

12 For comprehensive discussion of the mythology and the archaeology, see Adrienne Mayor, *The Amazons: Lives and Legends of Warrior Women Across the Ancient World,* Princeton: Princeton University Press, 2014.

13 V. I. Guliaev, "Amazons in the Scythia: new finds at the Middle Don, southern Russia," *World Archaeology* 35, no. 1 (2003).

14 Kuhrt, *The Persian Empire,* 137.

15 Column 5, which tells of later victories against Elam and the pointy-hatted Scythians, is only inscribed in Old Persian.

16 CMa, cf. CMb and CMc. Achaemenid royal inscriptions are cataloged according to a standard system whereby the first letter refers to the king (here Cyrus), the second to the place (here Murghab, the region of Pasargadae) and the third to a specific text.

17 Herodotus 3.88.2–3.

18 See, e.g., DSe §2, with Briant, *From Cyrus to Alexander,* 180.

19 DB §70, with Kuhrt, *The Persian Empire,* 157.

20 Thomas R. Trautmann, *Aryans and British India,* Berkeley: University of California Press, 1997, esp. 172–8.

21 Léon Poliakov, *The Aryan Myth: A History of Racist and Nationalist Ideas in Europe,* New York: New American Library, 1977, 183–214, 261–72; Trautmann, *Aryans and British India,* 184–7; Felix Wiedemann, "The Aryans: ideology and historiographical narrative types in the nineteenth and early twentieth centuries," in Helen Roche and Kyriakos N. Demetriou, eds., *Brill's Companion to the Classics, Fascist Italy and Nazi Germany,* Leiden: Brill, 2018.

22 For an earlier, and fragmentary, Assyrian ethnographic catalog, see the eighth- or seventh-century *Sargon Geography,* 51–2, 57–9, with Wayne Horowitz, *Mesopotamian Cosmic Geography,* Winona Lake: Eisenbrauns, 1998, 90–2; visual "catalogs" of foreign peoples can also be found in Bronze Age Egyptian art.

23 Herodotus 3.89.

24 Herodotus 4.93; Plutarch, *Alexander* 36.4.

25 Margaret C. Miller, *Athens and Persia in the Fifth Century B.C.: A Study in Cultural Receptivity,* Cambridge: Cambridge University Press, 1997, 97–113.

26 Alexandra Villing, "Persia and Greece," in John Curtis and Nigel Tallis, eds., *Forgotten Empire: The World of Ancient Persia,* London: British Museum Press, 2005, 237.
27 DSf §12; Miller, *Athens and Persia in the Fifth Century* B.C., 102.
28 Kuhrt, *The Persian Empire,* 785.
29 Herodotus 1.152–3.
30 Herodotus 5.73.
31 Attic exports: Susan Sherratt and Andrew Sherratt, "The growth of the Mediterranean economy in the early first millennium BC," *World Archaeology* 24, no. 3 (1993), 374. Immigrant artisans: Walter Burkert, *The Orientalizing Revolution: Near Eastern Influence on Greek Culture in the Early Archaic Age,* Cambridge, Mass.: Harvard University Press, 1992, 23 (Amasis, Lydos, Brygos).

15. The Persian Version

1 Plutarch, *Moralia* 225d.
2 https://pharos.vassarspaces.net/2021/01/14/capitol-terrorists-take-inspiration-from-ancient-world; other supporters of the insurrection carried posters encouraging the outgoing president to "cross the Rubicon," as Julius Caesar had done when he led an army against his own government.
3 Jonathan M. Hall, *Ethnic Identity in Greek Antiquity,* Cambridge: Cambridge University Press, 1997, 13; see also Helen Roche, "*Spartanische Pimpfe:* the importance of Sparta in the educational ideology of the Adolf Hitler Schools," in Stephen Hodkinson and Ian MacGregor Morris, eds., *Sparta in Modern Thought,* Swansea: Classical Press of Wales, 2012.
4 Herodotus 5.49–50, 97. Herodotus provides the main ancient account of the conflicts between Persia and Greek states, written about fifty years after the final battles. While partisan in its interpretations and unreliable on numbers, his account of the basic facts and events is well sourced, and probably in large part correct.
5 Herodotus 6.18–21.
6 Herodotus 6.48–9, 7.133–6.
7 Effect on the reputation of Athens: Lisa Kallet, "The fifth century: political and military narrative," in Robin Osborne, ed., *Classical Greece, 500–323* BC, Oxford: Oxford University Press, 2000, 172.
8 DNa §§28-29.
9 Herodotus 7.132 for a list.
10 Russell Meiggs and David Lewis, *A Selection of Greek Historical Inscriptions to the End of the Fifth Century* B.C., Oxford: Clarendon Press, 1969, 27, for the official list.
11 Herodotus 7.138.
12 Herodotus 8.142.
13 Composition of Persian fleet: Herodotus 7.89–99.
14 Herodotus 7.206–28, esp. 220. For a reality check on the myths that still surround this battle—as seen for instance in the film *300* (2006)—see https://www.badancient.com/claims/did-300-spartans-halt-persian-advance-thermopylae.
15 Herodotus 8.40 1.
16 Herodotus 8.140.
17 Herodotus 9.3, 13.

18 Pausanias 1.8.5; Arrian, *Anabasis* 7.19.2.

19 Drinking songs: Athenaeus, *Dinner Party Guests* 695. Meals: *IG* I^3 131. Statues (and much else): Vincent Azoulay, *The Tyrant-Slayers of Ancient Athens: A Tale of Two Statues,* Oxford: Oxford University Press, 2017.

20 Thucydides 6.54–7.

21 Survey: Robin Osborne, "Imaginary intercourse: an illustrated history of Greek pederasty," in Danielle Allen, Paul Christesen, and Paul Millett, eds., *How To Do Things with History: New Approaches to Ancient Greece,* Oxford: Oxford University Press, 2018.

22 Herodotus 1.135.

23 Council on Chios: Meiggs and Lewis, *Greek Historical Inscriptions,* 8; something similar is reported—much later—for contemporary Athens (*Constitution of Athens* 8.4; Plutarch, *Solon* 19.1). Popular government at Cyrene, Samos, and Athens: Herodotus 4.161, 3.142, 5.69.

24 Herodotus 6.43.

25 Herodotus 3.80; here he calls the concept *isonomia* (equality in law); at 6.43 with reference to the same conversation he calls it *demokratia.*

26 See *Constitution of Athens* 48.

27 Sara Forsdyke, *Exile, Ostracism, and Democracy: The Politics of Expulsion in Ancient Greece,* Princeton: Princeton University Press, 2005, 144–204, 285–8, for ostracism outside Athens, including at Syracuse.

28 Plutarch, *Aristides* 7.2–6; Philochorus *BNJ* 328 F 30.

29 Citizenship: *Constitution of Athens* 26. Slaves from the Levant: David Lewis, "Near Eastern slaves in Classical Attica and the slave trade with Persian territories," *Classical Quarterly* 61, no 1 (2011).

30 For sexual services expected of slaves see, among many examples, Xenophon, *Oeconomicus* 10.12; Lysias 1.12.

31 Maria Brosius, *Women in Ancient Persia, 559–331 B.C.,* Oxford: Clarendon Press, 1996; Maria Brosius, *The Persians: An Introduction,* London: Routledge, 2006, 41–3; Matt Waters, *King of the World,* Oxford: Oxford University Press, 2022, 48–54.

32 Artemisia: Herodotus 7.99, 8.87.

33 Brosius, *The Persians,* 53.

34 The classic work on women in ancient Greece is Sarah B. Pomeroy, *Goddesses, Whores, Wives, and Slaves: Women in Classical Antiquity,* London: Pimlico, 1994; see also David M. Schaps, *Economic Rights of Women in Ancient Greece,* Edinburgh: Edinburgh University Press, 1979.

35 Lloyd Llewellyn-Jones, *Aphrodite's Tortoise: The Veiled Woman of Ancient Greece,* Swansea: Classical Press of Wales, 2003.

36 Thucydides 2.45.

37 Thucydides 1.96. On the concept of Greek freedom, see Robin Seager and Christopher Tuplin, "The freedom of the Greeks of Asia: on the origins of a concept and the creation of a slogan," *Journal of Hellenic Studies* 100 (1980).

38 Herodotus 6.42.

39 Benjamin Dean Meritt, Malcolm Francis McGregor and H. T. Wade-Gery, *The Athenian Tribute Lists,* Princeton: American School of Classical Studies at Athens, 1939. Strictly speaking these listed the 1/60 of each contribution that was given to Athena herself.

40 *IG* I[3] 14, ll. 23–9, trans. Robin Osborne and Peter J. Rhodes, *Greek Historical Inscriptions 478–404 BC*, Oxford: Oxford University Press, 2017, no. 121.
41 Lisa Kallet-Marx, "Did tribute fund the Parthenon?," *Classical Antiquity* 8, no. 2 (1989).
42 Margaret Cool Root, "The Parthenon frieze and the Apadana reliefs at Persepolis: reassessing a programmatic relationship," *American Journal of Archaeology* 89, no. 1 (1985), 114–15.
43 Ibid.
44 Margaret C. Miller, *Athens and Persia in the Fifth Century BC: A Study in Cultural Receptivity*, Cambridge: Cambridge University Press, 1997, 110–11; John O. Hyland, *Persian Interventions: The Achaemenid Empire, Athens, and Sparta, 450–386 BCE*, Baltimore: Johns Hopkins University Press, 2018.
45 Hyland, *Persian Interventions*, 42–75.

16. Continental Thinking

1 Daniela Dueck and Kai Brodersen, *Geography in Classical Antiquity*, Cambridge: Cambridge University Press, 2012, 35–6. Hekataios is also said to have corrected or updated Anaximander's map (Agatheremus 1.1 = *BNJ* 1 T 12a).
2 Eric H. Cline, "Achilles in Anatolia: myth, history, and the Assuwa rebellion," in Gordon D. Young, Mark W. Chavalas, and Richard E. Averbeck, eds., *Crossing Boundaries and Linking Horizons: Studies in Honor of Michael C. Astour on His 80th Birthday*, Bethesda: CDL Press, 1996, 192; Naoíse Mac Sweeney, "Separating fact from fiction in the Ionian migration," *Hesperia* 86, no. 3 (2017), 383–4, with Homer, *Iliad* 2.461, Hesiod, *Catalogue of Women* 182 Most, and Archilochus 227 West. On the problems of identifying Assuwa see Ian Rutherford, "Diplomatic marriage as an engine for religious change: the case of Assuwa and Ahhiyawa," in Michele Bianconi, ed., *Linguistic and Cultural Interactions Between Greece and Anatolia: In Search of the Golden Fleece*, Leiden: Brill, 2021, 168–70.
3 Homeric Hymn to Pythian Apollo 251; Herodotus 6.43.
4 Herodotus 4.42–3.
5 Herodotus 4.44.
6 Trans-Saharan Route: Herodotus 4.181–5. Coastal trading: Herodotus 4.196, of debated reliability.
7 Herodotus 4.45.
8 Herodotus 3.115.
9 Herodotus 4.36; cf. 4.42, 45 for his own views on the comparative size of Asia and Europe.
10 Herodotus 4.45.
11 See further Martin W. Lewis and Kären Wigen, *The Myth of Continents: A Critique of Metageography*, Berkeley: University of California Press, 1997.
12 Diodorus Siculus 11.62.3; cf. Palatine Anthology 7.296; Aelius Aristides 2.215.
13 This strategy would represent a change in Persian rhetoric after 479, and the loss of European territories: for an earlier ideology of universal empire, see Johannes Haubold, *Greece and Mesopotamia: Dialogues in Literature*, Cambridge: Cambridge University Press, 101–14, and cf. Herodotus 1.209, 7.5, 8, 50, 54.
14 Herodotus 1.1–4.

15 Herodotus 1.4.4, 1.5.1; cf. 1.107.8, 9.116.3, and 9.122 for similar statements of the Persian claim to Asia.
16 Phiroze Vasunia, "Between east and west: mobility and ethnography in Herodotus' proem," *History and Anthropology* 23, no. 2 (2012), 184.
17 Johannes Haubold, "Xerxes' Homer," in Emma Bridges, Edith Hall, and Peter J. Rhodes, eds., *Cultural Responses to the Persian Wars: Antiquity to the Third Millennium,* Oxford: Oxford University Press, 2007, esp. 49–52.
18 Herodotus 7.43, with Haubold, "Xerxes' Homer," 54–6, for the interpretation advanced here.
19 Herodotus 7.150–1; I thank Alistair Blanshard for drawing my attention to this passage.
20 Jonathan M. Hall, *Hellenicity: Between Ethnicity and Culture,* Chicago: University of Chicago Press, 2002.
21 Speculation on the origins of the term *barbaros:* Strabo 14.2.28.
22 Aeschylus, *Persians,* 181–99; see also, e.g., 745–6, and 403 on "sons of Hellas" as a force of liberation.
23 Thucydides 6.2.6; Herodotus 5.57.
24 Thucydides 1.96.2. For post–Persian Wars panhellenism: Sofie Remijsen, "Only Greeks at the Olympics? Reconsidering the rule against non-Greeks at 'panhellenic' games," *Classica et Mediaevalia* 67 (2019), 15–16.
25 Hermippos frag. 63.
26 Trade with the Levant: Peter van Alfen, "Aegean–Levantine trade, 600–300 BCE: commodities, consumers, and the problem of autarkeia," in David M. Lewis, Edward M. Harris, and Mark Woolmer, eds., *The Ancient Greek Economy: Markets, Households and City-States,* Cambridge: Cambridge University Press, 2015. Trade with Persia: Amélie Kuhrt, *"Greeks" and "Greece" in Mesopotamian and Persian Perspectives,* Oxford: Leopard's Head Press, 2002, 13; Margaret C. Miller, *Athens and Persia in the Fifth Century BC: A Study in Cultural Receptivity,* Cambridge: Cambridge University Press, 1997, 65–74.
27 Edith Hall, *Inventing the Barbarian: Greek Self-Definition Through Tragedy,* Oxford: Clarendon Press, 1989; Margaret C. Miller, "Persians: the oriental other," *Source* 15, no. 1 (1995); Miller, *Athens and Persia in the Fifth Century BC.*
28 Miller, *Athens and Persia in the Fifth Century BC,* 141–3, 156–65, 218–42. Alexandra Villing, "Persia and Greece," in John Curtis and Nigel Tallis, eds., *Forgotten Empire: The World of Ancient Persia,* London: British Museum Press, 2005.
29 Plutarch, *Pericles* 13.9–11; Pausanias 1.20.4.
30 Ralph Anderson, "New gods," in Esther Eidenow and Julia Kindt, eds., *The Oxford Handbook of Ancient Greek Religion,* Oxford: Oxford University Press, 2015.
31 Denise Demetriou, *Phoenicians Among Others,* Oxford: Oxford University Press, 2023, chapter 1. Decree: *IG* II.2 141 (c. 365–360 BCE).
32 Diogenes Laërtius 7.3, 11.
33 Carolina López-Ruiz, *Phoenicians and the Making of the Mediterranean,* Cambridge, Mass.: Harvard University Press, 2021, 240.
34 Herodotus 9.122.3–4.
35 Cf. Haubold, *Greece and Mesopotamia,* 78–98, on the Mesopotamian roots of the Greek notion of a historical succession of empires.
36 Rosalind Thomas, *Herodotus in Context: Ethnography, Science and the Art of Persuasion,* Cambridge: Cambridge University Press, 2000, 86–98, for full

discussion, arguing that this is a product of the western Anatolian not mainland Greek intellectual milieu.

37 *Airs, Waters, Places,* 12.

38 Ibid., 16, 23. The rule of the environment is not absolute: freedom from tyranny, even in Asia, is another great prompt to courage (16).

39 Ibid., 12.

40 Aristotle, *Politics* 1327b, trans. Stephen Everson, *The Politics and the Constitution of Athens,* Cambridge: Cambridge University Press, 1996, 175, very slightly adapted.

41 Theopompus *BNJ* 115 F 204.

42 Aristotle, *Meteorology* 2.5, 362a32.

43 Subject to Persia before and during Persian Wars: Herodotus 5.18; DNa 3. Philip built on a family claim to Greek roots going back to the Olympics of 500 BCE. When fellow competitors there objected to the participation of the Macedonian king Alexander I on the grounds that he wasn't Greek, he successfully invented an Argive ancestor: Herodotus 5.22, 8.137–9.

44 Plutarch, *Alexander* 10.

45 Isocrates, *To Philip* 132; cf. *Helen* 67.

46 Isocrates, *Panegyricus* 17, 187, *To Philip* 9, *Helen* 51, and (for Europe's superiority to Asia) *Panathenaicus* 47, with Jacqueline de Romilly, "Isocrates and Europe," *Greece & Rome* 39, no. 1 (1992).

47 Demosthenes, *Philippics* 3.31, slightly adapted from the colorful translation by J. H. Vince in the Loeb Classical Library edition (London: Heinemann, 1930).

48 Diodorus Siculus 16.89.2; Polybius 3.6.13. Both are clear that this was a pretext for Philip's own imperial ambitions.

17. Of Elephants and Kings

1 Plutarch, *Alexander* 15.4–5.

2 Diodorus Siculus 17.39.1.

3 Arrian, *Anabasis* 2.14.4, 9.

4 Plutarch, *Alexander* 34.1.

5 Arrian, *Anabasis* 3.8.6, 3.11.6, with Michael B. Charles, "Alexander, elephants, and Gaugamela," *Mouseion* 52, no. 1 (2008).

6 The fragment is preserved at Aelian, *On the Nature of Animals* 4.21.

7 Arrian, *Anabasis* 3.16.4, 7.17.2; Strabo 16.1.15.

8 H. H. Scullard, *The Elephant in the Greek and Roman World,* London: Thames & Hudson, 1974, 65.

9 Diodorus Siculus 17.70.2.

10 Arrian, *Anabasis* 3.21.

11 Prostration: Arrian, *Anabasis* 4.10–12; Curtius 8.5.6; Plutarch, *Alexander* 54. I am in debt to Aneurin Ellis-Evans for my understanding of these events.

12 Andrew W. Collins, "The royal costume and insignia of Alexander the Great," *American Journal of Philology* 133, no. 3 (2012).

13 Arrian, *Anabasis* 4.4.1; Curtius 7.6.25–7; Justin 12.5.12; *EAH,* "Alexandria Eschate."

14 Curtius 8.13.5–6 (85); Diodorus Siculus 17.87.2 (130); Arrian, *Anabasis* 5.15.4 (200).

15 Arrian, *Anabasis* 5.15–17; Diodorus Siculus 17.87–8; Curtius 8.14.24–31.

16 Diodorus Siculus 17.89.2.
17 Plutarch, *Alexander* 62.2.
18 Diodorus Siculus 17.93–4.
19 Scullard, *The Elephant in the Greek and Roman World*, 73–4.
20 Arrian, *Anabasis* 7.4.
21 Plutarch, *On the Fortune of Alexander* 329c.
22 Ibid., 329a–b. Ancient cosmopolitanism: A. A. Long, "The concept of the cosmopolitan in Greek & Roman thought," *Daedalus* 137, no. 3 (2008).
23 See Anthony Pagden, "Stoicism, cosmopolitanism, and the legacy of European imperialism," *Constellations* 7, no. 1 (2000), 4–5, noting also that Zeno and other Stoics were said to have believed that only the good and the wise were candidates for world citizenship.
24 Plutarch, *Alexander* 14.
25 Diogenes Laërtius 6.63.
26 Cf. W. W. Tarn, *Alexander the Great and the Unity of Mankind*, London: H. Milford, 1933, with E. Badian, "Alexander the Great and the unity of mankind," *Historia* 7, no. 4 (1958).
27 See Jeremy Waldron, "What is cosmopolitan?," *Journal of Political Philosophy* 8, no. 2 (2000), for a spirited defense of cultural cosmopolitanism.
28 Diodorus Siculus 19.14.8.
29 Most recently, see Rachel Mairs, *The Graeco-Bactrian and Indo-Greek World*, London: Routledge, 2021, and https://www.carc.ox.ac.uk/gandharaconnections.
30 Daniel 11.3–5, trans. New International Version.
31 P. M. Fraser, *Ptolemaic Alexandria*, Oxford: Clarendon Press, 1972; Judith McKenzie, *The Architecture of Alexandria and Egypt, c. 300 BC to AD 700*, New Haven: Yale University Press, 2007.
32 Strabo 17.1.7.
33 DZc; Herodotus 2.158; Carol A. Redmount, "The Wadi Tumilat and the 'Canal of the Pharaohs,'" *Journal of Near Eastern Studies* 54, no. 2 (1995).
34 Posidippos 115 ed. Austin and Bastianini; Strabo 17.1.6; McKenzie, *The Architecture of Alexandria and Egypt*, 41–5.
35 Strabo 17.1.8, with Fraser, *Ptolemaic Alexandria* 1.312–19.
36 Roger S. Bagnall, "Alexandria: library of dreams," *Proceedings of the American Philosophical Society* 146, no. 4 (2002), 356 n. 36. This article usefully summarizes how little we really know about the library at Alexandria.
37 Archimedes, *The Sand-Reckoner* 4–5.
38 *EAH*, "Science, Mesopotamian."
39 Kleostrates: Pliny, *Natural History* 2.31. First surviving Greek discussion: Hypsicles, *On Rising-Times* (fl. c. 190 BCE), with Clemency Montelle, "The *Anaphoricus* of Hypsicles of Alexandria," in John M. Steele, ed., *The Circulation of Astronomical Knowledge in the Ancient World*, Leiden: Brill, 2016, for the subsequent integration of earlier Babylonian arithmetical astronomy with the Aegean geometrical tradition.
40 Walter Burkert, "Prehistory of Presocratic philosophy in an orientalizing context," in Patricia Curd and Daniel W. Graham, eds., *The Oxford Handbook of Presocratic Philosophy*, Oxford: Oxford University Press, 2008, 65.
41 Yossef Rapoport and Emilie Savage-Smith, *Lost Maps of the Caliphs: Drawing the World in Eleventh-Century Cairo*, Oxford: Bodleian Library, 2018, 75.

42 Klaus Geus, *Eratosthenes von Kyrene: studien zur hellenistischen Kultur- und Wissenschaftsgeschichte,* Munich: C. H. Beck, 2002.
43 Athenaeus, *Dinner Party Guests* 5.198e–f.
44 Tessa Rajak, *Translation and Survival: The Greek Bible of the Ancient Jewish Diaspora,* Oxford: Oxford University Press, 2009.
45 Denis C. Feeney, *Beyond Greek: The Beginnings of Latin Literature,* Cambridge, Mass.: Harvard University Press, 2016, 24.
46 J. Y. Empereur and Stéphane Compoint, *Alexandria Rediscovered,* London: British Museum Press, 1998; Franck Goddio and Manfred Clauss, *Egypt's Sunken Treasures,* Munich: Prestel, 2006; Jürgen Bischoff, Christoph Gerigk, and Lynda Matschke, *Diving to the Pharaohs: Franck Goddio's Discoveries in Egypt,* Göttingen: Steidl, 2016.
47 McKenzie, *The Architecture of Alexandria and Egypt,* 43–4.
48 Self-description: Pausanias 6.3.1, 10.7.8. Coronation of Ptolemy V: *Orientis Graeci Inscriptiones Selectae* 90, line 28 (the Rosetta Stone).
49 Greek population: Dorothy J. Thompson, "The multilingual environment of Persian and Ptolemaic Egypt: Egyptian, Aramaic, and Greek documentation," in Roger S. Bagnall, ed., *The Oxford Handbook of Papyrology,* Oxford: Oxford University Press, 2011, 401. Daybook of an official postal station: Sel. Pap. II 397, c. 255 BCE.
50 Diodorus Siculus 19.85.4. Cabbages: Athenaeus, *Dinner Party Guests* 9.369f.
51 Jane Rowlandson, "Town and country in Ptolemaic Egypt," in Andrew Erskine, ed., *A Companion to the Hellenistic World,* Oxford: Blackwell, 2003, 254–9.
52 Denis C. Feeney, *Caesar's Calendar: Ancient Time and the Beginnings of History,* Berkeley: University of California Press, 2007, 139; Paul J. Kosmin, *Time and Its Adversaries in the Seleucid Empire,* Cambridge, Mass.: Harvard University Press, 2018.
53 *EAH,* "Antioch."
54 Jeremy A. Black et al., *The Literature of Ancient Sumer,* Oxford: Oxford University Press, 2004, li; Maria Brosius, *The Persians: An Introduction,* London: Routledge, 2006, 81.
55 Strabo 15.2.9; Appian, *Syrian Wars* 55; Justin 15.4.20–1; Plutarch, *Alexander* 62.4; Pliny, *Natural History* 6.23.4. On this treaty see Paul J. Kosmin, *The Land of the Elephant Kings: Space, Territory, and Ideology in the Seleucid Empire,* Cambridge, Mass.: Harvard University Press, 2014, 32–7.
56 *Periplus* 3; Stanley M. Burstein, "Ivory and Ptolemaic exploration of the Red Sea: the missing factor," *Topoi* 6, no. 2 (1996), arguing that they sought ivory as well as live animals; Matthew Cobb, "The decline of Ptolemaic elephant hunting: an analysis of the contributory factors," *Greece & Rome* 63, no. 2 (2016).
57 Polybius 5.84.5–6, with Michael B. Charles, "Elephants at Raphia: reinterpreting Polybius 5.84–5," *Classical Quarterly* 57, no. 1 (2007), for the possibility that some of the elephants were Indian, captured decades earlier from the Seleucids.
58 Cobb, "The decline of Ptolemaic elephant hunting," 198 n. 31; cf. Adam L. Brandt, "The elephants of Gash-Barka, Eritrea: nuclear and mitochondrial genetic patterns," *Journal of Heredity* 105, no. 1 (2013). Future aDNA studies may clarify this issue.
59 Scullard, *The Elephant in the Greek and Roman World,* 100.

18. Clouds in the West

1 Christopher Brooke, "Eighteenth-century Carthage," in Béla Kapossy, Isaac Nakhimovsky, and Richard Whatmore, eds., *Commerce and Peace in the Enlightenment,* Cambridge: Cambridge University Press, 2017; Josephine Crawley Quinn, "Translating empire from Carthage to Rome," *Classical Philology* 112 (2017).

2 Adam Ferguson, *An Essay on the History of Civil Society,* Edinburgh: A. Kincaid and J. Bell, 1767, 291.

3 Milton: "The ready and easy way to establish a new Commonwealth" (1660), reprinted at Robert W. Ayers, ed., *Complete Prose Works of John Milton,* vol. 7, New Haven: Yale University Press, 1980, 422–3; Shaftesbury: *Grey's Debates of the House of Commons* II, p. 2: February 5, 1673.

4 J. A. van der Welle, *Dryden and Holland,* Groningen: J. B. Wolters, 1962, 23.

5 Polybius 6.51.1–2.

6 Polybius 6.25.11.

7 Polybius 3.22–3.

8 Etruscan treaties: Aristotle, *Politics* 3.1280a.

9 Quinn, "Translating empire from Carthage to Rome," 324.

10 See Sandrine Crouzet, "Les status civiques dans l'Afrique punique: de l'historiographie moderne à l'historiographie antique," *Mélanges de l'Ecole Française de Rome—Antiquité* 115 (2003), on the problems inherent in the long-running scholarly game of trying to map Roman institutions onto Carthaginian ones we know about in far less detail.

11 Judges: Reuven Yaron, "Semitic influence in early Rome," in Allan Watson, ed., *Daube Noster: Essays in Legal History for David Daube,* Edinburgh: Scottish Academic Press, 1974, 351–4. The word was used in Phoenician (and Hebrew) as a synonym for "ruler."

12 *Roman Statutes* 2.555–721.

13 Twelve Tables I.14, trans. *Roman Statutes.*

14 Codex Eshnunna 45, quoted and discussed at Raymond Westbrook, "III. The nature and origins of the Twelve Tables," *Zeitschrift der Savigny-Stiftung für Rechtsgeschichte: Romanistische Abteilung* 105, no. 1 (1988), 45.

15 For this argument and a comprehensive discussion of the Twelve Tables, see *OCD,* "Twelve Tables."

16 Polybius 3.24.

17 D. B. Harden, "The topography of Punic Carthage," *Greece & Rome* 9, no. 25 (1939), 6–7, with the Epitome of Livy 51; cf. Strabo 17.3.14, who gives an unrealistic figure of 360 stadia, over fifty-five kilometers. Harden suggests that Syracuse was the nearest rival with a wall circuit of perhaps seventeen miles (twenty-seven kilometers).

18 Josephine Crawley Quinn, *In Search of the Phoenicians,* Princeton: Princeton University Press, 2018, 82–3. Imports: Babette Bechtold, "Observations on the amphora repertoire of Middle Punic Carthage," *Carthage Studies* 2 (2008), with the caution advised in Mark Lawall's review in *Journal of Roman Archaeology* 23 (2010), 445–8. Exports: useful diagrams at Babette Bechtold, "The trade routes of Carthaginian amphorae," in Alfonsina Russo et al., eds., *Carthago: The Immortal Myth,* Rome: Electa, 2019. Trading enclaves or "fonduqs": Elizabeth B. Fentress, "Strangers in the city: élite communication in the Hellenistic central Mediterra-

nean," in Jonathan R. W. Prag and Josephine Crawley Quinn, eds., *The Hellenistic West: Rethinking the Ancient Mediterranean,* Cambridge: Cambridge University Press, 2013, 157–8. Athens and Corinth: Xenophon, *Oeconomicus* 8.11–19; Margaret C. Miller, *Athens and Persia in the Fifth Century* BC: *A Study in Cultural Receptivity,* Cambridge: Cambridge University Press, 1997, 64.

19 Ports: Pseudo-Skylax 111.9. Drowning: Strabo 17.1.19, with Pseudo-Aristotle, *On Wonders* 136 on Carthaginian control of the Gaditan tuna trade.

20 Joseph H. Marcus et al., "Genetic history from the Middle Neolithic to present on the Mediterranean island of Sardinia," *Nature Communications* 11 (2020); see also Daniel M. Fernandes et al., "The spread of steppe and Iranian-related ancestry in the islands of the western Mediterranean," *Nature Ecology & Evolution* 4 (2020).

21 Elizabeth A. Matisoo-Smith et al., "A European mitochondrial haplotype identified in ancient Phoenician remains from Carthage, north Africa," *PLOS ONE* 11, no. 5 (2016); Hannah M. Moots et al., "A genetic history of continuity and mobility in the Iron Age central Mediterranean," *Nature Ecology & Evolution* 7 (2023).

22 Emma Dench, *Romulus' Asylum: Roman Identities from the Age of Alexander to the Age of Hadrian,* Oxford: Oxford University Press, 2005, 164. For a survey of Roman cultural and social linkage with the rest of the Mediterranean in this era see Dan-el Padilla Peralta and Seth Bernard, "Middle republican connectivities," *Journal of Roman Studies* 112 (2022).

23 Plutarch, *Pyrrhus* 21.9.

24 Elephants in the triumph: Florus 1.13.28.

25 Diodorus Siculus 22.7.5, with Richard Miles, *Carthage Must Be Destroyed: The Rise and Fall of an Ancient Mediterranean Civilization,* London: Allen Lane, 2010, 415 n. 30, and Plutarch, *Pyrrhus* 24.1.

26 Polybius 1.10.5, 8. Carthaginian imperialism: Quinn, "Translating empire from Carthage to Rome"; Quinn, *In Search of the Phoenicians,* 87–8.

27 Polybius 1.20, 47, 59, 62.

28 509: Polybius 3.22.4; the same formulation is used in the mid-fourth-century treaty between Rome and Carthage (3.24.3), 241: Polybius 1.62.8.

29 Polybius 1.88.8–12.

30 Quinn, "Translating empire from Carthage to Rome," esp. 325–7.

31 Polybius 3.14–15.

32 Polybius 3.39–56.

33 Mercenaries: Livy 24.49.7–8, 25.33 (213–212 BCE).

34 Josephine Crawley Quinn, "North Africa," in Andrew Erskine, ed., *A Companion to Ancient History,* Oxford: Wiley Blackwell, 2009; Josephine Crawley Quinn, "Monumental power: 'Numidian royal architecture' in context," in Prag and Quinn, eds., *The Hellenistic West.*

35 For the battle and its aftermath, Polybius 15.12–18.

36 Polybius 5.104.10.

37 See most recently Seth Bernard et al., "An environmental and climate history of the Roman expansion in Italy," *Journal of Interdisciplinary History* 54, no. 1 (2023), emphasizing the local variability of the phenomenon in Italy, and human response to climate change. It cannot go without saying that the climate fluctuations that can be detected in the period covered by this book are insignificant by

comparison with the speed and extent of global warming we are experiencing in the current man-made environmental crisis, as temperatures rise more than ten times faster than the historical norm in the upswing from an ice age: see for instance https://royalsociety.org/topics-policy/projects/climate-change-evidence-causes/question-6.

38 For what follows, see Kyle Harper and Michael McCormick, "Reconstructing the Roman climate," in Walter Scheidel, ed., *The Science of Roman History*, Princeton: Princeton University Press, 2018.

39 Horace, *Epistles* 2.1.156–7.

40 Cicero, *Brutus* 72. See further Denis C. Feeney, *Beyond Greek: The Beginnings of Latin Literature*, Cambridge, Mass.: Harvard University Press, 2016, 122–38.

41 Feeney, *Beyond Greek*, 152–78.

42 Suetonius, *Terence* 1.

43 Temples: Charlotte R. Potts, *Religious Architecture in Latium and Etruria, c. 900–500 BC*, Oxford: Oxford University Press, 2015, 2.

44 Cicero, *On the Nature of the Gods* 3.60.

45 Polybius 6.23.6.

46 Livy 45.32.10.

47 Plutarch, *Aemilius Paulus* 29.4.

48 Strabo 14.5.2, also emphasizing the connection between piracy and slaving. See Dan-el Padilla Peralta, "Epistemicide: the Roman case," *Classica* 33, no. 2 (2020) on "the obliteration of epistemic diversity" across the growing empire, but especially in the western provinces (153), and Sailakshmi Ramgopal, "Connectivity and disconnectivity in the Roman empire," *Journal of Roman Studies* 112 (2022), 221–8, on the disconnectivities imposed by Roman imperial connectivity.

49 Liv Mariah Yarrow, *Historiography at the End of the Republic: Provincial Perspectives on Roman Rule*, Oxford: Oxford University Press, 2005, 37–44; Amy Richlin, "The traffic in shtick," in Matthew P. Loar, Carolyn MacDonald, and Dan-el Padilla Peralta, eds., *Rome, Empire of Plunder*, Cambridge: Cambridge University Press, 2017, 170.

50 Alexander Jones, *A Portable Cosmos: Revealing the Antikythera Mechanism, Scientific Wonder of the Ancient World*, New York: Oxford University Press, 2017.

51 Livy 36.4.

52 Roald Docter, "Urbanism," in Russo et al., eds., *Carthago*, 88; Ivan Fumadó Ortega, "Urban houses," in Russo et al., eds., *Carthago*, 89; Polybius 18.35.

53 Appian, *African Wars* 76.

54 Ibid., 127.

55 Ibid., 130; Cicero, *Tusculan Disputations* 3.53.

56 Polybius 38.22; Appian, *African Wars* 129.

57 Salt: R. T. Ridley, "To be taken with a pinch of salt: the destruction of Carthage," *Classical Philology* 81, no. 2 (1986), with https://www.badancient.com/claims/carthage-salted.

58 Appian, *African Wars* 135, with Cicero, *Verrines* 3.12; for the Carthaginian practice of charging taxes in towns and a tithe on land see Polybius 1.71–2.

59 Pliny, *Natural History* 18.22.

60 *Gazette nationale de France* 1798: Corps législatif, Conseil des cinq-cents, Séance de 24 Ventôse, with H. D. Schmidt, "The idea and slogan of perfidious Albion," *Journal of the History of Ideas* 14, no. 1 (1953).

19. Fighting for Freedom

1 Opera: Julian Rushton, "Mitridate, re di Ponto (Mithridates, King of Pontus)," in Stanley Sadie and Laura Macy, eds., *The Grove Book of Operas,* 2nd ed., Oxford: Oxford University Press, 2006. Play: Peter France, "Mithridate," in *The New Oxford Companion to Literature in French* (1995). King: Adrienne Mayor, *The Poison King: The Life and Legend of Mithradates, Rome's Deadliest Enemy,* Princeton: Princeton University Press, 2009, 378.

2 Christopher A. Stray, "Culture and discipline: classics and society in Victorian England," *International Journal of the Classical Tradition* 3, no. 1 (1996), 78–9 for this curriculum.

3 Name: Mayor, *The Poison King,* 27.

4 Duane W. Roller, *Empire of the Black Sea: The Rise and Fall of the Mithridatic World,* New York: Oxford University Press, 2020, 79–80, 84.

5 B. C. McGing, *The Foreign Policy of Mithridates VI Eupator, King of Pontus,* Leiden: Brill, 1986, 43–4.

6 Pliny, *Natural History* 7.24.

7 Sallust, *Histories* 2.73 Maurenbrecher; Justin 38.7.1; Tacitus, *Annals* 12.18; Appian, *Mithridatic Wars* 112. The claim to Achaemenid descent could be true: A. B. Bosworth and P. V. Wheatley, "The origins of the Pontic house," *Journal of Hellenic Studies* 118 (1998).

8 Strabo 11.9; Justin 41.4; Paul J. Kosmin, *Time and Its Adversaries in the Seleucid Empire,* Cambridge, Mass.: Harvard University Press, 2018, 98–9, on the Arsacid era.

9 Maria Brosius, *The Persians: An Introduction,* London: Routledge, 2006, 80, for the distribution of Parthian coinage.

10 Justin 41.3.

11 Cataphracts: e.g., Plutarch, *Life of Crassus* 24.1, 25.4. Parthian shot: e.g., Vergil, *Georgics* 3.31.

12 Barry W. Cunliffe, *By Steppe, Desert, and Ocean: The Birth of Eurasia,* Oxford: Oxford University Press, 2015, 98.

13 Sima Qian, *Shiji* 123 (c. 90 BCE, the earliest account), trans. Burton Watson, *Records of the Grand Historian of China,* New York: Columbia University Press, 1961, vol. 2, 264–89.

14 Sima Qian, *Shiji* 123, trans. Watson, *Records of the Grand Historian of China,* vol. 2, 268.

15 Appian, *Mithridatic Wars* 10.

16 Epitome of Livy 70; Plutarch, *Sulla* 5.4–5.

17 Memnon *BNJ* 434 F 1.38.8; Sallust, *Histories* 4.69.1–23; Appian, *Mithridatic Wars* 87; Dio 36.1–3; Plutarch, *Lucullus* 30.1.

18 Appian, *Mithridatic Wars* 10.

19 Cicero, *Pro lege Manilia* 19.

20 Cicero, *Pro Flacco* 60.

21 Appian, *Mithridatic Wars* 22–3; Plutarch, *Sulla* 24.4; Orosius 6.2.2–3; Eutropius 5.5.2.

22 Number of victims: Valerius Maximus 9.2.3; Memnon 22.9; cf. Plutarch, *Sulla* 24 (150,000). Credit crunch: Cicero, *Pro lege Manilia* 19, with Philip Kay, *Rome's Economic Revolution,* Oxford: Oxford University Press, 2014, 243–57.

23 Mayor, *The Poison King,* 21.
24 Appian, *Mithridatic Wars* 107–12.
25 Plutarch, *Pompey* 39; Appian, *Mithridatic Wars* 106.
26 Plutarch, *Pompey* 36.2, 39.3; Appian, *Mithridatic Wars* 106; Dio 37.5–7.
27 Plutarch, *Crassus* 2.
28 Gold: Dio 40.27.3. Banquet: Plutarch, *Crassus* 32–3.
29 Strabo 4.1.5; Valerius Maximus 2.6.7–8.
30 Christina Horst Roseman, *Pytheas of Massalia:* On the Ocean: *Text, Translation and Commentary,* Chicago: Ares, 1994, and Lionel Scott, *Pytheas of Massalia: Texts, Translation, and Commentary,* London: Routledge, 2022, for texts and translations of the fragments; Barry W. Cunliffe, *The Extraordinary Voyage of Pytheas the Greek,* London: Allen Lane, 2001, for further commentary. There is no clear evidence for the preservation of an even earlier "Massaliote Periplus" within Avienius' work, and reports of Carthaginian explorations of the Atlantic, while entirely plausible, may well in the versions we have of them be Greek fictions.
31 Pliny, *Natural History* 37.35–7; Cunliffe, *The Extraordinary Voyage of Pytheas the Greek,* 99–100; David J. Breeze and Alan Wilkins, "Pytheas, Tacitus and Thule," *Britannia* 49 (2018).
32 Polybius 34.5.3.
33 Karim Arafat and Catherine Morgan, "Athens, Etruria and the Heuneburg: mutual misconceptions in the study of Greek–barbarian relations," in Ian Morris, ed., *Classical Greece: Ancient Histories and Modern Archaeologies,* Cambridge: Cambridge University Press, 1994, 128; Alex Mullen, *Southern Gaul and the Mediterranean: Multilingualism and Multiple Identities in the Iron Age and Roman Periods,* Cambridge: Cambridge University Press, 2013, 98–110, 147–78; cf. Justin 43.4.1–2.
34 Strabo 4.1.5.
35 Barry W. Cunliffe, *Europe Between the Oceans: 9000 BC–AD 1000,* New Haven: Yale University Press, 2008, 372–4.
36 Elizabeth B. Fentress, "The Domitii Ahenobarbi and tribal slaving in Gaul," in Mirco Modolo et al., eds., *Una lezione di archeologia globale: studi in onore di Daniele Manacorda,* Bari: Edipuglia, 2019.
37 Diodorus Siculus 5.26.3.
38 Fentress, "The Domitii Ahenobarbi and tribal slaving in Gaul," 152.
39 Caesar, *Gallic War* 1.29.
40 Ibid., 2.28.
41 Ibid., 2.33.
42 Ibid., 4.14–15; Plutarch, *Cato the Younger* 51.1–2.
43 Appian, *Gallic War* 1.6.
44 Nico Roymans and Manuel Fernández-Götz, "Caesar in Gaul: new perspectives on the archaeology of mass violence," *Theoretical Roman Archaeology Journal* (2015), 74–7; Nico Roymans, "Conquest, mass violence and ethnic stereotyping: investigating Caesar's actions in the Germanic frontier zone," *Journal of Roman Archaeology* 32 (2019).
45 Suetonius, *Caesar* 54.2.
46 Caesar, *Civil War* 1.2 for the phrase.
47 Plutarch, *Caesar* 49.1 2.
48 Suetonius, *Caesar* 35.2, 37.2.

49 [Caesar], *Spanish War* 32.
50 Cicero, *Philippics* 2.110.

20. Rome, Open City

1 Augustus, *Res Gestae* 6.2; Dio 51.19.6; Suetonius, *Augustus* 56 for an example of the veto.
2 Augustus, *Res Gestae* 34; Suetonius, *Augustus* 7.
3 T. J. Cornell, "Aeneas and the twins: the development of the Roman foundation legend," *Proceedings of the Cambridge Philological Society* 21 (1975), 7–11.
4 Livy 1.3–6.
5 Emma Dench, *Romulus' Asylum: Roman Identities from the Age of Alexander to the Age of Hadrian*, Oxford: Oxford University Press, 2005, 15–20.
6 Livy 1.8.6; cf. Livy 5.53.9; Velleius Paterculus 1.8.5; Plutarch, *Romulus* 9.3.
7 Livy 1.9–13.
8 Cornell, "Aeneas and the twins," 16–22, on this and other early Greek tales of Rome.
9 Ibid., 15, with Cato, *Origines*, frag. 8–13; earlier versions are found in Ennius and Naevius.
10 Elena Isayev, "Tracing material endings of displacement," in Jan Driessen, ed., *An Archaeology of Forced Migration: Crisis-Induced Mobility and the Collapse of the 13th c.* BCE *Eastern Mediterranean*, Louvain-la-Neuve: Presses universitaires de Louvain, 2018, 84.
11 Patrick J. Geary, *The Myth of Nations: The Medieval Origins of Europe*, Princeton: Princeton University Press, 2002, 63–79.
12 Romulus: Livy 1.8.3.
13 Masks: Dio 56.34, with Harriet I. Flower, *Ancestor Masks and Aristocratic Power in Roman Culture*, Oxford: Clarendon Press, 1996, 245–6.
14 Ovid, *Fasti* 5.550–68; Velleius Paterculus 2.39.2; Suetonius, *Augustus* 29.2; Dio 55.10.2–5.
15 Augustus, *Res Gestae* 29. After Carrhae, Antony had lost even more Roman standards during an attempt to contain Persian expansion west during Rome's civil wars: Dio 48.24–7.
16 Dio 54.8.1.
17 Charles Brian Rose, "The Parthians in Augustan Rome," *American Journal of Archaeology* 109, no. 1 (2005), 23.
18 Justin 41.1.1.
19 Dio 55.10.6–8.
20 Amanda Claridge, *Rome: An Oxford Archaeological Guide*, 2nd ed., Oxford: Oxford University Press, 2010, is an excellent guide to the extant remains of the ancient city, liberally exploited here.
21 Strabo 5.3.8.
22 Vitruvius 2.8.11.
23 F. Coarelli and Y. Thebert, "Architecture funéraire et pouvoir: réflexions sur l'hellénisme numide," *Mélanges de l'École Française de Rome—Antiquité* 100, no. 2 (1988), 791–3. This was a replacement for the original tomb, and it was built by Ptolemy IV Philopater (r. 221–205).

24 Dio 51.16.5, with Suetonius, *Augustus* 17.2. Augustus also used an image of Alexander as his seal: Pliny, *Natural History* 37.10; Suetonius, *Augustus* 50.

25 Pliny, *Natural History* 36.69–70 on its transportation, and for a comprehensive study Molly Swetnam-Burland, "*Aegyptus Redacta:* the Egyptian obelisk in the Augustan Campus Martius," *Art Bulletin* 92, no. 3 (2010).

26 Grant Parker, "Monolithic appropriation? The Lateran Obelisk compared," in Matthew P. Loar, Carolyn MacDonald, and Dan-el Padilla Peralta, eds., *Rome, Empire of Plunder,* Cambridge: Cambridge University Press, 2017; Jennifer Trimble, "Appropriating Egypt for the Ara Pacis Augustae," in Loar, MacDonald, and Peralta, eds., *Rome, Empire of Plunder,* 116. On the Roman fascination in private as well as public contexts with Egypt and Egyptian art, see Miguel John Versluys, *Aegyptiaca Romana: Nilotic Scenes and the Roman Views of Egypt,* Leiden: Brill, 2002; Molly Swetnam-Burland, *Egypt in Italy: Visions of Egypt in Roman Imperial Culture,* New York: Cambridge University Press, 2015; Caitlín Eilís Barrett, *Domesticating Empire: Egyptian Landscapes in Pompeian Gardens,* Oxford: Oxford University Press, 2019; and Stephanie Pearson, *The Triumph and Trade of Egyptian Objects in Rome: Collecting Art in the Ancient Mediterranean,* Berlin: De Gruyter, 2021, comparing Roman attitudes to Egyptian art with their longer-standing embrace of Greek art.

27 Trimble, "Appropriating Egypt for the Ara Pacis Augustae," 117–19. Roman understanding of Egyptian obelisks: Pliny, *Natural History* 36.64–9.

28 Peter Heslin, "Augustus, Domitian and the so-called Horologium Augusti," *Journal of Roman Studies* 97 (2007), with Pliny, *Natural History* 36.72–3. Sections of this meridian come to light from time to time in excavations and basements, providing rather hazardous glimpses into the city's past well below the water table.

29 It is worth noting that the pavement was relaid in the later first century, and it is not certain that the old lettering was reproduced exactly.

30 Hannah Cornwell, *Pax and the Politics of Peace: Republic to Principate,* Oxford: Oxford University Press, 2017, 155–83.

31 Trimble, "Appropriating Egypt for the Ara Pacis Augustae," 121–8.

32 Ibid., 115–16, 126–8.

33 Pliny, *Natural History* 3.17, with Pascal Arnaud, "Texte et carte d'Agrippa," *Geographica Antiqua* 16–17 (2007–2008); Pascal Arnaud, "Marcus Vipsanius Agrippa and his geographical work," in Serena Bianchetti et al., eds., *Brill's Companion to Ancient Geography: The Inhabited World in Greek and Roman Tradition,* Leiden: Brill, 2015; Andrew Merrills, *Roman Geographies of the Nile: From the Late Republic to the Early Empire,* Cambridge: Cambridge University Press, 2017, 27–36.

34 Augustus, *Res Gestae* 23; Dio 55.10.7; Ovid, *Art of Love* 1.171.

35 Dio 55.10.8.

36 Mobility: Sailakshmi Ramgopal, "Mobility," in Carlos F. Noreña, ed., *A Cultural History of Western Empires in Antiquity,* London: Bloomsbury Academic, 2018, exploring the links between physical and social mobility. Migration to Rome: Neville Morley, "Migration and the metropolis," in Catharine Edwards and Greg Woolf, eds., *Rome the Cosmopolis,* Cambridge: Cambridge University Press, 2003 (a wonderful reimagining of the scholarly article); Laurens Ernst Tacoma, *Moving Romans: Migration to Rome in the Principate,* Oxford: Oxford University Press, 2016.

37 Roman population estimates: Andrew Wallace-Hadrill, "Imperial Rome: a city of

immigrants?," *Acta ad Archaeologiam et Artium Historiam Pertinentia* 29 (2017), 55–6, 68. Although the 1 million figure is commonly accepted in the scholarship, it is just an informed guess, and could easily be off by up to 50 percent either way. On the enslaved population, emphasizing the difficulty of estimation: Walter Scheidel, "Human mobility in Roman Italy, II: the slave population," *Journal of Roman Studies* 95 (2005).

38 Seneca, *Consolatio ad Helviam* 6.2–3.

39 aDNA: Margaret L. Antonio et al., "Ancient Rome: a genetic crossroads of Europe and the Mediterranean," *Science* 366, no. 6466 (2019).

40 Martin Goodman, *Rome and Jerusalem: The Clash of Ancient Civilizations*, London: Allen Lane, 2007, 385–8.

41 Arabic graffiti: Kyle Helms, "Pompeii's Safaitic graffiti," *Journal of Roman Studies* 111 (2021). Vagnari necropolis: Matthew V. Emery et al., "Ancient Roman mitochondrial genomes and isotopes reveal relationships and geographic origins at the local and pan-Mediterranean scales," *Journal of Archaeological Science: Reports* 20 (2018).

42 Short- and middle-distance migration: Greg Woolf, "Movers and stayers," in Luuk de Ligt and Laurens Ernst Tacoma, eds., *Migration and Mobility in the Early Roman Empire*, Leiden: Brill, 2016. Seasonal migration: Paul Erdkamp, "Seasonal labor and rural–urban migration in Roman Italy," in de Ligt and Tacoma, eds., *Migration and Mobility in the Early Roman Empire.*

43 Migration under Roman empire: de Ligt and Tacoma, eds., *Migration and Mobility in the Early Roman Empire*, and James Clackson, *Migration, Mobility and Language Contact in and Around the Ancient Mediterranean*, Cambridge: Cambridge University Press, 2020. Migration to Britain: Hella Eckardt, ed., *Roman Diasporas: Archaeological Approaches to Mobility and Diversity in the Roman Empire*, Portsmouth: Journal of Roman Archaeology, 2010; Hella Eckardt, Gundula Müldner, and Mary Lewis, "People on the move in Roman Britain," *World Archaeology* 46, no. 4 (2014); Hella Eckardt and Gundula Müldner, "Mobility, migration, and diasporas in Roman Britain," in Martin Millett, Louise Revell, and Alison Moore, eds., *The Oxford Handbook of Roman Britain*, Oxford: Oxford University Press, 2016.

44 Tacitus, *Annals* 1.11.

45 Dio 60.19–23.

46 Suetonius, *Claudius* 17.2.

47 On Roman Britain, see above all Martin Millett, *The Romanization of Britain: An Essay in Archaeological Interpretation*, Cambridge: Cambridge University Press, 1990, and David J. Mattingly, *An Imperial Possession: Britain in the Roman Empire, 54 BC–AD 409*, London: Allen Lane, 2006.

48 Lacey M. Wallace, *The Origin of Roman London*, Cambridge: Cambridge University Press, 2014. On Roman London see now Richard Hingley, *Londinium: A Biography: Roman London from Its Origins to the Fifth Century*, London: Bloomsbury Academic, 2018, and for a different interpretation of the foundation, Dominic Perring, *London in the Roman World*, Oxford: Oxford University Press, 2022.

49 Tacitus, *Annals* 14.33.

50 Roger Tomlin, *Roman London's First Voices: Writing Tablets from the Bloomberg Excavations, 2010–14*, London: Museum of London Archaeology, 2016.

51 Tab. Lond. Bloomberg WT 30, trans. Tomlin, *Roman London's First Voices.*

52 Luguseluus: Tab. Lond. Bloomberg WT 4; Martialis: Tab. Lond. Bloomberg WT 5; there are also Celtic names in the letters that are attested elsewhere in Britain like Mongontius (Tab. Lond. Bloomberg WT 6).

53 R.S.O. Tomlin, "'The girl in question': a new text from Roman London," *Britannia* 34 (2003).

54 Merchants: *RIB* [*Roman Inscriptions of Britain*] 9 & 29, with R.S.O. Tomlin and M.W.C. Hassall, "II. Inscriptions," *Britannia* 34 (2003), 364–5, for the Gaul.

55 J. Montgomery et al., "'Gleaming, white and deadly': using lead to track human exposure and geographic origins in the Roman period in Britain," in Eckardt, ed., *Roman Diasporas*, 217–19.

56 Rebecca C. Redfern et al., "Going south of the river: a multidisciplinary analysis of ancestry, mobility and diet in a population from Roman Southwark, London," *Journal of Archaeological Science* 74 (2016). More tentatively, study of the form of the skulls and teeth themselves suggested African and Asian ancestry for at least six of the individuals; as Kristina Killgrove has pointed out, the problem is that the comparison data comes from modern rather than ancient populations (https://www.forbes.com/sites/kristinakillgrove/2016/09/23/chinese-skeletons-in-roman-britain-not-so-fast).

57 Serapis temple at York: *RIB* 658.

58 "Middle Eastern" Man: Rui Martiniano et al., "Genomic signals of migration and continuity in Britain before the Anglo-Saxons," *Nature Communications* 7, no. 1 (2016). Ivory Bangle Lady: S. Leach et al., "A lady of York: migration, ethnicity and identity in Roman Britain," *Antiquity* 84, no. 323 (2010); craniometric study of her skull suggested that she was of partially African descent, but again the reference data is from the nineteenth and twentieth centuries CE, a far later period. For more apparent examples of migrants buried at York, see Gundula Müldner, Carolyn Chenery, and Hella Eckardt, "The 'headless Romans': multi-isotope investigations of an unusual burial ground from Roman Britain," *Journal of Archaeological Science* 38, no. 2 (2011).

59 Michael Kulikowski, "Constantine and the northern barbarians," in Noel Lenski, ed., *The Cambridge Companion to the Age of Constantine,* Cambridge: Cambridge University Press, 2005, 366. Refusal to cross the Alps: Ammianus Marcellinus 20.4.4.

60 Richard Hingley, "The Romans in Britain: colonization of an imperial frontier," in Christine D. Beaule, ed., *Frontiers of Colonialism,* Gainesville: University Press of Florida, 2017, 97, noting that some other cities were later given the honorary title of "colony" as well.

61 They were still there in the fourth century, recorded in a register of Roman military interests, the *Notitia dignitatum.*

62 *RIB* 1065.

63 Pepper at the fort of Vindolanda: Andrew Wilson, "A forum on trade," in Walter Scheidel, ed., *The Cambridge Companion to the Roman Economy,* Cambridge: Cambridge University Press, 2012, 290. Silk: https://www.mola.org.uk/discoveries/news/thirty-years-archaeological-work-reveal-incredible-detail-two-thousand-years.

21. Trade Winds

1 *RIB* [*Roman Inscriptions of Britain*] 1171.
2 Tamara Chin, "The invention of the Silk Road, 1877," *Critical Inquiry* 40, no. 1 (2013), discussing Ferdinand von Richthofen, *China: Ergebnisse eigener Reisen und darauf gegründeter Studien*, Berlin: Reimer, 1877–1912, and "Über die centralasiastischen Seidenstrassen bis zum 2. Jahrhundert n. Chr," *Verhandlungen der Gesellschaft für Erdkunde zu Berlin* 4 (1877), 96–122.
3 Marinos' account is preserved in a critical discussion by Ptolemy of Alexandria (1.11–12).
4 For references and quotations see Chin, "The invention of the Silk Road, 1877," 217.
5 Philippe Beaujard, "The Indian Ocean in Eurasian and African world-systems before the sixteenth century," *Journal of World History* 16, no. 4 (2005), 420.
6 On the myth of an overland "Silk Road" all the way from Rome to China, Warwick Ball, *Rome in the East: The Transformation of an Empire*, London: Routledge, 2000, 137–9.
7 Strabo 16.1.28.
8 Wilfred H. Schoff, *Parthian Stations by Isidore of Charax: An Account of the Overland Trade Route Between the Levant and India in the First Century* B.C., Philadelphia: Commercial Museum, 1914.
9 Isidorus of Charax, *Parthian Stations* 1.
10 Ibid., 19, with Fergus Millar, "Caravan cities: the Roman Near East and long-distance trade by land," in Michel Austin, Jill Harries, and Christopher Smith, eds., *Modus Operandi: Essays in Honour of Geoffrey Rickman*, London: Institute of Classical Studies, 1998, 120–1.
11 Barry W. Cunliffe, *By Steppe, Desert, and Ocean: The Birth of Eurasia*, Oxford: Oxford University Press, 2015, 272–5, 287–8.
12 Aegean silk: Tibullus 2.3.53–4, 2.4.29–30; Propertius 1.2.2, 2.1.5–6, 4.2.23, 4.5.23, 57; Horace, *Odes* 4.13.13; *Satires* 1.2.101; Ovid, *Art of Love* 2.298. Silk on trees: Vergil, *Georgics* 2.121; Seneca, *Phaedra* 389; cf. Pliny, *Natural History* 11.75–8 for a better-informed account. Earlier identifications of silk garments at Athens and in central Europe of the mid-first millennium BCE have been refuted by scientific analysis: Christina Margariti, Stavros Protopapas, and Vassiliki Orphanou, "Recent analyses of the excavated textile find from Grave 35 HTR73, Kerameikos cemetery, Athens, Greece," *Journal of Archaeological Science* 38, no. 3 (2011).
13 Florus 2.34.
14 Beaujard, "The Indian Ocean in Eurasian and African world-systems before the sixteenth century," 240.
15 Strabo 17.1.45, with Andrew Wilson, "Red Sea trade and the state," in Federico De Romanis and Marco Maiuro, eds., *Across the Ocean: Nine Essays on Indo-Mediterranean Trade*, Leiden: Brill, 2015, 13–18, and Matthew Cobb, "From the Ptolemies to Augustus: Mediterranean integration into the Indian Ocean trade," in Matthew Cobb, ed., *The Indian Ocean Trade in Antiquity: Political, Cultural and Economic Impacts*, Abingdon: Routledge, 2019, 26–7. One romantic account of the "discovery" of the monsoon winds in Egypt can be found at Strabo 2.3.4–5.
16 *SB* [*Sammelbuch griechischer Urkunden aus Äegypten*] III 7169.
17 Strabo 2.5.12; Cobb, "From the Ptolemies to Augustus," 25.

18 Beaujard, "The Indian Ocean in Eurasian and African world-systems before the sixteenth century," 447.
19 For overviews of ancient Indian Ocean trade with the Mediterranean see Roberta Tomber, *Indo-Roman Trade: From Pots to Pepper,* London: Duckworth, 2008; Kasper Grønlund Evers, *Worlds Apart Trading Together: The Organisation of Long-Distance Trade Between Rome and India in Antiquity,* Oxford: Archaeopress, 2017; and Matthew Cobb, *Rome and the Indian Ocean Trade from Augustus to the Early Third Century* CE, Leiden: Brill, 2018.
20 Cunliffe, *By Steppe, Desert, and Ocean,* 291–2. Over time the harbor at Myos Hormos silted up and Berenike to the south became a more important harbor: Wilson, "Red Sea trade and the state," 20.
21 Grant Parker, "Images of Mediterranean India: representing the subcontinent in ancient Greek and Roman art," in Grant Parker and Carla M. Sinopoli, eds., *Ancient India in Its Wider World,* Ann Arbor: University of Michigan Press, 2008, 173–8; Tomber, *Indo-Roman Trade,* 26–8. Excavations at Pattanam, probably the site of Muziris: P. J. Cherian et al., "Chronology of Pattanam: a multi-cultural port site on the Malabar Coast," *Current Science* 97, no. 2 (2009); Roberta Tomber, "The Roman pottery from Pattanam," in K. S. Mathew, ed., *Imperial Rome, Indian Ocean Regions and Muziris: New Perspectives on Maritime Trade,* New Delhi: Manohar, 2015.
22 Propertius 2.22.10.
23 Parker, "Images of Mediterranean India," 151–2, with Hippocrates, *Diseases of Women* 1.81.
24 Tacitus, *Annals* 2.33 (16 CE).
25 Andrew Wilson, "A forum on trade," in Walter Scheidel, ed., *The Cambridge Companion to the Roman Economy,* Cambridge: Cambridge University Press, 2012, 290; I thank Andrew Wilson for further discussion of this point.
26 Muziris Papyrus: P. Vindob. G. 40822 = *SB* XVIII 13167, with Federico De Romanis, *The Indo-Roman Pepper Trade and the Muziris Papyrus,* Oxford: Oxford University Press, 2020, trans. at 14–23. Implications for state revenues: Wilson, "Red Sea trade and the state," 23–4.
27 Dio Chrysostom, *Oration* 32.36.
28 Ibid., 32.39–40.
29 Cod. Pal. Gr. 398, 40v–54v; the modern edition is Lionel Casson, *The Periplus Maris Erythraei: Text with Introduction, Translation, and Commentary,* Princeton: Princeton University Press, 1989, whose translations I borrow here, but for discussion of the nature and dating of the text see Pascal Arnaud, "Le Periplus Maris Erythraei: une oeuvre de compilation aux préoccupations géographiques," in Jean-François Salles, Jean-Baptiste Yon, and Marie-Françoise Broussac, eds., *Autour du Périple de la mer Érythrée, Topoi* Supplement 11, 2012. A copy of this manuscript also exists: British Museum Add. Ms. 19391 ex Vatopedinus 655.
30 *Periplus* 6. For the exiguous archaeological evidence for Roman trade with the east African coast in this period: Mark Horton, Alison Crowther, and Nicole Boivin, "Ships of the desert, camels of the ocean: an Indian Ocean perspective on trans-Saharan trading systems," in David J. Mattingly et al., eds., *Trade in the Ancient Sahara and Beyond,* Cambridge: Cambridge University Press, 2017, 135–41.
31 *Periplus* 7, 6, 14.
32 *Periplus* 14; see Casson, *The Periplus Maris Erythraei,* 285–7, for the practicalities.

33 Casson, *The Periplus Maris Erythraei,* 289.
34 *Periplus* 52.
35 *Periplus* 49.
36 *Periplus* 63–4.
37 Richard J. A. Talbert. *Rome's World: The Peutinger Map Reconsidered,* Cambridge: Cambridge University Press, 2010.
38 Palmyra: John F. Matthews, "The tax law of Palmyra: evidence for economic history in a city of the Roman east," *Journal of Roman Studies* 74 (1984); Michael Gawlikowski, "Palmyra as a trading center," *Iraq* 56 (1994); Millar, "Caravan cities"; Rubina Raja, *Pearl of the Desert: A History of Palmyra,* New York: Oxford University Press, 2022.
39 Eivind Heldaas Seland, "Camels, camel nomadism and the practicalities of the Palmyrene caravan trade," *ARAM Periodical* 27 (2015); Jørgen Christian Meyer and Eivind Heldaas Seland, "Palmyra and the trade route to the Euphrates," *ARAM Periodical* 28 (2016).
40 Eivind Heldaas Seland, "The Persian Gulf or the Red Sea? Two axes in ancient Indian Ocean trade, where to go and why," *World Archaeology* 43, no. 3 (2011).
41 Eivind Heldaas Seland, "Networks and social cohesion in ancient Indian Ocean trade: geography, ethnicity, religion," *Journal of Global History* 8, no. 3 (2013), 38. Rome: Taco Terpstra, "The Palmyrene temple in Rome and Palmyra's trade with the west," in Jørgen Christian Meyer, Eivind Heldaas Seland, and Nils Anfinset, eds., *Palmyrena: City, Hinterland and Caravan Trade Between Orient and Occident,* Oxford: Archaeopress, 2016.
42 For the latest population estimates see Joan Campmany Jiménez et al., "Food security in Roman Palmyra (Syria) in light of paleoclimatological evidence and its historical implications," *PLOS ONE* 17, no. 9 (2022).
43 Pliny, *Natural History* 5.88.
44 *Inscriptions grecques et latines de la Syrie.*
45 Chinese silk in Palmyrene tombs of the first to third century CE: Craig Benjamin, *Empires of Ancient Eurasia: The First Silk Roads Era, 100 BCE–250 CE,* Cambridge: Cambridge University Press, 2018, 134–5.
46 Seland, "The Persian Gulf or the Red Sea?"
47 Bérénice Bellina et al., "Myanmar's earliest maritime Silk Road port-settlements revealed," *Antiquity* 92, no. 366 (2018).
48 Brigitte Borell, Bérénice Bellina and Boonyarit Chaisuwan, "Contacts between the Upper Thai–Malay Peninsula and the Mediterranean world," in Nicolas Revire and Stephen A. Murphy, eds., *Before Siam: Essays in Art and Archaeology,* Bangkok: River Books, 2014.
49 Charles Higham, *Early Mainland Southeast Asia: From First Humans to Angkor,* Bangkok: River Books, 2014, 279. For the broader picture of Roman connections with Vietnam see Nam C. Kim's essay at https://www.badancient.com/claims/romans-reach-vietnam.
50 Ambra Calo et al., "Sembiran and Pacung on the north coast of Bali: a strategic crossroads for early trans-Asiatic exchange," *Antiquity* 89, no. 344 (2015), discussed further by Miko Flohr at http://www.mikoflohr.org/blog/2020/01/21/global-romans-3-a-roman-bead-from-bali.
51 *Periplus* 4.
52 *Periplus* 5.

53 For an overview of ancient Axum see David W. Phillipson, *Foundations of an African Civilization: Aksum and the Northern Horn, 1000 BC–AD 1300*, London: Boydell & Brewer, 2012.
54 Eivind Heldaas Seland, "Early Christianity in east Africa and Red Sea/Indian Ocean commerce," *African Archaeological Review* 31, no. 4 (2014), 641.
55 Giusto Traina, "Central Asia in the late Roman mental map, second to sixth centuries," in Nicola Di Cosmo and Michael Maas, eds., *Empires and Exchanges in Eurasian Late Antiquity: Rome, China, Iran, and the Steppe, ca. 250–750*, Cambridge: Cambridge University Press, 2018.
56 *Hou Hanshu* 88, trans. at D. D. Leslie and K.H.J. Gardiner, *The Roman Empire in Chinese Sources*, Rome: Bardi, 1996, 42–55.
57 Leslie and Gardiner, *The Roman Empire in Chinese Sources*, 141–8, for sources and discussion.
58 *Hou Hanshu* 86, with commentary at Leslie and Gardiner, *The Roman Empire in Chinese Sources*, 151 n. 42.
59 *Hou Hanshu* 88.

22. Salt Roads

1 Alain de Lille, *Book of Parables (Patrologia Latina* 210, 591); Geoffrey Chaucer, *A Treatise on the Astrolabe* (1391), preface.
2 Herodotus 4.181–5.
3 Mario Liverani, "The Libyan caravan road in Herodotus IV.181–185," *Journal of the Economic and Social History of the Orient* 43, no. 4 (2000).
4 Herodotus 4.183.
5 David J. Mattingly, ed., *The Archaeology of Fazzān*, London: Society for Libyan Studies, 2003–2013, vol. 1, 88–9.
6 Garamantes: Mario Liverani, "The Garamantes: a fresh approach," *Libyan Studies* 31 (2000); Mattingly, *The Archaeology of Fazzān;* David J. Mattingly and Martin Sterry, "The first towns in the central Sahara," *Antiquity* 87, no. 336 (2013).
7 Ruth Pelling, "Garamantian agriculture and its significance in a wider North African context: the evidence of the plant remains from the Fazzan project," *Journal of North African Studies* 10, no. 3–4 (2005), 401.
8 Andrew Wilson, "Hydraulic engineering and water supply," in John Peter Oleson, ed., *The Oxford Handbook of Engineering and Technology in the Classical World*, Oxford: Oxford University Press, 2008, 291–3; Andrew Wilson, "Saharan trade in the Roman period: short-, medium- and long-distance trade networks," *Azania* 47, no. 4 (2012), 420–3.
9 Wilson, "Saharan trade in the Roman period," 410, 419.
10 Pelling, "Garamantian agriculture and its significance in a wider North African context"; Wilson, "Saharan trade in the Roman period," 419–20, 428; Mattingly, *The Archaeology of Fazzān*, vol. 4, 179–225.
11 Wilson, "Saharan trade in the Roman period," 428, 433; Faisal Almathen et al., "Ancient and modern DNA reveal dynamics of domestication and cross-continental dispersal of the dromedary," *Proceedings of the National Academy of Sciences* 113, no. 24 (2016).
12 Wilson, "Saharan trade in the Roman period," 413–14, 434.

13 David J. Mattingly and Franca Cole, "Visible and invisible commodities of trade: the significance of organic materials in Saharan trade," in David J. Mattingly et al., eds., *Trade in the Ancient Sahara and Beyond,* Cambridge: Cambridge University Press, 2017, exploiting comparative evidence from later periods.

14 Wilson, "Saharan trade in the Roman period"; David J. Mattingly, "The Garamantes and the origins of Saharan trade," in Mattingly et al., eds., *Trade in the Ancient Sahara and Beyond.*

15 Ibid., 417, 425.

16 H.A.R. Gibb and C. F. Beckingham, *The Travels of Ibn Battuta* A.D. *1325–1354,* London: Hakluyt Society, 1958–1994, 947, on Taghaza.

17 Andrew Wilson, "Saharan exports to the Roman world," in Mattingly et al., eds., *Trade in the Ancient Sahara and Beyond,* surveys the possibilities. Cf. for skepticism on regular trade south of the Fazzan, Sonja Magnavita, "Initial encounters: seeking traces of ancient trade connections between west Africa and the wider world," *Afriques* [Online] 4 (2013).

18 Pliny, *Natural History* 5.34, 37; E. Gliozzo et al., "In the footsteps of Pliny: tracing the sources of Garamantian carnelian from Fazzan, southwest Libya," *Journal of Archaeological Science* 52 (2014).

19 If any significant Saharan gold trade existed in antiquity, it only began in the very late third century CE, when gold coinage began to be minted at both Carthage and Alexandria: Timothy F. Garrard, "Myth and metrology: the early trans-Saharan gold trade," *Journal of African History* 23, no. 4 (1982); Wilson, "Saharan trade in the Roman period," 435–7; Wilson, "Saharan exports to the Roman world," 197–8.

20 Giraffe: David J. Mattingly et al., "Concluding discussion," in Mattingly et al., eds., *Trade in the Ancient Sahara and Beyond,* 435.

21 Wilson, "Saharan trade in the Roman period"; Wilson, "Saharan exports to the Roman world," 192–3.

22 *Expositio totius mundi* 60.

23 Elizabeth B. Fentress, "Slavers on chariots," in Aemilia Dowler and Elizabeth R. Galvin, eds., *Money, Trade and Trade Routes in Pre-Islamic North Africa,* London: British Museum, 2011, 66.

24 Wilson, "Saharan trade in the Roman period," 434.

25 Ibid., 433, with bibliography.

26 Ibid., 434–5.

27 David Cherry, "Armed resistance to Roman rule in North Africa, from the time of Augustus to the Vandal invasion," *Small Wars & Insurgencies* 31, no. 5 (2020).

28 David J. Mattingly, *Imperialism, Power, and Identity: Experiencing the Roman Empire,* Princeton: Princeton University Press, 2011, 162.

29 Wilson, "Saharan trade in the Roman period," 414; Pliny, *Natural History* 8.32.

30 David J. Mattingly, "Who shaped Africa? The origins of urbanism and agriculture in Maghreb and Sahara," in Niccolò Mugnai, Nicholas Ray, and Julia Nikolaus, eds., *De Africa Romaque: Merging Cultures Across North Africa,* London: Society for Libyan Studies, 2016.

31 Juvenal, *Satires* 10.78–81; cf. Fronto, *Principles of History* 17. For what follows, see Mattingly, *Imperialism, Power, and Identity,* 152–8.

32 Graeme Barker, *Farming the Desert: The UNESCO Libyan Valleys Archaeological Survey,* Paris: Unesco, 1996, 191–263.

33 Mason Hammond, "Composition of the Senate, A.D. 68–235," *Journal of Roman Studies* 47 (1957); this may be an underestimate, as the origins of only 114 of the 259 senators known to have served under the emperor Commodus are recorded; of those seventy-two are from Africa.
34 Orietta Dora Cordovana, "Between history and myth: Septimius Severus and Leptis Magna," *Greece & Rome* 59, no. 1 (2012).
35 Jean-Paul Rey-Coquais, "Une double dédicace de Lepcis Magna à Tyr," in Attilio Mastino, ed., *L'Africa romana: atti del IV convegno di studio, Sassari, 12–14 dicembre 1986*, Sassari: Università degli studi di Sassari, 1987.
36 *Historia Augusta: Septimius Severus* 15.7. Phoenician inscriptions are still found in the Libyan pre-desert in the fifth century CE, which is also when St. Augustine, the bishop of Hippo in modern Algeria, tells us that many African Christians spoke Phoenician rather than Latin: Augustine, *Epistles* 66.2, 209.3; *Sermons* 167.4.
37 Josephine Crawley Quinn, "The reinvention of Lepcis," in Alicia Jiménez, ed., "Colonizing a colonized territory: settlements with Punic roots in Roman times," in Martina Dalla Riva and Helga di Giuseppe, eds., *Meetings Between Cultures in the Ancient Mediterranean*, Rome: Ministero per i beni e le attività culturali, 2010.
38 David Gal, Hadas Saaroni, and Deborah Cvikel, "Mappings of potential sailing mobility in the Mediterranean during antiquity," *Journal of Archaeological Method and Theory* (2022).
39 *Historia Augusta: Heliogabalus* 20.6, 21.2 (poor treatment of parrots), 17.1–3, 33.7 (death).
40 Craig Benjamin, *Empires of Ancient Eurasia: The First Silk Roads Era, 100 BCE–250 CE*, Cambridge: Cambridge University Press, 2018, 272–4.
41 Joseph R. McConnell et al., "Lead pollution recorded in Greenland ice indicates European emissions tracked plagues, wars, and imperial expansion during antiquity," *PNAS* 115, no. 22 (2018).
42 Andrew Wilson, "Machines, power and the ancient economy," *Journal of Roman Studies* 92 (2002), 27.
43 Peter Sarris, *Empires of Faith: The Fall of Rome to the Rise of Islam, 500–700*, Oxford: Oxford University Press, 2011, 11.

23. The Rise of the Barbarians

1 Caesar, *Gallic War* 6.21–2.
2 Tacitus, *Germania* especially 7 and 11; an arbitrary claim at 2 that the Germans were an indigenous people who had never intermarried with others has also attracted much attention.
3 Montesquieu, *Spirit of the Laws* 11.6, trans. Anne M. Cohler, Basia Carolyn Miller, and Harold Samuel Stone, *Montesquieu: The Spirit of the Laws*, Cambridge: Cambridge University Press, 1989, 166. For the development of this perspective into an obsessive interest in the origins of the modern German race, see Patrick J. Geary, *The Myth of Nations: The Medieval Origins of Europe*, Princeton: Princeton University Press, 2002, 22–40, and Christopher B. Krebs, *A Most Dangerous Book: Tacitus's* Germania *from the Roman Empire to the Third Reich*, New York: W. W. Norton, 2011. Nazi ideology posited a combination of "Germanic," Greek, and Roman cultural roots to the modern German race: Johann Chapoutot, *Greeks,*

Romans, Germans: How the Nazis Usurped Europe's Classical Past, trans. Richard R. Nybakken, Berkeley: University of California Press, 2016.

4 Traders in Maroboduus' court: Tacitus, *Annals* 2.62.

5 Michael Kulikowski, "Constantine and the northern barbarians," in Noel Lenski, ed., *The Cambridge Companion to the Age of Constantine*, Cambridge: Cambridge University Press, 2005, 350–1, 368; Peter S. Wells, "Peoples beyond the Roman imperial frontiers," in Ed Bispham, ed., *Roman Europe*, Oxford: Oxford University Press, 2008, 303–9, 317; Peter Sarris, *Empires of Faith: The Fall of Rome to the Rise of Islam, 500–700*, Oxford: Oxford University Press, 2011, 9. Runes may have been based not on the Latin but on the Etruscan script: Giuliano Bonfante and Larissa Bonfante, *The Etruscan Language: An Introduction*, 2nd ed., Manchester: Manchester University Press, 2002, 117–20.

6 The best summary of the political and social history of the third- and fourth-century Roman empire is at Sarris, *Empires of Faith*, 8–32.

7 Ibid., 12, with Gregory Thaumaturgus, *Canonical Letter* 7.

8 For an overview of the Sasanians, see Touraj Daryaee, *Sasanian Persia: The Rise and Fall of an Empire*, London: I. B. Tauris, 2009.

9 Lactantius, *On the Deaths of the Persecutors* 5.

10 Palace: Anne Hunnell Chen, "Rival powers, rival images: Diocletian's palace at Split in light of Sasanian palace design," in Daniëlle Slootjes and Michael Peachin, eds., *Rome and the World Beyond Its Frontiers*, Leiden: Brill, 2016. Eunuchs: Lactantius, *On the Deaths of the Persecutors* 15.2. See Matthew P. Canepa, *The Two Eyes of the Earth: Art and Ritual of Kingship Between Rome and Sasanian Iran*, Berkeley: University of California Press, 2009, for an account of extensive contact, cultural exchange, and shared imperial technologies between Sasanian Persia and the late Roman empire much in sympathy with my own aims in this book.

11 Chronographer of 354 (*MGH Auctores Antiquissimi* 9, 148).

12 *Epitome de Caesaribus* 41.3.

13 Kulikowski, "Constantine and the northern barbarians," 357–9.

14 Olivier Hekster, *Caesar Rules: The Emperor in the Changing Roman World (c. 50 BC–AD 565)*, Cambridge: Cambridge University Press, 2023, 88–90.

15 See Timothy D. Barnes, *Constantine: Dynasty, Religion and Power in the Later Roman Empire*, Chichester: Wiley Blackwell, 2011, 93–7, on the evidence and on the problem of the so-called Edict of Milan.

16 Gavin Kelly, "Claudian's last panegyric and imperial visits to Rome," *Classical Quarterly* 66, no. 1 (2016).

17 P. J. Heather, *The Fall of the Roman Empire*, London: Macmillan, 2005, 76–80, with Philostorgius 2.5.

18 James Howard-Johnston, "The India trade in late antiquity," in Eberhard Sauer, ed., *Sasanian Persia: Between Rome and the Steppes of Eurasia*, Edinburgh: Edinburgh University Press, 2017, 286.

19 Douglas Boin, *Alaric the Goth: An Outsider's History of the Fall of Rome*, New York: W. W. Norton, 2020, 52.

20 Sarris, *Empires of Faith*, 32, with Ammianus Marcellinus 22.7.8 on the Gothic slave trade.

21 See the useful summary of Hunnic history at Mark Whittow, "Byzantium's Eurasian policy in the age of the Türk empire," in Nicola Di Cosmo and Michael Maas, eds., *Empires and Exchange in Eurasian Late Antiquity: Rome, China, Iran,*

and the Steppe ca. 250–750, Cambridge: Cambridge University Press, 2018, 275–9; see at greater length E. A. Thompson, *The Huns,* Oxford: Blackwell, 1999.

22 Ammianus Marcellinus 31.4.10–11.

23 Ibid., 31.13.19.

24 Sarris, *Empires of Faith,* 38, with Nov. Val. 10.1 (Law of Valentinian III). On late Roman taxation and the burdens it imposed, see also Chris Wickham, *Framing the Early Middle Ages: Europe and the Mediterranean, 400–800,* Oxford: Oxford University Press, 2005, 62–80.

25 *Codex Theodosianus* 14.10.2.

26 Orosius 7.40.1.

27 Jerome, *Letters* 127.12; *Commentary on Ezekiel,* preface.

28 Judith Herrin, *Ravenna: Capital of Empire, Crucible of Europe,* Princeton: Princeton University Press, 2020, 396.

29 Augustine, *City of God* 16.17; cf. Orosius 1.2 for a similar point.

30 G. W. Bowersock, "The east–west orientation of Mediterranean studies and the meaning of north and south in antiquity," in William V. Harris, ed., *Rethinking the Mediterranean,* Oxford: Oxford University Press, 2005, with, e.g., Cicero, *On the Nature of the Gods* 2.102; Vergil, *Aeneid* 7.95–101.

31 See Peter J. Heather, "Why did the barbarian cross the Rhine?," *Journal of Late Antiquity* 2, no. 1 (2009), and Michael Maas, "How the steppes became Byzantine: Rome and the Eurasian nomads in historical perspective," in Di Cosmo and Maas, eds., *Empires and Exchange in Eurasian Late Antiquity,* 22–3, for the importance of Hunnic movements under Attila in the disintegration of the Roman empire.

32 Marcellinus, Anno 476.

33 Boin, *Alaric the Goth,* 180.

34 Herrin, *Ravenna,* 123.

35 Ibid., 99, 102, 129.

36 Peter J. Heather, *The Goths,* Oxford: Blackwell, 1996, 181–94.

37 Andrew Merrills and Richard Miles, *The Vandals,* Oxford: Wiley Blackwell, 2010, 52–5.

38 David J. Mattingly, *An Imperial Possession: Britain in the Roman Empire, 54 BC–AD 409,* London: Allen Lane, 2006, 529–39, on the end of Roman Britain.

39 Large-scale study of early English genome-wide DNA: Joscha Gretzinger et al., "The Anglo-Saxon migration and the formation of the early English gene pool," *Nature* 610, no. 7930 (2022).

40 Kyle Harper, *The Fate of Rome: Climate, Disease, and the End of an Empire,* Princeton: Princeton University Press, 2017, 167–75; Mark Humphries, "Late antiquity and world history," *Studies in Late Antiquity* 1, no. 1 (2017), 27; Kyle Harper and Michael McCormick, "Reconstructing the Roman climate," in Walter Scheidel, ed., *The Science of Roman History,* Princeton: Princeton University Press, 2018.

41 Translated into English at Stephen A. Barney et al., *The Etymologies of Isidore of Seville,* Cambridge: Cambridge University Press, 2006. Popularity: Seb Falk, *The Light Ages: A Medieval Journey of Discovery,* London: Allen Lane, 2020, 83.

42 Chris Wickham, *Medieval Europe,* New Haven: Yale University Press, 2016, 18.

43 For a classic discussion with full references see Janet L. Nelson, "Queens as Jezebels: the careers of Brunhild and Balthild in Merovingian history," *Studies in Church History Subsidia* 1 (1978).

44 *Epistolae Austriacae* 26 (*MGH Epistolae Merovingici et Karolini aevi* 1, 139).

24. Kings of the World

1 Garth Fowden, *Quṣayr ʿAmra: Art and the Umayyad Elite in Late Antique Syria*, Berkeley: University of California Press, 2004.
2 https://www.wmf.org/sites/default/files/article/pdfs/2016_qusayr_amra_booklet.pdf (World Monuments Fund 2015).
3 Fowden, *Quṣayr ʿAmra*, 147–51.
4 *Kephalaia* 77, trans. Iain Gardner, *The Kephalaia of the Teacher: The Edited Coptic Manichaean Texts in Translation with Commentary*, Leiden: Brill, 1995, 197.
5 Ibn al-Balkhi, *Fars-nama* 97, 13–14.
6 Ibn al-Faqīh, *Kitab al-buldan* 429, with Fowden, *Quṣayr ʿAmra*, 216–17.
7 Fowden, *Qusayr ʿAmra*, 214–15.
8 What follows draws on the illuminating analysis offered at Richard E. Payne, "The Silk Road and the Iranian political economy in late antiquity: Iran, the Silk Road, and the problem of aristocratic empire," *Bulletin of the School of Oriental and African Studies* 81, no. 2 (2018).
9 On the Turks see Peter B. Golden, *An Introduction to the History of the Turkic Peoples: Ethnogenesis and State-Formation in Medieval and Early Modern Eurasia and the Middle East*, Wiesbaden: Harrassowitz, 1992, 127–53.
10 Sasanian coins: Touraj Daryaee, "The Persian Gulf trade in late antiquity," *Journal of World History* 14, no. 1 (2003), 12–14. Roman coins: Qiang Li, "Roman coins discovered in China and their research," *Eirene* 15 (2015).
11 Maria Brosius, *The Persians: An Introduction*, London: Routledge, 2006, 153–9, 165.
12 Douglas Boin, *Alaric the Goth: An Outsider's History of the Fall of Rome*, New York: W. W. Norton, 2020, 89.
13 Brosius, *The Persians*, 156, 185–6; Robert Hoyland, "Early Islam as a late antique religion," in Scott Fitzgerald Johnson, ed., *The Oxford Handbook of Late Antiquity*, Oxford: Oxford University Press, 2012, 1068.
14 *Abar Wizārišn ī Čatrang ud Nihišn Nēw-Ardaxšir* 9, trans. Touraj Daryaee, *On the Explanation of Chess and Backgammon*, Irvine, CA: Jordan Center for Persian Studies, 2016, 19.
15 Eivind Heldaas Seland, "Early Christianity in east Africa and Red Sea/Indian Ocean commerce," *African Archaeological Review* 31, no. 4 (2014).
16 Procopius, *Wars* 1.20.9–12.
17 Payne, "The Silk Road and the Iranian political economy in late antiquity," 233–4.
18 Peter Sarris, *Empires of Faith: The Fall of Rome to the Rise of Islam, 500–700*, Oxford: Oxford University Press, 2011, 140.
19 Judith Herrin, *Ravenna: Capital of Empire, Crucible of Europe*, Princeton: Princeton University Press, 2020, 164. The height is fifty-five meters, the diameter thirty-two meters.
20 Olivier Hekster, *Caesar Rules: The Emperor in the Changing Roman World (c. 50 BC–AD 565)*, Cambridge: Cambridge University Press, 2023, 169.
21 Procopius, *Wars* 8.17.1–8; Photius 26a.
22 Herrin, *Ravenna*, 151, 174, with Procopius, *Wars* 1.22.17–18 for the treaty.
23 Brosius, *The Persians*, 154.
24 Kyle Harper and Michael McCormick, "Reconstructing the Roman climate," in Walter Scheidel, ed., *The Science of Roman History*, Princeton: Princeton Univer-

sity Press, 2018, 20; Robert A. Dull et al., "Radiocarbon and geologic evidence reveal Ilopango volcano as source of the colossal 'mystery' eruption of 539/40 CE," *Quaternary Science Reviews* 222 (2019); Timothy Newfield, "Mysterious and mortiferous clouds: the climate cooling and disease burden of late antiquity," in Adam Izdebski and Michael Mulryan, eds., *Environment and Society in the Long Late Antiquity,* Leiden: Brill, 2018.

25 Procopius, *Wars* 4.14.5–6.

26 Ulf Büntgen et al., "Cooling and societal change during the late antique Little Ice Age from 536 to around 660 AD," *Nature Geoscience* 9, no. 3 (2016).

27 Peter Sarris, "New approaches to the 'Plague of Justinian,'" *Past & Present* 254, no. 1 (2022).

28 Simon Rasmussen et al., "Early divergent strains of *Yersinia pestis* in Eurasia 5,000 years ago," *Cell* 163, no. 3 (2015); Julian Susat et al., "A 5,000-year-old hunter-gatherer already plagued by *Yersinia pestis,*" *Cell Reports* 35, no. 13 (2021); see also Monica H. Green's thought-provoking essay at https://eidolon.pub/when-numbers-dont-count-56a2b3c3d07.

29 Monica H. Green, "Taking 'pandemic' seriously: making the Black Death global," in Monica H. Green, ed., *Pandemic Disease in the Medieval World: Rethinking the Black Death,* Kalamazoo: Arc Medieval Press, 2014, 32–3.

30 Ibid., 46–7; Sarris, "New approaches to the 'Plague of Justinian,'" 319.

31 Procopius, *Wars* 2.22–3; Procopius, *Anecdota* 4.1.

32 Sarris, "New approaches to the 'Plague of Justinian,'" 318, 320.

33 Yohannes Gebre Selassie, "Plague as a possible factor for the decline and collapse of the Aksumite empire: a new interpretation," *ITYOPIS—Northeast African Journal of Social Sciences and Humanities* 1 (2011); Sarris, "New approaches to the 'Plague of Justinian,'" 319.

34 Menander Protector 19.1, discussed at Mark Whittow, "Byzantium's Eurasian policy in the age of the Türk empire," in Nicola Di Cosmo and Michael Maas, eds., *Empires and Exchange in Eurasian Late Antiquity: Rome, China, Iran, and the Steppe, ca. 250–750,* Cambridge: Cambridge University Press, 2018, 282–3.

35 Whittow, "Byzantium's Eurasian policy in the age of the Türk empire," 272.

36 Herrin, *Ravenna,* 203–4.

37 James Howard-Johnston, *The Last Great War of Antiquity,* Oxford: Oxford University Press, 2021.

38 Harper and McCormick, "Reconstructing the Roman climate," 13.

39 Brosius, *The Persians,* 174.

40 Early Islam: Albrecht Noth with Lawrence I. Conrad, *The Early Arabic Historical Tradition: A Source-Critical Study,* 2nd ed., Princeton: Darwin Press, 1994, on the sources. For a lively account, see Karen Armstrong, *Islam: A Short History,* London: Weidenfeld & Nicolson, 2000, 3–65. For the fuller picture: Hugh Kennedy, *The Prophet and the Age of the Caliphates: The Islamic Near East from the Sixth to the Eleventh Century,* 4th ed., London: Routledge, 2023.

41 Early Islamic Levant: Hugh Kennedy, "Islam," in G. W. Bowersock, Peter Brown, and Oleg Grabar, eds., *Late Antiquity: A Guide to the Postclassical World,* Cambridge, Mass.: Harvard University Press, 1999.

42 Timothy Power, "The Red Sea under the Caliphal dynasties, c. 639–1171," *History Compass* 16, no. 10 (2018), 4.

43 Kennedy, "Islam," 221.

44 Hoyland, "Early Islam as a late antique religion," 1061, with translation.
45 Kennedy, "Islam," 228.
46 Fowden, *Quṣayr ʿAmra,* 179, 218.

25. The Father of Europe

1 Brian A. Catlos, *Kingdoms of Faith: A New History of Islamic Spain,* London: Hurst, 2018, is an up-to-date overview.
2 Latin Chronicle a. 754, 80, trans. Kenneth Baxter Wolf, *Conquerors and Chroniclers of Early Medieval Spain,* 2nd ed., Liverpool: Liverpool University Press, 1999, 91–128 at p. 117.
3 Sallust, *Jugurtha* 17.3. Only rarely is Europe placed first among equals by a Roman author. One example comes when the geographer Strabo, writing under Tiberius, explains that although there are three continents, he will begin with Europe because it has the most varied form, is best adapted to encourage excellence in manliness and citizenship, and has a greater store of goods than other continents (2.5.26). In a further innovation he also includes Greece as well as Rome within Europe. See Pliny, *Natural History* 3.1 for another claim to European primacy, on the grounds of its beauty and that it has fostered the conquerors of the world. And for a possible evocation of rivalry between Europe and Asia in private art of the Augustan period that may relate to distaste for Cleopatra, see Olivier Hekster, "Left behind in translation? The image of Augustus in Asia Minor," in Marjet Derks et al., eds., *What's Left Behind: The* Lieux de Mémoire *of Europe Beyond Europe,* Nijmegen: Vantilt, 2015, on the Tabula Chigi.
4 Isidore, *Etymologies* 14.2.3; Isidore, *De natura rerum* 48.2, with Suzanne Conklin Akbari, *Idols in the East: European Representations of Islam and the Orient, 1100–1450,* Ithaca: Cornell University Press, 2012, 40–1. For a classic account of the comparative rarity of references to "Europe" in medieval discourse, see Denys Hay, *Europe: The Emergence of an Idea,* 2nd ed., Edinburgh: Edinburgh University Press, 1968. For much more detail, Klaus Oschema, *Bilder von Europa im Mittelalter,* Ostfildern: Thorbecke, 2013.
5 Early usage: G. W. Bowersock, Peter Brown, and Oleg Grabar, *Late Antiquity: A Guide to the Postclassical World,* Cambridge, Mass.: Harvard University Press, 1999, Saracens.
6 See Kenneth Baxter Wolf, "*Convivencia* in medieval Spain: a brief history of an idea," *Religion Compass* 3, no. 1 (2009) for a critique of the overly enthusiastic account of al-Andalus as a model of tolerance and peaceful coexistence exemplified at Maria Rosa Menocal, *The Ornament of the World: How Muslims, Jews, and Christians Created a Culture of Tolerance in Medieval Spain,* Boston: Little, Brown, 2002.
7 Catlos, *Kingdoms of Faith,* 3.
8 *Indiculus luminosus* 35, trans. Jerrilynn D. Dodds, "Spaces," in María Rosa Menocal, Michael Sells, and Raymond P. Scheindlin, eds., *The Literature of al-Andalus,* Cambridge: Cambridge University Press, 2000, 83.
9 Karl J. Leyser, "Concepts of Europe in the early and high Middle Ages," *Past & Present* 137, no. 1 (1992), 32–4; Pim den Boer et al., *The History of the Idea of Europe,* 2nd ed., London: Routledge, 1995, 27; Oschema, *Bilder von Europa im*

Mittelalter, 134–60 for a synthetic treatment of the language of Europe in the late first millennium, emphasizing the variability of usage in this era and the ambivalence inherent in the association of the term with both the Carolingian realm and Christendom.

10 Einhard, *Life of Charlemagne,* 7.

11 Janet L. Nelson, *King and Emperor: A New Life of Charlemagne,* London: Allen Lane, 2019, 357; Judith Herrin, *Ravenna: Capital of Empire, Crucible of Europe,* Princeton: Princeton University Press, 2020, 370.

12 Nelson, *King and Emperor,* 367–74; Herrin, *Ravenna,* 377.

13 *Karolus magnus et Leo papa* (*MGH Poetae Latini Aevi Carolini 1,* 366–79), l. 504, with Leyser, "Concepts of Europe in the early and high Middle Ages," 34.

14 Nelson, *King and Emperor,* 384: *Karolus serenissimus augustus deo coronatus magnus pacificus imperator Romanum gubernans imperium qui et per misericordiam dei rex Francorum et Langobardorum.*

15 Ibid., on the evidence of the near-contemporary Lorsch Annals.

16 Much has been made of the fact that Irene occasionally used the masculine form "basileus" or king to describe herself, but the only evidence is a couple of legal documents, where the title may simply have been carried over from earlier usage without the scribe—or the queen—even noticing (Liz James, "Men, women, eunuchs: gender, sex and power," in John Haldon, ed., *The Social History of Byzantium,* Chichester: Wiley Blackwell, 2009, 45–6).

17 Glaciers: Kyle Harper and Michael McCormick, "Reconstructing the Roman climate," in Walter Scheidel, ed., *The Science of Roman History,* Princeton: Princeton University Press, 2018, 24. Ice cores: Joseph R. McConnell et al., "Lead pollution recorded in Greenland ice indicates European emissions tracked plagues, wars, and imperial expansion during antiquity," *PNAS* 115, no. 22 (2018).

18 Suzanne Conklin Akbari, "From due east to true north: orientalism and orientation," in Jeffrey J. Cohen, ed., *The Postcolonial Middle Ages,* New York: St. Martin's Press, 2000, 20–1.

19 Catlos, *Kingdoms of Faith,* 75–6.

20 Samuel Ottewill-Soulsby, "'Abbāsid-Carolingian diplomacy in early medieval Arabic apocalypse," *Millennium* 16 (2019), 213–14, 227–8; Herrin, *Ravenna,* 375.

21 Royal Frankish Annals a. 802 (*MGH Scriptores rerum Germanicarum 6,* 117).

22 Annals of St.-Bertin a. 865: text in Félix Grat, Jeanne Vielliard, and Suzanne Clémencet, eds., *Annales de Saint-Bertin,* Paris: Klincksieck, 1964, 124, trans. Janet L. Nelson, *The Annals of St.-Bertin,* Manchester: Manchester University Press, 1991, 129.

23 On all these exchanges, see Samuel Ottewill-Soulsby, "The camels of Charles the Bald," *Medieval Encounters: Jewish, Christian, and Muslim Culture in Confluence and Dialogue* no. 3 (2019). Sanhaja camel breeding: Richard W. Bulliet, *The Camel and the Wheel,* New York: Columbia University Press, 1990, 229.

24 Leyser, "Concepts of Europe in the early and high Middle Ages," 34–8.

25 Crete was recaptured by Constantinople in 960.

26 Low point: Chris Wickham, *Medieval Europe,* New Haven: Yale University Press, 2016, 135.

27 Cat Jarman, *River Kings: A New History of Vikings from Scandinavia to the Silk Roads,* London: William Collins, 2021, 74–5.

28 John Lind, "'Vikinger,' vikingetid og vikingeromantik," *Kuml* 61, no. 61 (2012);

Neil S. Price, *The Children of Ash and Elm: A History of the Vikings,* London: Allen Lane, 2020, 7–8, with Judith Jesch's essay at https://theconversation.com/what-does-the-word-viking-really-mean-75647.

29 On the continuities of the "viking" era with the recent past, see David Griffiths, "Rethinking the early Viking Age in the West," *Antiquity* 93, no. 368 (2019).

30 Trans. Michael Swanton, *The Anglo-Saxon Chronicle,* London: Dent, 1996, 54–6.

31 On the "charnel deposit" at Repton, Jarman, *River Kings,* 29–37.

32 Gillian Fellows-Jensen, "Scandinavian place names in the British Isles," in Stefan Brink and Neil Price, eds., *The Viking World,* London: Routledge, 2008.

33 "Republic of farmers": Price, *The Children of Ash and Elm,* 18, with 481–2 on the conversion.

34 Genetic study: Ashot Margaryan et al., "Population genomics of the Viking world," *Nature* 585, no. 7825 (2020), 392, based on samples taken in 2019 from 442 individuals who lived in Europe and Greenland between 2400 BCE and 1600 CE.

35 See Wladyslaw Duczko, *Viking Rus,* Leiden: Brill, 2004, 63, for the phrase.

36 For a concise account of the core role played by slavery in the viking world, see now Price, *The Children of Ash and Elm,* 141–54. For the vocabulary: Wickham, *Medieval Europe,* 94.

37 Orkney: Margaryan et al., "Population genomics of the Viking world." Iceland: Sara Goodacre et al., "Genetic evidence for a family-based Scandinavian settlement of Shetland and Orkney during the Viking periods," *Heredity* 95, no. 2 (2005); Maja Krzewińska et al., "Mitochondrial DNA variation in the Viking age population of Norway," *Philosophical Transactions of the Royal Society B* (2015); S. Sunna Ebenesersdóttir et al., "Ancient genomes from Iceland reveal the making of a human population," *Science* 360, no. 6392 (2018).

38 Joan N. Radner, ed. and trans., *Fragmentary Annals of Ireland,* Dublin: Dublin Institute for Advanced Studies, 1978, 120–1, with Caitlin R. Green's essay at https://www.caitlingreen.org/2015/09/a-great-host-of-captives.html—a blog with much of interest on long-distance trade and migration to Britain in general.

39 Price, *The Children of Ash and Elm,* 102.

40 Jarman, *River Kings,* 55–60.

41 Europe: Leyser, "Concepts of Europe in the early and high Middle Ages," 44–5, with Oschema, *Bilder von Europa im Mittelalter,* 155–8. Origins of Latin Christianity: Karl J. Leyser, "The ascent of Latin Europe," in Timothy Reuter, ed., *Communications and Power in Medieval Europe,* London: Hambledon Press, 1994; Conrad Leyser, "The memory of Gregory the Great and the making of Latin Europe, 600–1000," in Kate Cooper and Conrad Leyser, eds., *Making Early Medieval Societies: Conflict and Belonging in the Latin West, 300–1200,* Cambridge: Cambridge University Press, 2016.

42 Ottewill-Soulsby, "The camels of Charles the Bald," 273, 291–2.

26. The Translation Movement

1 The Translation Movement: Joel L. Kraemer, *Humanism in the Renaissance of Islam: The Cultural Revival During the Buyid Age,* 2nd ed., Leiden: Brill, 1992; Dimitri Gutas, *Greek Thought, Arabic Culture: The Graeco-Arabic Translation Movement in Baghdad and Early ʿAbbāsid Society (2nd–4th/8th–10th centuries),*

London: Routledge, 1998; Hans Daiber, "Die griechisch–arabische Wissenschaftsüberlieferung in der arabisch-islamischen Kultur in Übersetzungen des 8. bis 10. Jahrhunderts," in Harald Kittel et al., eds., *Übersetzung—Translation—Traduction*, Berlin: De Gruyter, 2007; Scott L. Montgomery, "Mobilities of science: the era of translation into Arabic," *Isis* 109, no. 2 (2018).

2 Hugh Kennedy, "Islam," in G. W. Bowersock, Peter Brown, and Oleg Grabar, eds., *Late Antiquity: A Guide to the Postclassical World*, Cambridge, Mass.: Harvard University Press, 1999, 224–5. Non-Muslims still had to pay an additional poll tax.

3 Mohsen Zakeri, "Translation from Middle Persian (Pahlavi) into Arabic to the early Abbasid Period (Persisch–arabische Übersetzungen im frühen Abbasidenreich)," in Kittlel et al., eds., *Übersetzung—Translation—Traduction*, 1199.

4 Gutas, *Greek Thought, Arabic Culture*, 24–5.

5 Ibid., 18–20.

6 Ibid., 13–16.

7 Jonathan Bloom, *Paper Before Print: The History and Impact of Paper in the Islamic World*, New Haven: Yale University Press, 2001, 42–56; Hyunhee Park, *Mapping the Chinese and Islamic Worlds: Cross-Cultural Exchange in Pre-Modern Asia*, New York: Cambridge University Press, 2012, 25–6. According to Arabic sources it came with prisoners of war taken at the Battle of Talas against China in 751.

8 Gutas, *Greek Thought, Arabic Culture*, 13; Robert Hoyland, "Early Islam as a late antique religion," in Scott Fitzgerald Johnson, ed., *The Oxford Handbook of Late Antiquity*, Oxford: Oxford University Press, 2012, 1068.

9 House of Wisdom: Sonja Brentjes and Robert Morrison, "The sciences in Islamic societies (750–1800)," in Robert Irwin, ed., *The New Cambridge History of Islam*, vol. 4: *Islamic Cultures and Societies to the End of the Eighteenth Century*, Cambridge: Cambridge University Press, 2010, 569.

10 Monthly salary as reported in Ibn an-Nadim's *al-Fihrist*: Franz Rosenthal, *The Classical Heritage in Islam*, London: Routledge, 1992, 49.

11 Gutas, *Greek Thought, Arabic Culture*, 136–7; Montgomery, "Mobilities of science," 315.

12 Kennedy, "Islam," 227.

13 Al-Khwarizmi, *Matifah al-'ulum*, trans. Rosenthal, *The Classical Heritage in Islam*, 54.

14 Gutas, *Greek Thought, Arabic Culture*, 193–6, provides a catalog of topics.

15 Examples at Rosenthal, *The Classical Heritage in Islam*, 18.

16 See Peter Adamson's essay at https://aeon.co/ideas/arabic-translators-did-far-more-than-just-preserve-greek-philosophy on the problems of translating the philosophical texts.

17 Simon Swain, *Economy, Family, and Society from Rome to Islam: A Critical Edition, English Translation, and Study of Bryson's* Management of the Estate, Cambridge: Cambridge University Press, 2013, 57–8.

18 Sebastian Brock, "The Syriac background to Hunayn's translation techniques," *ARAM Periodical* 3 (1991); Montgomery, "Mobilities of science," 315.

19 Gutas, *Greek Thought, Arabic Culture*, 32, 178–9.

20 Ibn an-Nadim, *al-Fihrist* 7.1 (Gustav Flügel, ed., *Kitab al-Fihrist*, Leipzig: Vogel, 1871–1872, I.243).

21 Gutas, *Greek Thought, Arabic Culture*, 179.

22 Barhebraeus (1226–86), trans. John Watt, reproduced at Swain, *Economy, Family, and Society from Rome to Islam,* 57.
23 For the important role of women in Carolingian literary culture: Felice Lifshitz, *Religious Women in Early Carolingian Francia: A Study of Manuscript Transmission and Monastic Culture,* New York: Fordham University Press, 2014.
24 Medical texts: Leigh Chipman, "Islamic medicine: refractions of the classical past," in Roberta Casagrande-Kim, Samuel Thrope, and Raquel Ukeles, eds., *Romance and Reason: Islamic Transformations of the Classical Past,* New York: Institute for the Study of the Ancient World, 2018; Montgomery, "Mobilities of science."
25 Aydın Sayılı, *The Observatory in Islam and Its Place in the General History of the Observatory,* 2nd ed., Ankara: Türk Tarih Kurumu Basımevi, 1988, 75–85.
26 See the essay by Christian Yates at http://theconversation.com/five-ways-ancient-india-changed-the-world-with-maths-84332.
27 For a digital reproduction, see https://treasures.bodleian.ox.ac.uk/treasures/bakhshali-manuscript.
28 Al-Farabi, *Ihsa' al-'ulum,* introduction, translated and discussed at Rosenthal, *The Classical Heritage in Islam,* 54–5.
29 Isidore: Seb Falk, *The Light Ages: A Medieval Journey of Discovery,* London: Allen Lane, 2020, 82–3. Charlemagne: *Admonitio Generalis* 72.
30 Walter Scheidel, "From the 'Great Convergence' to the 'First Great Divergence': Roman and Qin-Han state formation and its aftermath," in Walter Scheidel, ed., *Rome and China: Comparative Perspectives on Ancient World Empires,* Oxford: Oxford University Press, 2008, 20–3. China would retain primacy by comparison with western Eurasian powers until the Industrial Revolution.
31 Lynda Shaffer, "Southernization," *Journal of World History* 5, no. 1 (1994), 10–11.
32 John Gillis, *The Fadden More Psalter: The Discovery and Conservation of a Medieval Treasure,* Dublin: Worldwell, 2022.
33 Ibn Khordadbeh, *Kitab al-masalik* 153, trans. Adam Silverstein, "From markets to marvels: Jews on the maritime route to China, ca. 850—ca. 950 CE," *Journal of Jewish Studies* 58, no. 1 (2007), 96, with discussion at Timothy Power, "The Red Sea under the caliphal dynasties, c. 639–1171," *History Compass* 16, no. 10 (2018), 6–7.
34 Charles Burnett, "King Ptolemy and Alchandreus the Philosopher: the earliest texts on the astrolabe and Arabic astrology at Fleury, Micy and Chartres," *Annals of Science* 55, no. 4 (1998), 330.
35 John Crossley, "Old-fashioned versus newfangled: reading and writing numbers, 1200–1500," *Studies in Medieval and Renaissance History* 10 (2013), 86.
36 Chess in Córdoba in 822: Touraj Daryaee, *On the Explanation of Chess and Backgammon,* Irvine, CA: Jordan Center for Persian Studies, 2016, xxxiv.
37 For a full discussion of the Mediterranean economy in this period, which saw a "diversified but steady move toward economic complexity nearly everywhere" at odds with increasing fragmentation in the political realm, see Chris Wickham, *The Donkey and the Boat: Reinterpreting the Mediterranean Economy, 950–1180,* Oxford: Oxford University Press, 2023; quotation at 627.
38 Geniza merchants: Shelomo Dov Goitein, *A Mediterranean Society: The Jewish Communities of the Arab World as Portrayed by the Documents of the Cairo Geniza,* Berkeley: University of California Press, 1967; Jessica Goldberg, *Trade and*

Institutions in the Medieval Mediterranean: The Geniza Merchants and Their Business World, Cambridge: Cambridge University Press, 2012.

39 Brian A. Catlos, *Kingdoms of Faith: A New History of Islamic Spain,* London: Hurst, 2018, 139–72; Susanna A. Throop, *The Crusades: An Epitome,* Leeds: Kismet Press, 2018, 32.

40 Xénia Keighley et al., "Disappearance of Icelandic walruses coincided with Norse settlement," *Molecular Biology and Evolution* 36, no. 12 (2019).

41 This sequence of regions, arranged from north to south, is reproduced in the twelfth-century *Icelandic Geographical Treatise.* A somewhat different version of similar events is found in *Erik's Saga,* written down a couple of generations after the *Greenland Saga* in a higher epic style.

42 Margot Kuitems et al., "Evidence for European presence in the Americas in AD 1021," *Nature* 601, no. 7893 (2022); for a summary of the finds see Neil S. Price, *The Children of Ash and Elm: A History of the Vikings,* London: Allen Lane, 2020, 490–1.

27. The Sign of the Cross

1 Malta's Islamic governors were only removed in 1127.

2 Robert Bartlett, *The Making of Europe: Conquest, Colonization and Cultural Change, 950–1350,* Princeton: Princeton University Press, 1993, 249.

3 Vocabulary of the "Christian name" (or "stock"): ibid., 251.

4 Georg Strack, "Pope Urban II and Jerusalem: a re-examination of his letters on the First Crusade," *Journal of Religious History, Literature and Culture* 2, no. 1 (2016).

5 Fulcher of Chartres, *Historia Hierosolymitana* 3.37 (Heinrich Hagenmeyer, ed., *Fulcheri Carnotensis Historia Hierosolymitana,* Heidelberg: Carl Winters, 1913, 748–9).

6 Christopher Taylor, "Global circulation as Christian enclosure: legend, empire, and the nomadic Prester John," *Literature Compass* 11, no. 7 (2014).

7 David Abulafia, "The role of trade in Muslim–Christian contact during the Middle Ages," in Dionisius A. Agius and Richard Hitchcock, eds., *The Arab Influence in Medieval Europe,* Reading: Ithaca Press, 1994, 1; Ronald Findlay and Kevin H. O'Rourke, *Power and Plenty: Trade, War, and the World Economy in the Second Millennium,* Princeton: Princeton University Press, 2007, 97. For Islamic perspectives on the Crusades, see Paul M. Cobb, *The Race for Paradise: An Islamic History of the Crusades,* Oxford: Oxford University Press, 2014.

8 Giuseppe Petralia, "Le 'navi' e i 'cavalli,'" *Quaderni storici,* 103 (2000), 207–11; Chris Wickham, *Medieval Europe,* New Haven: Yale University Press, 2016, 131.

9 Pisa: Wickham, *Medieval Europe,* 131.

10 Date: Albert J. Ammerman, "Venice before the Grand Canal," *Memoirs of the American Academy in Rome* 48 (2003), 141.

11 Findlay and O'Rourke, *Power and Plenty,* 96.

12 Abulafia, "The role of trade in Muslim–Christian contact during the Middle Ages," 5; Wickham, *Medieval Europe,* 135–6.

13 Abulafia, "The role of trade in Muslim–Christian contact during the Middle Ages," 1.

14 Mohamed Ouerfelli, *Le sucre: production, commercialisation et usages dans la Méditerranée médiévale*, Leiden: Brill, 2008, 15–140.
15 Seb Falk, *The Light Ages: A Medieval Journey of Discovery*, London: Allen Lane, 2020, 86.
16 Steven J. Williams, *The* Secret of Secrets: *The Scholarly Career of a Pseudo-Aristotelian Text in the Latin Middle Ages*, Ann Arbor: University of Michigan Press, 2003.
17 Charles Burnett, "The coherence of the Arabic–Latin translation program in Toledo in the twelfth century," *Science in Context* 14, no. 1–2 (2001), for what follows.
18 Ibid., 249.
19 Bartlett, *The Making of Europe*, 249.
20 L. D. Reynolds and N. G. Wilson, *Scribes and Scholars: A Guide to the Transmission of Greek and Latin Literature*, 4th ed., Oxford: Oxford University Press, 2013, 121.
21 *Oxford Dictionary of National Biography*, "Bath, Adelard of."
22 John Crossley, "Old-fashioned versus newfangled: reading and writing numbers, 1200–1500," *Studies in Medieval and Renaissance History* 10 (2013), 86–90; Raffaele Danna, "Figuring out: the spread of Hindu-Arabic numerals in the European tradition of practical mathematics (13th–16th centuries)," *Nuncius* 36, no. 1 (2021); for the notaries, see Abulafia, "The role of trade in Muslim–Christian contact during the Middle Ages," 1.
23 Jeremy Johns, "I re normanni e i califfi fatimiti," in Biancamaria Scarcia Amoretti, ed., *Del nuovo sulla Sicilia musulmana*, Rome: Accademia nazionale dei Lincei, 1995, 9–50.
24 Karla Mallette, *The Kingdom of Sicily, 1100–1250: A Literary History*, Philadelphia: University of Pennsylvania Press, 2005, 29, 31.
25 S. Maqbul Ahmad, "Cartography of al-Sharif al-Idrisi," in J. B. Harley and David Woodward, eds.: *The History of Cartography*, vol. 2, part 1: *Cartography in the Traditional Islamic and South Asian Societies*, Chicago: University of Chicago Press, 1992.
26 Al-Idrisi, *Book of Roger*. All the selections given in what follows here are from sections 6–7 as translated at Mallette, *The Kingdom of Sicily*, 147. The work itself is edited at Enrico Cerulli, *Al-Idrisi: Opus geographicum: sive "Liber ad eorum delectationem qui terras peragrare studeant,"* Naples: Istituto Universitario Orientale di Napoli, 1970.
27 The full title is given here as translated at Mallette, *The Kingdom of Sicily*, 146.
28 Ahmad, "Cartography of al-Sharif al-Idrisi," 157.
29 Christopher Tyerman, *God's War: A New History of the Crusades*, London: Allen Lane, 2006, 225–40.
30 Hugh Kennedy, "Islam," in G. W. Bowersock, Peter Brown, and Oleg Grabar, eds., *Late Antiquity: A Guide to the Postclassical World*, Cambridge, Mass.: Harvard University Press, 1999, 228.
31 Customs records: Findlay and O'Rourke, *Power and Plenty*, 97.
32 See Bartlett, *The Making of Europe*, 15–23, for an overview.
33 Ibid., 106–32.
34 Ibid., 270–80.
35 Ibid., 255–60.

36 On the development of chivalry in this period, see Laura Ashe, *The Oxford English Literary History,* vol. 1: *1000–1350. Conquest and Transformation,* Oxford: Oxford University Press, 2017, 199–206.

37 Chrétien de Troyes, *Cligès* 30–6.

38 Sharon Kinoshita, "Medieval Mediterranean literature," *Publications of the Modern Language Association* 124, no. 2 (2009).

39 R. I. Moore, *The Formation of a Persecuting Society: Authority and Deviance in Western Europe, 950–1250,* 2nd ed., Oxford: Blackwell, 2007, 6.

40 Ibid., 12.

41 Ibid., with friendly updates at John H. Arnold, "Persecution and power in medieval Europe: the formation of a persecuting society, by R. I. Moore," *American Historical Review* 123, no. 1 (2018).

42 Roy Lowe and Yoshihito Yasuhara, *The Origins of Higher Learning: Knowledge Networks and the Early Development of Universities,* London: Routledge, 2017, 66–71.

43 Ibid., 40–7.

44 Philosophers: Alan Cameron, "The last days of the Academy at Athens," in his *Wandering Poets and Other Essays on Late Greek Literature and Philosophy,* Oxford: Oxford University Press, 2016. Nestorians: Wilhelm Baum and Dietmar W. Winkler, *The Church of the East,* London: RoutledgeCurzon, 2003, 23–5.

45 Lowe and Yasuhara, *The Origins of Higher Learning,* 100–3.

46 *BEI,* "Madrasa"; Jonathan P. Berkey, "Madrasas medieval and modern: politics, education, and the problem of Muslim identity," in Robert W. Hefner and Muhammad Qasim Zaman, eds., *Schooling Islam: The Culture and Politics of Modern Muslim Education,* Princeton: Princeton University Press, 2007, 42–4.

47 *Dizionario Biografico degli Italiani,* Costantino Africano (available online).

48 M. J. Toswell, *Today's Medieval University,* Kalamazoo, MI: ARC Humanities Press, 2017, 53.

49 Spread: Linda Walton, "Educational institutions," in Benjamin Z. Kedar and Merry E. Wiesner-Hank, *The Cambridge World History,* vol. 3. *Expanding Webs of Exchange and Conflict, 500 CE–1500 CE,* Cambridge: Cambridge University Press, 2015, 127.

50 Toswell, *Today's Medieval University,* 92.

51 Michael C. Weber, "The adoption of Al-Farabi's 'Mathematical Sciences' in the medieval west: a study in cross-cultural borrowing," *Scripta Mediterranea* 19–20 (1998–1999).

52 James A. Weisheipl, "Curriculum of the Faculty of Arts at Oxford in the early fourteenth century," *Medieval Studies* no. 26 (1964); Toby E. Huff, *The Rise of Early Modern Science: Islam, China, and the West,* 3rd ed., Cambridge: Cambridge University Press, 2017, 176; Leigh Chipman, "Islamic medicine: refractions of the Classical past," in Roberta Casagrande-Kim, Samuel Thrope, and Raquel Ukeles, eds., *Romance and Reason: Islamic Transformations of the Classical Past,* New York: Institute for the Study of the Ancient World, 2018, 69.

53 George Makdisi, *The Rise of Colleges: Institutions of Learning in Islam and the West,* Edinburgh: Edinburgh University Press, 1981, especially on the scholastic method in Islamic learning (105–52); note the useful reservations on other aspects of Makdisi's thesis expressed at Tim Geelhaar, "Did the medieval receive a 'complete model' of education from Classical Islam? Reconsidering George

Makdisi and his thesis," in Jörg Feuchter, Hoffmann Friedhelm, and Bee Yun, eds., *Cultural Transfers in Dispute: Representations in Asia, Europe and the Arab World Since the Middle Ages,* Frankfurt: Campus Verlag, 2011, and see also Charles Michael Stanton, *Higher Learning in Islam: The Classical Period, AD 700–1300,* Savage, MD: Rowman & Littlefield, 1990, 162–71.

54 Abulafia, "The role of trade in Muslim–Christian contact during the Middle Ages," 1.

55 David Abulafia, *Frederick II: A Medieval Emperor,* London: Allen Lane, 1992.

56 Thierry Buquet, "Hunting with cheetahs at European courts: from the origins to the end of a fashion," in Mark Hengerer and Nadir Weber, eds., *Animals and Courts,* Berlin: De Gruyter Oldenbourg, 2019. Cheetahs are often mistaken for leopards in contemporary European sources, but they are much easier to train.

57 Heather Dalton et al., "Frederick II of Hohenstaufen's Australasian cockatoo: symbol of detente between East and West and evidence of the Ayyubids' global reach," *Parergon* 35, no. 1 (2018). The name derived from the fact that Fustat was called Babillonia in Italian Latin, after the name of its Roman-era fort.

58 Mallette, *The Kingdom of Sicily,* 10.

59 Ibid., 72–83.

60 For brief scholarly interest in the idea around the same time, see Klaus Oschema, *Bilder von Europa im Mittelalter,* Ostfildern: Thorbecke, 2013, 188–91, with 261 n. 118 for a Christian West.

61 Matthew Paris, *Chronica Majora* a.1238; J. A. Giles, *Matthew Paris's English History: From the Year 1235 to 1273,* vol. 1, Bohn's Antiquarian Library, London: Henry G. Bohn, 1852, 131. The *Chronica Majora* is one of several chronicles by Matthew Paris, which overlap in their coverage.

62 Paris, *Chronica Majora* a.1241.

63 Ibid.

28. *Kalila wa-Dimna*

1 William of Rubruck, preface 2, all quotations trans. Peter Jackson, *The Mission of Friar William of Rubruck: His Journey to the Court of Great Khan Möngke, 1253–1255,* London: Hakluyt Society, 1990.

2 William of Rubruck 32.1. On Karakoram see Christoph Baumer, *The History of Central Asia,* vol. 3. *The Age of Islam and the Mongols,* London: I. B. Tauris, 2016, 194–9, and Jan Bemmann and Susanne Reichert, "Karakorum, the first capital of the Mongol world empire: an imperial city in a non-urban society," *Asian Archaeology* 4, no. 2 (2021).

3 William of Rubruck, 30.1–3.

4 Craig Benjamin, *Empires of Ancient Eurasia: The First Silk Roads Era, 100 BCE–250 CE,* Cambridge: Cambridge University Press, 2018, 266–7.

5 Baumer, *The History of Central Asia,* vol. 3, 171, 197–8.

6 William of Rubruck 33.7–22.

7 His story is told in the *Secret History of the Mongols,* the oldest known work of Mongolian literature, written down within a couple of decades of Temüjin's death and now surviving in slightly later Chinese versions. English translation: Igor de

Rachewiltz, *The Secret History of the Mongols: A Mongolian Epic Chronicle of the Thirteenth Century,* Leiden: Brill, 2004–2013.

8 Baumer, *The History of Central Asia,* vol. 3, 179.

9 Peter Frankopan, *The Silk Roads: A New History of the World,* London: Bloomsbury, 2015, 160.

10 Chinese weaponry: Baumer, *The History of Central Asia,* vol. 3, 196.

11 Ronald Findlay and Kevin H. O'Rourke, *Power and Plenty: Trade, War, and the World Economy in the Second Millennium,* Princeton: Princeton University Press, 2007, 105; Baumer, *The History of Central Asia,* vol. 3, 186. On the Mongols see now Marie Favereau, *The Horde: How the Mongols Changed the World,* Cambridge, Mass.: Belknap Press, 2021.

12 Peter Jackson, "The crisis in the Holy Land in 1260," *English Historical Review* 95, no. 376 (1980), 494–5.

13 Trans-Saharan gold trade: Sam Nixon, "Trans-Saharan gold trade in pre-modern times: available evidence and research agendas," in David J. Mattingly et al., eds., *Trade in the Ancient Sahara and Beyond,* Cambridge: Cambridge University Press, 2017.

14 Andrew Wilson, "Saharan trade in the Roman period: short-, medium- and long-distance trade networks," *Azania* 47, no. 4 (2012), 409, 437–40; Kevin MacDonald, "Complex societies, urbanism, and trade in the western Sahel," in Peter Mitchell and Paul J. Lane, eds., *The Oxford Handbook of African Archaeology,* Oxford: Oxford University Press, 2013, 835; Elizabeth Fentress and Andrew Wilson, "The Saharan Berber diaspora and the southern frontiers of Byzantine north Africa," in Susan T. Stevens and Jonathan P. Conant, eds., *North Africa Under Byzantium and Early Islam,* Washington, D.C.: Dumbarton Oaks, 2016.

15 Al-Idrisi, *Book of Roger,* First and Second Sections of the First Clime.

16 See Sarah Guérin, "Exchange of sacrifices: west Africa in the medieval world of goods," *Medieval Globe* 3, no. 2 (2017), for a summary, with MacDonald, "Complex societies, urbanism, and trade in the western Sahel," and Sam Nixon, ed., *Essouk-Tadmekka: An Early Islamic Trans-Saharan Market Town,* Leiden: Brill, 2017, 120–2, for the porcelain sherd, and 268–78, for the chronology and routes. Kathleen Bickford Berzock, *Caravans of Gold, Fragments in Time: Art, Culture, and Exchange Across Medieval Saharan Africa,* Evanston: Block Museum of Art, 2019, illustrates more archaeological evidence for trade in and around the medieval Sahara.

17 Chris Wickham, *The Donkey and the Boat: Reinterpreting the Mediterranean Economy, 950–1180,* Oxford: Oxford University Press, 2023, 42–3. Vast quantities have been found in excavations at Fustat.

18 Toby Green, *A Fistful of Shells: West Africa from the Rise of the Slave Trade to the Age of Revolution,* London: Allen Lane, 2019, 42–4.

19 Guérin, "Exchange of sacrifices," and Michael A. Gomez, *African Dominion: A New History of Empire in Early and Medieval West Africa,* Princeton: Princeton University Press, 2018, 92–143.

20 Al-ʿUmari, *Masalik al-absar fi mamalik al-amsar* ("Pathways of vision in the realms of the metropolises"), 10, as translated in J.F.P. Hopkins and Nehemia Levtzion, eds., *Corpus of Early Arabic Sources for West African History,* Cambridge: Cambridge University Press, 1981, 261–72. Tales of an earlier period of the kingdom's history survive in the local oral tradition preserved by professional

storytellers or *griots,* first collected for European readers by French travelers in the twentieth century. For an English translation of the *Sunjata Epic,* see David C. Conrad, *Sunjata: A New Prose Version,* Indianapolis: Hackett, 2016, with Gomez, *African Dominion,* 61–91.

21 Green, *A Fistful of Shells,* 39, citing a comparison calculated in *Time* magazine in 2015.

22 Al-Maqrizi, *Al-tibr al-masbuk fi man hajja min al-mulak* (Molded gold, on those kings who made the pilgrimage), trans. in Hopkins and Levtzion, *Corpus of Early Arabic Sources for West African History,* 351–2.

23 On this extended network of trade and culture the classic text is Janet L. Abu-Lughod, *Before European Hegemony: The World System* AD *1250–1350,* New York: Oxford University Press, 1989, describing it as the "first world system," though see Guérin, "Exchange of sacrifices" on Abu-Lughod's omission of African markets and trans-Saharan routes, and for a more recent exploration of the "globalizing" dynamic of the Mongol empire, Alexander Anievas and Kerem Nişancıoğlu, *How the West Came to Rule,* London: Pluto Press, 2015, 64–90. Abu-Lughod's is not the only attempt to apply to earlier eras insights from Immanuel Wallerstein's *The Modern World-System,* 4 vols., New York: Academic Press, 1974–1989, where interactions that comprise a world-system after c. 1400 are seen principally in terms of hierarchical relations of exchange between "cores" and "peripheries." For the Bronze and Iron Age, see Andrew Sherratt and Susan Sherratt, "From luxuries to commodities: the nature of Bronze Age trading systems," in Noel H. Gale, ed., *Bronze Age Trade in the Mediterranean,* Jonsered: Åström, 1991, and Susan Sherratt and Andrew Sherratt, "The growth of the Mediterranean economy in the early first millennium BC," *World Archaeology* 24, no. 3 (1993), with Toby C. Wilkinson, Susan Sherratt, and John Bennet, eds., *Interweaving Worlds: Systemic Interactions in Eurasia, 7th to the 1st Millennia* BC, Oxford: Oxbow, 2011. For the Indian Ocean in the first millennium CE, see Philippe Beaujard, "The Indian Ocean in Eurasian and African world-systems before the sixteenth century," *Journal of World History* 16, no. 4 (2005), who rejects a specific break or expansion within this existing world-system in the thirteenth (as argued by Abu-Lughod) or fifteenth (as argued by Wallerstein) century. For an even longer perspective see Andre Gunder Frank and Barry K. Gills, "The five thousand year world system: an interdisciplinary introduction," *Humboldt Journal of Social Relations* 18, no. 1 (1992). For a more recent exploration of the idea in relation to early medieval East Asia and the Islamic world, see Glen Dudbridge, "Reworking the world system paradigm," *Past & Present* 238, Supplement 13 (2018).

24 Hangzhou: Abu-Lughod, *Before European Hegemony,* 339. Cairo: Chris Wickham, *Medieval Europe,* New Haven: Yale University Press, 2016, 136. Great Zimbabwe: Shadreck Chirikure et al., "A Bayesian chronology for Great Zimbabwe: re-threading the sequence of a vandalized monument," *Antiquity* 87, no. 337 (2013).

25 E. E. Burke, ed., *The Journals of Carl Mauch, 1869–72,* Salisbury [Harare]: National Archives of Rhodesia, 1969, 190–1.

26 David Abulafia, "The role of trade in Muslim–Christian contact during the Middle Ages," in Dionisius A. Agius and Richard Hitchcock, eds., *The Arab Influence in Medieval Europe,* Reading: Ithaca Press, 1994, 8.

27 Findlay and O'Rourke, *Power and Plenty,* 94–6. Cloth of gold is frequently mentioned in Marco Polo's description of Mongol lands.

28 Guérin, "Exchange of sacrifices." Slaves: Wilson, "Saharan trade in the Roman period," 433.

29 Clove (*gharofano*): Dante, *Inferno* 29.128.

30 Porcelain in Europe: David Whitehouse, "Chinese porcelain in medieval Europe," *Medieval Archaeology* 16, no. 1 (1972). Clock technology: Donald R. Hill, "Arabic fine technology and its influence on European mechanical engineering," in Agius and Hitchcock, eds., *The Arab Influence in Medieval Europe.*

31 Text networks: Daniel Selden, "Text networks," *Ancient Narrative* 8 (2010).

32 Robert Irwin, *The Arabian Nights: A Companion,* London: Allen Lane, 1994, 16.

33 Sharon Kinoshita, "Translatio/n, empire, and the worlding of medieval literature: the travels of *Kalila wa Dimna,*" *Postcolonial Studies* 11, no. 4 (2008), with the Kalila and Dimna: AnonymClassic project based at the Freie Universität Berlin (https://www.geschkult.fu-berlin.de/en/e/kalila-wa-dimna/index.html).

34 English translation of the Arabic text: Michael Fishbein and James E. Montgomery, *Ibn al-Muqaffaʿ, Kalilah and Dimnah: Fables of Virtue and Vice,* New York: New York University Press, 2022.

35 Kinoshita, "Translatio/n, empire, and the worlding of medieval literature," 377; Touraj Daryaee, *On the Explanation of Chess and Backgammon,* Irvine, CA: Jordan Center for Persian Studies, 2016, xxxiii–xxxiv.

36 Linda Pellecchia, "From Aesop's Fables to the 'Kalila wa-Dimna': Giuliano da Sangallo's staircase in the Gondi palace in Florence," *I Tatti Studies* 14/15 (2011), 181.

37 Evolution of the text: https://www.geschkult.fu-berlin.de/en/e/kalila-wa-dimna/topics/Cultural-Translation.html.

38 Sharon Kinoshita, "Mediterranean literature," in Peregrine Horden and Sharon Kinoshita, eds., *A Companion to Mediterranean History,* Oxford: Wiley Blackwell, 2014, pointing out that this involves the devaluation of translated works in favor of more "authentic," if far less popular, texts.

39 Identifying non-Christians was more important than the precise nature of the heresy in these *chansons de geste:* Jews come under attack as well, and there is persistent confusion between Saracens and idol-worshipping pagans: Marianne Ailes, "The *Chanson de geste,*" in Anthony Bale, ed., *The Cambridge Companion to the Literature of the Crusades,* Cambridge: Cambridge University Press, 2018.

40 History of the text: excellent summary at Pellecchia, "From Aesop's Fables to the 'Kalila wa-Dimna,'" 171 n. 161; see also Beatrice Gruendler, "*Kalila wa-Dimna:* a unique work of world literature," in Verena M. Lepper, ed., *Arab and German Tales: Transcending Cultures,* Berlin: Kadmos, 2018.

41 See Geraldine Heng, "The romance of England: *Richard Coer De Lyon,* Saracens, Jews, and the politics of race and nation," in Jeffrey J. Cohen, ed., *The Postcolonial Middle Ages,* New York: St. Martin's Press, 2000, and Geraldine Heng, *The Invention of Race in the European Middle Ages,* Cambridge: Cambridge University Press, 2018, for the "racializing discourse" that emerges around the thirteenth century, associating both religion and skin color with medieval forms of nationalism.

42 Evidence for medieval population: Maria Ginatempo and Lucia Sandri, *L'Italia delle città. Il popolamento urbano tra Medioevo e Rinascimento (secoli XIII–XVI),* Florence: Le Lettere, 1990, 8[illegible].

43 Deborah Howard, *Venice & the East: The Impact of the Islamic World on Venetian*

Architecture 1100–1500, New Haven: Yale University Press, 2000; Thomas E. A. Dale, "Cultural hybridity in medieval Venice: reinventing the East at San Marco after the Fourth Crusade," in Henry Maguire and Robert S. Nelson, eds., *San Marco, Byzantium and the Myths of Venice*, Washington, D.C.: Dumbarton Oaks, 2010.

44 Albert J. Ammerman, "Venice before the Grand Canal," *Memoirs of the American Academy in Rome* 48 (2003), 141.

45 Ibid., 149 n. 44.

46 Marco Polo, *Description of the World*, 4; all translations are taken from Sharon Kinoshita, *Marco Polo: The Description of the World*, Indianapolis: Hackett, 2016, unless otherwise noted.

47 Ibid., 7–8.

48 Ibid., 15.

49 Sharon Kinoshita, "Medieval travel writing (2): beyond the pilgrimage," in Nandini Das and Tim Youngs, eds., *The Cambridge History of Travel Writing*, Cambridge: Cambridge University Press, 2019, 54–9, and Sharon Kinoshita, "Marco Polo and the world empire of letters," in Ken Seigneurie and Christine Chism, eds., *A Companion to World Literature*, vol. 2: *601 CE to 1450*, London: Wiley Blackwell, 2020, for context and analysis.

50 Polo, *Description of the World*, 1, translation slightly adapted.

51 Sharon Kinoshita, "Introduction," in ibid., xvii.

52 Polo, *Description of the World*, 117.

53 Ibid., 34, 38.

54 Kinoshita, "Medieval travel writing (2)," 56–9.

55 On the general authenticity of Marco's story, see Longxi Zhang, "Marco Polo, Chinese cultural identity, and an alternative model of East-West encounter," in Suzanne Conklin Akbari and Amilcare Iannucci, eds., *Marco Polo and the Encounter of East and West*, Toronto: University of Toronto Press, 2008.

56 Abu-Lughod, *Before European Hegemony*, 168–9; Findlay and O'Rourke, *Power and Plenty*, 107.

57 Compass: Philippe Beaujard, "The Indian Ocean in Eurasian and African world-systems before the sixteenth century," *Journal of World History* 16, no. 4 (2005), 430. The technology was known in Europe in the twelfth century; for this and a different perspective, see Seb Falk, *The Light Ages: A Medieval Journey of Discovery*, London: Allen Lane, 2020, 210–18.

29. The Land of Darkness

1 All translations of Ibn Battuta's text are taken from H.A.R. Gibb and C. F. Beckingham, *The Travels of Ibn Battuta AD 1325–1354*, London: Hakluyt Society, 1958–1994, Tim Mackintosh-Smith, *The Travels of Ibn Battutah*, abridged ed., London: Picador, 2003, is a more portable translation, and for the contexts see Ross E. Dunn, *The Adventures of Ibn Battuta*, Berkeley: University of California Press, 2012.

2 Secretary (Ibn Juzayy): Gibb and Beckingham, *The Travels of Ibn Battuta*, 6–7.

3 D. O. Morgan, "Ibn Battuta and the Mongols," *Journal of the Royal Asiatic Society* 11, no. 1 (2001), 3.

4 Gibb and Beckingham, *The Travels of Ibn Battuta,* 482–3.
5 Ibid., 955.
6 Graves: ibid., 969.
7 Ibid., 918, 925, 934.
8 Ibn al-Wardi, *An Essay on the Report of the Pestilence,* trans. Michael Dols, "Ibn al-Wardi's Risalah al-naba' 'an al-waba', a translation of a major source for the history of the Black Death in the Middle East," in Dickran K. Kouymjian, ed., *Near Eastern Numismatics, Iconograpy, Epigraphy and History: Studies in Honor of George C. Miles,* Beirut: American University of Beirut, 1974, 448, slightly adapted.
9 Monica H. Green, "The four Black Deaths," *American Historical Review* 125, no. 5 (2020), 1603.
10 Ibid., 1613; Monica H. Green, "Putting Asia on the Black Death map," *Medieval Globe* 8, no. 1 (2022).
11 Bruce M. S. Campbell, *The Great Transition: Climate, Disease and Society in the Late Medieval World,* Cambridge: Cambridge University Press, 2016; useful summary and bibliography at Dagomar Degroot, *The Frigid Golden Age: Climate Change, the Little Ice Age, and the Dutch Republic, 1560–1720,* Cambridge: Cambridge University Press, 2018, 31–2, with his essay at https://aeon.co/essays/the-little-ice-age-is-a-history-of-resilience-and-surprises.
12 Boris V. Schmid et al., "Climate-driven introduction of the Black Death and successive plague reintroductions into Europe," *Proceedings of the National Academy of Sciences* 112, no. 10 (2015).
13 Monica H. Green, "Taking 'pandemic' seriously: making the Black Death global," in Monica H. Green, ed., *Pandemic Disease in the Medieval World: Rethinking the Black Death,* Kalamazoo, MI: Arc Medieval Press, 2014, 41–5. China: Robert Hymes, "Epilogue: a hypothesis on the East Asian beginnings of the *Yersinia pestis* polytomy," in Green, ed., *Pandemic Disease in the Medieval World.* Southern Africa: Gérard Chouin, "Reflections on plague in African history (14th–19th c.)," *Afriques* 9 (2018); Monica H. Green, "Putting Africa on the Black Death map: narratives from genetics and history," *Afriques* 9 (2018).
14 See Gabriele de Mussi, *Istoria de morbo,* trans. T. Rosemary Horrox, *The Black Death,* Manchester: Manchester University Press, 1994, 17, with Hannah Barker, "Laying the corpses to rest: grain, embargoes, and *Yersinia pestis* in the Black Sea, 1346–48," *Speculum* 96, no. 1 (2021), for a bigger picture.
15 Green, "The four Black Deaths," 1606.
16 Monica H. Green, "Editor's Introduction to pandemic disease in the medieval world: rethinking the Black Death," in Green, ed., *Pandemic Disease in the Medieval World,* 9, 14.
17 Opinions vary as to the longer-term effects: for optimistic interpretations, see Chris Wickham, *Medieval Europe,* New Haven: Yale University Press, 2016, 214–16, and James Belich, *The World the Plague Made: The Black Death and the Rise of Europe,* Princeton: Princeton University Press, 2022.
18 Jerry H. Bentley, *Old World Encounters: Cross-Cultural Contacts and Exchanges in Pre-Modern Times,* New York: Oxford University Press, 1993, 163; cf. Wickham, *Medieval Europe,* 215, on economic integration within Europe.
19 Stuart J. Borsch, "Environment and population," *Comparative Studies in Society and History* 46 (2004); Stuart J. Borsch, "Plague depopulation and irrigation decay in medieval Egypt," *Medieval Globe* 1 (2014); Mohamed Ouerfelli, *Le sucre:*

production, commercialisation et usages dans la Méditerranée médiévale, Leiden: Brill, 2008, 94–9, 155–74.

20 David Nirenberg, *Communities of Violence*, 2nd ed., Princeton: Princeton University Press, 2015, 235–45; Green, "Editor's Introduction," 16. Excavation carried out from 2007 of a mass burial site at Tàrrega revealed that survivors later tried to give the deceased the appropriate rites.

21 See "Renaissance": Wickham, *Medieval Europe*, 3, with Mark Jurdjevic, "Hedgehogs and foxes: the present and future of Italian Renaissance intellectual history," *Past & Present* 195, no. 1 (2007), on the periodization and the state of the field. "Humanism" is also a nineteenth-century word.

22 Petrarch, *Familiar Letters* 20.8, with Theodor Mommsen, "Petrarch's conception of the Dark Ages," *Speculum* (1942). Later historians increasingly restricted the term to the second half of the first millennium CE.

23 Denys Hay, *Europe: The Emergence of an Idea*, 2nd ed., Edinburgh: Edinburgh University Press, 1968, 59.

24 On Petrarch's negative opinion of Greeks, ancient and modern, see Nancy Bisaha, *Creating East and West: Renaissance Humanists and the Ottoman Turks*, Philadelphia: University of Pennsylvania Press, 2004, 120–1.

25 David Rundle, *Humanism in Fifteenth-Century Europe*, Oxford: Society for the Study of Medieval Languages and Literature, 2012.

26 https://www.theguardian.com/books/2019/mar/07/surprise-as-unknown-irish-translation-of-ibn-sina-discovered-in-spine-of-book with https://www.isos.dias.ie/PRIVATE/Avicenna_Fragment.html.

27 Robert Irwin, *The Arabian Nights: A Companion*, London: Allen Lane, 1994, 96–7.

28 Boccaccio, *Decameron* IX.3, VII.9.

29 Saladin: ibid., I.3, X.9; Gerbino: ibid., IV.4.

30 Translations: Iain Macleod Higgins, ed., *The Book of John Mandeville, with Related Texts*, Indianapolis: Hackett, 2011 (from Old French); John Mandeville, *The Book of Marvels and Travels*, trans. Anthony Bale, Oxford: Oxford University Press, 2012 (from Middle English).

31 Sharon Kinoshita, "Medieval travel writing (2): beyond the pilgrimage," in Nandini Das and Tim Youngs, eds., *The Cambridge History of Travel Writing*, Cambridge: Cambridge University Press, 2019, 59.

32 Higgins, *The Book of John Mandeville, with Related Texts*, 157.

33 Kinoshita, "Medieval travel writing (2)," 61.

34 Keralan mathematics: George Gheverghese Joseph, *A Passage to Infinity: Medieval Indian Mathematics from Kerala and Its Impact*, New Delhi: Sage, 2009.

35 Zeina Klink-Hoppe, "Life in a coffee cup," *British Museum Magazine* 102 (Spring/Summer 2022).

36 Georges Grosjean, *Mapamundi, the Catalan Atlas of the Year 1375*, Zurich: Urs Graf, 1978.

37 Hay, *Europe*, 94–5; Klaus Oschema, *Bilder von Europa im Mittelalter*, Ostfildern: Thorbecke, 2013, 302–7.

38 Beatrice Forbes Manz, *The Rise and Rule of Tamerlane*, Cambridge: Cambridge University Press, 1989.

39 They brought with them another complication for the ideological purity of Christian Europe: a widespread notion that the Turks, like ancient Romans, Franks, and Britons, were descendants of Trojan refugees (Terence Spencer, "Turks and Trojans in the Renaissance," *Modern Language Review* 47, no. 3 (1952); Naoíse

Mac Sweeney, *Troy: Myth, City, Icon*, London: Bloomsbury Academic, 2018, 122–5). The idea that Franks and Turks shared a common Trojan heritage goes back to the Frankish Chronicle of Fredegar (c. 660 CE), and Britons got in on the act in the ninth-century *History of the Britons*. In the 1440s Mehmed II embraced the connection, visiting Troy like Xerxes and Alexander before him, and claiming the god-given right to avenge it (Kritovoulos, *History of Mehmed the Conqueror*, trans. Charles T. Riggs, Princeton: Princeton University Press, 1954, 181).

40 Noel Malcolm, *Useful Enemies: Islam and the Ottoman Empire in Western Political Thought, 1450–1750*, Oxford: Oxford University Press, 2019, 1.

41 Ibid., 2, 4.

42 Ibid., 4–6.

43 Hay, *Europe*, 84.

44 Toby Green, *A Fistful of Shells: West Africa from the Rise of the Slave Trade to the Age of Revolution*, London: Allen Lane, 2019, 56.

45 Malcolm, *Useful Enemies*, 26; Lisa Jardine and Jerry Brotton, *Global Interests: Renaissance Art Between East and West*, London: Reaktion, 2000, 8–9.

46 Continuing preference for "Christendom" over "Europe" until the late eighteenth century CE: Georgios Varouxakis, "When did Britain join the occident? On the origins of the idea of 'the West' in English," *History of European Ideas* 46, no. 5 (2020).

47 Hay, *Europe*, 73–95.

48 North African origins of Guanches: Ricardo Rodríguez-Varela et al., "Genomic analyses of pre-European conquest human remains from the Canary Islands reveal close affinity to modern north Africans," *Current Biology* 27, no. 21 (2017).

49 Raj Patel and Jason W. Moore, *A History of the World in Seven Cheap Things: A Guide to Capitalism, Nature, and the Future of the Planet*, Berkeley: University of California Press, 2017, 14–15.

50 Felix Brahm, "Guns in Africa," in *Oxford Research Encyclopedia of African History*, Oxford: Oxford University Press, 2020.

51 Green, *A Fistful of Shells*, 53. Akan goldfield: Sam Nixon, "Trans-Saharan gold trade in pre-modern times: available evidence and research agendas," in David J. Mattingly et al., eds., *Trade in the Ancient Sahara and Beyond*, Cambridge: Cambridge University Press, 2017, 169.

52 Green, *A Fistful of Shells*, 36.

53 Kenneth Baxter Wolf, "The 'Moors' of west Africa and the beginnings of the Portuguese slave trade," *Journal of Medieval and Renaissance Studies* 24, no. 3 (1994).

54 Bentley, *Old World Encounters*, 178.

55 Patel and Moore, *A History of the World in Seven Cheap Things*, 16–17.

56 Bentley, *Old World Encounters*, 179–80.

57 Michael L. Kunz and Robin O. Mills, "A Precolumbian presence of Venetian glass trade beads in Arctic Alaska," *American Antiquity* 86, no. 2 (2021).

58 Massimo Livi Bacci, "Return to Hispaniola: reassessing a demographic catastrophe," *Hispanic American Historical Review* 83, no. 1 (2003).

59 Joyce D. Chaplin, "Enslavement of Indians in early America: captivity without the narrative," in Elizabeth Mancke and Carole Shammas, eds., *The Creation of the British Atlantic World*, Baltimore: Johns Hopkins University Press, 2005, 48; Andrés Reséndez, *The Other Slavery: The Uncovered Story of Indian Enslavement in America*, Boston: Houghton Mifflin Harcourt, 2016, 8–10.

60 Green, *A Fistful of Shells*, 62; Joseph E. Inikori and Stanley L. Engerman, *The Atlantic Slave Trade: Effects on Economies, Societies, and Peoples in Africa, the Americas, and Europe*, Durham: Duke University Press, 1992.

30. A New World

1 A classic version can be found in Immanuel Wallerstein's *The Modern World-System*, 4 vols., New York: Academic Press, 1974–1989, with Philippe Beaujard, "The Indian Ocean in Eurasian and African world-systems before the sixteenth century," *Journal of World History* 16, no. 4 (2005), 439 and 448–9 for the problems, and Jan Nederveen Pieterse, "Ancient Rome and globalisation: decentring Rome," in Martin Pitts and Miguel John Versluys, eds., *Globalisation and the Roman World*, Cambridge: Cambridge University Press, 2014, 226–28, for other examples and alternatives. For the same concept in a "World Civ" textbook, see Jerry H. Bentley, Heather Streets-Salter, and Herbert F. Ziegler, *Traditions & Encounters: A Brief Global History*, 2nd ed., New York: McGraw-Hill, 2010, 344. This approach is also common in public scholarship in both Western contexts (e.g., https://www.history.com/news/columbian-exchange-impact-diseases) and Eastern ones. I found a particularly vivid example in the "Time Corridor" at the Macao Museum, where parallel cultural progress in Chinese and Western civilizations leads the visitor up to the arrival of the Portuguese on the island in the sixteenth century. The museum opened a year before the return of Macao to Chinese control in 1999, and the design is intended to highlight harmony between Chinese and Western cultures; for the differences between this and the Hong Kong Museum of History, which also opened in 1998, one year after the return of Hong Kong to China, see Kam-yee Law, "The red line over European colonialism: comparison of the Macao museum and Hong Kong museum of history after their return to China," *International Journal of Heritage Studies* 20, no. 5 (2014).

2 Sanjay Subrahmanyam, "Connected histories: notes toward a reconfiguration of early modern Eurasia," *Modern Asian Studies* 31, no. 3 (1997); Sanjay Subrahmanyam, *Three Ways to Be Alien: Travails and Encounters in the Early Modern World*, Waltham: Brandeis University Press, 2011; Charles H. Parker, *Global Interactions in the Early Modern Age, 1400–1800*, New York: Cambridge University Press, 2010; Jerry Bentley, Sanjay Subrahmanyam and Merry E. Wiesner-Hanks, eds., *The Cambridge World History*, vol. 6: *The Construction of a Global World, 1400–1800 CE*, Cambridge: Cambridge University Press, 2015; Alan Strathern, "Global early modernity and the problem of what came before," *Past & Present* 238, Supplement 13 (2018), 319–24.

3 Lisa Jardine and Jerry Brotton, *Global Interests: Renaissance Art Between East and West*, London: Reaktion, 2000, 58.

4 Toby Green, *A Fistful of Shells: West Africa from the Rise of the Slave Trade to the Age of Revolution*, London: Allen Lane, 2019, 8.

5 See, in a crowded field, Nancy Bisaha, *Creating East and West: Renaissance Humanists and the Ottoman Turks*, Philadelphia: University of Pennsylvania Press, 2004; Robert Markley, *The Far East and the English Imagination, 1600–1730*, Cambridge: Cambridge University Press, 2006; Timothy Brook, *Mr. Selden's Map of China: Decoding the Secrets of a Vanished Cartographer*, New York: Bloomsbury,

2013; Palmira Johnson Brummett, *Mapping the Ottomans: Sovereignty, Territory, and Identity in the Early Modern Mediterranean,* Cambridge: Cambridge University Press, 2015; Noel Malcolm, *Agents of Empire: Knights, Corsairs, Jesuits and Spies in the Sixteenth-Century Mediterranean World,* London: Allen Lane, 2015; Noel Malcolm, *Useful Enemies: Islam and the Ottoman Empire in Western Political Thought, 1450–1750,* Oxford: Oxford University Press, 2019; Jerry Brotton, *This Orient Isle: Elizabethan England and the Islamic World,* London: Allen Lane, 2016; Alexander Bevilacqua, *The Republic of Arabic Letters: Islam and the European Enlightenment,* Cambridge, Mass.: Harvard University Press, 2018; William Brandon, *New Worlds for Old: Reports from the New World and Their Effect on the Development of Social Thought in Europe, 1500–1800,* Athens: Ohio University Press, 1986; Anthony Grafton, April Shelford and Nancy G. Siraisi, *New Worlds, Ancient Texts: The Power of Tradition and the Shock of Discovery,* Cambridge, Mass.: Harvard University Press, 1992; Sarah H. Beckjord, *Territories of History: Humanism, Rhetoric, and the Historical Imagination in the Early Chronicles of Spanish America,* University Park: Pennsylvania State University Press, 2007; David Graeber and David Wengrow, *The Dawn of Everything: A New History of Humanity,* London, Allen Lane, 2021.

6 Joseph Jacobs, ed., *The Earliest English Version of the Fables of Bidpai, "The Morall Philosophie of Doni," by Sir Thomas North,* London: David Nutt, 1888, xi.

7 Giovanna Ceserani, *Italy's Lost Greece: Magna Graecia and the Making of Modern Archaeology,* Oxford: Oxford University Press, 2012, 102, with 131 n. 92.

8 Peter Burke, "Did Europe exist before 1700?," *History of European Ideas* 1 (1980), 23.

9 Montesquieu, *Spirit of the Laws* 17.16, emphasizing environmental factors; trans. at Anne M. Cohler, Basia Carolyn Miller, and Harold Samuel Stone, eds., *Montesquieu: The Spirit of the Laws,* Cambridge: Cambridge University Press, 1989, 284.

INDEX

Ptolemaic dynasty, 244–45, 247, 260, 286–88, 302

© FRAN MONKS

JOSEPHINE QUINN has been teaching Ancient History at Oxford University since 2003. In January 2025 she became the first woman to hold the Chair in Ancient History at Cambridge University. She has degrees from Oxford and the University of California, Berkeley; has taught in America, Italy, and the UK; and co-directed the Tunisian-British archaeological excavations at Utica. She is a regular contributor to the *London Review of Books* and *The New York Review of Books,* as well as to radio and television programs. She is the author of the award-winning *In Search of the Phoenicians.*